PHYSIOLOGY OF TREES

Edited by

A.S. Raghavendra
School of Life Sciences
University of Hyderabad
Hyderabad, India

A WILEY-INTERSCIENCE PUBLICATION

JOHN WILEY & SONS, INC.

New York • Chichester • Brisbane • Toronto • Singapore

Copyright © 1991 by John Wiley & Sons, Inc.

Library of Congress Cataloging in Publication Data:
Physiology of trees / edited by A.S. Raghavendra.
    p. cm.
"A Wiley-Interscience publication."
Includes index.
ISBN 0-471-50110-7
1. Trees—Physiology. I. Raghavendra, A.S.
QK711.2.P56 1991
582.16—dc20   91-7494
                                   CIP

Printed in the United States of America

10 9 8 7 6 5 4 3 2 1

PHYSIOLOGY OF TREES

CONTRIBUTORS

F.T. ADDICOTT, Department of Botany, University of California—Davis, Davis, California 95616-8537, USA

R. ALONI, Department of Botany, Tel Aviv University, Tel Aviv 69978, Israel

D. BARTHELEMY, Laboratoire de Botanique, Institut Botanique, 163 Rue Auguste Broussonet, 34000 Montpellier, France

R. BORCHERT, Department of Physiology and Cell Biology, University of Kansas, Lawrence, Kansas 66045-5321, USA

R. CEULEMANS, , Department of Biology, University of Antwerpen, Universiteitsplein 1, B-2610 Wilrijk-Antwerpen, Belgium

R.E. DICKSON, USDA Forest Service, North Central Forest Experiment Station, Forestry Sciences Laboratory, P.O. Box 898, Rhinelander, Wisconsin 54501, USA

C. EDELIN, Laboratoire de Botanique, Institut Botanique, 163 Rue Auguste Broussonet, 34000 Montpellier, France

T. ERICSSON, Department of Ecology and Environmental Research, Swedish University of Agricultural Sciences, Box 7072, S-75007 Uppsala, Sweden

A. HAGIHARA, Department of Forestry, Faculty of Agriculture, Nagoya University, Chikusa, Nagoya 464, Japan

F. HALLE, Laboratoire de Botanique, Institut Botanique, 163 Rue Auguste Broussonet, 34000 Montpellier, France

J.-E. HÄLLGREN, Department of Forest Genetics and Plant Physiology, Swedish University of Agricultural Sciences, S-90183 Umeå, Sweden

P. HARI, Department of Silviculture, University of Helsinki, Unioninkatu 40B, SF-00170 Helsinki, Finland

T.M. HINCKLEY, College of Forest Resources, University of Washington, Anderson Hall AR-10, Seattle, Washington 98195, USA

K. HOZUMI, Department of Forestry, Faculty of Agriculture, Nagoya University, Chikusa, Nagoya 464, Japan

v

T. INGESTAD,   Department of Ecology and Environmental Research, Swedish University of Agricultural Sciences, Box 7072, S-75007 Uppsala, Sweden

J. KALLARACKAL,   Plant Physiology Division, Kerala Forest Research Institute, Peechi 680653, Kerala, India

T. KELLER,   Swiss Federal Research Institute for Forest, Snow, and Landscape, CH-8903 Birmensdorf, Switzerland

E. KORPILAHTI,   Department of Silviculture, University of Helsinki, Unioninkatu 40B, SF-00170 Helsinki, Finland

P.P. KUMAR,   Botany Department, National University of Singapore, Lower Kent Ridge Road, Singapore 0511, Republic of Singapore

T. LUNDMARK,   Department of Forest Genetics and Plant Physiology, Swedish University of Agricultural Sciences, S-90183 Umeå, Sweden

A.J.S. MCDONALD,   Department of Ecology and Environmental Research, Swedish University of Agricultural Sciences, Box 7072, S-75007 Uppsala, Sweden

J.A. MILBURN,   Department of Botany, The University of New England, Armidale, N.S.W. 2351, Australia

L.G. NICKELL,   Nickell Research, Inc., P.O. Box 8487, Hot Springs Village, Arkansas 71909-0487, USA

E. NIKINMAA,   Department of Silviculture, University of Helsinki, Unioninkatu 40B, SF-00170 Helsinki, Finland

J.N. OWENS,   Department of Biology, University of Victoria, P.O. Box 1700 Victoria, B.C., Canada V8W 2Y2

A.S. RAGHAVENDRA,   School of Life Sciences, University of Hyderabad, Hyderabad 500 134, India

H. RICHTER,   Botany Institute, University of Agriculture, A-1100 Vienna, Austria

B. SAUGIER,   Centre d'Orsay, Labo d'Ecologie Vegetale (CNRS), Université of Paris-Sud, Bâtiment 362, F-91405 Orsay Cedex, France

P.J. SCHULTE,   Department of Biological Sciences, University of Nevada, Las Vegas, Nevada 89154, USA

M. STRAND,   Department of Forest Genetics and Plant Physiology, Swedish University of Agricultural Sciences, S-90183 Umeå, Sweden

T.A. THORPE,   Department of Biological Sciences, The University of Calgary, 2500 University Drive N.W., Calgary, Alberta, Canada T2N 1N4

Y. WAISEL,   Department of Botany, Tel Aviv University, Ramat Aviv, Tel Aviv 69978, Israel

C.T. WHEELER,   Department of Botany, University of Glasgow, Glasgow G12 8QQ, Scotland, UK

PREFACE

Trees are among the most fascinating objects of our world, because of their unique stature, importance, and complexity. Trees are the largest and oldest living organisms on the earth. The large variation in tree architecture is an essential component of our beautiful landscapes. Food, fiber, fuel, and other important products for both homes and industries are provided by trees.

In spite of their importance, studies on tree physiology are quite limited, mainly because of the large size of the trees, which imposes difficulties during experimentation. Besides, the internal factors of the tree make the situation for a tree physiologist more complex. Some of these factors are strong periodicity in growth and flowering, continuous shedding of plant parts, a complicated network of assimilate distribution, and often a very long interval between the environmental factor and the physiological response.

The interest in tree physiology has been renewed because of both an increase in the importance of trees and improvement in experimental techniques. Forests are capable of limiting the enrichment of carbon dioxide in our atmosphere, thus alleviating the problem of global warming. Agrosocial forestry and silviculture are a great help not only in improving the economy but also in conserving the environment and human life. Meanwhile, the increase in the expertise and sophistication in the equipment and techniques made it possible to conduct interesting experiments on trees. This led to an explosion in our knowledge of tree physiology in recent years, particularly during the last two decades.

The basic physiology of a tree is similar to that of any other plant. The trees are more complex in their structure and function. The main objective of this book is to provide a comprehensive review of all important aspects of tree physiology. Some of the chapters deal with the ecological components and certain applied topics, strongly related to physiological responses of trees. The book is aimed to be a resource of information for those interested in tree physiology. It should be useful to both graduate students and research workers in forestry, silviculture, horticulture, and plant physiology. I hope it would become an important addition to the already available classic monographs on tree physiology by Professors T.T. Kozlowski, P.J. Kramer, K.V. Thimann, and M.H. Zimmermann.

I take great pleasure to thank all the authors who responded to my invitation and contributed their review articles. I am grateful to Professor Bh. Krishnamurthy, Vice-Chancellor and Professor P.R.K. Reddy, Dean, School of Life Sciences of our University, for their encouragement and support. I thank the research students in my laboratory for their help in preparing the manuscript. Finally, I thank Virginia B. Martin and Philip Manor at John Wiley & Sons, Inc. for their efforts in publishing this book.

A.S. RAGHAVENDRA

Hyderabad, India
May 1991

CONTENTS

PHYSIOLOGY OF TREES

1 Canopy Architecture

D. BARTHELEMY, C. EDELIN, and F. HALLE

Laboratoire de Botanique, Institut Botanique, Montpellier, France

Contents

1.1. Introduction

The study of plant architecture is a recent discipline, and among the first works are the syntheses published in 1970 (1), 1974 (2), and 1978 (3). An original feature of architectural studies is that they were initiated in tropical regions and were at first concerned with the analysis of the aerial vegetative structure of tropical trees. Architectural concepts, however, provide a powerful tool for studying plant form, and investigations quickly spread to temperate species, herbs, and lianas. Even root systems were also investigated.

The architecture of a plant depends on the nature and relative arrangement of each of its parts. At any given time, the architecture is an expression of an equilibrium between endogenous growth processes and exogenous constraints exerted by the environment. The aim of architectural analysis is to identify these endogenous processes by means of observation (4). Considering the plant as a whole, from its germination to its death, architectural analysis is essentially a dynamic approach of plant development. For each species and each stage of development, observations are made on varying numbers of individuals, depending on the complexity of the architecture. When the plant is small, there is no particular problem and it can be analyzed and observed directly. As soon as it is several meters high, it becomes hard, and for a high adult tree, the problem seems insoluble except with the use of destructive methods. Observations, nevertheless, can be carried out on standing trees and most often they are made from ground level with the use of binoculars. This is a make-shift technique that will never replace direct observation; however, it is very efficient when the juvenile architecture is already known. When one is familiar, the skilled observer can recognize, even in a high crown, very precise structural details that would pass unnoticed otherwise. This technique must naturally be augmented with checks on the results and, in this respect, the analysis of dead fallen branches proves to be profitable. It allows the validation of the observations and often provides supplementary information. The results are summarized in a series of diagrams that symbolize successive growth stages. The validity of these diagrams is then checked by comparing them with reality: they must apply to the architecture of any individual of the same species encountered in the field for the analysis to be considered as completed.

Architectural analysis has proved to be probably one of the most efficient means that we have, at present, for the study of the organization of arborescent plants, and architectural concepts are of particular interest for the understanding of crown construction in trees. The present chapter gives up-to-date illustrations of thorough architectural analysis of crown construction in several species (see Section 1.5. of this Chapter). Nevertheless, a good understanding of tree development needs the previous knowledge of three major architectural concepts.

1.2. The concept of architectural model

For a tree, the growth pattern that determines the successive architectural phases is called its *architectural model*, or shorter, its model (1).

The architectural model is an inherent growth strategy that defines both the manner in which the plant elaborates its form, and the resulting architecture. It expresses the nature and the sequence of activity of the endogenous morphogenetic processes of the organism and corresponds to the fundamental growth program on which the entire architecture is established. The identification of the architectural model of any given plant is based on the observation of four major groups of simple morphological features that are well documented (1,3):

- The type of growth: rhythmic or continuous growth
- The branching pattern: presence or absence of vegetative branching; terminal or lateral branching; monopodial or sympodial branching; rhythmic, continuous, or diffuse branching
- The morphological differentiation of axes: orthotropy or plagiotropy
- The position of sexuality (terminal or lateral)

Each architectural model is defined by a particular combination of these morphological features and named after a well-known botanist. Although the number of these combinations is theoretically very high, there are apparently only 23 architectural models found in nature. These models apply equally to arborescent or herbaceous plants, from tropical or temperate regions, and belonging to closely related or distant taxa.

The reader will find much information on each architectural model in the books cited in the references, but Fig. 1.1 illustrates some of these models, each represented by hundreds, if not thousands, of species:

Corner's model (Fig. 1.1a) concerns unbranched plants with lateral inflorescences: e.g., the commonly cultivated tropical "paw-paw tree" (*Carica papaya* L.) or "coconut tree" (*Cocos nucifera* L.).

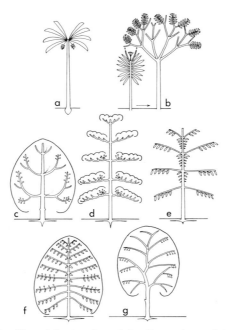

FIG. 1.1. Seven of the 23 architectural models: Corner's model (a), Leeuwenberg's model (b), Rauh's model (c), Aubreville's model (d), Massart's model (e), Roux's model (f), Troll's model (g). (Adapted from Ref. 5.)

Leeuwenberg's model (Fig. 1.1b) consists of a sympodial succession of equivalent units called "modules" (6–8), each of which is orthotropic and determinate in its growth by virtue of the ultimate production of an inflorescence. Branching is three-dimensional. Examples of this model are "cassava" (*Manihot esculenta* Crantz) and the "castor oil plant" (*Ricinus communis* L.).

Rauh's model (Fig. 1.1c) is represented by numerous woody plants from both tropical (e.g., the "rubber tree," *Hevea brasiliensis* Muell. Arg.) and temperate areas (e.g., most *Pinus* spp.); growth and branching are rhythmic on all the monopodial axes and sexuality is lateral.

Aubreville's model (Fig. 1.1d) is much less frequent than the previous ones and represented, for instance, by the tropical "pagoda tree" (*Terminalia catappa* L.): the trunk is monopodial and grows rhythmically, bearing whorled branch tiers. Branches grow rhythmically but are modular; each is plagiotropic by apposition.

Massart's model (Fig. 1.1e) differs only from the previous one in that the branches are plagiotropic by either leaf arrangement or symmetry but never by apposition. Numerous trees exhibit this growth strategy in both temperate (e.g., many gymnospermous genera like *Abies* Miller, *Araucaria* Juss.) and tropical areas (e.g., most species of Myristicaceae or Bombacaceae).

Roux's model (Fig. 1.1f) is very close to Massart's model, from which it differs only in the continuous or diffuse, not rhythmic, growth and branching of the trunk. This model is represented mainly by tropical species such as the "arabian coffee" (*Coffea arabica* L.).

Finally, in *Troll's model* (Fig. 1.1g), which seems to be the most frequent in both tropical and temperate woody species, axes are all plagiotropic, with the architecture built by their continual superposition. Many examples may be found in the Leguminosae family.

Growth patterns defined by the architectural models are genetically determined. Only under extreme ecological conditions is their expression affected by the environment (9–11). Different models can be represented by plants belonging to closely related species. Architectural analysis also shows that some plants frequently exhibit morphological features that are apparently related to two or three models (4,12,13). These intermediate forms prove that there is no real disjunction between the models. On the contrary, it must be considered that all architectures are theoretically possible and that there could be a gradual transition from one to the others. Among this architectural continuum, the models themselves represent the forms that are the most stable and the most frequent, that is to say the most probable biologically.

1.3. The concept of architectural unit

As we have seen, the architectural model represents the basic growth strategy of a plant. Nevertheless, the characters used in its identification are much too general to describe the complete and precise architecture of a plant. For any given plant, the specific expression of its model has been called its "architectural unit" (13).

This concept will be illustrated by the description of its progressive establishment in *Symphonia globulifera* L. (Linnaeus) f. (Clusiaceae), a tree, native from tropical South America and western Africa that conforms to Massart's architectural model (Fig. 1.2). This tree has an orthotropic, monopodial trunk (order 1 axis; A1) with decussate leaves and bears tiers of plagiotropic branches (order 2 axes; A2). When the tree is young (Fig. 1.2a), the trunk is irregularly branched. In the lower part of the tree, order 2 axes are unbranched, but progressively the branches inserted on the upper part of the trunk bear order 3 axes identical to the previous ones but shorter. As the tree grows, the trunk becomes regularly branched (Fig. 1.2b), and branches bear three branching orders (A2, A3, A4; Fig. 1.2c). When adult, the tree keeps its general architecture, conforming to its architectural model (Fig. 1.2d). The branches then have the following architecture (Fig. 1.2e): order 2, 3, and 4 axes are plagiotropic and are similar, except that their length decreases with respect to their increasing branching order; ultimate axes (order 5 axes) are numerous, short shoots that bear terminal inflorescences (1), represented in black in Fig.

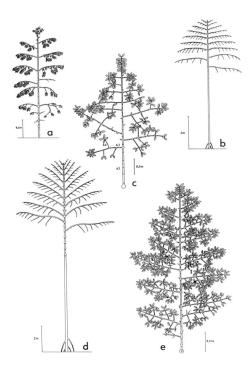

FIG. 1.2. Representation of the developmental sequence of *Symphonia globulifera* leading to the expression of its architectural unit. (Adapted from Ref. 14.)

1.2e. At this stage, the tree bears all its categories of axes: it expresses its specific elementary architecture, i.e., its architectural unit.

As illustrated, the architecture of a plant can be seen as a hierarchical branched system in which the axes can be grouped into categories. The structure and function of each category is characteristic of its rank and, for each species, the number of categories of axes is finite. The identification of the architectural unit is achieved by the complete diagnosis of the functional and morphological features of all of these categories of axes. For each of them the observation of all the architectural characteristics previously described is necessary, but the observations must be as exhaustive as possible and may concern any kind of morphological features, including precise growth direction, phyllotaxis, syllepsis or prolepsis, form and size of foliar organs, and presence or absence of sexuality. The results may be summed up in a table and, with the help of a diagram, they describe and define the specific elementary architecture of each plant, i.e., its architectural unit. Within the context of a general organization, the differences between specific architectural units are thus represented by the number of categories of axes, their functional and morphological features, and their relative positions.

This indicates that the architecture of a fully established branched system, whatever its complexity, can be summarized in terms of a very simple sequence of axes that represents its fundamental organization. In this sequence, leading from axis 1 to the ultimate axes following the specific branching pattern, each branch is the expression of a particular state of meristematic activity and the branch series as a whole can be considered to be tracking the overall activity. In this sense, the architectural unit represents the fundamental architectural and functional elementary unit of any given species.

1.4. The concept of reiteration

Some plants conform to their architectural unit during their whole lifespan; nevertheless, in many plants, especially most trees, this elementary architecture is repeated during ontogenesis.

As defined by Oldeman (2), *reiteration* is a morphogenetic process through which the organism duplicates totally or partially its own elementary architecture, i.e., its architectural unit. The result of this process is called a *reiterated complex*. Two situations illustrate this phenomenon:

- The traumas undergone by a plant throughout its whole life damage the vegetative structure more or less seriously. Generally the destruction of an axis, involving the disappearance of its terminal meristem, allows the development of some previously dormant or suppressed meristems subjacent to the injury. This gives rise to branched systems—reiterated complexes—which develop an architecture identical to that of the bearing axis.

• Within the crown of an old tree, it is common to observe small branched systems that look like the juvenile one and seem to be naturally "grafted" on the bearing plant.

Depending on whether the development of the reiterated complex is due to a trauma, the process is termed as *traumatic reiteration* or *adaptive reiteration*.

As already noted, the development of a plant conforming to its model implies the notion of a sequence in the activity of the whole set of meristems; one speaks of a differentiation sequence. The occurrence of reiterated complexes in this sequence seems to be a move backward within this sequence, a real dedifferentiation. A supernumerary trunk, resulting from the transformation of a growing branch (*sylleptic reiteration*), or from the development of a dormant meristem (*proleptic reiteration*), implies that the plant expresses all over again the juvenile growth pattern. This reversion in the growth pattern can be complete and thus involve again the total expression of the architectural unit leading from axis 1 to the ultimate branching order (*complete reiteration*), or it can be partial and duplicate only a part of the architecture of the plant (*partial reiteration*). This is well illustrated in cases of regeneration in which, when a trunk is cut, it produces sprouts that are identical to the bearing trees, whereas reiterated complexes that develop after a branch has been damaged have the same architecture as this branch.

In fact, reiteration encompasses several aspects (sprouts, root suckers, etc.) that have been known incidentally to botanists for a long time, but the fundamental interest of this concept is to regroup all these phenomena into a coherent whole, to bring out a common morphogenetic event.

Reiteration at first was considered as an opportunistic process. However, recent investigations (4) have demonstrated that this process, in the case of adaptive reiteration, is an automatic event that occurs after a definite threshold of differentiation during the "normal" development of a tree. This will be illustrated by the description of development and crown construction in some forest trees.

1.5. Crown construction of some forest trees

1.5.1. Araucaria hunsteinii *K. Schum.—Araucariaceae (Fig. 1.3)*

Araucaria hunsteinii is endemic in eastern New Guinea. This tree can reach a height of 89 m and 3 m in basal diameter, with a clean bole exceeding 40 m.

In the juvenile stage, *Araucaria hunsteinii* has an architecture conforming to Massart's model (Fig. 1.3a): a monopodial orthotropic trunk with a spiral phyllotaxis, growing rhythmically and producing tiers of dorsiventral plagiotropic branches. Each of these branches is a monopodium that branches rhythmically in a horizontal plane. The A3 branchlets, also plagiotropic, have limited growth and are self-pruning.

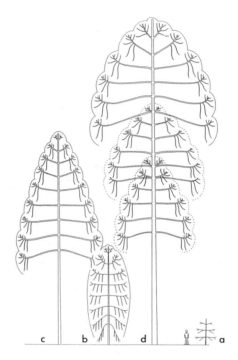

FIG. 1.3. Diagrammatic representation of the developmental sequence of *Araucaria hunsteinii*. (Adapted from Ref. 4.)

During its growth, the tree gradually changes its architecture (Fig. 1.3b,c). It acquires orthotropic branches with a radial symmetry, on which the A2 and A3 axes seem to have lost all rhythmicity of growth and branching, and bear leaves that are different from those found on plagiotropic branches.

The tree, thus modified, continues to grow (Fig. 1.3d). By means of a partial reiterative process, new proleptic branches are produced in the place of the old whorls; they contribute to the development of "nesting" crowns that are produced in succession regularly during the whole lifespan of the organism.

Sexuality only occurs when the tree has acquired its orthotropic branches. There seems to be an important spatial disjunction in sexual partitioning, the female cones being formed in the first crown of the tree and the male catkins in the later crowns.

1.5.2. Agathis dammara *(A.B. Lambert) L.C. Richard—Araucariaceae (Fig. 1.4)*

Agathis dammara is a native tree from tropical forests of Southeast Asia that can be found from Sumatra and Borneo to New Guinea.

When young (Fig. 1.4a), this tree conforms to Massart's architectural model: after a short stage with decussate leaves, the monopodial, orthotropic, and

FIG. 1.4. Diagrammatic representation of the developmental sequence of *Agathis dammara*. Adapted from Edelin (15). Ultimate axes are not represented.

rhythmically growing trunk has a spiral phyllotaxis. It bears tiers of plagiotropic branches showing two branching orders (order 3 axes not represented
in Fig. 1.4a) with decussate leaves.

As it grows, the tree becomes more branched and its architecture changes
(Fig. 1.4b). In the upper part of the tree, the general production of order 4
axes is accompanied by a turning up of the order 2 axes, which become
orthotropic with spiral phyllotaxis. During the development of the tree this
process goes on, and the whole architecture of the tree is modified (Fig. 1.4c).

When the tree is older, order 5 axes occur and, as previously, their formation is accompanied by a profound transformation of the architecture of
their bearing axis. The result is that order 3 axes become orthotropic with
spiral phyllotaxis, following the same metamorphosis as described previously
for order 2 axes. In the crown of such a tree (Fig. 1.4d), these two turned
up branching order axes have thickened in diameter and have the same architecture as the young tree, conforming to its architectural unit: they represent strong complete reiterated complexes (R).

1.5.3. Virola surinamensis Warb.—*Myristicaceae (Fig. 1.5)*

Virola surinamensis is native to the tropical rainforest of the northeastern
South America, where it is common along riverbanks and where it can reach
a height of 40–45 m.

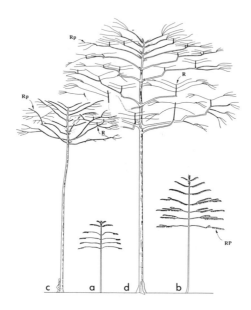

FIG. 1.5. Diagrammatic representation of the developmental sequence of *Virola sur-inamensis*. Ultimate axes are not represented.

The young tree conforms to Massart's architectural model (Fig. 1.5a): the monopodial, rhythmically growing and branching trunk has a spiral phyllotaxis and bears regular tiers of perfectly horizontal branches.

When the tree reach a height of 5–10 m, the architecture of the branches is modified (Fig. 1.5b); each branch has a determinate growth, by virtue of the death of its extremity, and forms a fork. Each element of the fork has the same architecture as the bearing branch and constitute a partial reiterated complex (Rp). Each fork may consist of two to five reiterated complexes.

As the tree grows, its branches become larger, and partial reiterated complexes are progressively more numerous.

As soon as the tree reaches a height of 15–25 m, its architecture is modified. On the larger branches some elements of the forks tend to turn up in their basal part (Fig. 1.5c), and finally complete reiterated complexes (R) arise from the basal part and upper side of the fork.

As the tree becomes older this process continues and the crown of an old tree (Fig. 1.5d) is built up by numerous forks that bear themselves numerous complete reiterated complexes, giving to the individuals of this species their characteristic crown.

1.5.4. Artocarpus elasticus *Reinw.—Moraceae (Fig. 1.6)*

Artocarpus elasticus is a tree frequently found in the Asiatic secondary forests, where it occurs in all lowland forest formations. It is known to grow up to 40 m and to have strong buttresses at the base of the trunk.

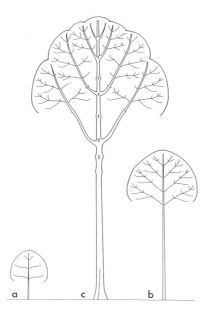

FIG. 1.6. Diagrammatic representation of the developmental sequence of *Artocarpus elasticus*. Adapted from Edelin (4). Ultimate axes are not represented.

The young *Artocarpus elasticus* has an orthotropic monopodial trunk with rhythmic growth and branching and spiral phyllotaxis. Its horizontal–oblique branches have erect distal ends and also grow rhythmically with spiral phyllotaxis. They at first consist of a single axis (A2) which is unbranched (Fig. 1.6a), slender and self-pruning, and subsequently some A3 axes, which are equally thin and short-lived (Fig. 1.6b). This production is rhythmical and is accompanied by the strengthening and turning up of axes 2.

The formation of supplementary A4 axes (Fig. 1.6c) accentuates this transformation. These are rare at first, but become more and more numerous, their development marking the establishment of large reiterated complexes (A2 + A3 + A4). The presence of these complexes on the trunk consolidates the crown structure of the tree.

The organism has then almost attained its maximal height and gradually self-prunes. Its final development (i.e., position of sexuality, possible formation of proleptic reiterated complexes) has not been observed.

1.5.5. Dipterocarpus costulatus *V. S1.—Dipterocarpaceae (Fig. 1.7)*

Dipterocarpus costulatus is native to Southeast Asia. This tree conforms to Massart's model. It has an orthotropic monopodial trunk with spiral phyllotaxis and rhythmic growth.

When juvenile (Fig. 1.7a), it branches (A2) are plagiotropic, distichous, and arranged in regular tiers. As it develops (Fig. 1.7b), the trunk produces increasingly larger and ramified branches. In the lower part of the tree, these

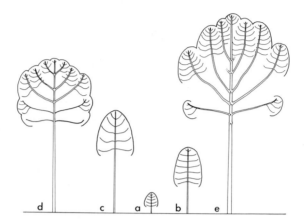

FIG. 1.7. Diagrammatic representation of the developmental sequence of *Diptero-carpus costulatus*. (Adapted from Ref. 4.) Ultimate axes are not represented.

axes bear lateral branches (A3) identical to axes 2. In the upper part of the tree, the production of order 4 branches is spasmodic and is accompanied by a profound transformation. Axis 2 tends toward orthotropy; its phyllotaxis becomes spirodistichous almost over its whole length, which has the imme-diate consequence of arranging the pseudowhorled A3 branches radially. The latter, just as axes 4, remain plagiotropic, distichous, and with an erect ex-tremity with spirodistichous phyllotaxis at their distal ends. In the middle part of the tree, the trunk bears branches whose structure is intermediate between the two preceding cases. These features of development become more pro-nounced as the tree grows (Fig. 1.7c). The branches then have the following architecture: A2 axes are orthotropic with spiral phyllotaxis throughout the whole length; A3 axes are plagiotropic, with rhythmically produced lateral branches arranged radially in tiers on A2; A4 axes are also plagiotropic, are subopposed, and develop on a horizontal plane.

This progressive development nonetheless occurs step by step. The ap-pearance of a new branching order is followed by an architecturally stable period of a variable duration that itself precedes and prepares for the following stage of the development. As the tree grows this process goes on and becomes more pronounced. The general production of order 5 branches (Fig. 1.7d and e) coincides with the formation of the syllleptic reiterated complexes, which represent the major limbs of the adult tree and on which sexuality occurs laterally among the ultimate axes.

1.5.6. Shorea leprosula Micq. — Dipterocarpaceae (Fig. 1.8)

Shorea leprosula is another Dipterocarpaceae native of Southeast Asia. This tree conforms to *Roux's* architectural model.

When juvenile *Shorea leprosula* has an orthotropic monopodial trunk with continuous branching and spiral phyllotaxis, bearing distichous plagiotropic

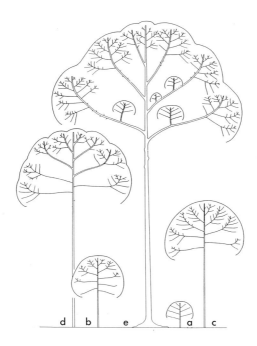

FIG. 1.8. Diagrammatic representation of the developmental sequence of *Shorea leprosula*. (Adapted from Ref. 4.) Ultimate axes are not represented.

branches that have two branching orders, A2 and A3 (at the stage shown in Fig. 1.8a).

As it grows, the tree becomes more branched and its architecture changes. The production of order 4 branches (at the stage shown in Fig. 1.8b,c) is accompanied by a turning up of the A2 axes, which become orthotropic, with spiral phyllotaxis. The A3 branches become orthotropic in turn when the ultimate A5 axes are formed (at the stage shown in Fig. 1.8d); and the whole branch, consequently strengthened, then becomes a reiterated complex.

The infrastructure of the tree is then established (Fig. 1.8e) and, on the most drooping limbs, some proleptic reiterated complexes of a modest size appear.

1.5.7. Shorea stenoptera *Burck.—Dipterocarpaceae (Fig. 1.9)*

Shorea stenoptera is a tree native to Southeast Asia that conforms to Roux's model.

Up to 1–2 m high (Fig. 1.9a), the trunk is not branched. Then (Fig. 1.9b), the orthotropic trunk, a continuously branching monopodium, bears plagiotropic distichous branches. Each of these consists of a single axis 2, rarely branched, which dies and self-prunes rapidly. Proleptic reiterated complexes grow out of some dormant buds borne on the trunk (Fig. 1.9c); they branch rapidly, and their plagiotropic branches are identical to those described above.

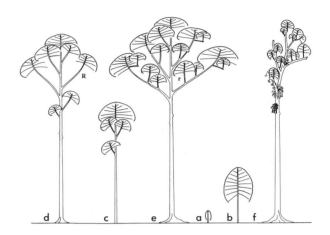

FIG. 1.9. Diagrammatic representation of the developmental sequence of *Shorea stenoptera*. (Adapted from Ref. 4.) Ultimate axes are not represented.

This reiteration occurs, although the tree is still in the shade of understorey; most of the time, these reiterated complexes do not exceed 4–5 m before precociously dying and falling. When the tree reaches the forest canopy, the same process goes on, but this time the reiterated complexes formed do not die (Fig. 1.9d). On the contrary, they produce strong limbs (R). Within the crown of the adult tree (Fig. 1.9e), new proleptic reiterated complexes (r) appear on the established infrastructure. Some of them, the longer ones, are formed on the upper side of the limbs. The others grow out from the branches and appear perpendicularly to them. The development and maintenance of the crown throughout the years is ensured by the constant renewal of these short-lived reiterated complexes.

This process continues on the old tree, which is marked by the death and gradual dislocation of the crown (Fig. 1.9f).

1.5.8. Tectona grandis *L.—Verbenaceae (Fig. 1.10)*

Teak (*Tectona grandis*) is an Asiatic tree. Its natural area of distribution consists of India, Sri Lanka, Burma, Thaïland, Vietnam, and possibly Indonesia, where it grows spontaneously. But it has been introduced to many other countries in Africa, South America, the West Indies, and Southeast Asia, particularly in Malaysia. The height of this middle-sized tree is on the average 35 m and exceptionally up to 50–60 m. It develops in tropical climates with a marked dry season and contributes to the formation of dry forests or moist forests and is always deciduous.

Teak has a rhythmical growth and schematically develops in two consecutive phases. During the first phase, the tree is monopodial. The trunk produces plagiotropic branches up to order 3 (not represented in the diagrams). The at first sparse, then generalized formation of order 4 axes, which is initially sparse, is later accompanied by a thickening and turning up of the affected

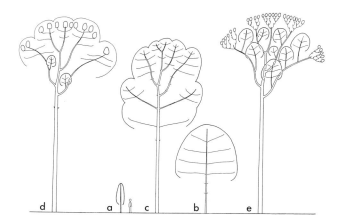

FIG. 1.10. Diagrammatic representation of the developmental sequence of *Tectona grandis*. (Adapted from Ref. 4.) Ultimate axes are not represented.

branches, the intensity of this phenomenon increasing with the number of these ultimate branches. These perennial reiterated complexes constitute the crown infrastructure (Fig. 1.10a–c).

Flowering, terminal on every axis, brings an end to this growth phase (Fig. 1.10d). A sympodial development is then established, with determinate modules having terminal inflorescences succeeding one another for a few years until this process itself becomes exhausted. In parallel with these events, more reiterated complexes grow on the limbs (Fig. 1.10e). They undergo a similar development that leads them to terminal reproduction and to death. The perennial character of the tree is ensured by the continuous replacement of these complexes.

1.5.9. Gmelina arborea L.—Verbenaceae (Fig. 1.11)

Gmelina arborea is a pioneer tree native to Asia. Its natural area spreads from India to Thaïland and from Sri Lanka to Assam, but it has been introduced into many Asiatic, African, or South American countries. This tree develops optimally in the humid semideciduous lowland forests. However, it also adapts very well to dry (central India) or wet (evergreen) forests. The tallest individuals recorded are in Burma; they exceed 35 m and their trunk diameters measure up to 1 m.

Gmelina arborea L. is a rhythmically growing tree. During the first part of its development, the trunk is an orthotropic monopodium with decussate leaves and it bears tiers of plagiotropic branches (A2 + A3) (Fig. 1.11a–c).

The progressive appearance of order 4 axes is accompanied by a modification in their architecture (Fig. 1.11d). They are more upwardly vertical and tend to acquire the structure of reiterated complexes; this ultimate stage is reached by only a rather low proportion of individuals.

Flowering (not represented on the diagrams) occurring at this stage, is firstly peripheral on the extremity of the ultimate axes. It progressively spreads

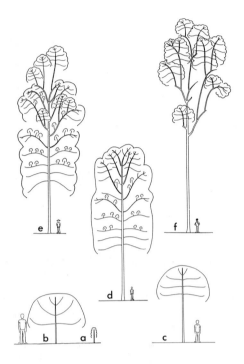

FIG. 1.11. Diagrammatic representation of the developmental sequence of *Gmelina arborea*. (Adapted from Ref. 4.) Ultimate axes are not represented.

to the branches of a lower order and then to the trunk which bends, the apex dying.

Proleptic reiterated complexes (Fig. 1.11e) then ensure continuity of growth. They appear on the branches or on the initial trunk, and their development leads to the formation of the new crown. The latter constitutes the sympodial superposition of such reiterated complexes throughout the years (Fig. 1.11f). These complexes become smaller and smaller and are affected in their turn by flowering, until the tree is exhausted.

1.5.10. Acacia auriculiformis *A. Cunn. ex Benth.—Mimosaceae (Fig. 1.12)*

Acacia auriculiformis is a pioneer tree native of southern New Guinea and northern Australia. This species has been introduced into numerous tropical countries in Africa and Asia because of its quick-growing capacity, its simple culture requirements, and the use of its wood as fuel. It is a small tree not exceeding 25 m in height and with a dense and generally very wide crown. Its trunk is short and bears limbs that can be inserted very low.

Acacia auriculiformis has an orthotropic monopodial trunk with spiral phyllotaxis bearing, when juvenile, plagiotropic A2 branches grouped in regularly spaced tiers (Fig. 1.12a,b).

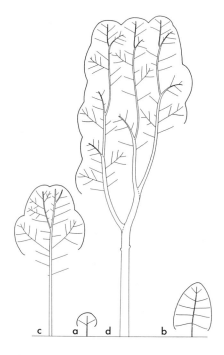

FIG. 1.12. Diagrammatic representation of the developmental sequence of *Acacia auriculiformis*. (Adapted from Ref. 4.) Ultimate axes are not represented.

As it develops, the branching pattern becomes progressively continuous; there is a sporadic production of ever more ramified branches (A3 and A4 axes) (Fig. 1.12c). The formation of the ultimate order 5 branches is accompanied by the establishment of reiterated complexes. As it reaches the end of its growth, the trunk curves over and flowering (not represented in the diagrams), which has started to occur a few years previously, spreads over the whole crown.

A trunk is maintained by the development of a series of reiterated complexes. These undergo the same process, flower, and then soon die. They are in their turn augmented by new reiterated complexes.

Thus, from the age of 3–4 years onward, the crown of *Acacia auriculiformis* is constructed by the sympodial superposition of trees naturally "grafted" to one another (Fig. 1.12d). This process ceases shortly before the death of the tree, a critical point in which every remaining vegetative axis is apparently involved in flowering.

1.6. Discussion

As already noticed, some arborescent plants may remain conform to their architectural unit during their lifespan, e.g., a large number of pioneer trees (8). The development of most of the trees, however, is marked by a progressive and profound modification of their initial architecture. Whether the crown of the tree is built up by partial reiteration (*Araucaria hunsteinii*), by complete reiteration (*Agathis dammara, Artocarpus elasticus, Dipterocarpus costulatus* etc.), or by a combination of both (*Virola surinamensis*), reiteration represents the fundamental process by which canopy *architecture* is established.

Even with a limited sample of tree species, one can appreciate that crown construction has some obvious internal consistency. When young, the tree expresses its architectural unit. Following a precise sequence of events, all the categories of axes are built up progressively and successively. The appearance of a new branching order is followed by an architecturally stable period of variable duration that itself precedes and prepares for the following stage of development. After a certain threshold of differentiation, the general production of some new-order branches coincides with the formation of reiterated complexes, which reproduce, totally or partially, the elementary architecture (i.e., the architectural unit) and represent the major limbs of the adult tree.

So, canopy architecture is built up by a profound morphogenetic transformation of the young tree and crown construction by means of reiteration represents a true "architectural metamorphosis" (4,12).

Whether the limbs of the old tree are established by proleptic reiteration (*Shorea stenoptera*) or sylleptic reiteration (*Agathis dammara, Dipterocarpus costulatus, Artocarpus elasticus* etc.), the crown of the old tree is a true colony of individuals of various sizes. The reiterated complexes, naturally "grafted" together, are relatively independent and exert a strong selective competition on each other (16).

Following a progressive and precise sequence of events, each species expresses its own "reiterative strategy" (5). However, these events are incorporated into a more general cycle that leads the "colonial tree" from germination to death.

The life of a forest tree (Fig. 1.13) is thus marked by three major architectural stages, which can be represented as:

- The "tree of the future" (Fig. 1.13a,b), corresponding to the growth in the understorey, and which possesses an architecture that strictly conform to the architectural unit. The tree expresses its architectural unit from axis 1 to ultimate axis (i.e., the threshold of reiteration).
- The "tree of the present" (Fig. 1.13c): the tree has reached the forest canopy and has developed a large crown by means of adaptive and traumatic reiteration. It is composed of the juxtaposition of progressively smaller reiterated complexes, which are termed *arborescent, frutescent,* and *herbaceous*.
- The "tree of the past" (Fig. 1.13d) is marked by the death and the gradual dislocation of the crown; the limbs start breaking, leaving stumps on the trunk on which populations of epiphytes become established. The crown progressively breaks up, heralding the death and fall of the tree.

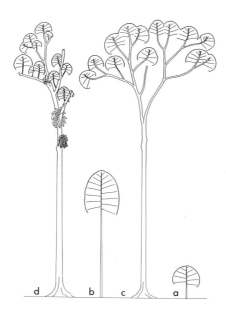

FIG. 1.13. Diagrammatic representation of the developmental sequence of the forest tree. (a,b) the tree of the future; (c) the tree of the present; (d) the tree of the past. (Adapted from Ref. 4.)

1.7. Concluding remarks

The discovery of the concepts of architectural model, architectural unit, and reiteration has provided botanists a powerful means of studying plant form and structure. Until the present day, more than 150 families have undergone architectural analysis, and these observations concern either herbaceous or woody plants from both temperate and tropical regions. All these studies have led to a general interpretation of the architecture and of the developmental sequences of plants, especially tropical woody plants.

Nevertheless, numerous problems remain unsolved. We have already a few examples of thorough architectural analysis of crowns in several tree species, but the sample of species is too narrow, and the diversity of the results is large. Therefore, any synthetic view of canopy architecture would be prematurate at the moment.

In our research group, the architectural analysis of crown construction, and canopy architecture is now in progress; we are working in the tropics and in temperate regions as well, but it could take some time before a synthesis to be achieved.

1.8. References

1. F. Hallé and R.A.A. Oldeman, *Essai sur l'architecture et la dynamique de croissance des arbres tropicaux*, Masson, Paris, 1970, p. 178.

2. R.A.A. Oldeman, *L'architecture de la forêt guyanaise*, Memo No. 73, O.R.S.T.O.M., Paris, 1974, p. 204.

3. F. Hallé, R.A.A. Oldeman, and P.B. Tomlinson, *Tropical Trees and Forests*, Springer-Verlag, Berlin, 1978, p. 441.

4. C. Edelin, *L'architecture monopodiale: l'exemple de quelques arbres d'Asie Tropicale*, Ph.D. thesis, Univ. Montpellier II, France, 1984, p. 258.

5. F. Hallé and C. Edelin, "L'analyse architecturale des arbres," in *6e Colloq. sur les Recherches Fruitières* (Bordeaux, France, C.T.I.F.L., Pont de la Maye et I.N.R.A.), Paris, 1987, pp. 5–19.

6. M.F. Prevost, *Bull. Soc. bot. Fr.*, **114** (lett. bot.), pp. 24–36 (1967).

7. M.F. Prevost, "Modular construction and its distribution in tropical woody plants," in P.B. Tomlinson and M.H. Zimmermann, eds., *Tropical Trees as Living Systems*, Cambridge Univ. Press, 1978, pp. 223–231.

8. F. Hallé, "Modular growth in seed plants," in J.L. Harper, B.R. Rosen, and J. White, eds, *The Growth and Form of Modular Organisms*, [*Philos. Trans. Roy. Soc. London, Ser. B*, **313**, 77–87 (1986)].

9. A. Temple, *Ericaceae. Etude architecturale de quelques espèces*, D.E.A. Botanique Tropicale, Univ. Montpellier II, 1975, p. 95.

10. F. Hallé, "Architectural variation at specific level of tropical trees," in P.B. Tomlinson and M.H. Zimmermann, eds., *Tropical Trees as Living Systems*, Cambridge Univ. Press, 1978, pp. 209–221.

11. D. Barthelemy, "Establishment of modular growth in a tropical tree: *Isertia coccinea* Vahl. (Rubiaceae)," in J.L. Harper, B.R. Rosen, and J. White, eds., *The Growth and Form of Modular Organisms* [*Philos. Trans. Roy. Soc. London, Sér. B*, **313**, 89–94 (1986)].

12. F. Hallé and F.S.P. Ng, *Malays. For*, 44(2–3), 222–223 (1981).

13. C. Edelin, *Images de l'architecture des Conifères*, Ph.D. thesis, 3rd cycle, Biologie végétale, Univ. Montpellier II, France, 1977, p. 255.

14. D. Barthelemy, *Architecture et sexualité chez quelques plantes tropicales: le concept de floraison automatique*, Ph.D thesis, Univ. Montpellier II., France, 1988, p. 262.

15. C. Edelin, "Stratégie de réitération et édification de la cime chez les Conifères," in *Comptes Rend. Colloq. Int. l'Arbre*, Montpellier, Sept. 9–14, 1985, Naturalia Monspeliensa, No. hors-sér., 1986, pp. 139–158.

16. E. Torquebiau, *The Reiteration of the Architectural Model. A Demographic Approach to the Tree*, Mém. D.E.A., Ecologie générale et appliquée, 1979, p. 51.

2 Photosynthesis

REINHART J. CEULEMANS
Department of Biology, University of Antwerpen, Wilrijk-Antwerpen,
Belgium

and
BERNARD SAUGIER
Université Paris-Sud, Ecologie Végétale (CNRS),
Orsay Cedex, France

Contents

2.1. Introduction

Forests represent 21% of the continental area, 76% of terrestrial biomass, and 37% of its bioproductivity (1,2). Thus, the trees in a forest stand form an essential part in the functioning of the terrestrial biosphere, especially in the carbon cycle. Yet tree photosynthesis is far less studied than crop photosynthesis for several reasons: the size of adult trees, which makes sampling very difficult; the large number of species; the difficulty in measuring photosynthesis of entire trees or of forest stands; and the quasi-absence of tree growth models based on photosynthesis and physiological processes.

The harvestable product of a tree—the stem—depends not only on photosynthetic carbon uptake by the foliage but also on respiration of the various organs and carbon investment into renewable organs (leaves, fine roots) and nonharvested organs (branches and large roots). Consequently, there is no obvious relationship between photosynthesis and wood production. However, a fast-growing tree needs a high photosynthesis, but the reverse is not necessarily true.

One of the first detailed and authoritative reviews on carbon dioxide gas exchange rates of trees and woody plants, including a list of average maximum rates of CO_2 uptake and dark respiration by Larcher (3) appeared in 1969. More recently, excellent reviews on photosynthesis-related topics in forest tree species were done by Schulze (4) and Jarvis and Sandford (5). The increased interest in integrated plant responses (mainly of trees) to environmental pollution, the fascinating possibilities of energy production from biomass plantations using fast-growing tree species, and the steady improvement in measuring techniques, have resulted in a new impetus to (eco)physiological studies on trees and woody plant species during the last two decades.

Schulze (4) and Jarvis and Sandford (5) have reviewed photosynthesis and growth of forest trees particularly in relation to growth form and productivity. This chapter mainly aims to review absolute data on tree photosynthesis during the past two decades, discuss the genetic variation in photosynthesis among different genera/species, and analyze the role of photosynthesis in growth and yield. The review further covers the relation between tree photosynthesis and related phenomena, namely, forest productivity, environment, canopy, and ecosystem.

In terms of competition and total carbon turnover, woody plants are classified into trees and bushes according to height (4). In this chapter, however, woody plants are rather separated into deciduous (broad-leafed) and evergreen (broad-leafed and coniferous) forms according to their leaf longevity. Larch (*Larix* spp.) is a deciduous rather than an evergreen coniferous species with a growing season significantly shorter than that of most other evergreens.

When compared to other land plants, trees have a number of unique characteristics such as their longevity and complexity, large size, and nonliving (and thus nonrespiring) components of biomass, which all result in a complex structure–function relationship. Moreover (and contrary to most agronomic crops), large natural stands provide sufficient genetic variability to be tapped during breeding and selection programs. In woody plants the biomass of stems and roots increases continually over time, although there is a superimposed seasonal variation because of shedding of various plant parts.

2.2. Variation in photosynthesis within and between species

Although tree photosynthesis is generally thought to be low (3,6,7), photosynthetic capacity values (on a leaf area basis) cover a rather large range, from ~2 μmol m^{-2} s^{-1} to >25 μmol m^{-2} s^{-1} (Table 2.1 and Fig. 2.1). The term *photosynthetic capacity* (A_m) is defined here as the net rate of CO_2 exchange measured under optimal conditions (i.e., saturating light, optimum temperature and low vapor-pressure deficit, except CO_2 and O_2 concentrations, which are at the normal atmospheric level). The data on absolute values of photosynthetic capacity and dark respiration for different genera and species of deciduous and evergreen broad-leafed and coniferous trees presented in Table 2.1 have been compiled primarily from the literature of the last two decades. For coniferous tree species, photosynthetic gas-exchange parameters

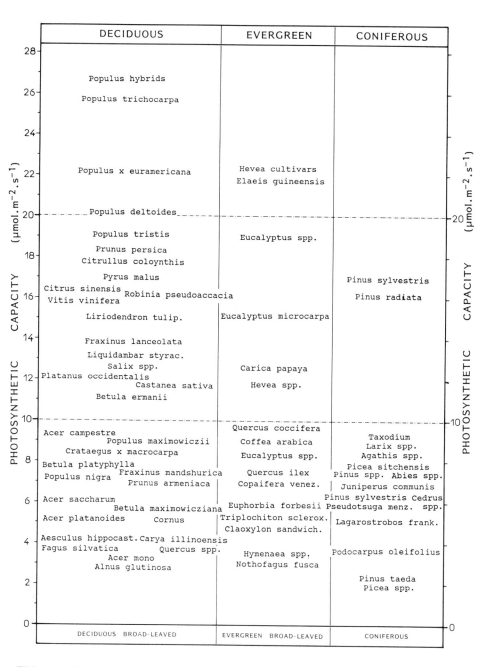

FIG. 2.1. Photosynthetic capacity for an important selection of different species and genera of deciduous and evergreen broad-leafed and coniferous woody plants. Information on growth conditions, experimental procedures, methods, exact data, and literature references can be found in Table 2.1.

Table 2.1. Average photosynthetic capacity $(A_m)^a$ and dark respiration rates (R_d) of different broad-leafed and coniferous tree species.[b] For a number of species without common name the family is indicated within brackets.

Tree species name	Common name	A_m^a	R_d	Conditions[b]	Method[c]	Ref.
Deciduous broad-leafed trees						
Acer campestre	Field maple	9		N/N	I	71
Acer mono		4–5	1–1.5	N/G	I	56
Acer platanoides	Maple	5				72
Acer pseudoplatanus	Sycamore	8		G/G	I	73
Acer saccharinum	Silver maple	6–7		N/N	I	68
Acer saccharum	Sugar maple	3		G/L	I	66
Aesculus hippocastanum	Horse-chestnut	5		N/N	I	57
Alnus glutinosa	Black alder	4		G/L	I	74
Alnus rubra	Red alder	6		G/L	I	44
Betula ermanii	Mountain birch	11	1.5	N/L	I	64,75
Betula maximowicziana	Birch	4–8	1–2	N/L	I	64,75,76
Betula pendula	White birch	9–15		N/N	I	57
Betula platyphylla	White birch	6–10	1.3–1.5	N/G	I	56
				F/L	I	76
Carya illinoensis	Pecan	5–7		G/G	I	77
		10		N/N	I	78
Castanea sativa	Sweet chestnut	8–16		N/N	R	79
		10–13		N/L	I	80
				N/N	C	81
Citrus sinensis	Orange	8–17		G/L	I	83
Crataegus × macrocarpa	Hawthorn	9–11		N/N	I	71,84
Fagus silvatica	European beech	2–6	0.7	N/L	I	65,85
Fraxinus lanceolata	Green ash	14		G/G	I	86
Fraxinus lanuginosa	Ash	4–8		N/G	I	56,64

Species	Common name					Ref.
Fraxinus mandshurica	Ash	6–10		N/G	I	64
Fraxinus pennsylvanica	Green ash	20–25	2	N/N	I	87
		5		N/N	I	57
Liriodendron tulipifera	Tulip tree	10–17		G/L	I	86,88
Liquidambar styraciflua	Sweetgum	6–11		G/L	I	89
		13		G/L	I	88
Malus domestica (Syn. *Py-*	Apple	6–19		N/N	R	25
rus malus)		13		N/L	I	90
						91
	Apple	8				92
Platanus occidentalis	London plane-tree	6–9		N/N	C	93,94
Populus deltoides	Eastern cottonwood	6–11 (13)		G/L	I	88
		19		N/N	R	29,95
				N/N		96
				N/L	I	67
Populus maximowiczii	Japanese poplar	9	0.13	G/L	I	97
Populus nigra	Black poplar	5–10	0.9–1	G/L	I	26,97
Populus tremula	European aspen	9		N/N	I	57
Populus tremuloides	Quaking aspen	20–22	0.7	N/N	I	31
						98
Populus trichocarpa	Black cottonwood	10–12		G/L	I	44,99
		14–15		N/N	I	29
		20–22		N/N	I	95
Populus tristis		25–30		N/N	R	7,100
				G/G; N/N	I	13
Populus euramericana	Euramerican poplar	10–16	0.6–1.5	G/L	I	26,99,101
				G/?		28
		20–25		N/N	I	13
				G/L	I	13,40
				N/N	R	7
P. nigra × *P. maximowiczii*		5	0.75	G/L	I	102

Table 2.1. (Continued)

Tree species name	Common name	A_m^a	R_d	Conditions[b]	Method[c]	Ref.
Deciduous broad-leafed trees						
P. trichocarpa × P. deltoides		23–25	1.2–1.9	G/G	I	103
				G/L	I	27,104
				N/N	I	29
Prunus armeniaca	Apricot	3–6		N/N	I	82,105
Prunus persica	Peach	20		N/N	I	106
		2.5 (?)		G/L	I	43
		3–6		G/G	R	107
Prunus spinosa	Blackthorn	10–12		N/N	I	84
		9–10		N/N	I	71
Pyrus communis	Pear	13	0.6	N/L	I	108
		18		N/N	I	108
Quercus macrocarpa		4	1–2	N/G	I	56
				G/L	I	66
Quercus mongolica	Oak	5–7	1	N/G	I	56
Quercus robur	Pedunculate oak	4				72
Quercus rubra	Northern red oak	5 (?)				109
Quercus sessiliflora	Chinese oak	3–8		G/L	I	86,110
				N/L	I	55
Quercus velutina	Black oak	7	1.5	N/G	I	56
				G/L	I	66
Robinia pseudoacacia	False acacia	13–17		G/L	I	88
Salix viminalis	Willow	13–16		G/G	I	45
S. purpurea × viminalis				N/N	I	111
Salix aquatica						
Vitis vinifera	Grapevine	5	1	G/L	I	14

				N/L	I	15
		7	2	N/N; G/G	I	15
		19		N/N	I	82
		17		N/N	R	47

Evergreen broad-leafed trees

Carica papaya	Papaya	13	0.9–1	G/L	I	112
Claoxylon sandwichense	(Hawaii)	3–7		G/G	I	16
Coffea arabica	Coffee	9		N/N		91
Copaifera venezuelana	(Caesalpinoideae)	7–8		G/G	I	113
Elaeis guineensis	Oil palm	20–25	1.4–2.1	N/N	R	52
				N/N	I	49
Eucalyptus behriana	Eucalyptus	8		N/N	I	114
Eucalyptus camaldulensis		2–6 (?)		N/N	R	115
Eucalyptus deglupta		18		N/N	I	116
Eucalyptus globulus		7		N/N	I	117
Eucalyptus maculata spp. *globoidea*		13		N/N	I	118
Eucalyptus microcarpa		15		G/L	I	119
Eucalyptus pauciflora		15–20		?/G	I	120
				N/N	I	114
Euphorbia forbesii	(Euphorbiaceae)	6–8		G/G	I	16
Hevea brasiliensis	Rubber tree	5–26	1.7–7.7	N/N	I	121
(selected clones)				G/L	I	122
Hevea spp.	Rubber tree	4–21	1.5–4.7	N/N	I	121
Hymenaea courbaril	(Caesalpinoideae)	4–5		G/G	I	113
Hymenaea parviflora	(Caesalpinoideae)	3–4		G/G	I	113
Nothofagus fusca	New Zealand red beech	4		G/G	I	123
Quercus coccifera	Kermes oak	10		N/N	I	124
Quercus ilex	Evergreen oak	3–7		N/N	C	125
Quercus suber	Cork oak	5–6	0.4	N/N	I	126
Triplochiton scleroxylon	Obeche	4–7	0.3–0.8	G/L	I	24

Table 2.1. (Continued)

Tree species name	Common name	A_m^a	R_d	Conditions[b]	Method[c]	Ref.
		Coniferous trees				
Abies alba	White fir	2–8		N/L	I	48
				N/L	I	41
Abies lasiocarpa	Subalpine fir	8.7		N/N	I	127
Agathis microstachya	(*Araucariaceae*)	4–6		G/G	I	113
Agathis robusta	(*Araucariaceae*)	6–10		G/G	I	113
				G/L	I	119
Cedrus atlantica	Atlas cedar	4–7.5			I	41
Cedrus brevifolia		9.6		G/L	I	128
Cedrus deodara	Himalaya cedar	3.8–4.0		G/L	I	128
Cedrus libani	Lebanon cedar	5.6		G/L	I	128
Juniperus communis	Juniper	7		N/N	I	127
Larix decidua	European larch	6–7	0.5	N/N	I	129
				N/N	I	8,9
Larix leptolepis	Japanese larch	8.3		N/N	I	8,9
		8.9		N/N	I	84
L. decidua × *leptolepis*	Hybrid larch	9.8		N/N	I	8,9
		8		N/N	I	84
Lagarostrobos franklinii	Huon pine	5–7	4	N/N	I	130
Picea abies	Norway spruce	2–3		N/N	I	12
				G/L	I	131
Picea engelmannii	Engelmann spruce	3–4	0.5	G/G	I	132
		4–5				124
Picea sitchensis	Sitka spruce	7–9		N/G	I	133
		3–6–8	1.6–2.1	G/G	I	50
				G/L; N/L	I	134

		A_m	R_d	Conditions	Method	Ref.
Pinus contorta	Lodgepole pine	3		G/G	I	135
		9		N/N	I	127
Pinus halepensis	Alep's pine	6–8		N/L; N/N	I	136
Pinus ponderosa	Ponderosa pine	—	2.8	N/N	I	137
Pinus radiata	Monterey pine	1.6–6		N/G	I	138
		10		N/N	I	114
		12		G/G	I	123
		16		N/N	I	11
Pinus sylvestris	Scots pine	3–7		Model	R	32
		12.5		N/N	I	35
		17		N/N	I	19,20
Pinus taeda	Loblolly pine	4–6		N/N; N/L	I	139
		2.5		G/L	I	10
		4		G/L	I	89
Podocarpus oleifolius	(*Coniferales*)	4		N/L	I	140
Podocarpus rospigliosii		2		N/L	I	140
Pseudotsuga menziesii	Douglas fir	2.3–3.5		N/G	I	141,142
		6–9		G/G	I	123
		4.5	0.7	N/L	I	33
Pseudotsuga macrocarpa	Fir	2.3				41
Taxodium distichum	Bald cypress	7.6		G/G	I	46

[a] Photosynthetic capacity values refer to maximum CO_2 exchange rates at saturating light, 20–25°C and 330 ppm CO_2. Dark respiration rates were measured at (or corrected to) atmospheric temperatures of 20–25°C. All values of A_m and R_d are expressed in µmol s^{-1}m^{-2} of single leaf area. For coniferous species A_m values were expressed per unit of projected leaf area.

[b] Growth and measurement conditions: first letter indicates growth conditions of plant material; the second letter indicates experimental measurement conditions. N = natural conditions (field, nursery, or *in situ*), G = controlled environment (growth chamber or greenhouse), L = laboratory.

[c] Method used: I = infrared gas-analysis, R = radioactive $^{14}CO_2$ technique, C = whole-plant enclosure technique.

as photosynthetic capacity (A_m), photosynthetic quantum efficiency, light compensation point, and dark respiration (R_d) were also comprehensively reviewed (3,5).

For reasons of uniformity and comparison the average values of photosynthetic capacity (A_m) of conifers were all normalized and expressed on a projected (one-sided) leaf area basis (Table 2.1). Photosynthetic capacities expressed on a dry-weight basis were converted to a leaf area basis using weight/area ratios specific for different genera. Similarly, A_m values expressed on a total needle area basis were converted using ratios of total to projected needle area, ranging from 2.23 for larch (8,9) and 2.24 for loblolly pine (10) to 2.5 for Monterey pine (11) or 2.6 for spruce (12). Unfortunately, data listed in Table 2.1 cannot present all information reported in the literature as several investigators use rather unusual parameters or units without mentioning conversion coefficients or exact reference basis. Nevertheless, both Table 2.1 and Fig. 2.1 would indicate the available information and the research that has been done on woody plant photosynthesis and respiration during the past two decades.

Photosynthesis values range between 2 and 25 μmol m^{-2} s^{-1} for deciduous broad-leafed trees and between ~2 and 10 μmol m^{-2} s^{-1} for coniferous trees (Table 2.1). Some important remarks should, however, be made about the correct interpretation of the absolute photosynthetic rates. First, growth conditions as well as the experimental methods have important implications on the gas-exchange rates that are measured. Plants raised under natural conditions and/or measured *in situ* tend to have higher A_m values than do plants grown under artificial (greenhouse or controlled-environment) conditions (3,13–15). Open or closed gas-exchange systems connected to an infrared gas analyzer measure different rates than, for example, radioactive $^{14}CO_2$ devices, which measure gross (or apparent) photosynthesis rather than net carbon dioxide uptake. Therefore, specifications on growth and measurement conditions and methods used are included in Table 2.1 in an abbreviated and simplified code. Further, most photosynthetic capacity values listed for the last two decades tend to be moderately higher than the values reported in the open literature before the mid-1970s. Part of the reason for the pre-1975 underestimations of A_m might be the fact that the effect of the leaf boundary layer has been neglected in the design of leaf or plant gas-exchange chambers, resulting in poor (and often limiting) boundary layer conductances. More recently, considerable improvements in the ventilation of gas-exchange cuvettes have resulted in an increased boundary layer conductance, and thus in increased gas-exchange rates.

So far all trees are known to have the C_3-type photosynthesis with only two exceptions (5). A tropical evergreen arborescent species, native to Hawaii, *Euphorbia forbesii* (*Euphorbiaceae*) as well as a few shrubby tree species of the *Chenopodiaceae* and *Polygonaceae* in the Russian steppes have been reported to show the C_4 metabolism (16,17).

Certain broad-leafed tree species such as oak (*Quercus*) and beech (*Fagus*) have photosynthetic capacities of only 3–6 μmol m^{-2} s^{-1}, which is much lower than the values for agronomic or horticultural species. Other species as poplar, green ash, oil palm and eucalypt, however, have rather high photosynthetic capacities attaining $A_m \geq 25$ µmol m^{-2} s^{-1}. While the ranges of A_m of evergreen and deciduous broad-leafed species are overlapping, most coniferous species form a slightly distinct group with mainly lower photosynthetic capacities (Fig. 2.1). On the basis of the data available from the literature, one might conclude that conifers are a group of trees with a poor photosynthetic capacity, i.e., 3–10 µmol m^{-2} s^{-1}, which is intrinsically lower than that of most broad-leafed (angiospermic) trees (5,18). However, photosynthetic capacities reported recently for two coniferous tree species are several times higher than the earlier measurements, although by no means remarkable for C$_3$ plants (5). For Monterey pine (*Pinus radiata*) and Scots pine (*Pinus sylvestris*) values of 16 and 17 µmol m^{-2} s^{-1} (expressed per projected needle area) have been reported by Benecke (11) and Troeng and Linder (19,20), respectively. These values indicate that A_m in conifers is not limited by some intrinsic incapacity (5,7).

Breeding programs in agronomy and horticulture have resulted in the selection of high-producing cultivars that have shown significantly lower photosynthetic capacities than the original wild species from which they originate (21–23). Indeed, photosynthesis per unit leaf area of modern cultivars of agronomic crops is not higher than that of older ones or of the original ancestors (23) and may even be noticeably lower as in wheat (21,22). The improved harvest index, i.e., the ratio of the weight of the harvestable product such as the grain in cereals and the nuts in peanuts, to total (above-ground) weight, explains the higher yields of modern agronomic cultivars. However, in a number of tree species and genera as apple, poplar, rubber tree, oil palm and eucalypt, intensive breeding and selection toward increased productivity (fruit or biomass) has resulted in fast-growing and high-producing hybrids or cultivars that also show improved A_m (24–27). So, with increasing degree of domestication and selection of cultivated tree crops the level of photosynthetic capacity also seems to have been improved. In terms of the harvestable product, certain tree crops (e.g., apple or oil palm) show many similarities with agronomic or horticultural crops, while in others (e.g., poplar or eucalypt) the product of harvest is vegetative rather than reproductive. Therefore, increasing yields of tree species where biological yield and economic yield are closely related via clonal selection for photosynthetic traits has shown certain prospects (26–29).

2.3. Photosynthesis and productivity

In many cases net photosynthesis has been found to be poorly or negatively correlated with growth rate (30). Failure to account for seasonal changes in net photosynthetic rate is one of the primary causes for such poor correlations (31). Other reasons could be the differences in leaf area, pattern of carbon partitioning, and variation in wood and root respiration rate. However, positive correlations between photosynthetic capacity and growth or productivity have been demonstrated for a number of tree species, such as poplar (27,29), larch (8,9), and loblolly pine (10).

When growth is related to total net photosynthesis integrated over the entire growing season and the total light intercepting leaf area, positive correlations are generally obtained (30,32). The relationship between net photosynthesis and growth (or productivity) in early growth stages of a tree species can, however, be entirely different from that in later stages of growth. Since few studies (e.g., Table 2.1) include information on plant growth or productivity, and since there is a large variability in experimental plant material and indices of growth or productivity used, comparative productivity data for tree species are often incomplete. In general, however, it has been found that woody species exhibit a tendency to low relative growth rate under optimal conditions (23).

When a comparison is made between different forest types, it is remarkable that coniferous forests of the temperate and boreal zone may reach and even exceed the total productivity of temperate and tropical broad-leafed forests (4,5). Despite a lower carbon gain per unit leaf weight and despite the large variability in the primary production of forest stands, which is related to differences in temperature and drought between the various study sites, the annual carbon gain is greater for conifers (wood production of $0.8-1.6$ kg m^{-2} yr^{-1}) than for broad-leafed deciduous trees (wood production of $0.6-0.9$ kg m^{-2} yr^{-1}) (4), except for certain species, such as poplar, which reaches 2.5 kg m^{-2} yr^{-1}.

Although coniferous forests are among those having the highest monthly primary production of all forest types (4), they generally have moderate photosynthetic capacities (Table 2.1). This disproportion is not due to a higher respiratory activity, since dark respiration rates (on a leaf area basis) of conifers are not significantly different from those of evergreen or deciduous broad-leafed species (Fig. 2.2). Nor is the moderate A_m of the coniferous needle sufficiently counterbalanced by a prolonged growing season, since a short photoperiod, low light intensity, and low temperatures restrict photosynthetic activity in autumn and spring in the European climate. Conditions are different, however, in summer-dry and winter-mild climates, as in the Pacific Northwest of North America (4,18,33). The low rates of photosynthesis by conifers when given optimal conditions in the middle of the winter are well known, but the reasons for this remain unclear (5,34).

Explanations for the apparent discrepancy between photosynthetic capacity and productivity in a number of coniferous species might be their higher leaf area index (LAI) and higher accumulation of total leaf biomass (4), their efficient crown structure (35,36), and their leaf longevity. Coniferous species with a rather poor A_m, such as *Pseudotsuga menziesii* and *Abies*, combine their low photosynthetic capacity with a very high LAI of ≤19 (4). Other, more sun-adapted species such as *Pinus radiata* and *Pinus sylvestris* show a high photosynthetic capacity (Table 2.1; Refs. 11,37), but a low LAI of $2-4$ (4). The high LAI of many coniferous stands is based on the clustering effect of their needles, which allows deep penetration of light into the stand (4,36).

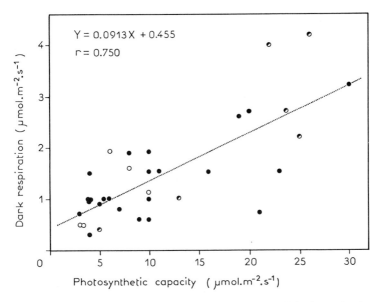

FIG. 2.2. Relationship between photosynthetic capacity and dark respiration rate for a total of 33 species of deciduous broad-leafed (closed circles), evergreen broad-leafed (half-open circles), and coniferous (open circles) trees. Linear regression significant at the 1% level.

Therefore, conifers can support a larger amount of leaves above a certain stem height without "parasite-leaves" than can deciduous trees. In view of the canopy architecture, evergreen needle-leafed trees are also more efficient in light capturing than are broad-leafed deciduous trees, since they disperse the total incoming light over a larger number of leaves (needles) and reduce the energy wastage that occurs under conditions of light saturation (Refs. 36,38; see also Chapter 1, this volume).

Specific differences between trees and agronomic crops affect the relationship between photosynthetic capacity and crop productivity. The photosynthetic carbon gain of a plant or a stand is a function of the rate of CO_2 assimilation per unit of time and leaf tissue, and the amount of leaf tissue. Thus, the development and deployment of a light-intercepting canopy is of utmost importance to the plant or crop. Contrary to agronomic crops forest canopies realize a complete ground cover during a major part of the growing season. Independent of the fertilization status of the site, tree canopies also attain their critical LAI, resulting in a canopy closure and complete ground cover. This is a consequence of the low annual increment in minerals stored in the tree biomass as compared to the high mineral uptake of annual crops. These factors result in an efficient light utilization at the forest canopy level. An oak stand growing on a poor site, for example, will attain its critical LAI after a certain period and fertilization would not increase LAI considerably. Agronomic crops growing on poor or unfertilized sites, however, will not be able to develop their full leaf area with consequent production losses. Fertilization in these agronomic crops will initially improve development of canopy leaf area and LAI and finally improve their allocation efficiency.

Photosynthetic capacity and dark respiration (both on a leaf area basis) are significantly intercorrelated for a wide variety of woody plant species (Fig. 2.2). The data in Fig. 2.2 are representative of more than 30 tree species (Table 2.1) and confirm a similar relationship shown by Givnish (39). Dark respiration always amounts to a 7–10% fraction of A_m. In terms of growth rate, species with a low growth rate seem to have high dark respiration rates per unit of leaf area (both in leaves and roots). On a dry-weight basis, however, species with a low (relative) growth rate have a lower dark respiration rate (less biomass, and thus less maintenance respiratory activity per unit of dry weight) (23).

2.4. Photosynthesis and environment

Abiotic factors such as light, temperature, CO_2 concentration, vapor-pressure deficit, and nutrient status have a major effect on net photosynthesis, and thus on growth and productivity (22,40–42). All environmental conditions that tend to reduce the photosynthetic rate (e.g., low light, low temperature, low nutrient availability) reduce the photosynthetic carbon gain (4,18). Plant water status, for example, influences the carbon relations of a tree at the gas-exchange and growth levels (Refs. 4,43,44; see also Chapter 6, this volume). Low nutrient uptake reduces the amount of nutrients available for incorporation into new living biomass. In particular, a shortage of phosphorus and nitrogen severely affects the photosynthetic capacity. In addition, the partitioning of carbohydrates will favor construction of a larger root biomas for nutrient uptake (Refs. 23,45,46; see also Chapter 3, this volume). The effects of water stress and temperature stress are discussed in detail in Chapters 6 and 13 (of this volume), respectively. All tree species, however, appear to have a large degree of adaptability to the climatic conditions of their habitat at the photosynthesis level.

The majority of trees are hypostomatous, or if amphistomatous, have very few stomata on the upper leaf surface (5,47,48). Consequently, the total conductance of all leaf surfaces is less than that for many herbaceous or agricultural plants. But photosynthetic capacity is more closely related to plant environment than to plant life form, although the success of a species in a given environment and in relation to its competitors may well be related to its total carbon gain (4).

Photosynthetic capacity varies not only with environment but also with age and position of the leaves (or needles) in the canopy. The evolution of photosynthesis as a function of leaf age differs according to the species or genus studied. Leaves of *Populus* and oil palm exhibited maximum photosynthetic rate immediately before maximum leaf size is attained (26,49). Stomatal conductance (and likely net photosynthesis) in *Quercus* reached a maximum several weeks after maximum leaf size was attained (50,51). Leaves of 10-

year-old oil palms remained photosynthetically active for 21 months, although with a decline in A_m after 11 months (49,52). This, of course, has important implications for the whole-tree photosynthetic CO_2 uptake.

Photosynthesis rates expressed per unit of leaf area or dry weight are very useful for extrapolations through appropriate models to the stand or canopy level and for calculations of carbon allocation and carbon balance. Photosynthesis values per unit of chlorophyll or per unit of leaf nitrogen content are more directly linked to photosynthetic efficiency and to the mechanism of the photochemical process. However, differences in total nitrogen content of leaves within and between species have been shown to be rather small. For a range of *Populus* clones, for example, total leaf nitrogen contents were only 2.3–2.7%. For tropical tree species values of 2.1% were reported versus values of 2.4% for sweet chestnut (53). In Scots pine the leaf nitrogen content was 0.8–1.1%, or 2.4–3.1 g N m^{-2} (20).

Pronounced differences in nitrogen content and in photosynthetic capacity per unit of nitrogen content can be found, however, among leaves grown under different light conditions. Specific leaf area, nitrogen content, photosynthetic quantum efficiency differed significantly among sun- and shade-adapted leaves (39,54–57). The variation in weight/area ratios of leaves of different evergreen and deciduous tree species is presented in Table 2.2. There exists a trade-off between leaf longevity and weight/area ratio; species that invest a great deal of time and carbon into leaf (or needle) formation (large weight/area ratios) have high leaf longevities (Table 2.2) and low photosynthesis (Table 2.1).

2.5. Photosynthesis at the stand or canopy level

The photosynthesis of a canopy (A_c) is basically the integration (or the sum) of the photosynthetic rates of all leaves that form the canopy (Fig. 2.3a). Thus, A_c depends on the characteristics of leaves (total area, orientation toward the light intensity, individual photosynthetic activity) as well as on different environmental factors, mainly the radiation. Photosynthetic response of a canopy to light is more linear than that of a single leaf (Fig. 2.3) (2,58). This results from the lower leaves in the canopy that are not light-saturated and may still benefit from an increase in light. Different photosynthetic parameters as photosynthetic quantum efficiency, photosynthetic capacity (A_m), dark respiration rate (R_d), and light compensation point, can be brought together into a single, empirical model of photosynthesis. Different models have already been built to calculate light penetration in a canopy and photosynthesis at the canopy level (see Chapter 18, this volume). These models are used to calculate canopy photosynthesis rates and to show the dependence of A_c on the values of individual parameters and their interactions. As an example, we show some results (Fig. 2.3a; Table 2.3) of the calculation of A_c using a simplified version of a Monteith-type model (59) for a LAI of 6.0. Crown architecture has been chosen in such a way that an horizontal layer with LAI = 1.0 transmits 60% of the incident light (m = 0.6). These results are

Table 2.2. Ratios of leaf weight per projected area (in g/m²) and average leaf longevity (in years) for various trees species (natural-environment conditions)

	Weight/Area Ratio (g/m²)	Longevity (years)	Ref.
Deciduous trees			
Broad-leafed			
Quercus petraea	50–108	0.5	65
Fagus silvatica	30–100	0.5	65
Castanea sativa	40–115	0.5	143
Populus spp. (clones)	57–80	0.5	Personal observation
Betula sp., *Fraxinus* sp.	49–75	0.5	144
Conifers			
Larix decidua	107	0.5	8,9
Evergreen broad-leafed trees			
Tropical			
Tropical rain forest species	100	2	22
Elaeis guineensis	80–120	2	52
Copaifera (*Caesalpinoideae*)	60		113
Hymenaea sp. (*Caesalpinoideae*)	75–91		113
Mediterranean			
Quercus ilex	160	1–2	22
Evergreen shrubs	200	1	145
Evergreen conifers			
Abies amabilis	70	15–20	36
Pinus sylvestris	250–300	2–3	19,20
Pinus taeda	184–209	2–3	10
Pinus ponderosa	242–286	2–3	137
Picea sitchensis	217	6	50
Picea abies	156–260	4–6–8	12

compared with a set of real measurements of net photosynthesis at the leaf level and of canopy CO_2 fluxes of a fast-growing (and high-producing) rubber tree (*Hevea brasiliensis*) clone (Fig. 2.3b). The photosynthesis–light-response curves show photosynthetic quantum efficiencies of 0.03 and 0.04 µmol µmol^{-1}, respectively at the leaf and canopy levels.

Values in Table 2.3 were obtained using a simplified version of the Monteith-type canopy photosynthesis model (59). The ratio between A_c (per unit soil surface area) and A_m may vary from 1.7 to >3.2 in a canopy with high LAI (Table 2.3), with species whose leaf photosynthesis reaches a plateau at low light levels. A 6- to 7-fold difference in A_m at the leaf level is reduced

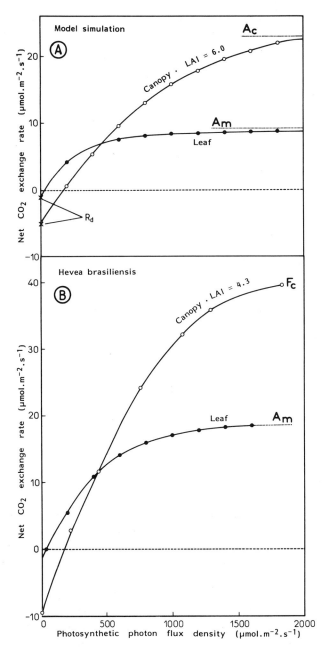

FIG. 2.3. Net CO_2 exchange rates at the leaf and canopy levels and CO_2 flux from the canopy as a function of photosynthetic photon flux density. (a) Simulated data from a simplified Monteith-type (59) model, describing a nonrectangular hyperbola, with α = 0.03, dark respiration = $0.8A_m$ and with 60% erect leaves; A_m = leaf photosynthetic capacity at light saturation, A_c = canopy photosynthetic capacity. (b) Measured data for *Hevea brasiliensis* clone GT 1, modified after Monteny (149) and Ceulemans et al. (121); F_c = CO_2 flux from the canopy with LAI = 4.3.

Table 2.3. Variation in gap between maximum photosynthetic capacity at leaf (A_m) and canopy (A_c) level.[a] Last column gives the ratio between maximum and minimum values of A_m and A_c, respectively.

Level		Rate						Ratio of extremes	
Leaf	A_m	24.1	19.6	13.2	8.9	5.4	3.6	Max/min	6.7
Canopy	A_c	41.4	38.8	31.2	23.7	16.1	11.7	Max/min	3.5
Ratio	A_m/A_c	1.72	1.98	2.36	2.66	2.98	3.25		

[a]Simulated using a simplified Monteith-type canopy photosynthesis model (59). Model parameters were leaf area index (LAI) = 5, saturating light intensity = 2 mmol m^{-2} s^{-1}, quantum efficiency (α) = 0.04, dark respiration rate (R_d) = $0.8A_m$. Values of A_m are expressed in μmol s^{-1} m^{-2} of single leaf area, A_c values in μmol s^{-1} m^{-2} of soil surface area.

to a factor of only 3–4 at the canopy level. With lower A_m rates, the canopy/leaf photosynthesis difference ratio becomes larger.

Contrary to agronomic crops, where fairly accurate measurements of gas exchange of entire vegetations or canopies can be made (using, e.g., micrometeorological or whole-plant enclosure techniques), the size and dimensions of a forest stand make accurate gas-exchange measurements at the canopy or stand level very difficult. A limited number of studies, however, have successfully attempted to get an idea of the CO_2 fluxes of forest stands (F_c) using different methods (Table 2.4). The CO_2 flux is equal to net canopy photosynthesis minus soil and wood respiration and thus underestimates canopy photosynthesis. Yet we see values of 18–25 μmol m^{-2} s^{-1} for deciduous forests, compared to leaf photosynthetic rates of 3–8 μmol m^{-2} s^{-1} for species such as oak or beech (compare Table 2.4 with Table 2.1). Similarly, the actual CO_2 flux (measured) above a rubber tree canopy is twice the rate of photosynthesis at the leaf level (Fig. 2.3b).

The arrangement of leaves within the foliage makes the canopy much more efficient than the leaf for converting light into dry matter. Values shown in Tables 2.3 and 2.4 are only slightly lower than those reported for crops: 34 μmol m^{-2} s^{-1} for sunflower (LAI = 1.8; Ref. 60), 38 μmol m^{-2} s^{-1} for rice and 63 μmol m^{-2} s^{-1} for maize (both dense canopies; Ref. 61). Sunflower and rice are C_3 species, and may be compared with tree species, whereas maize is a C_4 species.

Because of differences in crown architecture (see Chapter 1, this volume), competition, succession, and life form (4,54,62) the shape and structure of the canopy of various types of forests will be different. Striking differences exist, for example, in the roughness of the canopy of a climax tropical forest (with emergent and suppressed trees) and the canopy of a deciduous, monoclonal stand of poplars or rubber trees. These differences in canopy structure have important consequences for the coupling:decoupling ratio of the vegetation to the atmosphere (63) and the wind profile above the canopy. Rough forest canopies have a tendency to be better coupled to their surrounding

Table 2.4. Measured CO_2 fluxes above various forest canopies (F_c; expressed in μmol s^{-1} m^{-2} of soil surface area)

Type or Species	F_c	Method	Ref.
Mixed deciduous forest	18	Eddy correlation	146
Mixed deciduous forest	25	Eddy correlation	147
Mixed deciduous and evergreen forest	23	Eddy correlation	148
Chestnut coppice	17	Tree enclosure	22,81
Rubber-tree stand (young)	40	Energy balance	149
Scots pine	16	Model calculation	37
Scots pine	11–27	Energy balance	63
Sitka spruce	20	Energy balance	63
Ponderosa pine forest	12	Eddy correlation	150
Eucalypt forest stand	28	Canopy enclosure	118
Tropical rain forest	22	Momentum balance	151

environment than do uniform—and thus even and smooth—canopies. Further, important consequences include the overall light interception by the canopy, which is different for the situation of a dominant–suppressed mixture, versus a more uniform vegetation cover.

Differences also exist in growth or productivity between isolated trees and trees in a closed stand or canopy. Their carbon uptakes are different and related to the amount of intercepted light. A lot of wastage of light occurs in the isolated tree per unit soil area as compared to a canopy or vegetation situation. On the other hand, an isolated tree will grow faster than a canopy tree of the same leaf area, since—on average—leaves will receive a higher amount of light.

2.6. Ecological implications of photosynthesis

Because of the dependence on light and its direct relationship to plant survival and growth (54), the photosynthetic process has been emphasized in most ecological and successional research. Light is a major determinant in forest species replacement and succession. The degree of shade tolerance, sun or shade adaptation, structural arrangement of the foliage, and branching patterns are important in determining successional sequences in deciduous forest (38,54).

Rates of photosynthesis are higher in sun-adapted than in shade-adapted species (56,64) and the light compensation point is predictably lower for shade-adapted, late successional plants than those of sun-adapted, early successional ones. Moreover, the rate of photosynthesis (per unit of leaf area) generally declines with succession. If the broad-leafed species such as those listed in Table 2.1 are considered, late successional species typical for a climax-type situation (such as oak, beech, maple) have photosynthetic capacities of less than 10 μmol m^{-2} s^{-1} (and generally between 2 and 6 μmol m^{-2} s^{-1}). On the contrary, early successional or pioneer-type species and genera, having a rather high growth and regeneration rate and an invading nature (such as poplar, willow, green ash, eucalypt), always have photosynthetic capacities above 10 μumol m^{-2} s^{-1} (and $\leq$25 μmol m^{-2} s^{-1}). High regeneration rates of trees also tend to coincide with high photosynthetic capacities (54). Furthermore, the rate of photosynthesis in the late successional group tends to decline with increased shade tolerance (54).

Light saturation occurs at high light intensities in early successional plants and trees (54,58). In late successional trees, e.g., *Fagus grandifolia*, *Quercus rubra* (56,65), and *Acer saccharum* (66), however, light saturation occurs at much lower light intensities ($\sim$10–15% of full sunlight). In these species, photosynthetic rates may even decline under high light intensities. However, apparent quantum yield has been shown to be slightly higher for climax than for early successional trees. Mainly R_d is low in late successional, shade-adapted species, which makes them more efficient than early successional trees at low light intensities, and thus able to survive and strive in the understorey of forest canopies where photosynthetic production is limited by light intensity (54,58,67,68). Consequently, the ratio of photosynthesis to respiration decreases with succession.

2.7. Conclusions

Leaf photosynthesis in trees is fairly variable since its maximum value under natural conditions ranges from roughly 3 to 30 μmol m^{-2} s^{-1}. Forest canopy photosynthesis is likely to be less variable, with a maximum ranging from 15 to 40 μmol m^{-2} s^{-1}. Forests have low nutrient requirements, which enables them to establish full canopy cover even on relatively poor soils, and thus to play an important role in the regulation of biogeochemical cycles.

Leaf duration ranges from a few months in deciduous species to 7 years in spruce, with a trend toward decreased photosynthesis with increasing longevity. For each species there is a trade-off between its annual investment in leaf production and a return in terms of carbohydrate supply by the foliage. Leaf thickness and weight/area ratio decrease from the top of the canopy-down, shade-tolerant species presenting the largest variation. Gutschick and Wiegel (69) recently interpreted this variation in weight/area ratio as a way to maximize canopy photosynthesis for a given investment in foliage mass. It would be interesting to extend this study to leaves of various durations.

Photosynthesis by itself is only the requirement for growth, but it may be used in many ways as shown by the classical paper of Mooney (70) on carbon balance of plants, and more recently by the reevaluation of sun and shade adaptations by Givnish (39), taking into account the carbon gain of the whole plant to calculate a light compensation point that increases with the size of a tree.

Many aspects of the adaptive mechanisms of photosynthesis within trees are still not known. The whole research area is expanding rapidly because (a) field measurements have become much easier owing to portable infrared gas analyzers and data acquisition systems, (b) forest decline has received wider attention, and (c) forests play a central role in human conception of nature, regulation of the climate, and composition of the atmosphere.

We have ways of extrapolating photosynthesis from the leaf to the tree to the canopy, and we now need to go on to regional and global scales. To that end we need new models to compute carbon uptake from available environmental resources, satellite observations to understand the role played by the forests on our planet, and their evolution under the effect of the major changes that are to occur during the next century in the global environment. We have just started work in that direction that should prove to be stimulating for research in tree physiology.

Acknowledgments

The authors are grateful to M. Mousseau and T.M. Hinckley for fruitful discussions, J.Y. Pontailler for figure drawings, and J. Liebert for assistance with literature search. We also thank R.F. Stettler for some of the leaf longevity data of Table 2.2. Senior author (RC) is Research Associate of the Belgian NFWO.

2.8. References

1. G.L. Atjay, P. Ketner, and P. Duvigneaud, "Terrestrial primary production and phytomass," in B. Bolin, E.T. Degens, and S. Kempe, et al., eds., *The Global Carbon Cycle*, Scope 13, Wiley, New York, 1979, pp. 129–181.

2. B. Saugier, "Productivité des ecosystèmes naturels," *Biomasse actualités*, **9**, 42–49 (1986).

3. W. Larcher, "The effect of environmental and physiological variables on the carbon dioxide gas exchange of trees," *Photosynthetica*, **3**, 167–198 (1969).

4. E.D. Schulze, "Plant life forms and their carbon, water and nutrient relations," in O.L. Lange, P.S. Nobel, C.B. Osmond, and H. Ziegler, eds., *Physiological Plant Ecology. Encyclopedia of Plant Physiology* (New Series, Vol. 12/B), 2nd ed., Springer-Verlag, Berlin–New York, 1982, pp. 615–676.

5. P.G. Jarvis and A.P. Sandford, "Temperate forests," in N.R. Baker and S.P. Long, eds., *Photosynthesis in Contrasting Environments*, Elsevier Science Publishers B.V., The Netherlands, 1986, pp. 199–236.

6. P.G. Jarvis and M.S. Jarvis, "Growth rates of woody plants," *Physiol. Plant.*, **17**, 654–666 (1964).

7. N.D. Nelson, "Woody plants are not inherently low in photosynthetic capacity," *Photosynthetica*, **18**, 600–605 (1984).

8. R. Matyssek and E.D. Schulze, "Heterosis in hybrid larch (*Larix decidua* × *leptolepis*). I. The role of leaf characteristics," *Trees*, **1**, 219–224 (1987).

9. R. Matyssek and E.D. Schulze, "Heterosis in hybrid larch (*Larix decidua* × *leptolepis*). II. Growth characteristics," *Trees*, **1**, 225–231 (1987).

10. B.A. Boltz, B.C. Bongarten, and R.O. Teskey, "Seasonal patterns of net photosynthesis of loblolly pine from diverse origins," *Can. J. For. Res.*, **16**, 1063–1068 (1986).

11. U. Benecke, "Photosynthesis and transpiration of *Pinus radiata* D. Don under natural conditions in a forest stand," *Oecologia*, **44**, 192–198 (1980).

12. R. Zimmermann, R. Oren, E.D. Schulze, and K.S. Werk, "Performance of two *Picea abies* (L.) Karst. stands at different stages of decline. II. Photosynthesis and leaf conductance," *Oecologia*, **76**, 513–518 (1988).

13. N.D. Nelson and P. Ehlers, "Comparative carbon dioxide exchange for two *Populus* clones grown in growth room, greenhouse, and field environments," *Can. J. For. Res.*, **14**, 924–932 (1984).

14. P.E. Kriedemann, "Photosynthesis in vine leaves as a function of light intensity, temperature, and leaf age," *Vitis*, **7**, 213–220 (1968).

15. P.E. Kriedemann, W.M. Kliewer, and J.M. Harris, "Leaf age and photosynthesis in *Vitis vinifera* L.," *Vitis*, **9**, 97–104 (1970).

16. R.W. Pearcy, K. Osteryoung, and H.W. Calkin, "Photosynthetic responses to dynamic light environments by Hawaiian trees," *Plant Physiol.*, **79**, 896–902 (1985).

17. K. Winter, "C_4 plants of high biomass in arid regions of Asia. Occurrence of C_4 photosynthesis in Chenopodiaceae and Polygonaceae from the Middle East and USSR," *Oecologia*, **48**, 100–106 (1981).

18. R.B. Walker, D.R.M. Scott, D.J. Salo, and K.L. Reed, "Terrestrial process studies in conifers: A review," in J.F. Franklin, L.J. Dempster, and R.H. Waring, eds., *Proceedings Research on Coniferous Forest Ecosystems Symposium*, U.S. Dept. Agric. Forest Service, Portland, OR, 1972, pp. 211–225.

19. E. Troeng and S. Linder, "Gas exchange in a 20-year-old stand of Scots pine. I. Net photosynthesis of current and one-year-old shoots within and between seasons," *Physiol. Plant.*, **54**, 7–14 (1982).

20. E. Troeng and S. Linder, "Gas exchange in a 20-year-old stand of Scots pine. II. Variation in net photosynthesis and transpiration within and between within and between trees," *Physiol. Plant.*, **54**, 15–23 (1982).

21. L.T. Evans and R.L. Dunstone, "Some physiological aspects of evolution in wheat," *Aust. J. Biol. Sci.*, **23**, 725–741 (1970).

22. B. Saugier, "Plant growth and its limitation in crops and natural communities," in H.A. Mooney and M. Godron, eds., *Comparative Structural and Functional Characteristics of Natural versus Human-modified Ecosystems*, Ecological Studies, Vol. 44, Springer-Verlag, Berlin–New York, 1983, pp. 159–174.

23. H. Lambers, "Does variation in photosynthetic rate explain variation in growth rate and yield?" *Neth. J. Agric. Sci.*, **35**, 505–519 (1987).

24. D.O. Ladipo, J. Grace, A.P. Sandford, and R.R.B. Leakey, "Clonal variation in photosynthetic and respiration rates and diffusion resistances in the tropical hardwood *Triplochiton scleroxylon* K. Schum.," *Photosynthetica*, **18**, 20–27 (1984).

25. D.J. Avery, "Maximum photosynthetic rate—a case study in apple," *New Phytol.*, **78**, 55–63 (1977).

26. R. Ceulemans and I. Impens, "Leaf gas exchange processes and related characteristics of seven poplar clones under laboratory conditions," *Can. J. For. Res.*, **10**, 429–435 (1980).

27. R. Ceulemans and I. Impens, "Net CO_2 exchange rate and shoot growth of young poplar (*Populus*) clones," *J. Exp. Bot.*, **34**, 866–870 (1983).

28. J.C. Gordon and L.C. Promnitz, "Photosynthetic and enzymatic criteria for the early selection of fast-growing *Populus* clones," in M.G.R. Cannell and F.T. Last, eds., *Tree Physiology and Yield Improvement*, Academic Press, London, 1976, pp. 79–97.

29. J.G. Isebrands, R. Ceulemans, and B.M. Wiard, "Genetic variation in photosynthetic traits among *Populus* clones in relation to yield," *Plant Physiol. Biochem.*, **26**, 427–437 (1988).

30. F.T. Ledig and T.O. Perry, "Net assimilation rate and growth in loblolly pine seedlings," *For. Sci.*, **15**, 431–438 (1969).

31. K. Foote and M. Schaedle, "Seasonal field rates of photosynthesis and respiration in stems of *Populus tremuloides*," *Plant Physiol. Suppl.*, **53**, 352 (1974).

32. T. Lohammar, S. Larsson, S. Linder, and S.O. Falk, "FAST-simulation models of gaseous exchange in Scots pine," in T. Persson, ed., *Structure and Function of Northern Coniferous Forests—an Ecosystem Study*, Ecol. Bull., Stockholm, 1980, pp. 505–523.

33. D.C. Doehlert and R.B. Walker, "Photosynthesis and photorespiration in Douglas fir as influenced by irradiance, CO_2 concentration, and temperature," *For. Sci.*, **27**, 641–650 (1981).

34. W. Zelawski and R.B. Walker, "Photosynthesis, respiration and dry matter production," in J.P. Miksche, ed., *Modern Methods in Forest Genetics*, Springer-Verlag, Berlin, 1976, pp. 89–119.

35. C.L. Beadle, H. Talbot, R.E. Neilson, and P.G. Jarvis, "Stomatal conductance and photosynthesis in a mature Scots pine forest. III. Variation in canopy conductance and canopy photosynthesis," *J. Appl. Ecol.*, **22**, 587–595 (1985).

36. D.G. Sprugel, "The relationship of evergreenness, crown architecture, and leaf size," *Am. Nat.*, **133**, 465–479 (1989).

37. C.L. Beadle, R.E. Neilson, H. Talbot, and P.G. Jarvis, "Stomatal conductance and photosynthesis in a mature Scots pine forest. I. Diurnal, seasonal and spatial variation in shoots," *J. Appl. Ecol.*, **22**, 557–571 (1985).

38. H.S. Horn, *The Adaptive Geometry of Trees*, Princeton University Press, Princeton, NJ, 1971.

39. T.J. Givnish, "Adaptation to sun and shade: A whole-plant perspective," *Aust. J. Plant Physiol.*, **15**, 63–92 (1988).

40. J.P. Gaudillère and M. Mousseau, "Short term effect of CO_2 enrichment on leaf development and gas exchange of young poplars (*Populus euramericana* cv. I-214)," *Oecol. Plant.*, **10**, 95–105 (1989).

41. P. Grieu, J.M. Guehl, and G. Aussenac, "The effects of soil and atmospheric drought on photosynthesis and stomatal control of gas exchange in three coniferous species," *Physiol. Plant*, **73**, 97–104 (1988).

42. W. Zelawski, "Variation in the photosynthetic capacity of *Pinus sylvestris*," in M.G.R. Cannell and F.T. Last, eds., *Tree Physiology and Yield Improvement*, Academic Press, London, 1976, pp. 99–109.

43. J.M. Hand, E. Young, and A.C. Vasconcelos, "Leaf water potential, stomatal resistance, and photosynthetic response to water stress in peach seedlings," *Plant Physiol.*, **69**, 1051–1054 (1982).

44. S.R. Pezeshki and T.M. Hinckley, "The stomatal response of red alder and black cottonwood to changing water status," *Can. J. For. Res.*, **12**, 761–771 (1982).

45. A.J.S. McDonald, "Phenotypic variation in growth rate as affected by N- supply: Its effects on NAR, LWR and SLA," in H. Lambers, M.L. Cambridge, H. Konings, and T.L. Pons, eds., *Causes and Consequences of Variation in Growth Rate and Productivity of Higher Plants*, SPB Academic Publishing B.V., The Hague, The Netherlands, 1989, pp. 35–44.

46. S.R. Pezeshki, R.D. DeLaune, and W.H. Patrick, Jr., "Effect of salinity on leaf ionic content and photosynthesis of *Taxodium distichum* L.," *Am. Midl. Nat.*, **119**, 185–192 (1988).

47. A. Carbonneau and C. de Loth, "Influence du régime d'éclairement journalier sur la résistance stomatique et la photosynthèse brute chez *Vitis vinifera* L. cv. 'Cabernet-Sauvignon,' " *Agronomie*, **5**, 631–638 (1985).

48. J.M. Guehl and G. Aussenac, "Photosynthesis decrease and stomatal control of gas exchange in *Abies alba* Mill. in response to vapor pressure difference," *Plant Physiol.*, **83**, 316–322 (1987).

49. E. Dufrène and B. Saugier, "Field studies of leaf gas exchanges in oil palm trees (*Elaeis guineensis*)," *Ann. Sci. For.*, **46** (Suppl.), 439–442 (1989).

50. N.C. Turner and G.H. Heichel, "Stomatal development and seasonal changes in diffusive resistance of primary and regrowth foliage of red oak (*Quercus rubra* L.) and red maple (*Acer rubrum* L.)," *New Phytol.*, **78**, 71–81 (1977).

51. J. Nizinski, D. Morand and B. Saugier, "Dynamique de l'eau dans une chênaie (*Quercus petraea* (Matt.) Liebl.) en forêt de Fontainebleau," *Ann. Sci. For.*, **46** (Suppl.), 429–432 (1989).

52. R.H.V. Corley, "Photosynthesis and age of oil palm leaves," *Photosynthetica*, **17**, 97–100 (1983).

53. E. Dubroca and B. Saugier, "Effet de la coupe sur l'évolution saisonnière des réserves glucidiques dans un taillis de châtaigniers," *Bull. Soc. bot. Fr. Actual. bot.*, **135**, 55–64 (1988).

54. F.A. Bazzaz, "The physiological ecology of plant succession," *Ann. Rev. Ecol. Syst.*, **16**, 351–371 (1979).

55. G. Cornic and A. Schmitt, "Action de l'ombrage sur le dégagement de CO_2 à la lumière de *Quercus sessiliflora* Salisb.," *Physiol. Vég.*, **9**, 453–460 (1971).

56. T. Koike, "Photosynthetic responses to light intensity of deciduous broad-leaved tree seedlings raised under various artificial shade," *Environ. Control Biol.*, **24**, 51–58 (1986).

57. Y.L. Tsel'niker, "Resistances to CO_2 uptake at light saturation in forest tree seedlings of different adaptation to shade," *Photosynthetica*, **13**, 124–129 (1979).

58. W. Larcher, *Physiological Plant Ecology*, 2nd ed., Springer-Verlag, Berlin, 1980.

59. J.L. Monteith, "Light distribution and photosynthesis in field crops," *Ann. Bot.*, **29**, 17–37 (1965).

60. B. Saugier, "Sunflower," in J.L. Monteith, ed., *Vegetation and the Atmosphere*, Vol. 2, *Case Studies*, Academic Press, London–New York, 1976, pp. 87–119.

61. Z. Uchijima, "Maize and rice," in J.L. Monteith, ed., *Vegetation and the Atmosphere*, Vol. 2, *Case Studies*, Academic Press, London–New York, 1976, pp. 33–64.

62. H.H. Shugart, *A Theory of Forest Dynamics*, Springer-Verlag, Berlin–New York, 1984.

63. P.G. Jarvis, G.B. James, and J.J. Landsberg, "Coniferous forest," in J.L. Monteith, ed., *Vegetation and the Atmosphere*, Vol. 2, *Case Studies*, Academic Press, London–New York, 1976, pp. 171–240.

64. T. Koike, "Photosynthesis and expansion in leaves of early, mid, and late successional tree species, birch, ash, and maple," *Photosynthetica*, **21**, 503–508 (1987).

65. M. Ducrey, "Etude bioclimatique d'une futaie feuillue (*Fagus silvatica* L. et *Quercus sessiliflora* Salisb.) de l'est de la France. III. Potentialité photosynthétique des feuilles à différentes hauteurs dans le peuplement," *Ann. Sci. For.*, **38**, 71–86 (1981).

66. J.E. Wuenscher and T.T. Kozlowski, "Carbon dioxide transfer resistance as a factor in shade tolerance of tree seedlings," *Can. J. Bot.*, **48**, 453–456 (1970).

67. D.L. Regehr, F.A. Bazzaz, and W.R. Boggess, "Photosynthesis, transpiration and leaf conductance of *Populus deltoides* in relation to flooding and drought," *Photosynthetica*, **9**, 52–61 (1975).

68. D.L. Peterson and F.A. Bazzaz, "Photosynthetic and growth responses of silver maple (*Acer saccharinum* L.) seedlings to flooding," *Am. Midl. Nat.*, **112**, 261–272 (1983).

69. V.P. Gutschick and F.W. Wiegel, "Optimizing the canopy photosynthetic rate by patterns of investment in specific leaf mass," *Am. Nat.*, **132**, 67–86 (1988).

70. H.A. Mooney, "The carbon balance of plants," *Ann. Rev. Ecol. System.*, **3**, 315–346 (1972).

71. M. Küppers, "Carbon relations and competition between woody species in a Central European hedgerow. II. Stomatal responses, water use, and hydraulic conductivity in the root/leaf pathway," *Oecologia*, **64**, 344–354 (1984).

72. P. Holmgren, P.G. Jarvis, and M.S. Jarvis, "Resistances to carbon dioxide and water vapor transfer in leaves of different plant species," *Physiol. Plant.*, **18**, 557–573 (1965).

73. F.I. Woodward and F.A. Bazzaz, "The response of stomatal density to CO_2 partial pressure," *J. Exp. Bot.*, **39**, 1771–1781 (1988).

74. J.O. Dawson and J.C. Gordon, "Nitrogen fixation in relation to photosynthesis in *Alnus glutinosa*," *Bot. Gaz.*, **140**, S70–S75 (1979).

75. T. Koike, "The growth characteristics in japanese mountain birch (*Betula ermanii*) and white birch (*Betula platyphylla* var. *Japonica*), and their distribution in the northern part of Japan," in T. Fujimori and M. Kimura, eds., *Human Impacts and Management of Mountain Forests*, Forestry and Forest Products Research Institute, Ibaraki, Japan, 1987, pp. 189–200.

76. T. Koike and Y. Sakagami, "Comparison of the photosynthetic responses to temperature and light of *Betula maximowicziana* and *Betula platyphylla* var. *japonica*," *Can. J. For. Res.*, **15**, 631–635 (1985).

77. W.B. Sisson, J.A. Booth, and G.O. Throneberry, "Absorption of SO_2 by pecan (*Carya illinoensis* (Wang) K. Koch) and alfalfa (*Medicago sativa* L.) and its effect on net photosynthesis," *J. Exp. Bot.*, **32**, 523–534 (1981).

78. P.C. Andersen and B.V. Brodbeck, "Net CO_2 assimilation and plant water relations characteristics of pecan growth flushes," *J. Am. Soc. Hort. Sci.*, **113**, 444–450 (1988).

79. C. Deweirdt and G. Carlier, "Photosynthèse des feuilles de châtaigniers (*Castanea sativa* Mill.) mesurée *in situ* dans des taillis par incorporation de $^{14}CO_2$," *Oecol. Plant.*, 146–160 (1988).

80. S. Gonzalez-Valenzuela, *Les échanges de CO_2 des taillis de châtaigniers (Castanea sativa Mill.)*: *détermination de paramètres et évaluation du gain de matière organique des parties aeriennes d'après des mesures gazométriques faites en laboratoire*, Thesis D.E.A., Université de Grenoble, 1983.

81. J.Y. Pontailler, M. Leroux, and B. Saugier, "Evolution d'un taillis de châtaigniers après coupe: photosynthèse et croissance des rejets," *Oecol. Plant.*, **5**, 89–99 (1984).

82. E.D. Schulze, O.L. Lange, and W. Koch, "Ecophysiological investigations on wild and cultivated plants in the Negev desert. II. The influence of climatic factors on carbon dioxide exchange and transpiration at the end of the dry period," *Oecologia*, **8**, 334–355 (1972) (in German).

83. J. Lloyd, J.P. Syvertsen, and P.E. Kriedemann, "Salinity effects on leaf water relations and gas exchange of 'Valencia' orange, *Citrus sinensis* (L.) Osbeck, on rootstocks with different salt exclusion characteristics," *Aust. J. Plant Physiol.*, **14**, 605–617 (1987).

84. M. Küppers, R. Matyssek, and E.D. Schulze, "Diurnal variations of light-saturated CO_2 assimilation and intercellular carbon dioxide concentration are not related to leaf water potential," *Oecologia*, **69**, 477–480 (1986).

85. E. Masarovicòvà, *Gasometrical investigation into CO_2 exchange of the Fagus silvatica L. species under controlled conditions*, Biologicke Prace, Vol. 30/2, VEDA, Publishing House of the Slovak Academy of Sciences, Bratislava, 1984.

86. W.E. Williams, K. Garbutt, F.A. Bazzaz, and P.M. Vitousek, "The response of plants to elevated CO_2," *Oecologia*, **69**, 454–459 (1986).

87. J.E. Davis, T.J. Arkebauer, J.M. Norman, and J.R. Brandle, "Rapid field measurement of the assimilation rate *versus* internal CO_2 concentration relationship in green ash (*Fraxinus pennsylvanica* Marsh.): The influence of light intensity," *Tree Physiol.*, **3**, 387–392 (1987).

88. H.S. Neufeld, J.A. Jernstedt, and B.L. Haines, "Direct foliar effects of simulated acid rain. I. Damage, growth and gas exchange," *New Phytol.*, **99**, 389–405 (1985).

89. L.C. Tolley and B.R. Strain, "Effects of CO_2 enrichment and water stress on gas exchange of *Liquidambar styraciflua* and *Pinus taeda* seedlings grown under different irradiance levels," *Oecologia*, **65**, 166–172 (1985).

90. C. Lankes, "Effects of water deficit on photosynthesis, transpiration, and stomatal behaviour of the apple leaf," *Gartenbauwissenschaft*, **53**, 77–84 (1988).

91. M.A. Nunes and M.C. Matos, "Effect of light on gas exchange parameters of sun and shade adapted leaves of *Ceratonia siliqua*, *Coffea arabica* and *Malus domestica*," in J.D. Tenhunen, F.M. Catarino, O.L. Lange, and W.C. Oechel, eds., *Plant Response to Stress. Functional Analysis in Mediterranean Ecosystems*, Springer-Verlag, Berlin–New York, 1987, pp. 369–378.

92. A. Mika and R. Antoszewski, "Effect of leaf position and tree shape on the rate of photosynthesis in the apple tree," *Photosynthetica*, **6**, 381–386 (1972).

93. M.R. Thorpe, B. Saugier, S. Auger, A. Berger, and M. Methy, "Photosynthesis and transpiration of an isolated tree: Model and validation," *Plant, Cell Environ.*, **1**, 269–277 (1978).

94. S.P. Monselise and F. Lenz, "Effect of fruit load on photosynthetic rates of budded apple trees," *Gartenbauwissenschaft*, **45**, 220–224 (1980).

95. B.M. Wiard, *Growth of selected Populus clones as affected by leaf orientation, light interception, and photosynthesis*, M.S. thesis, University of Washington (USA), 1987.

96. J.G. Isebrands and D.A. Michael, "Effects of leaf morphology and orientation on solar radiation interception and photosynthesis in *Populus*," in T. Fujimori and D. Whitehead, eds., *Crown and Canopy Structure in Relation to Productivity*, Forestry and Forest Products Research Institute, Ibaraki, Japan, 1986, pp. 359–381.

97. O. Luukkanen and T.T. Kozlowski, "Gas exchange in six *Populus* clones, *Silvae Genetica*," **21**, 220–229 (1972).

98. O.A. Okafo and J.W. Hanover, "Comparative photosynthesis and respiration of trembling and bigtooth aspens in relation to growth and development," *For. Sci.*, **24**, 103–109 (1978).

99. R. Ceulemans, I. Impens, and V. Steenackers, "Variations in photosynthetic, anatomical, and enzymatic leaf traits and correlations with growth in recently selected *Populus* hybrids," *Can. J. For. Res.*, **17**, 273–283 (1987).

100. N.D. Nelson and D. Michael, "Photosynthesis, leaf conductance, and specific leaf weight in long and short shoots of *Populus* Tristis 1 grown under intensive culture," *For. Sci.*, **28**, 737–744 (1982).

101. F.E. Fasehun, "Effect of irradiance on growth and photosynthesis of *Populus* × *euramericana* clones," *Can. J. For. Res.*, **8**, 94–99 (1978).

102. A. Furukawa, "Photosynthesis and respiration in poplar plant," *J. Jap. For. Soc.*, **54**, 80–84 (1972).

103. P.B. Reich, "Relationships between leaf age, irradiance, leaf conductance, CO_2 exchange, and water use efficiency in hybrid poplar," *Photosynthetica*, **18**, 445–453 (1984).

104. R. Ceulemans and I. Impens, "ECOPASS—a multivariate model used as an index of growth performance of poplar clones," *For. Sci.*, **28**, 862–867 (1982).

105. E.D. Schulze, O.L. Lange, L. Kappen, M. Evenari, and U. Buschbom, "The role of air humidity and leaf temperature in controlling stomatal resistance of *Prunus armeniaca* L. under desert conditions. II. The significance of leaf water status and internal carbon dioxide concentration," *Oecologia*, **18**, 219–233 (1975).

106. T.M. DeJong, "Fruit effects on photosynthesis in *Prunus persica*," *Physiol. Plant.*, **66**, 149–153 (1986).

107. C.S. Tan and B.R. Buttery, "Photosynthesis, stomatal conductance, and leaf water potential in response to temperature and light in peach," *Hort. Sci.*, **21**, 1180–1182 (1986).

108. P.E. Kriedemann and R.L. Canterford, "The photosynthetic activity of pear leaves (*Pyrus communis* L.)," *Aust. J. Biol. Sci.*, **24**, 197–205 (1971).

109. N.C. Turner and G.H. Heichel, "Stomatal development and seasonal changes in diffusive resistance of primary and regrowth foliage of red oak (*Quercus rubra* L.) and red maple (*Acer rubrum* L.)," *New Phytol.*, **78**, 71–81 (1977).

110. P.J. Hanson, R.E. Dickson, J.G. Isebrands, T.R. Crow, and R.K. Dixon, "A morphological index of *Quercus* seedling ontogeny for use in studies of physiology and growth," *Tree Physiol.*, **2**, 273–281 (1986).

111. P. Pelkonen, "Carbon dioxide exchange in willow clones," in K. Perttu, ed., *Ecology and Management of Forest Biomass Production Systems*, Swedish University of Agric. Sciences, Report 15, Uppsala, Sweden, 1984, pp. 187–196.

112. K. Imai, F. Ogura, and Y. Murata, "Photosynthesis and respiration of papaya (*Carica papaya* L.) leaves," *Oecol. Plant.*, **3**, 399–407 (1982).

113. J.H. Langenheim, C.B. Osmond, A. Brooks, and P.J. Ferrar, "Photosynthetic responses to light in seedlings of selected Amazonian and Australian rainforest tree species," *Oecologia*, **63**, 215–224 (1984).

114. M. Küppers, A.G. Swan, D. Tompkins, W.C.L. Gabriel, B.I.L. Küppers, and S. Linder, "A field portable system for the measurement of gas exchange of leaves under natural and controlled conditions: Examples with field-grown *Eucalyptus pauciflora* Sieb. ex Spreng. ssp. *pauciflora*, *E. behriana* F. Muell. and *Pinus radiata* R. Don," *Plant, Cell Environ.*, **10**, 425–435 (1987).

115. S. Moreshet, "Physiological activity, in a semiarid environment, of *Eucalyptus camaldulensis* Dehn. from two provenances," *Aust. J. Bot.*, **29**, 97–110 (1981).

116. M.A. El-Sharkawy, J.H. Cock, and A.A. Held, "Water use efficiency of cassava. II. Differing sensitivity of stomata to air humidity in cassava and other warm-climate species," *Crop Science*, **24**, 503–507 (1984).

117. J.S. Pereira, J.D. Tenhunen, and O.L. Lange, "Stomatal control of photosynthesis of *Eucalyptus globulus* Labill. trees under field conditions in Portugal," *J. Exp. Bot.*, **38**, 1678–1688 (1987).

118. S.C. Wong and F.X. Dunin, "Photosynthesis and transpiration of trees in a eucalypt forest stand: CO_2, light and humidity responses, *Aust. J. Plant Physiol.*," **14**, 619–632 (1987).

119. T.D. Sharkey, "Transpiration-induced changes in the photosynthetic capacity of leaves," *Planta*, **160**, 143–150 (1984).

120. S.C. Wong, I.R. Cowan, and G.D. Farquhar, "Stomatal conductance correlates with photosynthetic capacity," *Nature*, **282**, 424–426 (1979).

121. R. Ceulemans, R. Gabriëls, I. Impens, P.K. Yoon, W. Leong, and A.P. Ng, "Comparative study of photosynthesis in several *Hevea brasiliensis* clones and *Hevea* species under tropical field conditions," *Trop. Agr.*, **61**, 273–275 (1984).

122. Z. Samsuddin and I. Impens, "Comparative net photosynthesis of four *Hevea brasiliensis* clonal seedlings," *Exp. Agr.*, **14**, 337–340 (1978).

123. D.Y. Hollinger, "Gas exchange and dry matter allocation responses to elevation of atmospheric CO_2 concentration in seedlings of three tree species," *Tree Physiol.*, **3**, 193–202 (1987).

124. J.D. Tenhunen, W. Beyschlag, O.L. Lange, and P.C. Harley, "Changes during summer drought in leaf CO_2 uptake rates of macchia shrubs growing in Portugal: Limitations due to photosynthetic capacity, carboxylation efficiency, and stomatal conductance," in J.D. Tenhunen, F.M. Catarino, O.L. Lange, and W.C. Oechel, eds., *Plant Response to Stress: Functional Analysis in Mediterranean Ecosystems*, Springer-Verlag, Berlin–New York, 1987, pp. 305–327.

125. F.E. Eckardt, G. Heim, M. Methy, and R. Sauvezon, "Interception de l'énergie rayonnante, échanges gazeux et croissance dans une forêt méditerranéene à feuillage persistant (*Quercetum ilicis*), *Photosynthetica*, **9**, 145–156 (1975).

126. J.D. Tenhunen, O.L. Lange, J. Gebel, W. Beyschlag, and J.A. Weber, "Changes in photosynthetic capacity, carboxylation efficiency, and CO_2 compensation point associated with midday stomatal closure and midday depression of net CO_2 exchange of leaves of *Quercus suber*," *Planta*, **162**, 193–203 (1984).

127. W.K. Smith, "Importance of aerodynamic resistance to water use efficiency in three conifers under field conditions," *Plant Physiol.*, **65**, 132–135 (1980).

128. G. Aussenac and D. Finkelstein, "Influence de la sècheresse sur la croissance et la photosynthèse du cèdre," *Ann. Sci. For.*, **40**, 67–77 (1983).

129. U. Benecke, E.D. Schulze, R. Matyssek, and W.M. Havranek, "Environmental control of CO_2 assimilation and leaf conductance in *Larix decidua* Mill. I. A comparison of contrasting natural environments," *Oecologia*, **50**, 54–61 (1981).

130. R.J. Francey, R.M. Gifford, T.D. Sharkey, and B. Weir, "Physiological influences on carbon isotope discrimination in huon pine (*Lagarostrobos franklinii*)," *Oecologia*, **66**, 211–218 (1985).

131. H. Schlegel, D.L. Godbold, and A. Huttermann, "Whole plant aspects of heavy metal induced changes in CO_2 uptake and water relations of spruce (*Picea abies*) seedlings," *Physiol. Plant.*, **69**, 265–270 (1987).

132. E.H. Delucia, "The effect of freezing nights on photosynthesis, stomatal conductance, and internal CO_2 concentration in seedlings of Engelmann spruce (*Picea engelmannii* Parry)," *Plant, Cell Environ.*, **10**, 333–338 (1987).

133. C.L. Beadle, R.E. Neilson, P.G. Jarvis, and H. Talbot, "Photosynthesis as related to xylem water potential and carbon dioxide concentration in Sitka spruce," *Physiol. Plant.*, **52**, 391–400 (1981).

134. R.E. Neilson and P.G. Jarvis, "Photosynthesis in Sitka spruce (*Picea sitchensis* (Bong.) Carr.). VI. Response of stomata to temperature," *J. Appl. Ecol.*, **12**, 879–891 (1975).

135. K.O. Higginbotham, J.M. Mayo, S. L'Hirondelle, and D.K. Krystofiak, "Physiological ecology of lodgepole pine (*Pinus contorta*) in an enriched CO_2 environment," *Can. J. For. Res.*, **15**, 417–421 (1985).

136. M.H. El Aouni, *Processsus déterminant la production du pin d'Alep (Pinus halepensis Mill.): Photosynthèse, croissance et répartition des assimilats*, Ph.D. thesis, Université de Paris, 1980.

137. P.I. Coyne and G.E. Bingham, "Variation in photosynthesis and stomatal conductance in an ozone-stressed Ponderosa pine stand: Light response," *For. Sci.*, **28**, 257–273 (1982).

138. K.J. Bennett and D.A. Rook, "Stomatal and mesophyll resistances in two clones of *Pinus radiata* D. Don known to differ in transpiration and survival rate," *Aust. J. Plant Physiol.*, **5**, 231–238 (1978).

139. J.A. Fites and R.O. Teskey, "CO_2 and water vapor exchange of *Pinus taeda* in relation to stomatal behavior: Test of an optimization hypothesis," *Can. J. For. Res.*, **18**, 150–157 (1988).

140. F. Meinzer, G. Goldstein, and M. Jaimes, "The effect of atmospheric humidity on stomatal control of gas exchange in two tropical coniferous species," *Can. J. Bot.*, **62**, 591–595 (1984).

141. F. Meinzer, "The effect of vapor pressure on stomatal control of gas exchange in Douglas fir (*Pseudotsuga menziesii*) saplings," *Oecologia*, **54**, 236–242 (1982).

142. F. Meinzer, "The effect of light on stomatal control of gas exchange in Douglas fir (*Pseudotsuga menziesii*) saplings," *Oecologia*, **54**, 270–274 (1982).

143. C. Sabatier-Tarrago, *Production de taillis de châtaigniers* (*Castanea sativa Mill.*) *en relation avec les caractéristiques stationelles*, Ph.D. thesis, Université Paris-Sud, 1989.

144. T. Koike, Y. Sakagami, and Y. Fujimura, "Characteristics of the leaf dynamics and the photosynthesis of the seedlings and saplings of *Betula maximowicziana* and *Fraxinus mandshurica* var. *japonica* in Hokkaido, Japan," in T. Fujimori and D. Whitehead, eds., *Crown and Canopy Structure in Relation to Productivity*, Forestry and Forest Products Research Institute, Ibaraki, Japan, 1986, pp. 396–408.

145. H.A. Mooney and S.L. Gulmon, "The determinants of plant productivity—natural versus man-modified communities," in H.A. Mooney and M. Godron, eds., *Disturbance and Ecosystems. Components of Response*, Ecological Studies 44, Springer-Verlag, Berlin, 1983, pp. 146–158.

146. G. den Hartog, H.H. Neumann, and K.M. King, "Measurements of ozone, sulphur dioxide and carbon dioxide fluxes to a deciduous forest," in *Proceedings of the 18th Conference on Agricult. and Forest Meteorol. and 8th Conference on Biometeorology and Aerobiology*, Sept. 14–18, 1987, W. Lafayette, IN; published by the American Meteorological Society, Boston, 1988, pp. 206–209.

147. D.D. Baldocchi, S.B. Verma, and D.E. Anderson, "Canopy photosynthesis and water-use efficiency in a deciduous forest," *J. Appl. Ecol.*, **24**, 251–260 (1987).

148. R.L. Desjardins, J.L. MacPherson, P. Alvo, and P.H. Schuepp, "Measurements of turbulent heat and CO_2 exchange over forests from aircraft," in B.A. Hutchinson and B.B. Hicks, eds., *The Forest–Atmosphere Interaction*, D. Reidel Publishing Company, Dordrecht–Boston, 1985, pp. 645–658.

149. B.A. Monteny, "Primary productivity of a *Hevea* forest in Ivory Coast," *Ann. Sci. Forest.*, **46** (Suppl.), 502–505 (1989).

150. O.T. Denmead and E.F. Bradley, "Flux-gradient relationships in a forest canopy," in B.A. Hutchinson and B.B. Hicks, eds., *The Forest–Atmosphere Interaction*, D. Reidel Publishing Company, Dordrecht–Boston, 1985, pp. 421–442.

151. L.H. Allen, Jr. and E.R. Lemon, "Carbon dioxide exchange and turbulence in a Costa Rican tropical rain forest," in J.L. Monteith, ed., *Vegetation and the Atmosphere*, Vol. 2, *Case Studies*, Academic Press, London–New York, 1976, pp. 265–308.

3 Assimilate Distribution and Storage

RICHARD E. DICKSON

USDA Forest Service, North Central Forest Experiment Station, Forestry Sciences Laboratory, Rhinelander, Wisconsin (USA)

Contents

3.1. Introduction

Trees as woody perennials have complex growth habits. Trees may live for thousands of years and become immense. Trees in natural stands are also members of complex plant and animal communities and must compete for all limited external resources. Because of competition, trees (and all other life-forms) have developed life-cycle strategies that enable them to acquire and conserve these resources in order to optimize competitive fitness, reproduction, and growth within the plant community (118). Allocation of these resources can be given an economic analogy (7) in which all resources within the plant are distributed to maximize marginal returns (yield per unit of resource invested). Carbon, with its photosynthetic fixation and allocation within the plant, is the currency used to acquire other resources.

Trees, as woody perennials, have seasonal growth cycles in which new leaves, roots, and structural tissue are produced. Trees are also able to convert new structural tissue into nonrespiring dry matter that continues to function in transport of nutrients and in physical support at a considerable savings in respiratory carbon costs. Trees, to grow and compete, must continuously balance the carbon costs of new leaf production, respiration, and acquisition and distribution of new resources. Thus, the distribution and utilization of carbon assimilates within trees determine their growth and survival.

In addition to the fairly direct fixation of carbon by photosynthetic tissue, its distribution to developing tissues, and its incorporation into structural and functional compounds, assimilate distribution patterns are complicated by the function of carbon and nitrogen assimilates in the biophysical and metabolic regulation of plant growth and development. Different sugars (e.g., sucrose, raffinose, stachyose), sugar alcohols (e.g., sorbitol, mannitol), and amino acids (e.g., arginine, proline) are involved (the exact mechanisms are largely unknown) in osmotic adjustment, the development of cold-hardiness, the metabolic adjustment to moisture and salt stresses, and many other regulatory functions. The differential production of these compounds and the selective distribution within the plant are regulated by feedback cycles that respond to genetic and environmental signals controlling growth. Several major aspects of assimilate distribution and utilization in trees are discussed in this chapter: (a) different tissues and cell types involved in distribution of assimilates within trees, (b) production of translocatable compounds such as sucrose and the sugar alcohols and their transport in leaves, (c) assimilate distribution within trees as regulated by leaf development and source–sink interactions, (d) storage of reserve assimilates and some of the major compounds involved in storage, and (e) use of assimilates in various aspects of tree growth and reproduction.

3.2. Tissues involved in distribution of assimilates

The structural and functional aspects of the different tissues involved in the distribution of assimilated carbon are discussed here, and some of the current literature is mentioned to help readers understand the other sections of this chapter. A detailed discussion of the work in this area, however, is beyond the scope of this chapter.

The distribution of assimilates within the plant involves two major and very complex tissue systems—the phloem and the xylem. In addition to these two major systems, several ancillary tissues and cell types such as rays, paraveinal mesophyll, and transfer cells are involved in movement and storage of assimilates. The phloem is the primary system for distribution of assimilated carbon—sugars and other organic nutrients—from leaves to all other parts of the plant. The xylem is the primary system for movement of water and minerals from roots to leaves and other parts of the plant. Some minerals and organic nutrients move readily from phloem to xylem and from xylem to phloem for circulation throughout the plant. Movement between xylem and phloem provides for the recycling of nutrients from senescing tissue to young developing tissues and is essential for the control of assimilate distribution in plants.

3.2.1. Phloem

The development of phloem tissue and the physiology of phloem function have been studied for many years. Numerous books (10,20,22) and review articles (21,53,100,125) have been written about phloem structure and function and should be consulted for in-depth coverage. To initiate transport, sucrose is synthesized in the mesophyll cells of the leaf and is transferred primarily in the symplast between mesophyll cells up to the minor veins. Near the minor veins, sucrose is transferred to the apoplast and then actively loaded into the sieve element–companion cell (SE–CC) complex of the phloem (53). Movement from symplast to apoplast is perhaps the most common route of transfer because it allows for the active uptake of sucrose and the development of high turgor pressure in the SE–CC complex. Symplastic transfer from mesophyll cells to the phloem, however, cannot be ruled out for some species (139). Active loading of sucrose into the SE–CC complex increases the osmotic potential and induces water flow into these cells (92). This water flux into the SE–CC complex increases the turgor pressure and initiates transport in the sieve tubes. Such pressure-induced flow in the sieve tubes forms the basis for the Munch hypothesis of phloem transport; that is, sucrose solution moves by mass flow from source to sinks along a pressure gradient maintained by sucrose production and loading at the source and unloading and utilization at sinks. In addition to sugars and sugar alcohols, many other organic compounds (amino acids, organic acids, plant growth regulators, etc.) and inorganic compounds (potassium, phosphorus, magnesium, etc.) move by mass flow in the phloem (20). Although moving in response to the sucrose-generated pressure gradient, these individual compounds may be removed from the phloem and utilized at any point along the way, depending on the needs of the plant (143).

3.2.2. Xylem

In the more classical sense, the function of xylem, other than its structural function as wood, is to conduct water and minerals from roots to shoots. In addition, a major function of xylem is the distribution of assimilates. In fact, the concentration of organic nutrients usually far exceeds that of mineral nutrients. Xylem sap commonly contains sugars, organic acids, amino acids, plant growth regulators, and many other organic compounds (28,157). Although usually a minor component in xylem sap during active plant growth, sugar may be found in high concentrations (2–3% w/v) in late winter and early spring in such genera as *Acer*, *Betula*, and *Salix* (16,42,111,152). Perhaps the most important function of xylem in assimilate distribution is the transport of organic nitrogen compounds (98).

Inorganic nitrogen taken up by roots is rapidly converted to organic nitrogen compounds for translocation within the plant. Sugars, organic acids, and amino acids are translocated from shoots to roots in the phloem, converted to organic nitrogen compounds, and retranslocated back to shoots in the xylem (28,96,97). The amount and kind of organic nitrogen compounds translocated in xylem differ with plant species (2,96), plant developmental stage or season of the year (75,110,135), amount or kind of inorganic nitrogen available to roots (102), and perhaps other environmental factors. The two amides, asparagine and glutamine, are major transport compounds in trees and many other plants and move readily in both xylem and phloem (35,96,117,143). Carbohydrate transport to roots, nitrogen uptake, production of amino acids, and transport back to shoots are closely controlled feedback cycles regulated by demand of both shoots and roots for carbohydrate and nitrogen necessary for growth. The differential production of amino acids and other transport compounds in roots and the different distributional patterns in shoots of these compounds provide metabolic mechanisms for regulation of the composition of both xylem and phloem; for uptake, distribution, and recycling within the plant; and for selective allocation to various sinks in the plant.

3.2.3. Rays, paraveinal mesophyll, and transfer cells

The ray parenchyma of woody plants is specialized for the seasonal storage, mobilization, and translocation of assimilates (65,112,113,157). Vertical xylem parenchyma around the vessels and the vertical and horizontal ray parenchyma form a three-dimensional storage and transport system that extends throughout the secondary tissues of the plant. Ray parenchyma cells in the xylem commonly develop a secondary wall with many pits through which plasmodesmata connect to other cells and form a continuous symplastic system. The frequencies of pit fields and plasmodesmata are such that radial transport between xylem and phloem is enhanced and leakage to the xylem apoplast is minimized (112). The major functions of the ray system are exchange of solutes with the tracheal elements of the xylem, radial transport between xylem and phloem, and seasonal storage of starch, sugar, amino acids, and proteins (115).

Another specialized tissue that functions in assimilate translocation and storage is the paraveinal mesophyll (PVM). The paraveinal mesophyll is an anatomically and physiologically specialized leaf tissue of certain legumes and many other plants (11,49,76). The PVM forms a cellular network, usually one cell layer thick, that extends between bundle sheaths of different veins and connects to both the spongy mesophyll and the palisade parenchyma. Because it is developmentally, structurally, and functionally part of the bundle sheath, this tissue has also been termed the extended bundle sheath system (76). The position of the PVM within the leaf lamina and the symplastic connections with the mesophyll cells indicate that most, if not all, assimilates produced in the spongy mesophyll and palisade parenchyma pass through the PVM before loading into the phloem. Although extensively described in early anatomical literature (76), the functional significance of the PVM in phloem loading, recovery of amino acids from the xylem stream, and storage of assimilates and protein has been appreciated only recently (11,49).

Transfer cells are specialized cells that appear to facilitate the movement of nutrients from one tissue to another. These cells are found in many plant species from ferns to trees. Transfer cells are not a specialized tissue, but are specialized versions of cells found in many different tissues (99). Transfer cells are recognized structurally by their highly convoluted secondary wall ingrowths that greatly increase cell wall surface area and plasma membrane surface area. The increase in membrane surface area should increase the number of specialized carrier on pump sites and thus the transfer of both organic and inorganic nutrients.

As stated above, transfer cells are found in a wide variety of plant tissues, such as minor veins, nodes, haustoria, glands, and root nodules, where the movement of nutrients from one tissue to another is required. For example, four types of transfer cells (A, B, C, and D cells) were described in minor veins of leaves (99). These four types of veinal transfer cells are common in herbaceous diocots, much less common in woody diocots, and quite rare in monocots. The transfer cells of minor veins function in the loading (A cell) and unloading (B cell) of sieve cells of the phloem, transfer from xylem to phloem (C cell), and transfer from xylem to bundle sheath parenchyma (D cell). The presence of transfer cells in different species of plants and in different tissues of a particular species is highly variable, and the stimuli required for development are unknown. Although the secondary wall ingrowths develop concomitantly with the initiation of transport, conclusive evidence for their function is lacking. Their specialized structure and their location bordering various tissue types involved in long-distance translocation, however, provide strong evidence for their function in short-distance transfer of nutrients.

3.3. Regulation within the leaf

In trees, as in all higher green plants, assimilate distribution begins with the fixation of carbon in the chloroplasts of the leaf. This carbon is then partitioned to starch in the chloroplast for temporary storage and to sucrose in the cytosol for transport to other plant parts. Sucrose may also be temporarily stored in the vacuole. Understanding sucrose metabolism and transport is a prerequisite for understanding assimilate distribution because sucrose is the primary sugar translocated in plants and is the initial carbon source used for energy and biosynthesis of all plant biomass (129). A detailed description of the pathways, enzymes, and molecules involved in sucrose synthesis and metabolism is beyond the scope of this chapter. A brief description will be presented, however, because of the importance of sucrose synthesis in initial phases of assimilate distribution. Readers are referred to references cited here for detailed descriptions of the various processes. In addition, much of the research cited involves herbaceous crop plants because comparable research on trees is not available. There is no reason to believe, however, that the results of research on crop plants cannot be applied to trees if similar time frames and plant ontogenetic stages are compared.

3.3.1. Partitioning between sucrose and starch

When carbon from CO_2 enters the Calvin–Bassham–Benson photosynthetic pathway, some is required for regeneration of compounds in the pathway and some is converted to various ancillary metabolites, but most of the carbon is rapidly moved out of the pathway into sucrose and starch (12). Sucrose synthesis accounts for a major portion of this carbon flow as 50–70% of the recently fixed carbon is incorporated into this neutral sugar (122). Most of the remaining carbon is temporarily incorporated into starch. Starch in the chloroplast is hydrolyzed primarily at night to provide additional carbon for sucrose synthesis. Carbon is actively transported out of the chlorplast as triose-P (D-phosphoglyceraldehyde, 3-phosphoglycerate, or dihydroxyacetone phosphate) by a protein carrier called the "triose-P" or "P_i (inorganic phosphate) translocator" (Fig. 3.1). Four molecules of triose-P are required to synthesize one molecule of sucrose. The P_i generated during sucrose synthesis may be carried back into the chloroplast. The triose-P, P_i carrier is reversible and driven by the concentration gradients of triose-P and P_i between the chloroplast stroma and the cytosol. In the cytosol, carbon flows from triose-P to fructose-1, 6-biphosphate (F16BP) to fructose-6-phosphate (F6P). Sucrose phosphate is then synthesized from F6P and uridine-diphosphoglucose (UDPG). For starch formation in the chloroplasts, carbon is diverted from the Calvin cycle through F6P to glucose-6-phosphate (G6P) and glucose-1-phosphate (G1P) to starch. This very simplified version of carbon flow to sucrose and starch is actually much more complicated and involves a number of alternative enzyme reactions, cofactors, and interacting control points. For detailed discussion of the regulation of sucrose and starch synthesis, see Refs. 6, 47, 68, 69, 127, 128, and 129.

Much of the research contributing to our understanding of sucrose and starch biosynthesis was conducted on isolated enzyme systems, plant organelles, and plant tissue. The processes and mechanisms elucidated by research on such isolated systems are essential for our understanding but tend to be relatively simple. Sucrose and starch metabolism becomes much more complicated when studied *in vivo* on whole plants (51) because the systems (e.g., the pathway of carbon from triose-P to sucrose) are adaptive, adjust to dif-

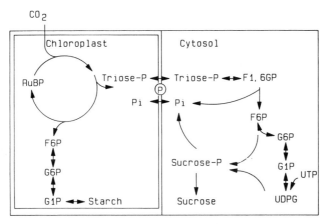

FIG. 3.1. Simplified diagram of carbon flow into the chloroplast, its cycling within the Calvin cycle, and partitioning to sucrose and starch. Symbol (P) denotes the P_i–triose-P carrier located in the chloroplast membrane.

ferent environmental requirements and are interactive, respond to changing requirements of the plant as a whole (129). For example, when Jablonski and Geiger (72) changed sugar beet (*Beta vulgaris* L.) plants from 14-h to 8-h days, the partitioning of carbon into starch more than doubled. The increased movement of carbon into starch, however, did not offset the decrease in total starch accumulation resulting from the 8-h days. Many other physiological and morphological changes also took place. Thus the change in response was not simply a shift in carbon flow from sucrose to starch but was an integrated response of the whole plant to changing environments. To understand the integrated control of carbon allocation, sucrose and starch synthesis, and translocation, the processes must be studied on intact and undisturbed plants (51).

Perhaps the best studies to date designed to determine the daily course of sucrose and starch synthesis under steady-state conditions were conducted on sugar beet and bean (*Phaseolus vulgaris* L.) (46,119,120). In these studies, ^{14}C was used as a tracer for carbon flow, plants were maintained under constant environmental conditions, and a sinusoidal light regime was imposed to simulate changing natural daylight. Under gradually changing light conditions, enzyme systems and regulatory mechanisms responded in a measured manner that did not set up oscillations in carbon flow to sucrose and starch (46). Photosynthetic rate or net carbon exchange (NCE) closely followed the changing light intensity. Leaf starch normally accumulates during the light period and degrades during the dark to maintain sucrose levels and transport rates. In these studies on sugar beet and bean, starch degradation and synthesis closely followed NCE. Starch levels decreased in the morning and evening as starch was degraded to provide carbon to supplement the synthesis of sucrose. Starch accumulation or degradation began when NCE was approximately 50% of maximum. The rate of sucrose synthesis from newly fixed carbon increased and decreased during the day, closely following NCE. Incorporation of carbon in starch was not directly controlled by sucrose levels in leaf tissue because both starch and sucrose accumulated concurrently during the day. This result contrasts with other studies that indicated that starch synthesis or degradation began with some specific concentration of sucrose in the mesophyll (52).

Studies of the changes in concentrations of other metabolites and enzyme systems in relation to NCE in sugar beet leaves indicated that with low-light conditions, most of the carbon fixed was used in maintaining the Calvin cycle (119,120). In addition, concentrations of triose-P were low and fructose-2, 6-bisphosphate (F26BP) were high. Because triose-P is presumed to be the major carrier of carbon from chloroplast to cytosol (Fig. 3.1) and F26BP is a strong inhibitor of the conversion of F16BP to F6P (68,127), relatively little carbon should move through this pathway into sucrose. Starch degradation and sucrose synthesis, however, take place rapidly under low light, indicating there must be considerable transport of carbon from chloroplast to cytosol. Such carbon could be transported as hexose-P although details of such pathways are lacking. The major points to be made here are (1) sucrose synthesis continued even though environmental conditions changed, (2) the path of carbon differed considerably depending on whether starch or newly fixed CO_2 was the source, and (3) multiple enzyme systems and different pathways of carbon flow could be phased in or out depending on environmental conditions and the needs of the plant. These alternative pathways provide redundancy in systems so that the plant can adapt to different environmental conditions. The relative partitioning of newly fixed carbon between starch storage and sucrose for transport has important implications for plant growth and development because allocation within the plant can change diurnally and in response to different environmental conditions.

3.3.2. Production of other transport compounds

It is generally accepted that sucrose is the major carbohydrate involved in translocation of assimilates in the phloem of most higher plants (20). Other sugars and sugar alcohols, however, are common transport and storage compounds in certain plant families. (For an introduction to this literature, see Refs. 20, 84, and references cited therein.) Sorbitol is the major photosynthetic product and translocated compound in many species of the Rosaceae—for example, *Malus* (apple), *Pyrus* (pears), and *Prunus* (peach, cherry, plum), and may constitute 60–90% of the soluble carbohydrates stored in and translocated from leaves of plants in this family (84,85). Similarly, mannitol is an important translocation product in several plant families (e.g., Oleaceae) in which *Fraxinus* (ash) and *Syringa* (lilac) are important woody species (133). In addition to these sugar alcohols or polyols, several other nonreducing sugars are translocated in some woody plants. Trip et al. (133) found after $^{14}CO_2$ labeling of leaves of lilac (*Syringa vulgaris* L.) and white ash (*Fraxinus americana* L.) that sucrose and mannitol were the major translocated compounds and that raffinose, stachyose, and verbascose were also labeled and translocated. Similarly, Costello et al. (17) found that stachyose (53%), raffinose (18%), sucrose (13%), and verbascose (6%) were the major carbohydrates in phloem exudation of evergreen ash (*Fraxinus uhdei Wenz*). No mention was made of mannitol content in that study. Raffinose, stachyose, and verbascose are also major transport sugars in *Curcurbita* (cucumber, squash, etc.) (20). Although these polyols and sugars may be present in young, developing leaves, they are imported primarily from older, mature source leaves. Major increases in synthetic enzymes, leaf pools, and translocation rates are associated with leaf maturity (85). Davis et al. (23) found in a series of $^{14}CO_2$ labeling studies with celery (*Apium graveolens* L.) that the total concentration of mannitol in leaves was always greater than that of sucrose, particularly in young, developing leaves (20–45 times greater in younger leaves). When those developing leaves were labeled with ^{14}C, however, only 4–8% of the water-soluble ^{14}C was found in mannitol, in contrast to 30% in sucrose, indicating considerable import of mannitol. When the leaves matured and transport of mannitol and sucrose began, the percentage of ^{14}C in mannitol increased to 20–35% and ^{14}C sucrose decreased to 15–20% of the water-soluble ^{14}C. These data indicate that sucrose is produced and utilized in leaves of all ages while mannitol is synthesized primarily in mature leaves and utilized in young, developing leaves and other sinks. Thus, mannitol and probably sorbitol and the raffinose sugars serve primarily as nonreducing long-distance transport compounds. The polyols and raffinose sugars also have additional roles in plant metabolism and are worthy of more intensive study.

3.3.3. Diurnal storage and change in transport

Allocation of carbon within the plant is a major determinant of growth and is influenced by such factors as sink strength, vascular connections between source and sink, and carbon flow between transport and storage products in the source leaf (29). Recently fixed carbon in source leaves is partitioned primarily to sucrose and to starch. Both sucrose and starch synthesis and carbon allocation within the plant have distinct diurnal patterns that are quite reproducible under constant environmental conditions, but may change rapidly if environmental conditions change (72). Different species may also have different partitioning patterns under the same environmental conditions. Fondy et al. (46) found that sucrose concentration doubled during the light period in sugar beet leaves but increased over five times in bean. Sugar beet also used more starch during the dark period than bean (90% vs. 25–45% in sugar beet and bean leaves, respectively). Similar diurnal changes in sucrose and starch were found in cottonwood (*Populus deltoides* Bart. Marsh.) leaves (Fig. 3.2). Sucrose concentration rapidly increased to about 25% of residue dry weight, remained constant through the light period, then decreased after dark. Starch concentration also began to increase at full light and continued to increase throughout the light period. Sucrose concentration decreased during the dark period to about 50% of that present in the light, whereas more

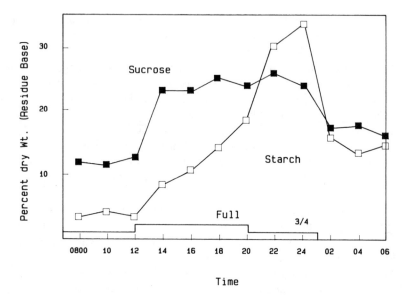

FIG. 3.2. Diurnal changes in sucrose and starch concentrations in mature cottonwood (*Populus deltoides*) leaves. Percent dry weights are based on residue dry weights, primarily structural carbohydrates that remain after soluble sugars and starch are removed from the tissue. The light regime was stepped from three-fourths to full light in the growth room. (Adapted from Ref. 30.)

than 80% of the starch was lost (30). Starch is degraded during the dark period, and the free sugars are converted to sucrose to maintain translocation.

Within-plant transport patterns may also change diurnally. Sink strength is probably the major controlling factor in photosynthate distribution within the plant. Rapidly expanding leaves on vegetative plants are strong sinks and receive most of the assimilate exported from the primary source leaf (nearest source leaf with direct vascular connections to the sink leaves). In a study on assimilate distribution in cottonwood, Dickson (30) found that the total amount of recently fixed ^{14}C translocated from a source leaf decreased during the light period (Fig. 3.3a). This decrease was associated with a shift in partitioning of ^{14}C from sugar to starch. At the same time, ^{14}C translocated upward to developing leaves and stem decreased from 81 to 55% of the total ^{14}C translocated. In contrast, ^{14}C translocated downward to lower stem and roots increased from 13 to 37%. The transport of recently fixed ^{14}C to expanding leaves (LPIs 2 and 4) declined during the light period from about 40–20% of the total ^{14}C translocated (Fig. 3.3b). This shift in allocation was probably mediated by a buildup of substrate (both imported and fixed *in situ*) in the expanding leaves during the light period.

Studies of competition for assimilate between expanding leaves and roots have shown that leaves are the stronger sinks. The import rate by expanding leaves is fairly constant for both day and night (45,67). In contrast, roots

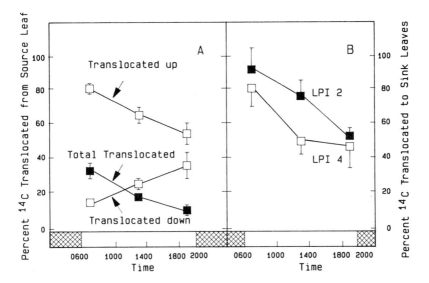

FIG. 3.3. Translocation of ^{14}C at different times during the light period within cottonwood (*Populus deltoides*) plants. The source leaf at leaf plastochron index (LPI) LPI 7, the first fully expanded leaf on the plant, was treated with $^{14}CO_2$ (0.5-h pulse and 3.5-h chase) at 0700, 1300, and 1900 h. Then the whole plant was harvested and subdivided, and ^{14}C was determined in the different fractions. (a) Percent total ^{14}C fixed that was translocated from the source leaf (total translocated) in 4 h, and allocation (up or down) of the translocated ^{14}C. (b) Percent translocated ^{14}C recovered in sink leaves LPI 2 and LPI 4. Bars show standard error of the mean. (Adapted from Ref. 30.)

import most of their photosynthate during the day for two major reasons. During the light period, CO_2 fixation is high, export rates are high, and excess photosynthate is available for transport to roots. During the dark period, export rates from source leaves usually decrease by 30–50% (45). If import to expanding leaves remains constant, export to roots must decrease. If leaf expansion rates increase at night, import by the leaf may increase, further limiting supply to the roots (9). Leaf growth at night may be sustained also by export from stem or roots of carbohydrate accumulated during the previous light period (67).

3.4. Regulation within the plant

The distribution of assimilate within the plant is regulated by source–sink interactions. Sources are exporters of assimilates and sinks are net importers of assimilate (63). The major sources in vegetative plants are the mature leaves.

Mature leaves fix carbon dioxide and export assimilates, primarily sucrose, to other parts of the plant. Stem and root storage tissue may also act as either source or sink, depending on season of the year and needs of the rest of the plant. Young, developing leaves have high metabolic rates and expansion rates and thus are strong sinks. These developing leaves compete with other sinks of the plant and strongly influence allocation patterns. The conversion of developing leaves from sinks to sources involves profound structured and physiological changes.

3.4.1. Sink–source conversion

Structural development and physiological processes change continuously from leaf initiation to full maturity. These changes are not uniform throughout the lamina but progress from tip to base in most plants. The onset of translocation from a particular lamina region indicates tissue maturity. Translocation begins after the SE–CC complex matures and a translocatable product is produced in the tissue (34). The simple leaf of cottonwood provides a good example of this developmental pattern. Both anatomical and ^{14}C transport studies show that leaf maturity begins at the lamina tip and progresses basipetally. In contrast to cottonwood, the compound leaves of green ash (*Fraxinus pennsylvanica* Marsh.) and honeylocust (*Gleditsia triacanthos* L.) mature first at the base. Basal leaflets may translocate both to developing distal leaflets and out of the leaf (82).

Northern red oak (*Quercus rubra* L.) has a simple leaf with yet another developmental pattern. Red oak leaf and stem growth is episodic with one or several flushes of growth each season. Within a flush, all the leaves of that flush expand and mature at about the same time, although there is an acropetal developmental gradient within the flush. Northern red oak leaves become autotrophic (no longer importing photosynthate from older leaves) at about 50% of full expansion. Transport of photosynthate out of the leaf begins at the lamina base at about 40–50% of full leaf expansion and progresses toward the tip. Transport out of the whole leaf begins at about 60–70% of full leaf expansion (132).

Most initial studies on sink–source transition in leaves were concerned primarily with the general patterns of changes in structure and function within the leaf (29). More recent studies were concerned with the mechanisms regulating the sink–source transition (138). These mechanisms involve both biochemical and structural changes. Carbon fixed by young, developing leaves is incorporated primarily into pigments, protein, and structural carbohydrates, chemical fractions associated with the rapidly developing photosynthetic capacity and structural components of the leaf. In a study of carbon flow during cottonwood leaf development, Dickson and Shive (34) found that in young leaves, more than 50% of recently fixed ^{14}C was incorporated into protein and pigments while only 10% was found in sugar. The percentage of ^{14}C incorporated into sugars increased almost linearly with leaf age. At leaf maturity, more than 50% of the ^{14}C was found in the sugar fraction. Thus, carbon flow into different biochemical pathways changes dramatically during leaf development (29,138). Translocation from a maturing portion of the leaf lamina does not begin until all other carbon requirements of the tissue are met and an excess of sugar is available for export.

Important structural changes also take place during the sink–source transition. The minor veins (classes IV and V) mature during this period and are used only for export. The phloem of the minor veins does not mature until the import phase is over (36,138). Associated with minor vein maturity is the development of the capacity to load sugar into the phloem against a concentration gradient (41). In addition, with maturity, the phloem in minor veins appears to lose the ability to unload imported sugars. This phenomenon probably is associated with blockage of the symplastic pathways between phloem and mesophyll cells. Partial separation of the cell walls during expansion of the maturing lamina tissue and blockage of the plasmodesmatal connections between the SE–CC complex and the adjoining mesophyll cells are probable mechanisms (36,138). The loss of the ability of mature leaves to unload imported assimilates has important implications for plant growth, which will be discussed later. The switch in carbon flow to neutral sugars and sugar alcohols for translocation and the anatomical and physiological maturation of the phloem in minor veins are closely synchronized in time and space, but one does not necessarily follow the other, as was clearly shown with albino tobacco (*Nicotiana tabacum*) leaves (137). In that study, albino shoots grafted on green stock plants produced new leaves for months with assimilate from the green stock plant. When the albino leaves were fully expanded, however, they were no longer able to import ^{14}C assimilates from the stock plant and soon died. In mature albino leaves, the minor veins lost the ability to unload sugars; and without an *in situ* source of photosynthate, the leaves soon died.

3.4.2. Source–sink interactions

To understand assimilate distribution in plants, one must have some knowledge of source–sink interaction. The movement of carbon from chloroplast to cytosol is the first source–sink movement in assimilate distribution. The chloroplast is the ultimate source of fixed carbon, and the chloroplast membranes are the primary barrier to movement. The intercellular movement from chloroplast to cytosol is perhaps the most important control point in source–sink interactions. Control of carbon flow at the chloroplast, however, has been discussed earlier in this chapter and by others (47,48,51). Here, source–sink interactions of plants are discussed at the whole-plant level. Sources are green leaves or other photosynthetic tissues that fix carbon and produce more assimilate than that required for their own growth and maintenance. Sinks are net importers of assimilate. The allocation of assimilate to different sinks is largely independent of assimilate production but is related to relative sink strength (63). Sink strength is the ability of the sink organ to import assimilate relative to other sinks in the plant and is related to sink size, growth rate, metabolic activity, and respiration rate. Developing leaves and developing fruit are relatively strong sinks; stem and root storage tissue are weak sinks. Thus, little carbon would be stored during early seasonal vegetative growth in trees. In fact, previously stored assimilates are depleted during rapid vegetative growth (31). Source leaves largely control the supply of sucrose and the loading of sucrose into the phloem. Once loaded, however, sink strength regulates allocation within the plant. The movement of assimilates is directly related to the sucrose gradient between source and sink. Rapidly growing sinks rapidly unload and utilize sucrose to maintain a steep gradient in the phloem (100).

Source–sink interactions were recently reviewed (50,51), and much research on whole plants showed that there are active feedback systems between source and sink tissue. High sink demand may increase photosynthetic rates and phloem loading in source leaves. Conversely, low sink demand may decrease photosynthetic rates, sucrose production, and phloem loading and may increase carbon partitioning into starch. The factors that control or mediate feedback between source and sink are largely unknown but may involve plant growth regulator transport, phloem turgor changes, enzymatic changes, and changes in source leaf structure. Because of the complexity of the systems involved and the different experimental time frames, much conflicting experimental results have been reported (50). Nevertheless, experiments with whole-plant systems, conducted over several days or weeks to allow for system adjustments, have shown that photosynthetic rates and translocation rates increase and decrease in response to changes in sink strength. The capacity for CO_2 fixation, carbon movement into sucrose or starch, and sucrose loading and transport are in constant adjustment, depending on the requirements of assimilate sinks.

A striking example of this source–sink interaction was found in northern red oak. Northern red oak has a semideterminate growth habit in which cyclic or episodic flushes of new leaf and stem growth occur. Because all leaves of a flush are expanding and developing at about the same time, the new flush is a major sink, particularly in small seedlings. Studies of carbon fixation and transport in northern red oak seedlings showed that carbon exchange rates, ^{14}C fixation, and translocation from the first-flush source leaves increased and then decreased dramatically during both the second and third flush (Fig. 3.4) (71). According to the *Quercus* morphological index (QMI), the second flush is rapidly expanding during the 2-stem linear and 2-leaf linear phase of shoot development (61). Carbon fixed in and carbon transported from the first-flush source leaves increased in response to the strong sink of the developing shoot (Fig. 3.4). During the 2-lag phase, leaves of the second flush are fully expanded, exporting assimilates, and are no longer sinks. The decrease in demand for assimilate decreased both carbon fixed and carbon translocated from the source leaves. This cycle was repeated during the third flush.

The distribution of assimilate within plants with determinate or semideterminate growth habit also responds to the flush cycle. During a flushing

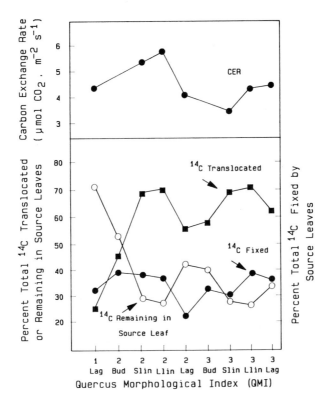

FIG. 3.4. Changes in carbon fixation and transport during flushing episodes in northern red oak (*Quercus rubra*). A first-flush source leaf was treated with $^{14}CO_2$ for 30 min, and the percentage of ^{14}C fixed and translocated was determined. (Adapted from Ref. 71.)

episode (e.g., 2-leaf linear; Fig. 3.5), more than 90% of the ^{14}C translocated from first-flush leaves was directed upward to developing second-flush leaves and stem, while about 5% was found in lower stem and roots. During the lag phase when second-flush leaves were fully expanded, only about 5% of the ^{14}C exported from first-flush leaves was translocated upward while 95% was translocated downward to lower stem and roots. First-flush leaves responded again during the third flush of growth with upward translocation of ^{14}C, even though the mature leaves of the second flush were also translocating upward. Such shifts in the direction of translocated photosynthate is probably a major contributing factor in the out-of-phase periodicity of shoot and root growth commonly observed in trees (37,64,123).

The distribution of assimilates within trees with indeterminate growth habit (trees that produce individual leaves at regular intervals during the growing season) such as cottonwood follows a consistent pattern throughout the growing season. Transport from mature leaves depends on vascular connections

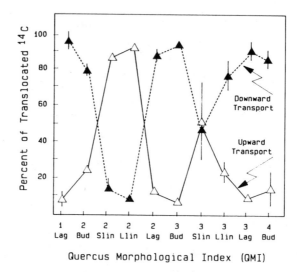

FIG. 3.5. Distribution of translocated ^{14}C within northern red oak (*Quercus rubra*) seedlings during two flushes of growth. Percentages are based on total ^{14}C recovered in different plant parts 48 h after ^{14}CO$_2$ treatment of a first-flush source leaf. Upward transport—sum of all ^{14}C found in leaves and stem above the first flush. Downward transport—sum of all ^{14}C found in first-flush stem and roots. Developmental stages are based on the *Quercus* morphological index (Ref. 61), i.e., 2Bud, developing bud of the second flush 2 cm long; 2Llin, leaf linear growth stage—middle leaves of the second flush rapidly expanding; 2Lag, second-flush leaves are fully expanded. (Adapted from Ref. 31.)

between source and sink leaves and proximity to major sinks (29,142). For example, a recently mature source leaf (a mature leaf capable of exporting assimilates) on a 16-leaf cottonwood plant has direct vascular connections to sink leaves (developing leaves that are importing assimilates) located three and five positions above the source leaf. Thus a leaf at leaf plastochron index (LPI) 7 would transport primarily to sink leaves LPI 4 and LPI 2 (Fig. 3.6). Recently mature leaves (LPI 7, 8, and 9) translocate upward to developing leaves and apex as well as downward to lower stem and roots. Older leaves (LPI 12–15) transport primarily downward to lower stem and roots. In larger plants (e.g., with 45 leaves), essentially the same transport patterns hold except more leaves (ca. 15) are in each leaf zone. The developmental and transport patterns described above should be found in all trees with indeterminate growth.

Developing lateral branches are also strong sinks. Assimilate for early development of proleptic branches (branches that develop from dormant buds on older shoots) comes from stem storage in deciduous trees and from both storage and current photosynthate in evergreen trees. Photosynthate for early development of sylleptic branches (branches that develop from current-year buds) is supplied primarily by the axillant leaf associated with the branch

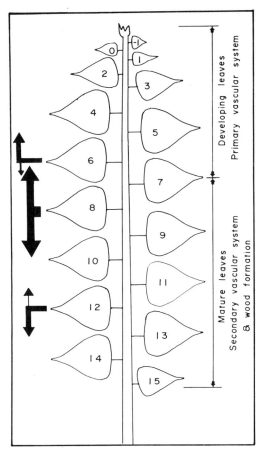

FIG. 3.6. Diagram of a 16-leaf cottonwood (*Populus deltoides*) plant showing the leaf plastochron index (LPI) numbering system, developing and mature leaf zones and the relative direction and amounts of photosynthate transported from different leaves. (Adapted from Ref. 29.)

(44). Branch sink strength decreases as more foliage leaves are produced. In cottonwood, sylleptic branches become photosynthetically independent of the main plant after 10–15 mature leaves have developed (29). Photosynthate produced by individual leaves on a branch is distributed within that branch in the same pattern described above for the main shoot of a seedling or current terminal of a larger tree. Photosynthate not required for branch growth and maintenance is transported to the main stem and moves primarily downward to lower stem and roots.

3.4.3. Leaf and branch autonomy

Assimilate from a particular source leaf or branch is not freely available to all other parts of the plant. Plants are composed of modular units that increase in complexity from tiny intercellular organelles to whole shoot or root systems. These units combine into subsystems that tend to function semiindependently with respect to the whole plant. Such subsystems function autonomously, particularly with respect to the assimilation and use of carbon (150).

As leaves expand and mature, they change from sinks to sources of assimilates. This maturation process involves both structural and physiological changes. Mature source leaves fix carbon, use some for internal respiration and tissue maintenance (ca. 20–30%), and export the remainder (ca. 70–80%) (51). Mature leaves under normal conditions do not import photosynthate via the phloem from other mature leaves, even if directly connected by vascular traces. Mature leaves can be induced to import small quantities of photosynthate, e.g., if severely stressed by aphid attack (154) or by experimental manipulation of light and CO_2 levels (39,43,130). If mature leaves are induced to import assimilate by light exclusion or other severe treatment, the imported assimilate remains mostly in the veins. Mature leaves are usually incapable of using imported sugars because of active phloem reloading from the apoplast (outside the plasmolemma in nonliving cell walls, etc.) or blockage of symplastic (inside the plasmolemma or living protoplasts) transport pathways away from the phloem (138). Thus, shading or other environmental stress leads to senescence and shedding of mature leaves that cannot maintain a favorable carbon balance.

Branches, as assemblages of leaves, are more complex subsystems. During early development, as the axillary bud elongates and foliage leaves expand from the preformed leaf primordia in the bud, the branch is a strong sink (44). The sink strength of the branch decreases as more foliage leaves develop. When the new branch has enough mature leaves to supply developing leaves, it becomes photosynthetically independent of the main shoot (29). Assimilate produced by branch leaves is distributed within the branch just as it is in the main shoot; thus, upper mature leaves supply the developing leaves, and lower mature leaves supply the lower portions of the branch. Excess assimilate produced by mid- and lower-branch leaves is translocated to the main stem. Thus, branch assimilate is important for lower main stem and root growth, particularly after budset and maturation of the branch leaves. However, this excess branch assimilate contributes little to height growth (29,70). Leaves of mid- and lower-crown branches export little assimilate to the current terminals or upper crown of the main stem or to other lower-crown branches. Also, leaves on current terminals and upper branches do not export to the lower branches. Thus, the leaves on any particular branch are responsible for production of assimilate for branch and leaf respiration, for cambial development, for vascular tissue development in that branch, and for development and maintenance of vascular connections between branch and mainstem. If excess photosynthate is not produced by leaves on the branch because of shading or some other stress, cambial activity in the branch stops, vascular connections between the branch and newly developing xylem of the main stem are not maintained, and the branch is soon isolated from the water and mineral nutrient flow of the main stem (86). When water and nutrient flow is disrupted, leaves on the branch senesce and the whole branch dies.

3.5. Seasonal storage of assimilates

Woody plants store reserves during times of excess assimilate production and use these reserves when demand exceeds current production. In perennial plants, excess photosynthate is stored as carbohydrate, lipids, and other chemical compounds. Storage of reserves is particularly important for plants growing in areas with large seasonal climatic changes. Reserves are used for respiration and plant maintenance during the dormant season and for new growth in spring. Stored products are also used for episodic growth flushes during the growing season (123).

Reserves are stored in living parenchyma cells of small twigs, branches, stems, and roots. In addition, needles or leaves of evergreen plants also store reserve assimilates. Most living parenchyma cells are capable of storage. Major storage tissues are the vertical and ray parenchyma of bark and xylem and the pith cells (156,157). In addition, living fibers in the xylem play a significant role in storage in *Acer* and certain other tree genera (146).

3.5.1. Carbohydrates

Carbohydrates are the major storage compounds in perennial plants. The seasonal variation in concentration and location of carbohydrates has been examined in many tree species (8,40,54,66,79,80,94). The seasonal cycles of carbohydrate storage and depletion are most clearly defined in single-flush deciduous trees. In branches and stems of such trees, the concentration of total nonstructural carbohydrates increases in late summer and fall, decreases slightly during the winter, then decreases rapidly in early spring during the spring growth flush. Starch concentration usually has two maxima, one in fall and one in spring. Starch is stored in late summer and fall as growth demands of the tree decrease. Associated with cool temperatures in late fall, the stored starch is hydrolyzed to soluble sugar (e.g., sucrose, raffinose, stachyose), which may increase cold-hardiness (94). Starch is again formed in early spring with warm temperatures before bud break and is then depleted during the spring growth flush.

The patterns of starch storage in roots differ from that found in stems because starch in roots is usually not hydrolyzed during the winter (Fig. 3.7). The seasonal pattern of starch storage in sugar maple (*Acer saccharum* Marsh.) roots and in several species of *Quercus* has been studied in some detail (146). The seasonal patterns of storage and depletion also differ among carbohydrate fractions (e.g., starch, sucrose, glucose) (8,66), among different species (19,73), and among different parts of the same plant (55). Conifers and other evergreens also differ from deciduous species in that there is less seasonal fluc-

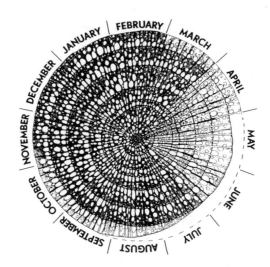

FIG. 3.7. Diagram of a cross section of a sugar maple (*Acer saccharum*) root showing the annual cycle of starch depletion, storage, and new xylem growth. Note that starch was depleted in April and May during new shoot growth and then was accumulated late in the growing season. Xylem formation in the new annual ring (July–August) did not deplete starch in the older rings. In the new ring, starch was first deposited in rays and then in xylem fibers in sequence with the maturity of this tissue. (Adapted from Ref. 146.)

tuation in conifer reserves because current photosynthate can supplement reserves during flushes of growth (31,54).

3.5.2. Nitrogen compounds

Nitrogen compounds are also a major form of assimilate storage in perennial plants. The major cycles of nitrogen storage and utilization are seasonal and associated with changes in tree growth. These seasonal nitrogen cycles have been studied mainly in fruit trees (75,126,131,134). Nitrogen storage usually begins as soon as new leaf and shoot growth slows in early summer. The initiation of storage is often indicated by an increase in arginine concentration in small branches and bark tissue. Both soluble nitrogen and protein nitrogen gradually increase during the summer as growth slows, then rapidly increase as leaves begin to senesce. Leaves on small trees may contain up to 50% of the total nitrogen in the plant, and 75–80% of that nitrogen may be retranslocated back into stems before leaf abscission (13,18,140). Nitrogen accumulation continues late into the fall in the main stem and roots as soluble nitrogen moves from twigs to main stem, and newly absorbed inorganic nitrogen is converted to organic nitrogen and stored in roots (75,134).

In perennial plants, nitrogen is stored both as soluble amino compounds and protein. In apple trees, when protein accumulation in bark peaked in late November, Kang and Titus (74) found about 90% of the nitrogen in protein and about 10% in soluble amino compounds. The relative proportions of soluble versus insoluble nitrogen compounds vary with season, within different parts of the tree, with fertilization, with different extraction methods, and with changing environmental conditions (75).

The presence of storage proteins in tree tissue has been recognized for a long time. Until the recent development of better extraction techniques, however, few detailed studies were conducted. Studies on *Salix* (115) and on several other forest tree species (114,121,151) have shown that storage proteins are located in vacuoles of ray and phloem parenchyma cells. Storage proteins are rich in arginine and other basic amino acids, accumulate in the fall, and disappear in the spring. The concentration of storage protein is greater in bark than in wood, decreases from fine twigs to branches to stems, then increases in roots. Protein content may exceed 2–3% in bark of small twigs, although it is usually less than 1% of total dry weight in stems and roots (114).

In evergreen trees, leaves and needles as well as stem and roots are important sites for nitrogen storage. Nitrogen is stored during periods of inactive growth and then retranslocated to new developing leaves and shoots during flushing. In *Citrus*, a tropical evergreen tree with an episodic flushing growth habit, nitrogen used in the new flush comes largely from storage. By measuring the nitrogen content of different tree parts before and after the spring growth flush, Kato (75) found that nitrogen in the new flush came from mature leaves (20%), stem (40%), roots (30%), and the soil (10%). Similarly, Nambiar and Fife (93) found that up to 54% of the nitrogen in mature needles was translocated to the developing flush in *Pinus radiata*.

3.5.3. *Lipids and other compounds*

Other chemical compounds may act as assimilate storage reserves in trees and other perennial plants, but their concentrations are generally insignificant compared to that of storage carbohydrate. Lipids have long been considered important storage compounds in forest trees and may reach high concentrations in specific structures such as buds and fruit (80). Lipid concentrations in stems have also been shown to increase in the fall and decrease in spring (54,156). Lipid concentrations as high as 5–6% of dry weight have been reported in the older literature (see references cited in Ref. 80). These high concentrations are suspect, however, because the analytical methods were not specific for storage lipids. Nelson and Dickson (94) found that triglycerides, the major form of storage lipid, increased from 1 to 3% of residue dry weight in cottonwood (*Populus deltoides*) stems as the plants became dormant under 8-h days. In contrast, total nonstructural carbohydrates increased to more than 35% of residue dry weight. The ability to store lipids as assimilate reserves varies widely among different tree species: in some deciduous trees and conifers lipids may form significant reserves. Even though the energy content of storage lipids is approximately twice that of carbohydrates, the amount of storage lipid in most tree species would need to increase about 10 times to equal the energy found in carbohydrate reserves. Hemicelluloses may also act as assimilate reserves, although there is considerable debate about the extent to which hemicellulose once incorporated into cell walls can be remobilized (54). Hemicelluloses are common reserves in some seeds and may be stored in parenchyma cells of leaves, stems, and roots and used during new growth (78). Because the hemicelluloses are such heterogenous polysaccharides with wide ranges in solubilities, some labile fractions may be useful as reserves. Analytical techniques for their extraction and analyses must be carefully standardized before their true role as reserve carbohydrate in trees can be established.

3.6. Tree growth and use of assimilates

All plants allocate carbon to maximize competitive fitness, reproduction, and growth within their various plant communities. Plants in different environments have different "strategies" for allocation, depending on their life-forms (118). Annual plants have basically four seasonal growth phases—early vegetative, flowering, seed fill, and senescence—and thus their allocation patterns are relatively simple. In comparison, trees may live from 50 years to more than 5000 years. During their lives, trees go through several different growth stages: seedlings, saplings, pole stage, mature flowering and fruiting, and senescence. Each stage is characterized by increasingly complex crown morphology and allocation patterns. In addition, seasonal growth phases also alter allocation patterns (33,124). Additional complexities and differences arise between deciduous and evergreen trees. Deciduous and evergreen trees use different strategies to maximize carbon gain and utilization of both internal and external resources (118). Deciduous trees rapidly renew all their leaves in the spring at a relatively low carbon cost per unit leaf area but at a high cost of stored carbohydrate. Deciduous leaves are also very productive per unit leaf area, and much of the carbon fixed after leaf development is available for growth of stems and roots or for storage. In contrast, carbon costs of evergreen leaves are relatively high (101). In most evergreen species, however, only a small portion of total leaf mass is renewed each year. Carbon fixation continues in older leaves, and overall carbon gain may be similar to that in rapidly growing deciduous trees (88). Although patterns of carbon fixation, allocation within the plant, and cycling within the plant may differ in many details between and among deciduous and evergreen trees, the major seasonal patterns of carbon allocation are very similar.

3.6.1. Reserves versus current assimilates

Stored assimilates are used for new leaf growth and shoot growth in the spring and for regrowth of leaves after defoliation (57,58,155). However, the degree to which current photosynthate versus stored assimilate contributes to new growth is not at all clear. In deciduous trees, stored assimilates must be used for the initial flush of new growth. As soon as mature leaves are present, however, the use of reserves stop, and current photosynthate is used for subsequent growth. Wargo (146), in his work on the seasonal starch storage patterns and growth of sugar maple, clearly showed that new root growth used current photosynthate (Fig. 3.7). During flushing in May, roots were depleted of starch content. Starch began to accumulate by late June after new leaf growth ceased, and most of the root parenchyma and fiber cells were filled with starch by late July. These root starch reserves were not depleted when new xylem formed in the root, indicating that the new radial root growth resulted largely from current photosynthate.

In conifers and other evergreens, assimilate for new growth comes both from reserves and current photosynthate (31). The relative contribution from these two sources of assimilates is not clear and may vary with species and environmental conditions (38,81,83). New root growth may be particularly sensitive to current photosynthate supply. Roots are functionally weak sinks and usually receive assimilate only after developing leaf demand is met, thus the commonly observed periodicity of root growth (37). Van den Driessche (141) found that assimilate used in new root growth in planted Douglas fir (*Pseudotsuga menziesii*) and Sitka spruce (*Picea sitchensis*) came largely from current photosynthate. Philipson (104) extended these observations with ringing studies and found that girdled Sitka spruce could produce new roots from stored carbohydrate in the root system but at considerably decreased rates. In contrast, Douglas fir could not use stored carbohydrate in the root system and produced no new root growth when girdled.

3.6.2. Defoliation, growth, and the use of assimilates

The use of assimilates in response to defoliation by plant herbivores or other causes can have dramatic effects on subsequent growth of trees. Plants respond to defoliation with compensatory growth, increased assimilation of carbon, and production of antiherbivore defense compounds (14). A partial or even complete defoliation of vigorously growing plants with adequate reserves usually has little effect on overall growth. In vigorous nursery-grown *Populus* hybrids, 75–80% defoliation was required to decrease growth by 20% (4). Similar defoliation of plants that are already under other stresses, however, may cause death. Defoliated plants usually respond by decreases in lower stem and root growth, increases in new foliage and lateral branch growth, and increases in photosynthesis in both residual foliage and newly produced foliage (3,136). Such changes in carbon allocation and increases in carbon fixation rates may partially compensate for lost foliage. Repeated defoliation of trees can lead to severe decreases in number of buds and new leaves and eventually to branch dieback or death of the whole tree (62,147).

Specific response to defoliation may be highly variable because of genetic makeup, physiological states, and quantity of reserves. The timing of defoliation can also be important. Defoliation in July and August can be particularly damaging because this is a time of rapid assimilate storage. Buds and new shoots formed after such late-season defoliation are often killed during the winter, and carbohydrate depletion may limit regrowth the following year

(57,58). New branch and foliage growth of deciduous plants in the spring depends entirely on stored carbohydrates, and new branches may abscise soon after initiation if carbohydrate is limiting. More important for tree growth, defoliation may initiate a cycle involving many stress factors. For example, low carbohydrate reserves in stems and roots increase susceptibility to cold winter temperatures, decrease foliage regrowth, decrease root growth, increase water stress, and increase susceptibility to root rots and other pathogens (58,148,149). Such multiple stresses may cause top dieback, general progressive decline, and eventual death of the tree.

3.6.3. Flowering and fruiting

The use of assimilates in flower and fruit production in trees has been extensively studied and reviewed (79). Much of the work on assimilates and fruit production involved commercial fruit trees and other horticultural crops (24,106,109,116,153), although some conifers have been studied (26,17). In fruit crops, the large amount of fruit produced imposes a severe drain on both carbohydrate reserves and current photosynthate. These reproduction costs are reflected in alternate-bearing trees in which a large fruit crop in one year results in little or no fruit the next year (116). Such large fruit crops may also decrease vegetative growth in both the "on" and "off" years because of reserve depletion. Decreases in vegetative growth and fruit production following high-seed-production years are also common in forest trees and other perennial plants (1,59,79). Such heavy mast years may severely deplete carbohydrate reserves (153). However, depletion of reserves is probably not the main cause of erratic seed years in most forest trees because many environmental and physiological factors are involved in flower and fruit production.

Differences in resource allocation and assimilate required for reproduction have been implicated in the sexual dimorphism of dioecious plants. Males often exceed females in total plant size, plant height, growth rates, and frequencies in populations (105). Assimilate allocation to reproduction, however, is only one factor of many that control growth and development of male or female plants in different environments (107). There is little experimental evidence for how flower and fruit production alters growth, individual mortality, and future fecundity in perennial plants because of problems in experimental design, phenological differences between sexes, and lack of in-depth seasonal studies of assimilate allocation (1,105,107).

The relative contribution of stored assimilate versus current photosynthate for fruit production is also highly variable for different species and during the seasonal course of fruit development. During early stages of leaf and flower development, most carbon for growth comes from reserves. With leaf maturity, however, essentially all assimilate for fruit development comes from current photosynthate of nearby leaves. Hansen (60) estimated that about 200 mg of stored assimilate was needed to produce functional leaves and flowers on a spur shoot of apple (*Malus domestica*). Subsequent growth to about 2500 mg for the mature leaves and fruit came from current photosynthesis. Thus, only about 8–10% of this final dry weight came from reserves. Green fruit may also photosynthetically fix carbon and contribute to seed development. In a study of fruit gas exchange in 15 different tree species, Bazzaz et al. (5) found that the contribution of fruit photosynthesis to fruit respiration and growth ranged from 64% (*Acer platanoides*) to 2% (*Quercus macrocarpa*) of the total carbon required. In contrast to the above information, some forest trees that are summer drought deciduous or shade deciduous develop large seed crops after leaf fall. Assimilate for seed production in these trees comes almost entirely from reserves (25,91).

3.6.4. Fine roots and mycorrhizae

The assimilate required for the production of fine roots (<2 mm in diameter) and their associated microflora and microfauna is a significant portion of the total carbon fixed in photosynthesis (90). Estimates commonly range from 50 to 70% of net primary production (95,108). Surprisingly, research on root growth and carbon costs has received relatively little attention until quite recently. Because of the technical difficulty involved in sampling and the variability found in root growth, good information on the assimilate required for fine-root growth and mycorrhizae development is largely lacking. This lack creates a major gap in our understanding of carbon allocation in trees.

Fine-root biomass, as a percentage of leaf or total above-ground biomass, increases until canopy closure and then either remains constant or decreases as the stand ages (145). Annual production of fine roots in different stands after closure varies widely ($1-11$ tons ha^{-1} yr^{-1}; see Ref. 89 and references cited therein). Seasonal patterns of growth also vary from constant growth rates to one or two major growth peaks during the year. Such variation in fine-root growth should be expected because root growth is affected by species, climate, soil type, fertility, moisture, temperature, shoot growth patterns, management system, and methods for sampling and calculating root biomass (89). The percentage of net primary production (NPP) required for fine-root growth also varies widely. Estimates range from 8 to 80% of NPP with 50–60% the most common values (89,108). Fine-root production is generally greater on poor sites (15,77,95,145). For example, Keys and Grier (77) found that fine-root production was only 8% of total dry matter production on a good Douglas fir site but was 36% on a poor site. Total production did not differ that greatly between the sites (2.4 tons ha^{-1} more on the good site); thus more carbon was allocated to root growth on the poor site. Similar changes in allocation to root growth may be induced by fertilization. Gower and Vitousek (56) found that fertilization of nitrogen limited forest stands on the island of Hawaii reduced the total fine-root biomass from 800 to 425 g m^{-2} within 2 years after initiation of the fertilization trials.

Assimilates flowing into and out of fine roots support a dense community of soil organisms. Probably all forest trees form mycorrhizal symbiotic associations (103). However, it is difficult to quantify the amount of assimilates allocated to either fine roots or the mycorrhizal fungi and other rhizosphere organisms. Estimates of assimilate allocation to mycorrhizae range from 10 to 40% of the total photosynthetically fixed carbon (103). Studies with ^{14}C have shown that 40% of the photosynthetically fixed $^{14}CO_2$ was found in mycorrhizal roots, while only 10% of the ^{14}C was translocated to nonmycorrhizal roots (87). In field studies on *Abies amabilis* ecosystems, Vogt et al. (144) estimated that 15% of NPP was allocated to mycorrhizae and 60% of NPP was allocated to fine roots in mature stands. Thus, 75% of NPP of these stands was required to maintain these fine-root systems. The allocation of such massive amounts of carbon to fine roots and associated mycorrhizae points out the importance of these systems in the various "strategies" trees use to compete in their respective communities.

3.7. Concluding Remarks

Throughout this chapter, there have been somewhat detailed descriptions of how assimilates from current photosynthate move from chloroplast to phloem and xylem and are distributed throughout the tree and how assimilates are stored as reserves and then subsequently used in new growth. Most of the information used in this chapter comes from studies on trees and other plants grown in controlled environments or under optimum conditions in the field. Forest trees and many horticultural crops do not grow in optimum environments but under conditions of frequent and multiple stresses. Trees respond to stress by changes in assimilation and allocation of carbon and other resources within the plant. Because of changes in carbon allocation, tree growth changes to compensate for the stress. Such changes in growth involves compensatory feedback between many parts of the tree. Environmental stresses are sensed primarily by leaves (32). With the initiation of stress (e.g., water stress), leaf growth slows, decreasing leaf sink strength. Then, photosynthate builds up in source leaves, and transport is redirected to lower stem and roots. The increase in supply of current photosynthate to roots may increase root growth; increased root growth results in an increase in water uptake, and the cycle repeats. Tree response to defoliation, an additional example of a stress response, is given in some detail in Section 3.6.2.

Each tree species has a different strategy or inherent response to stresses normally encountered in its ecological community. Unfortunately, relatively little is known about how a particular species will respond to a single well-defined stress, much less to multiple stresses. In addition, response to short-term stresses is often quite different from response to long-term stresses because of the ability of trees to acclimate to stress. Much more multidisciplinary research is needed with important tree species to develop basic biological information on how water, nutrient, and other environmental stresses affect carbon fixation; assimilate distribution and utilization; leaf, stem, and root growth; and shoot–root feedback.

3.8. References

1. J. Ågren, "Sexual differences in biomass and nutrient allocation in the Dioecious *Rubus chamaemorus*," *Ecology*, **69**, 962–973 (1988).

2. R.L. Barnes, "Organic nitrogen compounds in tree xylem sap," *For. Sci.*, **9**, 98–102 (1963).

3. J. H. Bassman and D.I. Dickmann, "Effects of defoliation in the developing leaf zone on young *Populus × euramericana* plants. I. Photosynthetic physiology, growth, and dry weight partitioning," *For. Sci*, **28**, 599–612 (1982).

4. J. Bassman, W. Myers, D. Dickmann, and L. Wilson, "Effects of simulated insect damage on early growth of nursery-grown hybrid poplars in northern Wisconsin," *Can. J. For. Res.*, **12**, 1–9 (1982).

5. F.A. Bazzaz, R.W. Carlson, and J.L. Harper, "Contribution to reproductive effort by photosynthesis of flowers and fruits," *Nature*, **279**, 554–555 (1979).

6. E. Beck and P. Ziegler, "Biosynthesis and degradation of starch in higher plants," *Ann. Rev. Plant Physiol. Plant Mol. Biol.*, **40**, 95–117 (1989).

7. A.J. Bloom, F.S. Chapin III, and H.A. Mooney, "Resource limitation in plants—an economic analogy," *Ann. Rev. Ecol. Syst.*, **16**, 363–392 (1985).

8. A. Bonicel, G. Haddad, and J. Gagnaire, "Seasonal variations of starch and major soluble sugars in different organs of young poplars," *Plant Physiol. Biochem.*, **25**, 451–459 (1987).

9. J.A. Bunce, "Effects of water stress on leaf expansion, net photosynthesis, and vegetative growth of soybeans and cotton," *Can. J. Bot.*, **56**, 1492–1498 (1978).

10. M.J. Canny, *Phloem Translocation*, Cambridge Univ. Press, London, 1973.

11. M.J. Canny, "Bundle sheath tissues of legume leaves as a site of recovery of solutes from the transpiration stream," *Physiol. Plant.* **73**, 457–464 (1988).

12. M.L. Champigny, "Regulation of photosynthetic carbon assimilation at the cellular level: A review," *Photosyn. Res.*, **6**, 273–286 (1985).

13. F.S. Chapin III and R.A. Kedrowski, "Seasonal changes in nitrogen and phosphorus fractions and autumn retranslocation in evergreen and deciduous taiga trees," *Ecology*, **64**, 376–391 (1983).

14. P.D. Coley, J.P. Bryant, and F.S. Chapin III, "Resource availability and plant antiherbivore defense," *Science*, **230**, 895–899 (1985).

15. P.G. Comeau and J.P. Kimmins, "Above- and below-ground biomass and production of lodgepole pine on sites with differing soil moisture regimes," *Can. J. For. Res.*, **19**, 447–454 (1989).

16. P.M. Cortes and T.R. Sinclair, "The role of osmotic potential in spring sap flow of mature sugar maple trees (*Acer saccharum* Marsh.)," *J. Exp. Bot.*, **36**, 12–24 (1985).

17. L.R. Costello, J.A. Bassham, and M. Calvin, "Enhancement of phloem exudation from *Fraxinus uhdei* Wenz. (Evergreen ash) using ethylenediaminetetraacetic acid," *Plant Physiol.*, **69**, 77–82 (1982).

18. B. Côté and J.O. Dawson, "Autumnal changes in total nitrogen, salt-extractable proteins and amino acids in leaves and adjacent bark of black alder, eastern cottonwood and white basswood," *Physiol. Plant.*, **67**, 102–108 (1986).

19. P.I. Coyne and C.W. Cook, "Carbohydrate reserve cycles in eight desert range species," *J. Range Management*, **23**, 438–444 (1970).

20. A.S. Crafts and C.E. Crisp, *Phloem Transport in Plants*, Freeman, San Francisco, 1971.

21. J. Cronshaw, "Phloem structure and function," *Ann. Rev. Plant Physiol.*, **32**, 465–484 (1981).

22. J. Cronshaw, W.J. Lucas, and R.T. Giaquinta, eds., *Phloem Transport*, Alan R. Liss, New York, 1986.

23. J.M. Davis, J.K. Fellman, and W.H. Loescher, "Biosynthesis of sucrose and mannitol as a function of leaf age in celery (*Apium graveolens* L.)," *Plant Physiol.*, **86**, 129–133 (1988).

24. T.M. Dejong, J.F. Doyle, and K.K. Day, "Seasonal patterns of reproductive and vegetative activity in early and late maturing peach, *Prunus persica* cultivars," *Physiol. Plant.*, **71**, 83–88 (1987).

25. C.W. DePamphilis and H.S. Neufeld, "Phenology and ecophysiology of *Aesculus sylvatica*, a vernal understory tree," *Can. J. Bot.*, **67**, 2161–2167 (1989).

26. D.I. Dickmann and T.T. Kozlowski, "Mobilization by *Pinus resinosa* cones and shoots of C^{14}-photosynthate from needles of different ages," *Am. J. Bot.*, **55**, 900–906 (1968).

27. D.I. Dickmann and T.T. Kozlowski, "Mobilization and incorporation of photo-assimilated ^{14}C by growing vegetative and reproductive tissues of adult *Pinus resinosa* Ait. trees," *Plant Physiol.*, **45**, 284–288 (1970).

28. R.E. Dickson, "Xylem translocation of amino acids from roots to shoots in cottonwood plants," *Can. J. For. Res.*, **9**, 374–378 (1979).

29. R.E. Dickson, "Carbon fixation and distribution in young *Populus* trees," in T. Fujimori and D. Whitehead, eds., *Proceedings Crown and Canopy Structure in Relation to Productivity*, Forest and Forest Products Research Institute, Ibaraki, Japan, 1986, pp. 409–426.

30. R.E. Dickson, "Diurnal changes in leaf chemical constituents and ^{14}C partitioning in cottonwood," *Tree Physiol.*, **3**, 157–171 (1987).

31. R.E. Dickson, "Carbon and nitrogen allocation in trees," *Ann. Sci. For.*, **46** (suppl.), 631s–647s, in E. Dreyer et al., eds., *Forest Tree Physiology*, Elsevier/INRA, Paris, 1989.

32. R.E. Dickson and J.G. Isebrands, "Leaves as regulators of stress response in plants," in H.A. Mooney, E.J. Pell, and W.E. Winner, eds., *Integrated Response of Plants to Stress*, Academic Press, New York, in press.

33. R.E. Dickson and E.A. Nelson, "Fixation and distribution of ^{14}C in *Populus deltoides* during dormancy induction," *Physiol. Plant.*, **54**, 393–401 (1982).

34. R.E. Dickson and J.B. Shive, Jr., "$^{14}CO_2$ fixation, translocation, and carbon metabolism in rapidly expanding leaves of *Populus deltoides*," *Ann. Bot.*, **50**, 37–47 (1982).

35. R.E. Dickson, T.C. Vogelmann, and P.R. Larson, "Glutamine transfer from xylem to phloem and translocation to developing leaves of *Populus deltoides*," *Plant Physiol.*, **77**, 412–417 (1985).

36. B. Ding, M.V. Parthasarathy, K. Niklas, and R. Turgeon, "A morphometric analysis of the phloem-unloading pathway in developing tobacco leaves," *Planta*, **176**, 307–318 (1988).

37. A.P. Drew and F.T. Ledig, "Episodic growth and relative shoot:root balance in loblolly pine seedlings," *Ann. Bot.*, **45**, 143–148 (1980).

38. A. Ericsson, "Effects of low temperature and light treatment, following winter cold storage, on starch accumulation in scots pine seedlings," *Can. J. For. Res.*, **14**, 114–118 (1984).

39. W. Eschrich and B. Eschrich, "Control of phloem unloading by source activities and light," *Plant Physiol. Biochem.*, **25**, 625–634 (1987).

40. S. Essiamah and W. Eschrich, "Changes of starch content in the storage tissues of deciduous trees during winter and spring," *IAWA Bull.*, **6**, 97–106 (1985).

41. R.J. Fellows and D.R. Geiger, "Structural and physiological changes in sugar beet leaves during sink to source conversion," *Plant Physiol.*, **54**, 877–885 (1974).

42. A.R. Ferguson, J.A. Eiseman, and J.A. Leonard, "Xylem sap from *Actinidia chinensis:* Seasonal changes in composition," *Ann. Bot.* **51**, 823–833 (1983).

43. D.G. Fisher and W. Eschrich, "Import and unloading of ^{14}C assimilate into mature leaves of *Coleus blumei*," *Can. J. Bot.*, **63**, 1700–1707 (1985).

44. D.G. Fisher, P.R. Larson, and R.E. Dickson, "Phloem translocation from a leaf to its nodal region and axillary branch in *Populus deltoides*," *Bot. Gaz.*, **144**, 481–490 (1983).

45. B.R. Fondy and D.R. Geiger, "Diurnal patterns of translocation and carbohydrate metabolism in source leaves of *Beta vulgaris* L.," *Plant Physiol.*, **70**, 671–676 (1982).

46. B.R. Fondy, D.R. Geiger, and J.C. Servaites, "Photosynthesis, carbohydrate metabolism, and export in *Beta vulgaris* L. and *Phaseolus vulgaris* L. during square and sinusoidal light regimes," *Plant Physiol.*, **89**, 396–402 (1989).

47. C.H. Foyer, "The basis for source–sink interaction in leaves," *Plant Physiol. Biochem.*, **25**, 649–657 (1987).

48. C.H. Foyer, "Feedback inhibition of photosynthesis through source–sink regulation in leaves," *Plant Physiol. Biochem.*, **26**, 483–492 (1988).

49. V.R. Franceschi and R.T. Giaquinta. "Specialized cellular arrangements in legume leaves in relation to assimilate transport and compartmentation: Comparison of the paraveinal mesophyll," *Planta*, **159**, 415–422 (1983).

50. D.R. Geiger, "Effects of translocation and assimilate demand on photosynthesis," *Can. J. Bot.*, **54**, 2337–2345 (1976).

51. D.R. Geiger, "Understanding interactions of source and sink regions of plants," *Plant Physiol. Biochem.*, **25**, 659–666 (1987).

52. R. Gerhardt, M. Stitt, and H.W. Heldt, "Subcellular metabolite levels in spinach leaves: Regulation of sucrose synthesis during diurnal alterations in photosynthetic partitioning," *Plant Physiol.*, **83**, 399–407 (1987).

53. R.T. Giaquinta, "Phloem loading of sucrose," *Ann. Rev. Plant Physiol.*, **34**, 347–387 (1983).

54. C. Glerum, "Food sinks and food reserves of trees in temperate climates," *NZ J. For. Sci.*, **10**, 176–185 (1980).

55. C. Glerum and J.J. Balatinecz, "Formation and distribution of food reserves during autumn and their subsequent utilization in jack pine," *Can. J. Bot.*, **58**, 40–54 (1980).

56. S.T. Gower and P.M. Vitousek, "Effects of nutrient amendments on fine root biomass in a primary successional forest in Hawaii," *Oecologia*, **81**, 566–568 (1989).

57. R.A. Gregory and P.M. Wargo, "Timing of defoliation and its effect on bud development, starch reserves, and sap sugar concentration in sugar maple," *Can. J. For. Res.*, 16, 10–17 (1986).

58. R.A. Gregory, M.W. Williams, Jr., B.L. Wong, and G.J. Hawley, "Proposed scenario for dieback and decline for *Acer saccharum* in northeastern U.S.A. and southeastern Canada," *IAWA Bull.*, **7**, 357–369 (1986).

59. H.L. Gross, "Crown deterioration and reduced growth associated with excessive seed production by birch," *Can. J. Bot.*, **50**, 2431–2437 (1972).

60. P. Hansen, "^{14}C-studies on apple trees VII. The early seasonal growth in leaves, flowers and shoots as dependent upon current photosynthesis and existing reserves," *Physiol. Plant.*, **25**, 469–473 (1971).

61. P.J. Hanson, R.E. Dickson, J.G. Isebrands, T.R. Crow, and R.K. Dixon, "A morphological index of *Quercus* seedling ontogeny for use in studies of physiology and growth," *Tree Physiol.*, **2**, 273–281 (1986).

62. G.H. Heichel and N.C. Turner, "Branch growth and leaf numbers of red maple (*Acer rubrum* L.) and red oak (*Quercus rubra* L.): Response to defoliation," *Oecologia*, **62**, 1–6 (1984).

63. L.C. Ho, "Metabolism and compartmentation of imported sugars in sink organs in relation to sink strength," *Ann. Rev. Plant Physiol. Plant Mol. Biol.*, **39** 355–378 (1988).

64. Von G. Hoffmann and H. Lyr. "Charakterisierung des Wachstumsverhaltens von Pflanzen durch Wachstumsschemata," *Flora*, **162**, 81–98 (1973).

65. W. Höll, "Radial transport in rays," in M.H. Zimmermann and J.A. Milburn, eds., *Encyclopedia of Plant Physiology*, New Series, Vol. I, *Transport in Plants. I. Phloem Transport*, Springer-Verlag, Berlin–New York, 1975, pp. 432–450.

66. W. Höll, "Seasonal fluctuation of reserve materials in the trunkwood of spruce (*Picea abies* (L.) Karst.)," *J. Plant Physiol.*, **117**, 355–362 (1985).

67. S.C. Huber, "Relation between photosynthetic starch formation and dry-weight partitioning between the shoot and root," *Can. J. Bot.*, **61**, 2709–2716 (1983).

68. S.C. Huber, "Biochemical mechanisms for regulation of sucrose accumulation in leaves during photosynthesis," *Plant Physiol.*, **91**, 656–662 (1989).

69. S.C. Huber, P.S. Kerr, and W. Kalt-Torres, "Regulation of sucrose formation and movement," in R.L. Heath and J. Preiss, eds., *Regulation of Carbon Partitioning in Photosynthetic Tissue*, Proceedings 8th Annual Symposium in Plant Physiology, Riverside, CA, American Society of Plant Physiologists, Waverly Press, Baltimore, 1985, pp. 199–214.

70. J.G. Isebrands, "Toward a physiological basis of intensive culture of poplar," *Proceedings TAPPI Research and Development Division Conference*, Asheville, NC (USA), 1982. pp. 81–90.

71. J.G. Isebrands, P.T. Tomlinson, and R.E. Dickson, "Carbon fixation and allocation in northern red oak," *Monograph of Northern Red Oak* (*Quercus rubra* L.), INRA, Bordeaux, France, in press.

72. L.M. Jablonski and D.R. Geiger, "Responses of sugar beet plant morphology and carbon distribution to shortened days," *Plant Physiol. Biochem.*, **25**, 787–796 (1987).

73. Y. Kanazawa, "Growth analysis of seedlings of two deciduous broad-leaved tree species, *Quercus acutissima* Carr. and *Fagus crenata* Blume, from the viewpoint of dry matter and 'soluble' carbohydrate economy," *Jap. J. Ecol.*, **31**, 147–153 (1981).

74. S-M. Kang and J.S. Titus, "Qualitative and quantitative changes in nitrogenous compounds in senescing leaf and bark tissues of the apple," *Physiol. Plant.*, **50**, 285–290 (1980).

75. T. Kato, "Nitrogen metabolism and utilization in citrus," *Hort. Rev.*, **8**, 181–216 (1986).

76. K.G. Kevekordes, M.E. McCully, and M.J. Canny, "The occurrence of an extended bundle sheath system (*Paraveinal mesophyll*) in the legumes," *Can. J. Bot.*, **66**, 94–100 (1988).

77. M.R. Keys and C.C. Grier, "Above- and below-ground net production in 40-year-old douglas-fir stands on low and high productivity sites," *Can. J. For. Res.*, **11**, 599–605 (1981).

78. G.A. Kile, "Annual variations in soluble sugars, starch, and total food resources in *Eucalyptus obliqua* roots," *For. Sci.*, **27**, 449–454 (1981).

79. T.T. Kozlowski and T. Keller, "Food relations of woody plants," *Bot. Rev.*, **32**, 293–382 (1966).

80. P.J. Kramer and T.T. Kozlowski, *Physiology of Woody Plants*. Academic Press, New York, 1979.

81. K.W. Krueger and J.M. Trappe, "Food reserves and seasonal growth of Douglas-fir seedlings," *For. Sci.*, **13**, 192–202 (1967).

82. P.R. Larson and R.E. Dickson, "^{14}C translocation pathways in honeylocust and green ash: Woody plants with complex leaf forms," *Physiol. Plant.*, **66**, 21–30 (1986).

83. K. Loach and C.H.A. Little, "Production, storage, and use of photosynthate during shoot elongation in balsam fir (*Abies balsamea*)," *Can. J. Bot.*, **51**, 1161–1168 (1973).

84. W.H. Loescher, "Physiology and metabolism of sugar alcohols in higher plants," *Physiol. Plant.*, **70**, 553–557 (1987).

85. W.H. Loescher, G.C. Marlow, and R.A. Kennedy. "Sorbitol metabolism and sink–source interconversion in developing apple leaves," *Plant Physiol.*, **70**, 335–339 (1982).

86. D.A. MaGuire and D.W. Hann. "A stem dissection technique for dating branch mortality and reconstructing past crown recession," *For. Sci.*, **33**, 858–871 (1987).

87. F. Martin, M. Ramstedt, and K. Söderhäll, "Carbon and nitrogen metabolism in ectomycorrhizal fungi and ectomycorrhizas," *Biochimie*, **69**, 569–581 (1987).

88. R. Matyssek, "Carbon, water and nitrogen relations in evergreen and deciduous conifers," *Tree Physiol.*, **2**, 177–187 (1986).

89. H.M. McKay and D.C. Malcolm, "A comparison of the fine root component of a pure and a mixed coniferous stand," *Can. J. For. Res.*, **18**, 1416–1426 (1988).

90. R. McMurtrie and L. Wolf, "Above- and below-ground growth of forest stands: A carbon budget model," *Ann. Bot.*, **52**, 437–448 (1983).

91. H.A. Mooney and R.I. Hays, "Carbohydrate storage cycles in two Californian Mediterranean-climate trees," *Flora*, **162**, 295–304 (1973).

92. R. Murphy, "Water flow across the sieve–tube boundary: Estimating turgor and same implications for phloem loading and unloading. III. Phloem in the leaf," *Ann. Bot.*, **63**, 561–570 (1989).

93. E.K.S. Nambiar and D.N. Fife, "Growth and nutrient retranslocation in needles of radiata pine in relation to nitrogen supply," *Ann. Bot.*, **60**, 147–156 (1987).

94. E.A. Nelson and R.E. Dickson, "Accumulation of food reserves in cottonwood stems during dormancy induction," *Can. J. For. Res.*, **11**, 145–154 (1981).

95. T.R. Nisbet and C.E. Mullins, "A comparison of live and dead fine root weights in stands of Sitka spruce in contrasting soil water regimes," *Can. J. For. Res.*, **16**, 394–397 (1986).

96. J.S. Pate, "Transport and partitioning of nitrogenous solutes," *Ann. Rev. Plant Physiol.*, **31**, 313–340 (1980).

97. J.S. Pate, "Patterns of nitrogen metabolism in higher plants and their ecological significance," In J.A. Lee, S. McNeill and I.H. Rorison, eds., *Nitrogen as an Ecological Factor*, Blackwell Scientific Publ., Oxford, 1983, pp. 225–255.

98. J.S. Pate and C.A. Atkins, "Xylem and phloem transport and the functional economy of carbon and nitrogen of a legume leaf," *Plant Physiol.*, **71**, 835–840 (1983).

99. J.S. Pate and B.E.S. Gunning, "Transfer cells," *Ann. Rev. Plant Physiol.*, **23**, 173–196 (1972).

100. J.W. Patrick, "Sieve element unloading: Cellular pathway, mechanism and control," *Physiol. Plant.*, **78**, 298–308 (1990).

101. R.W. Pearcy, O. Björkman, M.M. Caldwell, J.E. Keeley, R.K. Monson, and B.R. Strain, "Carbon gain by plants in natural environments," *BioScience*, **37**, 21–29 (1987).

102. M.B. Peoples, J.S. Pate, C.A. Atkins, and F.J. Bergersen, "Nitrogen nutrition and xylem sap composition of peanut (*Arachis hypogaea* L. cv. Virginia Bunch)," *Plant Physiol.*, **82**, 946–951 (1986).

103. D.A. Perry, M.P. Amaranthus, J.G. Borchers, S.L. Borchers, and R.E. Brainerd, "Bootstrapping in ecosystems," *BioScience*, **39**, 230–237 (1989).

104. J.J. Philipson, "Root growth in Sitka spruce and Douglas-fir transplants: Dependence on the shoot and stored carbohydrate," *Tree Physiol.*, **4**, 101–108 (1988).

105. P.F. Ramp and S.N. Stephenson, "Gender dimorphism in growth and mass partitioning by box-elder (*Acer negundo* L.)," *Am. Midl. Nat.*, **119**, 420–430 (1988).

106. T.R. Roper, J.D. Keller, W.H. Loescher, and C.R. Rom, "Photosynthesis and carbohydrate partitioning in sweet cherry: Fruiting effects," *Physiol. Plant.*, **72**, 42–47 (1988).

107. A.K. Sakai, "Sex ratios of red maple (*Acer rubrum*) populations in northern lower Michigan," *Ecology*, **71**, 571–580 (1990).

108. D. Santantonio and J.C. Grace, "Estimating fine root production and turnover from biomass and decomposition data: A compartment-flow model," *Can. J. For. Res.*, **17**, 900–908 (1987).

109. A. Sanz, C. Monerri, J. Gonzalez-Ferrer, and J.L. Guardiola, "Changes in carbohydrates and mineral elements in *Citrus* leaves during flowering and fruit set," *Physiol. Plant.*, **69**, 93–98 (1987).

110. J.J. Sauter, "Seasonal variation of amino acids and amides in the xylem sap of *Salix*," *Z. Pflanzenphysiol.*, **101**, 399–411 (1981).

111. J.J. Sauter, "Efflux and reabsorption of sugars in xylem. II. Seasonal changes in sucrose uptake in *Salix*," *Z. Pflanzenphysiol.*, **111**, 429–440 (1983).

112. J.J. Sauter and S. Kloth, "Plasmodesmatal frequency and radial translocation rates in ray cells of poplar (*Populus* × *canadensis* Moench 'robusta')," *Planta*, **168**, 377–380 (1986).

113. J.J. Sauter and S. Kloth, "Changes in carbohydrates and ultrastructure in xylem ray cells of *Populus* in response to chilling," *Protoplasma*, **137**, 45–55 (1987).

114. J.J. Sauter, B. van Cleve, and S. Wellenkamp, "Ultrastructural and biochemical results on the localization and distribution of storage proteins in a poplar tree and in twigs of other tree species," *Holzforschung*, **43**, 1–6 (1989).

115. J.J. Sauter and S. Wellenkamp, "Protein storing vacuoles in ray cells of willow wood (*Salix caprea* L.)," *IAWA Bull.*, **9**, 59–65 (1988).

116. A.A. Schaffer, E.E. Goldschmidt, R. Goren, and D. Galili, "Fruit set and carbohydrate status in alternate and nonalternate bearing *Citrus* cultivars," *J. Am. Soc. Hort. Sci.*, **110**, 574–578 (1985).

117. K.R. Schubert, Products of biological nitrogen fixation in higher plants: Synthesis, transport, and metabolism. *Ann. Rev. Plant Physiol.*, **37**, 539–574 (1986).

118. E.-D. Schulze, "Plant life-forms and their carbon, water and nutrient relations," in *Encyclopedia of Plant Physiology*, New Series, Vol. 12B, Springer-Verlag, Berlin, New York, 1982, pp. 616–676.

119. J.C. Servaites, B.R. Fondy, and D.R. Geiger, "Sources of carbon for export from spinach leaves throughout the day," *Plant Physiol.*, **90**, 1168–1174 (1989).

120. J.C. Servaites, D.R. Geiger, M.A. Tucci, and B.R. Fondy, "Leaf carbon metabolism and metabolite levels during a period of sinusoidal light," *Plant Physiol.*, **89**, 403–408 (1989).

121. K.-K. Shim and J.S. Titus, "Accumulation and mobilization of storage proteins in ginkgo shoot bark," *J. Kor. Soc. Hort. Sci.*, **26**, 350–360 (1985).

122. R.C. Sicher, "Sucrose biosynthesis in photosynthetic tissue: Rate controlling factors and metabolic pathway," *Physiol. Plant.*, **67**, 118–121 (1986).

123. P.A. Sleigh, H.A. Collin, and K. Hardwick, "Distribution of assimilate during the flush cycle of growth in *Theobroma cacao* L.," *Plant Growth Regulation*, **2**, 381–391 (1984).

124. J.L. Smith and E.A. Paul, "Use of an *in situ* labeling technique for the determination of seasonal ^{14}C distribution in ponderosa pine," *Plant and Soil*, **106**, 221–229 (1988).

125. D.C. Spanner, "Transport in the phloem," *Nature*, **232**, 157–160 (1971).

126. P.J.C. Stassen, H.W. Stindt, D.K. Strydom, and J.H. Terblanche, "Seasonal changes in nitrogen fractions of young kakamas peach trees," *Agroplantae*, **13**, 63–72 (1981).

127. M. Stitt, "Fructose 2,6-bisphosphate and plant carbohydrate metabolism," *Plant Physiol.*, **84**, 201–204 (1987).

128. M. Stitt and W.P. Quick, "Photosynthetic carbon partitioning: Its regulation and possibilities for manipulation," *Physiol. Plant.*, **77**, 633–641 (1989).

129. S-J.S. Sung, D.-P. Xu, C.M. Galloway, and C.C. Black Jr., "A reassessment of glycolysis and gluconeogenesis in higher plants," *Physiol. Plant.*, **72**, 650–654 (1988).

130. S.L. Thrower and L.B. Thrower, "Translocation into mature leaves—the pathway of assimilate movement," *New Phytol.*, **86**, 145–154 (1980).

131. J.S. Titus and S.-M. Kang, "Nitrogen metabolism, translocation, and recycling in apple trees," *Hort. Rev.*, **4**, 204–246 (1982).

132. P.T. Tomlinson, R.E. Dickson, and J.G. Isebrands, "Acropetal leaf differentiation in *Quercus rubra* L," *Am. J. Bot.*, (in press).

133. P. Trip, C.D. Nelson, and G. Krotkov, "Selective and preferential translocation of ^{14}C-labeled sugars in white ash and lilac," *Plant Physiol.*, **40**, 740–747 (1965).

134. J. Tromp, "Nutrient reserves in roots of fruit trees, in particular carbohydrates and nitrogen," *Plant and Soil*, **71**, 401–413 (1983).

135. J. Tromp and J.C. Ovaa, "Response of young apple trees to time of nitrogen fertilization with respect to the nitrogen, potassium, and calcium levels in xylem sap, new growth, and the tree as a whole," *J. Plant Physiol.*, **119**, 301–309 (1985).

136. T.J. Tschaplinski and T.J. Blake, "Photosynthetic reinvigoration of leaves following shoot decapitation and accelerated growth of coppice shoots," *Physiol. Plant.*, **75**, 157–165 (1989).

137. R. Turgeon, "Termination of nutrient import and development of vein loading capacity in albino tobacco leaves," *Plant Physiol.*, **76**, 45–48 (1984).

138. R. Turgeon, "The sink–source transition in leaves," *Ann. Rev. Plant Physiol. Plant Mol. Biol.*, **40**, 119–138 (1989).

139. R. Turgeon and P.K. Hepler, "Symplastic continuity between mesophyll and companion cells in minor veins of mature *Curcurbita pepo* L. leaves," *Planta*, **179**, 24–31 (1989).

140. L.E. Tyrrell and R.J.E. Boerner, "*Larex laricina* and *Picea mariana*: Relationships among leaf life span, foliar nutrient patterns, nutrient conservation, and growth efficiency," *Can. J. Bot.*, **65**, 1570–1577 (1987).

141. R. Van den Driessche, "Importance of current photosynthate to new root growth in planted conifer seedlings," *Can. J. For. Res.*, **17**, 776–782 (1987).

142. T.C. Vogelmann, P.R. Larson, and R.E. Dickson, "Translocation pathways in the petioles and stem between source and sink leaves of *Populus deltoides* Bartr. ex Marsh," *Planta*, **156**, 345–358 (1982).

143. T.C. Vogelmann, R.E. Dickson, and P.R. Larson, "Comparative distribution and metabolism of xylem-borne amino compounds and sucrose in shoots of *Populus deltoides*," *Plant Physiol.*, **77**, 418–428 (1985).

144. K.A. Vogt, C.C. Grier, and C.E. Meier. "Mycorrhizal role in net primary production and nutrient cycling in *Abies amabilis* ecosystems in western Washington," *Ecology*, **63**, 370–380 (1982).

145. K.A. Vogt, D.J. Vogt, E.E. Moore, B.A. Fatuga, M.R. Redlin, and R.L. Edmonds, "Conifer and angiosperm fine-root biomass in relation to stand age and site productivity in Douglas-fir forests," *J. Ecol.*, **75**, 857–870 (1987).

146. P.M. Wargo, "Starch storage and radial growth in woody roots of sugar maple," *Can. J. For. Res.* **9**, 49–56 (1979).

147. P.M. Wargo, "Defoliation and tree growth," in C.C. Doane and M.L. McManus, eds., *The Gypsy Moth: Research toward Integrated Pest Management*. U.S. Department of Agriculture, Washington, DC, 1981, pp. 225–240.

148. P.M. Wargo, "Defoliation, dieback, and mortality," in C.C. Doane and M.L. McManus, eds., *The Gypsy Moth: Research toward Integrated Pest Management*, U.S. Department of Agriculture, Washington, DC, 1981, pp. 240–248.

149. P.M. Wargo and M.E. Montgomery, "Colonization by *Armillaria mellea* and *Agrilus bilineatus* of oaks injected with ethanol," *For. Sci.* **29**, 848–857 (1983).

150. M.A. Watson and B.B. Casper, "Morphogenetic constraints on patterns of carbon distribution in plants," *Ann. Rev. Ecol. Syst.* **15**, 233–258 (1984).

151. S. Wetzel, C. Demmers, and J.S. Greenwood, "Seasonal fluctuating bark proteins are a potential form of nitrogen storage in three temperate hardwoods," *Planta*, **178**, 275–281 (1989).

152. B.W. Wood, "Carbohydrate composition of vascular system exudates and characterization of their uptake by leaf tissue of pecan," *J. Am. Soc. Hort. Sci.*, **112**, 346–351 (1987).

153. B.W. Wood, "Pecan production responds to root carbohydrates and rootstock," *J. Am. Soc. Hort. Sci.*, **114**, 223–228 (1989).

154. A. Wu and L.B. Thrower, "Translocation into mature leaves," *Plant Cell Physiol.*, **14**, 1225–1228 (1973).

155. T. Yamashita, "Mobilization of carbohydrates, amino acids and adenine nucleotides in hardwood stems during regrowth after partial shoot harvest in mulberry trees (*Morus alba* L.)," *Ann. Bot.*, **57**, 237–244 (1986).

156. H. Ziegler, "Storage, metabolism and distribution of reserve material in trees," in M.H. Zimmermann, ed., *The Formation of Wood in Forest Trees*, Academic Press, New York, 1964, pp. 303–320.

157. M.H. Zimmermann and C.L. Brown, *Trees: Structure and Function*, Springer-Verlag, New York, 1971.

4 Respiration

AKIO HAGIHARA and KAZUO HOZUMI

Department of Forestry, Faculty of Agriculture, Nagoya University, Nagoya, Japan

Contents

4.1. Introduction

Forest stands are characterized by a large amount of biomass in comparison with biomass in other terrestrial communities. Leaf biomass tends to remain constant for a fairly long period after the complete closure of canopies, but woody biomass is steadily accumulated with the progress of stand growth (1,2). Although the respiration rate of woody organs, such as stems, branches, and roots, is much smaller than that of leaves, the dry-matter budget of forest stands is remarkably affected by the respiratory consumption of the woody organs because of their vast accumulation of biomass. Wood–leaf ratio ascending from younger to older stands can cause the corresponding rise in the ratio of respiration loss to gross production, i.e., the decline of net production (1).

Kira and Shidei (1) stressed that the net production alone cannot be a stable measure of the potential primary productivity of forest stands, but the best measure of forest productivity should be the gross production (net production plus respiration loss). The measurement of respiration loss is therefore indispensable in view of the dry-matter economy of forest stands.

Measuring the accurate rate of respiration offers a great technical difficulty, mainly because of the tree's inherent huge biomass. Various methods have been employed to overcome this difficulty: a simplified flux technique applying temperature inversions (3), *in situ* measurement of CO_2 gas exchange by enclosing small parts of trees (e.g., 4–8) or whole top-parts of a tree (9,10), indirect estimation of average leaf and wood respiration from destructive sampling data (11,12), and the summation of CO_2 release from detached samples of different sizes (13,14) and its elaboration (15–18).

Although information on the respiration of trees has been accumulated (19,20), available estimates in regard to stand respiration are still limited in both number and reliability. The present chapter describes the characteristics of respiration at three important levels of organization: organs, trees, and stands. The mechanism and regulation of respiration at these three levels are discussed further.

4.2. Temperature dependence of respiration

Although stem respiration can occasionally be reduced independently of temperature during the daytime because of water stress and/or the transport of CO_2 by sap flows (21,22), the respiration can be expected to correspond to temperature change (6,23–27). Since chemical reactions are generally described in Arrhenius's equation, it is approximately the case that the respiration rate r increases exponentially with increasing temperature T:

$$r = r_0 \exp(kT) \tag{4.1}$$

where r_0 is the respiration rate at $T = 0°C$ and k is a coefficient (28,29).

In biological processes a temperature increase of 10°C increases the velocity of the chemical reactions by a constant multiple. This multiple is denoted by the temperature coefficient Q_{10}. By assuming Eq. 4.1, we can define the Q_{10} in the form (30,31)

$$Q_{10} = \exp(10k). \tag{4.2}$$

For stems of *Pinus sylvestris* the Q_{10} value was close to 2.0 throughout the year except for the high values in the winter months when stems were frozen most of the time (8).

In a greenhouse, Butler and Landsberg (32) measured dark respiration by enclosing the aerial parts of apple trees. They presumed that a Q_{10} value of

2.32 was relatively conservative over 8 months of the year. The authors (33–35) performed the CO_2 gas-exchange measurement of the aboveground parts of a hinoki (Japanese; fire tree) (*Chamaecyparis obtusa*) forest tree ca. 5.0 m high during a 3-year period using an open gas-exchange system (36), which allowed *in situ* measurement to be carried out throughout a year. Carbon dioxide gas-exchange rates and air temperatures were simultaneously recorded at 3-min intervals. The relationship between nighttime respiration and air temperature was examined at monthly intervals, and the investigators confirmed that the relationship was an exponential function of air temperature (Fig. 4.1). As illustrated in Fig. 4.2, there existed an apparent seasonal fluctuation in Q_{10}, whose value ranged from 1.4 to 3.4 and was higher in the winter season than in the summer season. As a result, the monthly Q_{10} value linearly corresponded to the monthly mean air temperature (Fig. 4.3).

According to Larcher (30), respiration increases with a Q_{10} value of ca. 2.0 at 5–25°C; below 5°C the Q_{10} value is high, around 3.0 or even more; above 25–30°C it falls slowly to 1.5 or less. This tendency of the Q_{10} value has been experimentally observed for detached samples of stems (26,37) or leaves (38,39). It is thought that the temperature dependence of the Q_{10} value is due to the shift of the activation energy of enzymes (40).

4.3. Dark respiration of leaves

There is a considerable difference in the activity of the leaf dark respiration between sun and shade leaves (41). The depth-dependent change in the leaf dark respiration is influenced by external factors such as microclimates within the canopy and internal factors such as aging of leaves (42). Yoda et al. (43) first pointed out that the gradient of the activity from upper-layer leaves down to lower-layer leaves depends mainly on the corresponding profile of the

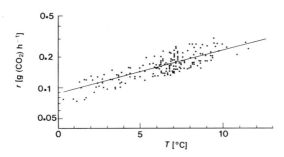

FIG. 4.1. Dependence of the nighttime respiration rate r of the aerial parts of a hinoki, *Chamaecyparis obtusa*, forest tree on air temperature T in March (34). The temperature inside the chamber was adjusted to that outside the chamber. The straight line is an approximation based on Eq. 4.1, where the values of r_0 and k are respectively 0.086 g (CO_2) h^{-1} and 0.098°C^{-1}.

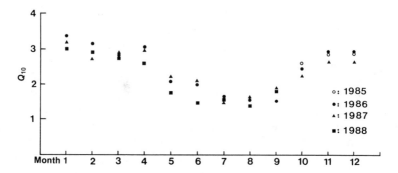

FIG. 4.2. Monthly variation in the Q_{10} value of the aerial parts of a whole-hinoki tree over a 3-year period from October 1985 to September 1988 (35). The Q_{10} value is calculated from Eq. 4.2 for the nighttime respiration.

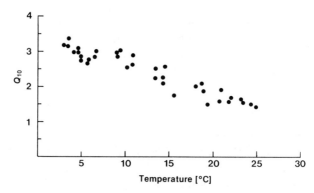

FIG. 4.3. Change in the Q_{10} value in accordance with the monthly mean air temperature. The monthly Q_{10} value in Fig. 4.2 is plotted against the corresponding monthly mean air temperature in the nighttime.

radiation regime under which leaves exist within canopies. To describe the decrease of leaf dark respiration from the top toward the bottom of the canopy, the following three empirical equations (Eqs. 4.3, 4.7, and 4.9) have been proposed (17,44,45).

The first approximation was proposed by Hozumi (44) for estimating the total dark respiration by a canopy. He formulated the respiration rate r_F relating to the relative radiation I'/I_0 in a hyperbolic equation

$$\frac{1}{r_F} = \frac{a_1}{I'/I_0} + b_1 \qquad (4.3)$$

where a_1 and b_1 are coefficients and I' and I_0 are respectively the radiation intensity to which leaves were exposed at original positions within the canopy and the radiation above the canopy.

On the other hand, the relative radiation I'/I_0 on a horizon within a canopy decreases exponentially with increasing cumulative leaf area density F from the top of the canopy downward (46):

$$\frac{I'}{I_0} = \exp(-KF) \tag{4.4}$$

where K is the light extinction coefficient. The canopy dark respiration R_F is given by integrating the resulting equation $r_F(F)$, where Eq. 4.4 is substituted into Eq. 4.3, with respect to F:

$$R_F = \int_0^F r_F(F)dF. \tag{4.5}$$

The result of the integral (44) is

$$R_F = \frac{1}{Kb_1} \ln \frac{a_1 + b_1}{a_1 + b_1 \exp(-KF)}. \tag{4.6}$$

This method has been applied to warm-temperate evergreen oak forests (47–49).

The second approximation was described in a beech forest (17):

$$r_F = a_2 \left(\frac{I'}{I_0} \right)^{b_2} \tag{4.7}$$

where a_2 and b_2 are coefficients. The same relationship was reported by Yoda (18) for a tropical rain forest. If Eqs. 4.4 and 4.7 hold, then the total canopy respiration is calculated from

$$R_F = \frac{a_2}{Kb_2} [1 - \exp(-Kb_2F)]. \tag{4.8}$$

The third approximation was the case proposed by Hagihara and Hozumi (45) in a *Chamaecyparis obtusa* plantation:

$$r_F = a_3 \left(\frac{I'}{I_0} \right) + b_3 \tag{4.9}$$

where a_3 and b_3 are coefficients. An example sustaining Eq. 4.9 in a 27-year-old *c. obtusa* plantation (50) is illustrated in Fig. 4.4. This relationship was also recognized in *Larix leptolepis* plantations (52,53). It seems that Eq. 4.9,

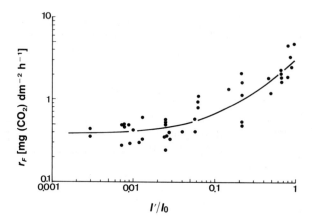

FIG. 4.4. Dependence of the respiration rate of leaves r_F on the relative radiation I'/I_0, to which leaves were exposed at their original positions within the canopy of a hinoki plantation in August. The respiration rate of detached samples was determined by IRGA at 21.5°C of the monthly mean air temperature. An improved anthracene actinometer (51) was used to observe the light profile within the canopy. The data are fitted to Eq. 4.9, where the values of a_3 and b_3 are 2.95 mg (CO_2) dm^{-2} h^{-1} and 0.383 mg (CO_2) dm^{-2} h^{-1}, respectively. (Adapted from Ref. 50.)

rather than Eqs. 4.3 and 4.7, results in a closer fit especially to the data obtained in pure stands. On the assumption that Eqs. 4.4 and 4.9 are valid, the total canopy respiration is given in the form (45)

$$R_F = \frac{a_3}{K}\left[1 + \frac{Kb_3F}{a_3} - \exp(-KF)\right]. \tag{4.10}$$

4.4. Respiration of woody organs

4.4.1. Respiration rates of detached samples as related to their diameter

The respiration rate per unit weight of woody tissues is closely related to the thickness of the woody organs (13). Yoda et al. (15) proposed an elaborate method to estimate the total woody respiration in a tree, taking the dependence of the respiration rate on the diameter of a sample segment into consideration. This generalization made it possible to estimate the total respiration of woody organs with a relatively small number of measurements for the calculation.

The relationship between the respiration rate r_w per unit weight of woody segments and their diameter D has been formulated in the following two cases:

Case 1 (15,16):

$$\frac{1}{r_w} = A_1 D + B_1. \tag{4.11}$$

Case 2 (17,18):

$$\frac{1}{r_w} = A_2 D^2 + B_2. \tag{4.12}$$

Here A_1, B_1, A_2, and B_2 are coefficients specific to species, seasons, and mother trees from which sample segments are taken. The $r_w - D$ (case 1) or $r_w - D^2$ (case 2) curve on log–log coordinates has two asymptotes respectively having gradient values of 0.0 and -1.0. The respiration rate r_w therefore becomes constant irrespective of D in the range of smaller diameters, while it is inversely proportional to D (case 1) or D^2 (case 2) in the range of larger diameters. In other words, CO_2 release from segments having a constant length is proportional to their weight in very fine woods, whereas CO_2 release from very thick woods is proportional to their surface area in case 1 or is constant irrespective of their thickness in case 2. Since the physiological activity of woods is concentrated mostly on a thin cambial zone just below bark (54), these relationships seem to be quite reasonable.

Respiration rates are represented not only on a weight basis but also on a surface area basis. On the assumption that the bulk density of woods is constant irrespective of their thickness, the respiration rate per unit weight, r_w of Eq. 4.12, can be converted into the respiration rate r_s per unit surface area as follows:

$$\frac{1}{r_s} = A_2' D + \frac{B_2'}{D} \tag{4.13}$$

where A_2' and B_2' are coefficients relating to the bulk density. The comparison between the $r_w - D^2$ and the $r_s - D$ trajectory is exemplified in Fig. 4.5. It should be noted that we must distinguish between dimensions of respiration rates (13,55,56).

4.4.2. Total respiration of a woody organ per tree

On the basis of the pipe model theory (57), Shinozaki et al. (58) found that the frequency distribution density $\psi(D)$ of diameters in the trunk, branches, and roots of a tree can be formulated by a definite power function with the exponent of $-a$:

$$\psi(D) = f D^{-a} \tag{4.14}$$

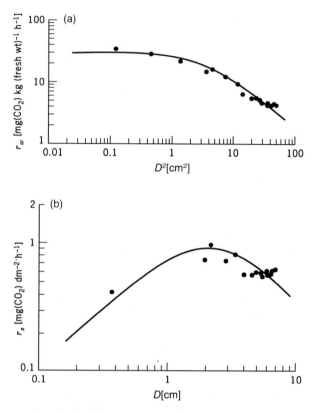

FIG. 4.5. Dependence of the respiration rate (at ca. 8.5°C) of stem sections on their diameter of a 26-year-old hinoki plantation in November. (a) Relationship between the respiration rate per unit weight r_w and the diameter D. The curve corresponds to Eq. 4.12, where the values of A_2 and B_2 are respectively 0.00632 cm^{-2} mg $(CO_2)^{-1}$ kg (fresh weight) h and 0.0324 mg $(CO_2)^{-1}$ kg (fresh weight) h. (b) Relationship between the respiration rate per unit surface area r_s and the diameter D. The curve corresponds to Eq. 4.13, where the values of A_2' and B_2' are respectively 0.253 cm^{-1} mg $(CO_2)^{-1}$ dm^2 h and 1.30 mg $(CO_2)^{-1}$ cm dm^2 h; each was calculated from the corresponding parameter value in Eq. 4.12 using a constant bulk density of 1.0 kg (fresh weight) dm^{-3}. (Adapted from Ref. 56.)

where f is a factor whose value depends on tree size. In the case of trunks the shape of the whole organ is roughly approximated by a cone, and hence the value of a is nearly equal to zero. In roots and branches the value of a is very near to 2.0, although in branches the value is somewhat variable.

The total respiration r_T of a certain woody organ per tree can be calculated by combining Eq. 4.11 or 4.12 with Eq. 4.14. The respiration rate $r_w(D)$ per unit weight of sample segments with a diameter of D is first multiplied by the total weight $dw(D)[=\psi(D)dD]$ of sample segments having the same diameter D, and then the resulting product is integrated over the whole diameter range (15,17,18):

$$r_T = \int r_w(D)dw(D) = \int_{D_{min}}^{D_{max}} r_w(D)\psi(D)dD$$

$$= \frac{(3 - a)w}{D_{max}^{3-a} - D_{min}^{3-a}} \int_{D_{min}}^{D_{max}} r_w(D)D^{2-a}dD \qquad (4.15)$$

where $w\,[= \int dw(D)]$ is the total weight of a woody organ per tree and D_{max} and D_{min} are respectively the maximum and the minimum diameters of the woody organ.

The concrete form of Eq. 4.15 differs according to both the value of a and the $r_w(D)-D$ relationship. If the value of a is equal to zero (for stems), then the concrete form is on one hand

$$r_T = \frac{3w}{A_1^3(D_{max}^3 - D_{min}^3)} \left[\frac{(A_1D + B_1)^2}{2} - 2B_1(A_1D + B_1) \right.$$

$$\left. + B_1^2 \ln(A_1D + B_1) \right]_{D_{min}}^{D_{max}} \qquad (4.16)$$

where Eq. 4.11 is assumed (15), and on the other hand

$$r_T = \frac{3w}{A_2(D_{max}^3 - D_{min}^3)} \left[D - \left(\frac{B_2}{A_2}\right)^{1/2} \arctan\left(\frac{A_2}{B_2}\right)^{1/2} D \right]_{D_{min}}^{D_{max}} \qquad (4.17)$$

where Eq. 4.12 is assumed (17,18). Equation 4.16 was applied to tropical forests (16) and a warm-temperate evergreen oak forest (49); and Eq. 4.17, to a *Chamaecyparis obtusa* plantation (59) and a tropical rain forest (18).

If the value of a equals 2.0 (for roots and/or branches), then the solution based on Eq. 4.11 takes the form (15)

$$r_T = \frac{w}{A_1(D_{max} - D_{min})} \left[\ln(A_1D + B_1) \right]_{D_{min}}^{D_{max}} \qquad (4.18)$$

and the solution based on Eq. 4.12 takes the form (17,18)

$$r_T = \frac{w}{(A_2B_2)^{1/2}(D_{max} - D_{min})} \left[\arctan\left(\frac{A_2}{B_2}\right)^{1/2} D \right]_{D_{min}}^{D_{max}}. \qquad (4.19)$$

Equation 4.18 was applied to tropical forests (16), a warm-temperate evergreen oak forest (49), roots of a *Chamaecyparis obtusa* plantation (59), and branches of a tropical rain forest (18). On the other hand, Eq. 4.19 was applied to roots of a tropical rain forest (18).

4.4.3. *Respiration rates within woody tissues*

Yoda et al. (60) tried to estimate the respiration rate inside bark. If we denote the respiration rate at the distance x from bark inward by $\eta(x)$, we can write the respiration rate r_w (on a weight basis) of the segment whose length and diameter are respectively L and D in the integral equation

$$r_w = \frac{\int_0^{D/2} \eta(x)(D - 2x)L\omega dx}{\int_0^{D/2} (D - 2x)L\omega dx} \qquad (4.20)$$

where ω is the bulk density. If the value of ω is constant irrespective of x and r_w is as in case 1, then the explicit solution of $\eta(x)$ becomes

$$\eta(x) = \frac{1}{B_1(1 + 2A_1x/B_1)^3}. \qquad (4.21)$$

This equation shows that the respiration rate inside bark decreases abruptly with increasing distance from the bark. Yoda et al. (60) pointed out that this tendency of the change in inward respiration rates agrees with the results obtained for the stems of *Fraxinus nigra* by Goodwin and Goddard (54).

4.5. Tree size dependence of whole-forest tree respiration

4.5.1. *Respiration among forest trees different in size*

Ninomiya and Hozumi (9,10) made a nondestructive measurement of the aboveground parts respiration of forest trees using an enclosed standing tree method. As a result, they found that the annual amount of the respiration of individual trees is related to their corresponding weight.

The relationship between the respiration r and the weight w satisfied the power function for a young stand of *Pinus densi-thunbergii*

$$r = gw^h \qquad (4.22)$$

where g and h are constants (9). This relationship is illustrated in Fig. 4.6. The value of h was nearly equal to 1.0. Ogawa et al. (61) also demonstrated that in a seedling population of *C. obtusa* the value of the exponent h was fairly close to unity over all seasons. It may be concluded that the respiration of individual trees is directly proportional to their weight.

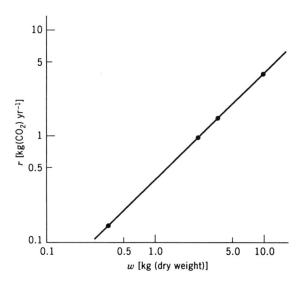

FIG. 4.6. Dependence of the annual respiration of the aboveground parts of a tree r on the corresponding weight w in a young *Pinus densi-thunbergii* plantation (9). The CO_2 accumulation in air inside chamber was hourly assessed from the gas sampling with syringes. The straight line is an approximation based on Eq. 4.22, where the values of g and h are respectively 0.42 kg (CO_2) yr^{-1} kg (dry weight)$^{-h}$ and 1.03.

On the other hand, the $r-w$ relation for a 24-year-old stand of *C. obtusa* was given by a generalized power function

$$r = g(w - w_{min})^h \qquad (4.23)$$

where g and h are constants and w_{min} is the critical value of aboveground parts weight below which forest trees cannot survive (10,62). This relationship is illustrated in Fig. 4.7. The value of the exponent h was around $2/3$. It may be concluded that the respiration per tree is directly proportional to their surface areas in the range where w is sufficiently larger than w_{min}. Equation 4.23 contrasts with Eq. 4.22 strikingly and may reflect a respiration property of populations under self-thinning.

Dividing both sides of Eq. 4.23 by w results in

$$SRR = \frac{r}{w} = g\frac{(w - w_{min})^h}{w} \qquad (4.24)$$

where SRR represents the specific annual respiration rate (62). As is obvious from Fig. 4.8, SRR has a maximum value at the value of weight $w^*[= w_{min}/(1 - h)]$ because the value of h is less than unity. Ninomiya and Hozumi (62) concluded that the forest trees having weights less than w^* are destined to suffer natural thinning.

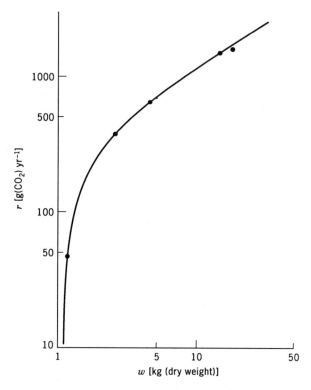

FIG. 4.7. Dependence of the annual respiration on the top parts of individual trees r on their estimated top weight w in a 24-year-old hinoki plantation. The curve is given by Eq. 4.23, where the values of g, h, and w_{min} are respectively 322.5 g (CO_2) yr^{-1} kg (dry weight)$^{-h}$ and 0.634, and 1.10 kg (dry weight). (Adapted from Refs. 10 and 62.)

4.5.2 Time trajectory of whole-tree respiration to its size

Equations 4.22 and 4.23 describe the relationship between the respiration and size of individual trees at a given instant of time. We must compare this respiration–size relationship at a given time instant to that over a time continuum, or with the progress of time.

More recently, Hagihara et al. (35) made a continuous and long-term measure of the aerial-parts respiration of a tree in a young *C. obtusa* plantation. Figure 4.9 shows that, with time, the annual amount of respiration tends to increase with an increase in stem volume. They formulated the relationship between the respiration r and the stem volume v in the power function

$$r = pv^q \tag{4.25}$$

where p and q are constants. The value of q was nearly equal to $\frac{2}{3}$. It may thus be likely that the respiration of a tree is directly proportional to its own

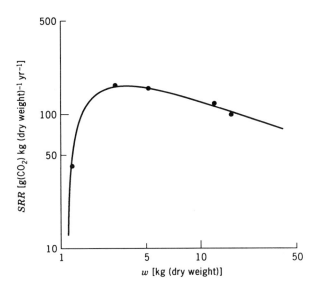

FIG. 4.8. Relationship between the specific annual respiration rate of individual trees *SRR* and the corresponding weight *w* in a hinoki plantation (62). The curve is given by Eq. 4.24, where the parameter values are the same as those determined for Eq. 4.23 in Fig. 4.7.

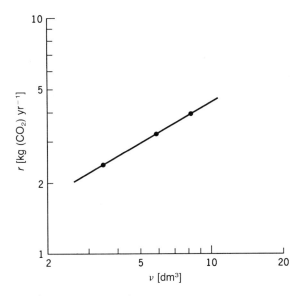

FIG. 4.9. Time trajectory of the relationship between the aerial-parts respiration *r* and the stem volume *v* of a whole-hinoki tree. Dark respiration in the daytime was estimated by taking account of the measurements of nighttime respiration and the Q_{10} value (Figs. 4.1 and 4.2). The data are fitted to Eq. 4.25, where the values of *p* and *q* are respectively 1.16 kg (CO_2) yr^{-1} dm^{-3q} and 0.616. (Adapted from Ref. 35.)

surface area. This result is in formal agreement with that obtained by Ninomiya and Hozumi (10,62) for the relationship between the respiration of individual trees and their size, although Eq. 4.25 is materially different from Eq. 4.23.

4.6. Respiration of forest stands

4.6.1. The sum of the respiration of individual trees

The stand respiration is the total amount of the respiration by individual trees composing a forest stand. The respiration of individual trees depends on their body size on one hand and the stand is consisted of trees different in size on the other hand. Hozumi and Shinozaki (63) suggested obtaining the functional amount of a stand by combining the size distribution of individual trees with the size dependence of the functional amount of individual trees.

If we denote the distribution density function of the weight w of individual trees by $\phi(w)$ and the functional relationship of the respiration of individual trees to their weight by $r(w)$, the total respiration of a stand R can be obtained from the integral (63)

$$R = \int_{w_{min}}^{w_{max}} r(w)\phi(w)dw \tag{4.26}$$

where w_{max} and w_{min} denote the maximum and minimum weight of trees, respectively. Different types of distribution function of the weight of individual trees have been derived from the observed data (64–66).

The Weibull distribution density function is widely used to describe the size distribution with respect to diameters (67–71). If the distribution density function of the diameters is given by the Weibull distribution and the allometric relationship lies between diameter and weight, then the distribution density function of weight can also be written in the Weibull form

$$\phi(w) = \frac{\rho b}{\alpha}\left(\frac{w}{\alpha}\right)^{b-1} \exp\left\{ -\left(\frac{w}{\alpha}\right)^{b} \right\} \tag{4.27}$$

where ρ is the tree density and α and b are coefficients (positive values) specific to the stand concerned. Figure 4.10 illustrates that the frequency distribution of the weight of individual trees in a *Chamaecyparis obtusa* plantation was closely fitted to Eq. 4.27.

Inserting Eqs. 4.22 and 4.27 into Eq. 4.26, and assuming that the values of w_{max} and w_{min} are respectively infinite and zero, we obtain

$$R = \rho g \alpha^{h}\Gamma\left(1 + \frac{h}{b}\right) \tag{4.28}$$

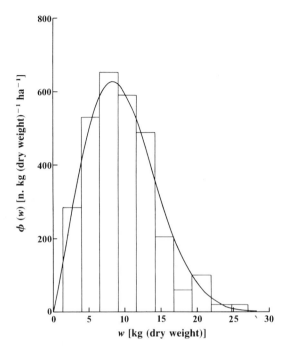

FIG. 4.10. Histogram of the whole-tree weight w in a 18-year-old hinoki plantation. The smooth curve represents the distribution density function designated by $\phi(w)$ in Eq. 4.27, where the tree density ρ is 7617 ha^{-1} and the values of α and b are respectively 11.0 kg (dry weight) and 2.17. (Adapted from Ref. 69.)

where $\Gamma(x)$ stands for the gamma function. We can assess the total amount of the respiration of a stand from Eq. 4.28.

In a more general formulation, the Weibull includes the smallest possible weight w_{min}:

$$\phi(w) = \frac{\rho b}{\alpha} \left[\frac{w - w_{min}}{\alpha} \right]^{b-1} \exp \left[-\left\{ \frac{w - w_{min}}{\alpha} \right\}^{b} \right]. \qquad (4.29)$$

The stand respiration based on Eqs. 4.23 and 4.29 can also be given by Eq. 4.28.

4.6.2. Respiration of whole stands

Table 4.1 shows the respiration amounts of respective components to the stand respiration in an 18-year-old *C. obtusa* plantation (69). The total respiration was 25.7 tons (dry matter) ha^{-1} yr^{-1}, of which 60% resulted from foliages. In *Abies sachalinensis* stands (15), two-thirds of the stand respiration was by the leaves; in tropical forests (14,18), in a warm-temperate evergreen oak forest (49), and in European beech plantations (72) about half of the

Table 4.1. Annual respiration, biomass, and its annual increment on a ground area (1.0-ha) basis in an 18-year-old *Chamaecyparis obtusa* plantation (69)

	Leaves	Branches	Stems	Roots	Total
Respiration R,[a] tons (dry matter) yr^{-1}	15.3	1.58	6.06	2.77	25.7
Biomass y, tons (dry weight)	14.2	6.09	37.3	15.4	72.9
Biomass increment Δy, tons (dry weight) yr^{-1}	0.0[b]	1.39	7.75	3.74	12.9

[a]Respiration rates were converted into the corresponding rates of organic matter consumption, assuming a conversion factor of 0.614 ton of dry matter per ton of CO_2.
[b]Assuming that an equilibrium of the canopy biomass has been established.
The net production of 15.4 tons ha^{-1} yr^{-1} added to the respiration consumption makes the gross production of 41.2 tons ha^{-1} yr^{-1}.

stand respiration was by the leaves, whereas in a loblolly pine plantation (73) only one-third of the total was due to the leaves.

Ogawa et al. (61), by combining their results with previous research (50,69,74), graphically represented the annual stand respiration of *C. obtusa* plantations related to forest development (Fig. 4.11). The annual stand respiration shows a rapid rise with increasing biomass at the earliest stage of stand development and then increases somewhat to reach a more or less constant level, which is likely to be maintained for quite a long period. Sprugel (75), although estimating respiration on the basis of the foregoing data reported by Yoda et al. (15), found in balsam fir forests that the above-ground woody respiration increases with stand age up to about age 20, after which it declines somewhat and then remains fairly constant throughout the life of the stand.

Kira and Shidei (1) suggested that stand respiration continues to increase monotonously with increasing biomass of woody organs after the complete closure of a canopy, assuming that the stand respiration increases proportionally with increasing biomass. Oohata and Shidei (76) pointed out that the total amount of the surface area of woody organs remains constant after the closure of a canopy, assuming both the similarity in form among trees and the 3 over 2 power law of natural thinning (77). In addition to this conclusion, they assumed that the respiration of woody organs per tree is proportional to its surface area. As a result, they drew a hypothetical interpretation that the stand respiration reaches an equilibrium over a long period of time once the canopy has been closed. As already mentioned, in individual trees the respiration was nearly proportional to the surface area (10,35,62). The trend of the annual stand respiration illustrated in Fig. 4.11 seems to substantiate the model proposed by Oohata and Shidei (76).

4.6.3. Relationship between stand respiration, biomass, and biomass increment

On the basis of the data published for evergreen forest stands, Hagihara and Hozumi (69) found a hyperbolic relationship between the ratio of annual stand respiration R to annual biomass increment Δy and the relative growth

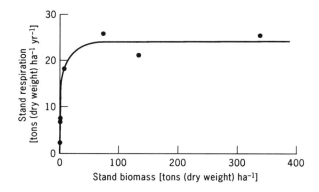

FIG. 4.11. Change in the annual amount of stand respiration as related to the biomass in hinoki plantations. (Adapted from Ref. 61.)

rate $\Delta y/y$. It appears from Fig. 4.12 that the $R/\Delta y$ ratio decreases with increasing $\Delta y/y$. The formula derived from the figure was

$$\frac{R}{\Delta y} = \frac{m}{\Delta y/y} + c \qquad (4.30)$$

where m and c are constants. The estimated values of m and c were 0.0632 yr^{-1} and 1.44, respectively (69).

Equation 4.30 states that the ratio of annual stand respiration to annual biomass increment becomes constant irrespective of the relative growth rate in young stands with higher relative growth rates, whereas it is inversely proportional to the relative growth rate in climax stands with smaller relative growth rates. In other words, the annual stand respiration of young stands is proportional to the annual biomass increment, whereas that of climax forests is directly proportional to the biomass.

It is expected that the consumption due to respiration is connected with biomass and its increment to a great extent (86). Thornley (87) considered that the respiration can be divided into both constructive and maintenance respiration; the former results from the synthesis of new material and the latter is connected with the maintenance of already existing material. Equation 4.30 can be transformed as

$$R = my + c\Delta y. \qquad (4.31)$$

This equation suggested that respiration is partitioned into two terms. The first term on the right-hand side of Eq. 4.31 means the portion resulting from biomass, and the second term means the portion resulting from the biomass increment. Although the respiration resulting from biomass depends on temperature (88), Eq. 4.30 seems to give roughly the interrelationship between annual stand respiration, biomass, and its annual increment.

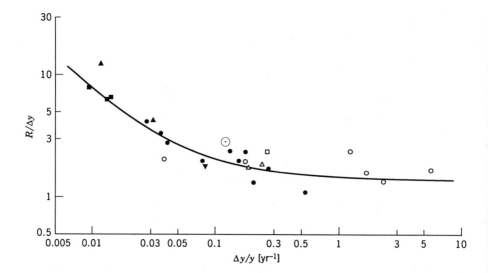

FIG. 4.12. Relationship between the ratio of annual stand respiration to annual biomass increment $R/\Delta y$ and the relative growth rate $\Delta y/y$ in evergreen forest stands. The curve corresponds to Eq. 4.30, $R/\Delta y = 0.0632/(\Delta y/y) + 1.44$. Data sources: ●, *Abies* forests (12,78); △, *Castanopsis cuspidata* forests (11,79); ○, hinoki plantations (69,80–82); ⊙, loblolly pine plantation (73); ▼, oak–pine forest (83); □, *Cryptomeria japonica* plantation (74); ▲, tropical forests (14,84); ■, warm-temperate evergreen oak forests (85). (Adapted from Ref. 69.)

4.7. Concluding remarks

Organic growth can be considered a result of an interaction of the synthesis and degradation, the anabolism and catabolism, of the building materials of the body. Organisms can grow positively so long as building up prevails over breaking down, and can reach a steady state if and when both processes are equal to each other in velocity. As a result, the growth velocity of any organism is expressed as the difference between the velocities of the synthetic and degradative processes; each velocity is given by a power function of the body weight (89).

Although the relationship between the metabolic rate and the body size belongs to the classical topics of physiology, there are few data as far as trees are concerned. This is due mainly to methodological difficulties caused from the huge size inherent to trees. Recently direct measurement of the CO_2 gas exchange of a whole-forest tree became possible by means of technical improvements (see Refs. 36, 90; cf. Refs. 5,92–94). We will thus be able to assess the values of the two processes from the measurements. This approach, together with biometrical and functional approaches (95,96), give us a better understanding of the growth process of trees from a physiological viewpoint (97–99).

ACKNOWLEDGMENTS

We wish to express our thanks to Messrs. S. Mori, Forestry & Forest Products Research Institute, and S. A. Paembonan, Nagoya University, for their invaluable help during the preparation of this manuscript. Our own research with respect to the CO_2 gas-exchange measurement of a hinoki forest tree cited in this chapter was supported in part by a Grant-in-Aid Scientific Research (Nos. 60480063, 62560146) from the Ministry of Education, Science and Culture, Japan.

4.8. References

1. T. Kira and T. Shidei, "Primary production and turnover of organic matter in different forest ecosystems of the Western Pacific," *Jpn. J. Ecol.*, **17**, 70 (1967).
2. R.E. McMurtrie and L. Wolf, "Above- and below-ground growth of forest stands: A carbon budget model," *Ann. Bot.*, **52**, 437 (1983).
3. G.M. Woodwell and W.R. Dykeman, "Respiration of a forest measured by CO_2 accumulation during temperature inversions," *Science*, **154**, 1031 (1966).
4. G.M. Woodwell and D.B. Botkin, "Metabolism of terrestrial ecosystems by gas exchange techniques: The Brookhaven approach," in D.E. Reichle, ed., *Analysis of Temperate Forest Ecosystems* (*Ecological Studies*, Vol. 1), Springer-Verlag, Berlin-Heidelberg, 1970, pp. 73–85.
5. E.-D. Schulze and W. Koch, "Measurement of primary production with cuvettes," in P. Duvigneaud, ed., *Productivity of Forest Ecosystems*, UNESCO, Paris, 1971, pp. 141–157.
6. R.S. Kinerson, "Relationship between plant surface area and respiration in loblolly pine," *J. Appl. Ecol.*, **12**, 965 (1975).
7. W. Tranquillini, *Physiological Ecology of the Alpine Timberline. Tree Existence at High Altitudes with Special Reference to the European Alps* (*Ecological Studies*, Vol. 31), Springer-Verlag, Berlin–Heidelberrg, 1979.
8. S. Linder and E. Troeng, "The seasonal variation in stem and coarse root respiration of a 20-year-old Scots pine (*Pinus sylvestris* L.)," *Mitt. Forstl. Bundes-Vers. Wien*, **142**, 125 (1981).
9. I. Ninomiya and K. Hozumi, "Respiration of forest trees. I. Measurement of respiration in *Pinus densi-thunbergii* Uyeki by an enclosed standing tree method," *J. Jpn. For. Soc.*, **63**, 8 (1981).
10. I. Ninomiya and K. Hozumi, "Respiration of forest trees. II. Measurement of nighttime respiration in a *Chamaecyparis obtusa* plantation," *J. Jpn. For. Soc.*, **65**, 193 (1983).
11. Y. Tadaki, "Studies on the production structure of forest. XIV. The third report on the primary production of a young stand of *Castanopsis cuspidata*," *J. Jpn. For. Soc.*, **50**, 60 (1968).
12. Y. Tadaki, K. Hatiya, K. Tochiaki, H. Miyauchi, and U. Matsuda, "Studies on the production structure. XVI. Primary productivity of *Abies veitchii* in the subalpine zone of Mt. Fuji," *Bull. For. Forest Prod. Res. Inst.*, **229**, 1 (1970).

13. C.M. Möller, D. Müller, and J. Nielsen, "Respiration in stem and branches of beech," *Forstl. Forsögsv. Danmark*, **21**, 273 (1954).

14. D. Müller and J. Nielsen, "Production brute, pertes par respiration et production nette dans la forêt ombrophile tropicale," *Forstl. Forsögsv. Danmark*, **29**, 69 (1965).

15. K. Yoda, K. Shinozaki, H. Ogawa, K. Hozumi, and T. Kira, "Estimation of the total amount of respiration in woody organs of trees and forest communities," *J. Biol. Osaka City Univ.*, **16**, 15 (1965).

16. K. Yoda, "Comparative ecological studies on three main types of forest vegetation in Thailand. III. Community respiration," *Nature Life in SE Asia*, **5**, 83 (1967).

17. K. Yoda, *Forest Ecology (Ecological Studies*, Vol. 4), Kyōritsu-Shuppan, Tokyo, 1971.

18. K. Yoda, "Community respiration in a lowland forest in Pasoh, Peninsular Malaysia," *Jpn. J. Ecol.*, **33**, 183 (1983).

19. S. Linder, *Photosynthesis and Respiration in Conifers. A Classified Reference List 1891–1977 (Studia Forestalia Suecica* 149), Swed. Univ. Agric. Sci., Uppsala, 1979.

20. S. Linder, *Photosynthesis and Respiration in Conifers. A Classified Reference List, Supplement 1 (Studia Forestalia Suecica* 161), Swed. Univ. Agric. Sci., Uppsala, 1981.

21. K. Negisi, "Respiration in Forest Trees," in T. Shidei and T. Kira, eds., *Primary Productivity of Japanese Forests. Productivity of Terrestrial Communities (JIBP Synthesis*, Vol. 16), Univ. Tokyo Press, Tokyo, 1977, pp. 86–93, 96–99.

22. K. Negisi, "Diurnal fluctuations of the stem bark respiration in relationship to the wood temperature in standing young *Pinus densiflora, Chamaecyparis obtusa* and *Quercus myrsinaefolia* trees," *J. Jpn. For. Soc.*, **64**, 315 (1982).

23. G.M. Woodwell and R.H. Whittaker, "Primary production in terrestrial communities," *Am. Zool.*, **8**, 19 (1968).

24. W. Tranquillini and W. Schütz, "Über die Rindenatumung einiger Bäume an der Waldgrenze," *Zentralbl. Ges. Forstwes.*, **87**, 42 (1970).

25. D.A. Rook and M.J. Corson, "Temperature and irradiance and the total daily photosynthetic production of a *Pinus radiata* tree," *Oecologia (Berl.)*, **36**, 371 (1978).

26. K. Negisi, "Diurnal and seasonal fluctuations in the stem bark respiration of a standing *Quercus myrsinaefolia* tree," *J. Jpn. For. Soc.*, **63**, 235 (1981).

27. Y. Kakubari, "Diurnal and seasonal fluctuations in the bark respiration of standing *Fagus sylvatica* trees at Solling, West Germany," *J. Jpn. For. Soc.*, **70**, 64 (1988).

28. P.G. Jarvis and J.W. Leverentz, "Productivity of Temperate, Deciduous and Evergreen Forests," in O.L. Lange, P.S. Nobel, C.B. Osmond, and H. Ziegler, eds., *Ecosystem Processes: Mineral Cycling, Productivity and Man's Influence (Physiological Plant Ecology*, Vol. IV), Springer-Verlag, Berlin–Heidelberg, 1983, pp. 233–280.

29. J.J. Landsberg, *Physiological Ecology of Forest Production*, Academic Press, Orlando, FL, 1986.

30. W. Larcher, *Physiological Plant Ecology*, 2nd ed., Springer-Verlag, Berlin–Heidelberg, 1980.

31. A.H. Fitter and R.K.M. Hay, *Environmental Physiology of Plants*, 2nd ed., Academic Press, London–San Diego, 1987.

32. D.R. Butler and J.J. Landsberg, "Respiration rates of apple trees, estimated by CO_2-efflux measurements," *Plant Cell Environ.*, **4**, 153 (1981).

33. A. Hagihara and K. Hozumi, "Respiration of a hinoki (*Chamaecyparis obtusa*) tree," *Trans. Mtg. Jpn. For. Soc.*, **99**, 365 (1988).

34. S.A. Paembonan, A. Hagihara, and K. Hozumi, "Seasonal trends of the nighttime respiration of a hinoki tree," *Trans. Mtg. Chubu Br. Jpn. For. Soc.*, **37**, 39 (1989).

35. A. Hagihara, S.A. Paembonan, and K. Hozumi, "Respiration measurement of a hinoki forest-tree over a three-year-period," *Trans. Mtg. Jpn. For. Soc.*, **100** 443 (1989).

36. A. Hagihara, K. Hozumi, and S. Handa, "An apparatus for determining the CO_2 gas-exchange of a forest tree in the field," *Bull. Nagoya Univ. For.*, **9**, 32 (1987).

37. K. Negisi, "Diurnal fluctuation of CO_2 release from the stem bark of standing young *Pinus densiflora* trees," *J. Jpn. For. Soc.*, **57**, 375 (1975).

38. A. Hagihara, "Study on photosynthesis and respiration of forest tree. I. Relation between leaf age and photosynthetic activity in *Pinus Thunbergii*," *J. Jpn. For. Soc.*, **55**, 71 (1973).

39. A. Hagihara, T. Koike, and K. Hozumi, "Photosynthesis of *Larix leptolepis* trees," *Trans. Mtg. Chubu Br. Jpn. For. Soc.*, **27**, 129 (1979).

40. J.M. Lyons, "Chilling injury in plants," *Ann. Rev. Plant Physiol.*, **24**, 445 (1973).

41. T. Kusumoto, "Photosynthesis and respiration in leaves of main component species," In T. Kira, Y. Ono, and T. Hosokawa, eds., *Biological Production in a Warm-Temperate Evergreen Oak Forest of Japan (JIBP Synthesis*, Vol. 18), Univ. Tokyo Press, Tokyo, 1978, pp. 88–98, 139–142.

42. P.J. Kramer and T.T. Kozlowski, *Physiology of Woody Plants*, Academic Press, New York, 1979.

43. K. Yoda, K. Hozumi, T. Nakai, and K. Shinozaki, "Estimation of community respiration. I. Leaves," *Proc. 15th Mtg. Ecol. Soc. Japan*, p. 207 (1968).

44. T. Kira, K. Shinozaki, and K. Hozumi, "Structure of forest canopies as related to their primary productivity," *Plant Cell Physiol.*, **10**, 129 (1969).

45. A. Hagihara and K. Hozumi, "Estimation of canopy respiration and its seasonal change in a *Chamaecyparis obtusa* plantation," *J. Jpn. For. Soc.*, **59**, 405 (1977).

46. M. Monsi and T. Saeki, "Über den Lichtfaktor in den Pflanzengesellschaften und seine Bedeutung für die Stoffproduktion," *Jpn. J. Bot.*, **14**, 22 (1953).

47. K. Hozumi, H. Kirita, and M. Nishioka, "Estimation of canopy photosynthesis and its seasonal change in a warm-temperate oak forest at Minamata (Japan)," *Photosynthetica*, **6**, 158 (1972).

48. M. Nishioka, K. Hozumi, H. Kirita, and M. Nagano, "Estimation of canopy photosynthesis and respiration," in T. Kira, Y. Ono, and T. Hosokawa, eds., *Biological Production in a Warm-Temperate Evergreen Oak Forest of Japan (JIBP Synthesis*, Vol. 18), Univ. Tokyo Press, Tokyo, 1978, pp. 99–111, 142–143.

49. K. Yoda, "Estimation of community respiration," in T. Kira, Y. Ono, and T. Hosokawa, eds., *Biological Production in a Warm-Temperate Evergreen Oak Forest of Japan (JIBP Synthesis*, Vol. 18), Univ. Tokyo Press, Tokyo, 1978, pp. 112–131, 143–144.

50. S. Mori, A. Hagihara, and K. Hozumi, "Respiration on an individual tree basis in a hinoki plantation," *Proc. 31st Mtg. Ecol. Soc. Japan*, p. 142 (1984).

51. A. Hagihara, I. Ninomiya, and K. Hozumi, "Evaluation of the light climate in a *Chamaecyparis obtusa* plantation by a chemical light-meter," *J. Jpn. For. Soc.*, **64**, 220 (1982).

52. Y. Asami, A. Hagihara, and K. Hozumi, "Photosynthesis of a *Larix leptolepis* plantation," *Trans. Mtg. Chubu Br. Jpn. For. Soc.*, **29**, 13 (1981).

53. N. Kurachi, *Production Structure of a Larix leptolepis Plantation*, Ph.D. thesis, Nagoya Univ., 1989.

54. R.H. Goodwin and D.R. Goddard, "The oxygen consumption of isolated woody tissues," *Am. J. Bot.*, **27**, 234 (1940).

55. S. Oohata, T. Yamakura, H. Saito, and T. Shidei, "A study on the vertical distribution of respiratory activity of a 40-year-old stand of *Chamaecyparis obtusa*," *Bull. Kyoto Univ. For.*, **42**, 103 (1971).

56. S. Mori and A. Hagihara, "Respiration in stems of hinoki (*Chamaecyparis obtusa*) trees," *J. Jpn. For. Soc.*, **70**, 481 (1988).

57. K. Shinozaki, K. Yoda, K. Hozumi, and T. Kira, "A quantitative analysis of plant form—the pipe model theory. I. Basic analysis," *Jpn. J. Ecol.*, **14**, 97 (1964).

58. K. Shinozaki, K. Yoda, K. Hozumi, and T. Kira, "A quantitative analysis of plant form—the pipe model theory. II. Further evidence of the theory and its application in forest ecology," *Jpn. J. Ecol.*, **14**, 133 (1964).

59. A. Hagihara and K. Hozumi, "Respiration consumption by woody organs in a *Chamaecyparis obtusa* plantation," *J. Jpn. For. Soc.*, **63**, 156 (1981).

60. K. Yoda, K. Shinozaki, K. Hozumi, and T. Nakai, "Estimation of community respiration. IV. A model of the respiration rate–diameter relationship," *Proc. 15th Mtg. Ecol. Soc. Japan*, p. 213 (1968).

61. K. Ogawa, A. Hagihara, and K. Hozumi, "Growth analysis of seedling community of *Chamaecyparis obtusa*. I. Respiration consumption," *J. Jpn. For. Soc.*, **67**, 218 (1985).

62. I. Ninomiya and K. Hozumi, "Respiration of forest trees. II. Estimation of community respiration," *J. Jpn. For. Soc.*, **65**, 275 (1983).

63. K. Hozumi and K. Shinozaki, "Studies on the frequency distribution of the weight of individual trees in a forest stand. IV. Estimation of the total function of a forest stand and a generalized mean plant," *Jpn. J. Ecol.*, **24**, 207 (1974).

64. K. Hozumi, K. Shinozaki, and Y. Tadaki, "Studies on the frequency distribution of the weight of individual trees in a forest stand. I. A new approach toward the analysis of the distribution function and the $-3/2$th power distribution," *Jpn J. Ecol.*, **18**, 10 (1968).

65. K. Hozumi and K. Shinozaki, "Studies on the frequency distribution of the weight of individual trees in a forest stand. II. Exponential distribution," *Jpn. J. Ecol.*, **20**, 1 (1970).

66. K. Hozumi, "Studies on the frequency distribution of the weight of individual trees in a forest stand. III. A beta-type distribution," *Jpn. J. Ecol.*, **21**, 152 (1971).

67. R.L. Bailey and T.R. Dell, "Quantifying diameter distributions with the Weibull function," *For. Sci.*, **19**, 97 (1973).

68. J.L. Clutter and B.J. Allison, "A growth and yield model for *Pinus radiata* in New Zealand," in J. Fries, ed., *Growth Models for Tree and Stand Simulation*, IUFRO Org. Working Party S4.01-4, Stockholm, 1974, pp. 136–160.

69. A. Hagihara and K. Hozumi, "Studies on the primary production in a *Chamaecyparis obtusa* plantation," *J. Jpn. For. Soc.*, **65**, 357 (1983).

70. D.M. Hyink and J.W. Moser, Jr., "A generalized framework for projecting forest yield and stand structure using diameter distributions," *For. Sci.*, **29**, 85 (1983).

71. Y. Ueno and Y. Ōsawa, "The applicability of the Weibull and the expanded Weibull distributions," *J. Jpn. For. Soc.*, **69**, 24 (1987).

72. C.M. Möller, D. Müller, and J. Nielsen, "Graphic presentation of dry matter production of European beech," *Forstl. Forsögsv. Danmark*, **21**, 327 (1954).

73. R.S. Kinerson, C.W. Ralston, and C.G. Wells, "Carbon cycling in a loblolly pine plantation," *Oecologia (Berl.)*, **29**, 1 (1977).

74. Y. Tadaki and Y. Kawasaki, "Studies on the production structure of forest. IX. Primary productivity of a young *Cryptomeria* plantation with excessively high stand density," *J. Jpn. For. Soc.*, **48**, 55 (1966).

75. D.G. Sprugel, "Density, biomass, productivity, and nutrient-cycling changes during stand development in wave-regenerated balsam fir forests," *Ecol. Monogr.*, **54**, 165 (1984).

76. S. Oohata and T. Shidei, "A study on the annual change of net productivity in the forest communities," *Bull. Kyoto Univ. For.*, **46**, 40 (1974).

77. K. Yoda, T. Kira, H. Ogawa, and K. Hozumi, "Intraspecific competition among higher plants. XI. Self-thinning in overcrowded pure stands under cultivated and natural conditions," *J. Biol. Osaka City Univ.*, **14**, 107 (1963).

78. M. Kimura, I. Mototani, and K. Hogetsu, "Ecological and physiological studies on the vegetation of Mt. Shimagare. VI. Growth and dry matter production of young *Abies* stand," *Bot. Mag. Tokyo*, **81**, 287 (1968).

79. Y. Tadaki, "Studies on the production structure of forest. VII. The primary production of a young stand of *Castanopsis cuspidata*," *Jpn. J. Ecol.*, **15**, 142 (1965).

80. Y. Tadaki, N. Ogata, Y. Nagatomo, and T. Yoshida, "Studies on the production structure of forest. X. Primary productivity of an unthinned 45-year-old stand of *Chamaecyparis obtusa*," *J. Jpn. For. Soc.*, **48**, 387 (1966).

81. K. Ogawa, A. Hagihara, and K. Hozumi, "Growth analysis of a seedling community of *Chamaecyparis obtusa*. II. Primary production," *J. Jpn. For. Soc.*, **68**, 135 (1986).

82. K. Ogawa, *Growth and Matter Economy of Hinoki Seedling Populations Grown under Nursery Conditions*, Ph.D. Thesis, Nagoya Univ., 1989.

83. R. H. Whittaker and G.M. Woodwell, "Structure, production and diversity of the oak-pine forest at Brookhaven, New York," *J. Ecol.*, **57**, 155 (1969).

84. T. Kira, "Primary production and carbon cycling in a primeval lowland rainforest of peninsular Malaysia," in M.R. Sethuraj and A.S. Raghavendra, eds., *Tree Crop Physiology*, Elsevier Science Publ. B.V., Amsterdam, 1987, pp. 99–119.

85. T. Kira and K. Yabuki, "Primary production rates in the Minamata Forest," in T. Kira, Y. Ono, and T. Hosokawa, eds., *Biological Production in a Warm-*

Temperate Evergreen Oak Forest of Japan (*JIBP Synthesis*, Vol. 18), Univ. Tokyo Press, Tokyo, 1978, pp. 131–138, 145.

86. K.J. McCree, "An equation for the rate of respiration of white clover plants grown under controlled conditions," in I. Šetlik, ed., *Production and Measurement of Photosynthetic Productivity*, PUDOC, Wageningen, 1970, pp. 221–229.

87. J.H.M. Thornley, *Mathematical Models in Plant Physiology. A Quantitative Approach to Problems in Plant and Crop Physiology*, Academic Press, New York, 1976.

88. Y. Yokoi, M. Kimura, and K. Hogetsu, "Quantitative relationships between growth and respiration. I. Components of respiratory loss and growth efficiencies of etiolated red bean seedlings," *Bot. Mag. Tokyo*, **91**, 31 (1978).

89. L. v. Bertalanffy, *General System Theory. Foundations, Development, Applications*, George Braziller, New York, 1968.

90. Y. Matsumoto, "A method for measuring photosynthesis and respiration rates of an intact crown in the field," *Trans. Mtg. Jpn. For. Soc.*, **96**, 723 (1985).

91. P.G. Jarvis, J. Čatský, F.E. Eckardt, W. Koch, and D. Koller, "General principles of gasmetric methods and the main aspects of installation design," in Z. Šesták, J. Čatský, and P.G. Jarvis, eds., *Plant Photosynthetic Production. Manual of Methods*, W. Junk N.V. Publ., The Hague, The Netherlands, 1971, pp. 49–110.

92. H.A. Mooney, "Carbon dioxide exchange of plants in natural environments," *Bot. Rev.*, **30**, 455 (1972).

93. S. Linder, B. Nordström, J. Parsby, E. Sundbom, and E. Troeng, *A Gas Exchange System for Field Measurements of Photosynthesis and Transpiration in a 20-year-old Stand of Scots Pine* (*Technical Report* 23), Swed. Univ. Agric. Sci., Uppsala, 1980.

94. K. Maruyama, "The Shimadzu climatized chamber for measuring photosynthesis, respiration and transpiration in pot grown Japanese beech seedlings," *Bull. Niigata Univ. For.*, **13**, 1 (1980).

95. D.R. Causton and J.C. Venus, *The Biometry of Plant Growth*, Edward Arnold, London, 1981.

96. R. Hunt, *Plant Growth Curves. The Functional Approach to Plant Growth Analysis*, Edward Arnold, London, 1982.

97. K. Hozumi, "Phase diagrammatic approach to the analysis of growth curve using the $u–w$ diagram—basic aspects," *Bot. Mag. Tokyo*, **98**, 239 (1985).

98. K. Hozumi, "Analysis of growth curve of stem volume in some woody species using the $u–w$ diagram," *Bot. Mag. Tokyo*, **100**, 87 (1987).

99. K. Hozumi, "Biomass duration in growth models," *Bot. Mag. Tokyo*, **102**, 75 (1989).

5 Symbiotic Nitrogen Fixation

C. T. WHEELER

Department of Botany, University of Glasgow, Glasgow, Scotland

Contents

5.1. Introduction

Trees and shrubs that form symbiotic associations with nitrogen-fixing organisms have been utilized for plant production worldwide for many centuries. The improvements in soil nutrient status that result from the recycling of their litter ensures an important role for many species in land reclamation and as nurse or amenity species. Others are important forestry species, used for the production of sawlogs, fiber, pulp, and fuelwood (1). They are also valuable in agroforestry, where through the application of appropriate silvicultural and management techniques they can help maintain or increase soil fertility (2). There is an enormous diversity of species, varying widely in morphology and physiology and in the nature of their microsymbionts, that makes available trees suitable for planting in a wide range of habitats.

Table 5.1. The range of nodulated woody plants

Family or subfamily	Genera	
	Mainly nodulated	Nonnodulated

Leguminosae

Family or subfamily	Mainly nodulated	Nonnodulated
Caesalpinioideae	*Sclerolobium, Dimorphandra, Chamaecrista*	*Gleditsia, Delonix, Cassia, Bauhinia*
Mimosoideae	*Acacia, Inga, Mimosa*	*Adenanthera, Newtonia*
Papilionoideae (stem nodulation)	*Dalbergia, Robinia, Erythrina (Aeschynomene, Sesbania)*	*Dipteryx, Inocarpus*

Nonlegumes nodulated by Rhizobiaceae

Ulmaceae	*Parasponia*	

Actinorhizal plants

Nodulated genera

Coriariaceae	*Coriaria*
Rosaceae	*Cercocarpus, Chamaebatia, Cowania, Dryas, Purshia, Rubus(?)*
Datiscaceae	*Datisca*
Myricaceae	*Myrica, Comptonia*
Betulaceae	*Alnus*
Elaeagnaceae	*Elaeagnus, Hippophae, Shepherdia*
Rhamnaceae	*Ceanothus, Colletia, Discaria, Kentrothamnus, Retamnilla, Talguenea, Trevoa*
Casuarinaceae	*Allocasuarina, Casuarina, Gymnostoma*

Cycads nodulated by cyanobacteria

Bowenia, Ceratozamia, Cycas, Dioon, Encephalartos, Macrozamia, Microcycas, Stangeria, Zamia.

5.2. The macro- and microsymbionts

There are three groups of microorganisms that fix nitrogen in symbiotic associations with plants. The Gram-negative bacteria *Rhizobium, Azorhizobium* and *Bradyrhizobium* (genera showing fast or slow growth, respectively, on yeast mannitol agar) that belong to the Rhizobiaceae, filamentous actinomycetes of the genus *Frankia*, and heterocystous cyanobacteria of the genera *Anabaena* and *Nostoc*. The range of woody plants that are hosts for these microorganisms is shown in Table 5.1. Many leguminous species have a broad spectrum of infectivity and nodulation of woody legumes by both slow- and fast-growing rhizobia has been described (3). Slow-growing bacteria also nodulate the nonlegume *Parasponia*. These are placed in a separate group in the genus *Bradyrhizobium* since they do not readily nodulate other tropical legumes and *Parasponia* itself is not readily nodulated by Bradyrhizobia from other legumes (4).

The wealth of legume trees that are available for exploitation has begun to be appreciated fully only in recent years. Most species in the Caesalpinoideae and Mimosoideae Families and more than one-third of the Papilionoideae are woody. The greatest number of these species occur in the tropics and the subtropics, although many ecologically and economically important species grow in temperate regions. Of those species examined, 97% of Papilionoid, 90% of Mimosoid, and 23% of Caesalpinoid species are nodulated (3). A large proportion of legume tree species still await examination for nodules, and various characteristics of the root systems of woody legumes can render observation of nodulation difficult. For example, in dry areas nodules on *Prosopis* (mesquite) occur at a depth of several meters so that a search of only superficial soil layers could easily lead to a false record of nonnodulation (5). Mature trees may be sparsely nodulated, especially in tropical or subtropical regions subject to periodic drought. For example, it took Hogberg 5 days to find nodules on *Xeroderris* in the savannah of Tanzania (6)! Various sources may be consulted concerning the taxonomy of the Rhizobiaceae and the current nodulation status of these trees (3,7,9).

Frankia-nodulated species are all nonleguminous and are usually referred to as "actinorhizal" plants, to distinguish them from *Parasponia* or other *Rhizobium*-nodulated nonlegumes that may be discovered. These plants are taxonomically diverse, with species distributed among 24 genera and eight plant families. They are most prominent in temperate and warm-temperate climates, but there are many important species in the tropics, notably members of the Casuarinaceae. Since the first confirmed isolation of *Frankia*, many hundreds of isolates have been obtained from different actinorhizal genera, utilizing a variety of isolation techniques. Many strains have been subject to chemotaxonomic analysis utilizing criteria of serology, cell wall type, and whole-cell sugar patterns, DNA homology, isozyme variation, and soluble protein patterns (10,11). The continued accumulation of critical taxonomic data should soon permit speciation of the genus. At present, strains are designated according to a numerical system (12).

The host plant specificity of strains is also being elucidated slowly. On the basis of cross-inoculation studies, isolates from six of the actinorrhizal genera have been divided into four groups that nodulate (1) *Alnus* and *Myrica*, (2) *Casuarina* and *Myrica*, (3) the three Elaeagnaceous genera (*Elaeagnus*, *Hippophae*, and *Shepherdia*) and *Myrica*, and (4) the Elaeagnaceae alone (13). Even from study of this limited range of plant genera, it is clear that the specificity of infection of actinorhizal genera by *Frankia* is more flexible than the infection of legumes by *Rhizobium*. It is hoped that this feature may encourage more intensive study of the molecular genetics of *Frankia* by those researchers interested in extending the range of host plant nodulation by nitrogen-fixing organisms.

The Cycads belong to the Gymnosperms and are the only group of woody plants known to form nitrogen-fixing symbioses with cyanobacteria, although the lichen associations that festoon many trees provide an important source of nitrogen for many forest ecosystems (14). The Cycadales consists of some nine genera with about 90 species that occur in tropical and subtropical regions of the southern hemisphere. Both *Anabaena* and *Nostoc* have been isolated from the coralloid cycad root nodules. While cycads are not important as timber species in their own right, they can be important as a source of nitrogen in some forest ecosystems, such as the Jarrah forests of western Australia, where they provide a significant input of nitrogen following burning of the undergrowth (15). Their unique association with the Gymnosperms is starting to attract more attention; for example, DNA hybridization studies have shown recently the association of a wide range of *Nostoc* strains with cycad nodules (16).

5.3. Infection and nodule development

5.3.1. The processes

All actinorhizal nodules and the vast majority of the perennial nodules of woody legumes are branched structures of indeterminate growth. They can be heavily pigmented, and some legume tree nodules are very hard because of the formation of a layer of sclereids in the cortex (17). In most legume nodules, the infected cells characteristically are central with peripheral vascular tissue. However, in the woody legume *Andira* and the *Bradyrhizobium*-nodulated nonlegume *Parasponia*, the vascular tissue is central and the infected cells are located in the cortex, thus resembling the modified lateral root structure of *Frankia* nodules.

Overall, the nodulation process involves the following sequence of complex interactions between the host plant and microsymbiont:

1. *Infection.* Recognition, binding, and penetration.
2. *Nodule initiation.* Stimulation of cell division in the host root cortex ahead of invading microsymbiont; initiation of prenodule and/or nodule primordium.
3. *Nodule development.* Invasion of newly divided cells; development of vascular tissue; development of nitrogen-fixing activity by microsymbiont within nodule cells.

Within this broad framework of events, there is a diversity of developmental patterns that may be followed in different genera of legumes and actinorhizal plants, both during host plant root penetration and later during nodule initiation and development.

The bacteria can invade the host plant root by a variety of routes—through the root hairs, through the epidermis via cracks or wounds, or through the middle lamella. Following root hair infection, both rhizobia and *Frankia* are contained within structures of host plant origin—the former by the walls of the infection thread and the latter by a polysaccharide encapsulation layer (18–20). The infection thread or the encapsulated hyphae grow down into the cortex to infect cells whose division has been stimulated ahead of the invading bacteria. In legumes, this group of cells forms the nodule primordium. In roothair-infected actinorhizal plants, the nodule primordium, originates from the pericycle of the stele and the initial corticular divisions give rise to a prenodule. This becomes infected first and from here hyphae grow out to infect the developing nodule.

Root hair infection was thought to be the route followed in most nodulated species. However, infection via the epidermis of the host root is now known to be common in both legumes and nonlegumes and is a process found in many woody legumes. Indeed, root hairs are few or are absent from the roots of many legumes and actinorhizal plants. In some species, entry takes place through weak points in the epidermis induced by the emergence of lateral root, such as in the nodulation of peanut (*Arachis hypogea*) or *Stylosanthes*. In *Parasponia*, rhizobia stimulate random division of the outer cortical cells near the base of a root hair, thus rupturing the epidermis and permitting entry of the bacteria. In *Mimosa* and in *Elaeagnus*, where root hairs are few or absent, rhizobia or *Frankia*, respectively, digest their way through the middle lamella of radial cell walls. In all these modes of infection, further invasion of the cortex also proceeds by an intercellular route and in rhizobium infections, threads are formed only following entry of the invading bacteria into cells differentiated within the nodule primordium. In intercellular infections of actinorhizal plants, a prenodule is not formed as in root hair infection but the hyphae ramify through the intercellular spaces of the cortex, eventually invading the cells of a nodule primordium. It is known that the mode of infection is dictated by the genome of the actinorhizal plant since some individual strains of *Frankia* are capable of root hair or intercellular infection depending on the host plant genus, for example, with *Myrica* or Elaeagnaceous species, respectively (21,22).

Traditionally in the legume symbiosis, it was held that nitrogen fixation occurred only following release of rhizobia from the infection threads. Following release, they are separated from the host cytoplasm by the peribacteroid membrane, which originates from the plasmalemma. In *Parasponia* and in many woody legumes, however, the bacteria are not released from the infection thread and nitrogen fixation occurs within these structures. It has been suggested that it is only in the more evolutionarily advanced legumes that rhizobia are transformed into nitrogen-fixing bacteroids following release from the infection thread. *Frankia* is also separated from the host cell cytoplasm by encapsulation with material believed to be mainly of host plant origin, during both intercellular and intracellular penetration. In actinorhizal nodules, where the microsymbiont is separated by the encapsulation layer from the host cytoplasm, vesicles or swollen hyphal tips develop in which nitrogen fixation occurs. Further details of the process of infection and nodule development are available in various reviews (17,23,24).

5.3.2. Regulation of nodulation

Elegant analysis of *Rhizobium*, using molecular biological techniques, has begun to elucidate the molecular signals whose exchange regulates the transcription of the genes controlling the formation of nitrogen-fixing nodules in herbaceous legumes. Host plant lectins are involved in the recognition and binding process, although their overall role is not yet clearly defined (25). Recent research has shown the importance of root lectin as determinants of host specificity. Introduction of the pea lectin gene into white clover, using *Agrobacterium* as a vector, resulted in the production of "hairy" roots that could be nodulated by *Rhizobium* specific for peas (26). This gain of ability to nodulate was incomplete, however, showing that other factors are involved in the recognition process. A role for *Rhizobium* polysaccharides in determining host plant compatibility has been shown by the poor infectivity and nodulation given by mutants defective in their production (27). It has been suggested that one function of bacterial exopolysaccharides may be to mask the bacteria from agglutination by some plant root lectins (23). In *Frankia*, specific binding of fluorescein-labeled lectins to particular groups of strains has been demonstrated (28), but further definitive study of carbohydrates and proteins that may be involved in specific interactions with the actinorhizal plant root are awaited.

Regulation of the development of the symbiosis involves numerous bacterial and host plant genes. Many of the symbiotic genes, particularly the *nodABC* and *nodD* genes, are highly conserved in those organisms that have been studied. They seem to be central to the formation of nodules, at least in legumes, and are involved in the control of early events such as root hair curling, invasion, and the stimulation of cell division in the host plant.

Specific flavonoids in legume root exudates control the transcription of the bacterial *nodD* gene, which in turn activates the *nodABC* genes that control the nodulation process. Other phenylpropanoid compounds antagonize the action of the stimulatory compounds, and the balance between these substances may determine whether nodule initiation is successful. The maintenance of such balance involves interaction with the host plant genes that control the synthesis of the enzymes involved in the phenylpropanoid biosynthesis. Many plant mutants, defective in some part of the nodulation process, have been obtained and are being analyzed to understand the contribution of the host plant to the development of the symbiosis. Rapid advances are being made toward elucidating the genes that are involved in the control of nodulation, but to date, details of function have emerged only for the bacterial *nodD* gene (23,27).

At present, there is little specific information concerning the regulation of nodulation at a molecular level in woody nitrogen-fixing plants. One notable difference among the microsymbionts is that whereas many of the *nod* genes in *Rhizobium* are clustered on large plasmids, in *Bradyrhizobium* and *Frankia* they tend to be located on chromosomes. A novel nodulation gene (*nodK*) has been detected between the *nodD* and *nodABC* operons in several bradyrhizobia, including the strains that nodulate *Parasponia* (29). A recent finding of interest for understanding the process of nodulation of nonlegumes by bradyrhizobia is that the *nodDI* genes from *Rhizobium* are key determinants in extending the host range to *Parasponia* (30).

In *Frankia*, preliminary research has shown some homology of the *nodABC* genes with those of *Rhizobium* (see references quoted in Ref. 31). Homology has been reported between a *Frankia* DNA fragment, located close to the *nifH* gene, and three of the genes coding for pectate lyase in *Erwinia chrysanthemi* (32); it is presumed that the production of hydrolytic enzymes such as pectinases and cellulases is necessary for penetration of the microbe into the host plant tissues.

5.3.3. Control of nitrogenase synthesis

The *nif* gene system that codes for the biosynthesis of nitrogenase has been studied for a number of years, and much information is now available concerning its structural organisation and control. The *nif* genes from many different diazotrophs show considerable homology. One notable difference between groups is that while in many species of *Rhizobium* the *nif* genes are located on plasmids, in genera such as *Bradyrhizobium* and *Frankia* and in the cyanobacteria they are usually of chromosomal location. In *Rhizobium*, the structural genes for nitrogenase (*nifHDK*) form a single cluster whereas in the *nif* gene clusters of *Bradyrhizobium* and of *Frankia*, both of which can nodulate woody species, *nifH* is separated from *nifDK* (29,33). The control genes for the *nif* operon, *nifAL*, interact with the *ntr* genes that control nitrogen assimilation into organic form. These systems respond to changes in oxygen levels and, in free living forms, to changes in mineral nitrogen levels in the environment. Rhizobial bacteroids are unable to take up ammonia and inhibition of nitrogen fixation in nodules by combined nitrogen occurs by other means, such as diversion of host plant photoassimilates away from the nodules and changes in cell membrane potentials. In the case of nitrate uptake and its reduction to ammonia, nitrite formation may inhibit bacteroid function although it is a matter of debate whether nitrate reduction occurs in the bacteroid ozone (34,35).

The techniques of molecular genetics currently are facilitating rapid advances in our understanding of the complexity of the processes of infection, nodule development and nitrogen fixation in symbiotic systems. Further information on the nature and control of these gene systems may be obtained from recent reviews (23,27,36,37).

5.4. Nitrogenase and its function

The biochemistry of the nitrogen-fixing process has been summarized recently in several books (38–40) and will be considered briefly. The nitrogenase complex contains two proteins: (1) dinitrogenase reductase, a dimer containing two identical subunits, each of about 30,000 Da and containing a single [4Fe–4S] cluster bridging the subunits; and (2) dinitrogenase, a tetramer containing two pairs of dissimilar subunits, each of about 60,000 Da and containing iron and molybdenum. Recent studies suggest that molybdenum can be replaced by vanadium under conditions of molybdenum starvation to produce an alternative, vanadium-based nitrogen-fixing system (41). The overall reaction catalyzed by nitrogenase is

$$N_2 + 8[H^+ + e^-] + 16\ ATP \rightarrow 2NH_3 + H_2 + 16[ADP + Pi] \quad (5.1)$$

5.4.1. Reduction of acetylene

Nitrogenase will also reduce many other triple-bonded substrates, the best known of which is acetylene:

$$C_2H_2 + 2[H^+ + e^-] \rightarrow C_2H_4 \quad\quad\quad (5.2)$$

The ethylene evolved during this reaction can be measured readily by gas chromatography, and the reaction forms the basis of the well-known acetylene reduction assay for nitrogenase activity. Unfortunately, the ratio between the number of electrons used to reduce nitrogen to ammonia and acetylene to ethylene, when measured experimentally, is rarely 4 : 1, as suggested by Equations 5.1 and 5.2. A variety of factors, including differences in permeability of the gases involved, differences in hydrogen evolution, effects on respiration and nodule permeability, affect the ratios that may be obtained between acetylene-reduced and nitrogen-fixed substances. Consequently, while the assay has proved invaluable, particularly for some laboratory experiments, applicability to nodulated plants and to field samples is restricted. Readers should study reports of critical investigations of acetylene reduction in root nodules before proceeding with its use (42).

5.4.2. Hydrogen evolution

Equation 5.1 depicts two notable properties of nitrogenase: the hydrolysis of large amounts of ATP and the production of hydrogen during the reduction process. The latter process represents a considerable loss of energy, some of which may be recouped through the action of an uptake hydrogenase. This enzyme reoxidizes the liberated hydrogen, passing the electrons down an electron transport pathway to oxygen and regaining ATP through oxidative phosphorylation:

$$H_2 \rightarrow 2H^+ + 2e^- \left(\begin{array}{l} \tfrac{1}{2}O_2 \\ + n(ADP + Pi) \\ H_2O + nATP \end{array}\right. \quad (5.3)$$

There is considerable variation in the amount of hydrogen evolved from the nodules of different species of legumes and nonlegumes. Under some circumstances, substantial improvements in yields of nitrogen fixed can be obtained in associations where hydrogen evolution is low. Schubert and Evans (44) introduced the concept of relative efficiency, RE, which quantifies the relationship between nitrogen fixation and hydrogen evolution:

$$RE = 1 - \frac{\text{rate of } H_2 \text{ evolution in air}}{\substack{\text{rate of } H_2 \text{ evolution in 20\% } O_2 + 80\% \text{ Ar} \\ \text{(or rate of } C_2H_2 \text{ reduction)}}} \qquad (5.4)$$

The rate of hydrogen evolution in the absence of nitrogen gives the total activity of the enzyme, as does the rate of reduction of acetylene to ethylene since hydrogen is seldom evolved then and all electrons are donated to acetylene. However, exposure to acetylene may inactivate endophytic uptake hydrogenase in some species, including *Alnus*, and consequently give false assays of relative efficiency (44). From Eq. 5.1, it can be seen that $RE = 0.75$ in organisms with a fully efficient nitrogenase but with no uptake hydrogenase activity. Hydrogen recycling by an efficient uptake hydrogenase will give values higher than this, while lower values indicate wastage through hydrogen evolution of a proportion of the energy going to the nitrogenase system. Although the uptake hydrogenases of wild-type organisms show much diversity in effectivity (see Section 5.6) in many instances, relative efficiency is often high for the nodules of wild plants, whereas nodules on crop plants more often contain strains of microsymbiont with low-uptake hydrogenase activity. Agricultural practices, involving application of combined nitrogen to crops, may have removed some of the evolutionary pressure for survival of the most efficient strains.

5.4.3. Oxygen relations

Nitrogenase is highly sensitive to and is rapidly inactivated by oxygen. Various strategies have evolved to protect the enzyme from inactivation in the functional nodule, where good aeration is necessary to support the aerobic respiration of both root nodule cells and the endophytes. In actinorrhizal nodules, with ample intercellular spaces to facilitate the ready diffusion of air into infected regions of the cortex, the specialized, lipoidal wall of the endophyte vesicles within which nitrogenase is located is believed to help control ingress of oxygen (45). At the same time, *Frankia* has unusually high superoxide dismutase activity that will help scavenge highly reactive oxygen radicals (46). In legume nodules, the nodule endodermis restricts ingress of gases in those nodules where the endophyte mass is centrally situated. Indeed, the permeability of the nodule seems to be flexible and may change in response to alterations in gas composition (47). Other control measures include respiratory scavenging of available oxygen and possibly oxygen utilization during hydrogen oxidation via the hydrogenase system (47).

Perhaps most attention has been given to the occurrence and role of hemoglobin in the regulation of oxygen flux in nitrogen-fixing nodules. This protein facilitates the supply of oxygen to the terminal oxidase of symbiotic bacteria. It has a high oxygen affinity and a rapid oxygen turnover rate that keeps free oxygen at levels sufficient for the functioning of the oxidases but low enough to prevent inactivation of nitrogenase (48). Hemoglobins are ubiquitous in legume nodules and in *Parasponia* and occur in at least some actinorhizal nodules (48). In *Casuarina*, an actinorrhizal plant where hemoglobin has been detected in both nodules and roots, molecular-weight differences of the hemoglobins present, suggest that different genes may code for the proteins. It seems that gene sequences coding for hemoglobin may be more widespread in the plant kingdom than thought previously since DNA sequences that hybridize with soybean legume hemoglobin probes not only hybridize with DNA from nonnodulating legumes, such as *Colutea arborescens* (Carob), but also to DNA from the roots of nonlegumes such as *Trema* and *Celtis*, related to *Parasponia* and to birch, related to *Alnus* (49). It is not known what function these genes may serve in the species where they occur or whether they can be "switched on" under the influence of particular environmental conditions.

5.5. Assay of nitrogen fixation

Standard techniques for the assay of nitrogen fixation, such as assessment of nitrogen accumulation in plants grown in media free of combined nitrogen, comparison of nitrogen accumulation with nonnodulated controls, or mass spectrometric measurement of enrichment with ^{15}N following the supply of labelled gas, can be applied fairly readily to young, pot-grown woody plant species (50). However, the variability of nodulation distribution, the size of woody plants, the depth of penetration of perennial root systems and the large amounts of woody, inactive tissue that develops on perennial nodule clusters all exacerbate the difficulties of quantifying nitrogen fixation in the field and of expressing rates of nitrogen fixation on an area or per-plant nodulation basis (51,52).

As discussed in Section 5.4.1, the acetylene reduction assay is suitable only for qualitative demonstration of nitrogen fixation in the field. One alternative approach is to use nitrogen balance techniques. Here, accretion of fixed nitrogen in an ecosystem is assessed from a balance sheet of change in the total nitrogen content of the ecosystem over a period of time. Accurate measurement of the nitrogen content of the different components of the system and of leaching and denitrification losses (good quantitative techniques for the last are still not available) is essential if meaningful results for symbiotic fixation are to be obtained. Other errors can be due to variations in the nature and extent of mycorrhizal and other microbial associations of experimental and control plants, which may facilitate the transfer of nitrogen between nodulated and nonnodulated plants.

Rates of nitrogen accretion in the nitrogen fixing species are often compared with those of nonnodulating nonlegumes, or with a nonnodulating isoline of the same species. Nonnodulating isolines have been developed mainly for herbaceous legumes, and little work has been carried out as yet to identify such lines for woody plant species. Even if available, developmental differences between the root systems of nitrogen-fixing plants and either mutant or nonnodulating species can result in the exploration of different volumes of soil and thus give rise to errors in the assessment of nitrogen fixation.

Techniques using ^{15}N undoubtedly provide the most precise methods for assay of nitrogen fixation. However, major problems of handling, experimental design, and cost make it impossible to assay nitrogen fixation in large field plants by measurement of isotopic enrichment following the feeding of ^{15}N gas. One alternative is to assay nitrogen fixation by dilution of isotopic mineral N, added to the soil as salts enriched with ^{15}N-labeled NH_4^+ or NO_3^- in amounts that will not affect nitrogen fixation. This technique permits the integration of nitrogen fixation over a period of time, but its application requires comparisons with control, nonnodulated plants, grown in soil similar to that of the nodulated plants. Variability in mineral salt distribution, differences between the root systems of control and nodulated plants, mycorrhizal transfer of ^{15}N, leaching, and denitrification losses can all cause variations in ^{15}N uptake and enrichment. Methods to help overcome these problems, such as screening control species to select those in which mineral uptake is most similar to the nodulated plant, have been suggested (53).

Another isotope technique that has particular attraction for use with large woody species is the measurement of variation in natural abundance of ^{15}N in the plant tissue. Biological reactions tend to discriminate in favor of ^{14}N. This discrimination is particularly marked during denitrification so that the pool of mineral nitrogen in the soil is enriched with ^{15}N. In comparison, discrimination during nitrogen fixation is much less so that the abundance of ^{15}N in plant nitrogen that has been derived directly from nitrogen fixation is smaller than when assimilated from the soil. The main constraint on the use of natural abundance techniques is the requirement that the $^{15}N : {}^{14}N$ ratio of the soil nitrogen of the ecosystem under investigation should be consistent as well as significantly different from air. This often is not the case and heterogeneity of discrimination for ^{15}N in the soil of the ecosystem has rendered unreliable the use of the natural abundance assay in many ecosystems (54,55). The technique may be the only one that is applicable in certain situations, however, and it has been applied with some success to *Prosopis*, nodulated at depth in the Sonoran desert, where it is suggested that fixation provides 43–61% of the plant nitrogen (56).

A different assay, which has generated much interest, involves measurement of the xylem sap nitrogenous compounds that are involved in the transport of fixed nitrogen from root to shoot. Depending on the plant genus, the amide nitrogen of glutamine, formed from the ammonia produced during nitrogen fixation, is utilized to synthesize asparagine, or the ureides allantoin and allantoic acid, or citrulline. These compounds are then used to transport nitrogen to the host plant (39). In some crop plants, such as soybean or *Phaseolus*, the ureides originate mainly from fixed molecular nitrogen while assimilation of combined nitrogen results mainly in the transport of asparagine. Assays of the ureide content of the xylem sap of such species, relative to the content of other nitrogenous compounds, has thus been used to assay for nitrogen fixation (57–59). The potential for application of the technique to tree species is rather limited for two main reasons: (1) many trees that do not fix nitrogen nevertheless do produce and translocate ureides and (2) in many legume trees that do translocate ureides, their contribution to the nitrogen content of the xylem sap is small relative to that of the amino acids. Indeed, in some species the amount of ureides can be higher in NH_4NO_3-fertilized than in nitrogen-fixing trees. It is not applicable to plants, including tree legumes such as *Acacia*, that synthesize and translocate amides both when fixing nitrogen and when assimilating combined forms of nitrogen (54,60).

The ureido–amino acid citrulline also occurs in actinorhizal species such as *Alnus* or *Casuarina*. However, the xylem sap content of this compound is of limited use for the estimation of nitrogen fixation since it is also synthesized during the assimilation of both fixed and combined nitrogen (61). The association of particular problems with all of these techniques emphasizes the importance of employing at least two different methods to determine rates of nitrogen fixation in the field to permit results to be cross-checked.

5.6. Endophyte effectivity and competitivity

Infective microsymbionts for both legumes and actinorhizal plants are often widespread in soils within the normal geographic range of the host plants, although adverse environmental conditions, such as high temperature or drought, can eliminate compatible bacteria from the soil (62). Variation in the effectivity of nitrogen fixation in the microsymbionts found in a particular soil may be due to differences in competitivity between strains, in their ability to support good nodulation, and/or in their nitrogenase activity. For example, variations in the relative efficiency of nitrogen fixation in six species of tropical leguminous trees, grown in the same pasture soil in Mexico, suggested an energy loss due to hydrogen evolution of 15–30% in the different symbioses (63). Wide variation in the effectivity for nodulation and nitrogen fixation in alders has been shown for strains of *Frankia* in soils from a range of sites in Scotland (64). Superior strains of endophyte, isolated from host nodules, can be selected and used to inoculate seedlings to enhance nodulation and nitrogen fixation (65). The most effective strains for supporting plant growth combine good, but not necessarily the best, rates of symbiotic nitrogen fixation together with the ability to stimulate superior nodulation (Fig. 5.1).

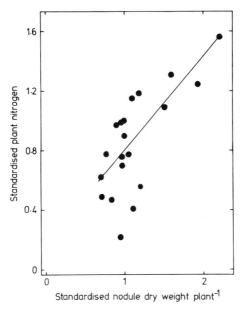

FIG. 5.1. Variation in the effectivity of *Frankia* strains, isolated from *Alnus* nodules, for nodulation and nitrogen fixation in *Alnus rubra*. Data for the weight of nodules induced per plant and for nitrogen fixed per unit weight of nodules are shown relative to the values obtained for plants inoculated with *Frankia* strain ArI4, for which both values are unity. (Data redrawn from Ref. 65).

A special feature of actinorhizal plant nodulation is the occurrence of two types of *Frankia* that differ in their ability to sporulate *in vivo*—so-called spore (+) and spore (−) strains (66). Spore (+) strains tend to be more infective than spore (−), but symbiotic nitrogen fixation in the latter is more energetically efficient so that nitrogen fixation with spore (−) types often is the most effective (67,68). The predominance in the field of certain endophytic types may be related to environmental conditions such as soil disturbance or moisture content, but clear answers to this question await the development of better techniques for the isolation and culture of the more recalcitrant spore (+) strains (69).

The relative competitivity of introduced and indigenous endophyte strains is a major factor governing the success of field inoculation practices. However, whereas many legume crops are sown direct into the field where inoculum strains have to compete with indigenous microorganisms for root nodulation of the emerging seedlings, tree seedlings are usually nursery-grown and competition can be reduced or eliminated by sterilization of seed beds. Because of the perennial nature of the nodules, the introduced strains will persist for some years in the developing nodule clusters, although indigenous strains may be responsible for some of the new infections that occur after transplantation.

5.7. Environmental effects

The close interdependence of the symbiotic partners ensures that any factor in the environment which affects plant growth will also affect root nodule development and function. It is, therefore, difficult to separate the effects of environmental change on the host plant from specific effects on the development and function of the symbiosis. In general, the microsymbiont is less tolerant of extremes of pH than the host plant and the limits for infection in particular are narrower than for plant growth with combined nitrogen. Soil pH interacts markedly with the availability and uptake of minerals. However, laboratory and field experiments have shown special requirements for mineral nutrients such as cobalt, which is incorporated into cobalamin-containing coenzymes. Adequate supplies of calcium are necessary for the infection process, while good supplies of iron, molybdenum, and phosphate are all essential for the synthesis and function of nitrogenase. Ectomycorrhizal and endomycorrhizal infections enhance nodulation and nitrogen fixation by assisting the uptake of minerals, especially of phosphate (70). Light, temperature, and water supply all interact in the field to determine host plant growth rate and the success of the symbiosis. Strains of endophyte that nodulate woody legumes or actinorhizal plants show adaption to a broad range of environmental stress, such as temperature, drought, salinity, and these may be selected for inclusion in inocula to be applied to nursery plants (62).

5.7.1. Diurnal and seasonal effects

Diurnal fluctuations in nitrogen fixation woody species in the field are often due mainly to changes in temperature but may be reinforced, particularly in seedlings, by fluctuations in light and the supply of photosynthates. In more mature plants, the carbohydrate reserves of the plant will help buffer the effect of changes in photosynthate supply on nitrogenase activity (62). Changes in temperature, photoperiodicity and light intensity also reinforce each other in their effect on the seasonality of nitrogen fixation. Utilizing the acetylene reduction assay as a comparative measure of nitrogenase activity, studies with *Alnus rubra* in Scotland, where periodic droughting effects seldom are experienced, showed that fixation commences in the spring as soil temperatures rise (71). Increases in temperature and day length induce budbreak, the development of new photosynthetic tissue, renewed nodule cell division and the differentiation of new endophytic nitrogen-fixing vesicles. The seasonality of nitrogen fixation closely follows the seasonal growth of the tree, with the maximum potential for nitrogenase activity being reached during the main period of shoot elongation and declining with the approach of autumn (Fig. 5.2).

5.7.2. Drought and salinity

Drought can play a major role in restricting nitrogen fixation in both temperate and tropical species. In many crop legumes, large inhibitions of nitro-

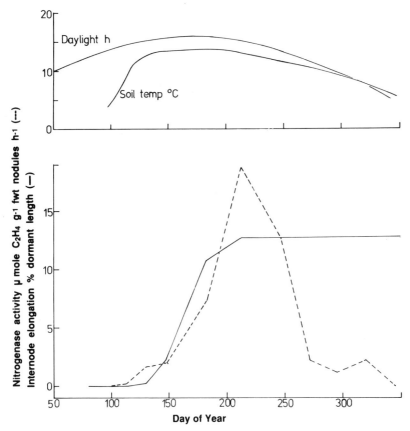

FIG. 5.2. Seasonal changes in tree growth (shoot elongation, expressed as a percentage of the dormant shoot length) and nitrogenase activity (assayed at a constant temperature of 20°C) for a stand of *Alnus glutinosa* in western Scotland. Annual changes in photoperiod and in soil temperature to a depth of 10 cm are also shown. (Data adapted from Refs. 64 and 71.)

genase activity have been observed when leaf moisture stress exceeds -0.5 MPa (62). Similar results are observed for some actinorhizal species. For example, in *Alnus incana* nitrogenase activity was halved when stress reduced plant water potentials to -0.6 to -0.8 MPa and was nearly zero when potentials were around -1 MPa (72). A greater decrease in water potential may be required to affect nitrogen fixation in plants showing xerophytic characteristics. For example, the critical plant water potential has been observed to be as low as -2 MPa in *Purshia tridentata*, a xerophytic shrub in North Western America subject to summer drought (73,74). Drought is an important factor governing the seasonality of nitrogen fixation; Fig. 5.3 shows how nitrogenase activity in both *Purshia* and the legume *Cytisus scoparius* diminished during summer drought, although fruit development may have contributed to the decline in the latter species (75).

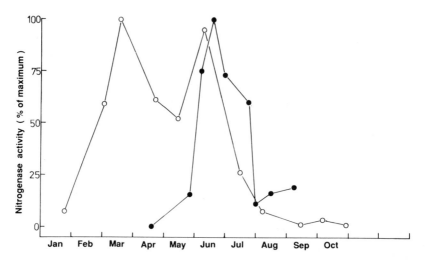

FIG. 5.3. Seasonal changes in nitrogenase activity in *Cytisus scoparius* (O) and *Purshia tridentata* (●) in relation to the onset of summer drought. In *Cytisus*, growing on a lowland site in western Oregon with high annual rainfall, the decline in activity in April was associated with the commencement of flowering and fruit formation. The decline during July occurred during a dry period and was associated with a decrease in predawn xylem pressure potential to less than −5 bars. *Purshia* was growing in central Oregon, where there is only slight summer rainfall and consequently is more drought tolerant than *Cytisus*. In *Purshia*, decreased nitrogenase activity in July was associated with a decrease in predawn xylem potential from −6 to −15 bars. (Data redrawn from Refs. 73 and 75.)

    Drought inhibition of nodule activity arises both from effects on the host plant, such as limitation of photosynthesis through stomatal closure (76), and through more direct effects on the nodules, such as increasing resistance to oxygen diffusion (72,77). Waterlogging can also reduce nitrogen fixation through effects on gaseous diffusion. For example, a soil moisture content of 12% reduced the rate of acetylene reduction in seedlings of the drought resistant *Allocasuarina verticillata*, grown in a sandy loam with a field capacity of 16% moisture (78). Some actinorhizal plants, such as *Myrica gale* or *Casuarina*, produce negatively geotropic roots in waterlogged conditions that assist nodule aeration (79). The ultimate method of avoidance of stress due to waterlogging must be the development of stem nodules on those few legumes, such as *Sesbania*, which grow on waterlogged soils during the rainy season (80).

    Tolerance of soil salinity is a feature increasingly sought for tree planting in areas subject to high rates of soil water evaporation. In herbaceous legumes such as beans, salt is known to inhibit infection and early nodulation. Often the host plant is more sensitive to saline conditions than is the microsymbiont (81,82). Legume trees vary considerably in their ability to tolerate saline conditions, and programs of genetic improvement have been established to select for this trait (83). Many species of *Casuarina* are tolerant of saline conditions and variation in the salinity tolerance of effective *Frankia* strains has made it possible to select both tree species and microsymbiont strains adapted to saline environments (84).

5.8. Nutrient cycling and soil improvement

Nutrient poor soils invariably show improvements in nitrogen content following the growth of well-nodulated trees. Even on more fertile soils, where the benefits for tree growth of nitrogen fixation may not be obvious, an improvement in soil nitrogen content can become evident during the life of the stand. Thus, while after 18 years the growth on a moderately fertile clay soil of *Picea sitchensis* intermixed with *Alnus rubra* was not improved compared with a monoculture, the upper soil nitrogen content nevertheless increased substantially. The phosphorus content of the upper soil layers also increased, possibly because of the deposition via the leaf litter of soil phosphorus scavenged by alder mycorrhizas or of phosphorus brought up from the subsoil by the deep-rooting alder (85).

Annual nitrogen uptake and annual return of nitrogen were found to be three and six times greater, respectively, in red alder than in Douglas fir ecosystems in the American Northwest (86). Whereas in Douglas fir about 19% of the annual nitrogen requirement was met by recycling from older foliage, in alder only 3% of the nitrogen was recycled, presumably because of the additional nitrogen available from fixation. Non-nitrogen-fixing deciduous stands in temperate regions on average recycle more than 20% of their nitrogen for growth. It has been suggested that the lower requirement for recycling of nitrogen in nitrogen-fixing alders permits the retention of physiologically active leaves well in the winter so that the photosynthetic period is significantly longer than is typically available to other deciduous species (86–88). In *Acacia holoserica*, growing in Australia on an area restored after surface mining, the nitrogen content of shed litter constituted 7.5% of the gross annual demand for nitrogen, again suggesting a low level of recycling of tree nitrogen. However, in this case only 19% of the demand was estimated to be supplied by nitrogen fixation and much of the remaining nitrogen was thought to come from mineralisation of soil organic material (89).

Both nodulation and nitrogen fixation are inhibited by the uptake of combined nitrogen, although the levels that affect these processes vary greatly between species and with the stage of development of the plant (62). These effects have led to suggestions that the buildup in soil nitrogen that occurs during the growth of nitrogen-fixing trees may reduce both nodulation and the rates of nitrogen fixation found late in the life of such stands. Direct tests of this suggestion are not available, however, and it should be noted that fairly high levels of combined nitrogen are required to inhibit nodulation in species such as alder. Other factors may come into play as stands age; for example, pathogenic microorganisms have been held responsible for nodule deterioration in aging stands of *Hippophae rhamnoides* (90).

Various aspects of nutrient cycling, nodulation, and nitrogen accretion in relation to stand age of *Alnus nepalensis*, growing in the Himalayas, have been studied by Sharma and Ambasht (91–93) (Fig. 5.4). Tree densities were highest in a 7-year plantation and were reduced progressively by thinning to 40% of the maximum in a 56-year stand. Average annual litterfall reached its maximum about 30 years, after canopy closure, and was accompanied by the largest increase in soil nitrogen (91). There were only small differences in the annual production per tree of active nodules in 7- and 56-year trees. However, the rate of fixation per tree was 60% lower in the older trees, so that the amount of nitrogen fixed per unit weight of active nodules apparently decreased substantially as the trees aged (92). It was suggested that decreased activity might result from changes in the pattern of photoassimilate partitioning to the root system of the older trees. As soil nitrogen levels increased with stand age, the contribution of fixed nitrogen to the total nitrogen uptake fell, by about 22% between the 7-year and the 56-year-old stand (93). Thus, uptake of recycled mineral nitrogen by the root systems replaced the high-energy processes of nitrogen fixation and nodule production.

5.9. Mixed plantations

The establishment of mixed plantations of nitrogen-fixing and non-nitrogen-fixing trees poses many silvicultural problems. The choice of tree species and their respective densities in the stand must permit fixed nitrogen to be recycled at a rate sufficient to support good growth of the nonfixing partner. At the

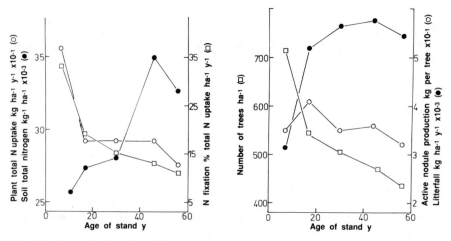

FIG. 5.4. Tree density, litterfall, nodulation, and nitrogen accretion in different aged stands of *Alnus nepalensis* growing in the eastern Himalayas. (Data redrawn from Refs. 91–93.)

same time, interspecies competitive effects that may suppress tree growth must be minimized. The effects of stand density and site fertility on species interactions and productivity have been studied for a variety of pure and mixed plantations and in intercropped agroforestry systems. For example, *Alnus rubra* or *A. glutinosa*, grown in mixed stands with *Populus* for high yield, short rotation forestry, have shown significant improvements in tree growth over the first 3 or 4 years compared with pure *Populus* stands (94,95). However, increased productivity in an *A. rubra–Populus* mix established on a nitrogen-poor alluvial soil was observed only with slow-growing *Populus* clones. Overtopping and shading of the alder by the higher yielding clones reduced nitrogen fixation and yield (96). In another trial of intermixed poplar and *A. glutinosa*, yields superior to pure poplar stands were achieved after only 3 years, presumably as recycled minerals became available to support poplar growth (97).

On fertile sites, addition of red alder to Douglas fir plantations reduced growth and productivity (98). However, on less fertile sites, where the maximum tree size and density relationships of the conifer were well below those of fertile plots, greater availability of space and resources for the added alder facilitated yield improvement. Competition for resources resulted in heavy mortality in densely planted, mixed plots. There is a need for further research to separate clearly density-related and species interaction effects. It is also clear from all the studies that there has been little research to compare the allocation of resources to the developing root systems of trees in pure and mixed plantations on sites of different fertility.

In conclusion, the rapid advances in present knowledge of the basic processes involved in nitrogen fixation have created opportunities for the enhancement of forest productivity through the use of relatively pollution-free, biological techniques. Further improvements in their utilization can be expected from better information on rates of nitrogen fixation in the field, which requires the development of rapid and precise assay procedures, by greater knowledge of resource allocation to nitrogen-fixing trees in plantations and through improvements and the further development of silvicultural practices. It is to be hoped that the coming years will see these gaps closed.

5.10. References

1. J.C. Gordon and C.T. Wheeler, eds., *Biological Nitrogen Fixation in Forest Ecosystems: Foundations and Applications*, Martinus Nijhoff/W. Junk, The Hague, 1983.

2. P.K.R. Nair, E.C.M. Fernandes, and P.N. Wambugu, "Multipurpose leguminous trees and shrubs for agroforestry," *Agrofor. Syst.*, **2**, 145–163 (1984).

3. S.M. de Faria, G.P. Lewis, J.I. Sprent, and J.M. Sutherland, "Occurrence of nodulation in the Leguminosae," *New Phytol.*, **111**, 607–619 (1989).

4. M.J. Trinick and P.A. Hadobas, "Biology of the *Parasponia–Bradyrhizobium* symbiosis," *Plant Soil*, **110**, 177–185 (1988).

5. P. Felker and P.R. Clark, "Position of mesquite (*Prosopis* spp.) nodulation and nitrogen fixation (acetylene reduction) in 3-m-long phraeophytically simulated soil columns," *Plant Soil*, **64**, 297–305 (1982).

6. P. Hogberg, "Nitrogen fixation and nutrient relations in Savannah woodland trees," *J. Appl. Ecol.*, **23**, 675–688 (1986).

7. O.N. Allen and E.K. Allen, *The Leguminosae: A Source Book of Characteristics*, Macmillan, London, 1981.

8. G. Lim and J.C. Burton, "Nodulation status of the Leguminosae," in W.J. Broughton, ed., *Nitrogen Fixation 2—Rhizobium*, Clarendon Press, Oxford, 1982, pp. 1–34.

9. D.C. Jordan, "Rhizobiaceae," in J.G. Holt and N.R. Kreig, eds., *Bergey's Manual of Systematic Bacteriology*, Vol I, 9th ed., Williams & Wilkins, Baltimore, 1984.

10. D. Callaham, P. delTredici, and J.G. Torrey, "Isolation and cultivation 'in vitro' of the actinomycete causing root nodulation in *Comptonia*," *Science*, **199**, 899–902 (1978).

11. H.A. Lechevalier and M.P. Lechevalier, "Systematics, isolation and culture of *Frankia*," in C.R. Schwintzer and J.D. Tjepkema, eds., *The Biology of Frankia and Actinorhizal Plants*, Academic Press, New York, 1990.

12. M.P. Lechevalier, "The taxonomy of the genus *Frankia*," *Plant Soil*, **78**, 1–6 (1984).

13. D. Baker, "Relationships among pure cultured strains of *Frankia* based on host specificity," *Physiol. Plant.*, **70**, 245–248 (1987).

14. J.W. Millbank, "Nitrogen fixation by lichens," in N.S. Subba Rao, ed., *Current Developments in Biological Nitrogen Fixation*, Oxford International Book House (IBH), New Delhi, 1984, pp. 197–218.

15. A.P. Hansen, J.S. Pate, A. Hansen, and D.T. Bell, "Nitrogen economy of post-fire stands of shrub legumes in Jarrah (*Eucalyptusmarginata*) forest of S.W. Australia," *J. Exp. Bot.*, **186**, 26–41 (1987).

16. P. Lindblad, R. Haselkorn, B. Bergman, and S. Nierzwicki-Bauer, "Comparison of DNA restriction fragment length polymorphisms of *Nostoc* strains in and from cycads," *Arch. Microbiol.*, **152**, 20–24 (1989).

17. J.I. Sprent and J.A. Raven, "Evolution of nitrogen-fixing symbioses," *Proc. Roy. Soc. Edin.*, **85B**, 215–237 (1985).

18. J.I. Sprent and M. de Faria, "Mechanisms of infection of plants by nitrogen fixing organisms." *Plant Soil,*

19. M. Lalonde and A. Quispel, "Ultrastructural and immunological demonstration of the nodulation of the European *Alnus glutinosa* (L.) Gaertn. host plant by the North American *Alnus crispa* var. Mollis Fern. root nodule endophyte," *Can. J. Microbiol.*, **23**, 1529–1547 (1977).

20. A.M. Berry, L. McIntyre, and M. McCully, "Fine structure of root hair infection leading to nodulation in the *Frankia–Alnus* symbiosis," *Can. J. Bot.*, **64**, 292–305 (1986).

21. I.M. Miller and D.D. Baker, "The initiation, development and structure of root nodules of *Elaeagnus angustifolia* L. (Elaeagnaceae)," *Protoplasma* **128**, 107–119 (1985).

22. I.M. Miller and D.D. Baker, "Nodulation of actinorhizal plants by *Frankia* strains capable of both root hair infection and intercellular penetration," *Protoplasma*, **131**, 82–91 (1986).

23. B.G. Rolfe and P.M. Gresshoff, "Genetic analysis of legume nodule initiation," *Ann. Rev. Plant Physiol.*, **39**, 297–319 (1988).

24. A.M. Berry and L.A. Sunell, "The infection process and nodule development," in C.R. Schwintzer and J.D. Tjepkema, eds., *The Biology of Frankia and Actinorhizal Plants*, Academic Press, New York, 1990.

25. F.B. Dazzo and G.L. Truchet, "Attachment of nitrogen fixing bacteria to roots of host plants," in N.S. Subba Rao, ed., *Current Developments in Biological Nitrogen Fixation*, Oxford IBH, New Delhi, 1984.

26. C.L. Diaz, L.S. Melchers, P.J.J. Hooykas, B.J.J. Lugtenberg, and J.W. Kijne, "Root lectin as a determinant of host-plant specificity in the Rhizobium-legume symbiosis," *Nature*, **338**, 579–581 (1989).

27. J.A. Downie and A.W.B. Johnstone, "Nodulation of legumes by Rhizobium," *Plant Cell Environ.*, **11**, 403–412 (1988).

28. A. Chaboud and M. Lalonde, "Lectin binding on surfaces of *Frankia* strains," *Can. J. Bot.*, **61**, 2889–2897 (1983).

29. K.F. Scott, "Conserved nodulation genes from the non-legume symbiont *Bradyrhizobium* sp. (*Parasponia*)," Nucleic Acids Res., **14**, 2905–2915 (1986).

30. G.L. Bender, M. Nayudu, K.K. LeStrange, and B.G. Rolfe, "The *nodDI* gene from *Rhizobium* strain NGR234 is a key determinant in the extension of host range to the nonlegume *Parasponia*," *Mol. Plant–Microbe Interact.*, **1(7)**, 259–266 (1988).

31. M.A. Djordevic, D.W. Gabriel, and B.G. Rolfe, "Rhizobium—the refined parasite of legumes," *Ann. Rev. Phytopathol.*, **25**, 145–168 (1987).

32. P. Simonet, P. Normand, and R. Bardin, "Mapping of a symbiosis involved region in *Frankia*," Abstracts, 9th. Int. Conf. Nitrogen Fixation, Koln, Germany, 1988.

33. J.M. Ligon and J.P. Nakas, "Isolation and characterisation of *Frankia* sp. strain FaC1 genes involved in nitrogen fixation," *Appl. Env. Microbiol.*, **53**, 2321–2327 (1987).

34. M. Becana and J.I. Sprent, "Nitrogen fixation and nitrate reduction in the root nodules of legumes," *Physiol. Plant.*, **70**, 757–765 (1987).

35. J. Streeter, "Inhibition of legume nodule formation and N_2 fixation by nitrate," *CRC Crit. Rev. Plant Sci.*, **7**, 1–23 (1988).

36. A. Quispel, "Bacteria–plant interactions in symbiotic nitrogen fixation," *Physiol. Plant.*, **74**, 783–790 (1988).

37. C.P. Vance, M.A. Egli, S.M. Griffith, and S.S. Miller, "Plant regulated aspects of nodulation and nitrogen fixation," *Plant Cell Environ.*, **11**, 413–427 (1988).

38. J.R. Postgate, *Nitrogen Fixation*, 2nd ed., Edward Arnold, London, 1986.

39. R.O.D. Dixon and C.T. Wheeler, *Nitrogen Fixation in Plants*, Blackie, Glasgow, 1986.

40. J.R. Gallon and A.E. Chapman, *An Introduction to Nitrogen Fixation*, Cassell, London, 1987.

41. R.D. Joerger and P.E. Bishop, "Bacterial alternative nitrogen fixation systems," *CRC Crit. Rev. Microbiol.*, **16**, 1–14 (1988).

42. F.R. Minchin, J.F. Witty, J.E. Sheehy, and M. Muller, "A major error in the acetylene reduction assay: Increases in nodular nitrogenase activity under assay conditions," *J. Exp. Bot.*, **34**, 641–649 (1983).

43. K.R. Schubert and H.J. Evans, "Hydrogen evolution: A major factor affecting the efficiency of nitrogen fixation in nodulated symbionts," *Proc. Natl. Acad. Sci., U.S.A.*, **73**, 1207–1211 (1976).

44. L.J. Winship, K.J. Martin, and A. Sellstedt, "The acetylene reduction assay inactivates root nodule uptake hydrogenase in some actinorhizal plants," *Physiol. Plant.*, **70**, 361–366 (1987).

45. R. Parsons, W.B. Silvester, S. Harris, W.T.M. Gruijyer, and S. Bullivant, "*Frankia* vesicles provide inducible and absolute oxygen protection for nitrogenase," *Plant Physiol.*, **83**, 728–731 (1987).

46. B.D. Steele and M.D. Stowers, "Superoxide dismutase and catalase in *Frankia*," *Can. J. Microbiol.*, **32**, 409–413 (1986).

47. M. Becana and C. Rodriguez-Barrueco, "Protective mechanisms of nitrogenase against oxygen excess and partially-reduced oxygen intermediates," *Physiol. Plant.*, **75**, 429–438 (1989).

48. C.A. Appleby, D. Bogusz, E.S. Dennis, and W.J. Peacock, "A role for haemoglobin in all plant roots?," *Plant Cell Environ.*, **11**, 359–367 (1988).

49. J. Hattori and D.A. Johnson, "The detection of leghemoglobin-like sequences in legumes and non-legumes," *Plant Mol. Biol.*, **4**, 285–292 (1985).

50. W.B. Silvester, "Analysis of nitrogen fixation," in J.C. Gordon and C.T. Wheeler, eds., *Biological Nitrogen fixation in Forest Ecosystems: Foundations and Applications*, Martinus Nijhoff/W. Junk, The Hague, 1983, pp. 173–212.

51. P. Hogberg and M. Kvarnstrom, "Nitrogen fixation by the woody legume *Leucaena leucocephala* in Tanzania," *Plant Soil*, **66**, 21–28 (1982).

52. P. Linblad and R. Russo, "Acetylene reduction by *Erythrina poepigiana* in a Costa Rican coffee plantation," *Agrofor. Syst.*, **4**, 33–37 (1986).

53. S.F. Ledgard, J.R. Simpson, J.R. Freney, F.J. Bergersen, and J.R. Simpson, "Assessment of the relative uptake of added and indigenous soil nitrogen by nodulated legumes and reference plants in the nitrogen-15 dilution measurement of notrogen fixation: Glasshouse application of the method," *Soil Biol. Biochem.*, **17**, 323–328 (1985).

54. A.P. Hansen and J.S. Pate, "Evaluation of the ^{15}N natural abundance method and xylem sap analysis for assessing N_2 fixation of understorey legumes in Jarrah (*Eucalyptusmarginata* Donn ex Sm.) forest in S.W. Australia," *J. Exp. Bot.*, **38**, 1446–1458 (1987).

55. D. Binkley, P. Sollins, and W.A. McGill, "Natural abundance of nitrogen-15 as a tool for tracing alder-fixed nitrogen," *Soil Sci. Soc. Am. J.*, **49**, 444–447 (1985).

56. G. Shearer, D.H. Kohl, R.A. Virginia, B.A. Bryan, J.L. Skeeters, E.T. Nilsen, M.R. Sharifi, and P.W. Rundel, "Estimates of nitrogen fixation from variation in the natural abundance of N-15 in a Sonoran desert ecosystem," *Oecologia (Berl.)*, **56**, 365–373 (1983).

57. D.F. Herridge, "Relative abundance of ureides and nitrate in plant tissues of soybean as a quantitative assay of nitrogen fixation," *Plant Physiol.*, **70**, 1–6 (1982)

58. P.R. McClure, D.W. Israel, and R.J. Volk, "Evaluation of the relative ureide content of xylem sap as an indicator of N_2 fixation in soybeans," *Plant Physiol.*, **66**, 720–725 (1980).

59. C. Argillier, J.-J. Drevon, M. Zengbe, and L. Salsac, "Relation between nitrogenase activity and stem or xylem sap ureide content of soybean plants (*Glycine max* L. Merr)," *Plant Sci.*, **61**, 37–42 (1989)

60. C. van Kessel, J.P. Roskoski, and K. Keane, "Ureide production by N_2-fixing and non-N_2-fixing leguminous trees," *Soil Biol. Biochem.*, **20**, 891–897 (1988).

61. G.S. Tonin, C.T. Wheeler, and A. Crozier, "Effect of N nutrition on amino acid composition of xylem sap and stem wood in *Alnus glutinosa*," *Physiol. Plant.*, **79**, 506–511 (1990).

62. R.O.D. Dixon and C.T. Wheeler, "Biochemical, physiological and environmental aspects of symbioptic nitrogen fixation," in J.C. Gordon and C.T. Wheeler, eds., *Biological Nitrogen Fixation in Forest Ecosystems: Foundations and Applications*, Martinus Nijhoff/W. Junk, The Hague, 1983, pp. 108–172.

63. C. van Kessel, J.P. Roskski, T. Wood, and J. Montano, "Nitrogen fixation and hydrogen evolution by six species of leguminous trees," *Plant Physiol.*, **72**, 909–910 (1983).

64. C.T. Wheeler, M.E. McLaughlin, and P. Steele, "A comparison of symbiotic nitrogen fixation in Scotland in *Alnus glutinosa* and *Alnus rubra*," *Plant Soil*, **61**, 169–188 (1981).

65. J.E. Hooker and C.T. Wheeler, "The effectivity of *Frankia* for nodulation and nitrogen fixation in *Alnus rubra* and *Alnus glutinosa*," *Physiol. Plant.*, **70**, 333–341 (1987).

66. J.G. Torrey, "Endophyte sporulation in root nodules of actinorhizal plants," *Physiol. Plant.*, **70**, 279–288 (1987).

67. A. Houwers and A.D.L. Akkermans, "Influence of inoculation on yield of *Alnus glutinosa* in the Netherlands," Plant Soil, **61**, 189–202 (1981).

68. K.A. vandenBosch and J.G. Torrey, "Consequences of sporangial formation for nodule function in root nodules of *Comptonia peregrina* and *Myrica gale*," *Am. J. Bot.*, **72**, 99–108 (1984).

69. J.D. Tjepkema, D. Benson, and C. Schwintzer, "Physiology of actinorhizal plants," *Ann. Rev. Plant Physiol.*, **37**, 209–232 (1986).

70. M.J. Daft, D.M. Clelland, and I.C. Gardner, "Symbiosis with endomycorrhizas and nitrogen fixing organisms," *Proc. Roy. Soc. Edin.*, **85B**, 283–298 (1985).

71. C.T. Wheeler, S.H. Watts, and J.R. Hillman, "Changes in carbohydrates and nitrogenous compounds in the root nodules of *Alnus glutinosa* in relation to dormancy," *New Phytol.*, **95**, 209–218 (1983).

72. K.-R. Sundstrom and K. Huss-Danell, "Effects of water stress on nitrogenase activity in *Alnus incana*," *Physiol. Plant.*, **70**, 342–348 (1987).

73. D.A. Dalton and D.B. Zobel, "Ecological aspects of nitrogen fixation by *Purshia tridentata*," *Plant Soil*, **48**, 57–80 (1977).

74. T.L. Righetti, C.H. Chard, and R.A. Backhaus, "Soil and environmental factors related to nodulation in *Cowania* and *Purshia*," *Plant Soil*, **91**, 147–160 (1986).

75. C.T. Wheeler, O. Helgerson, D.A. Perry, and J.C. Gordon, "Nitrogen fixation and biomass accumulation in plant communities dominated by *Cytisus scoparius* in Oregon and Scotland," *J. Appl. Ecol.*, **24**, 231–237 (1987).

76. C. Huang, J.S. Boyer, and L.N. Vanderhoef, "Limitation of acetylene reduction (nitrogen fixation) by photosynthesis in soybeans having low water potentials," *Plant Physiol.*, **56**, 228–232 (1975).

77. P.R. Weisz, R.F. Denison, and T.R. Sinclair, "Response to drought stress of nitrogen fixation (acetylene reduction) rates by field-grown soybeans," *Plant Physiol.*, **78**, 525–530 (1985).

78. P. Hopmans, L.A. Douglas, P.M. Chalk, and S.G. Delbridge, "Effects of soil moisture content, mineral nitrogen and salinity on nitrogen fixation (acetylene reduction) by *Allocasuarina verticillata* (Lam.) L. Johnson seedlings," *Aust. For. Res.*, **13**, 189–196 (1983).

79. J.D. Tjepkema, "Oxygen concentration within the nitrogen fixing root nodules of *Myrica gale* L.," *Am. J. Bot.*, **70**, 59–63 (1983).

80. B. Dreyfus and Y. Dommergues, "Nitrogen fixing nodules induced by *Rhizobium* on the stem of the tropical legume *Sesbania rostrata*," *FEMS Microbiol. Lett.*, **10**, 313–317 (1981).

81. P.W. Singleton and B.B. Bohlool, "Effect of salinity on nodule formation by soybean," *Plant Physiol.*, **74**, 72–76 (1984).

82. H.H. Zahran and J.I. Sprent, "Effects of sodium chloride and polyethylene glycol on root hair infection and nodulation of *Vicia faba* L. plants by *Rhizobium leguminosarum*," *Planta*, **167**, 303–309 (1986).

83. O.S. Tomar and R.K. Gupta, "Performance of some forest tree species in saline soils under shallow and saline water table conditions," *Plant Soil*, **87**, 329–335 (1985).

84. J.O. Dawson and A.H. Gibson. "Sensitivity of selected *Frankia* isolates from *Casuarina Allocasuarina* and North American host plants to sodium chloride," *Physiol. Plant.* **70**, 272–278 (1987).

85. D.C. Malcolm, J.E. Hooker, and C.T. Wheeler, "*Frankia* symbiosis as a source of nitrogen in forestry: A case of study of symbiotic nitrogen fixation in a mixed *Alnus–Picea* plantation in Scotland," *Proc. Roy. Soc. Edin.*, **85B**, 263–282 (1985).

86. D.W. Cole and M. Rapp, "Elemental cycling in forest ecosystems," in D.E. Reichle, ed., *Dynamic Properties of Forest Ecosystems*, Cambridge University Press, **23**, 1981, pp. 341–409.

87. J.O. Dawson and D.T. Funk, "Seasonal changes in foliar nitrogen concentration of *Alnus glutinosa*," *For. Sci.*, **27**, 239–243 (1981).

88. B. Cote and J.O. Dawson, "Autumnal changes in total nitrogen, salt-extractable protein and amino acids in leaves and adjacent bark of black alder, eastern cottonwood and white basswood," *Physiol. Plant.*, **67**, 102–108 (1986).

89. P.J. Langkamp, G.K. Farnell, and M.J. Dalling, "Nutrient cycling in a stand of *Acacia holosericea* A. Cunn. ex Don. I. Measurements of precipitation, interception, seasonal acetylene reduction, plant growth and nitrogen requirement," *Aust. J. Bot.*, **30**, 87–106 (1982).

90. P.A.I. Oremus, "Occurrence and infective potential of the endophyte of *Hippophae rhamnoides* L. ssp. Rhamnoides in coastal sand-dune areas," *Plant Soil*, **56**, 123–139 (1980).

91. E. Sharma and R.S. Ambasht, "Litterfall, decomposition and nutrient release in an age sequence of *Alnus nepalensis* plantation stands in the Eastern Himalayas," *J. Ecol.*, **75**, 997-1010 (1987).

92. E. Sharma and R.S. Ambasht, "Root nodule age–class transition, production and decomposition in an age sequence of *Alnus nepalensis* plantation stands in the Eastern Himalayas," *J. Appl. Ecol.*, **23**, 689–701 (1986).

93. E. Sharma and R.S. Ambasht, "Nitrogen accretion and its energetics in the Himalayan alder," *Funct. Ecol.*, **2**, 229–235 (1988).

94. D.S. Debell and M.A. Radwan, "Growth and nitrogen relations of coppiced black cottonwood and red alder in pure and mixed plantings," *Bot. Gaz.*, **140** (suppl), 97–101 (1979).

95. E.A. Hansen and J.O. Dawson, "Effect of *Alnus glutinosa* on hybrid poplar height growth in a short-rotation intensively cultured plantation," *For. Sci.*, **28**, 49–59 (1981).

96. P.C. Heilman and R.F. Stettler, "Phytomass production in young mixed plantations of *Alnusrubra* Bong. and cottonwood in Western Washington," *Can. J. Microbiol.*, **29**, 1007–1013 (1983).

97. E. Teissier du Cros, G. Jung, and M. Bariteau, "Alder–*Frankia* interaction and alder–poplar association for biomass production," *Plant Soil*, **78**, 235–243 (1984).

98. D. Binkley, "Importance of size-related relationship in mixed stands of Douglas-fir and red alder," *For. Ecol. Management*, **9**, 81–85 (1984).

6 Water Relations

THOMAS M. HINCKLEY

College of Forest Resources, University of Washington, Seattle, Washington, USA

HANNO RICHTER

Botany Institute, University of Agriculture, Vienna, Austria

and

PAUL J. SCHULTE

Department of Biological Sciences, University of Nevada, Las Vegas, Nevada

Contents

6.1. Introduction

Environmental factors, such as water and temperature, affect trees both directly and indirectly, occasionally singly, but most often in combination with other factors. Therefore, water relations will be presented with the understanding that water supply rarely affects trees independently of other environmental factors and that the interaction between water and temperature or water and nutrients may more often or under more critical circumstances affect tree growth and survival. With that cautionary note, many authors regard water as the single most important environmental factor affecting the occurrence and growth of trees. Gradients in precipitation, contrasts in exposure, and changes in soil texture or soil depth, all of which have an appreciable impact on the water balance of a plant, will have a dramatic, visible effect on vegetation cover, stature, and type. Kramer (1) and Boyer (2) argue that water supply affects productivity of forest plantations and agronomic crops more than all other environmental factors combined. In addition to its direct effects, water plays an important role in decomposition, weathering, and nutrient fluxes in the soil; consequently, water and nutrient relations are tightly bound. Fluxes of water within the plant have impacts on the distribution of nutrients and plant growth regulators, factors that affect plant function.

There is a relatively long history of ecological and physiological interest in the water relations of plants. Experimental studies on water uptake, transport, and loss in plants by the Reverend Stephen Hales (3), the recognition by Hellriegel in 1883 (4) of the trade-off between water and carbon dioxide exchange and his introduction of the concept of Transpirationskoeffizient (transpiration ratio: liters of water consumed per kilogram of dry matter produced), the experiments of de Vries (5) to isolate the function of the casparian strip in the roots, and Pfeffer's (6) use of an artificial semipermeable membrane from which he was able to calculate very precisely the osmotic potential of solutions are all examples of the historical foundation on which current ideas in plant water relations are grounded. Indeed, in manuscripts by Darwin (7), Dixon (8), and Huber (9), one discovers concepts, experiments, and results dealing with many of the topics that are currently popular in plant or tree water relations.

Three breakthroughs in instrumentation appear critical in the development of the present interest in the water relations of woody plants and forest trees: (1) the infrared gas analyzer, (2) the Scholander-Hammel pressure chamber, and (3) the portable diffusion porometer. As an excellent example of the ecological application of such new technologies, Waring and coworkers (10) used soil water status, as estimated by predawn water potential of *Pseudotsuga menziesii* saplings, to describe the relative abundance of three major tree species of southwestern Oregon (Fig. 6.1). Others have noted relationships between water status and species distribution (11,12), leaf area index (13), and productivity (14,15). However, a number of authors have shown that nutrient supply alone or nutrient supply interacting with water supply can affect the distribution and productivity of forest species and communities (16,17). Other environmental factors, such as high and low temperatures, may also be more critical to species distribution than water stress.

Figure 6.2 illustrates the relationship between water potential and physiological processes while highlighting some areas of current discussion or debate. In this figure, decreases in leaf water potential of the *Populus* hybrid result in decreases in both net photosynthesis and leaf conductance. The decrease in leaf conductance appears to be associated with the point of turgor loss in the leaf. In contrast, decreases in water potential of *Populus trichocarpa* affected only net photosynthesis while leaf conductance remained unchanged even after leaf wilting. Only by drought stressing the root system of *P. trichocarpa* or by direct application of abscisic acid to the foliage did stomata respond to atmospheric or leaf water deficits (19). These results highlight a number of current issues, including (a) the role of leaf turgor and water potential versus relative water content in affecting processes within a leaf

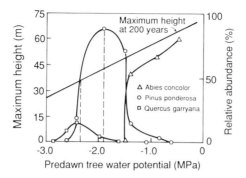

FIG. 6.1. Predawn water potentials of 2-m-tall *Pseudotsuga menziesii* defining a water stress gradient developed during summer droughts in a mountainous region of southwestern Oregon. The water potential gradient so defined related closely to (1) the maximum height reached by Douglas fir; (2) the relative frequency of ponderosa pine and other tree species; and (3) the rate of height growth over a range of environments, varying from class I (height of 30 m at 100 years) to class IV (height of 20 m at 100 years). (Reproduced with permission from Ref. 10.)

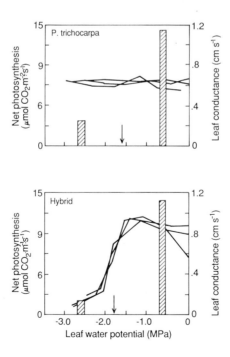

FIG. 6.2. Leaf conductance and net photosynthesis as affected by leaf water potential for *Populus trichocarpa* and a hybrid between *P. trichocarpa* and *P. deltoides*. Arrows indicate the point of turgor loss in the leaf. (Modified from Refs. 18 and 19.)

(20–24), (b) the role of the leaf versus the root in sensing water deficits and thus controlling processes in the leaf (25–27), and (c) whether or not stomatal behavior during periods of desiccation results in an optimization of water use efficiency (28,29). These issues will be developed in this chapter.

Plant water relations have been among the most widely studied aspects of plant physiology, environmental physiology, and physiological ecology. As a result, a large number of excellent books and reviews exist on the subject of water relations, and readers are referred to these (30–39). We will not review the entire field of plant or woody plant water relations. Many of these texts or review articles do so. Instead, we will discuss some of the fascinating and, perhaps, controversial areas of plant water relations and, in particular, those areas originating from research on woody plants. Although this chapter is part of a book on tree physiology, we will frequently rely on non-woody plant literature.

6.2. Water relations terminology and units

Readers interested in acquiring a theoretical background on water relations should read Nobel (35). For our purposes, water potential may be presented from two perspectives: (1) how water in the various compartments of a plant responds to water potential and its changes presented by the soil–plant–atmosphere continuum and (2) what causes water potential at any point in this continuum to change. The second part will be presented in Section 6.3. Water potential in a cell or tissue can be expressed as

$$\Psi = \Psi_o + \Psi_p \qquad (6.1)$$

where Ψ_o is the partial potential describing the osmotic effects of dissolved solutes and Ψ_p describes the pressure effects. In this equation, Ψ_o is always negative; solutes will always reduce total water potential, while Ψ_p can assume negative values when the solution is in a state of tension; for example, in xylem conduits; or positive values, such as those found in vacuoles of living cells. Of these two terms, osmotic potential cannot change as rapidly as pressure potential, which will therefore be the main factor responsible for fine-tuning potentials in response to transient, fluctuating demands from the continuum.

Equation 6.1 forms the basis by which the behavior of water potential and its components in a shoot of *Abies amabilis* (Fig. 6.3) can be readily described by the use of a Höfler diagram (40). Where the osmotic potential line intersects the Y axis depends on the concentration of solutes or the osmotic potential at full saturation, while how steeply the osmotic potential line bends upward depends upon the interaction between the concentration of solutes and the volume of the symplast. The shape of the pressure or turgor potential line is largely a function of the elasticity of the cell wall and the counterpressure of the surrounding tissue. Such diagrams or relationships are readily constructed for whole organs with a technique for creating pressure–volume curves. The theory and application of this technique are described elsewhere (42–45).

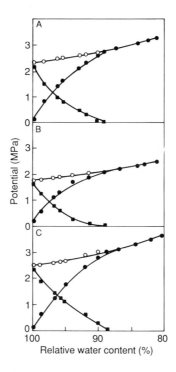

FIG. 6.3. Höfler diagrams for 1-year-old foliage samples from March 14, 1981 (A), August 8, 1981 (B), and March 19, 1982 (C). Samples were collected from *Abies amabilis* trees used for diurnal water relation measurements. Values of Ψ (●) and osmotic potential (O) are negative. Values of turgor potential (■) are positive. The minimum Ψ measured on each date was -1.34 (A), -1.42 (B), and -1.39 MPa (C). (Reproduced with permission from Ref. 41.)

6.3. The pathway of water movement in trees

Water movement from the soil, through the plant and to the atmosphere, must be treated as a series of interrelated, interdependent processes. For example, the rate of water absorption from the soil is affected by both the rate of water loss from the leaves to the atmosphere and the rate at which water can move from the soil to the root surface. Water movement is then related to differences in water potential, and resistance to water flow and water potential at a given location is related to how fast water is moving toward and away from it.

This movement of water may be described with water transport equations analogous to the Ohm's law in electrical engineering, where

$$\text{Flux} = \frac{\text{driving force}}{\text{resistance}} \text{ or water flux} = \frac{\Delta\Psi}{R} \tag{6.2}$$

where $\Delta\Psi$ is the difference in water potential and R is the resistance between the two points where water potential is being considered. In 1948, based on

Eq. 6.2 and earlier work of Huber (9), van den Honert (46) proposed equations for describing water flow from the soil to the atmosphere in a linear fashion; that is, flow is from points *a* to *b* to *c*. A major weakness in modeling flow with such an equation is that flow is described in terms of a catena or unbranched chain, whereas a tree is a branched system that also may store water.

Richter (47) reexamined the original work of Huber (9) and concluded that the unbranched catena model and its associated equations (46,48) represented both a misinterpretation of Huber's conclusions and a gross oversimplification of water flow through a plant, particularly a plant as complex as a tree. Richter's equation is

$$\Psi = \Psi_s - \rho\, gh - \sum_{i=s}^{p} J_i r_i \tag{6.3}$$

where total water potential at a given point in the plant is the sum of soil water potential, gravitational potential, and frictional potential. The frictional potential is equal to the sum, along the branched pathway from the bulk soil *s*, to a point *p* in the plant, of the products of partial fluxes J_i and partial resistances r_i. An unbranched model would treat the friction term as the product of two single variables (i.e., $QR_{soil-leaf}$, where Q is flow or transpiration and R is resistance).

Figure 6.4 shows how, in a steady-state situation, the three components of Richter's equation interact to produce a set of values for total water potential in a tree. If there is no water flow through the tree ($J_i = 0$), then the line labeled "hydrostatic gradient" will represent the water potential at any point *x* in this tree. However, if there is flow (friction is now an important factor in affecting Ψ), water potentials more negative than the hydrostatic gradient line will be observed. Because friction is appreciable at branch junctions, water potentials decrease more rapidly along the branch than the stem (discussed later).

As pointed out by van den Honert (46) and Jarvis (50), water loss from the plant is controlled at the liquid–air interface in the leaves and is, therefore, affected by changes in the resistance to water-vapor loss only through stomata and cuticle and not the various resistances encountered by water passing from the soil to the leaf. Changes in the resistances between the soil and leaf will affect Ψ. It should be noted that the relative importance of various resistances in the liquid pathway or the importance of the resistance at the liquid–air interface has been argued both by those examining flow through the components of a single individual (41,51–54) and by those scaling from the leaf to the landscape (55). However, resistances in the liquid pathway from the soil to the leaf and in the vapor pathway from the leaf to the atmosphere are important in determining leaf water potential. These resistances will be discussed in the section on water-deficit formation.

Historically, two models, based on the catenary theory of water flow, have been used to describe flow through the soil–plant–atmospheric continuum: unbranched (48) and branched (47,51). Current models have been expanded

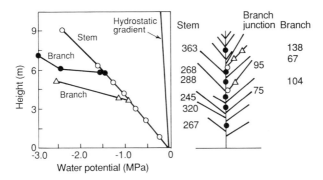

FIG. 6.4. Water potential gradients were calculated assuming equal transpiration rates and assuming soil water potential to be -0.05 MPa. Leaf-specific conductivities along the main stem ($\bullet$), at the branch junction (O), and in the branch ($\triangle$) are shown to the right for *Populus grandidentata*. (Modified from Ref. 49.)

to incorporate the presence of stored water or capacitance (Fig. 6.5). Such considerations become important whenever we deal with a more realistic non-steady-state situation. The presence of hysteresis in curves of water potential and transpiration has been cited as an example of the effect of stored water on the water flow equation (57,58). The importance of stored water in plant water relations is most obvious for succulent plants (59), but has also been considered for trees. Diurnal changes in the diameter of tree stems (60) and time lags between changes in transpiration from leaves and changes in stem water flow or water potential (61–64) provide evidence for water movement from storage in trees. Most of the diurnal flow of water from storage is provided by the phloem and the bark (56), while on a seasonal basis, the sapwood is the most important source (65). Since most of this stored water appears to come from the sapwood and from tracheids in the sapwood, questions of if and how tracheids may be refilled once they have been emptied seem important.

6.4. The formation of water deficits

In order to discuss the effect of water status on physiological processes in trees, one must first understand how water deficits are formed and how they may reach a level sufficient to induce a negative response in the tree. The terms "water deficit" and "water stress" are related; a water deficit occurs following any decrease in plant water content below full saturation. Water stress may be defined as a decrease in water content or water potential, which decreases plant form or function below some optimum. Water deficits can develop from (a) a decrease in soil water content and potential, which sets the highest potential level the tree can reach; and (b) an increase in atmospheric demand and/or resistance to water flow from source to sink, i.e., from soil to atmosphere. The rate of change in plant water potential and content

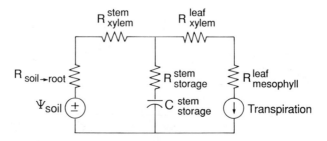

FIG. 6.5. Modified diagram of the resistance–capacitance model for coniferous trees proposed by Milne (56) (R = resistance, Ψ = water potential, and C = capacitance). By incorporating capacitance, the model is capable of considering water flow under non-steady-state conditions.

induced by these factors will depend on plant properties such as tissue capacitance, xylem resistance, and stomatal conductance. As an example of the formation of a water deficit, an increase in transpiration leads to increased water movement through all the flow resistances and, therefore, to reduced water potentials and a larger water potential gradient between the leaf tissue and the soil. A reduced water potential may lead to different water contents in various organs or tissues, because the relationship between water potential and water content depends strongly on the elasticity of the tissue (Fig. 6.3).

Water deficits can also develop from a decline in soil moisture content (long-term) and from the localized depletion of water around the absorbing root (short-term). In the first case, depth of the soil and texture (i.e., soil water storage capacity), the quantity of input through precipitation, groundwater or overland flow, the vertical and horizontal extent of roots, and root competition all influence the frequency, severity, and duration of water deficits. For example, Manning and Barbour (66) observed that minimum values of predawn water potentials in *Haplopappus cooperi* (a shallow-rooted species) ranged from -3.78 to -6.27 MPa depending on the extent and nature of intra- and interspecific root competition. In the deep-rooted *Chrysothamnus teretifolius* growing on the same site, leaf water potential ranged from -1.58 to -1.97 MPa and there was no apparent pattern related to root competition. A deep-root system plays an important role in moderating soil water deficits (67).

Recent work of Caldwell and Richards (68) and Corak et al. (69) suggests that roots of both desert xerophytes and deep-rooted agricultural species such as *Medicago sativa* may absorb water from deep soil layers and transport it back into the soil near the surface at night, thus altering the pattern of water distribution within the soil profile. This water is then available for uptake by shallow roots and transport to the shoot during the subsequent day. Water near the surface may serve a number of functions such as increasing surface fine-root longevity, promoting surface mineralization and decomposition, decreasing the resistance to water flow from the soil to the root (a greater proportion of the profile is now moist), and decreasing the resistance to water absorption by fine roots since more fine roots are now involved in water uptake. Similarly, mycorrhizal fungi may enhance the movement of water from the soil to the root surface and perhaps even into the root (70). Further work in quantifying the hydraulic properties of both transport systems would be interesting, for our purposes, with special emphasis on trees.

The ability of roots to absorb water affects the development of plant water deficits. Water encounters a resistance in passing from the root surface to the root xylem that is often expressed per unit root surface area [root resistivity (MPa sm^{-1}) or the reciprocal, root conductivity (Lp; m MPa^{-1} s^{-1})]. Root Lp varies with soil temperature (41,71,72), root growth (53,73–75), and soil oxygen (76,77). For example, Teskey et al. (41) noted that as soil temperature decreased from 15 to 2°C, Lp in *Abies amabilis* decreased slowly and in proportion to changes in the viscosity of water. As soil or root temperature decreased below 2°C, Lp decreased very rapidly.

Other topics of current interest in water uptake by roots have not been considered for trees with the detail found in studies of agriculturally-important plants. For example, the active uptake of nutrients by roots provides a driving force for water uptake that varies in importance depending on water flow rate (78,79). Also, the distribution of water uptake along individual roots has been described for wheat and corn (80) and for barley (81). These studies indicate that the relative contribution of apoplastic (within cell walls) versus symplastic (through cytoplasm of cells) pathways for water crossing the root varies with distance from the root tip and hence with root age.

The vascular tissue of plants was regarded historically as a series of low-resistance pipes connecting the roots to the foliage (41). Its role in affecting water potential, plant function (e.g., leaf growth), or plant form was largely dismissed. However, as Hellkvist et al. (64) noted, significant gradients in water potential exist in the stems and branches of *Picea sitchensis*, indicating that hydraulic resistance in the xylem has a role in determining leaf water potential. Recent work suggests a much greater influence of the xylem anatomy and hydraulic architecture of the crown on the water relations of trees (49,51,54,83–90). As shown in Fig. 6.4, hydraulic conductivity (1/resistivity) is relatively high in the main stem, intermediate in branches, and lowest at junctions between the stem and branches or between primary and secondary branches (constriction zones). These conductivities then affect the gradients of water potential that exist within a plant. For the *Populus grandidentata* example shown, lower water potentials exist in leaves on branches than in leaves on the main stem under conditions of equal transpiration. Based on these results and similar results with other species, Zimmermann (49) hypothesized that trees are segmented such that branches and individual leaves are shed preferentially to the main axis or apex of the tree. Thus as water stress develops during periods of high transpiration, vascular constrictions at branches or leaf petiole junctions lead to lethal water stress in these lateral plant structures before the main axis of the tree is endangered. As these leaves or branches are lost, less demand is placed on the root system to supply water to the shoot, and water stress in the more vital regions of the tree is minimized. Zimmermann's concept of segmentation is further supported by recent work on the loss of xylem function by cavitation of water columns in the xylem and embolism of the conducting pathway.

The role of these vascular constrictions between branches and the stem deserves more conceptual as well as experimental work. While transpiration is occurring, Ψ values in the xylem between leaves on a branch and the constriction zone will be more negative than Ψ in the stem, possibly inducing stomatal closure in that branch and a reduction in transpiration, thus protecting the remainder of the tree from potentially lethal water potentials. However, under conditions of soil drought and tightly closed stomata, the role of the constriction zone may be reduced: water potential gradients within the tree tend to decrease as transpiration decreases. We might hypothesize that vascular constrictions serve two roles: (a) reducing transpiration during the time of highest evaporative demand and potentially poorest water use efficiency by midday stomatal closure and (b) leading to an accumulation of abscisic acid (ABA) during stress periods and an induction of abscission in repeatedly stressed (and thus less efficient) leaves or branches.

Although it has long been acknowledged that embolism of xylem conduits has an important effect on the ability of the xylem to conduct water (8), the degree to which cavitation occurs within a given species and the relative vulnerabilities of various species with different tissue types (tracheid or vessel) and different element diameters is less clear. The cavitation of tracheids or vessels appears to result from the entry of air into the xylem element through pores in pit membranes (86). Although it has often been assumed that large-diameter elements are more vulnerable to cavitation than narrower elements (91), recent estimates of relative vulnerability suggest that, compared across species, vessels are not necessarily more likely to cavitate than tracheids (92). However within a species, wider elements appear more likely to cavitate (Fig. 6.6). Comparisons between different species may need to consider anatomical characteristics such as the size of pores in pit membranes (87) as well as xylem element diameter in evaluating relative vulnerabilities to cavitation. As observed by Salleo and LoGullo (84), a given species may contain a range of vessel diameters, with wide vessels having high conductance but also a high risk of cavitation, and narrow vessels that are safer but have lower hydraulic conductance. These authors also emphasize the importance of knowing the distribution of element diameters at various points in the conducting system of a tree—for example, in nodes and internodes and in distal and proximal parts of the crown. Finally, they summarize the current status of work in cavitation by noting the lack of a solid theoretical basis to explain cavitation, the lack of information on how plants tolerate or recover from cavitation and the presence of weaknesses in all of the current techniques by which cavitation is studied (acoustical, hydraulic, anatomic, and densiometric). Cavitation is further discussed in the next chapter (Chapter 7, this book).

Two important hypothetical situations are indicated by the work of the authors cited above: (a) all species may operate near the brink of what Tyree terms "catastrophic xylem dysfunction" and (b) because of the constriction

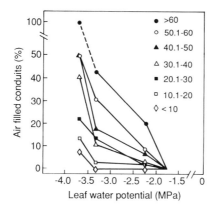

FIG. 6.6. Relationship between leaf water potential and percentage of air-filled conduits in a range of conduit diameter size classes (from <10 to >60 μm) for *Ceratonia siliqua*. (From S. Salleo and M. LoGullo, unpublished data.)

zone, branches of a tree might be regarded as a collection of small independent trees, each "rooted" in the bole. Catastrophic xylem dysfunction is defined as the water potential at which major portions of the vascular system cavitate, which then increases the resistance to flow and necessitates the development of more negative water potentials in order to maintain similar rates of flow. These more negative water potentials then induce more cavitation, etc. Of course, trees seldom die because of such dynamic stress (however, twigs, branches, and even considerable portions of the crown do die), and we can assume that stomatal regulation plays a major role in keeping xylem water potential above the threshold value for catastrophic dysfunction. Richter (12) and others have observed that many species close their stomata near the water potential when turgor will be zero (e.g., Fig. 2 in Ref. 93). An interesting research topic would be a study of the interaction between the point of catastrophic xylem dysfunction, the lethal water potential or relative water content (after 24), and the osmotic potential at the turgor loss point especially as periods of diurnal or seasonal osmotic adjustment are noted. The presence of xylem-tapping mistletoes in which stomatal opening has been observed while the stomata of the host's foliage are closed and its impact on hydraulic architecture and catastrophic dysfunction would be another topic (36,94). The second hypothetical situation of regarding a branch as a small, independently rooted tree has interesting parallels with the concept of autonomous branches based on a carbon budget (95) or into the broader discussion of modular growth (96) or independent physiological units (97). Additional work is needed to elucidate the conditions under which a branch may be regarded as independent.

6.5. The sensing of stress episodes

Turner (98) evaluated a number of hypotheses regarding how stress episodes could be sensed. He identified two variables that could be sensed, turgor pressure and cell volume, and two locations where the sensing might occur, the leaf and the root. We have added an additional consideration, the point of catastrophic xylem dysfunction.

Hsiao (99) and Steponkus (100) hypothesized that turgor prssure is the transducer of water deficits. Stomatal closure at zero turgor, ABA accumulation near zero turgor, changes in ABA accumulation, the active accumulation of solutes during drought exposure, and stomatal closure with stress hardening are all used as evidence of the turgor transducer hypothesis. However, the work of Blackman and Davies (101) and Gollan et al. (102) demonstrated that leaf turgor and stomatal aperture are not always well correlated. In the experiments by Gollan et al. (102), full turgor was artificially maintained in the leaves while the soil dried, and yet stomata closed. Others have observed a better relationship between stomatal activity and soil water status than between stomatal activity and leaf water potential (22,27,75,103).

The second hypothesized sensor of stress episodes is found in the root. In a series of very elegant experiments, Borchert (104) demonstrated an important controlling relationship between root and shoot growth. By constantly removing leaves after a certain number had been produced on a *Quercus palustris* shoot, he was able to maintain continuous shoot growth rather than the more typically noted response of alternating root and shoot growth (105). He hypothesized that root area, and thus water uptake capacity, must be in balance with leaf area and that by maintaining this balance he could sustain shoot growth. The studies of Blackman and Davies (101) and Gollan et al. (102) have clearly shown a strong interaction between the status of the root and stomatal aperture independent of leaf water potential or turgor. Masle and Passioura (106) demonstrated that leaf growth in wheat seedlings changed as (a) bulk density of the soil changed and (b) soil water content decreased. There have been a number of recent papers suggesting that, although hormones such as ABA may originate in the roots, it is not hormones produced in the roots that are responsible for the noted aboveground responses (27,107). Munns and King (108) observed that root-stressed plants had altered stomatal behavior as others have shown. However, they were able to extract the sap coming from the roots in the xylem, treat unstressed plants, and observe a response similar to that noted in the stressed plant. When they removed all the ABA from the extracted sap, a response, although not as strong, was still observed.

In contrast to the importance of metabolic messages, Teskey et al. (109) stressed the importance of a much more rapid message coming from a distant point in the conducting system to the foliage. They placed the base of a 1-m-long foliated shoot of *Abies amabilis* into water, allowed time for equilibration to occur, and then cut 50% of the way through the shoot. Rapid stomatal closure was observed within 10 min with no change in bulk needle water potential. A very different response was noted when the branch was completely cut through. In that case, water potential declined and stomata remained open until water potential approached the turgor loss point and then stomata gradually closed.

As argued by both Boyer (23) and Schulze et al. (27), plants respond to both hydraulic and metabolic signals. Current work with herbaceous material emphasizes the metabolic responses, while work with trees emphasizes the hydraulic (51,109). It is important to note that the experimental protocol used by Gollan and others (102), which artificially maintains high turgor in the foliage, has not been applied to trees. Perhaps a continuum exists where plant anatomy and plant size and the type of stress and how it is imposed affect the hydraulic and metabolic signals originating along the flow pathway and arriving at the foliage. Similarly, Turner (98) hypothesized that plants with a high hydraulic conductance would show small changes in leaf water potential and the leaf would be sensitive to root water relations. In contrast, plants with low hydraulic conductance would have large changes in leaf water potential and would be more sensitive to shoot water relations. The nature and location of hydraulic constrictions in the flow path of different species need to be described and related to this potential continuum. In addition, the potential for a rapid, reversible, unmonitored hydraulic signal cannot be dismissed (110).

Changes in cell volume have been hypothesized to act as the third proposed sensor of water deficits (20). Critical, then, is the elasticity of the cell wall as estimated by either the pressure probe or the pressure–volume technique:

$$\varepsilon = \left(\frac{dP}{dV}\right)V \tag{6.4}$$

where ε is the volumetric elastic modulus (the more elastic the cell wall, the smaller the value of ε). Although ε is often cited as a constant or only for tissues at full saturation, it is clear that ε varies with cell turgor pressure. For cells at zero turgor, ε is small or near zero and increases, perhaps linearly, with cell turgor pressure (111,112). Nonlinear patterns of change in ε have been observed in conifers (113) and deciduous trees (114). Unfortunately, this parameter is not particularly easy to determine with certainty, especially using bulk tissue samples. More work is needed with woody plants using a pressure probe to study elasticity for individual cells.

Sinclair and Ludlow (20) suggested that relative water content is a superior parameter for understanding the impact of drought stress on physiological processes. What is the evidence supporting their conclusion? First, Ludlow (24) has noted a close relationship between cell or plant death and lethal relative water content. Second, Kaiser (21) noted, by using leaf discs from three ecologically very different species (*Arbutus unedo*—xerophyte, *Spinacia oleracea*—mesophyte, and *Impatiens valeriana*—hydrophyte), that the response of photosynthesis to changes in RWC (or relative cell volume) was very similar in these species. Surprisingly, he found that even at a RWC of 50% (which is well below the turgor loss point) positive rates of photosynthesis were still observed. As a result of these observations, he concluded that the response of photosynthesis to low air humidity or to only minor water deficits, as reported in the literature, must be solely due to reduced stomatal opening. However, there exist two very strong counterarguments to his conclusion. Scarascia-Mugnozza et al. (18) observed that net photosynthesis decreased to less than 20% of maximum in *Populus trichocarpa* while stomata were still open and leaf water potential was slightly less than the turgor loss point (Fig. 6.2). Relative water content was greater than 80%. Second, Sen Gupta and Berkowitz (115) showed that chloroplasts are capable of osmotic adjustment as leaf water content declines, suggesting that bulk leaf estimates of turgor may not be as useful for correlating with photosynthesis as would be estimates of chloroplast turgor. In addition, they observed nonstomatal inhibition of photosynthesis at much higher relative water contents than those noted by Kaiser (21). As explained previously, total leaf water potential and its osmotic and pressure components are related to relative water content (Fig. 6.3). Therefore, changes in relative water content do not occur independently of changes in either water potential or the components of water potential. We will return to this discussion when considering the effects of plant water relations on physiological processes.

As discussed earlier, Tyree (51) would argue that stomata of a leaf merely respond to water potentials that would lead to cavitation and loss of xylem function. Although the data shown in Fig. 6.7 illustrate a close coupling between the initiation of decreases in xylem hydraulic conductivity and stomatal closure, the transducer for this hypothesized sensor of water deficits needs to be identified. In addition, we might hypothesize that only an intrinsic variable (such as pressure, temperature, concentration) can act as a direct sensor of water deficits. It is not clear how cells could directly sense extrinsic variables such as volume or mass and changes in these variables may be sensed only when they affect an intrinsic variable.

6.6. Tree water status and physiological processes

In his 1973 review, Hsiao (2) concluded that growth (particularly cell elongation) was the process most sensitive to water deficits. Lockhart (116) proposed that the rate of cell expansion (E defined by dV/dt) was linearly related to cell turgor pressure (P) above a threshold turgor pressure or yield threshold (Y):

$$E = m(P - Y) \qquad (6.5)$$

where m is the cell wall extensibility or "yielding tendency." Boyer (117,118) and Zahner (119) have clearly shown that growth is severely reduced by moderate water deficits in both herbaceous plants and trees (see Fig. 6.1). Although cell turgor may be important for leaf growth, the two are not always correlated. For example, Munns and Termaat (120) found in salt-stressed plants that leaf growth could cease in spite of the maintenance of cell turgor. Roden et al. (121) observed a decrease in leaf growth for droughted *Populus*

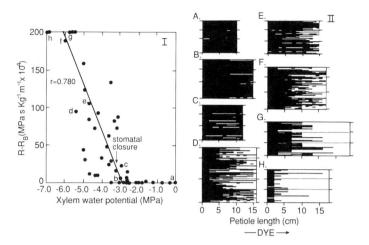

FIG. 6.7. (I) Xylem water potential at maximum dehydration versus xylem flow resistance above base level ($R - R_B$) for petioles. Each point represents a single *Rhapis excelsa* petiole. Petioles labeled a to h were used in dye studies summarized in II. Xylem water potential of laminae at stomatal closure (-3.20 ± 0.18 MPa) is indicated. (II) Penetration of dye in vascular bundles (black lines) of petioles under different xylem water potentials. Dye movement was from left to right. (Reproduced with permission from Ref. 138.)

regardless of osmotic adjustment and the maintenance of turgor. The decrease in leaf growth was related to changes in cell wall extensibility and not to changes in leaf turgor. One way that the foliage may respond to changes in the water status or metabolic conditions of the root is through changes in cell wall extensibility. This change probably occurs as the result of a metabolic signal from the root to the shoot.

Cell expansion is also clearly under the control of growth substances and the effects of auxin on expansion have been studied extensively, as reviewed by Brummell and Hall (122). Therefore, it should not be unexpected that the effects of water deficits on cell growth would involve changes in the concentrations of, or sensitivity to, various growth substances. Trewavas (123) and Firn (124) provide a review of the current debate on the role of growth substances in plant development. Perhaps the greatest weakness in tree physiology is the difficulty in linking the hydraulic and metabolic realms over the short and long term. The interaction between multiple stresses, between the stressing of one part, for example, of the root system and the rest of the tree and between when a stress is imposed and the growth phase of the tree are just a few of the situations in which a whole tree focus is necessary but lacking.

Photosynthesis is affected by plant water status, with water deficits eventually leading to some reduction in photosynthesis (Fig. 6.2). The degree of stomatal opening is a prime factor in determining the relationship between water deficits and photosynthesis, but water deficits can affect photosynthesis through other mechanisms as well. Thus the role of water deficits on photosynthesis has often been subdivided between stomatal and nonstomatal limitations (125,126). Any environmental factor that reduces stomatal opening without damaging the actual photosynthetic machinery will reduce the rate at which carbon dioxide can diffuse into the leaf and, at least under some conditions, reduce the rate of photosynthesis. Although many have argued that the parallel declines in photosynthesis and stomatal conductances are indicative of stomatal regulation, others have suggested that some other factor, such as the activity of sinks for photosynthate, has reduced photosynthesis and that stomata have closed in response to reduced photosynthesis, thus optimizing water use efficiency (see 28, 29 for more complete discussions of stomatal optimization). Photosynthesis is discussed in detail in Chapter 2 (this book) by Ceulemans and Saugier.

6.7. Regulation of plant water status and transpiration

When discussing stomatal function in forest trees, there are a number of important factors. First, from the view of the leaf or the whole tree, the stomata represent the single location where transpiration may be regulated (changes in cuticular conductance, foliage morphology, and crown structure also play important roles in altering water loss, but they provide no means of short-term regulation). However, when one scales from the leaf or the tree to the whole stand, the relative importance of stomatal conductance versus canopy or stand boundary-layer conductance may change significantly (55,127). Second, there are many hypotheses regarding what factors regulate stomatal activity. Many of these hypotheses are related to experimental conditions rather than true differences in the response of stomata to environmental factors. For example, under conditions of rapid growth (i.e., high sink strength), stomata of *Malus* spp. will be very sensitive to absolute humidity differences, while under conditions of no growth, stomata will be insensitive (128). There are a number of excellent reviews describing stomatal function (36,129–133).

In general, the key to a vastly improved understanding of the role of stomatal activity in plants has been the acknowledgment that properties of the water potential equation measured at the bulk leaf level are at best correlated with stomatal aperture and that the entire plant has an impact on the response of a given leaf's stomata (47,51,54,106,108,134). Key generalizations made at this level include (a) the importance of isolating the water potential of the guard cell complex from that of the bulk leaf, (b) the hydraulic and metabolic role that roots have in sensing the soil environment, and (c) the hydraulic and perhaps metabolic role that shoots play in sensing their environment. It would be useful if considerations of root vs. shoot control (22–27) were extended to tree species where plant size and transport distances might alter the interactions between roots and shoots as described for agronomic plants.

6.8. Drought resistance

An overview of stress concepts in plant physiology is presented by Larcher (135). The well-developed and widely accepted treatment by Levitt (34) analyzes components of stress resistance and concentrates on the connection between a stress factor and the response of the organism. By employing an avoidance mechanism, the plant can alleviate the disruptive influence of the stress, and, thereby, the full influence of the stress factor does not reach the site of stress reaction, the protoplasm. The protoplasm, on the other hand, has to tolerate those influences not eliminated or reduced by avoidance. In Larcher's view, this concept has great merit in opening insights into the reaction chains following stress impact. Its main flaws are its static nature and the labeling of stress as something inherently negative. For example, stress can elicit responses that make an organism fitter for survival.

Larcher (135) separates the response of a plant to stress into three phases: (a) alarm, (b) resistance, and (c) exhaustion. Stress is emphasized as being dynamic in both time and space, having a dual nature with both destructive and constructive components, affecting typically just one organ immediately, but the entire organism eventually, and resulting always in net energy expenditure. The long-term development of an equilibrium leaf area index for a site and the short-term responses of stomata and leaf and root osmotic potential are clear illustrations of the dynamic nature of the response of trees to stress (10,13–16).

Historically, drought resistance (or the response of plants to water stress and/or shortage) has been examined by treating the mechanisms separately (e.g., stomatal closure) or in small groups (e.g., deep roots, stomatal closure). Ludlow (24) proposes that responses to water stress do not occur independently, but coincide in combinations or groups that he calls "strategies." He defines a strategy as a combination or grouping of mechanistically linked responses and characteristics that manifest a particular type of behavior during periods of water stress. According to Ludlow (24) there are three types of strategies: (a) escape—survival only in the most dehydration-tolerant form, a seed; (b) avoidance—because tissues are very sensitive to dehydration, there must be mechanisms to avoid dehydration; and (c) tolerance—tissues that can tolerate dehydration need not avoid dehydration. The most important determinant of which strategy a plant species uses is its dehydration tolerance, which in seed plants is seldom absolute. Only in a relatively few species is there a possibility for the survival of the plant in water equilibrium with the surrounding air (i.e., resurrection plants). Dehydration tolerance is determined by the leaf water potential or relative water content of the last surviving leaf on a plant subjected to a low continuous soil drying cycle.

Based on work in Australia, Ludlow (24) ranked a large number of crop and forage species according to whether a tolerance or avoidance strategy is most apparent. Lethal water potentials for his study species ranged from greater than -2.0 MPa in *Vigna ungulculata* to less than -12.0 MPa in 32 different C$_4$ grasses. Species with a relatively high lethal water potential (i.e., −2.5 MPa) demonstrated the avoidance strategy, while those with a low lethal water potential showed the tolerance strategy. Larsen (136), using a different definition of lethal water potential (the water potential where 50% of the buds on a seedling died during a controlled dehydration period), noted a range from −6.6 MPa in a provenance of *Pseudotsuga menziesii* from western Oregon to −10.4 MPa in a provenance from New Mexico. In contrast, Hinckley et al. (93) observed a much narrower range of lethal water potentials in leaves of six diverse, co-occurring woody shrub species from near Vienna, Austria. Lethal water potential values ranged from −4.5 MPa in the shallow-rooted *Viburnum lantana* and the deep-rooted *Quercus pubescens* to −5.4 MPa in the deep-rooted *Crataegus monogyna*. In defining drought tolerance of a tree, we should be careful to describe what organ we are examining (e.g., leaf vs. bud), how we are treating the tree (e.g., whole tree vs. part, rapid vs. gradual dehydration) and what phase we are examining (e.g., alarm, resistance, or exhaustion).

The usefulness of various measures of water status is a topic of debate (22–27). Although a water relations parameter such as relative water content may be useful from a predictive standpoint, it may be less useful in mechanistic studies. The concept of water potential based in thermodynamics has proved quite useful in understanding the movement of water from the soil and through plants. What is necessary now is to acknowledge that interactions between the purely hydraulic realm, forming the basis for water potential, and physiological processes must include the metabolic realm found in control mechanisms that involve growth substances.

Ludlow (24) has developed a list of responses to water deficits and their consequences to plant function. When one examines the species studied by Ludlow (23), such a classification scheme works very nicely. Unfortunately, the strategies or combinations described by Ludlow (24) do not seem so readily and broadly applicable when one examines other data sets (93,137). For example, LoGullo and Salleo (137) examined three Mediterranean species (*Olea oleaster*, *Ceratonia siliqua*, and *Laurus nobilis*) that appeared to be part of a homogeneous group (sclerophylls); however, the strategies they adopted to withstand drought were different from those proposed by Ludlow (24). Application of Ludlow's lethal water potential or relative water content to the classification of these three species may have allowed for a more critical examination and classification of their strategies. In all likelihood, a continuous spectrum of response exists within most woody species, and these responses probably change with stage of development. Finally, it may be fruitful to use the proposed response pattern of Larcher (135) to examine the response of trees to water deficits.

6.9. Concluding remarks

Although many characteristics of trees make them difficult research subjects, these same features provide a unique opportunity for future studies of plant water relations. In this chapter we have not tried to review exhaustively the water relations of trees, but instead have sought to describe several areas of contemporary interest in this field. Many of these topics are of interest because they address the unique nature of the tree form. For example, the presence of a long-distance pathway for water transport that must either be maintained for many years or regenerated has led to interesting work on water movement through tracheids and vessels as well as on the relationships between water stress and cavitation of water in the xylem. Trees also provide an opportunity to test some of the hypotheses for the control of stomata by roots through the action of growth substances. Are roots able to regulate processes in leaves of large trees as they may in agriculture crops? Would this hypothesis conflict with the notion of branches as autonomous units? Such studies make increasingly clear the difficulty in restricting the study of plant water relations to physical considerations not incorporating the metabolic realm. On one hand, our understanding of plant process has been strongly aided by the development of new instruments and methods for studying this physical realm. On the other hand, we are still faced with basic questions about how water deficits are sensed by various plant structures and even what physical variables are involved and may be useful for predicting water status. Hopefully the current work we have attempted to highlight will provide some insight into these and other questions concerning the water relations of trees.

Acknowledgments

The authors thank Drs. R. Ceulemans and Jan-Erik Halgren for critical comments. Funds for writing this chapter were partially provided by the Institute für Forstökologie, Universität für Bodenkultur, Wien and NSF Grant BSR 87-17450.

6.10. References

1. P.J. Kramer, "The role of physiology in forestry," *Tree Physiol.*, **2**, 1–16 (1986).
2. J.S. Boyer, "Plant productivity and environment," *Science*, **218**, 443–448 (1982).
3. S. Hales, in W. Innys, J. Innys, and T. Woodward, eds., *Vegetable Staticks*, Scientific Book Guild, London, 1727.
4. F. Hellriegel, *Beiträge zu den naturwissenschaftlichen Grundlagen des Ackerbaues*, Vieweg und Sohn, Braunschweig, 1883.
5. H. de Vries, "Studiën over Zuigwortels," *Maandblad voor Natuurwetenschappen* **4**, 53 (1886).
6. W. Pfeffer, *Pflanzenphysiologie. Ein Handbuch der Lehre vom Stoffwechsel in der Pflanze*, Verlag von Wilhelm Engelmann, Leipzig, 1897, p. 620.
7. F. Darwin, "Observation on stomata," *Phil. Trans. Roy. Soc. London B.*, **190**, 531–621 (1898).

8. H.H. Dixon, *Transpiration and the Ascent of Sap in Plants*, Macmillan, London, 1914.

9. B. Huber, "Die Beurteilung des Wasserhaushaltes der Pflanze. Ein Beitrag zur vergleichenden Physiologie," *Jb. Wiss. Botan.*, **64**, 1–120 (1924).

10. R.H. Waring and W.H. Schlesinger, *Forest Ecosystems: Concepts and Management*, Academic Press, Orlando, FL, 1985, p. 340.

11. H. Walter, *Die Hydratur der Pflanze und ihre physiologisch ökologische Bedeutung*, Fischer, Jena, 1931, pp. 118–121.

12. H. Richter, "The water status in the plant—experimental evidence," in O.L. Lange, L. Kappen, and E.-D. Schulze, eds., *Water and Plant Life*, Ecological Studies Vol. 19, Springer-Verlag, Berlin, 1976, p. 42–58.

13. C.C. Grier and S.W. Running, "Leaf area of mature northwestern coniferous forests: Relation to site water balance," *Ecology*, **58**, 893–899 (1977).

14. H. Gholz, "Environmental limits on aboveground net primary production, leaf area, and biomass in vegetation zones of the Pacific Northwest," *Ecology*, **63**, 469–481 (1982).

15. B.J. Myers, "Water stress integral—a link between short-term processes and long-term growth," *Tree Physiol.*, **4**, 315–324 (1988).

16. P.B. Reich and T.M. Hinckley, "Water relations, soil fertility, and plant nutrient composition of a pygmy oak ecosystem," *Ecology*, **61**, 400–416 (1980).

17. J.D. Aber, K.J. Nadelhoffer, P. Steudler, and J.M. Melillo, "Nitrogen saturation in northern forest ecosystems," *BioScience*, **39**, 378–386 (1989).

18. G. Scarascia-Mugnozza, T.M. Hinckley, and R.F. Stettler, "Evidence for non-stomatal inhibition of net photosynthesis in rapidly dehydrated shoots of *Populus*," *Can. J. For. Res.*, **16**, 1371–1375 (1986).

19. P.J. Schulte and T.M. Hinckley, "Abscisic acid relations and the response of *Populus trichocarpa* stomata to leaf water potential," *Tree Physiol.*, **3**, 103–113 (1987).

20. T.R. Sinclair and M.M. Ludlow, "Who taught plants thermodynamics? The unfulfilled potential of plant water potential," *Aust. J. Plant Physiol.*, **12**, 213–217 (1985).

21. W.M. Kaiser, "Effects of water deficit on photosynthetic capacity," *Physiol. Plant.*, **71**, 142–149 (1987).

22. J.B. Passioura, "Response to Dr. P.J. Kramer's article, 'Changing concepts regarding plant water relations', Volume 11, Number 7, pp. 565–568," *Plant, Cell Environ.*, **11**, 569–571 (1988).

23. J.S. Boyer, "Water potential and plant metabolism: Comments on Dr. P.J. Kramer's article, 'Changing concepts regarding plant water relations', Volume 11, Number 7, pp. 565–568," and Dr. J.B. Passioura's Response, pp. 569–571, *Plant, Cell Environ.*, **12**, 213–216 (1989).

24. M.M. Ludlow, "Drought resistance, an examination of different strategies," in W. Kreeb, H. Richter, and T.M. Hinckley, eds., *Structural and Functional Responses to Environmental Stresses*, SPB Publ, The Hague, 1989, pp. 269–281.

25. P.J. Kramer, "Changing concepts regarding plant water relations," *Plant, Cell Environ.*, **11**, 565–568 (1988).

26. R. Munns, "Why measure osmotic adjustment?," *Aust. J. Plant Physiol.*, **15**, 717–726 (1988).

27. E-D. Schulze, E. Steudle, T. Gollan, and U. Schurr, "Response to Dr. P.J. Kramer's article, 'Changing concepts regarding plant water relations', Volume 11, number 7, pp. 565–568," *Plant, Cell Environ.*, **11**, 573–576 (1988).

28. D.W. Sheriff, E.K.S. Nambiar and D.N. Fife, "Relationships between nutrient status, carbon assimilation and water use efficiency in *Pinus radiata* (D. Don) needles," *Tree Physiol.*, **2**, 73–88 (1986).

29. J.A. Fites and R.O. Teskey, "CO_2 and water vapor exchange of *Pinus taeda* in relation to stomatal behavior: Test of an optimization hypothesis," *Can. J. For. Res.*, **18**, 150–157 (1988).

30. T.C. Hsiao, "Plant responses to water stress," *Ann. Rev. Plant Phys.*, **24**, 519–570 (1973).

31. H.G. Jones, A.N. Lakso, and J.P. Syvertsen, "Physiological control of water status in temperate and subtropical trees," *Hort. Rev.*, **7**, 301–352 (1985).

32. T.T. Kozlowski, ed., *Water Deficits and Plant Growth*, Vols. I–VII, Academic Press, New York, 1968–1983.

33. P.J. Kramer, *Plant and Soil Water Relationships*, Academic Press, New York, 1983, p. 483.

34. J. Levitt, *Responses of Plants to Environmental Stress*, Vol. I, Academic Press, New York–London, 1980, p. 607.

35. P.S. Nobel, *Physicochemical and Environmental Plant Physiology*, Academic Press, New York, 1991, 635 pp.

36. E.-D. Schulze, "Carbon dioxide and water vapour exchange in response to drought in the atmosphere and in the soil," *Ann. Rev. Plant Physiol.*, **37**, 247–274 (1986).

37. B. Slavik, *Methods of studying Plant Water Relations*. Springer-Verlag, Berlin–New York, 1974, p. 449.

38. N.C. Turner, "Adaptation to water deficits: A changing perspective," *Aust. J. Plant Physiol.*, **13**, 175–190 (1986).

39. N.C. Turner, "Measurement of plant water status by the pressure chamber technique," *Irrig. Sci.*, **9**, 289–308 (1988).

40. K. Höfler, "Ein Schema für die osmotische Leistung der Pflanzenzelle," *Ber. Dtsch. Bot. Ges.*, **38**, 288–298 (1920).

41. R.O. Teskey, T.M. Hinckley, and C.C. Grier, "Temperature-induced change in the water relations of *Abies amabilis* (Dougl.) Forbes," *Plant Physiol.*, **74**, 77–80 (1984).

42. M.T. Tyree and H. Richter, "Alternative methods of analyzing water potential isotherms: Some cautions and clarifications. I. The impact of non-ideality and of some experimental errors," *J. Exp. Bot.*, **32**, 643–653 (1981).

43. P.J. Schulte and T.M. Hinckley, "A comparison of pressure–volume curve data analysis techniques," *J. Exp. Bot.*, **36**, 1590–1602 (1985).

44. S.B. Kikuta and H. Richter, "Graphical evaluation and partitioning of turgor responses to drought in leaves of durum wheat," *Planta*, **168**, 36–42 (1986).

45. M.D. Abrams, "Sources of variation in osmotic potentials with special reference to North American tree species," *For. Sci.*, **34**, 1030–1046 (1988).

46. T.H. van den Honert, "Water transport in plants as a catenary process," *Disc. Faraday Soc.*, **3**, 146–153 (1948).

47. H. Richter, "Frictional potential losses and total water potential in plants: A reevaluation," *J. Exp. Bot.*, **24**, 983–994 (1973).

48. D.C. Elfving, M.R. Kaufmann, and A.E. Hall, "Interpreting leaf water potential measurements with a model of the SPAC," *Physiol. Plant.*, **27**, 161–168 (1972).

49. M.H. Zimmermann, *Xylem Structure and the Ascent of Sap*, Springer, Berlin–New York, 1983, p. 143.

50. P.G. Jarvis, "Water transfer in plants," in D.A. deVries and N.K. vanAlfen, eds., *Heat and Mass Transfer in the Environment of Vegetation*. Scripta Book Co., Washington, D.C., 1975, pp. 369–394.

51. M.T. Tyree, "A dynamic model for water flow in a single tree: evidence that models must account for hydraulic architecture," *Tree Physiol.*, **4**, 195–217 (1988).

52. S.W. Running, "Field estimates of root and xylem resistances in *Pinus contorta* using root excision," *J. Exp. Bot.*, **31**, 555–569 (1980).

53. J.P. Passioura, "Water transport in and to roots," *Ann. Rev. Plant Phys. Mol. Biol.*, **39**, 245–265 (1988).

54. M.T. Tyree and J.S. Sperry, "Do woody plants operate near the point of catastrophic xyem dysfunction caused by dynamic water stress?: Answers from a model," *Plant Physiol.*, **88**, 574–580 (1988).

55. P.G. Jarvis and K.G. McNaughton, "Stomatal control of transpiration; scaling up from leaf to region," *Adv. Ecol. Res.*, **15**, 1–49 (1986).

56. R. Milne, "Diurnal water storage in the stems of *Picea sitchensis* (Bong.) Carr.," *Plant, Cell Environ.*, **12**, 63–72 (1989).

57. T.M. Hinckley, S.W. Running, and J.P. Lassoie, "Temporal and spatial variations in the water status of forest trees," *For. Sci. Monogr.*, **20**, 1–72 (1978).

58. D. Whitehead, "A review of processes in the water relations of forests," in J.J. Landsberg and W. Parsons, eds., *Research for Forest Management*, CSIRO, Melbourne, 1985, pp. 94.

59. P.J. Schulte and P.S. Nobel, "Responses of a CAM plant to drought and rainfall: Capacitance and osmotic pressure influences on water movement," *J. Exp. Bot.*, **40**, 61–70 (1989).

60. J.P. Lassoie, "Diurnal dimensional fluctuations in a Douglas-fir stem in response to tree water status," *For. Sci.*, **19**, 251–255 (1973).

61. R.H. Waring, D. Whitehead, and P.G. Jarvis, "Comparison of an isotopic method and the Penman–Monteith equation for estimating transpiration from Scots pine," *Can. J. For. Res.*, **19**, 555–558 (1980).

62. N.J. Legge and D.J. Conner, "Hydraulic characteristics of mountain ash (*Eucalyptus regnans* F. Muell.) derived from in situ measurements of stem water potential," *Aust. J. Plant Physiol.*, **12**, 77–88 (1985).

63. R.H. Waring, D. Whitehead, and P.G. Jarvis, "The contribution of stored water to transpiration in Scots pine," *Plant, Cell Environ.*, **2**, 223–230 (1979).

64. J. Hellkvist, G.P. Richards, and P.G. Jarvis, "Vertical gradients of water potential and tissue water relations in Sitka spruce trees measured with the pressure chamber." *J. Appl. Ecol.*, **11**, 637–668 (1974).

65. R.H. Waring and S.W. Running, "Sapwood water storage: Its contribution to transpiration and effect upon water conductance through the stems of old-growth Douglas-fir," *Plant, Cell Environ.*, **1**, 131–140 (1978).

66. S.J. Manning and M.G. Barbour, "Root systems, spatial patterns, and competition for soil moisture between two desert subshrubs," *Am. J. Bot.*, **75**, 885–893 (1988).

67. J.W. Stringer, P.J. Kalisz, and J.A. Volpe, "Deep tritiated water uptake and predawn xylem water potentials as indicators of vertical rooting extent in a *Quercus-Carya* forest," *Can. J. For. Res.*, **19**, 627–631 (1989).

68. M.M. Caldwell and J.H. Richards, "Hydraulic lift: Water efflux from upper roots improves effectiveness of water uptake by deep roots," *Oecologia*, **79**, 1–5 (1989).

69. S.J. Corak, D.G. Blevins, and S.G. Pallardy, "Water transfer in an alfalfa/maize association," *Plant Physiol.*, **84**, 582–586 (1987).

70. C.P. Andersen, A.H. Markhart, III, R.K. Dixon, and E.I. Sucoff, "Root hydraulic conductivity of vesicular–arbuscular mycorrhizal green ash seedlings," *New Phytol.*, **109**, 465–471 (1988).

71. T.A. Day, E.H. DeLucia, and W.K. Smith, "Influence of cold soil and snow cover on photosynthesis and conductance in two Rocky Mountain conifers," *Oecologia*, **80**, 546–552 (1989).

72. S.C. Grossnickle, "Planting stress in newly planted jack pine and white spruce. 1 Factors influencing water uptake," *Tree Physiol.*, **4**, 71–84 (1988).

73. R. Sands, E.L. Fiscus, and C.P.P. Reid, "Hydraulic properties of pine and bean roots with varying degrees of suberization, vascular differentiation and mycorrhizal infection," *Aust. J. Plant Physiol.*, **9**, 559–569 (1982).

74. S.J. Colombo and M.F. Asselstine, "Root hydraulic conductivity and root growth capacity of black spruce (*Picea mariana*) seedlings," *Tree Physiol.*, **5**, 73–82 (1989).

75. B. Smit, M. Stachowiak, and E. Van Volkenburgh, "Cellular processes limiting leaf growth in plants under hypoxic root stress," *J. Exp. Bot.*, **40**, 27–32 (1989).

76. J.D. Everard and M.C. Drew, "Mechanisms controlling changes in water movement through the roots of *Helianthus annuus* L. during continuous exposure to oxygen deficiency," *J. Exp. Bot.*, **40**, 95–104 (1989).

77. B. Smit and M. Stachowiak, "The effects of hypoxia and elevated carbon dioxide levels on water flux through *Populus* roots," *Tree Physiol.*, **4**, 153–165 (1988).

78. E.L. Fiscus, "Diurnal changes in volume and solute transport coefficients of *Phaseolus* roots," *Plant Physiol.*, **80**, 752–759 (1986).

79. K. Katou, T. Tauru, and M. Furumoto, "A biophysical model for water movement in roots: Root exudation and root pressure," *Plant and Soil*, **111**, 213–216 (1988).

80. H. Jones, R.A. Leigh, R.G. Wyn Jones, and A.D. Tomos, "The integration of whole-root and cellular hydraulic conductivities in cereal roots," *Planta*, **174**, 1–7 (1988).

81. J. Sanderson, "Water uptake by different regions of the barley root. Pathways of radial flow in relation to development of the endodermis," *J. Exp. Bot.*, **34**, 240–253 (1983).

82. K. Shinozaki, K. Yoda, K. Hozumi, and T. Kira, "A quantitative analysis of plant form—the pipe model theory. I. Basic analyses," *Jpn. J. Ecol.*, **14**, 97–105 (1964).

83. R.E. Dickson and J.G. Isebrands, "Role of leaves in regulating structure–functional development in plant shoot," in H.A. Mooney, W.E. Winner, and E.J. Pell, eds., *Integrated Response of Plants to Stress*, Academic Press, New York, 1991.

84. S. Salleo and M.A. LoGullo, "Xylem cavitation in nodes and internodes of *Vitis vinifera* L. plants subjected to water stress. Limits of restoration of water conduction in cavitated xylem conduits," in W. Kreeb, H. Richter, and T.M. Hinckley, eds., *Structural and Functional Responses to Environmental Stresses*, SPB Academic, The Hague, 1989, pp. 33–42.

85. P.J. Schulte and A.C. Gibson, "Hydraulic conductance and tracheid anatomy in six species of extant seed plants," *Can. J. Cot.*, **66**, 1073–1079 (1988).

86. J.S. Sperry and M.T. Tyree, "Mechanism of water stress-induced xylem embolism," *Plant Physiol.*, **88**, 581–587 (1988).

87. H.R. Schultz and M.A. Matthews, "Resistance to water transport in shoots of *Vitis vinifera* L.," *Plant Physiol.*, **88**, 718–724 (1988).

88. M.T. Tyree and J.S. Sperry, "Vulnerability of xylem to cavitation and embolism," *Ann. Rev. Plant Phys. Mol. Biol.*, **40**, 19–38 (1989).

89. M.H. Zimmermann, "Hydraulic architecture of some diffuse-porous trees," *Can. J. Bot.*, **56**, 2286-2295 (1978).

90. T. Ikeda and T. Suzaki, "Distribution of xylem resistance to water flow in stems and branches of hardwood species," *J. Jpn. For. Soc.*, **66**, 229–236 (1984).

91. D.W. Woodcock, "Climate sensitivity of wood-anatomical features in a ring-porous oak (*Quercus macrocarpa*)," *Can. J. For. Res.*, **19**, 639–644 (1989).

92. M.T. Tyree and M.A. Dixon, "Water stress induced cavitation and embolism in some woody plants," *Physiol. Plant.*, **66**, 397–405 (1986).

93. T.M. Hinckley, F. Duhme, A.R. Hinckley, and H. Richter, "Drought relations of shrub species: Assessment of the mechanisms of drought resistance," *Oecologia*. **59**, 344–350 (1983).

94. G. Glatzel, "Mineral nutrition and water relations in hemiparasitic mistletoes: A question of partitioning. Experiments with *Loranthus europaeus* on *Quercus petraea* and *Quercus robur*," *Oecologia*, **56**, 193–201 (1983).

95. D.G. Sprugel and T.M. Hinckley, "The branch autonomy concept," in W.E. Winner and L.G. Phelps, eds., *Response of Trees to Air Pollution: The Role of Branch Studies*, Proceedings Workshop National Forest Response Program, Boulder, CO, Nov. 5–6, 1987, 1988, pp. 7–23.

96. R.C. Hardwick, "Physiological consequences of modular growth in plants," *Phil. Trans. Roy. Soc. London*, **313**, 161–173 (1986).

97. M.A. Watson, "Integrated physiological units in plants," *Trends Ecol. Evol.*, **1**, 119–123 (1986).

98. N.C. Turner, "Crop water deficits; a decade of progress," *Adv. Agron.*, **39**, 1–51 (1987).

99. T.C. Hsiao, E. Acevedo, E. Fereres, and D.W. Henderson, "Stress metabolism water stress, growth and osmotic adjustment," *Phil. Trans. Roy. Soc. London B*, **273**, 479–500 (1976).

100. P.L. Steponkus, "A unified concept of stress in plants," in D.W. Rains, R.C. Valentine, and A. Hollaender, eds., *Genetic Engineering of Osmoregulation*, Plenum Press, New York, 1980, pp. 235, 1980.

101. P.G. Blackman and W.J. Davies, "Root to shoot communication in maize plants of the effects of soil drying," *J. Exp. Bot.*, **36**, 39–48 (1985).

102. T. Gollan, J.B. Passioura, and R. Munns, "Soil water status affects the stomatal conductance of fully turgid wheat and sunflower leaves," *Aust. J. Plant. Physiol.*, **13**, 459–464 (1986).

103. J. Zhang and W.J. Davies, "Abscisic acid produced in dehydrating roots may enable the plant to measure the water status of the soil," *Plant, Cell Environ.*, **12**, 73–81 (1989).

104. R. Borchert, "Endogenous shoot growth under constant conditions," *Physiol. Plant.*, **35**, 152–157 (1975).

105. J.B. Wilson, "A review of evidence on the control of shoot:root ratio, in relation to models," *Ann. Bot.*, **612**, 433–449 (1988).

106. J. Masle and J.B. Passioura, "The effect of soil strength on the growth of young wheat plants," *Aust. J. Plant Physiol.*, **14**, 643–656 (1987).

107. M.B. Jackson, S.F. Young, and K.C. Hall, "Ethylene and the response of roots of maize (*Zea mays* L.) to physical impedance," *J. Exp. Bot.*, **39**, 1631–1637 (1988).

108. R. Munns and R.W. King, "Abscisic acid is not the only stomatal inhibitor in the transpiration stream of wheat plants," *Plant Physiol.*, **88**, 703–708 (1988).

109. R.O. Teskey, T.M. Hinckley, and C.C. Grier, "Effect of interruption of flow path on stomatal conductance of *Abies amabilis*," *J. Exp. Bot.*, **34**, 1251–1259 (1983).

110. P.M. Schildwacht, "Is a decreased water potential after withholding oxygen to roots the cause of the decline of leaf-elongation rates in *Zea mays* L. and *Phaseolus vulgaris* L.?," *Planta*, **177**, 178–184 (1989).

111. E. Steudle, U. Zimmermann, and U. Lüttge, "Effect of turgor pressure and cell size on the wall elasticity of plant cells," *Plant Physiol.*, **59**, 285–289 (1977).

112. E.J. Stadelmann, "The derivation of the cell wall elasticity function from the cell turgor potential," *J. Exp. Bot.*, **35**, 859–868 (1984).

113. K. Gross and T. Pham-Nguyen, "Pressure-volume analyses on shoots of *Picea abies* and leaves of *Coffea liberica* at various temperatures," *Physiol. Plant.*, **70**, 189–195 (1987).

114. S.G. Pallardy, J.S. Pereira, and W.C. Parker, "The state of water in tree systems," in J.P. Lassoie and T.M. Hinckley, eds., *Techniques and Methodologies in Tree Ecophysiology*, CRC Press, New York, 1991, pp. 27–75.

115. A. Sen Gupta and G.A. Berkowitz, "Chloroplast osmotic adjustment and water stress effects on photosynthesis," *Plant Physiol.*, **88**, 200–206 (1988).

116. J.A. Lockhart, "An analysis of irreversible plant cell elongation," *J. Theor. Biol.*, **8**, 264–276 (1965).

117. J.S. Boyer, "Leaf enlargement and metabolic rates in corn, soybean, and sunflower at various leaf water potentials," *Plant Physiol.*, **46**, 233–235 (1970).

118. J.S. Boyer, "Cell enlargement and growth-induced water potentials," *Physiol. Plant.*, **73**, 311–316 (1988).

119. R. Zahner, "Water deficits and growth of trees," in T.T. Kozlowski, ed., *Water Deficits and Plant Growth*, Vol. II, Academic Press, London, 1968, p. 191.

120. R. Munns and A. Termaat, "Whole-plant responses to salinity," *Aust. J. Plant Physiol.*, **13**, 143–160 (1986).

121. J. Roden, E. Van Volkenburgh, and T.M. Hinckley, "The response of hybrid poplar trees to mild water deficit," *Tree Physiol.*, **6**, 211–219 (1990).

122. D.A. Brummell and J.L. Hall, "Rapid cellular responses to auxin and the regulation of growth," *Plant, Cell Environ.*, **10**, 523–543 (1987).

123. A.J. Trewavas, "Understanding the control of plant development and the role of growth substances," *Aust. J. Plant Physiol.*, **13**, 447–457 (1986).

124. R.D. Firn, "Growth substance sensitivity: The need for clearer ideas, precise terms and purposeful experiments," *Physiol. Plant.*, **67**, 267–272 (1986).

125. M. Havaux, M. Ernez, and R. Lannoye, "Tolerance of poplar (*Populus* sp.) to environmental stress. I. Comparative study of poplar clones using the *in vivo* chlorophyll fluorescence method," *Oecol. Plant.*, **9**, 161–172 (1988).

126. P. Grieu, J.M. Guehl, and G. Aussenac, "The effects of soil and atmospheric drought on photosynthesis and stomatal control of gas exchange in three coniferous species," *Physiol. Plant.*, **73**, 97–104 (1988).

127. T.A. Black and F.M. Kelliher, "Processes controlling understory evapotranspiration," *Phil. Trans. Roy. Soc. Lond. B*, **324**, 207–231 (1989).

128. A.N. Lakso, "The effects of water stress on physiological processes in fruit crops," *Acta Horticulturae*, **171**, 275–293 (1985).

129. E. Zeiger, G.D. Farquhar, and I.R. Cowan, eds., *Stomatal Function*, Stanford University, California, 1987, p. 503.

130. P. Eliás, "Stomata in forest communities: Density, size and conductance," *Acta Universitatis Carolinae–Biologica*, **31**, 27–41 (1988).

131. K. Raschke, R. Hedrich, U. Reckmann, and J.I. Schroeder, "Exploring biophysical and biochemical components of the osmotic motor that drives stomatal movement (review)," *Botanica Acta*, **101**, 283–294 (1988).

132. C.M. Willmer, "Stomatal sensing of the environment," *Biol. J. Linn. Soc.*, **34**, 205–217 (1988).

133. M.R. Kaufmann, "Ecophysiological processes affecting tree growth: Water relationships," in R.K. Dixon, R.S. Meldahl, G.A. Ruark, and W.G. Warren, eds., *Process Modeling of Responses to Environmental Stress*, Timber Press, Portland, 1990, pp. 64–78.

134. P.J. Schulte and T.M. Hinckley, "The relationship between guard cell water potential and the aperture of stomata in *Populus*," *Plant, Cell Environ.*, **10**, 313–318 (1987).

135. W. Larcher, "Stress bei Pflanzen" *Naturwissenschaften*, **74**, 158–167 (1987).

136. J.B. Larsen, "Geographic variation in winter drought resistance of Douglas-fir (*Pseudotsuga menziesii* Mirb. Franco)," *Silvae Genetica*, **30**, 109–114 (1981).

137. M. LoGullo and S. Salleo, "Different strategies of drought resistance in three Mediterranean scherophyllous trees growing in the same environmental conditions," *New Phytol.*, **108**, 267–276 (1988).

138. J.S. Sperry, "Relationship of xylem embolism to xylem pressure potential, stomatal closure, and shoot morphology in the palm *Rhapis excelsa*," *Plant Physiol.*, **80**, 110–116 (1986).

7 Cavitation and Embolisms in Xylem Conduits

J.A. MILBURN

Department of Botany, The University of New England, Armidale, New South Wales, Australia

Contents

7.1. Cavitation and the disruption of sap flow in plants

The ancients appreciated the enormous quantities of water consumed and indeed elevated within plants. Gradually the problem of the mechanism of this process has been more clearly formulated requiring fundamental reappraisal of convential notions of hydraulic mechanisms. Thus, since formulated in 1894 by Dixon and Joly (5), the principle of cohesion has gradually been accepted, and this, in combination with the intricate anatomy of the plant, is now universally accepted as the major mechanism driving sap flow in plants. However, the overall concept of water transport has also been modified. Once seen primarily as the *ascent* of sap, the problem is now viewed primarily as a problem of water extraction against unfavorable gradients of water potential, especially from drying and saline soils.

Fortunately, the understanding of hydraulic transport is now quantifiable with an array of increasingly more convenient instruments. Water potentials can be measured directly using psychrometers. Pressure components can be measured using the Scholander pressure chamber, and osmotic components can be measured with increasing ease using both freezing-point and vapor-pressure osmometers. Cavitation can be detected by several means: micro-

163

scopic observation, audiodetection and, most recently, ultrasonic methods. These allow increasingly precise quantitative data to be collected that have revealed essentially *minor* inconsistencies in our original preconceptions.

Another important contributory cause of sap disruption is not cavitation itself but rather the introduction of gas embolisms into the system. Embolisms are produced naturally in the aftermath of cavitation, but they are enormously important in horticulture when plant organs are excised for propagation or as cut flowers. They are also a natural consequence of the maturing of sapwood that first must cavitate then become embolized before it is converted into heartwood.

In this chapter the main focus of attention will be on cavitation and embolization. Other causes of disruption, such as tyloses and pathogen infection, will be covered only in outline.

7.2. Cavitation and embolism—definition and incidence in plants

In plants *cavitation* (Latin *cavus*, hollow) is the formation of a cavity or hollow within a body of water usually as plant sap. The initiation of cavitation can either be produced dynamically, e.g., by centrifugation or shock waves, such as might be induced by explosives, or in a static condition. If water is heated near boiling point, it forms small voids (bubbles) that spontaneously collapse, a familiar phenomenon in a "singing" kettle. At lower temperatures static cavitation can only be induced if the liquid is contained in some form of rigid envelope. In the case of the Berthelot tube the envelope is glass. In plants one or more cells, acting in combination, form the container from rigid lignified cell walls. Sap cavitating is usually almost pure water; however, in the case of fungal spores, cavitation occurs in either the cytoplasm or vacuolar sap, which are sufficiently supplied with solutes to have an osmotic potential of about -2 MPa (9).

An *embolism* is an obstruction (Greek *embolus*, stopper) to the flow of plant sap. When cavitation occurs in fungal spores, bryophyte elators or fern sporangia there are bubbles but there is no embolism because these are no conducting channels. However, cavitation in a vessel or other vascular conduit in causing a bubble to emerge also causes embolism because it tends to arrest flow. When initiated a cavitation bubble is virtually at vacuum. It is then quickly invaded by water vapor (vapor pressure of water at 20°C is 2.33×10^{-3} MPa) and then more slowly by gases dissolved in the plant sap and most cell walls. Gases, at atmospheric pressure outside, continue to dissolve in the cell wall moisture and then emerge in the near-vacuum embolism. This process continues until both gas pressures equilibrate. At this stage the embolism is gas-filled and is difficult to remove because it must be redissolved, e.g., by pressurisation. Since this is the reverse of the previous process it tends to be protracted. In nature if it were to be reversed within a few hours a considerable root pressure would be required.

One minor yet significant force can promote the dissolution of an embolism; this is the "excess pressure" in a bubble. Thus the surface tension of water tends to raise the pressure in a bubble. The smaller the bubble, the greater the curvature and hence the greater the gas pressure (ca. 0.02MPa for a typical vessel). Normally bubbles are confined in narrow tubes: these have the effect of increasing the pressure of what might be a large spherical bubble to that of the diameter of the tube (Fig. 7.1). For this effect to operate, a bubble must be scrupulously clean; minute traces of surfactant cause bubbles to resist dissolution strongly. Further interference is caused by the gas-saturated unstirred liquid layer surrounding a bubble. This probably explains the rapid dissolution of small bubbles of gas when they are being swept along a vessel. Experimental details were given by Dickson and Blackman (4); bubbles can be observed to disappear in a few minutes while being transported through vessels.

7.3. Chronology

The ascent of water in plants has long fascinated humans. The chronology (Table 7.1) shows the search was mainly directed toward the familiar positive-pressure pumps. Next, with the establishment of the cohesion hypothesis the negative pressure system was assumed quite stable.

   With the detection of cavitation the water pipeline was recognized to be far more vulnerable than previously supposed.

   We still need however to fill in an immense amount of detail. Thus we are concerned to locate restrictions in vascular hydraulic pathways (27). We are also still discovering the ranges of water potential in which cavitation occurs in many groups of species (19,21,22).

7.4. Detection of cavitation

Many methods can be used to detect cavitation. Cavitation was observed by Berthelot (1) using a thick-walled glass tube completely filled with water. As

FIG. 7.1. Embolized vessel in a conduit (vessel, tracheid, or fiber). The excess pressure in the bubble is a function of the diameter (*d*) of the unit, which controls the curvature of the ends of the bubble, rather than its total volume. Cavitation may be initiated by entry of a tiny bubble through the wall, which then "explodes." However, cavitation can occur below liquids in fungal spores showing that there are other methods of initiation. The bubble typically shrinks from one end until it becomes spherical (dotted outline) when it becomes detached as it shrinks further.

Table 7.1. A chronology of research findings on cavitation and embolisms[a]

1669	Ray: Sap circulates in plants like blood in animals
1717	Hales: Quantitative approach to sap transport in plants
1850	Berthelot: Cavitation of water in glass (1)
1884	Godlewski: Cells must pump sap to generate movement
1894	Dixon and Joly: Cohesion theory proposed to explain sap ascent (5)
1914	Dixon: Transpirational friction and gravity affect sap ascent equally (6)
1920	Bode: Observed cavitation in vascular xylem (2)
1927	Bose: Sap ascent caused by pulsation of cortical cells
1935	Priestly: Cohesion mechanism impossible, xylem air-filled
1936	Pierce: *Ricinus* stems air or water filled depending on season (15)
1938	Dickson and Blackman: Air bubbles absored by xylem (4)
1939	Handley: Stem cooling *above freezing point* causes wilting
1964	Zimmermann: Handley's claim disproved by improved methods (26)
1965	Scholander et al.: Measurement of large sap tensions by pressure chamber (19)
1966	Milburn: Cavitation predicted in *Ricinus* (7)
1966	Miburn and Johnson: Acoustic detection of sap cavitation (8)
1973	Milburn: Cavitation in excised *Ricinus* leaves (10)
1973	Milburn: Cavitation in whole plants of *Ricinus* under stress (11)
1974	Milburn and McLaughlin: Acoustic detection on vascular bundles (12)
1983	Tyree and Dixon: Ulatrasonic detection used on *Thuja* (25)
1985	Crombie, Hipkins and Milburn: Gas penetration causes cavitation (3)
1987	Sperry, Holbrook, Zimmermann and Tyree: Root pressure restores conduction in vines (20)
1988	Ritman and Milburn: Ultrasonic and audible methods compared (16,17,18)
1988	Sperry, Donnelly and Tyree: Methods for measuring conductivity/embolism (22)
1989	Tyree and Sperry: Xylem cavitation and embolism reviewed (27)

[a]The numbers in parentheses correspond to those in the list of references.

the tube was cooled, because the enclosed water contracted more than the enveloping glass, a point was reached when there was a sharp "click" and a cloud of tiny bubbles emerged that quickly rose and coalesced into a single bubble. By careful warming, the tube could be restored to its original condition and the cycle repeated.

Effectively therefore we are limited to *three* basic methods. These are *vision*, *sound* and also what might be termed *consequential* in that we can observe the results of cavitation. The first two methods will be examined in more detail below. Theoretically other methods might also be used, e.g., the emission of light during cavitation, but to date there have been no reports of success using, say, scintillation counters, and tests by the author have been unsuccessful.

7.4.1. Vision

The anatomy of a plant is such that cells and xylem elements have to be observed microscopically. A bared stem is initially translucent but becomes more whitish and opaque to the naked eye as water is lost, but this is not a useful way to monitor cavitation. Under the microscope cavitation can be detected quite easily in small objects such as fungal spores (9), liverwort elators, and fern sporangia, but it is much more difficult to monitor vascular plants in this way. Owing to the multiplicity of tubes and opaque investing tissues one is limited to surface illumination rather than transmitted light. When cavitation occurs, the initial process is very rapid, and this is followed by a subsequent, often rapid, process: the emptying of sap from the cavitated conduit into adjoining sap-filled conduits. The need for anatomical incisions to expose the tissue (perhaps introducing weaknesses or punctures), the high speed of cavitation events become a problem. Also the haphazard effect of viewing a small part of the whole vasculature makes optical methods generally impractical.

It should be noted, however, that observations of these systems have greatly increased our knowledge of cavitation. Thus we know that the first bubble appearing probably represents a volume equivalent to the elastic recoil of the walls of the container. A *subsequent* enlargement of the bubble is a function of both hydraulic resistance via the container walls and also the water potential gradient drawing water from the cavitated unit at now near-vacuum pressure. Cavitation itself may arise from a microscopic bubble entrained in a micro-crack (14,29).

7.4.2. Acoustic detection

The use of electronic amplification to detect cavitation acoustically (8) was a direct development of the Berthelot tube observation, scaled down to match the microscopic anatomy of the plant. A plant organ, usually a leaf, was suspended from an electrical transducer, using a wire or sharp pin to wrap or impale the tissue. As water evaporated from the specimen the water in the xylem was subjected to increasing stress, which eventually induced cav-itation in the form of a succession of clicks. These were amplified, recorded and monitored via headphones. The subsequent plot was initially zero and then rose irregularly to one or more peaks, which then fell to a second silent period as the ability to cavitate was lost.

A number of benefits were immediately obvious. The amount of surgical preparation was minimal. A whole plant or organ could be monitored si-multaneously, and information could be gained of invisible events deeply embedded within tissues. It disadvantages were that the audioamplifier had to be very powerful and the manual recording system, first used, was very tedious.

Over the course of time many environmental effects were tested because there was no independent way to measure cavitation with such precision. This circumstantial evidence supported the idea that cavitation, rather than me-chanical strain, produced the clicks. It could be stopped by supplying water or preventing water loss from the tissues. Similarly, it could be induced by introducing particulate suspensions into the water supply of an excised leaf. Accelerating water loss by supplying radiant energy accelerated the sequence considerably. No effect of radioactive radiation could be detected: this is surprising since a similar system is used in physics to detect ionization tracks (bubble chamber).

It was shown that the technique could be used not only to study whole organs but also excised tissues, e.g., excised vascular bundles of *Plantago* (12). Such systems were much more akin to a Berthelot tube in that they could be restored and experiments repeated. In this way several important findings were made. Thus the effects of cavitation could best be reversed by evacuating the tissue to remove emboli; positive pressure could dissolve entrapped emboli, but the process was comparatively slow. In addition, it became clear that cavitation was incomplete in intact tissues. Only links in the entire chain were broken. When the tissue was surgically stripped, a large additional number of conduits now cavitated. It also became apparent that cavitation occurred at comparatively modest negative pressures (-0.5 to -1.5 MPa) in plants such as *Ricinus* and *Plantago*.

Measurement of the sap tensions at which cavitation has been initiated is a potentially difficult exercise. The ideal device for measurement of negative sap pressures is unquestionably a pressure chamber. But how will a pressure chamber affect cavitation? Theoretically the bubbles in sap could be reformed by sap forced from living cells into the adjoining xylem. Also mechanical shock could induce cavitation in stressed, but as yet uncavitated, conduits.

The quantitative measurement of sap cavitation now normally proceeds in two stages. First, the fully hydrated organ is subjected to a net water loss program while cavitation is monitored electronically. Periodically the organ is removed and weighed: this gives a reference state to link relative water content to totals of acoustic signals. Finally, when cavitation has virtually ceased, the tissue is again restored to full hydration. In a second cycle of dehydration the tissue is periodically weighed and the balancing pressure for sap exudation is determined using a pressure chamber. To complete the procedure the organ dry weight is determined for the calculation of relative water contents (see Fig. 2 in Ref. 30). Using these and similar technique it is possible to elucidate the range of tensions in which cavitation is induced in different plant species. These indicate adaptations to meet ecological requirements (Table 7.2).

It is not easy to monitor cavitation in whole field-grown plants. Wind and other environmental changes produce false signals from leaves or twigs rubbing together. The wavelength of audioacoustic signals allows them to be transmitted long distances through plant vascular tissues (up to several meters). Such signals are difficult to distinguish from background noise; a problem compounded by the slow rate at which signals are generated by whole plants. Unlike excised organs, whole plants are able to martial diminishing water reserves very effectively by stomatal closure and protracted uptake from soils. Such constraints have tended to limit the application of the technique of audiodetection (0.2–2.0 kHz) to an acoustically insulated laboratory, unlike ultrasonic signals (50–1000 kHz).

Table 7.2. Cavitation and water potentials in a range of plants

Plant (genus)	Type of plant	"Normal range" of water potentials, $-$MPa	Approximate water potentials of cavitation, $-$MPa		
			Begins	Maximum	Ends
Plantain (*Plantago*)	Rosette herb	0–0.5	0.5	1.0	1.5
Banana (*Musa*)	Giant herb	0–0.2	0.4	0.8	1.2
Castor bean (*Ricinus*)	Shrubby herb	0.15–0.35	0.5	1.2	2.0
—(*Rhododendron*)	Shrub	0.2–1.2	1.7	2.2	3.0
Gum (*Eucalyptus*)	Tree (dicot)	0.1–1.5	1.8	2.7	4.0
Sycamore (*Acer*)	Tree "	0.5–1.5	1.5	1.9	3.0
Ash (*Fraxinus*)	Tree "	0.5–1.0	1.0	5.2	10.0
Wattle (*Acacia*)	Tree "	0.5–1.3	1.5	2.5	5.0
—(*Thuja*)	Tree—conifer	0.3–0.8	0.9	2.1	—

[a]Examples of different plant types and the range of water potentials in which they commonly live. Approximate water potentials are indicated for initiation of cavitation in well-watered plants, maximum incidence of cavitation, and termination of cavitation. There is considerable variation from plant to plant. (From various sources, some unpublished.)

Work in 1976 by Milburn and Walding (unpublished observations), using piezoelectric transducers devices showed that fragments of wood dried on the probe continued to produce high frequency signals when so small that the units were very unlikely to function as sap-conducting conduits in nature. This program was therefore curtailed.

7.4.3. Ultrasonic detection

Ultrasonic detectors were used first by Tyree and Dixon (25) to study cavitation in drying shoots of *Thuja* and other genera. Vast numbers of signals were detected, thousands in comparison with hundreds by the audio technique. As with earlier audio methods, the rate of production of acoustic signals began slowly with hydrated tissue, increased to a high value and then decreased.

The method has a number of advantages over the audio methods. The short wavelength detected is not transmitted for long distances through the tissues, allowing accurate location of signal generation. Audio signals (e.g, speech) do not interfere, and interference from wind or twigs and leaves rubbing together can be eliminated by removing such sources of noise a few centimeters' distance from the probe. Thus the method has been used successfully to detect cavitation in such crops as maize (26). It has also been used to monitor cavitation in samples of wood quite successfully (23,24). The large numbers of signals gives a less erratic trace than the audio method.

This work raised the question of the apparent difference between audio and ultrasonic methods in monitoring cavitation. Although a number of circumstantial observations *do* support the idea that ultrasonic methods monitor cavitation, there is not yet the same body of supporting data as for audio techniques. If the number of signals is very high can these represent cavitation in conducting xylem units? Recently Ritman and Milburn (16,17,18) tackled the issue using both audio and ultrasonic techniques to monitor the same experimental subject. The latter included vascular tissues of many kinds and also fern sporangia. They concluded that the ultrasonic technique did indeed detect cavitation but that the cavitation was occurring in fibers, which would normally be strengthening in function, as well as vessels and tracheids, which would normally conduct sap. Hence the system seems to be very useful for indicating cavitation as a whole. However, since cavitation in fibers is not so relevant to sap flow, this should be recognized in performing the analysis. The system has been reviewed by Tyree and Sperry (27).

7.5. Embolism: its relevance to survival

For trees the occurrence of embolisms must be so commonplace as to be considered quite normal. There is a continual tendency for wood to develop embolisms and this seems to be countered in most species by simply producing new water-filled conduits from the cambium. Some genera (e.g., *Vitis*, *Acer*) seem to have developed special methods to control the development of emboli, such as following drought or as a consequence of freezing (13,20). In most, however, the development of embolisms seems to permanently incapacitate the conduits. This development is made permanent through the development of tyloses, which are essentially balloonlike out-growths from adjoining living cells. After only a few hours, tyloses fill the conduits and through condensation processes they become mummified. Wood thus preserved is the familiar heartwood.

A simple test can be used to illustrate the degree of embolization in tree trunks. Pieces of wood are cut radically at different depths through the sapwood toward the center of a trunk and dropped into vials of water. The outermost samples sink quite soon, but the inner layers remain buoyant for a considerable time before they too become waterlogged and sink. This delay coincides with redissolution of the gas embolisms.

Apparently this natural onset of embolization can be augmented in a number of semicatastrophic ways. Obviously, water stress, in inducing cavitation, can precipitate embolization, the bubbles becoming more permanent through gas permeation and evolution. If the walls remain wet, the process is slowed by the need to dissolve and evolve. However, if the walls lose moisture to the extent that surface tension no longer blocks some pores, gas can then enter directly and rapidly via these "dry" pores and so invade the conduits and fibers rapidly. Embolisms are difficult to remove by resoaking because water supplied quickly reblocks the pores in the walls with new fluid films and thus entrapping the gas within the conduits. It is for this reason that vacuum infiltration of water is so much more effective in removing embolisms than mere soaking or pressurisation (12). Cavitation is reduced in species that have been subjected to water stress and can be presumed to be severely embolized (see Fig. 7.2).

It is critical for tree survival that embolization be contained, if not actually prevented. If plants were served by a single integral pipeline, a single puncture would totally disrupt the vascular system. Probably for this reason the length of many conduits (e.g., tracheids) in leaves is short, probably as a defense against attack by, for example, leaf-eating caterpillars. As explained in the next section, the invasion of gas is thus contained as a consequence of the wood anatomy.

In a similar manner any shoot, when cut in air, immediately undergoes a severe degree of embolization. Air is drawn into the cut shoot until it reaches the vessel endings, where there are pit membranes. Many genera, e.g., *Acacia*, seem to be adversely affected by this drastic treatment. Other genera seem relatively immune. Those engaged in propagation, floriculture, and horticulture are particularly concerned with minimizing such damage. It is indeed

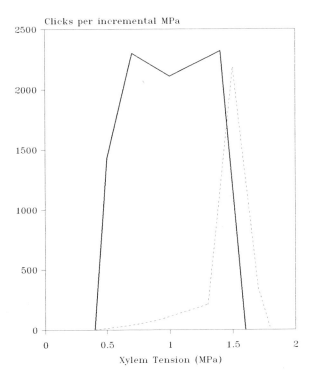

FIG. 7.2. Cavitation profile for leaves of a *Ricinus* plant over the range 0.2 MPa before (continous trace "a") and after (dotted trace "b") severe wilting to -1.0 MPa. After wilting the profile is reduced because only the more resistant conduits are water-filled; the remainder are embolized. This absence of cavitation has been dubbed a "cavitation scar."

remarkable that so many cut flowers and shoots are able to withstand cutting in air and yet survive on standing in water for many days. The reason for this is that the embolisms are restricted to conduits (principally vessels and tracheids) that are severed. A few adjoining the incision will remain unsevered and so remain free from embolization adjacent to the site of cutting. By entering these water-filled units, water is able to circumvent the embolisms and providing uptake keeps pace with transpiration the shoot continues to live. Over a period of time surface-tension forces tend to drive embolisms into solution so that vascular disruption decreases. This effect seems entirely physical because it can even take place at low temperatures (1°C; see Ref. 7).

7.6. Anatomic and ultrastructural considerations

Apparently low wide conduits offer great advantages in having a frictional low drag on the flow of xylem sap. However, if these are lost, severe disruption must result. Tracheids and fibers, on the other hand, are shorter and probably much less liable to disrupt. If they become embolized, only a small part of the total conducting system is lost. Hence it seems that plants operate an "insurance policy" through having relatively secure conduction via tracheids and fibers. They also gamble for high stakes in having vessels that are more efficient but easy to disrupt and therefore vulnerable. The different designs, proportions, and population sizes of conduits all reflect the ability of a plant to protect its pipeline, such as by stomatal function, or the efficiency of root uptake and so suit different species to their ecological situations.

7.7. References

1. M. Berthelot, "Sur quelques phénomenenes de dilatation forcee des liquids," *Am. Chim. Phys. 3e Ser.*, **30**, 232 (1850).
2. H.R. Bode, "Beiträge. zur Dynamik der Wasserbewegungen in der Gefasspflanzen," *Jahrb. Wiss. Bot.*, **62**, 92–127 (1923).
3. D.S. Crombie, M.F. Hipkins, and J.A. Milburn, "Gas penetration of pit membranes in the xylem of *Rhododendron* as the cause of acoustically detectable sap cavitation," *Aust. J. Plant Physiol.*, **12**, 445–453 (1985).
4. H. Dickson and V.H. Blackman, "The absorption of gas bubbles present in xylem vessels," *Ann. Bot. (London) New Series*, **2**, 293–299 (1938).
5. H.H. Dixon and J. Joly, "On the ascent of sap," (abstract) *Proc. Roy. Soc. London*, **57**, 3 (1894).
6. H.H. Dixon, *Transpiration and the Ascent of Sap in Plants*, Macmillan, London, 1914.
7. J.A. Milburn, "The conduction of sap I. Water conduction and cavitation in water stressed leaves," *Planta (Berl.)*, **69**, 43–52 (1966).
8. J.A. Milburn and R.P.C. Johnson, "The conduction of sap. II. Detection of

vibrations produced by sap cavitation in *Ricinus* xylem," *Planta (Berl.)*, **69**, 43–52 (1966).

9. J.A. Milburn, "Cavitation and osmotic potentials of *Sordaria* ascospores," *New Phytol.*, **69**, 133–141 (1970).

10. J.A. Milburn, "Cavitation in *Ricinus* by acoustic detection: induction in excised leaves by various factors," *Planta (Berl.)*, **110**, 253–265 (1973a).

11. J.A. Milburn, "Cavitation studies on whole *Ricinus* plants by acoustic detection," *Planta (Berl.)*, **112**, 333–342 (1973b).

12. J.A. Milburn and M.E. McLaughlin, "Studies of cavitation in isolated vascular bundles and whole leaves of *Plantago major* L." *New Phytol.*, **73**, 861–871 (1974).

13. J.A. Milburn, "*Water Flow in Plants*," Longman Group, London–New York, 1979.

14. W.F. Pickard, "The ascent of sap in plants," *Progr. Biophys. Mol. Biol.*, **37**, 181–229 (1981).

15. G.J. Pierce, "The state of water in ducts and tracheids," *Am. J. Bot.*, **4**, 623–628 (1936).

16. K.T. Ritman and J.A. Milburn, "Acoustic emissions from plants: ultrasonic and audible compared," *J. Exp. Bot.*, **39**, 1237–1248 (1988).

17. K.T. Ritman and J. A. Milburn, "The acoustic detection of cavitation in fern sporangia." *J. Exp. Bot.*, **41**, 1157–1160 (1990).

18. K.T. Ritman and J.A. Milburn, "Monitoring of ultrasonic and audible emissions from plants with and without vessels," *J. Exp. Bot.*, **42**, 123–130 (1991).

19. P.F. Scholander, H.T. Hammel, E.D. Bradstreet and E.A. Hemmingsen, "Sap pressures in vascular plants," *Science*, **148**, 339–346 (1965).

20. J.S. Sperry, N.M. Holbrook, M.H. Zimmermann and M.T. Tyree. "Spring filling of xylem vessels in wild grapevine," *Plant Physiol.*, **83**, 414–417 (1987).

21. J.S. Sperry and M.T. Tyree, "Mechanism of water stress-induced xylem embolism," *Plant Physiol.*, **88**, 581–587 (1988).

22. J.S. Sperry, J.R. Donnelly and M.T. Tyree, "A method for measuring hydraulic conductivity and embolism in xylem," *Plant, Cell Environ.*, **11**, 35–40 (1988).

23. J.S. Sperry, J.R. Donnelly and M.T. Tyree, "Seasonal occurrence of xylem embolism in sugar maple (*Acer saccharum*)," *Am. J. Bot.*, **75**, 1212–1218 (1988).

24. J.S. Sperry, M.T. Tyree and J.R. Donnelly, "Vulnerability of xylem to embolism in a mangrove vs. an inland species of rhizophoraceae," *Physiol. Plant.*, **74**, 276–283 (1988c).

25. M.T. Tyree and M.A. Dixon, "Cavitation events in *Thuja occidentalis* L.? Ultrasonic acoustic emissions from the sapwood can be measured," *Plant Physiol.*, **72**, 1094–1099 (1983).

26. M.T. Tyree, E.L. Fiscus, S.D. Wullschleger and M.A. Dixon, "Detection of xylem cavitation in corn under field conditions," *Plant Physiol.*, **82**, 597–599 (1986).

27. M.T. Tyree and T.S. Sperry, "Vulnerability of xylem to cavitation and embolism," *Ann. Rev. Plant Phys.*, **40**, 19–38 (1989).

28. M.H. Zimmermann, "The effect of low temperature on the ascent of sap in trees," *Plant Physiol.*, **39**, 568–572 (1964).

29. M.H. Zimmermann, "Hydraulic architecture of some diffuse-porous trees," *Can. J. Bot.*, **56,** 2286–2295 (1978).

30. M.H. Zimmermann and J.A. Milburn, "Transport and storage of water," in O.L. Lare, P.S. Nobel, C.B. Osmond, and H. Ziegler, eds., *Physiological Plant Ecology,* II. *Encyclopedia of Plant Physiology New Series*, Vol. 12B, Springer-Verlag, Berlin–New York, 1982, pp. 135–151.

31. M.H. Zimmerman. *Xylem Structure and the Ascent of Sap.* Springer Verlag, Berlin (1983).

8 Wood Formation in Deciduous Hardwood Trees

RONI ALONI

Department of Botany, Tel Aviv University, Tel Aviv 69978, Israel

Contents

8.1. Introduction

This chapter provides an overview of the mechanisms that control wood formation in trees, especially in temperate deciduous hardwoods. Special attention is paid to explain a major topic in xylogenesis, namely, the control of vessel size within the whole tree as affected by internal and external factors. The vessel diameter has a very important functional significance in water conduction. In ideal capillaries, conductivity is proportional to the fourth power of the radius, or the diameter (1), which means that at a given pressure gradient the relative volumes of water flowing through capillaries, or vessels, of diameters 1, 2, 4, and 5 are 1, 16, 256, and 625, respectively. A typical cross section of a ring-porous wood (Fig. 8.1) demonstrates that most of the

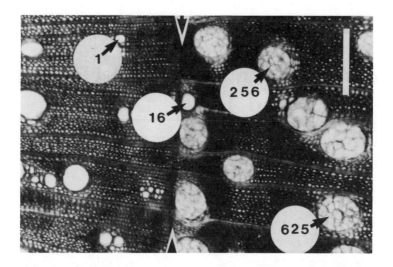

FIG. 8.1. Photomicrograph of a transverse section of a ring-porous wood taken at the border (opposite arrows) region between the annual xylem rings of a 2-year-old stem of *Robinia pseudacacia* harvested in winter. The latewood of the first formed annual xylem ring (left) is characterized by narrow vessels, whereas the earlywood of the annual ring formed in the second year (right) has typical wide vessels. The numbers marked near the vessels indicated by arrows show the relative volumes of water that would have flown through these four vessels. The photomicrograph also demonstrates that the large and efficient earlywood vessels of a ring-porous tree (values: 256, 625) are not safe since they function during only one growing season and are embolized at the end of the season and are plugged with tyloses. In contrast, the narrow vessels (values: 1, 16), which are not efficient in water conduction, are safe vessels and remain conductive for 2 to several years (bar = 250 μm).

water would have flown through the wide earlywood vessels, whereas the narrow latewood vessels would be inefficient.

This chapter provides a summary of the role of growth regulators in xylogenesis as a preamble to a discussion of the control of vessel and fiber differentiation in hardwood trees. For additional information regarding the hormonal control of vascular differentiation, the reader is directed to earlier reviews (2–5) and to a book on vascular differentiation and plant growth regulators (6).

This chapter focuses on three major aspects of wood formation: the endogenous control of vessel size and density along the axis of a tree, vascular adaptation and the role of external growth conditions on xylogenesis, and the control of ring-porous versus diffuse-porous wood formation in temperate deciduous hardwood trees. In Section 8.5, I put forward a new hypothesis regarding the growth regulator control of wide earlywood vessel formation in ring-porous trees and the control of narrow vessels and fibers in the latewood.

Finally, the effect of gall-forming aphids on wood differentiation in tree branches is discussed, in the hope that the study of this phenomenon might reveal a novel control mechanism for wood formation.

8.2. Hormonal aspects of xylogenesis

8.2.1. Role of young leaves and auxin in vessel differentiation

Developing buds and young, growing leaves induce vessel differentiation that extends from the developing leaves toward the root tips. The auxin indole-3-acetic acid (IAA), produced mainly by the young and fast-growing leaves, is the major stimulus and limiting factor that induces and controls vessel differentiation (2,4,5,7,9). The basipetal polar movement of auxin from the young leaves toward the roots through parenchyma cells, procambium, cambium, and differentiating wood elements results in the formation of xylem tissue along the flow of auxin. This continuous flow of auxin ensures a continuous pattern of vessels or tracheids that connects the leaves with the roots (2,5). When the plant axis is wounded, the basipetal flow of auxin is interrupted, resulting in the diffusion of auxin in a horizontal direction. Such diffusion of auxin induces cell to cell transport of auxin along a new horizontal axis. This change in auxin polarity results in the horizontally oriented differentiation of new vessels and fibers (2). Above a transverse wound, auxin can be forced to move in circular patterns, which result in the differentiation of tracheids or vessels in the form of closed rings (8). Closed circular vessels and associated narrow vessels occur normally in branch junctions of trees, where the size and frequence of the circular vessels increases continuously with stem width and age (64). We propose that these nonfunctional circular vessels decrease water conductivity through the branch junction and increase the hydraulic segmentation of a lateral branch from the main stem.

8.2.2. Role of roots and cytokinin in vessel and fiber formation

Roots do not induce wood formation nor must they be present in order to obtain xylem in stem tissues. However, the root apices are sources of inductive stimuli that promote xylem development, with cytokinin as the major stimulus from the root. Most of our knowledge concerning the role of cytokinin in xylem differentiation comes from tissue culture studies (6). Very little knowledge about the role of cytokinin in wood formation has been gained from studies performed with intact plants.

Cytokinin was a controlling factor in vessel regeneration around a wound in an *in vivo* system (*Coleus* internodes) in which the endogenous cytokinin level was minimized (10). At appropriate concentrations, zeatin, kinetin, and 6-benzylamino-purine (BAP) induced a significant increase in vessel regeneration. This study also showed an increase in cambium responsiveness along the stem from leaves to roots. We suggested that such a basipetal increase in cambium sensitivity in a large tree would enable the cambial initials at the base of the trunk and at the roots to respond to basipetally decreasing supply of inductive stimuli originating in the leaves (10).

Cytokinin is required during the early stages of xylem fiber differentiation in intact young plants of *Helianthus* (11). Later stages of fiber maturation can occur in the absence of cytokinin (12). This regulator probably brings the meristematic initials and their derivative cells to an advanced stage of differentiation, in which the cells show a stronger response to auxin and gibberellin stimulation.

8.2.3. Role of mature leaves and gibberellin in fiber differentiation

For a long time, it was recognized that gibberellin promotes fiber formation. Spraying the leaves of intact plants with gibberellin increased the number of fibers in jute (13), increased the length of fibers in hemp (14), and increased the number and size of fibers in other genera (15,16).

Mature leaves stimulate cambial activity and fiber differentiation (17,18). The effect of mature leaves on secondary xylem fiber differentiation can be replaced by an exogenous application of a high level of gibberellin combined with a low level of auxin. A combination of both growth regulators induces the xylem formation composed almost entirely of secondary fibers (18). In *Populus*, for example, the application of gibberellin effects the elongation of xylem fibers only in the presence of auxin (19).

Excision experiments have shown that the stimuli for fiber differentiation originating in mature (20,21) as well as young leaves (21,22), move in a polar manner along the plant axis, inducing fibers along their pathway. The role of the leaves in the differentiation of phloem fibers can be replaced by an exogenous application of gibberellin plus auxin (5,23). When various combinations of both growth regulators were applied to decapitated and excised stems of *Coleus*, high concentrations of auxin stimulated the rapid differentiation of relatively small fibers with thick secondary walls, whereas high levels of gibberellin produced long fibers with thin walls (23,65).

8.2.4. Effect of stress and ethylene on xylogenesis

Plant tissues synthesize ethylene in response to stress conditions such as flooding, drought, or bending of shoots. These stress conditions regulate cambial activity and modify the quality and quantity of wood formation in trees (6,24).

The application of ethrel (2-chloroethylphosphonic acid), an ethylene-releasing compound, to the stems of trees augmented tracheid production in *Pinus halepensis* (25) and increased the number of vessels while reducing their diameters in *Ulmus americana* (26). In both species, ethrel substantially increased the amount of ray tissue in the treated region and retarded fiber differentiation, which resulted in the observation of immature fibers.

When *Eucalyptus gomphocephala* seedlings are placed horizontally, they produce higher amounts of ethylene in their upper halves, where reaction wood (tension wood) is induced (27). This tension wood, which is formed by hardwood trees in the upper side of a bent branch, is induced by ethylene plus auxin. This hormonal combination induces numerous narrow vessels in the tension wood, while few wider vessels differentiate in the lower side of the branch (R. Aloni, unpublished observations). Similarly, in a flooded stem, the xylem that is induced below the water level by a combination of ethylene plus auxin is locally characterized by numerous narrow vessels; the vessels formed above the water level are much wider (T. Plotkin and R. Aloni, unpublished observations).

8.3. Control of vessel size and density along the tree axis

Along the axis of a tree from the leaves to the roots, there is a continual increase in the size of individual wood elements. This general increase is observed in both tracheid length and diameter, as one proceeds from branches to trunk and down into the roots of *Sequoia sempervirens* trees (28). A similar increase in tracheid size can also be observed in a transverse section of a stem or a branch of a tree. Proceeding outward from the inner growth ring through a number of annual growth rings, tracheid size increases until a constant size is usually attained. However, in the oldest stems of *Pinus longaeva*, tracheid length has steadily increased over the last 2200 years, with no signs of leveling off (29).

In hardwoods, similar polar pattern of gradual increase is found in vessel diameter and length from twigs, down along the shoot and extending into the roots of *Acer rubrum* trees (30). This basipetal increase in vessel diameter is associated with a decrease in vessel density, i.e., the number of vessels per unit of transverse-sectional area. Thus, vessel density is greater in branches where the vessels are narrow than it is in the trunk and roots where they are wider. A similar pattern of basipetal increase in element length was reported for fibers in *Fraxinus excelsior* trees (31).

In the first hypothesis regarding the control of vascular element size it was proposed that the diameter of tracheids (32) as well as of vessels (19) is "positively" regulated by auxin level. However, this concept of a positive correlation between auxin level and tracheid (32) or vessel (19) diameter is contrary to what one would expect from the overall pattern of vascular element size along the axis of the tree. The smallest vascular elements differentiate near the leaves, where the highest auxin levels are expected, while the largest elements are formed in the roots, at the greatest distance from the auxin sources. To resolve this contradiction and to explain both the general increase in conduit size and the decrease in vessel density that occurs from leaves to roots, Aloni and Zimmermann (33) have proposed the following "six-point" hypothesis:

1. Basipetal polar flow of auxin establishes a gradient of decreasing auxin concentration from leaves to roots.

2. Local structural or physiological obstruction of auxin flow results in a local increase in auxin concentration.

3. The distance from the source of auxin to the differentiating cells controls the amount of auxin flowing through the differentiating cells at any given time, thus determining the cells' position in the gradient.

4. The rate of conduit differentiation is positively correlated with the amount of auxin that the differentiating cells receive; consequently, the duration of the differentiation process increases from leaves to roots.

5. The final size of a conduit is determined by the rate of cell differentiation. Because cell expansion ceases after the secondary wall is deposited, rapid differentiation results in narrow vascular elements, while slow differentiation permits more cell expansion before secondary wall deposition and therefore results in wide vascular elements. Hence, decreasing auxin concentrations from leaves to roots lead to an increase in conduit size in this direction.

6. Conduit density is controlled by, and positively correlated with, auxin concentration; consequently, vessel density decreases from leaves to roots.

Experimental evidence that supports this six-point hypothesis (33) has recently been summarized (5,6). The rates of vessel differentiation (Fig. 8.2)

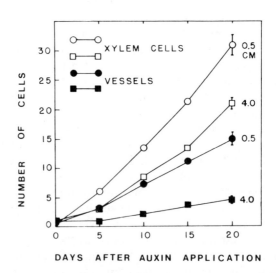

DAYS AFTER AUXIN APPLICATION

FIG. 8.2. Effect of distance (0.5 to 4.0 cm shown) from 0.1% naphthaleneacetic acid (NAA) application site on the rate of formation of secondary vessels (solid circles and squares) and total number of secondary xylem cells (open circles and squares) along a radius in the same internode of *Phaseolus vulgaris*. Each point represents the average of ten measurements. Vertical bars indicate standard errors. (Reproduced with permission from Ref. 33.)

and tracheid formation (34) are constant at any given distance from the auxin source. Application of auxin to decapitated stems induces the differentiation of numerous narrow vessels immediately below the site of application (Fig. 8.3) and a progressive decrease in the number of vascular elements and increase in their diameter with increasing distance from the auxin source toward the roots (5,6,33).

8.4. Adaptation of the xylem to the tree's environment

Comparative anatomic studies reveal similarities in the structure of the wood in plants grown in extreme habits versus ones grown in mesomorphic environments (35). The safer conduit (with respect to freezing and gas-induced cavitation or embolism) in the xylem of trees is the tracheid. Therefore, conifers, which are dependent on tracheids for water transport, are very effective competitors in cold and dry habitats.

The vessel system in hardwood trees is well adapted to their environment. In extreme habitats, dwarf trees develop and their xylem shows high density of narrow vessels. Such vascular systems, which are typical of extreme habitats, are safe adaptive mechanisms against drought and freezing. Conversely,

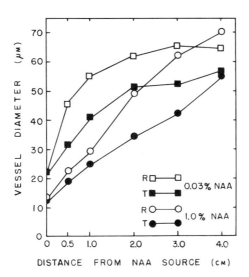

FIG. 8.3. Effect of low (0.03% NAA, squares) and high (1.0% NAA, circles) auxin concentrations on the radial (R) and tangential (T) diameters of late-formed vessels produced along decapitated internodes of *Phaseolus vulgaris*. Both concentrations induced a substantial gradient of increasing vessel diameter with increasing distance from the site of application. The high concentration yielded the narrowest vessels immediately below the site of application. (Reproduced with permission from Ref. 33.)

well-developed forest trees grown in comfortable conditions have wide vessels (1,35,36).

Aloni (5) suggested that the environment influences the size of the vessels through its control of the development, height, and shape of the tree. The height and extent of branching determine levels of the polar flow of auxin and probably other growth regulators along the tree. The following vascular adaptation hypothesis (5) explains the ecological control of the size and frequency of vessels and fibers in hardwood trees:

1. Limiting conditions in the environment curtail the development of the tree and result in small and suppressed shoots, whereas optimal conditions allow the tree to reach its maximum potential size.

2. The duration of the growth period determines the total development of the tree. In extreme and limiting habitats, the active growth period is relatively short and allows the development of only small trees. In stable and moderate conditions, growth activity is allowed throughout the year, resulting in large and well-developed trees.

3. The height of the tree and the extent of its branching determines gradients of auxin along the axis of the tree. Increase in tree height and decrease in the extent of branching enhance the gradients of auxin from the young leaves (which are the sources of auxin) to the lower parts of the trunk. In small trees typical of both dry and cold habitats, as well as locations where there is insufficient soil for root growth, the distances from the young leaves to the roots are very short and no substantial gradient of auxin can be formed. Therefore, auxin levels are relatively high along these small trees and result in the differentiation of numerous very narrow vessels in the greatest densities, as predicted by the six-point hypothesis (33). These plants also have relatively small fibers with thick secondary walls, induced by the high auxin levels (23). On the other hand, in large trees, the very long distances from young leaves to the roots allows a substantial decrease in auxin levels in the lower parts of the stem and in the roots, resulting in the differentiation of very wide vessels in lower densities at these locations. The decrease in auxin level in the basal parts of a large tree also results in the formation of large fibers with relatively thin secondary walls.

Although there is some experimental evidence that supports the adaptation hypothesis (5,6), it should be tested further in various experimental systems and under different growth conditions.

8.5. Regulation of xylem differentiation in temperate deciduous hardwoods

8.5.1. The problem of earlywood vessel formation

Although Hartig (37) and Russow (38) observed long ago that wide vessels form in the trunk of a *Quercus* tree at a very early stage of bud development, the mechanisms controlling vessel differentiation in earlywood are still not clearly understood. There is a vast literature on cambial reactivation in the spring and on earlywood vessel differentiation (e.g., see Refs. 3, 39–48 and the literature cited therein). Many correlative phenomena were recognized in these studies. In broad-leafed trees, the size differences of the vessels, or pores, in the early- and latewoods are quite marked and two categories of deciduous trees are determined: diffuse-porous species and ring-porous species (Fig. 8.4).

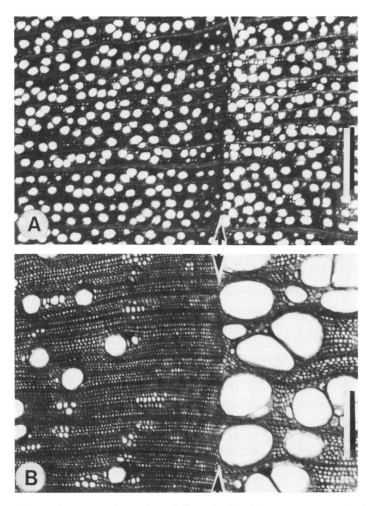

FIG. 8.4. Size and pattern of vessels and fibers in the diffuse-porous wood of a *Pyrus malus* tree (A), compared with the ring-porous wood of a *Melia azedarach* tree (B). Both photomicrographs are oriented in the same direction (the earlywood of the last formed annual xylem ring is on the right) and are in the same magnification (bar = 250 μm). The border lines between the annual xylem rings are marked by arrows.

Priestley and Scott (41) made a clear distinction between the pattern of cambial reactivation in the spring in diffuse-porous and ring-porous angiosperms. They found that in the diffuse-porous group the spread of cambial reactivation is a relatively slow process, commencing at the base of swelling buds and proceeding gradually downward toward the base of the tree. In other words, it takes several weeks for the "wave" of cambial activity to extend from the twigs of a large tree to the base of its trunk. In contrast, the reactivation of the cambium in ring-porous species is so rapid throughout the entire tree that it occurs almost simultaneously in the branches and the trunk. This is why the bark of ring-porous trees may slip a few days before any bud swelling can be observed in the spring. During the growing season, in diffuse-porous species, there is a close correlation between cambial activity and extension growth. In ring-porous trees, however, extension growth frequently stops early in the season while cambial activity continues for a long period (42,44). Generally, the diffuse-porous species seem to possess a greater growth intensity than do the ring-porous ones (39). Forest trees in which leaf emergence consistently occurs in early spring are diffuse-porous species, while ring-porous species are late-leafing trees (49). Furthermore, there is a report on a diffuse-porous tree (*Acer pseudoplatanus*) in which the buds of the lower branch whorls tend to open earlier than those of the upper crown (47).

In ring-porous species, the first vessels are very wide and are formed at, or just prior to, the breaking of buds. Conversely, in diffuse-porous trees the earlywood vessels are formed much later and appear in the trunk when the leaves are one-fourth to fully expanded (39). Furthermore, in a ring-porous species the initial wide vessels develop almost simultaneously all along the main stem (48), whereas in a diffuse-porous tree they are restricted to the base of the buds, appearing first in the lower branches and later in the upper ones (47). The wide earlywood vessels of ring-porous species are also very long and extend for the length of the stem itself (50,51), whereas the earlywood vessels of the diffuse-porous species are narrow and much shorter, usually less than 1 m (51).

When young trees are completely debudded in later winter, before any bud activity can be observed, new earlywood vessels differentiate in ring-porous trees but are entirely absent in diffuse-porous species (43,52). Young growing leaves are known to produce auxin that moves basipetally and induces cambial divisions and the differentiation of vessels along its pathway (5,9,53). Therefore, it was difficult to explain the cambial reactivation and vessel formation in both normal and debudded ring-porous trees. Wareing (43,44) suggested that in the cambium of ring-porous trees there is a high initial reserve of an auxin precursor that enables early cambium reactivation and rapid spread of earlywood vessel formation at an early stage of bud development. He also suggested that the very wide earlywood vessels of ring-porous species are induced by a high supply of auxin in the spring (43,44). Presumably, in ring-porous species this reserve of auxin precursor is accumulated during the previous season, whereas in diffuse-porous species little or no such reserve is formed. Digby and Wareing (54) found an auxin precursor in a ring-porous tree (*Ulmus glabora*) prior to and during bud swelling, but were unable to detect either an auxin precursor, or auxin activity in a diffuse-porous tree (*Populus trichocarpa*) prior to bud swelling. However, results contradicting Wareing's hypothesis (43,44) were obtained in experiments with two ring-porous species: *Robina pseudacacia* and *Melia azedarach* (p. 189 in Ref. 5). In these experiments, the trees were debudded in early spring about 1 month before bud break. Application of moderate or high auxin concentrations to the terminal bud area inhibited the formation of wide vessels and yielded narrow vessels in the earlywood. These contradicting results point out a need for a new general hypothesis to account for the fundamental differences in wood formation between ring-porous and diffuse-porous species.

8.5.2. Wood formation control in ring-porous vs. diffuse-porous species: The limited-growth hypothesis

It is postulated here that in the course of the evolution of temperate deciduous hardwood trees, there have undoubtedly been continuous selective pressures in limiting environments to shorten the duration of the growing season and to limit vegetative growth. These selective environmental pressures finally resulted in the development of the specialized ring-porous wood that maximized the efficiency of water conduction. In ring-porous trees, the highly efficient, very wide and long vessels are formed before most of the leaves develop, providing the leaves an advantage in water supply compared to the leaves of diffuse-porous trees. During the growing season the mature leaves of a ring-porous tree stimulate formation of a wood that consists mostly of well-developed fibers with narrow, short vessels. Conversely, in the original group, namely, the less specialized diffuse-porous trees, there is a less efficient vascular system comprised of numerous narrow vessels, usually with softer fibers that differentiate in a uniform pattern throughout the entire growing season.

It is further postulated that the natural selection for ring-porous wood has led to a decrease in the intensity of vegetative growth, accompanied by reduced levels of growth regulators. The latter was followed by an increase in the sensitivity of the cambium to a relatively low level of internal stimulation. These internal changes created the special conditions that enabled the differentiation of very wide earlywood vessels during a limited period of time in the spring, in the ring-porous trees. On the basis of the foregoing, I propose the following limited growth hypothesis:

1. The growth of diffuse-porous trees developing under favourable conditions is vigorous. Comfortable environments promote active root systems and consequently high cytokinin production. The latter may stimulate early bud break in spring in an acropetal direction, that is, first in the lower branches

at the base of the tree and later in the upper branches. An actively growing root system also favors the development of many lateral branches. In contrast, in ring-porous species that had been exposed in the course of evolution to limiting pressures, bud break is delayed and the active growing season is shorter. These trees exhibit a less intensive vegetative growth as their root systems produce relatively low levels of cytokinin for stem growth and development. Consequently, ring-porous trees often show some basipetal pattern of bud break and somewhat stronger apical dominance, which leads to the production of fewer lateral branches and to retardation of these branches at an early stage when they emerge. In young, short trees, the bud break will be faster than in old or large trees of the same species, as the distances are shorter between the root apices and the buds in the former. In old trees, however, branches near the roots may have early bud break as a result of high local cytokinin levels.

2. The vigorous growth of diffuse-porous species is associated with high hormone levels,whereas in ring-porous trees, the lesser growth intensity is accompanied by low levels of growth regulators.

3. Diffuse-porous trees form young and actively growing leaves throughout most of the growing season. They therefore show a continuous and extensive growth of the annual shoot. Their young : mature leaves ratios are relatively high throughout the growing season. Conversely, in ring-porous trees most of the young leaves are produced during a relatively limited period (early in the growing season). Consequently, in the summer their young : mature leaf ratios are low and their extension growth is of short duration.

4. The young : mature leaf ratios during the growing season lead to corresponding auxin : gibberellin ratios. In diffuse-porous species high auxin : gibberellin ratios are expected through most of the growing season, while low auxin : gibberellin ratios are expected in the summer in the ring-porous species.

5. In the ring-porous species, the cambium has become highly sensitive owing to decreased levels of hormonal stimulation. On the other hand, in diffuse-porous trees the cambium has remained less sensitive and therefore requires high levels of stimulation for its operation.

6. In diffuse-porous trees, earlywood vessels differentiate after bud break in response to the highly supply of auxin produced by the young growing leaves. Since the cambium of these trees is not sensitive and needs high stimulation levels for vessel differentiation, their very first earlywood vessels are restricted to the bases of the buds, where the highest auxin levels occur. On the other hand, in ring-porous species, enhanced cambium sensitivity to very low auxin levels creates the special conditions needed for the differentiation of very wide vessels, which start to expand along the stem before and during bud break. According to the six-point hypothesis (33), low auxin supply at the very early stages of bud break induces slow differentiation, which permits more cell expansion before secondary wall deposition and leading to

the formation of wide and long vessels. As explained in the first point of the present hypothesis, a decrease in the number of lateral branches in ring-porous species enhances the auxin gradients from the swelling buds toward the root, which means that very low auxin levels are expected in the basal parts of the tree where earlywood vessels of the widest diameter occur.

7. In those diffuse-porous species that show an acropetal pattern of bud break, the earlywood vessel formation appears first in the lower branches and later in the upper ones. Conversely, in ring-porous trees that display a basipetal pattern of bud development, the first lignified vessels appear immediately below the apical bud, which is the first one to show leaf emergence.

8. During the growing season, in diffuse porous species, there are relatively high young : mature leaf ratios and consequently high auxin : gibberellin ratios. This hormonal stimulation induces numerous narrow vessels with fibers throughout most of the growing season in diffuse-porous trees. Only toward the end of the growing season, when the last formed leaves become mature, is there a decrease in auxin level. At this stage the effect of gibberellin predominates leading to the production of long fibers together with vessels of smaller diameter (Fig. 8.5). On the other hand, in ring-porous trees, after the wide earlywood vessels are formed, the low young : mature leaf ratio and consequently the low auxin : gibberellin ratio results in the differentiation of numerous well-developed fibers together with narrow, short vessels during most of the growing season.

The limited-growth hypothesis explains the pattern of divergence of ring-porous trees from the group of origin, namely, diffuse-porous trees. Obviously, intermediate patterns of tree development result in semi-ring-porous

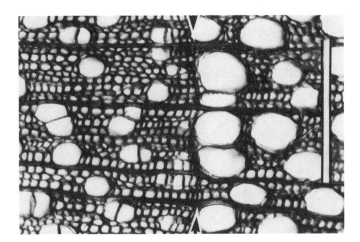

FIG. 8.5. A magnified view of vessels and fibers in the latewood (left) and earlywood (right) of a diffuse-porous tree (*Populus canadensis*). Note that in the latewood there is a decrease in vessel diameter and an increase in the fiber number. The borderline between the annual rings is marked with arrows (bar = 250 μm).

types of wood. It is hoped that the limited growth hypothesis will provide a better understanding of how wood porosity can be influenced or even altered by experimentally induced environmental changes.

8.5.3. Supporting evidence for the limited growth hypothesis

Observations and experiments made on *Populus euphartica* (55,56) and *Adesmia horrida* (57) support the limited-growth hypothesis. In both these species, conditions that limit the duration of growth and the intensity of stem development favor the formation of a ring-porous type of wood. *Populus euphartica* is a diffuse-porous tree that grows in Israel near riverbanks. Under favorable conditions the tree exhibits vigorous shoot growth, which is associated with wide annual xylem rings of diffuse-porous wood. However, in limiting environments such as dry sites, shoot elongation is restricted and is associated

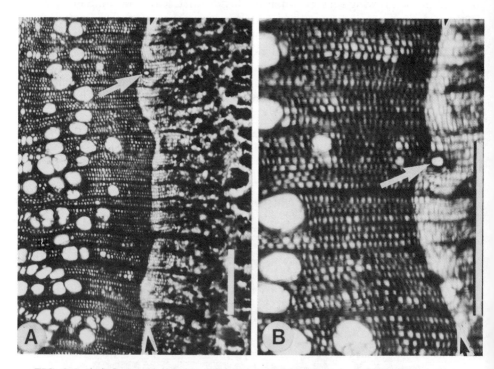

FIG. 8.6. (A) Cross section through a control, debudded stem of the ring-porous tree *Melia azedarach* taken 50 mm below the location of the apical bud. The photomicrograph shows a single, very narrow earlywood vessel (white arrow) that differentiated after debudding. This very narrow vessel was probably induced by a very limited amount of auxin produced by the stem tissues. This stem served as a control of the experiment presented in Fig. 8.7. (B) The same vessel (white arrow) is also shown in higher magnification. The vascular cambium is marked by the black arrows (bar = 250 μm).

with narrow annual rings and ring-porous wood (55). Similarly, when a highly concentrated salt (NaCl) solution was experimentally applied to the roots of *P. euphartica*, the duration of stem growth was reduced and narrow annual rings with a ring-porous type of wood were formed. In control trees, however, which were not exposed to the salt stress, diffuse-porous wood was formed (56).

The type of wood porosity in *Adesmia horrida* trees grown on the slopes of the Sierra de Uspallata in Argentina is determined by rainfall values. In dry habitats where tree growth is limited, a ring-porous wood differentiates, while in the more humid locations where more vigorous shoot development is possible, a semi-ring-porous wood is found (57).

In the central hardwoods region of the eastern deciduous forest of West Virginia, ring-porous species dominate the xeric sites, while diffuse-porous trees occupy the hidric environments (58). Thus, the fast growing diffuse-porous trees are more successful in competition for the relatively high-moisture habitats and the ring-porous ones are adapted to the limiting locations.

Experiments by the present author on the effect of auxin levels on early-wood vessel diameter in ring-porous trees (p. 189 in Ref. 5) also support the limited growth hypothesis, since they have shown that the wide earlywood vessels in ring-porous species are induced by very low auxin levels. For example, when the stems of the ring-porous tree *Melia azedarach* are debudded about a month prior to bud break, a few isolated very narrow vessels differentiate in their stems (Fig. 8.6). These isolated vessels appear somewhat wider in the base of the stem, thus confirming Wareing's early observations (50). Buds are necessary for the differentiation of many wide earlywood vessels as can be seen in the intact untreated stems (Fig. 8.7A). When a very low auxin level (0.003% NAA) replaced the terminal bud, after all the buds were removed from the ring-porous tree, wide earlywood vessels were induced (Fig. 8.7B). Increasing the auxin supply (0.01% NAA) resulted in a moderate decrease in vessel size (Fig. 8.7C), while a further auxin boost (0.1% NAA) yielded a marked diminution in vessel diameter (Fig. 8.7D). Clearly, the moderate or relatively high levels of auxin when applied to ring-porous trees at the time of bud break are seen to limit the size of the earlywood vessels and result in a diffuse-porous type of wood.

These findings, in sum, point to the fact that in ring-porous trees, the differentiation of wide earlywood vessels depends on a low auxin supply. The application of moderate or high levels of auxin at the time of bud break accelerates vessel differentiation, therefore resulting in narrow vessels, as predicted by the six-point hypothesis (33). In intact ring-porous trees the first formed wide earlywood vessels are induced by exposure to the very low supply of auxin, produced by the buds at the incipient stages of their development. This is possible only because the cambium has become very sensitive. This experimental evidence thus contradicts the long-held view (43) that the widest earlywood vessels in a ring-porous tree are induced by a high initial supply of auxin.

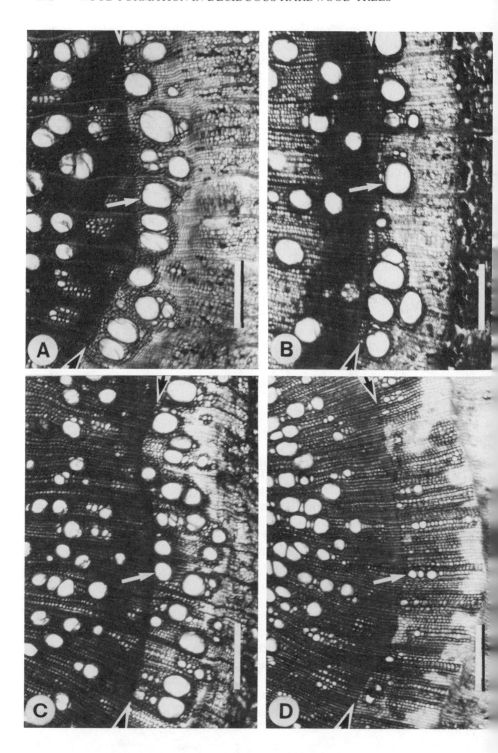

←**FIG. 8.7.** The effect of auxin (NAA) concentration on earlywood vessel differentiation is shown in transverse sections through stems of the ring-porous tree *Melia azedarach*. All photomicrographs were taken from the same experiment, run in Tel Aviv from February 15 to March 15, 1986, and are presented in the same orientation and magnification, (bar = 250 μm). All the sections were taken 50 mm below the apical bud, which was left intact (A) or was replaced by a range of auxin concentrations: 0.003% NAA (B), 0.01% NAA (C), or 0.1% NAA (D). The auxin was applied in the form of a lanolin paste, which was renewed every 3 days. The photomicrographs show a substantial decrease in the diameter of the earlywood vessels (white arrows) with increasing auxin concentration (B, C, D). The low auxin concentration induced wide vessels (B). The two higher auxin concentrations induced many more xylem cells along a radius with narrower vessels (C, D). The highest auxin concentration tested (0.1% NAA) resulted in very narrow earlywood vessels (D). The borderline between the latewood of 1985 (left) and the new earlywood of 1986 (right) is marked with black arrows. The experiment was repeated three times (in 1984, 1985, and 1986) with 5–10 stems per treatment.

8.6. Effect of gall-forming aphids on xylogenesis

The study of xylem differentiation, such as that induced by aphids below a gall is of particular interest to those seeking to improve wood production and quality because such studies may possibly reveal yet unknown control mechanism. Aloni et al. (60) discovered that gall-forming aphids induce both qualitative and quantitative changes in xylem differentiation within the branch below the gall. A gall (Fig. 8.8), induced by aphids, serves as a reproductive incubator within which a single genotype is reproduced parthenogenetically and a few hundred of aphids are formed before dispersal.

FIG. 8.8. A branch of *Pistacia palaestina* bearing a gall (arrow) induced by the gall-forming aphid *Bizongia pistaciae* photographed at the end of the growing season (bar = 25 mm).

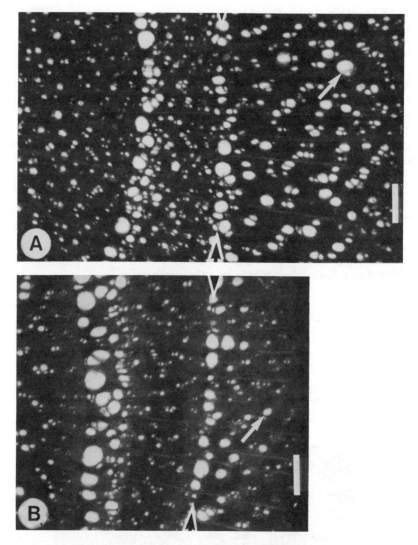

FIG. 8.9. Transverse sections of 3-year-old branches of *Pistacia palaestina*, both taken from the same tree at the end of the growing season, 100 mm below a gall (A) and at an equivalent location in an ungalled branch (B). Both sections are shown in the same direction and magnification (bar = 250 μm). Note that the more xylem, characterized by numerous wide vessels (e.g, white arrow) throughout the growing season, differentiated in the last formed annual ring (right) under the gall (A). In contrast, the last formed annual xylem ring of the ungalled branch (B) had narrow vessels in the latewood (e.g., white arrow). In both branches the two older annual xylem rings (left) showed a typical pattern of a ring-porous wood with wide vessels in the earlywood and narrow ones in the latewood. The earlywood vessels of the last formed annual ring are marked with black arrows.

Branches of *Pistacia atlantica* carrying galls induced by the gall-forming aphid *Slavum wertheimae* show enhanced xylem differentiation below the gall site (60). Usually, there is no effect on the xylem above the gall. Aphid-induced xylem below a gall in *Pistacia atlantica* as well as in *P. palaestina* is characterized by the differentiation of numerous wide vessels differentiated throughout the growing season, whereas in ungalled control branches, the latewood has a few narrow vessels typical of a ring-porous tree (Fig. 8.9). The differentiation of numerous wide vessels at the end of the growing season, when the population of aphids in the gall reaches its maximum size, makes possible a substantial increase of sap movement into the gall tissues. We (D.A. Katz, C. Döring, and R. Aloni, unpublished results) have found a substantial increase in water movement in the branches carrying galls as compared to ungalled control branches of the same size in *Pistacia palaestina* trees. During autumn, when the aphids leave the gall, the wide vessels below the gall become embolized, causing serious damage to the branch.

In the galls formed on branches of *Pistacia palaestina* trees (Fig. 8.8) by the gall-forming aphids *Bizongia pistaciae*, higher levels of IAA were found in the gall tissues in autumn (more than a month before the aphids leave the gall) than in intact mature leaves of control branches (D.A. Katz and R. Aloni, unpublished results). It remains to be ascertained whether this higher auxin level in the gall tissues at the end of the growing season is contributed directly by the gall-forming aphids (i.e., perhaps the aphids synthesize and secrete auxin precursor or an auxin) as suggested by Miles (61), or whether it is produced by the plant tissues in response to stimulation by the aphids. Certainly there is a need to study the levels of gibberellin and other regulators as well.

8.7. Concluding remarks

Experimental evidence shows that the cellular complexity of the xylem is controlled by fluxes of signals originating in leaves and root apices. The major signal involved in all aspects of xylogenesis is auxin. In the present chapter, I have focused on the role of low-level streams of auxin in controlling the differentiation of wide and hence efficient vessels in trees, especially in the earlywood of ring-porous species. The role of gibberellin in fiber differentiation was discussed with respect to latewood formation. However, current knowledge on the control of xylogenesis stems from studies made on a few species only, and thus large gaps and many unsolved questions on the role of growth regulators in wood formation still exist.

The author hopes that the three proposed hypotheses, especially the limited-growth hypothesis, will stimulate the reader's interest in the field of arboreal xylem differentiation, a field of vast economic importance in terms of improving wood productivity and quality. Clearly the three hypotheses need to be tested on a wider variety of tree species and under different experimental conditions in order to elucidate the possible role of both internal and external factors influencing the formation of wood in trees. Finally, although insects normally damage wood formation by interrupting xylogenesis (62,63), gall-forming aphids promote xylogenesis and induce wood that is more efficient. The control of differentiation in such aphid-induced xylem should pose a challenge for the imaginative student.

ACKNOWLEDGMENT

The author thanks Professor Carol A. Peterson and Miss Michelle Blais for critical reading of the manuscript and Springer-Verlag for permission to reproduce Figures 8.2 and 8.3.

8.8. References

1. M.H. Zimmermann, "Xylem Structure and the Ascent of Sap," in T.E. Timmell, ed., *Springer Series in Wood Science*, Springer-Verlag, Berlin–New York, 1983.

2. T. Sachs, "The control of the patterned differentiation of vascular tissues," *Adv. Bot. Res.*, **9**, 152–255 (1981).

3. R.A. Savidge and P.F. Wareing, "Plant-growth regulators and the differentiation of vascular elements," in J.R. Barnett, ed., *Xylem Cell Development*, Castle House Publications, Kent, UK, 1981, p. 192–235.

4. R. Aloni, "The induction of vascular tissues by auxin," in P.J. Davies, ed., *Plant Hormones and Their Role in Plant Growth and Development*, Martinus Nijhoff, Dordrecht, Boston, London, 1987, p. 363–374.

5. R. Aloni, "Differentiation of vascular tissues," *Annu. Rev. Plant Physiol.*, **38**, 179–204 (1987).

6. L.W. Roberts, P.B. Gahan, and R. Aloni, *Vascular Differentiation and Plant Growth Regulators*, in T.E. Timell, ed., *Springer Series in Wood Science*, Springer-Verlag, Berlin–New York, 1988.

7. W.P. Jacobs, "Functions of hormones at tissue level of organization," in T.K. Scott, ed., *Encyclopedia of Plant Physiology: Hormonal Regulation of Development*. Vol. 2, *The Functions of Hormones from the Level of the Cell to the Whole Plant* (new series), Springer-Verlag, Berlin–New York, 1984, pp. 149–171.

8. T. Sachs and D. Cohen, "Circular vessels and the control of vascular differentiation in plants," *Differentiation*, **21**, 22–26 (1982).

9. W.P. Jacobs, "The role of auxin in differentiation of xylem around a wound," *Am. J. Bot.*, **39**, 301–309 (1952).

10. S.F. Baum, R. Aloni, and C.A. Peterson, "Role of cytokinin in vessel regeneration in wounded *Coleus* internodes," *Ann. Bot.* in press (1991).

11. Y. Saks, P. Feigenbaum, and R. Aloni, "Regulatory effect of cytokinin on secondary xylem fiber formation in an *in vivo* system," *Plant Physiol.*, **76**, 638–642 (1984).

12. R. Aloni, "Role of cytokinin in differentiation of secondary xylem fibers," *Plant Physiol.*, **70**, 1631–1633 (1982).

13. S.M. Sircar and R. Chakraverty, "The effect of gibberellic acid on jute (*Corchorus capsularis*)," *Sci. Cult.*, **26**, 141–143 (1960).

14. C.K. Atal, "Effect of gibberellin on the fibers of hemp," *Econ. Bot.* **15**, 133–139 (1961).

15. M.Y. Stant, "The effect of gibberellic acid on fibre-cell length," *Ann. Bot.*, **25**, 453–462 (1961).

16. M.Y. Stant, "The effect of gibberellic acid on cell width and cell-wall of some phloem fibres," *Ann. Bot.*, **27**, 185–190 (1963).

17. P.F. Wareing and D.L. Roberts, "Photoperiodic control of cambial activity in *Robina pseudoacacia* L.," *New Phytol.*, **55**, 289–388 (1956).

18. T. Hess and T. Sachs, "The influence of a mature leaf on xylem differentiation," *New Phytol.*, **71**, 903–914 (1972).

19. J. Digby and P.F. Wareing, "The effect of applied growth hormones on cambial division and the differentiation of the cambial derivates," *Ann. Bot.*, **30**, 539–548 (1966).

20. R. Aloni, "Polarity of induction and pattern of primary phloem fiber differentiation in *Coleus*," *Am. J. Bot.*, **63**, 877–889 (1976).

21. R. Aloni, "Source of induction and sites of primary phloem fibre differentiation in *Coleus blumei*," *Ann Bot.*, **42**, 1261–1269 (1978).

22. T. Sachs, "The induction of fibre differentiation in peas," *Ann. Bot.*, **36**, 189–197 (1972).

23. R. Aloni, "Role of auxin and gibberellin in differentiation of primary phloem fibers," *Plant Physiol.*, **63**, 609–614 (1979).

24. L.W. Roberts and A.R. Miller, "Ethylene and xylem differentiation," *What's New in Plant Physiol.*, **13**, 13–16 (1982).

25. F. Yamamoto and T.T. Kozlowski, "Effect of ethrel on growth and stem anatomy of *Pinus halepensis* seedlings," *IAWA Bull.* (new series), **8**, 11–19 (1987).

26. F. Yamamoto, G. Angeles, and T.T. Kozlowski, "Effect of ethrel on stem anatomy of *Ulmus americana* seedlings," *IAWA Bull.* (new series), **8**, 3–9 (1987).

27. N.D. Nelson and W.E. Hillis, "Ethylene and tension wood formation in *Eucalyptus gomphocephala*," *Wood Sci. Technol.*, **12**, 309–315 (1978).

28. I.W. Bailey, "The structure of tracheids, in relation to the movement of liquids, suspensions and undissolved gases," in K.V. Thimann, ed., *The Physiology of Forest Trees*, Ronald Press, New York, 1958, pp. 71–82.

29. P. Baas, R. Schmid, and B.J. Van Heuven, "Wood anatomy of *Pinus longaeva* (bristlecone pine) and the sustained length-on-age increase of its tracheids," *IAWA Bull.*, (new series), **7**, 221–228 (1986).

30. M.H. Zimmermann and D. Potter, "Vessel-length distribution in branches, stem and root of *Acer rubrum* L.," *IAWA Bull.* (new series), **3**, 103–109 (1982).

31. M.P. Denne and V. Whitbread, "Variation of fibre length within trees of *Fraxinus excelsior*," *Can. J. For. Res.*, **8**, 253–260 (1978).

32. P.R. Larson, *Wood Formation and the Concept of Wood Quality*, School of Forestry Bulletin No. 74, Yale Univ., New Haven, CT, 1969.

33. R. Aloni and M.H. Zimmermann, "The control of vessel size and density along the plant axis—a new hypothesis," *Differentiation*, **24**, 203–208 (1983).

34. M.P. Denne, "A comparison of root and shoot-wood development in conifer seedlings," *Ann. Bot.*, **36**, 579–587 (1972).

35. S. Carlquist, *Comparative Wood Anatomy, Systematic, Ecological, and Evolutionary Aspects of Dicotyledon Wood*, in T.E. Timell, ed., *Springer Series in Wood Science*, Springer-Verlag, Berlin–New York, 1988.

36. A. Fahn, E. Werker, and P. Baas, *Wood Anatomy and Identification of Trees and Shrubs from Israel and Adjacent Regions*, Israel Academy of Science, Jerusalem, 1986.

37. T. Hartig, "Über die Entwicklung des Jahresringes der Holzpflanzen," *Bot. Z.*, **11**, 553–560, 569–579 (1853).

38. E.I. Russow, "Ueber Tüpfelbildung und Inhalt der Bastparenchym-und Basts-trahlzellen der Dikotylen und Gymnospermen. 2. Ueber den Inhalt der paren-chymastrischen Elemente der Rinde vor und während des Knospenaustriebes und Beginns der Cambiumthätigkeit in Stamm und Wurzel der einheimischen Lig-nosen," *Bot. Centralblatt*, **13**, 271–275 (1883).

39. J.E. Lodewick, "Seasonal activity of the cambium in some northeastern trees," *Bull. NY State College For. Tech. Publ.*, 23 (1928).

40. J.H. Priestley, "Studies in the physiology of cambial activity. 3. The seasonal activity of the cambium," *New Phytol.*, **29**, 316–354 (1930).

41. J.H. Priestley and L.I. Scott, "A note upon summer wood production in the tree," *Proc. Leeds. Phil. Soc.*, **3**, 235–248 (1936).

42. G.S. Jr. Avery, P.R. Burkholder, and H.B. Creighton, "Production and distri-bution of growth hormone in shoots of *Aesculus* and *Malus*, and its probable role in stimulating cambial activity," *Am. J. Bot.*, **24**, 51–58 (1937).

43. P.F. Wareing, "Growth studies in woody species. 4. The initiation of cambial activity in ring-porous species," *Physiol. Plant.*, **4**, 546–562 (1951).

44. P.F. Wareing, "The physiology of cambial activity," *J. Inst. Wood Sci.*, **1**, 34–42 (1958).

45. J.C. Zasada and R. Zahner, "Vessel element development in the earlywood of red oak (*Quercus ruba*)," *Can. J. Bot.*, **47**, 1965–1971 (1969).

46. L.W. Roberts, *Cytodifferentiation in Plants, Xylogenesis as a Model System*, Cambridge Univ. Press, London, 1976.

47. M.P. Denne and C.J. Atkinson, "Reactivation of vessel expansion in relation to budbreak in sycamore (*Acer pseudoplatanus*) trees," *Can. J. For. Res.*, **17**, 1166–1174 (1987).

48. C.J. Atkinson and M.P. Denne, "Reactivation of vessel production in ash (*Fraxinus excelsior* L.) trees," *Ann. Bot.*, **61**, 679–688 (1988).

49. M.J. Lechowicz, "Why do temperate deciduous trees leaf out at different times? Adaptation and ecology of forest communities," *Am. Nat.*, **124**, 821–842 (1984).

50. K.N.H. Greenidge, "An approach to the study of vessel length in hardwood species," *Am. J. Bot.*, **39**, 570–574 (1952).

51. M.H. Zimmermann and A. A. Jeje, "Vessel-length distribution in stems of some American woody plants," *Can. J. Bot.*, **59**, 1882–1892 (1981).

52. M. Reines, "The initiation of cambial activity in black cherry," *For. Sci.*, **5**, 70–73 (1959).

53. C.A. Reinders-Gouwentak, "Physiology of the cambium and other secondary

meristems of the shoot," in W. Ruhland, ed., Handbuch der Pflanzenphysiologie XV/1, Springer-Verlag, Berlin, 1965, pp. 1077–1105.

54. J. Digby and P.F. Wareing, "The relationship between endogenous hormone levels in the plant and seasonal aspects of cambial activity," *Ann. Bot.*, **30**, 607–622 (1966).

55. N. Liphschitz and Y. Waisel, "Effects of environment on relations between extension and cambial growth of *Populus euphratica* Oliv," *New Phytol.*, **69**, 1059–1064 (1970).

56. N. Liphschitz and Y. Waisel, "The effect of water stresses on radial growth of *Populus euphratica* Oliv," *La-Yaaran*, **20**, 80–84 (1970).

57. F.A. Roig, Jr., "The wood of *Adesmia horrida* and its modifications by climatic conditions," *IAWA Bull.* (new series), **7**, 129–135 (1986).

58. R.L. Guthrie, "Xylem structure and ecological dominance in a forest community," *Am. J. Bot.*, **76**, 1216–1228 (1989).

59. P.F. Wareing, "Extension and radial growth in trees," *Nature*, **166**, 278 (1950).

60. R. Aloni, D.A. Katz, and D. Wool, "Effect of the gall-forming aphid *Slavum wertheimae* on the differentiation of xylem in branches of *Pistacia atlantica. Ann. Bot.*, **63**, 373–375 (1989).

61. P.W. Miles, "Studies on the salivary physiology of plant bugs: Experimental induction of galls," *J. Insect Physiol.*, **14**, 97–106 (1968).

62. N. Liphschitz and Z. Mendel, "Histological studies of *Pinus halepensis* stem xylem affected by *Matsucoccus josephi* (Homoptera: Margarodidae)," *IAWA Bull.* (new series), **8**, 369–376 (1987).

63. Z. Mendel and N. Liphschitz, "Unseasonale latewood and incrusted pits are the cause of drying in *Pinus halepensis* and *P. eldarica* infested with *Matsucoccus josephi*," *J. Exp. Bot.*, **39**, 951–959 (1988).

64. S. Lev-Yadun and R. Aloni, "Vascular differentiation in branch junction: circular patterns and functional significance," Trees, **4**, 49–54 (1990).

65. R. Aloni, M.T. Tollier, and B. Monties, "The role of auxin and gibberellin in controlling lignin formation in primary phloem fibers and in xylem of *Coleus blumei* stems," Plant Physiol., **94**, 1743–1747 (1990).

9 Growth and Nutrition of Tree Seedlings

A.J.S. McDONALD, T. ERICSSON and T. INGESTAD

Department of Ecology and Environmental Research, Swedish University of Agricultural Sciences, Uppsala, Sweden

Contents

9.1. Introduction

In this chapter, some nutritional aspects of plant growth are considered, with particular emphasis on the quantitative nitrogen, phosphorus, and potassium requirements for dry-matter production. The examples and discussion are almost entirely confined to seedling growth at steady-state nutrition, that is, to plants whose internal nutrient concentrations remain constant with time. Many of the theoretical considerations associated with the concept of "steady-state" nutrition have been discussed by Ågren (1). The reasoning behind such an emphasis is discussed in detail in Section 9.2, and, indeed, one of the main aims of this chapter is to advocate the usefulness of the steady-state approach in studies of seedling nutrition. Because many of the published studies with this approach have been carried out by the authors, the examples given and the literature cited in Section 9.3 are inevitably biased in favor of the authors' own work. The emphasis on steady-state nutrition has precluded discussion of many other nutritional aspects that may be important or even crucial to the growth of a tree seedling. These include the occurrence of nitrogen fixation and mycorrhizal associations. A vast literature pertains to these areas, but, in the context of the steady-state concept, only a few studies have been done (2,3).

Much of the following discussion on nutrition is appropriate to seedling establishment. Many other variables are, of course, important in determining the success or otherwise of seedling establishments, and some of these are the subject of other chapters. However, in all instances, it may be assumed that climatic and edaphic variables interact with plant nutrition. Many climatic variables (including air pollutants and carbon dioxide concentration) will affect photosynthesis and the subsequent translocation and accumulation of metabolites. On the other hand, soil properties such as temperature, pH, and degree of compaction may affect root growth and the uptake of nutrients and water. Likewise, availability of water about the root surface may affect nutrient uptake, and, indeed, it would seem almost inevitable that experiments designed to investigate the effects of soil water depletion on plant growth have a nutritional component.

By way of illustrating how plant nutrition may interact with other growth variables, the dependence of nitrogen nutrition on photon flux density is discussed in Section 9.4.

Finally, growth response under conditions of well-defined depletion in nutrient availability is considered in Section 9.5.

9.2. Nutrient Usage

Nutrient requirements may depend to some extent on the genotype, although a remarkably small range of nutrient proportions may be adequate to the growth of a wide range of tree species. This presumably reflects the central role of the incorporated nutrients in metabolic processes, which is common to most plants. The reader is referred to some of the standard texts on mineral nutrition for a summary of some of the main uses of mineral nutrients in plants (4–6).

9.2.1. Nutrients and dry-matter production

The importance of nutrient supply and uptake to crop production has resulted, over many years, in a vast experimentation and literature pertaining to plant nutrition and growth. A great deal of publication has related to experiments with small plants in laboratory studies, where the underlying assumption is that under controlled environments the effects of different mineral nutrients on plant growth can be more easily studied than in the field. This approach is equally true of studies with tree seedlings as with any other type of plant.

The traditional approach has been to grow plants in solutions of different nutrient concentration or to grow potted plants to which defined (often constant) amounts of nutrient have been added on one or more occasions during the investigation. Conceptually, this approach has its counterpart in the field where nutrient availability (in terms of nutrient concentration) has been perceived in terms of amount of nutrient per soil volume and where addition (mineral fertilization) is defined in terms of amount to be added per unit soil area. Normally, little account has been taken of the standing biomass and its current nutrient requirement at the time of fertilization. Indeed, field practice has probably influenced both the development of laboratory procedure and, inevitably, the type of result and conclusions that have been reached concerning the growth and nutrition of seedlings.

In recent years, this traditional approach to studies in plant nutrition has been criticized. The main grounds for criticism are that the choice of concentration variable, or regular addition of constant amounts of nutrient, are inappropriate to maintaining nutrient supply proportional to increasing plant weight. This is perhaps best illustrated with respect to plants growing with initially adequate nutrient supply for maximum growth (Fig. 9.1). In the example shown, it is apparent that during the first 3 weeks with the traditional supply, the amount of nutrient taken up by the plant each week was less than that supplied. This means that during the first 3 weeks of the experiment, plant growth rate was maximal. In small plants this is equivalent to a constant maximum relative growth rate or maximum exponential growth. During the fourth week of the experiment, however, the amount of nutrient in solution was inadequate to meet the quantitative requirement for maximum growth. This means that nutrient deficiency had occurred by the end of week 4. Thus, depending on the time at which harvests were made, the solution concentration (as measured at the start of each week) would have been considered either adequate for maximum growth or to have represented a nutrient deficiency.

The criticisms leveled at the traditional approach have been concerned primarily with dry-matter productivity and dry-matter allocation in response to nutrient supply. However, it is also apparent that the ion concentration often used in studying mechanisms of nutrient uptake (and indeed the measured uptake capacity of the root) are quite in excess of the requirements for maximum growth. In fact, it has been demonstrated that, where nutrient concentration in the root solution has been maintained constant, the same maximum plant relative growth rate could be maintained for all solution concentrations investigated (8).

9.2.2. Steady-state nutrition

The preceding observations on nutrient uptake and growth provide a useful starting point for an appreciation of the alternative steady-state approach to

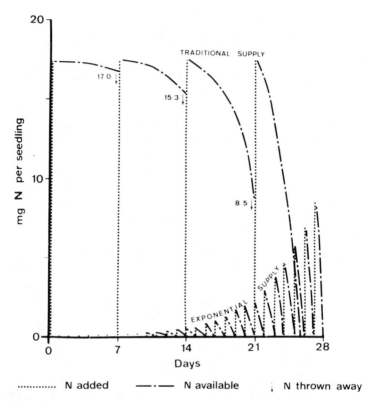

FIG. 9.1. Time course of nitrogen depletion from a nutrient solution renewed at weekly intervals (traditional supply = 17.5 mg N available each week), compared with the exponential increase in nitrogen addition and uptake required for maximum growth. The data pertain to birch seedlings (*Betula pendula* Roth.) with the same initial plant size; see Linder and Ingestad (Ref. 7).

nutritional studies. When a small plant has free access to nutrients, it will take up nutrients exponentially at a rate associated with maximum exponential increase in plant weight for a given genotype and growth environment. A constant maximum relative growth rate is maintained, associated with a constant maximum relative rate of increase in nutrient uptake. At stable, maximum conditions, the exponent of nutrient uptake is equal to that of plant weight increase. Thus, the nutrient concentration in the plant also remains constant with time. It is this constancy in plant nutrient concentration which characterizes steady-state nutrition.

The finesse with the steady-state approach and its main contribution to stress physiology has been the observation that, by choosing and maintaining an exponent of nutrient addition below the maximum value, plant growth acclimates, such that the exponent of plant weight gain is equal to that of nutrient addition. In other words, plant relative growth rate (RGR) is equal to the relative addition rate of nutrient (RAR). This is true, irrespective of species and growth climate (Fig. 9.2) and has been demonstrated separately for most of the macronutrients and a number of trace elements, where free access to all other nutrients has been maintained. After a lag phase in which nutrient and dry-matter distribution within the plant acclimates to the particular rate of exponential increase in nutrient addition, plant nutrient concentrations and dry-matter distributions tend to stabilize. Values that are characteristic of genotype, growth climate, and rate of nutrient addition may thus be determined (9–13).

A large part of this chapter is concerned with presenting and discussing characteristic responses to limited supply of macro and trace elements in tree seedlings. However, before that, it seems appropriate to discuss further some implications of inadequate nutrient supply and why the steady-state approach may provide more useful information in studies of seedling nutrition.

9.2.3. Implications of inadequate nutrient supply

In order to demonstrate the possible experimental artifacts associated with nonstable nutrition, plant growth, and uptake of nitrogen at a constant rate

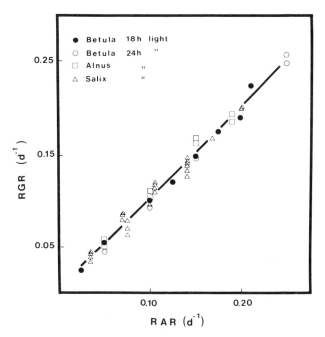

FIG. 9.2. Dependence of plant relative growth rate, RGR (day^{-1}), on the relative addition rate of nutrient, RAR (day^{-1}). The data are for birch (*Betula pendula* Roth.) grown at 18- and 24-hr photoperiods (adapted from Refs. 9, 10); grey alder (*Alnus incana* L.) (adapted from Ref. 10); willow (*Salix*) (adapted from Ref. 11).

of nitrogen addition may be considered. In Fig. 9.3, simulated changes in fresh weight, plant nitrogen concentration, and relative growth rate are illustrated. The effect of an addition rate of 1000 μmol day^{-1} is compared with that of the addition rate required to maintain optimum nutrition and maximum relative growth rate (about 122 μmol day^{-1} on day 2 and about 100,000 μmol day^{-1} on day 28). The optimum internal fresh-weight concentration was 0.6% nitrogen and the maximum relative growth rate in continuous light was 0.25 day^{-1}. The initial fresh weight was taken as 1.0 g, giving an initial nitrogen content of 428 μmol.

Figure 9.3a shows that a constant addition rate of 1000 μmol day^{-1} is sufficient for optimum nutrition and maximum growth for about 10 days. Later, plant nitrogen concentration and relative growth rate decline continuously (Fig. 9.3b). This is because the nitrogen in solution is insufficient to

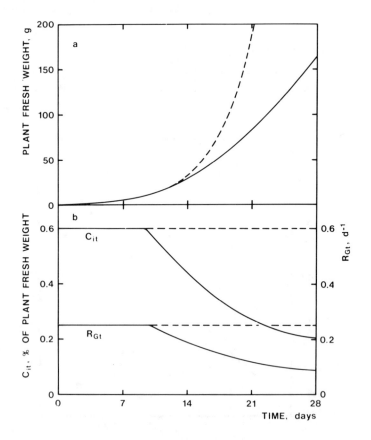

FIG. 9.3. Simulated change with time of (a) plant fresh weight, g, and (b) plant nitrogen concentration, C_{it} (% N of fresh weight) and plant relative growth rate, R_{Gt} (day^{-1}). The broken lines indicate an exponential increase in nitrogen supply associated with maximum growth and the solid lines a constant supply of 1000 μmol N day^{-1}. The simulations were based on data for birth (*Betula pendula* Roth.); see Ingestad (Ref. 7).

meet the requirement for constant exponential growth. It should be noted that growth seems to be exponential even after day 10 with constant nitrogen addition in Fig. 9.3a. Thus, a fitted curve of the form $y = a[\exp(bx)]$ gives b ($=$RGR) $= 0.14$ day^{-1} with an r^2 value of 0.98 for the period day 10–day 28. However, because both plant nitrogen concentration and plant relative growth rate have changed considerably during the same period (Fig. 9.3b), it is obvious that nutritional stability cannot be assumed from the goodness of fit in the exponential expression of plant weight increase.

The influence of plant nitrogen concentration (Fig. 9.4a) or different constant addition rates (Fig. 9.4b) on plant fresh weight are shown after growth periods of different lengths, using the same data as in Fig. 9.3.

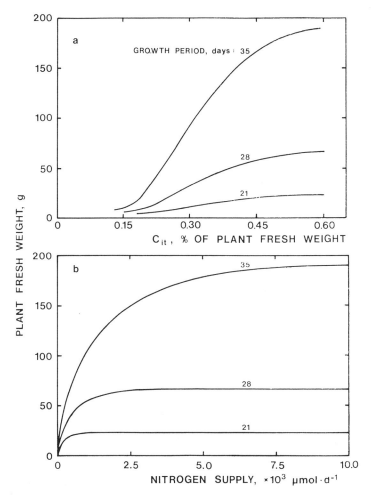

FIG. 9.4. Simulated influence of (a) internal nitrogen concentration, C_{it} (% N of fresh weight), and (b) different constant nitrogen addition rates on plant fresh weight, g. The simulations are based on data for birch (*Betula pendula* Roth.); see Ingestad (Ref. 7).

During the simulated decrease in plant relative growth rate and in internal nitrogen concentration (Fig. 9.3b), changes in the uptake and allocation of carbon and nitrogen will occur continuously after day 10. This means that the dependence of dry-matter production on the treatment variable (1000 μmol N day^{-1}) is also changing. Thus, the results obtained, and conclusions reached in such an experiment, are dependent on the time at which sampling is made.

One important implication of this discussion is that, even in treatments that are considered to represent high nitrogen availability, plants may eventually start to run out of nitrogen and end up with low internal nitrogen concentrations. This argument may be taken further by simulating the time course of changes in plant relative growth rate and internal nitrogen concentration that would be obtained for plants with different nitrogen productivities (rate of dry-matter increase per plant nitrogen) and the same constant nitrogen addition rate (Fig. 9.5). The different nitrogen productivities may be attributable to genotype or growth environment. For example, the dependencies

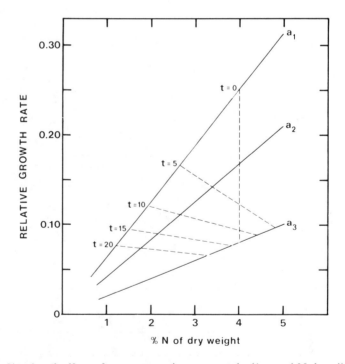

FIG. 9.5. Simulated effect of a constant nitrogen supply (1 mmol N day^{-1}) on plant nitrogen concentration (% N of dry weight) and relative growth rate of birch seedlings (*Betula pendula* Roth.) with different nitrogen productivities (a_1, a_2, a_3); see Linder and Rook (Ref. 14) for details of calculation.

shown in Fig. 9.5 are typical of plants grown at different photon flux densities. All the treatments are initially assumed to be at optimal nutrition (ca. 4% N of dry weight in birch). In treatments with the highest nitrogen productivities (a_1 and a_2), relative growth rates and plant nitrogen concentrations start to decrease immediately, whereas in the treatment a_3, with the lowest nitrogen productivity, no decrease would occur until about day 15. This is because the constant nitrogen addition rate is sufficient to maintain maximum growth at this growth environment. By day 20, all the relative growth rates are approximately the same and plant nitrogen concentrations are negatively correlated with plant size. This is the opposite of what is found in situations where plant nutrition is stable, as in the steady-state approach.

Having emphasized the importance of maintaining stability of response in quantitative studies in plant nutrition, we now consider some examples of growth response to limited supplies of N, P, and K.

9.3. Growth response to nitrogen, phosphorus, and potassium supply

All the results presented in this section are for birch plants that have been grown in solution culture with exponentially increasing availability of either N, P, or K and with free access to all other mineral nutrients. Growth conditions are similar in all experiments and full details have been published elsewhere (15–17).

The first observation to be made is that, irrespective of whether N, P, or K is most limiting to growth, a stability of growth response in terms of increase in biomass and nutrient uptake is reached. This is indicated by the equality of acclimated values of plant relative growth rate and relative rate of increase in the limiting nutrient (Fig. 9.6). What is not shown in Fig. 9.6 is that this stability of response is attained only after a lag phase of several days or weeks during which uptake and subsequent allocation and usage of carbon, water, and other nutrients acclimates to the given rate of supply. This lag phase is discussed in more detail in Section 9.5, and the extent to which growth climate may affect the acclimated response is discussed in Section 9.4.

9.3.1. Shoot growth analysis

Relative growth rate may be considered in terms of its component parts LAR (leaf area ratio = total leaf area per unit of plant dry weight) and NAR (net assimilation rate = rate of plant dry-matter increase per unit of leaf area):

$$RGR = LAR \times NAR \qquad (9.1)$$

The usefulness of this approach is in separating the development of structure (LAR = dry-matter allocation to different plant organs and development of total leaf area) from the functional components of carbon exchange (NAR

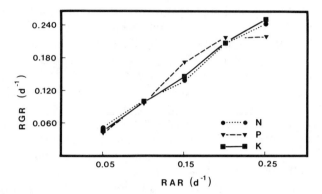

FIG. 9.6. Dependence of plant relative growth rate, RGR (day^{-1}), on the relative rate of increase, RAR (day^{-1}), of either nitrogen, phosphorus, or potassium. Symbols pertain to the limiting nutrient and all other nutrients are available in nonlimiting amounts for growth.

= photosynthesis, respiration, exudation, and mortality). It provides little information of a physiological nature but, importantly, does provide some information on the extent to which either carbon exchange or structural development is affected by nutrient supply and thus limiting to growth. By dividing NAR and LAR into further components, the processes and physiology that are most limiting to growth may be identified. This provides a logical framework for emphasizing certain types of physiological research.

In Section 9.3.1.1, LAR is considered in terms of leaf weight ratio (LWR = the fraction of total plant dry matter belonging to leaves) and specific leaf area (SLA = leaf area produced per leaf dry weight):

$$LAR = LWR \times SLA \qquad (9.2)$$

Only two components of net assimilation rate are discussed in Section 9.3.1.2—photosynthetic rate (P_n) and dark respiration rate (R_D)—and then only with respect to nitrogen supply.

9.3.1.1 Structural development, LAR. From Fig. 9.7a, it may be seen that LAR is positively correlated with the supply rate of the most limiting nutrient. The dependencies on N and P supply are similar. However, at the poorest rate of supply, plants of similar dry weight have twice the leaf area where K is limiting compared with plants in which either N or P is limiting. This is partly attributable to a larger fraction of plant dry matter being allocated to leaves (LWR in Fig. 9.7b) and also to higher values of specific leaf area in K-limited plants than in N- or P-limited plants (Fig. 9.7c). The general expectation is that often, under conditions of nutrient limitation, less dry matter is allocated to leaves (18,19). This is true of N and P limitation, but in plants with limited supplies of K, dry matter allocation to roots is apparently no

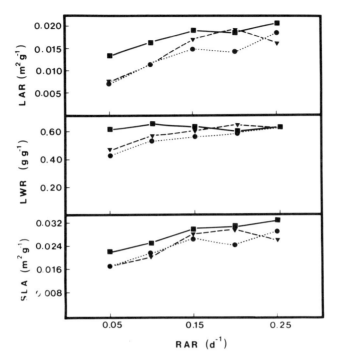

FIG. 9.7. Dependence of leaf area ratio, LAR (m² g plant DW⁻¹ (dry weight⁻¹)), leaf weight ratio, LWR (g leaf DW g plant DW⁻¹), and specific leaf area, SLA (m² g leaf DW⁻¹), on the relative rate of increase, RAR (day⁻¹), of either nitrogen, phosphorus, or potassium. Symbols as in Fig. 9.6.

greater (and may even be slightly less) at poorer rates of supply than at more optimal K supply.

The increment in leaf area associated with an increment in plant nutrient is shown in Fig. 9.8. In general, the increment ratio (area per nutrient amount) is greater where the limiting nutrient is in poor supply. This is most obvious in the case of phosphorus and potassium in Fig. 8b,c, respectively, and, to a much lesser extent, is true of nitrogen in Fig. 9.8a. Indeed, where leaf area is related to nitrogen amount (dL/dN in Fig. 9.8a), the difference between N-, P-, and K-limited plants is small. This may reflect a central role for nitrogen in the regulation of leaf area growth, irrespective of which nutrient is most limiting. If this is true, then the higher values of dL/dP and dL/dK associated, with poor P and K supplies, respectively (Fig. 9.8b,c), would be more attributable to enhanced N/P and N/K ratios at poor P and K supplies than to any increased efficiency of using P or K as such in leaf area growth.Indeed, in the experiments to which these data pertain, higher ratios of N/P and N/K have been measured at poorer P and K supplies, respectively (16,17).

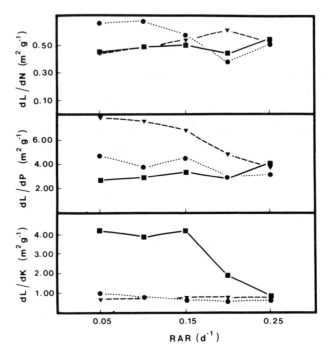

FIG. 9.8. Dependence of leaf area growth per plant nitrogen, dL/dN (m² g plant N⁻¹), per plant phosphorus, dL/dP (m² g plant P⁻¹) and, per plant potassium, dL/dK (m² g plant K⁻¹), on the relative rate of increase, RAR (day⁻¹), of either nitrogen, phosphorus, or potassium. Symbols as in Fig. 9.6.

9.3.1.2. Carbon exchange, NAR. With all of N-, P-, and K-limited supplies, NAR is positively correlated with supply rate (Fig. 9.9). Nitrogen and phosphorus-limitations show similar dependencies of NAR on supply at most rates. On the other hand, because LAR in Fig. 9.7a was shown to be higher at poor K supply than in plants with poor N or P supply, lower values of NAR are to be expected at poor K supply than at equivalent N or P supplies (see Eq. 9.1). This is confirmed in Fig. 9.9, where NAR in K-limited plants is approximately half that in N- or P-limited plants.

Higher values of NAR at better nutrient supply are consistent with other findings, although the extent to which the dependence exists will depend on other environmental factors and, in some instances, it may be quite small (20). The occurrence of higher values of NAR at better nutrient supply may be attributable to higher photosynthetic rates per unit of leaf area or to reduced carbon losses. In the case of N, the evidence is somewhat contradictory. In leaves and shoots belonging to plants that have acclimated to an exponentially increasing supply of N, the value of P_n, as measured at the growth climate, is rather constant (20–22). Values of $P_{n,max}$ at light saturation may, however, be higher at better N supply. Other workers have reported

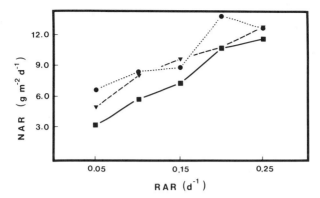

FIG. 9.9. Dependence of net assimilation rate, NAR (m^2 g leaf DW^{-1} day^{-1}), on the relative rate of increase, RAR (day^{-1}), of either nitrogen, phosphorus, or potassium. Symbols as in Fig. 9.6.

higher values of NAR and P_n at better N supply, but the extent to which the result is characteristic of stable response to N supply or reflects response to N deficiency, is often unknown.

Carbon losses may take the form of respiration, exudation, and mortality. In the experiments with N, P, and K in culture solution as described, mortality is low. In experiments with N-limitation, dark respiration rates, when related to the amount of nitrogen in the plant, tend to be constant (unpublished data of the authors). Both these considerations, when combined with apparent constancy in P_n, suggest that at least part of the dependence of NAR on nutrient supply may be accounted for by exudation losses at poorer rates of supply. This suggestion has not, however, been confirmed.

Lower values of NAR at poor K supply compared with equivalent rates of N and P supply may be associated with lower values of P_n. This is supported by the observation that at low values of N supply, concentrations of leaf starch are large whereas starch is largely absent from leaves belonging to plants with poor K supply (Refs. 21, 22; also unpublished data of the authors). Higher starch concentrations are also generally found in leaves of plants with poor P supply.

9.3.1.3. Categories of response.   The discussion here has been confined to N, P, and K supply, but the results may be indicative of two major types of response. In the case of N and P, large amounts of carbohydrate are found when the limiting nutrient is in poor supply. Where this is the case, photosynthesis is arguably unlikely to be growth-limiting and an increased proportion of dry matter is allocated to root growth. In experiments with N and P, carbon storage is found in roots only at extremely poor rates of supply. Most of the carbon allocated to roots is apparently incorporated in new root structure or may possibly contribute to exudation loss. A similar growth response to that observed for N and P is found with respect to limited S supply (un-published data of the authors).

On the other hand, response to limiting K supply does not involve any large shift in dry-matter allocation between shoots and roots. Because carbon storage is absent, it seems likely that the current growth of K-limited plants may be limited by carbon uptake. A similar lack of response in dry-matter allocation has been shown with respect to other limiting nutrients. These include Mg supply (unpublished data of the authors) and Fe and Mn supplies (Göransson, personal communication). Where nutrient supply is limiting to carbon uptake, growth response at poor rates of supply apparently does not involve the same shift in dry-matter allocation in preference of roots as is found with other nutrients.

The explanation for the difference in response has not been established, but it may reflect the central role of certain nutrients in carbon uptake as opposed to other growth processes (6,18).

9.3.2. Root growth analysis

In all the preceeding discussion, the emphasis has been on shoot growth. However, at steady-state nutrition, it is to be expected that characteristic responses of root growth to limiting supplies of different nutrients will occur. For the types of experiment described here, with root systems growing in culture solution, the root environment is obviously very different from that encountered in any soil. However, the simplified and well-defined root environment in these experiments allows study of certain basic types of growth response that would otherwise prove impossible. In many soils, increases in root length and surface area may be extremely important for exploring a soil volume and for the continued acquisition of nutrients. Thus, characteristic responses of root growth in relation to nutrient uptake may be critical in determining the subsequent availability of any limiting nutrient. In this context, a solution culture system can be advantageous where, despite extremely good contact between nutrients and the root surface, characteristic responses of root growth to limiting supplies of different nutrients are observed.

In Fig. 9.10, root growth is expressed in terms of weight increase in relation to the amounts of N, P, and K taken up at different rates of N, P, and K supply. Obviously, weight increase alone gives an incomplete picture of root response and, where available, information on length and area increase is desirable (23). In all instances (N, P, and K), where the limiting nutrient is in poor supply, root growth with respect to uptake of the limiting nutrient is greater than at better availability (Fig. 9.10a–c). However, the consistently low values of dw_r/dN and dw_r/dP in plants that are K-limited (Fig. 9.10a,b) reflects an uptake of N and P that is in excess of growth requirement. This is consistent with the high values of nutrient uptake per root weight (dN/dw_r and dP/dw_r in Fig. 9.11a,b) in K-limited plants. Apparently, the uptake of N and P in K-limited plants is not closely regulated by growth requirement. This contrasts with the trends in Fig. 9.10c, where dw_r/dK is affected by all N, P,

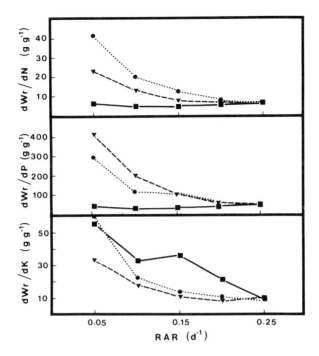

FIG. 9.10. Dependence of root growth per plant nitrogen, dw_r/dN (g root DW g plant N^{-1}), per plant phosphorus, dw_r/dP (g root DW g plant P^{-1}) and per plant potassium, dw_r/dK (g root DW g plant K^{-1}), on the relative rate of increase, RAR (day^{-1}), of either nitrogen, phosphorus, or potassium. Symbols as in Fig. 9.6.

and K supplies. It may be concluded that, in plants with limited N and P supplies, the uptake of potassium is linked to the growth requirement (Fig. 9.11c).

9.4 Nutrition and climate

In Section 9.3, all the results and discussion pertained to plants grown in the same climate. This is justifiable on the grounds that only by standardizing the growth climate would it be possible to identify characteristic growth responses to limiting supplies of nutrient. In the natural world, climate not only will vary from one site to another but, in terms of its component weather, may also be a highly variable quantity. In this section, it is assumed that the plant has a large time constant when compared with the variation in driving variables and that it essentially operates as an integrator. In other words, growth response to fluctuations in weather will, within certain limits, be similar to that for a constant, average climate.

In Section 9.4.1, the discussion has been confined to only one example of interaction between plant growth, nutrition, and climate. Many different in-

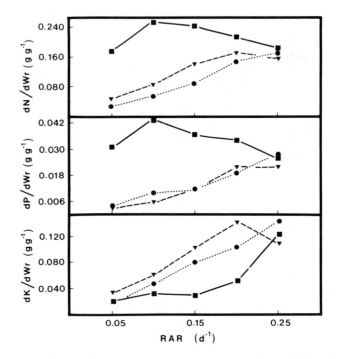

FIG. 9.11. Dependence of (a) nitrogen uptake per root weight, dN/dw_r (g plant N g root DW^{-1}), (b) phosphorus uptake per root weight, dP/dw_r (g plant P g root DW^{-1}), and (c) potassium uptake per root weight, dK/dw_r (g plant K g root DW^{-1}), on the relative rate of increase, RAR (day^{-1}), of either nitrogen, phosphorus, or potassium. Symbols as in Fig. 9.6.

teractions between nutrition and climate occur, but by way of example, the following discussion is confined to growth response with respect to N supply and photo flux density (Q). In order to characterize the response, the discussion is confined to plants grown at different, constant values of photon flux density and with nitrogen supplies that are increasing at different exponential rates (15).

9.4.1. Growth analysis

From Fig. 9.12 it may be seen that the maximum value of RGR is dependent on Q. However, the value of Q at which maximum RGR first saturates with respect to Q is quite low (250 μmol m^{-2} s^{-1}). This is associated with light-saturated values of nitrogen productivity [$(dw/dt)/N$ as shown in Fig. 9.13]. Thus, the rate of dry matter gain per amount of plant nitrogen does not assume higher values, although the photosynthetic light-response curve of leaves grown at high values of Q might first be expected to show saturation only at much higher values of photon flux density (20).

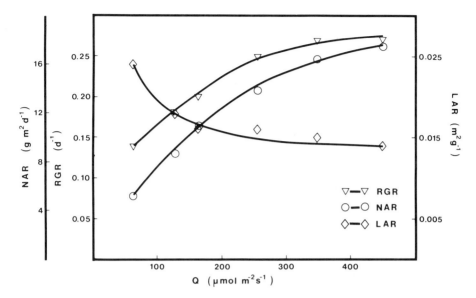

FIG. 9.12. Dependence of maximum values, at optimal nutrition, of plant relative growth rate, RGR (day^{-1}), net assimilation rate, NAR (g plant DW m^{-2} day^{-1}) and leaf area ratio, LAR (m^2 g plant DW^{-1}), on photon flux density during growth, Q (μmol m^{-2} s^{-1}).

From Fig. 9.12, it is apparent that net assimilation rate (NAR) has not saturated with respect to Q over the range for which Q has been investigated. However, if structural growth is analyzed as in the previous section, it is apparent from Fig. 9.12 that leaf area ratio (LAR) is higher in plants grown at lower values of Q. Elsewhere, it has been shown that this is not associated with a shift in dry-matter partitioning between leaves and roots but is accounted for by much higher values of specific leaf area (SLA) at lower values of Q (20). Although a number of factors may be important, one of the main reasons for lower values of SLA at high values of Q is a large amount of starch (21,22). As shown in Fig. 9.13, the increment in leaf area per increment in plant nitrogen (dL/dN) is greater at lower values of Q.

In conclusion, the potentially higher values of RGR and nitrogen productivity, which might have been expected at higher values of Q on the basis of NAR and P_n alone, are apparently offset by lower values of leaf area production.

Interestingly, with respect to plants grown at different photon flux densities, it has been shown that the extent, but not the nature, of plant growth response to limited nutrient supply is affected (15). Thus, the types of dependence discussed for N supply in Section 9.3 are applicable to any photon flux density. However, the actual values of structural variables are dependent on photon flux density as illustrated for optimum nutrition in Figs. 9.12 and 9.13. In passing, it may be noted that the values of root growth variables in

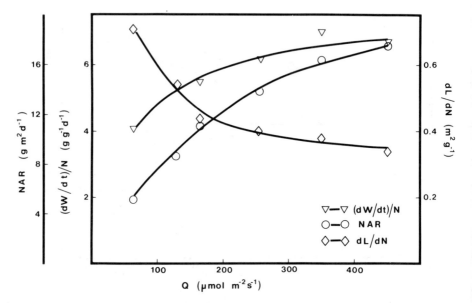

FIG. 9.13. Dependence of maximum values, at optimal nutrition, of nitrogen productivity, $(dw/dt)/dN$ (g plant DW g plant N^{-1} day^{-1}), net assimilation rate, NAR (g plant DW m^{-2} day^{-1}) and leaf area per plant nitrogen, dL/dN (m^2 g plant N^{-1}), on photon flux density during growth, Q (μmol m^{-2} s^{-1}).

relation to nitrogen uptake, as discussed in Section 9.3 (Figs. 9.10 and 9.11), are largely unaffected by photon flux density (15).

9.5. Fluctuation in nutrient supply

Throughout the preceding discussion, the importance of maintaining nutrient supply proportional to increasing plant size in studies of seedling growth was emphasized. This allows for unambiguous conclusions concerning the effect of nutritional or climatic variables on plant growth. However, nutrient availability at the root surface in the soil may be a highly variable quantity. What, then, are the likely effects of variable nutrient supply on seedling growth? One approach to addressing this question is to observe the sequence of events that take place in the plant following a well-defined change in nutrient supply. One example of this is in moving between two rates of addition at different rates of exponential increase. The advantage of such an approach is that the start and finish conditions are well defined in terms of steady-state concentration of nutrients in the whole plant. This constitutes a very simplified type of variability, but it does provide possibilities for appreciating what happens in plants that start to run out of nutrients or, as is the case following an application of mineral fertilizer, in plants that suddenly receive more nutrients.

In experiments with changes in nutrient supply, growth analysis as outlined in the previous sections may still be applicable. Again, the thrust of the argument is in identifying which process is likely to be most limiting to the subsequent growth of the plant. Having made such an observation, the relevant physiology may then be studied in more detail. Experiments in which nutrient supply has either been suddenly increased or decreased have been made with birch seedlings grown in culture solution. The following discussion, by way of example, is confined to nitrogen and to the situation of decreased supply (24).

9.5.1. Growth analysis

Immediately following a step decrease in relative addition rate of N, there is apparently a rapid decrease in the flow of N to the shoot, with eventually no net transport of N from roots to leaves (Fig. 9.14a). This is indicated by the extremely low values of relative rate of increase in the amount of N found in leaves. With time, the transfer of N to leaves recovers, and, as would be expected from a consideration of steady-state nutrition, the relative rate of increase in the amount of N belonging to leaves tends to stabilize at the new, reduced rate of exponential increase in N addition.

Following the decrease in net transfer of N to leaves, a rapid decrease in leaf area growth is observed (Fig. 9.14c). This tends to stabilize rapidly at the new rate of addition and does so before the relative root and whole-plant growth rates. Thus, here is further evidence that the development of leaf area would appear to be tightly coupled to the availability of N.

The relative growth rate of the root decreases more slowly than that of the whole plant and thus, by implication, more slowly than that of the shoot (Fig. 9.14c). This results in a shift in dry-matter allocation in favor of roots, as would be expected from the discussion of lower leaf weight ratio (LWR) at lower, steady-state values of N nutrition in Section 9.3.1.1.

Immediately following the decrease in N addition is a large increase in the relative rate of increase in the amount of starch to be found in leaves (Fig. 9.14b). This peaks, drops rapidly and subsequently stabilizes in accordance with the new rate of N supply. This results in a rapid increase in the starch concentration of leaves, which is then maintained high throughout the subsequent exponential phase of growth, again, as might be expected from the previous discussion of steady-state values (see Section 9.3.1.2).

9.6. Concluding remarks

Plant nutrition is arguably one of the most important considerations in seedling establishment. In Section 9.2, growth response in plants at steady-state nutrition was compared with that in plants where nutrient supply was inadequate for maintaining relative growth rate and plant nutrient concentrations con-

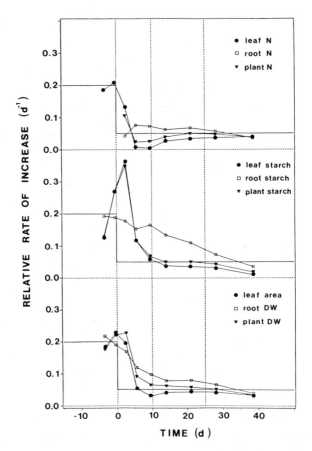

FIG. 9.14. Time series of relative rates of increase (day^{-1}) in 9a) total amounts of nitrogen in leaves, roots, and whole plant; (b) total amounts of starch in leaves, roots, and whole plant; and (c) leaf area and dry weight of roots and whole plant. At time $= 0$, the relative rate of increase in nitrogen supply decreased from 0.20 to 0.05 day^{-1}.

stant. The types of problem associated with interpreting growth response at anything other than steady-state nutrition have been highlighted. Inevitably, from the standpoint of steady-state nutrition, results pertaining to experiments in which a constancy in plant nutrient concentration has not been maintained are difficult to interpret as characteristic of defined nutrient supply. An increased awareness of this argument is desirable (and necessary) if progress is to be made in quantifying aspects of plant nutrition.

Where steady-state nutrition is achieved, responses of leaf and root growth to, for example, N, P, and K supplies can be determined (Section 9.3). An important distinction may be made between responses to nutrient stress that involve accumulation of carbohydrate (N and P supplies) and those resulting in low carbohydrate content (K supply). Dry-matter distribution between leaves and roots is unaffected by K supply, whereas an increased allocation to roots at poorer supplies of N and P is found. This may reflect differences in the extent to which carbon uptake and carbohydrate availability are affected by the limited supply of a nutrient. Thus, no general response of increased allocation of dry matter to roots at poor nutrient supply can be assumed.

The example of interaction between nitrogen supply and photon flux density presented in Section 9.4 is one of many possible environmental interactions with plant nutrition. However, because many of the growth variables that respond to photon flux density also respond to nitrogen supply, the example is illustrative of the requirement for steady-state nutrition in assessing the effects of other environmental variables on seedling growth.

Finally, the steady-state approach allows for clearly defined start and end conditions in assessing growth response to a change in nutrient supply. Hopefully, the approach outlined in Section 9.5 will be of relevance to those interested in defining sequences of growth response following a change in any nutritional variable.

9.7. References

1. G. Ågren, "Theory for growth of plants derived from the nitrogen productivity concept," *Physiol. Plant.*, **64**, 17–28 (1985).
2. T. Ingestad, "Growth, nutrition, and nitrogen fixation in grey alder at varied rate of nitrogen addition," *Physiol. Plant.*, **50**, 353–364 (1980).
3. T. Ingestad, A.S. Arveby, and M. Kähr, "The influence of ectomycorrhiza on nitrogen nutrition and growth of *Pinus silvestris* L. seedlings," *Physiol. Plant.*, **68**, 575–582 (1986).
4. E. Epstein, *Mineral Nutrition of Plants: Principles and Perspectives*, Wiley, New York, 1972.
5. H. Gauch, *Inorganic plant nutrition*, Dowed, Hutchinson and Ross, Stoudsburg, PA, 1972.
6. F.B. Salisbury and C.W. Ross, *Plant Physiology*, 3rd ed., Wadsworth Publishing Co., Belmont, CA, 1985.
7. S. Linder and T. Ingestad, "Ecophysiological experiments under limiting and non-limiting conditions of mineral nutrition in field and laboratory," *Bicentenary Celebration of C.P. Thunberg's visit to Japan*. Royal Swedish Embassy and the Botanical Society of Japan, Tokyo, 1977, pp. 69–76.
8. T. Ingestad, "Relative addition rate and external concentration; driving variables used in plant nutrition research," *Plant, Cell Environ.*, **5**, 443–453 (1982).
9. T. Ingestad and A.-B. Lund, "Nitrogen stress in birch seedlings. 1 Growth technique and growth," *Physiol. Plant.*, **45**, 137–148 (1979).
10. T. Ingestad, "Nutrition and growth of birch and grey alder seedlings in low conductivity solutions and at varied relative rates of nutrient addition," *Physiol. Plant.*, **52**, 454–466 (1981).
11. T. Ericsson, "Effects of varied nitrogen stress on growth and nutrition of *Salix*," *Physiol. Plant.*, **51**, 429–432 (1981).

12. H. Jia and T. Ingestad, "Nutrient requirement and stress response of *Populus simonii* and *Paulownia tomentosa*," *Physiol. Plant.*, **62**, 117–124 (1984).
13. T. Ingestad and M. Kähr, "Nutrition and growth of coniferous seedlings at varied relative nitrogen addition rate," *Physiol. Plant.*, **65**, 109–116 (1985).
14. S. Linder and D.A. Rook, "Effects of mineral nutrition on carbon dioxide exchange and partitioning of carbon in trees," in G.D. Bowen and E.K.S. Nambiar, eds., *Nutrition of Plantation Forests*, Academic Press, London, 1984, pp. 211–236.
15. T. Ingestad and A.J.S. McDonald, "Interaction between nitrogen and photon flux density in birch seedlings at steady-state nutrition," *Physiol. Plant.*, **77**, 1–11 (1989).
16. T. Ericsson and T. Ingestad, "Nutrition and growth of birch seedlings at varied relative phosphorus addition rate," *Physiol. Plant.*, **72**, 227–235 (1988).
17. T. Ericsson and M. Kähr, "Effects of varied relative potassium addition rate on growth and nutrition of birch seedlings (*Betula pendula* Roth.)," *Trees* (submitted).
18. D.T. Clarkson and J.B. Hanson, "The mineral nutrition of higher plants," *Ann. Rev. Plant Physiol.*, **32**, 239–298 (1980).
19. J. Moorby and R.T. Besford, "Mineral nutrition and growth," in A. Läuchli and R.L. Bieleski, eds., *Inorganic Plant Nutrition (Encyclopedia of Plant Physiology, New Series, Vol. 15B)*, Springer-Verlag, Berlin–New York, 1983, pp. 481–527.
20. A.J.S. McDonald, T. Lohammar, and T. Ingestad, "Net assimilation rate and shoot area development in small birch plants (*Betula pendula* Roth.) at different values of stable nutrition and photon flux density," *Trees* (in press).
21. A.J.S. McDonald, A. Ericsson, and T. Lohammar, "Dependence of starch storage on nutrient availability and photon flux density in small birch (*Betula pendula* Roth.)," *Plant, Cell Environ.*, **9**, 433–438 (1986).
22. R.H. Waring, A.J.S. McDonald, S. Larsson, T. Ericsson, A. Wiren, E. Arwidsson, A. Ericsson, and T. Lohammar, "Differences in chemical composition of plants grown at constant relative growth rates with stable mineral nutrition," *Oecologia (Berlin)*, **66**, 157–160 (1985).
23. D.T. Clarkson, "Factors affecting mineral nutrient acquisition by plants," *Ann. Rev. Plant Physiol.*, **36**, 77–115 (1985).
24. A.J.S. McDonald, T. Lohammar, and A. Ericsson, "Growth response to step-decrease in nutrient availability in small birch (*Betula pendula* Roth.)," *Plant, Cell Environ.*, **9**, 427–432 (1986).

10 Growth Periodicity and Dormancy

ROLF BORCHERT

Department of Physiology and Cell Biology, University of Kansas, Lawrence, Kansas, USA

Contents

10.1. Shoot growth in tropical and temperate trees

Periodic (or episodic, intermittent, rhythmic) rather than continuous growth is almost universal among trees (1,2). Periods of rapid shoot growth (*flushing*)

usually alternate with periods of rest. In seasonal climates, environmental control of growth periodicity is indicated by the synchronized bud break and flushing observed in deciduous temperate or tropical trees in response to favorable temperatures or the first heavy rains, respectively. However, unexpectedly, most mature trees complete a single, relatively short, annual period of shoot growth well before the end of the growing season, and growth remains arrested for the remainder of the year (Fig. 10.1).

Many young trees grow continuously for several months in favorable environments, but saplings of trees such as *Hevea* (rubber; Fig. 10.2C,D), *Theobroma* (cacao; Fig. 10.6 inset), *Quercus* (oak; Fig. 10.3) or *Pinus* (pine; Fig. 10.1e) pass through as many as 15 growth cycles per year (3–5). Periodic shoot growth under such conditions is asynchronous among the trees of a population (6), and, in the wet tropics, flushes of shoot growth may be asynchronous even within the crown of individual trees (2). The arrest of shoot growth and the duration of the rest period are therefore not determined by changes in environment, but must be regulated by physiological changes within the tree. Trees passing through repeated cycles of growth and rest unrelated to environmental changes thus manifest an endogenous growth periodicity, often referred to as *rhythmic growth* (Figs. 10.2C,D, 10.4).

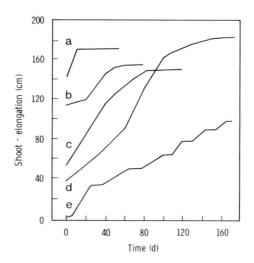

FIG. 10.1. Patterns of seasonal shoot growth in 5–10-year-old temperate trees. (a) *Aesculus* (buckeye). (b) *Carya* (hickory): single flush of determinate shoot growth with expansion of the leaves (preformed in the winter bud) followed by growth cessation and formation of a terminal bud early in the growing season. (c) *Fraxinus* (ash). (d) *Salix* (willow): indeterminate shoot growth during which newly initiated leaves expand during a prolonged growth period. (e) *Pinus palustris* (longleaf pine): recurrent flushes of determinate shoot growth with terminal bud formation at the end of each flush. (Redrawn from Refs. 1,11.)

10.1.1. Tree growth periodicity: a new perspective

Most research on tree growth has focused on the environmental control of periodicity and the mechanism of dormancy in a few temperate fruit and timber tree species. Consequently, all earlier discussions of tree growth periodicity have considered annual tree development including a period of winter dormancy as the normal situation, rather as a specific developmental pattern adapted to cold-temperate climates (7,8).

Our increased knowledge of growth patterns in tropical trees provides the opportunity to review tree development from a new, broader perspective. In a radical departure from the past, growth periodicity in trees will be considered here to be primarily an inherent consequence of the developmental constraints of trees as large, long-lived plants pursuing a characteristic adaptive strategy (Section 10.8).

Because of the present limited understanding of the causal factors responsible for the induction and breaking of rest periods in trees, too many terms have been coined in the past to describe different types of dormancy (9). To simplify matters, only two operationally defined "states" of apical meristems will be distinguished here: (a) *resting buds* or meristems, which resume growth within 1–2 weeks after being transferred to favorable growing conditions and (b) *dormant buds* or meristems, which do not resume growth within this time period. Unless exposed to a specific set of environmental conditions, such buds—like dormant seeds—may remain inactive even under favorable conditions for several weeks or months.

10.2. Shoot morphogenesis

Much of the current knowledge on periodic shoot growth has been gained not by measurements of extension growth (Figs. 10.1, 10.2D), but from phenological observations on the timing of bud break, leaf expansion, flowering, and leaf fall (Section 10.5), as well as from analyses of tree morphology. Because of the distinct morphogenetic changes usually associated with the onset and termination of shoot growth, stem sections formed during a period of shoot extension can be easily recognized. Morphology and architecture of a tree thus provide a lasting record of its developmental history (10).

10.2.1. Periodic growth in Hevea

The pattern of developmental changes occurring during one period of shoot growth in *Hevea brasiliensis*, the rubber tree, and the resulting morphological record are representative for most temperate and many tropical trees and, therefore, will be described in detail (Fig. 10.2) (4). The resting terminal bud, enclosed by bud scales, contains the inactive apical meristem with the primordia of nectaries (scalelike, reduced leaves bearing nectary glands) and the first foliage leaves (= preformed leaves). As the apical meristem enlarges,

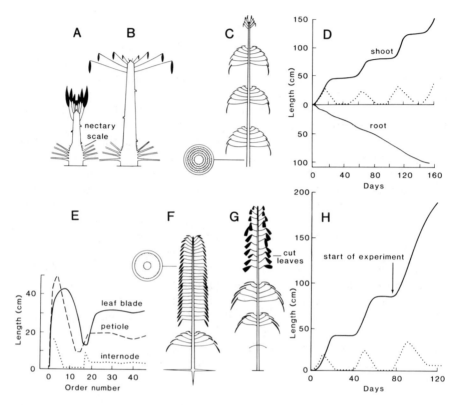

FIG. 10.2. Periodic, indeterminate shoot growth in saplings of the tropical tree *Hevea brasiliensis* (rubber tree). (A,B) Rapid elongation of stem internodes between the nectaries and the first foliage leaves, and incipient expansion of new foliage leaves. (C) Sapling with four consecutive flushes of shoot growth and a stem cross section showing the corresponding periodicity in cambium growth (growth rings). (D) Periodic shoot elongation (_____), shoot growth rate (. . . .), and continuous root elongation during three flushes of shoot growth lasting approximately 40 days each. (E,F) Spontaneous transition from periodic to continuous shoot growth (lampbrush) and the corresponding changes in length of petioles, leaf blades, and internodes. (G,H) Transition from periodic to continuous shoot growth resulting from experimental reduction in leaf area. (Redrawn from Ref. 4.)

the bud opens and the bud scales eventually abscise. Their closely spaced scars mark the limit between consecutive shoot increments (Fig. 10.2A,B). Nectaries, the first new foliar organs to appear on the elongating shoot, are separated by very long internodes indicative of rapid shoot extension (Fig. 10.2A,B). They are followed without transition forms by the first, largest foliage leaves of the flush (Fig. 10.2B). Subsequent leaves have progressively smaller blades and shorter petioles and internodes (Fig. 10.2B,C,E). An abrupt transition from the last foliage leaf to bud scales marks the end of shoot growth and formation of the new terminal bud.

The progressive reduction in internode length between the foliage leaves reflects a marked decline in the rate of shoot elongation. Young leaves thus begin expanding during a period of declining shoot elongation, and petiole elongation and leaf blade expansion are completed well after the arrest of shoot growth. Periodic shoot growth is accompanied by periodic activity of the cambium, as indicated by the formation of growth rings in the wood (Fig. 10.2C), while simultaneous root growth is continuous (Fig. 10.2D).

The periodic shoot growth in *Hevea* thus involves not only an alternation between periods of rest and cell growth in the apical meristem but also a precisely timed, reversible transition between fully developed foliage leaves and reduced leaf organs such as bud scales and nectaries. The transition from foliage leaves to bud scales is developmentally similar to the transition from foliage leaves to bracts and flower organs, which precedes flowering. The reversibility of this developmental sequence is, however, unique to trees of the *Hevea*-type of development, which probably represents the most advanced and most adaptable of the many known patterns of tree growth (see also Chapter 1, this volume).

10.2.2. Variation in shoot morphogenesis

The temporal relations between rest, extension growth, and leaf morphogenesis are highly variable (1,7,11). During *determinate shoot growth* of temperate, broad-leafed trees, all leaves unfolding during the relatively short period of shoot growth arise from primordia preformed in the resting bud (Fig. 10.1a,b). Primordia for leaves expanding during the next growth episode, usually 1 year later, develop soon after the arrest of shoot growth within the resting bud. The prolonged, *indeterminate shoot growth* of trees such as *Populus* (poplar) or *Salix* (willow; Fig. 10.1d) also involves the expansion of leaves newly initiated at the apical meristem.

Different shoot growth patterns are observed among trees of the same species or even within the same individual tree. Saplings, stem sprouts, and vigorous leaders often exhibit relatively long periods of indeterminate shoot growth (Sections 10.3 and 10.4), whereas lateral shoots, such as short or spur shoots, have only a brief period of determinate growth. Similar variation in shoot morphogenesis exists among conifers (12,13); in *Pinus* and other genera foliar primordia may be preformed within the terminal bud as much as two seasons before they expand.

Many other tree species are unable to undergo reversion from foliage leaves to bud scales and hence do not form terminal buds enclosed by bud scales. In such trees, the shoot apex may be protected by the leaf bases or stipules of older leaves or may be naked, as in leguminous trees. Periods of shoot growth are terminated by irreversible morphogenetic changes in the apical meristem such as formation of a terminal inflorescence (e.g., *Aesculus* and many hapaxanthic tropical trees), abortion of the shoot tip [e.g., *Ulmus* (elm) and leguminous trees with naked buds], or parenchymatization of the apical meristem, as common in tropical trees. Subsequent shoot growth originates from lateral buds subtending the transformed or aborted shoot tip, often resulting in characteristic branching patterns (Ref. 10; See also Chapter 1 in this book).

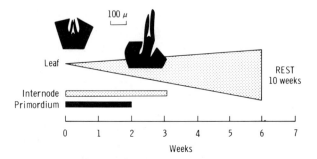

FIG. 10.3. Development of the apical bud in *Gnetum africanum*. After a rest period of 10 weeks, the internode, the existing pair, and the next pair of leaf primodia begin to grow simultaneously, but growth of the internode and the new primordia is arrested, presumably by correlative inhibition, long before leaves are fully expanded. (Redrawn from Ref. 14.)

10.2.3. Continuous shoot growth

Evergreen trees of slow, continuous growth are confined to the wet tropics (1,2,10). Trees such as palms, *Rhizophora mangle* (mangrove), *Schefflera*, and *Gnetum africanum* (10,14) may produce a leaf or leaf pair every few months, and periods of extension growth and morphogenesis alternate with relatively long periods of rest (Fig. 10.3). Continuous shoot growth is thus characterized by the lack of morphogenetic changes at the shoot apex, but not necessarily by a constant rate of shoot extension.

10.3. Correlative growth inhibition in constant environments

10.3.1. The regulation of periodic shoot growth

The most puzzling aspect of periodic growth in trees is the cessation of shoot growth under environmental conditions that permit continued growth of herbaceous plants and seedlings of many tree species. Only when we understand the inhibitory factors involved will we be able to define the state of the inactive meristem and the conditions required for the resumption of growth. We must therefore address the following questions: Which physiological factors arrest extension growth, alter the morphogenetic pattern, and induce rest in the apical meristem? How do these factors arise in trees growing under favorable conditions? What causes the inhibitory factors to eventually disappear and permit the resumption of shoot growth in the absence of apparent environmental triggers? How is the duration of the rest period determined?

10.3.2. Experimental modification of shoot growth patterns

A priori, one would expect the maintenance of a functional equilibrium between growing shoots and other organs to be a prerequisite for continuous growth. For instance, the remarkably constant dry-weight ratios between root and shoot found in many seedling populations (15,16) suggest the existence of mechanisms regulating the balance of growth between root and shoot. Indeed, most experimental treatments modifying shoot growth periodicity affect the root : shoot ratio or the functional equilibrium between a tree's root and shoot system.

A spontaneous transition from periodic to continuous shoot growth, re-sulting in the "lampbrush" growth form, is occasionally observed in young *Hevea* trees. Lampbrush trees have relatively small leaves and short inter-nodes, indicative of a low rate of shoot extension (Fig. 10.2E,F) (4). Similarly, in the wet tropics, the main shoot (leader) of several species of *Pinus* may grow continuously and form unbranched "foxtails" more than 10 m in length (11). Transition from periodic to continuous growth can be induced experi-mentally in *Hevea* by reducing each expanding leaf to one-third its normal size (Fig. 10.2G,H). Successive removal of immature leaves results in con-tinuous growth in saplings of other species (14,17,18).

Defoliation of temperate trees during the summer by experimental ma-nipulation, severe drought, insect attack, or hailstorms, may cause renewed growth of arrested terminal and lateral buds in late summer (7), and occasional dry periods in tropical rain forests result in leaf shedding and subsequent flushing in evergreen trees (Refs. 2,19; Section 10.5.2). Potted saplings of *Hevea* and several temperate trees grow continuously for many months in the high humidity of the greenhouse environment (7).

The arrest of shoot growth by restriction of root growth is illustrated by the well-known slowdown and eventual cessation of growth in *pot-bound* plants. Shoot growth in potted saplings of *Quercus* is arrested whenever they reach a certain leaf area but resumes after transplanting into larger containers (6). The effect of an increased root : shoot ratio is dramatically illustrated by the rapid, continuous growth of stem sprouts or coppice shoots; e.g., sprouts of *Quercus* may grow continuously, rather than periodically, for several months (5).

10.3.3. Periodic root growth

In contrast to the continuous root growth of *Hevea* saplings (Fig. 10.2D), periods of root growth alternate in the majority of trees with periods of shoot growth. In temperate trees root growth begins in spring several weeks before bud break, slows down or stops during flushing, and resumes after the arrest of shoot growth (20). In tree seedlings, the temporal, and implicitly functional, relations between periodic root and shoot growth are precise: each period of rapid root growth is immediately followed by the resumption of shoot growth. Inversely, root growth appears to be inhibited by shoot growth, as indicated by its rapid decline during the initiation of shoot growth (Fig. 10.4) (16,18,20).

10.3.4. Arrest of shoot growth by water deficits

The establishment or maintenance of a relatively large root : shoot ratio by reduction of leaf area or increased root growth enables continued shoot growth

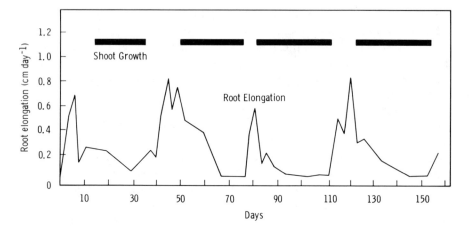

FIG. 10.4. Periodicity of shoot and root growth in 2-year-old seedlings of *Quercus alba*. (Redrawn from Ref. 20.)

or the resumption of growth in resting buds of small trees (Section 10.3.2). Implicitly, these events relieve the restriction of shoot growth imposed earlier by a functional imbalance between root and shoot. This type of inhibition of one organ by another is defined as *correlative inhibition* (1,7). The resulting bud rest will be referred to as *correlative rest*.

When pot-bound tree seedlings are transplanted to larger containers, shoot growth resumes without defoliation (6). Leaves thus inhibit shoot growth only if deficient in a factor provided by the root system in proportion to its size. The most important substance supplied by the roots and continuously required by leaves in substantial amounts is water. *Internal water deficits resulting from an unbalanced root : shoot ratio thus constitute the most likely physiological basis for the correlative inhibition of shoot growth by leaves and the cause for*

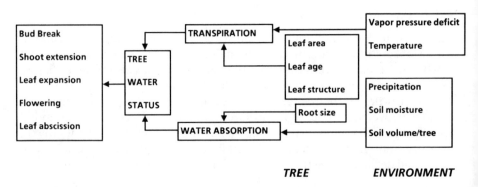

FIG. 10.5. Biotic, environmental, and climatic factors affecting the water status and development of trees.

Table 10.1. Effects of root restriction on growth correlations and water relations of alder seedlings[a]

Variable	Treatments			
Root volume (ml)	500	16	6	1
Leaf area/plant (cm^2)	1050	800	400	160
Transpiration/plant (mg s^{-1})	13	17	5	1
Water potential, 5th leaf (mPa)	-0.7	-1.1	-1.35	-1.8
Noon diffusive resistance (s cm^{-1})	10		10	25
Root : shoot ratio (dry weights)	0.25		0.1	0.13

[a]The roots of seedlings of *Alnus glutinosa* (48 days old, 4.5 cm height) were placed into perforated polypropylene test tubes (1.5, 6, 16 ml), which prevented roots from growing out, and were set into a 500-ml container containing aerated nutrient solution. Roots of "unrestricted" control seedlings grew directly in the 500-ml container. Measurements were taken after 70 days of treatment. (Data adapted from Ref. 21.)

the arrest of shoot growth during periodic growth. Defoliation or cultivation of tree seedlings in high humidity (Section 10.3.2) would thus permit continuous shoot growth by preventing the development of water deficits causing arrest of shoot growth (Fig. 10.5).

In seedlings of *Alnus* (alder) growing in nutrient solution, progressive restriction of root volume results in a lowered root : shoot ratio, decreasing leaf water potentials, and arrest of shoot growth (Table 10.1) (21). Inversely, removing one-third of the stem and its leaves from the top of *Populus* seedlings reduces water stress in the remaining shoot and releases lateral buds from correlative inhibition (22). The reduced growth of lateral tree branches as compared to that of the leader has been attributed to a reduced water supply of the laterals (23). There is thus good experimental evidence for the role of water deficits in various types of correlative inhibition in trees.

Correlative inhibition by the root is unlikely to be the result of deficiencies in root-produced plant hormones such as cytokinins. However, abscisic acid formed in water-stressed leaves might mediate the inhibitory effect of internal water deficits (Section 10.7).

10.3.5. Computer simulation

The dynamic interaction among several variables, as involved in any type of correlative inhibition, cannot be verified by experiments such as those described, which necessarily involve destructive sampling. Correlative inhibition of shoot growth by the root system was therefore computer-simulated (Fig. 10.6) (24). Simulation yields patterns of periodic shoot growth remarkably similar to those observed in young trees of *Theobroma* grown under constant conditions. Shoot and leaf growth are arrested simultaneously in *Theobroma*, presumably by an internal water deficit. Reducing leaf size in the simulation decreases transpiration and results in continuous shoot growth, as achieved experimentally in *Hevea* (Fig. 10.2G,H).

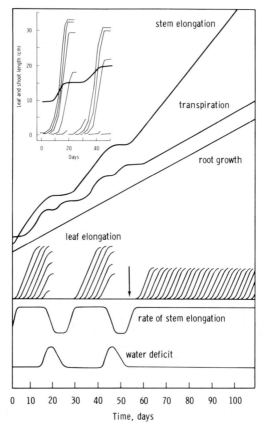

FIG. 10.6. Computer simulation of rhythmic shoot growth. During the beginning of each flush the stem elongates and leaves expand in rapid sequence, causing a rapid increase in leaf area and transpiration. When water loss by transpiration exceeds water absorption by the continuously growing root, a water deficit develops and causes termination of stem and leaf growth. Shoot growth resumes when the water balance has been restored by root growth. Reduction of leaf length by 45% after day 50 reduces the rate of increase in leaf area and transpiration to the rate of root growth, achieving a balanced water economy and continuous growth of the tree (compare Fig. 10.2G). Inset: Periodic shoot elongation (thick line) and leaf growth (thin lines) in saplings of *Theobroma cacao* under constant environmental conditions. (Redrawn from Refs. 3,24.)

The computer model illustrates how periodic growth under constant environmental conditions can result from interaction between *any* two, potentially continuous partial processes, if the slower process is rate-limiting for the faster one. The repeated alternation between feedback inhibition and growth will manifest itself as an endogenous growth rhythm of constant period length (Figs. 10.2D, 10.3, 10.6). Feedback inhibition by internal water deficits represents only one of several conceivable mechanisms. However, the model explains many observed periodic growth patterns, if the various biotic and environmental factors affecting a tree's water balance are adequately considered (Fig. 10.5), and predicts changes in growth patterns resulting from gradual variation in individual components of the feedback mechanism (Sections 10.4 and 10.5).

10.3.6. Correlative inhibition within growing shoots

In contrast to *Theobroma* (Fig. 10.6), leaf expansion in *Hevea* and *Quercus* continues well after the arrest of shoot extension (Fig. 10.2B) (6). Similarly, in the tropical liana *Gnetum*, growth of the internode, the next pair of leaf primordia, and a single leaf pair are initiated simultaneously after a period of rest. Whereas shoot extension and morphogenesis are arrested early, expansion of the large leaves continues for 6 weeks; removal of the expanding leaves prevents inhibition of the other growth processes (Fig. 10.4) (14). These examples strongly suggest correlative inhibition of shoot meristems by expanding leaves, which might be the result of a growth-induced water potential, the lowered water potential providing the force to attract water for the growth process (25).

Assimilate reserves of deciduous and evergreen temperate trees are rapidly depleted during flushing in spring (11,20). Experimental evidence for the arrest of rapid shoot growth early in the growing season due to assimilate depletion is ambiguous, but lack of adequate assimilate supply is definitely not the inhibitory factor preventing the resumption of shoot growth later in the growing season.

10.4. The effect of tree size

With increasing tree size, the number of growing shoots, and hence the internal competition for water and other resources, increases exponentially. A progressively larger fraction of shoots will be subject to some kind of correlative inhibition, and root expansion may be restricted by physical limits of the rhizosphere or competition with other roots. Maintaining a functional balance between root and shoot will thus become progressively more difficult, and periods of shoot growth should become shorter relative to periods of correlative rest. Without exception, the observed age-dependent changes in shoot growth periodicity reflect the predicted trend toward shorter growth flushes and longer periods of rest (26).

Saplings of many tropical trees such as *Bombax*, *Ceiba*, and *Tectona* (teak) remain evergreen and grow continuously until they reach a height of several meters. As tree size increases further, there is a transition to periodic growth; trees will branch, shed their leaves during the dry season, and cease growing for progressively longer periods. In tropical trees with periodic growth of seedlings, the interval between consecutive growth flushes tends to lengthen with age, and the number of annual growth flushes declines from 8 to 10

(*Hevea*, *Theobroma*; Figs. 10.2, 10.6) to 4 in mature *Theobroma* and *Camellia thea* (tea), and to 1 or 2 in most other trees.

Similar age-related changes in growth–periodicity occur in temperate trees. In *Quercus* the number of seasonal flushes declines from 3–4 in seedlings to 1–2 in mature trees. In *Acer*, *Fraxinus* (ash), and *Prunus seedlings* grow continuously, but *saplings* may undergo temporary reductions in growth rate accompanied by partial transformation of leaves into bud scales, then resume rapid growth, and finally form a resting bud in fall. In mature trees shoot growth usually ceases by midsummer (Fig. 10.1) but may resume after defoliation by insect damage or drought (Section 10.3.2).

10.5. Seasonal drought

10.5.1. Tree development and seasonal drought

In many tropical regions, seasonal variations in temperature and photoperiod are small, but fluctuations in rainfall are great. In Costa Rica, at a latitude of 10°N, the variation of monthly temperatures from the annual mean is about 1°C and the photoperiod varies less than 30 min annually, but more than 95% of the annual precipitation falls between late April and early November (Fig. 10.7) (27). Considering climate, the major determinant of periodic growth, one would predict synchronized flushing of trees with the advent of rains in May, and no shoot growth during the 5 months of drought.

The annual course of development and water status in *Cochlosperum* and *Spondias* (Fig. 10.7) is representative of most trees in tropical deciduous forests (27). Changes in stem circumference (girth) are correlated with tree water potential and therefore indicate changes in tree water status (28). As expected, rapid rehydration of leafless trees after the first rains causes bud break, and the cessation of rainfall results in a rapid decline in soil moisture and tree water potential accompanied by leaf fall.

The phenological records in Fig. 10.8 describe the growth periodicity of several populations within two tropical tree species, *Erythrina poeppigiana* and *Tabebuia rosea*, growing along an altitudinal gradient on the Pacific slope of Costa Rica ranging from 40 to 1340 m (29,30). These populations differ in tree size, water availability, and evapotranspiration during the dry season. There is thus wide variation with respect to the biotic and environmental factors affecting tree water status (Fig. 10.5).

Even a glance at the phenological records reveals that seasonal patterns of shoot development among the different tree populations of these species are far from synchronous and poorly correlated with seasonal climatic changes. Such a lack of predicted correlations between climate and tree development was noted in many studies of tropical tree phenology and led to speculations considering slight fluctuations in temperature and photoperiod as causes for growth periodicity (2,27). However, a critical reanalysis shows that the observed growth patterns correlate well with temporal changes in tree water status, supporting the role of water deficits in correlative rest (Section 10.3.4).

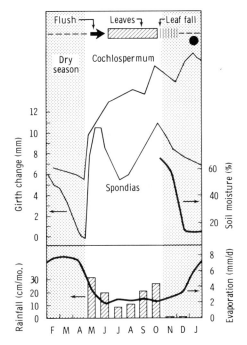

FIG. 10.7. Seasonal development and water status of *Cochlospermum vitifolium* and *Spondias purpurea* as a function of climate in the tropical deciduous lowland forest of Costa Rica. Relative change in girth of stem reflects changes in tree water potential. Seasonal changes in climate are indicated by changes in rainfall (bars), evaporation (lower curve) and soil moisture (curve: center right). The black dot indicates flowering in *Cochlospermum*. (Redrawn from Ref. 27.)

10.5.2. Leaf fall and bud break

Whenever *Erythrina* or *Tabebuia* shed their leaves during the wet season, new shoot growth starts before or immediately after leaf fall is complete (Figs. 10.8A–C,E,H,I; 10.9). This habit of *leaf exchange* has been described for many evergreen tropical trees (2). Watering of potted *Theobroma* saplings after a period of imposed drought causes renewed flushing only if preceded by partial shedding of leaves (19,26). The *induction of bud break by defoliation, considered exceptional in temperate trees* (Section 10.3.4), *thus represents the normal developmental sequence in tropical trees*.

Defoliation enables shoot growth by eliminating internal water deficits (Section 10.2.4). During the dry season, water stress in two large *Erythrinas* increased with leaf expansion and caused the abscission of young leaves. When water stress was relieved with the onset of the rains, new shoots emerged before leaf fall was complete (Fig. 10.9) (29). Resumption of growth in resting vegetative buds thus constitutes a reliable biological indicator for the elimination of water stress after leaf shedding. Inversely, a delay in the resumption of shoot growth after leaf fall indicates that drought has prevented full relief

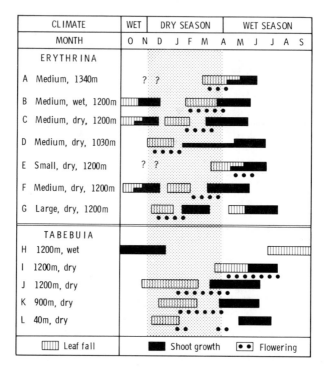

FIG. 10.8. Periods of seasonal development in *Erythrina poeppigiana* and *Tabebuia rosea* along an altitudinal gradient on the Pacific slope of Costa Rica ranging from 40 to 1340 m. Wet sites were within 10 m of a river; dry sites were at least 15 m away from a river. Tree size ranged from 2 to 3 m (small) to >20 m (large). After shoot growth and leaf expansion, trees were in full foliage until leaf fall occurred. (Redrawn from Refs. 30,32.)

from water stress (Fig. 10.7) or that fully hydrated buds are dormant (Section 10.6.1).

Like leaf expansion, the opening of flower buds (anthesis) involves cell expansion and is therefore sensitive to water stress. In *Erythrina*, *Tabebuia*, and many other tropical trees, flowers open during or immediately after leaf fall. Opening of flower buds is thus correlatively inhibited by senescent foliage and triggered by the elimination of water stress after leaf shedding (31). In *Cochlospermum*, drought-induced leaf shedding results in a reduction of water stress followed by anthesis (Fig. 10.7). Flowering, in turn, enhances water stress, as is also observed during flowering in leafless *Tabebuia* (28). The delayed bud break in trees flowering during the dry season (Fig. 10.8C,D,J,K) is probably due to water stress resulting from the unfolding of the large and relatively long-lived flowers of *Erythrina* and *Tabebuia* (30,32); flowers would thus inhibit bud break correlatively.

In conclusion, the developmental sequence *leaf fall → flowering → flushing*, observed in evergreen and deciduous tropical trees, represents a *bona fide* causal sequence regulated in time by the successive correlative changes af-

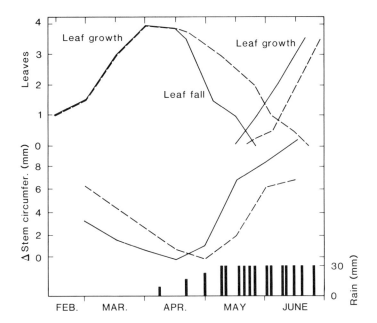

FIG. 10.9. Relations between leaf growth and tree water status (indicated by changes in stem diameter) in *Erythrina* (compare Fig. 10.7G). Stages in leaf development range from small, light green leaves (1) to mature, dark green foliage (4), and from 10% leaf fall (3.5) to complete leaf shedding (0). (Redrawn from Ref. 29.)

fecting tree water status. The central role of leaf fall in breaking correlative bud rest is obscured in temperate trees by the temporal separation of leaf fall and bud break by the cold season, and thus has not been adequately recognized in the past. This raises the question concerning the control of leaf fall as the first step in this sequence.

10.5.3. Leaf longevity

Leaves have a finite, species-specific life expectancy, which in tropical trees ranges from less than 6 months for delicate leaves to more than 2 years for coriaceous leaves (2,33). Toward the end of their life span, leaves become inefficient in photosynthesis and stomatal control; e.g., weeks before they are shed, older leaves in *Tabebuia* (Fig. 10.8H) and other species lose stomatal control, resulting in considerable water stress (34). In tropical rainforests, occasional dry spells cause massive abscission of such senescent leaves and subsequent flushing on individual branches of evergreen trees (Section 10.5.2).

Irrespective of site, *Erythrina* sheds leaves and then flushes twice a year as compared to only one annual growth cycle in *Tabebuia*. Lack of environmental triggering of leaf fall is apparent in *Erythrina* during the wet season (Fig. 10.8B,C,G) and in *Tabebuia* at dry and riparian sites (Fig. 10.8H–J). *In the absence of seasonal environmental stress, the longevity of leaves thus determines the duration of bud rest caused by correlative inhibition, and hence the endogenous growth periodicity.*

10.5.4. Changes in growth periodicity with increasing drought

Along the permanently humid Atlantic slope of Costa Rica, *Erythrina* is evergreen and the phases of seasonal development occur asynchronously in individual branches (29). On the Pacific slope, trees growing in the premontane moist forest flower and exchange leaves during the late dry season; i.e., they are evergreen (Fig. 10.8A). With decreasing elevation and increasing evapotranspiration during the dry season, leaf fall begins progressively earlier (Fig. 10.8A–D), and flowering and flushing occur in succession rather than simultaneously, resulting in a period during which flowering trees stand leafless. At 1030 m, leaf fall and flowering early in the dry season is followed by bud break, but new leaves remain small and fail to expand fully until the advent of rains (Fig. 10.8D).

At the same location, small, pruned *Erythrina* change leaves and flower late in the dry season (Fig. 10.8E), while leaf shedding and subsequent flowering and flushing occur progressively earlier with increasing tree size (Figs. 10.8F,G; 10.9). This pattern parallels the trend along the altitudinal gradient of increasing drought (Fig. 10.8A–D) and confirms the effect of tree size on growth periodicity (Section 10.4).

Within the same species, increasing seasonal drought thus causes characteristic changes in growth periodicity. In an aseasonal climate, development is asynchronous within the crown of evergreen trees, slight seasonal drought synchronizes leaf exchange and flowering (Fig. 10.8a,b), and moderate drought imposes a deciduous habit with temporal separation of successive developmental phases (Fig. 10.8C,D). Throughout the range of *Erythrina*, leaf fall is the primary developmental and correlative change triggering anthesis and bud break by reducing water stress.

Increasing drought affects growth periodicity in opposite ways: on one hand, it accelerates leaf shedding and thus rehydration, flowering, and flushing; on the other hand, drought depletes soil water and prevents buildup of the high water potential required for shoot growth. These trends are apparent over the range of *Tabebuia* (Fig. 10.8I–L). At higher elevations anthesis occurs after leaf fall, but flushing is delayed by seasonal drought (Fig. 10.8I–K). At 40 m, release from water stress by leaf shedding permits only partial anthesis. The remaining flower buds open after the first rains just before the resumption of shoot growth (Fig. 10.8L; compare *Cochlospermum* in Fig. 10.7). In *Tabebuia neochrysantha* and other species isolated, heavy rain during the dry season causes rapid rehydration of trees and mass flowering in tropical deciduous forests (28). With increasing seasonal drought the interval between leaf shedding and bud break becomes progressively longer (Figs. 10.8K,L; 10.7). Leaf shedding is insufficient to relieve water stress, and drought prevents rehydration and bud break in leafless trees, which thus remain in a state of *drought-imposed rest.*

10.6. Bud dormancy

10.6.1. Tropical trees

In a few tropical tree species, leaf shedding is not immediately followed by the resumption of shoot growth under favorable environmental conditions. *Bombax, Bombacopsis, Cedrela*, and *Cordia* remain bare for several months even in areas without a pronounced dry season. Similarly, bud break in detached, leafless twigs of most drought-deciduous tropical trees can be induced at any time by standing them in water, but branches of *Bombax* and similar species resume growth only at certain times (2). Apical meristems in these species are thus temporarily dormant, i.e., unable to resume growth even in the absence of correlative or environmental inhibition.

10.6.2. Temperate trees

The growth periodicity of temperate trees during the growing season and its regulation are the same as in tropical trees (Section 10.3). Temperate trees differ from the latter mainly in their potential to become *dormant* and *cold-hardy* during the winter. This is strikingly illustrated by seedlings of *Corylus* (hazelnut), in which adaptation to cold climates can be suppressed by a single recessive gene controlling the sensing of changes in photoperiod (35). In autumn, *nondormant mutants* of *Corylus* become neither dormant nor cold-hardy. In spite of low temperature and short daylength, terminal shoots continue to grow slowly, bud break occurs in lateral buds, and plants are eventually killed by freezing temperatures (Fig. 10.10).

Bud break or *bud rest* can be monitored by simple observation of morphogenetic changes (Figs. 10.1, 10.2), but cold-hardiness and the loss of

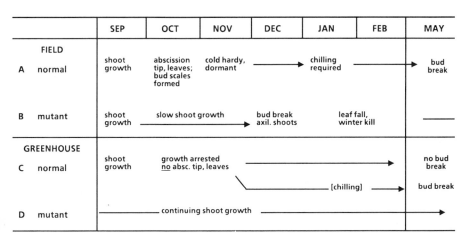

FIG. 10.10. Seasonal development in normal saplings and in nondormant mutants of *Corylus avellana* (hazelnut) (Adapted from Ref. 35.)

growth potential associated with dormancy must be assessed experimentally. *Bud dormancy* is evaluated by transferring entire, defoliated tree seedlings, stem cuttings, or isolated internodes bearing a single bud to optimum growing conditions (Fig. 10.11). Under such conditions *resting buds* will resume growth within 10 days (Fig. 10.11B, Sep., March). With increasing intensity of dormancy, the time to bud break increases to several weeks or months (Fig. 10.11B, Oct.–Jan.).

The growth pattern in potted seedlings of *Fraxinus* growing in Europe illustrates the course of seasonal development in most temperate, broad-leafed trees (Fig. 10.11A,B). After a flush of shoot growth in spring, by midsummer terminal buds of the seedlings enter a state of *correlative rest*, which can be broken by defoliation as late as September. Thereafter, short photoperiods and declining temperatures of autumn cause a rapid transition from *rest* to intensive *dormancy* (Fig. 10.11B, Sep.–Oct.). The intensity of dormancy declines from October to January, and by February dormant buds have returned to a state of rest. This time course suggests that the main adaptive value of dormancy is to prevent bud break in fall, which would result in the death of the new shoots during winter (compare Fig. 10.10B). During February and March, resumption of shoot growth under field conditions is

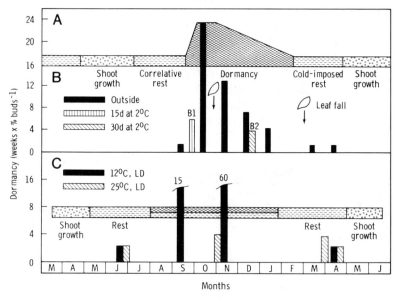

FIG. 10.11. Seasonal development and bud dormancy in seedlings of *Fraxinus excelsior* (ash). (A) Annual course of shoot growth, bud rest, and dormancy in potted seedlings exposed to climatic conditions of central France. (B) Changes in the growth potential of terminal buds of defoliated seedlings transferred from the outside to a growth chamber (25°C, 16 h light). Dormancy units were calculated by dividing weeks to budbreak by the fraction of plants on which budbreak occurred. (B1, B2) Seedlings transferred to growth chamber after receiving the indicated treatment. (C) Seedlings maintained at 12 or 25°C and 16-h photoperiod (LD). (Redrawn from Refs. 36–38.)

delayed by low temperature (Fig. 10.11A,B), and buds are thus in a state of *cold-imposed rest*, analogous to the *drought-imposed rest* of tropical trees during drought (Section 10.5.4).

10.6.3. The effect of chilling

A low-temperature treatment of *Fraxinus* seedlings early in the winter enhances the *induction of dormancy*, but cold exposure at a later time causes the *breaking of dormancy* [Fig. 10.11, B1, B2). The effect of chilling thus varies with the physiological state of the dormant bud. Under natural conditions, breaking of dormancy in temperate trees requires an exposure to low temperatures for a minimum period. This *chilling requirement*, the intensity of dormancy, and cold-hardiness are correlated within species, ecotypes, and cultivars of woody plants, reflecting the adaptive nature of these characters. Temperate fruit trees range from a high chilling requirement, good cold-hardiness, and late bud break in varieties suited for the northern temperate zone to varieties with low chilling requirements for warm temperate and subtropical climates (39).

10.6.4. Role of photoperiod

If dormancy and cold-hardiness are to protect temperate trees against freezing damage, physiological changes must occur before trees are actually exposed to the first frost. *A priori*, the progressively shorter photoperiods of autumn, rather than declining temperature, should thus be the principal environmental signal inducing dormancy and cold-hardiness in anticipation of the coming of winter (7,17). This is in marked contrast to drought adaptation, where water stress itself causes the adaptive developmental changes such as enhanced leaf shedding and arrest of shoot growth (Section 10.5).

  In mature temperate trees, shoot growth is arrested long before fall (Fig. 10.1) and bud rest is therefore *not* caused by exposure to short photoperiods. Because of the difficulty of working with such trees, the relative contribution of photoperiod versus low temperature to the induction of dormancy is not known. Saplings of both tropical and temperate trees respond to short photoperiods (8–10 h) with a reduction in shoot extension, which may or may not be followed by the formation of resting buds (7,17). In many species, growth is immediately resumed when plants are returned to long photoperiods, but some temperate species become dormant and require chilling before growth can be resumed. Similarly, exposure to long photoperiods prevents the induction of dormancy in many, but not all, temperate species (e.g., Fig. 10.11C). In *Corylus* seedlings short photoperiods without simultaneous cold exposure cause an arrest of shoot growth and dormancy, but do not trigger the morphogenetic changes normally associated with dormancy induction (Fig. 10.10A,C).

  Photoperiod thus plays an important role in the control of seasonal development in temperate trees, but responses to photoperiod vary widely among species and do not permit a distinction as to whether photoperiod induces bud rest, dormancy, or cold-hardiness. Photoperiodism, like hormonal control (Section 10.7), is thus only one among several regulatory mechanisms.

10.6.5. Induction of dormancy under constant conditions

Dormancy has been observed in equatorial forests around the world (Section 10.6.1). In equatorial Kenya and Java, bud dormancy in apple trees (*Malus*) can be prevented by defoliation soon after harvesting the fruit (39,40). Dormancy develops and then disappears when *Fraxinus* seedlings are grown under long days at 12°C, but not at 25°C (Fig. 10.11C). Trees can thus become dormant without exposure to variations in photoperiod or temperature, and the biochemical changes associated with the transition of buds from rest to dormancy are primarily endogenous in nature, but can be affected by the environment.

10.7. Hormonal regulation

The hypothesis that bud dormancy in trees might be caused by inhibitory plant hormones, such as abscisic acid (ABA), was introduced 40 years ago, since the level of growth inhibitors in extracts from dormant *Fraxinus* buds declined during winter in parallel with bud dormancy. Later, it was proposed that short photoperiods cause an increase in the ABA content of buds, while chilling reduces ABA levels and thus enables bud break in spring. None of these hypotheses withstood experimental testing (41,42), and the following assessment of hormonal control of bud dormancy, written 25 years ago, remains valid (7): "Our knowledge of endogenous growth regulators (including morphogenetic receptor pigments), and their interactions under various conditions, is so inadequate that intelligent discussion of the subject is not yet possible." Indeed, neither shoot growth periodicity nor any other aspect of plant development involving correlations between organs (e.g., apical dominance, flower induction, or tuber formation) has been satisfactorily explained in terms of hormone interactions (43). The genetic and physiological control of morphogenesis is so complex even in a relatively simple system such as the isolated shoot meristem of tobacco (44) that any attempt to deduce hormonal control of shoot growth periodicity in woody plants from crude correlations between extracted hormones and shoot development appears overly simplistic. There can be little doubt that plant hormones are involved in the regulation of growth periodicity. However, the complex interrelations between environmental (photoperiod, drought, and cold), nutritional, and hormonal factors remain to be unraveled.

Much of the evidence for the involvement of plant hormones in the regulation of dormancy is of limited value, because the physiological state of the analyzed buds has seldom been defined. Observed hormonal changes claimed to be correlated with the onset and breaking of bud dormancy are more likely to be associated with bud rest. During periodic shoot growth in *Citrus* and *Quercus* seedlings the ABA level is lowest just before flushing (5), and bud break caused by defoliation in *Theobroma* and *Malus* grown in the tropics is preceded by a decline in ABA content (45). In many temperate trees, endogenous levels of ABA are lowest immediately before bud break in spring, i.e., months after the chilling requirement has been met and dormancy has ended (41). In *Prunus cerasus* (sour cherry), defoliation in autumn prevents an increase in ABA, but not bud dormancy. Levels of growth-promoting hormones such as auxin, gibberellins, and cytokinins generally increase before bud break, suggesting that the ratio between ABA and growth-promoting hormones might control the induction and breaking of dormancy or rest.

The arrest of shoot growth and formation of terminal buds by an ABA treatment of seedlings of *Betula* and other species under long-day conditions (41) represents an induction of rest rather than dormancy, because growth resumes soon after the treatment ends. Inversely, treatments with gibberellins can stimulate the growth of resting buds that have partly emerged from dormancy, but do not break dormancy. For every example describing a specific effect of externally applied hormones, there are others in which applied hormones were ineffective in inducing or breaking bud rest, or in which no correlation between hormone content and activity of the apical meristem was found. None of the proposed hypotheses has thus been conclusively confirmed.

Water deficits, the major factor involved in the induction of correlative rest (Sections 10.3.4 and 10.3.6) cause elevated levels of ABA in leaves. This growth inhibitor is then transported to sinks such as growing apical meristems (46). The implicit correlation between the disappearance of water deficits and decreased ABA concentration prior to bud break induced by defoliation raises the unexplored question of whether internal water deficits affect apical meristems directly or indirectly via the induction of ABA synthesis.

In many instances, the chilling requirement for the breaking of bud dormancy in woody plants as well as tubers and corms can be eliminated by bud scale removal, soaking in warm water, anaerobiosis, or treatments with various chemicals, including metabolic poisons. Changes in respiration and nucleotide metabolism associated with the breaking of bud dormancy indicate a reduced energy metabolism during dormancy (8,38), but such changes might be the consequence rather than the cause of dormancy.

10.8. Periodic growth and the adaptive strategy of trees

Periodic shoot growth of trees, characterized by the temporary arrest of growth under favorable growing conditions (correlative bud rest), results primarily from the interaction among the organs of a tree. As a tree increases in size and hence in the number of interacting organs, the pattern of shoot growth periodicity changes as a consequence of changing functional correlations. Water deficits resulting from an excess of transpiration over water absorption appear to be the principal cause of shoot growth cessation. Elimination of water deficits, and thus correlative inhibition, by shedding of leaves causes the termination of correlative bud rest and the resumption of shoot growth. In nonseasonal climates, the interval between consecutive episodes of leaf fall and shoot growth, i.e., the period length of shoot growth rhythmicity, is therefore a function of the species-specific longevity of a tree's leaves, and shoot growth periodicity is ultimately the consequence of the periodic, simultaneous replacement of a tree's foliage. Only trees that form and replace leaves slowly and gradually are able to sustain continuous, but slow, growth.

Adverse environmental conditions such as drought or cold may prevent the resumption of shoot growth even after leaf fall. Consequently, trees are leafless during periods of drought- or cold-imposed bud rest, and shoot growth resumes as soon as environmental stress is relieved. The endogenous shoot growth rhythmicity may thus be adapted secondarily to seasonal changes in climate. Finally, resting buds may become dormant, i.e., temporarily lose the potential to resume growth when exposed to favorable growing conditions. Periodic growth patterns *per se* are therefore not genetically determined, but result from the interaction among a variety of endogenous and environmental factors.

Earlier attempts to explain the adaptive significance of growth periodicity and rest periods have considered these phenomena in isolation rather than viewing trees as large, long-lived plants with a characteristic strategy for maximizing carbon gain (47,48). At the beginning of each episode of shoot growth, reserve assimilates are invested in the growth of branches and leaves, resulting in the rapid establishment of a full complement of leaves. Carbon gain from the mature foliage is then used for growth in girth, to replenish assimilate reserves for the next phase of shoot growth and, eventually, to produce seeds. In trees with a full crown of productive leaves, shoot growth is arrested to reduce self-shading and should resume soon after leaf fall. In view of the trade-off between carbon gain and water loss, the central role of water stress in the proximate mechanisms regulating tree growth periodicity is to be expected.

Periods of imposed rest and dormancy in leafless trees reflect delays imposed on the normal reestablishment of photosynthetic surfaces by environmental stress such as drought or cold; environmentally imposed bud rest thus represents tolerance of, rather than adaptation to, environmental stress. In contrast, bud dormancy and cold-hardiness are truly adaptive, because these temporarily acquired physiological states enable temperate trees to survive cold winters.

ACKNOWLEDGMENTS

The author gratefully acknowledges critical review of the manuscript by Dr. C. Martin and careful execution of the illustrations by S. Hagen.

10.9. References

1. M.H. Zimmermann and C.L. Brown, *Trees. Structure and Function*, Springer-Verlag, New York, 1971.

2. K.A. Longman and J. Jenik, *Tropical Forest and Its Environment*, 2nd ed. Longman, London, 1988.

3. D.C. Greathouse, W.M. Laetsch, and B.O. Phinney, "The shoot-growth rhythm of a tropical tree, *Theobroma cacao*," *Am. J. Bot.*, **58**, 281 (1971).

4. F. Hallé and R. Martin, "Étude sur la croissance rythmique chez l'Hévéa (*Hevea brasiliensis*)," *Adansonia*, **8**, 475 (1968).

5. S. Lavarenne-Allary, "Recherches sur la croissance des bourgeons de chêne et de quelques autres espèces ligneuses," *Ann. Sci. For. (Paris)*, **22**, 1 (1965).

6. R. Borchert, "Endogenous shoot growth rhythms and indeterminate shoot growth in oak," *Physiol. Plant.*, **35**, 152 (1975).

7. J.A. Romberger, *Meristems, Growth, and Development in Woody Plants*, U.S. Dept. Agric. Tech. Bull. No. 1293, 1963.

8. A. Vegis, "Ruhezustände bei höheren Pflanzen," in W. Ruhland, ed., *Encyclopedia of Plant Physiology*, Vol. 15/2, Springer-Verlag, Berlin, p. 499, 1965.

9. G.A. Lang, J.D. Early, G.C. Martin, and R.L. Darnell, "Endo-, para-, and ecodormancy: Physiological terminology and classification for dormancy research," *HortiScience*, **22**, 371 (1987).

10. F. Hallé, R.A.A. Oldeman, and P.B. Tomlinson, *Tropical Trees and Forests. An Architectural Analysis*," Springer-Verlag, Berlin, 1978.

11. T.T. Kozlowski, *Growth and Development of Trees*, Vol. I, Academic Press, New York, 1971.

12. M.G.R. Cannell, S. Thompson, and R. Lines, "An analysis of inherent differences in shoot growth within some north temperate conifers," in M.G.R. Cannell and F.T. Last, eds., *Tree Physiology and Yield Improvement*, Academic Press, London, 1976, p. 173.

13. R.M. Lanner, "Patterns of shoot development in *Pinus* and their relationship to growth potential," in M.G.R. Cannell and F.T. Last, eds., *Tree Physiology and Yield Improvement*, Academic Press, London, 1976, p. 223.

14. F. Mialoundama, M. Lauzac, and P. Paulet, "The periodic induction of dormancy during the rhythmic growth of *Gnetum africanum*," *Physiol. Plant.*, **61**, 309 (1984).

15. D. Richards, "Root–shoot interactions: A functional equilibrium for water uptake in peach [*Prunus persica* (L.) Batsch.]," *Ann. Bot.*, **41**, 279 (1976).

16. A.P. Drew and F.T. Ledig, "Episodic growth and relative shoot : root balance in loblolly pine seedlings," *Ann. Bot.*, **45**, 143 (1980).

17. K.A. Longman, "Control of shoot extension and dormancy: External and internal factors," in P.B. Tomlinson and M.H. Zimmermann, eds., *Tropical Trees as Living Systems*, Cambridge Univ. Press, Cambridge, 1978, p. 465.

18. M. Vogel, "Recherche du déterminisme du rhythme de croissance du cacaoyer," *Café, Cacao, Thé*, **19**, 265 (1975).

19. P. de T. Alvim and R. Alvim, "Relation of climate to growth periodicity in tropical trees," in P.B. Tomlinson and M.H. Zimmermann, eds., *Tropical Trees as Living Systems*, Cambridge Univ. Press, Cambridge, 1978, p. 445.

20. P.B. Reich, R.O. Teskey, P.S. Johnson, and T.M. Hinckley, "Periodic root and shoot growth in oak," *Forest Sci.*, **26**, 590 (1980).

21. T.J. Tschaplinski and T.J. Blake, "Effects of root restriction on growth correlations, water relations and senescence of alder seedlings," *Physiol. Plant.*, **64**, 167 (1985).

22. T.J. Blake and T.J. Tschaplinski, "Role of water relations and photosynthesis in the release of buds from apical dominance and the early invigoration of decapitated poplars," *Physiol. Plant.*, **68**, 287 (1986).

23. F.W. Ewers and M.H. Zimmermann, "The hydraulic architecture of balsam fir (Tsuga canadensis)," *Canad. J. Bot.*, **62**, 940 (1984).

24. R. Borchert, "Simulation of rhythmic tree growth under constant conditions," *Physiol. Plant.*, **29**, 173 (1973).

25. J.S. Boyer, "Cell enlargement and growth-induced water potentials," *Physiol. Plant.*, **73**, 311 (1988).

26. R. Borchert, "Feedback control and age-related changes of shoot growth in seasonal and nonseasonal climates," in P.B. Tomlinson and M.H. Zimmermann, eds., *Tropical Trees as Living Systems*, Cambridge Univ. Press, Cambridge, 1978, p. 497.

27. P.B. Reich and R. Borchert, "Water stress and tree phenology in a tropical dry forest in the lowlands of Costa Rica," *J. Ecol.*, **72**, 61 (1984).

28. P.B. Reich and R. Borchert, "Phenology and ecophysiology of the tropical tree, *Tabebuia neochrysantha* (Bignoniaceae)," *Ecology*, **63**, 294 (1982).

29. R. Borchert, "Phenology and ecophysiology of tropical trees: *Erythrina poeppigiana* O.F. Cook," *Ecology*, **61**, 1065 (1980).

30. R. Borchert, "Tabebuia," in A.H. Halevy, ed., *CRC Handbook of Flowering*, Vol. 5, CRC Press, Boca Raton, FL, 1986, p. 347.

31. R. Borchert, "Phenology and control of flowering in tropical trees," *Biotropica*, **15**, 81 (1983).

32. R. Borchert, "Erythrina," in A.H. Halevy, ed., *CRC Handbook of Flowering*, Vol. 5, CRC Press, Boca Raton, FL, 1986, p. 95.

33. B.F. Chabot and D.J. Hicks, "The ecology of leaf life span," *Ann. Rev. Ecol. Syst.*, **13**, 229 (1982).

34. P.B. Reich and R. Borchert, "Changes with leaf age in stomatal function and water status of several tropical tree species," *Biotropica*, **20**, 60 (1988).

35. M.M. Thompson, D.C. Smith, and J.E. Burgess, "Nondormant mutants in a temperate tree species, *Corylus avellana* L.," *Theor. Appl. Genet.*, **70**, 687 (1985).

36. S. Lavarenne, P. Champagnat, and P. Barnola, "Influence d'une même gamme de températures sur l' entrée et la sortie de dormance des bourgeons du frêne (*Fraxinus excelsior* L.)," *Physiol. vég.*, **13**, 215 (1975).

37. S. Lavarenne, P. Barnola, M. Gendraud, and N. Jallut, "Caractérization biochimique de la periode de repos au cours de la croissance rhythmique du Frêne cultivé á température élevée et constante," *CR Acad. Sci. Paris ser. III*, **303**, 139 (1986).

38. P. Barnola, S. Lavarenne, M. Gendraud, and N. Jallut, "Étude biochimique d'une dormance rythmique chez le Frêne (*Fraxinus excelsior* L.) cultivé en conditions contrôlées," *CR Acad. Sci. Paris ser. III*, **303**, 239 (1986).

39. M.C. Saure, "Dormancy release in deciduous fruit trees," *Horticult. Rev.*, **7**, 239 (1985).

40. S. Notodimedjo, H. Danoesastro, S. Sastrosumarto, and G.R. Edwards, "Shoot growth, flower initiation and dormancy of apple in the tropics," *Acta Horticult.*, **120**, 179, 256 (1981).

41. D.P. Lavender and S.N. Silim, "The role of growth regulators in dormancy in forest trees," *Plant Growth Regul.*, **6**, 171 (1987).

42. L.E. Powell, "The hormonal control of bud and seed dormancy in woody plants," in P.J. Davies, ed., *Plant Hormones and Their Role in Plant Growth and Development*, Nijhoff, Dordrecht, 1987, p. 539.

43. P.J. Davies, ed., *Plant Hormones and their Role in Plant Growth and Development*, Nijhoff, Dordrecht, 1987.

44. D.R. Meeks-Wagner, E.S. Dennis, K.T. Thanh Van, and W.J. Peacock, "Tobacco genes expressed during in vitro floral initiation and their expression during normal plant development," *Plant Cell*, **1**, 25 (1989).

45. J.S. Taylor, P.P. Pharis, B. Loveys, S. Notodimedjo, and G.R. Edwards, "Changes in endogenous hormones in apple during bud burst induced by defoliation," *Plant Growth Regul.*, **2**, 117 (1984).

46. J.A.D. Zeevart and R. A. Creelman, "Metabolism and physiology of abscisic acid," *Ann. Rev. Plant Physiol. Plant Mol. Biol.*, **39**, 439 (1988).

47. T.J. Givnish, ed., *On the Economy of Plant Form and Function*, Cambridge Univ. Press, Cambridge, 1986.

48. K.A. Longman, "The dormancy and survival of plants in the humid tropics," *Symp. Soc. Exp. Biol.*, **23**, 471 (1969).

11 Flowering and Seed Set

JOHN N. OWENS

Department of Biology, University of Victoria, Victoria, British
Columbia, Canada

Contents

11.1. Introduction

Flowering and seed set in trees have received far less attention than that in
herbaceous plants, as demonstrated by the five volumes edited by Halevy

(1). This is because many trees are too large to be easily studied, have long juvenile periods before they flower, have long reproductive cycles, have complex bud structure, and have an unpredictable pattern of floral initiation. Nevertheless, the desire to increase fruit production in horticulture and seed production in forestry has stimulated more interest in tree sexual reproduction. A recent book (2) covers most aspects for hardwoods and conifers. Although physiological and developmental approaches are essential, both are rarely covered in a single study. This chapter attempts to synthesize the physiology and development of flowering and seed set in hardwood and coniferous forest trees with only occasional reference to fruit trees.

11.2. Flowering periodicity

Most information on flowering periodicity comes from data on forest stands or fruit crops rather than individual trees. Trees pass through a variable juvenile stage, ranging from 1 to over 40 years (Table 11.1). The mature, reproductive, stage is a condition called "ripeness to flower," and the transition to this stage is known as "phase change" (3). The capacity to flower is retained thereafter. The periodicity of flowering varies among and within species. In temperate forest trees, good seed-set occurs every 3–7 years (Table 11.1). In fruit trees biennial crops are common because frequent flowering is a genetically selected trait. The frequency of flowering in tropical trees is extremely variable.

Three types of temperate zone plants have been distinguished based on their flowering features: (a) most herbaceous plants have a *direct flowering* habit in which floral initiation and development through anthesis occur without interruption, (b) *indirect flowering* occurs in most woody perennials in which there is a period of rest (dormancy) at some stage between floral initiation and anthesis, and (c) many herbaceous species undergo *cumulative flowering* in which floral primordia form over a long time but anthesis of all flowers occurs at one time (3).

Four types of periodicity in the flowering of tropical plants are recognized (3):

1. In *ever-flowering* species flower initiation occurs throughout the year, e.g., *Fiscus* spp.
2. In *nonseasonal flowering* plants flowering periodicity occurs among plants and from branch to branch.
3. *Gregarious flowering* plants have regular initiation of floral buds that remain closed for weeks or months until environmental conditions are favorable, sometimes resulting in synchronous anthesis over a wide area, e.g., *Coffea* spp.
4. *Seasonal flowering* occurs in response to alteration in seasons (rainy or dry) or day length.

Table 11.1. Bud types, age, and frequency of flowering in selected hardwood and conifer trees[a]

Family/botanical name	Common name	Buds simple (S) or mixed (M)	Buds terminal (T) or axillary (A)	First good seed crops (years)	Intervals between good seed crops (years)
Aceraceae					
Acer platanoides	Norway maple	M	T,A	25–30	1–3
Platanus occidentalis	American sycamore	M	A	25–30	1–3
Betulaceae					
Alnus glutinosa	Common alder	S	A	15–20	2–3
Betula pendula	Silver birch	S	T,A	15	1–3
Fagaceae					
Fagus sylvatica	Common beech	M	A	50–60	5–15
Quercus petraea	Sessile oak	M	A	40–50	2–5
Saliaceae					
Populus tremuloudes	Quaking aspen	S	A	50–70[b]	4–5
Salix nigra	Black willow	S	A	25–75[b]	1–3
Oleaceae					
Fraxinus excelsior	Common ash	M	A	25–30	3–5
Cupressaceae					
Chamaeyparis lawsoniana	Lawson cyress	S	T	20–25	4–5
Thuja plicata	Western redcedar	S	T	20–25	2–3
Pinaceae					
Abies grandis	Grand fir	S	A	40–45	3–5
Larix decidua	European larch	S	T	25–30	3–5
Picea abies	Norway Spruce	S	T,A	30–35	3–5
Pinus contorta	Lodgepole pine	M	A	15–20	2–3
Pseudotsuga menziesii	Douglas fir	S	A	30–35	5–7
Tsuga heterophylla	Western hemlock	S	A,T	25–30	3–4

[a]Data compiled from various sources.
[b]Optimum.

Thus, there is a tremendous diversity in flowering of angiosperms, especially in tropical trees. The diversity is much less in conifers.

Long-term fluctuations in production of cone crops have been demonstrated in conifers (4–6) and in fruit crops and hardwoods (7,8) (Table 11.1). Cone, fruit, and seed production represent the climax of long reproductive cycles and can be influenced by many factors. Although periodicity is generally well documented, the causes are poorly understood because of the complex interactions of many endogenous and exogenous factors.

11.3. Reproductive cycles

The reproductive cycles in conifers are better known than that in hardwoods (9), while little is known about the reproductive cycles of most tropical trees.

Three reproductive cycles represent the ranges of those found in most temperate-zone trees. The most common cycle in hardwoods and conifers spans 2 years from floral initiation through a period of winter dormancy until seed release. Reproductive buds are initiated in the summer, and pollination occurs the next spring. The time between pollination and fertilization is brief, usually only a few weeks. Embryo and seed development are rapid and continuous. The mature seeds may be released as early as late summer of the year of pollination. Retention of seed beyond that time is often determined by climatic or biotic requirements unique to a species and to its method of seed dispersal. A second reproductive cycle is found in most species of *Pinus*, several other conifers, and some hardwoods. This cycle is the same as that described above except that there is about a 1-year delay between pollination and fertilization. A third reproductive cycle is found in a few conifers and hardwoods. This cycle is similar to the first cycle except that embryo and seed development begin but are arrested in late summer or autumn. Seeds that are immature during winter resume development the next spring and mature by late summer or autumn (9). Occasional combinations of the latter two cycles occur and result in very prolonged cycles (10).

There is much variation in the phenology of floral development owing to the long reproductive cycles of most trees. The longer the process, the greater the possibility for fruit or seed losses to occur. The cause of losses in many trees is not determined since there is very limited information on stage of development at which the fruit or seed loss occurred (9,11,12).

11.4. Floral initiation, induction, and enhancement

Floral initiation describes the transition of an indeterminate vegetative terminal or axillary apical meristem (apex) into a determinate reproductive apex that develops into an angiosperm flower or flowering shoot or a conifer strobilus (cone). Floral induction in juvenile or otherwise nonreproductive trees and the enhancement of flowering in poor-flowering trees are valuable tools in agriculture and forestry. For a complete discussion of the flowering process and the terminology in current use for herbaceous angiosperms, the reader is referred to Bernier's reviews (13,14), although this terminology may not always be applicable to woody perennials.

Floral initiation, the first step in any reproductive cycle, appears to be similar in angiosperms and conifers. The classical view of floral initiation in herbaceous plants is that the flowering stimulus (evocation) originates in various plant parts and is transmitted over a period of hours or days to the apex where a transition occurs from a vegetative to a floral apex (13). Most plants flower in response to specific environmental changes, such as photoperiod and temperature. This classical view has never been accepted for woody perennials, where flowering appears to result from a series of developmental stages, each sequentially determined by the hormone and/or substrate balance at the initiation site and modulated by different environmental factors acting on various plant organs (11,13,14).

Most cultural treatments to induce or enhance flowering involve alteration of environmental factors that may initiate flowering. The number of combinations of cultural treatments is almost limitless and their results are often inconclusive or contradictory. In addition various growth regulators have been applied often with cultural treatments to induce or enhance flowering. Several extensive reviews have been written on these subjects (6,7,9,11,15–18).

11.4.1. Types of reproductive buds

In most trees, reproductive buds are enclosed by bud scales, whereas in some they are completely exposed. Buds may be simple, containing only floral parts as in most conifers (Figs. 11.1d,f) or mixed, containing leaves and flowers as in most hardwoods but few conifers. Flowers or strobili may also be located either terminally or in the axils of leaves or bracts (Table 11.1, Fig. 11.2).

In conifers normally all reproductive buds are unisexual [separate male (Fig. 11.1f) and female strobili (Fig. 11.1d)], but bisexual (hermaphroditic) strobili are not uncommon (19). Hardwood flowers may be bisexual (perfect) as in most species of *Acer*; unisexual (imperfect) as in *Quercus, Populus,* and *Betula*; or polygamous, having both unisexual and bisexual flowers as in some species of *Acer* (20). Those that have unisexual flowers may have both male and female on the same plant (monoecious) or on separate plants (dioecious). Most conifers and hardwoods are monoecious. However, the control of gender is not necessarily fixed within a genus (e.g., *Populus*; Ref. 20), species, or even an individual (e.g., *Acer*, Ref. 21).

11.4.2. Time and site of floral initiation

11.4.2.1. Conifers. There have been several reviews of times and sites of floral initiation in conifers (9,15,22). Of the seven families of conifers only the Pinaceae and Cupressaceae have been extensively studied. Generally,

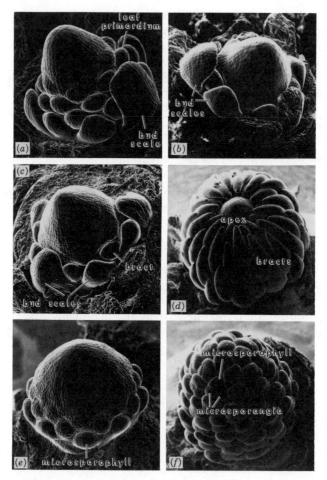

FIG. 11.1. Scanning electron micrographs of differentiating *Pseudotsuga* apical meristems and buds: (a) vegetative apical meristem, ×79; (b) undetermined axillary apex, ×75; (c) seed-cone apex at onset of bract initiation, ×60; (d) seed-cone bud after bud scales were removed; ×24; (e) pollen-cone apex at onset of microsporophyll initiation, ×60; (f) pollen-cone bud after bud scales were removed, ×30.

seed cones occur on vigorous lower order shoots in upper regions of the crown and pollen cones occur on less vigorous higher order shoots lower in the crown (22,23).

In most conifers pollen cones and seed cones are initiated from terminal or axillary apices during the spring or summer before pollination. Only in the soft pines are seed cones initiated after dormancy, a few weeks before pollination (Fig. 11.2). In the Pinaceae, reproductive apices (terminal or axillary) produce a series of bud scales (Fig. 11.1c) and then undergo a brief period of apical enlargement and differentiation before beginning to initiate leaves (Fig. 11.1a), bracts (Fig. 11.1c,d) or microsporophylls (Fig. 11.1e,f).

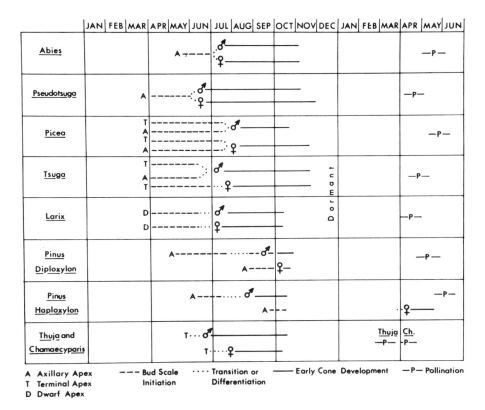

FIG. 11.2. Times and sites of cone-bud initiation in several conifers.

The development of apices is determined by their position on the shoot and in the crown as well as the physiological status of the shoot and the tree. Apices may abort during bud-scale initiation, resulting in death of the apex and termination of growth of the potential shoot. Apices may initiate some or all of their bud scales before development is arrested. These remain as small latent buds that may resume growth, often years later. Other apices initiate all bud scales and then differentiate as vegetative, pollen cone, or seed cone apices (Fig. 11.3) (9). In many conifers pollen- and seed-cone buds differentiate at the same time while in others (*Pinus, Tsuga, Thuja, Chamaecyparis*) pollen cones differentiate before seed cones (Fig. 11.2). Patterns and times of cone-bud differentiation are surprisingly uniform within a species in north temperate regions.

11.4.2.2. Hardwoods.   Floral initiation in hardwoods is complex and has not been studied as much as in conifers. In north temperate hardwoods, floral buds are initiated before winter dormancy, but the extent to which buds develop before dormancy varies. The anatomy of floral initiation has been studied in only a few genera such as *Betula* (24) and *Juglans* (25).

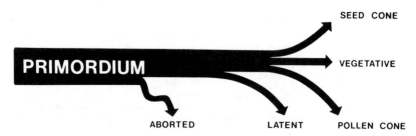

FIG. 11.3. Pathways of axillary bud development in *Pseudotsuga*.

11.4.3. Environmental factors

Potential reproductive apices undergo several weeks of undetermined growth (Fig. 11.3) during which their development is very malleable. At this time environmental and endogenous factors interact to control bud development. Many studies have tried to demonstrate a relationship between environmental factors and flowering in geographic regions, in forest stands, and on individual trees, but it is difficult to identify causal mechanisms, as mentioned in several reviews (7,9,11,15,16).

11.4.3.1. Temperature. High summer temperatures generally favor increased flowering. This was first mentioned for *Fagus* in 1751 by Linnaeus. Warm June and July temperatures enhance flower production in *Fagus*, especially male flowering, while cool autumns enhance female flowering (8). High summer temperatures have also been implicated in enhanced flowering in *Betula* (26), *Pinus* (16), *Abies* (27), *Picea* (28,29), and *Pseudotsuga* (6,27). High temperatures during floral initiation may affect metabolic processes, but we know little about these processes in reproductively mature trees.

The placing of potted trees in warm environments such as greenhouses or the tenting of field-grown trees are commonly used floral enhancement techniques for hardwoods (30) and conifers (31). Several treatments are commonly applied in conjunction with plant growth regulator (PGR) treatments (9). The timing of greenhouse treatment is important in conifers. Recent studies in *Picea* demonstrate that the elevated temperatures, with drought and gibberellin acid$_{4/17}$ (ga$_{4/7}$), are most effective during the period of lateral shoot elongation (32,33). The most effective treatments in *P. engelmannii* were those that inhibited shoot elongation and retarded bud development temporarily, delaying the time of cone-bud differentiation (34). The effect of such treatments on metabolites and PGRs are poorly understood.

11.4.3.2. Light intensity and photoperiod. Most studies indicate that effects of light intensity on flowering are indirect, relating to crown exposure, slope, shading, and floral distribution within the crown. Generally, branches exposed to high light intensity flower more abundantly than shaded branches, as has been shown in *Pseudotsuga* (35) and *Tectona* (36). Thinning has enhanced flowering in *Pinus* and *Pseudotsuga* (9) and certain fruit trees (11). Crown closure altered light intensity and proportion of male and female flowers (gender expression) in *Acer* (21).

Photoperiod has not been demonstrated to have the direct effect on flowering in trees that it has in many herbaceous plants (13,14). In three species of *Pinus* flowering was not affected by daylength (23,37). However, it has been suggested for *Picea* (38) and *Pinus contorta* (39,40) that daylength may effect development and numbers of seed cones produced. In *Thuja, Chamaecyparis* and *Tsuga* (9) it was demonstrated that under natural conditions pollen cones differentiated under increasing daylengths while seed cones differentiated under decreasing daylengths.

Photoperiod does affect shoot elongation, and it may be through the complex interaction of shoot elongation and bud differentiation (34) that photoperiod has an indirect influence on flowering. Greenwood (41), using short days to create an "out-of-phase dormancy" treatment, demonstrated that this was an effective indirect use of photoperiod for cone induction in *Pinus taeda*.

It is difficult to separate the effects of increased light and temperature on flowering in experiments carried out under otherwise natural conditions. A more specific use of light has been the growth of seedlings in continuous light or long days. *Betula* (42), *Picea* (43), and *Pinus* (44) seedlings grown under continuous light or long days flowered much earlier (at age 10–12 months and 4 and 5 years, respectively) than trees grown under natural conditions, which is commonly 15–20 years of age (see Table 11.1). Longman and Wareing (42) concluded from experiments in which *Betula* and *Larix* seedlings were grown in heated greenhouses under long photoperiods that sexual maturity of trees results from an attainment of a certain size rather than number of annual growth cycles.

11.4.3.3. Moisture stress and roots.

Positive correlations have been shown between low rainfall and increased cone production in *Pinus* (45), *Picea* (46), *Abies*, and *Pseudotsuga* (5,27). However, most of the early correlations were done without a knowledge of the time of floral initiation and did not separate effects on floral initiation from subsequent floral development. Also, in nature it is difficult to separate moisture availability from the effects of temperature and light intensity. In *Fagus* dry summers were correlated with increased seed production over a 100-year period (8). Subsequent experiments have shown that low moisture availability, separate from high temperature, affect flowering in *Fagus* (47) and *Picea* (32,33).

The promotive effect of natural moisture stress on flowering led to many attempts to induce or enhance flowering by various treatments, many of which halt or diminish root activity. Recently there has been increased evidence that roots play a more direct role in flowering of conifers than simply through water and mineral absorption (48,49). This role may be the synthesis and export to shoots of PGR or other substances that inhibit flowering, as demonstrated in *Ribes* (50). Similar inhibitory substances have not been demonstrated in conifers and hardwoods, although it has been speculated that gibberellins and cytokinins (51) from roots have a role in flowering. Despite the lack of a clear understanding of the role of roots in flowering, many treatments affecting roots affect flowering.

Carefully controlled drought treatments are difficult to carry out, especially in field-grown trees, and many attempts have not been accompanied by water potential measurements. In field-grown *Pseudotsuga* root pruning increased moisture stress and promoted flowering (62). Experiments using potted trees can be more easily controlled and monitored (33). Predawn moisture stresses of -1.4 to -2.0 MPa (52) appear adequate for cone induction or enhancement. Root pruning may alter the cycle of root activity in addition to affecting water uptake (49). Similarly, flooding of roots promoted flowering in potted *Pseudotsuga* (48). Philipson (32,49) suggested that high soil temperatures, which promoted flowering in *Picea sitchensis* potted grafts, did so by reducing root activity. As in all floral induction treatments, timing of drought or root inhibition is critical and must be related to time of floral initiation in each species (see Section 11.4.2.2).

11.4.3.4. Nitrogen and other mineral nutrients.   All other factors being equal, trees growing in fertile sites produce more seed than those growing on less fertile sites (7). The application of nitrogenous fertilizers is one of the oldest and most widely used floral induction–enhancement treatments. A summary of effects on flowering in hardwoods and conifers is tabulated by Owens and Blake (9). Fertilization may be important mainly in contributing to rapid growth leading to earlier onset of flowering (53). Nitrogen (N) is the only mineral that will promote flowering in conifers (18). Sweet and Hong (54) regard the major roles of nitrogen are to improve tree vigor and increase crown size and number of potential flowering sites. Others proposed that specific products of N metabolism, amino acids, and arginine in particular play a direct role in flowering (55). The form of N is important. Nitrate-N was the preferred source for *Pseudotsuga* (55), whereas ammonium-N was most effective in *Pinus elliotti* (56) and hardwoods in general (11). Results from fertilizer treatments are often extremely variable and inconclusive (9). In many studies the form of N is not specified and the time of application with relation to floral differentiation is not adequately considered. Other minerals such as phosphorus and potassium are frequently applied with N, making it difficult to determine their specific effects (11).

11.4.3.5. Other stress factors.   In general, any injury that imposes a stress on the tree may enhance flowering. These are commonly called *stress crops*, and many stress treatments are used in floral induction and enhancement (9).

Girdling, banding, and strangulation have long been used successfully to induce flowering in fruit trees (11), conifers, and some hardwoods (9). These treatments are intended to increase carbohydrate concentration in the crown by impeding its downward movement. This is based on the theory that high C/N (carbon/nitrogen) ratios promote flowering and low ratios favor vegetative growth. However, there is only a mixed support for this hypothesis. Floral induction–enhancement may also occur as a result of branch pruning, grafting, bending, wounding, resin tapping, defoliation, and frost and root damage (9), but no single convincing explanation is available.

11.4.4. Endogenous cycles

The lack of a consistent positive relationship between environmental factors and flowering may be because of the endogenous cycles within individual trees. Although all the factors controlling reproductive bud differentiation are not known, we know that in most trees abundant crops do not occur in consecutive years. An abundant crop on a tree is usually followed by no crop or a small crop regardless of how favorable environmental conditions may be.

The times of reproductive bud differentiation and subsequent development usually coincide with rapid growth of shoots and maturation of the fruits or cones of the current season, all of which have high nutrient requirements (57). Consequently, shoot elongation and reproductive bud development may be inhibited by the current (subtending) fruits or cones that are strong metabolic sinks (60). In mature *Pinus radiata*, pollen, seeds, and cones can account for up to 16% of total dry weight of the tree (58). Appreciable quantities of minerals and nitrogen also accumulate in fruits and seeds (59). Therefore, it may take one or more years following a heavy crop before endogenous conditions are suitable for reproductive bud development. Added to this must be favorable environmental conditions. It is no wonder that seed crops in many trees, which have not been genetically selected for frequent crops, are very cyclic and infrequent in their seed and cone crops (Table 11.1).

11.4.5. Plant growth regulator (PGR) treatments

A recent and comprehensive review of the effects of PGR on flowering of hardwoods and conifers is made by Owens and Blake (9). Only a brief survey of the most promising PGR treatments is presented here. The modes of action of PGRs in flowering are still speculative but are discussed elsewhere (9). A comprehensive account of growth regulators tested for their effect on flowering is given in Chapter 20 of this book.

In general, gibberellins (GAs) promote flowering in conifers but inhibit flowering in woody angiosperms (11,18,61). Cones have been induced in several species of Cupressaceae, Taxodiaceae, and Pinaceae using GA_3 or the less polar GAs, namely, GA_4, GA_7, and GA_9 (Table 11.2).

The timing of GA application is very important and must precede reproductive bud differentiation. Biochemical changes no doubt begin before anatomic differentiation is visible (Fig. 11.2). Commonly, the optimal times of treatment are determined empirically or through anatomic study (9,34). The percentage of lateral shoot elongation is a good indicator of the best treatment time in most conifers. There is an inverse relationship between flowering and

Table 11.2. Trees in which cone induction has been achieved with gibberellins

GA$_3$		GA$_{4/7}$
Cupressaceae (15 species)	Taxodiaceae (4 species)	Pinaceae (17 species)
Callitris (1)[a]	Cryptomeria (1)	Larix (2)
Chamaecyparis (4)	Metasequoia (1)	Picea (4)
Cupressus (5)	Sequoiadendron (1)	Pinus (9)
Juniperus (P)[b] (1)	Taxodium (1)	Psuedotsuga (1)
Thuja (3)		Tsuga (1)
Thujopsis (P) (1)		

[a]Numbers in parentheses indicate number of species in which cones have been induced.
[b]P indicates only pollen cones were induced.

shoot elongation. Activation of the subapical meristem in woody dicots by GAs stimulates shoot elongation but inhibits flowering, whereas substances that retard subapical activity and shoot growth may promote flowering (61). Cone-induction–enhancement treatments enhance (62), retard (63), or have no effect on shoot elongation (33), but these variable results appear to depend on time of treatment in relation to shoot development. Unfortunately, the dynamics of shoot elongation are not completely understood especially in relation to bud development and flowering (34).

Auxins and cytokinins may enhance or modify the response to exogenous GAs but alone are ineffective (51,64). The synthetic auxin, naphthaleneacetic acid (NAA), when applied alone does not promote flowering, except possibly in *Larix leptolepis* (65). However, when applied in combination with GAs, NAA may enhance flowering (66). Auxin and abscissic acid may affect ethylene production, as do many adjunct treatments; this "stress ethylene" may stimulate flowering. However, few attempts have been made to use ethylene directly to induce or enhance flowering. Ethel (2-chloroethyl-phosphonic acid) enhanced the effectiveness of GA$_3$ in promoting flowering in *Cupressus* and *Chamaecyparis* and doubled the number of seed cones but not pollen cones produced in *Picea abies* grafts (67). The growth retardants Cycocel (CCC) enhanced cone induction in *Picea abies* when applied with GA$_3$ (68,69). In their review Bonnet-Masimbert and Zaerr (66) acknowledge that timing of treatments can be an important factor in the variable results obtained using growth retardants as well as GAs. Because GAs have been so successful in conifers, it is now commonly used commercially in many seed orchards. However, methods of application vary (66).

At the time of reproductive bud differentiation, levels of endogenous GAs and other PGRs in shoots and especially buds are poorly understood. Endogenous PGRs at time of flowering have been related to tree age or cone induction treatments in conifers (17,51,70–72). Work is now beginning using immunologic methods for quantification of abscissic acid, indolacetic acid, and cytokinins and GAs in small samples of tissue (buds) as opposed to whole shoots (66). Results from these studies should give a clearer picture of the complex relationship of various PGRs to floral bud differentiation. Studies of hardwoods are even less definitive at this time. Juvenile and mature flowering *Betula varrucosa* trees were compared in their content of PGRs (GAs, abscissic acid, cytokinin) in buds and apical portions of shoots (73). Presently, these types of studies in conifers and hardwoods suggest correlations between levels of PGRs and flowering but do not demonstrate a direct causal relationship to flowering.

Seeds from floral induced trees are of comparable quality to those from noninduced trees (49). Induction–enhancement treatments need only be of short duration to be effective and the treatments do not necessarily affect subsequent floral and seed development. However, excessive flowering may result in ovule, seed, or cone abortion due to a variety of causes as will be discussed in subsequent sections.

11.5. Floral development

Floral buds in most temperate-zone trees are formed before winter dormancy. Conifer buds overwinter after all microsporangia and most ovuliferous scales are initiated, but the stage of sporogenous tissue development may vary from premeotic to fully developed pollen. In most pollen- and seed-cone buds meiosis occurs after winter dormancy (9,74). Similarly, in most hardwoods meiosis within the anthers occurs in the spring (74). Floral or mixed buds in temperate trees have a winter chill requirement, but the duration of chilling is generally not known. Conifer cone buds begin development before vegetative buds, suggesting a difference in chilling requirement (9).

11.5.1. Temperature effects

Severe winter and spring frosts may cause abortion of reproductive buds or cause subtle damage to ovules (75) or pollen (76). Low temperatures have caused meiotic irregularities and pollen abortion in *Larix leptolepsis* (76). High temperatures have also caused damage to cones and affected production and viability of pollen in *P. engelmannii* (52), *P. abies* (76), *P. sitchensis* (77), and *Tsuga heterophylla* (78).

Once winter chill requirements are satisfied and dormancy ends, floral development is promoted by warm temperatures (74,79). The stage of buds during winter along with the rate of postdormancy development (9) determine the variations in time between the winter dormancy and anthesis, which may range from 1 week to several months in conifers (9). In the hardwoods *Alnus*, *Betula*, and *Corylus* daylength rather than temperature modulated the timing of meiosis (74).

11.6. Pollination

All conifers and most temperate hardwoods are wind-pollinated, whereas most fruit and tropical trees are insect pollinated. Wind pollination (anemophily) is a "primitive" feature exhibited in gymnosperms and an "advanced" or "reduced" characteristic exhibited in angiosperms (80). Wind pollinated species are characterized by production of large quantities of pollen, specialized stigmatic surfaces for pollen collection and anthesis tuned to environmental cues (81). Pollen can be carried at great distances by wind. The aerodynamics of wind pollination around floral structures is complex (82). In insect pollinated trees pollination is largely an incidental by-product of nectar collection, quantities of pollen are generally low, and the time of anthesis is less tuned to environmental cues (81).

In angiosperms the stigma may be variously lobed, be wet or dry, and bear secretions and/or hairlike projections (papillae). The attachment of pollen to the stigma may involve complex pollen–stigma recognition mechanisms (83). The pollen wall contains proteins and other molecules, while the stigma has a recognition system. Both systems operate under control of a complex genetic system, the S locus, and the acceptance or rejection is analogous to many antigen–antibody, lectin–sugar residue and enzyme–substrate interactions. Acceptance (compatibility) or nonacceptance (incompatibility) may occur at various times, resulting in adhesion or nonadhesion of pollen to the stigma, hydration or failure to hydrate pollen, or inhibition at various phases of pollen tube growth through the stigma and style (84). There is often a callose formation in the stigma or style that physically seals off the pollen from the female tissue, prevents tissue hydration, or ties up nutrients used for pollen tube growth; any of these processes could prevent fertilization (83). In *Populus* both structural and cytochemical features of the stigma accounts for the interspecific incompatibility (85). At later stages pollen tubes may also become arrested near the ovules. Secretions from the obturator (a placental protuberance) in some species may cause resumption of pollen tube growth (86), and fertilization may then occur.

Conifers have no known pollen recognition systems, but they do have variable and interesting pollen-collecting structures (9). The ovule may be flask-shaped with a narrow opening (micropyle) in the integument tip as in the Cupressaceae and Taxodiaceae (Fig. 11.4a), or the integument tip around the micropyle may be large and funnel-shaped as in *Abies* and *Cedrus* (Fig. 11.4b). Integument tips of other species have long arms or flaps as in *Pinus* and *Picea* (Fig. 11.4c) or a stigmatic surface covered with hairs as in *Pseudotsuga* and *Larix* (Fig. 11.4e). In most conifers a pollination drop, which is a nectar-like secretion from the nucellus, is exuded from the ovule (Figs. 11.4a,d). There it collects pollen that may have adhered to minute secretions on the arms or flaps (Fig. 11.4c) or landed directly on the pollination drop (Fig. 11.4a). The drop then recedes into the micropyle, apparently by evaporation, carrying pollen to the nucellus in which the egg is located (Fig. 11.5b). In others, the integument tip grows inward, carrying into the micropyle pollen

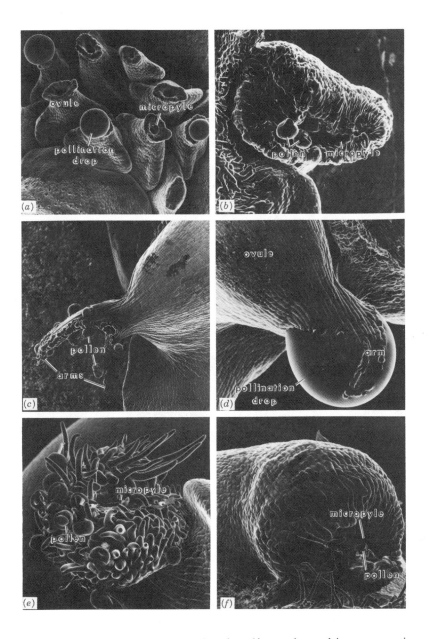

FIG. 11.4. Scanning electron micrographs of conifer ovules and integument tips at pollination: (a) *Chamaecyparis* ovule at pollination, ×50; (b) integument tip of *Abies* at pollination showing pollen being taken into the micropyle, ×75; (c) integument tip of *Picea* at pollination showing micropylar arms with secretory droplets to which pollen has become attached, ×36; (d) integument tip of *Picea* with a pollination drop, ×54; (e) integument tip of *Pseudotsuga* at pollination showing pollen among the stimatic hairs, ×90; (f) integument tip of *Pseudotsuga* after pollen has been engulfed into the micropyle, ×90.

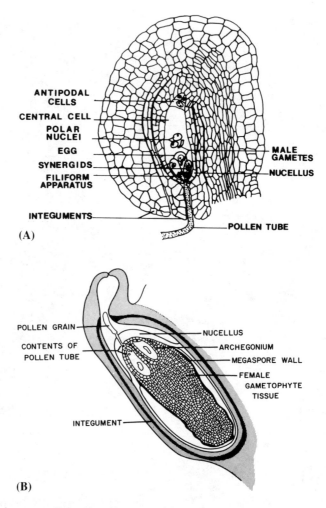

ANTIPODAL
CELLS

CENTRAL CELL

POLAR
NUCLEI

EGG

SYNERGIDS

FILIFORM
APPARATUS

INTEGUMENTS

(A)

MALE
GAMETES

NUCELLUS

POLLEN TUBE

POLLEN GRAIN

CONTENTS OF
POLLEN TUBE

NUCELLUS

ARCHEGONIUM

MEGASPORE WALL

FEMALE
GAMETOPHYTE
TISSUE

INTEGUMENT

(B)

FIG. 11.5. A comparison of angiosperm (a) and conifer (b) ovules at the time of fertilization.

adhering to secretory droplets (Fig. 11.4b) or hairs (Fig. 11.4f). Pollen then germinates and the pollen tubes penetrate the nucellus (Fig. 11.5b). In a few conifers pollen forms long tubes that grow from the bract as in *Tsuga heterophylla* (78) or scale as in *Araucaria* (87) into the micropyle. Conifer pollen contains stored starch and/or lipid and usually does not grow the long distances common in angiosperms (9). Conifer pollen tube growth usually occurs in weeks or months rather than hours or days as in angiosperms, and growth may be arrested in the scale (*Araucaria*) (87) or nucellus (*Pinus*) for several months (12). The physiology of pollen tube growth in conifers is poorly understood. There are complete reviews of general pollen physiology (84,88) and those with emphasis on conifers (9,89).

11.7. Fertilization

Angiosperm ovules are simpler in structure (Fig. 11.5a) and generally smaller than conifer ovules (Fig. 11.5b) at fertilization. In angiosperms each ovary may contain several ovules; each ovule has one or two integuments and a thin nucellus. The embryo sac (megagametophyte) within the nucellus is quite variable among plant groups but commonly contains one egg cell and two adjacent synergids with a filiform apparatus, three nonfunctional antipodal cells, and a large vacuolate central cell that contains two polar nuclei (Fig. 11.5b). The pollen tube commonly enters the filiform apparatus and then a synergid where the two male gametes are released. One male gamete then enters and fuses with the egg and the second fuses with the two central cell nuclei (Fig. 11.5a) to form the primary endosperm nucleus. This process is called double fertilization (9). The endosperm may have several structural forms, and it supplies nutrients for the embryo and stimulates embryo development. In most trees the endosperm is used up during embryo development, and seed storage products are contained within the cotyledons of the embryo (90).

Mature conifer ovules (Fig. 11.5b) have a single integument and a thick nucellus. The megagametophyte is large, usually consisting of thousands of cells. Each usually contains several eggs, commonly 4–6, but as few as 1 and up to 100 eggs have been reported for some species (10). One pollen tube may enter each egg. Although each pollen tube contains two male gametes, only one fertilizes the egg. The second male degenerates, and there is no double fertilization. The large megagametophyte functions as the endosperm does in angiosperms but is not used up during embryo development. It remains as storage tissue for germinating seeds (9). Cytologic and biochemical events during fertilization are active research areas especially in angiosperms at the present time (91). The reader is referred to the articles of Singh (10) and Owens and Blake (9) for a more complete list of references.

11.8. Seed development

Nutrient transfer during embryogenesis is better understood in angiosperms than in conifers. In many angiosperms the synergids have a filiform apparatus, characteristic of transfer cells, which may aid in short-distance nutrient transport. After fertilization the central cell and antipodal cell wall surfaces aid in transport of nutrients to the embryo sac from the surrounding ovule tissue. The embryo suspensor cells also facilitate the movement of nutrients from ovule tissue. Maturing ovules undergo considerable growth during seed development.

In most conifers, seeds are nearly fully enlarged and many have separated from the ovuliferous scales by the time fertilization occurs (9). Subsequent embryo and seed development is dependent on various forms of storage products already in the seed. There are no known specialized transfer cells for nutrients from the ovule to the megagametophyte (10). Storage products are soluble organic compounds (simple sugars, fatty acids, and amino acids) that are gradually changed to less soluble forms in large storage organelles (92). Both lipids and proteins accumulate during seed development. Mature conifer seeds are high in fat as large lipid bodies, moderate in protein as distinct protein bodies, and low in carbohydrate with relatively little starch, mostly stored in the megagametophyte (93). In contrast, most hardwoods are high in carbohydrate (especially starch) and low in protein with moderate levels of fat, mostly stored in the large cotyledons (92). At fertilization the seed has a high moisture content, as much as 700% based on oven-dry weight in *Pinus lambertiana*, which is reduced to 30% in the embryo and 60% in the megagametophyte in the mature seed (92).

11.8.1. Control of embryogenesis

Regulation of gene expression during plant embryogenesis is a rapidly developing area in selected agricultural crops (94), but studies of forest trees are only beginning (95). Most studies deal with genes that are active during later embryonic development. Seed proteins (93) are the area of focus because they provide distinct markers of embryogenic events. Genes that encode prevalent mRNAs related to specific developmental events are being identified. These genes are being studied because they are an excellent model for dissecting the regulatory process controlling plant gene expression (94). This information will be important to our understanding of zygotic embryogenesis and seed development and in developing somatic polyembryogenic systems.

11.8.2. Polyembryony

Polyembryony is common in conifers and is of two types. Simple (archegonial) polyembryony results when more than one egg is fertilized and often several embryos begin to develop. Cleavage polyembryony results when a young embryo separates into four filaments, each of which can develop into a separate embryo. Simple polyembryony occurs in most conifers if enough pollen is present. Cleavage polyembryony occurs in many conifers. Consequently, developing conifer seeds often contain many young embryos (up to four times the number of archegonia), but normally only one fully develops. This is the postzygotic selection mechanism characteristic of gymnosperms. See Singh (10) and Owens and Blake (9) for complete references.

   Polyembryony occurs in angiosperms but has been found in few hardwoods. True polyembryony (more than one embryo per embryo sac) occurs by budding or cleavage of the proembryo, from synergids, from antipodal cells in *Ulmus* (96), and from suspensor budding in *Acer* and several unspecified types in *Alnus, Fraxinus, Jugulans,* and *Populus* (20). False polyembryony occurs when more than one embryo arises per ovule because more than one embryo sac is present. Adventive embryos arise from tissues outside the embryo sac (e.g., nucellus or integument) as in citrus (97). Polyembryony has been of practical importance in propagating certain tree species by providing uniform genetic material (3).

11.8.3. Factors affecting seed development

The number of ovules produced per cone or flower (seed potential) usually far exceeds that of mature seeds. Losses occur throughout ovule and seed development—at prezygotic and postzygotic stages (98). An obvious cause is failure to be pollinated. The percentage of ovules pollinated (pollination success) varies from one flower or cone to another, between plants, and among years. Many ovules abort even when abundant pollen is available because of low pollen viability or vigor, incompatibility, or competition for resources (9). Woody species under natural pollinations tend to be outcrossers, which have lower seed:ovule and fruit:flower ratios than do inbreeders (99). Woody perennials must allocate resources between vegetative and reproductive functions and yet store reserves for the next growing season. This often reduces flower, fruit, cone, and seed numbers (100), thus lowering the percentage of fertile ovules that develop into viable seed (seed efficiency). Another cause for loss is that outcrossers suffer high genetic loads, causing abortions of ovule, embryo, or seed (99).

Cone drop in *Pinus* is common. The physiological causes for this have been reviewed (9,12). Sarvas (79) estimated that 80% of naturally occurring cone drop in *P. sylvestris* resulted from low levels of pollination and that if 20% of potentially fertile ovules aborted due to lack of pollen, the cone aborted. In some conifers (e.g., *Picea*, *Thuja*) low pollination success results in low seed efficiency and small cones (101), while in others (*Pseudotsuga*, *Tsuga*) seed efficiency is reduced but cones develop normally (78). The loss of cones after fertilization is not common and may occur with insect attack.

Loss of seeds in conifers can occur at several stages. Ovules abort at about the time of pollination, often because of low temperatures (75) or lack of pollen (101). As little as one pollen grain in the micropyle may be sufficient to prevent ovule abortion (101). The incidence of ovule abortion is usually low until the time of fertilization. Pollinated ovules may fail to be fertilized because of low pollen viability or vigor, but dead (mentor) pollen may only temporarily promote ovule development (101). The second major loss of potential seeds, after poor pollination, is early embryo abortion, which usually results from selfing in conifers (9,99). Early ovule abortion results in small empty seeds. Embryo abortion results in normal size but empty or partially filled seeds (78,101). Such losses, which appear to be characteristic of a species, can be improved by cultural treatments.

Woody angiosperm flowers have varying numbers of ovules depending on species. In *Quercus* six ovules form but only one matures into a seed, whereas in *Betula* only one of four ovules develops into a seed. Although ovule abortion decreases seed production, it may be an important means of selection or survival of remaining ovules. The position of the remaining ovule(s) is fixed in many inbreeders and random in many outcrossing hardwoods (99).

Premature abscission of flowers is also common, but the causes are uncertain. Most flowers of *Tectonia grandis* and several species of *Quercus* may abscise prematurely. A complete review of flower and fruit abortion and their causes and functions is given by Stephenson (102).

The premature drop of cones, flowers, and fruits may result from competition for metabolites between vegetative and reproductive shoots. In others abortion is seen as a trade-off between seed number and seed quality that permits the parent plant to match fruit production with available resources (101).

During the relatively long reproductive cycles in conifer and hardwood trees, there are many possible causes for failure in sexual reproduction. The relative importance of each may vary from species to species and result from failure at floral initiation or pollination or from bud, cone, flower, embryo, or seed abortion. In many species flowering and seed set can be increased through an understanding of these processes and by determining the causes for the losses.

ACKNOWLEDGMENTS

The author wishes to thank Dr. Conor O'Reilly for careful review of recent literature and critical review of the manuscript, Diane Gray for expert typing and assistance, and Sheila Morris and Tom Gore for photographic assistance. This chapter was partially supported by a Natural Sciences and Engineering Research Council of Canada Grant (A-1982).

11.9. References

1. A.H. Halevy, ed., *Handbook of Flowering*, Vols. I–V, CRC Press, Boca Raton, FL, 1985.
2. M. Sedgley and A.R. Griffin, *Sexual Reproduction of Tree Crops*, Academic Press, New York, 1989.
3. P.J. Kramer and T.T. Kozlowski, *Physiology of Woody Plants*, Academic Press, New York, 1979.
4. R. Daubenmire, "A seven-year study of cone production as related to xylem layers and temperature in *Pinus ponderosa*," *Am. Midl. Nat.*, **64**, 187–193 (1960).
5. W.P. Lowry, "Apparent meteorological requirements for abundant cone crop in Douglas-fir," *For. Sci.*, **12**, 185–192 (1966).
6. C.L.H. Van Vredenburch and J.G.A. La Bastide, "The influence of meteorological factors on the cone crop of Douglas fir in the Netherlands," *Silvae Genet.*, **18**, 182–186 (1969).
7. J.D. Matthews, "Factors affecting the production of seed by forest trees," *For. Abstr.*, **24**, i (1963).
8. E. Holmsgaard and H.C. Olson, "The influence of weather on beech mast," *Forogsv. Danm*, **26**, 345–370 (1960).

9. J.N. Owens and M.D. Blake, *Forest Tree Seed Production*, Forestry Canada Information Report P1-X-53, 1985.

10. H. Singh, *Embryology of Gymnosperms*, Gebrüder Borntraeger, Berlin, 1978.

11. D.I. Jackson and G.B. Sweet, "Flower initiation in temperate woody plants," *Horti. Abstr.*, **42**, 9–24 (1972).

12. G.B. Sweet, "Shedding of reproductive structures in forest trees," in T.T. Kozlowski, ed., *Shedding of Plant Parts*, Academic Press, New York, 1973, pp. 341–382.

13. G. Bernier, "The flowering process as an example of plastic development," *Symp. Soc. Exp. Biol.*, **40**, 257–286 (1986).

14. G. Bernier, "The control of floral evocation and morphogenesis," *Ann. Rev. Plant Physiol.*, **39**, 175–219 (1988).

15. G.S. Puritch, *Cone Production in Conifers. A Review of the Literature and Evaluation of Research Needs; with an Economic Analysis by A. H. Vyse*, Dept. Environ. Can., Can. Forestry Serv., Pacific Forest Res. Centre, Report BC-X-65, (1972, revised 1977).

16. K.J. Lee, "Factors affecting cone initiation in pines: A review," *Korean Inst. For. Genet. Res. Rep.*, **15**, 45–85 (1979).

17. R.P. Pharis and S.D. Ross, "The hormonal promotion of flowering in the Pinaceae," in A.H. Halevy, ed., *Handbook of Flowering*, Vol. 5, CRC Press, Boca Raton, FL, 1986, pp. 2–41.

18. S.D. Ross and R.P. Pharis, "Flower induction in crop trees: Different mechanisms and techniques with special reference to conifers," in M.G.R. Cannell, J.E. Jackson, and J.C. Gordon, eds., *Attributes of Trees as Crop Plants*, Institute of Terrestrial Ecology, Monks Wood Exp. Sta., Abbots Ripton, Huntingdon, UK, 1985, pp. 383–397.

19. K.J. Tosh and G.R. Powell, "Proliferated, bisporangiate, and other atypical cones occurring on young, plantation-grown *Larix laricina*," *Can. J. Bot.*, **64**, 469–475 (1986).

20. G.L. Davis, *Systematic Embryology of the Angiosperms*, Wiley, New York, 1966.

21. D.E. Hibbs and B.C. Fischer, "Sexual and vegetative reproduction of striped maple (*Acer pensylvanicum* L.)," *Bull. Torr. Bot. Club.*, **106**, 222–227 (1979).

22. K.A. Longman, "Variability in flower initiation in forest trees," in M.G.R. Cannell and J.E. Jackson, eds., *Attributes of Trees as Crop Plants*, NERC Press, UK, Institute of Terrestrial Ecology, Penicuik, Midlothian, Scotland, 1985, pp. 398–408.

23. P.F. Wareing, "Reproductive development in *Pinus sylvestris*," in K.V. Thimann, ed., *The Physiology of Forest Trees*, Ronald Press, New York, 1958, pp. 643–654.

24. A.D. Macdonald, D.H. Mothersill, and J.C. Caesar, "Shoot development in *Betula papyrifera*. III. Long-shoot organogenesis," *Can. J. Bot.*, **62**, 437–445 (1984).

25. V.S. Polito and N.-Y. Li, "Pistillate flower differentiation in English walnut (*Juglans regia* L.): A developmental basis for heterodichogamy," *Scientia Hortic* (*Amst.*), **26**, 333–338 (1985).

26. K.A. Longman, "Physiological studies in birch," *Proc. Roy. Soc. Edinburgh*, **85B**, 97–113 (1984).

27. S. Eis, "Cone production of Douglas-fir and grand fir and its climatic requirements," *Can. J. For. Res.*, **3**, 61–70 (1973).

28. K. Lindgren, I. Ekberg, and G. Eriksson, "External factors influencing female flowering in *Picea abies* (L.) Karst," *Stud. For. Suec*, **142**, 53 (1977).

29. G.E. Caron and G.R. Powell, "Patterns of seed-cone and pollen-cone production in young *Picea mariana* trees," *Can. J. For. Res.*, **19**, 359–364 (1989).

30. M. Lepisto, "Accelerated birch breeding in plastic greenhouses," *For. Chron.*, **49**, 172–173 (1973).

31. P.B. Tompsett and A.M. Fletcher, "Increased flowering of Sitka spruce (*Picea sitchensis* (Bong.) Carr.) in a polythene house," *Silvae Genet.*, **26**, 84–86 (1977).

32. J.J. Philipson, "The role of gibberellin $A_{4/7}$, heat and drought in the induction of flowering in Sitka spruce," *J. Exp. Bot.*, **34**, 291–302 (1983).

33. S.D. Ross, "Promotion of flowering in potted *Picea engelmannii* (Perry) grafts: Effects of heat, drought, gibberellin $A_{4/7}$ and their timing," *Can. J. For. Res.*, **15**, 618–624 (1985).

34. J.N. Owens and S.J. Simpson, "Bud and shoot development in *Picea engelmannii* in response to cone induction treatments," *Can. J. For. Res.*, **18**, 231–241 (1988).

35. R.R. Silen, "July-stimulated flowering in Douglas fir," *For. Sci.*, **19**, 288–290 (1973).

36. K.K. Nanda, "Some observations on growth, branching behaviour and flowering of teak (*Tectona grandis* L.F.) in relation to light," *Indian Forester*, **88**, 207–218 (1962).

37. R.M. Lanner, *Growth and Cone Production of Knobcone Pine under Interrupted Nights*, USDA Forest Serv. Res. Paper No. PSW-38, 1963.

38. D.J. Durzan, R.A. Campbell, and A. Wilson, "Inhibition of female cone production in white spruce by red light treatment during night under field conditions," *Env. Exp. Bot.*, **19**, 133–144 (1979).

39. K.A. Longman, "Effects of gibberellin, clone and environment on cone initiation, shoot growth and branching in *Pinus contorta*," *Ann. Bot.*, **50**, 247–257 (1982).

40. C. O'Reilly and J.N. Owens, "Reproductive growth and development in seven provenances of lodgepole pine," *Can. J. For. Res.*, **18**, 43–53 (1988).

41. M.S. Greenwood, "Flowering induced on young loblolly pine grafts by out-of-phase dormancy," *Science*, **201**, 443–444 (1978).

42. K.A. Longman and P.F. Wareing, "Early induction of flowering in birch seedlings," *Nature (Lond.)*, **184**, 2037–2038 (1959).

43. E. Young and J.W. Hanover, "Accelerating maturity in *Picea* seedlings," *Acta Hort.*, **56**, 105–114 (1976).

44. N.C. Wheeler, C.C. Ying, and J.C. Murphy, "Effect of accelerating growth on flowering in lodgepole pine seedlings and grafts," *Can. J. For. Res.*, **12**, 533–537 (1982).

45. G.E. Rehfeldt, A.R. Stage, and R.T. Bingham, "Strobili development in western white pine: Periodicity, prediction and association with weather," *For. Sci.*, **17**, 454–461 (1971).

46. J.G.A. La Bastide and C.L.H. Van Vredenburch, "The influence of weather conditions on the seed production of some forest trees in the Netherlands," *Meded. Bosbouwproefstation*, **102**, 1–12 (1970).

47. E. Holmsgaard and H.C. Olson, "On the influence of the weather on beech mast and the employment of artificial drought as a means to produce beech mast," in *IUFRO 13th Congress*, Vienna, Part 2(1), 1961, (Section 22, paper 19).

48. M. Bonnet-Masimbert, P. Delanzy, G. Chanteloup, and J. Coupaye, "Influence de l'état d'activité des racines sur la floraison induite pardes gibbérellines 4 et 7 chez *Pseudotsuga menziesii* (Mirb.) Franco," *Silvae Genet.*, **31**, 178–183 (1982).

49. J.J. Philipson, "A review of coning and seed production in *Picea sitchensis*," in D.M. Henderson and R. Faulkner, eds., *Proc. Roy. Soc. Edinburgh, B*, **93(1–2)**, 183–195 (1987).

50. W.W. Schwabe and A.H. Al-Doori, "Analysis of a juvenile-like condition affecting flowering in the black current (*Ribes nigrum*)," *J. Exp. Bot.*, **82**, 969–981 (1973).

51. S.D. Ross, R.P. Pharis, and W.D. Binder, "Growth regulators and conifers: Their physiology and potential uses in forestry," in L.G. Nickell, ed., *Plant Growth Regulating Chemicals*, Vol. 2, CRC Press, Boca Raton, FL, 1983, pp. 35–78.

52. S.D. Ross, "Pre- and post-pollination polyhouse environment effects on pollen and seed development in potted *Picea engelmannii* grafts," *Can. J. For. Res.*, **18**, 623–627 (1988).

53. R.H. Zimmerman, "Juvenility and flowering in woody plants: A review," *HortScience*, **7(5)**, 447–455 (1972).

54. G.B. Sweet and S.O. Hong, "The role of nitrogen in relation to cone production in *Pinus radiata*," *NZ J. For. Sci.*, **8**, 225–238 (1978).

55. L.F. Ebell and E.E. McMullan, "Nitrogenous substances associated with differential cone production responses of Douglas fir to ammonium and nitrate fertilization," *Can. J. Bot.*, **48**, 2169–2177 (1970).

56. R.L. Barnes and G.W. Bengston, "Effects of fertilization, irrigation, and cover cropping on flowering and on nitrogen and soluble sugar composition of slash pine," *For. Sci.*, **14**, 172–180 (1968).

57. T.T. Kozlowski and T. Keller, "Food relations of woody plants," *Bot. Rev.*, **32**, 293–382 (1966).

58. J.M. Fielding, "Branching and flowering characteristics of Monterey pine," *Aust. For. Timber Bur. Bull.*, **37**, 59 (1960).

59. H.K. Bell and N.F. Childers, "Peach nutrition," in H.F. Childers, ed., *Mineral Nutrition of Fruit Crops*, Hort. Publ., Rutgers Univ., New Brunswick, NJ, 1954.

60. D.I. Dickmann and T.T. Kozlowski, "Mobilization and incorporation of photoassimilated ^{14}C by growing vegetative and reproductive tissues of adult *Pinus resinosa* Ait. trees," *Plant Physiol.*, **45**, 284–288 (1970).

61. K. Singh and S. Kumar, "Manipulation of flowering in wood plants by the use of gibberellins," *Indian J. For.*, **9**, 331–336 (1986).

62. S.D. Ross, "Enhancement of shoot elongation in Douglas fir by gibberellin $A_{4/7}$ and its relation to the hormonal promotion of flowering," *Can. J. For. Res.*, **13**, 986–994 (1983).

63. J.E. Webber, S.D. Ross, R.P. Pharis, and J.N. Owens, "Interaction between gibberellin $A_{4/7}$ and rootpruning on the reproductive and vegetative process in Douglas fir. II. Effects on growth," *Can. J. For. Res.*, **15**, 348–353 (1985).

64. R.P. Pharis and C.G. Kuo, "Physiology of gibberellins in conifers," *Can. J. For. Res.*, **7**, 299–325 (1977).

65. H. Hashizume, "Experimental induction of female flowers in young Japanese larch (*Larix leptolepsis* Gordon)," *J. Jpn. For. Soc.*, **49**, 405–408 (1967).

66. M. Bonnet-Masimbert and J.B. Zaerr, "The role of plant growth regulators in promotion of flowering," *Plant Growth Regul.*, **6**, 13 (1987).

67. M. Bonnet-Masimbert, "Induction florale précoce chez *Cupressus arizonica* et *Chamaecyparis lawsoniana*," *Silvae Genet.*, **20**, 82–90 (1971).

68. H. Bleymüller, "Investigations on the dependence of flowering in Norway spruce (*Picea abies* (L.) Karst) upon age," *Acta Hort.*, **56**, 169–172 (1976).

69. W. Chalpuka, "Effect of growth regulators on flowering of Norway spruce (*Picea abies* (L.) Karst.) grafts," *Silvae Genet.*, **28**, 125–127 (1979).

70. R.P. Pharis, "Interaction of native or exogenous plant hormones in the flowering of woody plants," in H.R. Schuttle and D. Gross, eds., *Proc. Conf. Regulation of Developmental Processes in Plants*, Halle, Germany, 1977, pp. 343–360.

71. A.R. Dunberg, "Flower induction in Norway spruce," in *IUFRO Norway Spruce Meeting S.2.03.11–S.2.02.11*, Bucharest, 1979, pp. 139–157.

72. W. Chalupka, M. Giertych, and J. Kopcewicz, "Effect of polythene covers, a flower inducing treatment, on the content of endogenous gibberellin-like substances in grafts of Norway spruce," *Physiol. Plant.*, **54**, 79–82 (1982).

73. E. Galoch, "Comparison of the content of growth regulators in juvenile and adult plants of birch (*Betula verrucosa* Ehrh.)," *Acta Physiologiae Plant*, **7(4)**, 205–215 (1984).

74. A. Luomajoki, "The latitudinal and yearly variation in the timing of microsporogenesis in *Alnus*, *Betula* and *Corylus*," *Hereditas*, **104**, 231–243 (1986).

75. J.N. Owens and M. Molder, "Sexual reproduction in western redcedar (*Thuja plicata*)," *Can. J. Bot.*, **58**, 1376–1396 (1980).

76. G. Eriksson, I. Ekberg, and A. Jonsson, "Meiotic investigations in pollen mother cells of Norway spruce cultivated in a plastic greenhouse," *Hereditas*, **66**, 1–20 (1970).

77. J.J. Philipson, J.N. Owens, and M.A. O'Donnell, "The production and development of seed and pollen in *Picea sitchensis* grafts treated with gibberellin $A_{4/7}$ to induce coning and the effect of forcing treatments," *New Phytol.*, **116**, 695–703 (1990).

78. A.M. Colangeli and J.N. Owens, "Postdormancy seed-cone development and the pollination mechanism in western hemlock," *Can. J. For. Res.*, **19**, 44–53 (1989).

79. R. Sarvas, "Investigations on the flowering and seed crop of *Pinus sylvestris*," *Commun. Inst. For. Fenn.*, **53**, 1–198 (1962).

80. P. Dowding, "Wind pollination mechanisms and aerobiology," *Int. Rev. Cytol.*, **107**, 421–437 (1987).

81. D.R. Whitehead, "Wind pollination: Some ecological and evolutionary perspectives," in L. Real, ed., *Pollination Biology*, Academic Press, New York, 1983, pp. 97–108.

82. K.J. Niklas, "Aerodynamics of wind pollination," *Sci. Am.*, **257**, 72–77 (1987).

83. C. Dumas and R.B. Knox, "Callose and determination of pistil viability and incompatibility," *Theor. Appl. Genet.*, **67**, 1–10 (1983).

84. J. Heslop-Harrison, "Pollen germination and pollen-tube growth," in G.H. Bourne, ed., *International Review of Cytology*, Vol. 107, *Pollen Cytology and Development*, Academic Press, Orlando, FL, 1987, 1–78.

85. M. Villar, M. Gaget, C. Said, R.B. Knox, and C. Dumas, "Incompatibility in *Populus*: Structural and cytochemical characteristics of the receptive stigmas of *Populus alba* and *P. nigra*," *J. Cell Sci.*, **87**, 483–490 (1987).

86. M. Herrero, A. Arbeloa, and M. Gascon, "Pollen pistil interaction in the ovary in fruit trees," in M. Cresti, P. Gori, and E. Pacini, eds., *Sexual Reproduction in Higher Plants*, Springer-Verlag, New York, 1988, pp. 297–302.

87. R.J. Haines, N. Prakash, and D.G. Nikles, "Pollination in *Araucaria* Juss," *Aust. J. Bot.*, **32**, 583–594 (1984).

88. H.G. Dickinson, "The physiology and biochemistry of meiosis in the anther," in G.H. Bourne, ed., *International Review of Cytology*, Vol. 107, *Pollen: Cytology and Development*, Academic Press, Orlando, FL, 1987, pp. 79–110.

89. W.D. Binder, G.M. Mitchell, and D.J. Ballantyne, *Pollen Viability, Testing, Storage, and Related Physiology. Review of the Literature with Emphasis on Gymnosperm Pollen*, Dept. Environ., Can. Forest Serv., Pacific Forest Research Centre Report BC-X-105, 1974.

90. C.S. Schopmeyer, *Seeds of Woody Plants in the United States*, USDA Forest Service Handbook No. 450, 1974.

91. R.B. Knox and M.B. Singh, "New perspectives in pollen biology and fertilization," *Ann. Bot. (Lond.)*, **60** (Suppl. 4), 15–37 (1987).

92. S.L. Krugman, W.I. Stein, and D.M. Schmitt, "Seed Biology," in C. Schopmeyer, ed., *Seeds of Woody Plants in the United States*, USDA Forest Service Handbook 450, 1974, pp. 1–40.

93. D.J. Gifford, "An electrophoretic analysis of the seed proteins from *Pinus monticola* and eight other species of pine," *Can. J. Bot.*, **66**, 1808–1812 (1988).

94. R.B. Goldberg, S.J. Barker, and L. Perez-Grau, "Regulation of gene expression during plant embryogenesis," *Cell*, **56**, 149–160 (1989).

95. F.W. Whitmore and H.B. Kriebel, "Expression of a gene in *Pinus strobus* ovules associated with fertilization and early embryo development," *Can. J. For. Res.*, **17**, 408–412 (1987).

96. J.L. Guignard and J.C. Mestre, "Sur le développement d'embryons à partir des antipodes chez *l'Ulmus campestris* L.," *Bull. Bot. Fr.*, **113**, 227–228 (1966).

97. C.W. Wardlaw, *Embryogenesis in Plants*, Wiley, New York, 1955.

98. M.F. Willson and N. Burley, *Mate Choice in Plants*, Princeton Univ. Press, Princeton, NJ, 1983.

99. D. Weins, C.L. Calvin, C.A. Wilson, C.I. Davern, D. Frank, and S.R. Seavey, "Reproductive success, spontaneous embryo abortion, and genetic load in flowering plants," *Oecologia*, **71**, 501–509 (1987).

100. D. Charlesworth, "Why do plants produce so many more ovules than seeds," *Nature (Lond.)*, **338**, 21–22 (1989).

101. J.N. Owens, A.M. Colangeli, and S.J. Morris, "The effect of self, cross and no pollination on ovule, embryo, seed and cone development in western redcedar (*Thuja plicata* Donn.)," *Can. J. For. Res.*, **20**, 66–75 (1990).

102. A.G. Stephenson, "Flower and fruit abortion: Proximate causes and ultimate functions," *Ann. Rev. Ecol. Syst.*, **12**, 253–279 (1981).

12 Abscission: Shedding of Parts

FREDRICK T. ADDICOTT

Department of Botany, University of California—Davis, California,
USA

Contents

12.1. Introduction

This chapter surveys the abscission phenomena of trees and the underlying physiology. Pertinent literature includes innumerable observations of botanists, horticulturalists, and foresters in the many temperate and tropical regions of the world. References cited in the text were selected as representative of recent publications, in which reference lists will lead the interested reader to more details than could be included here. References for unsupported statements in the text can be found in earlier reviews (1–5).

12.1.1. Scope of abscission in trees

Abscission is the process whereby parts of an organism are separated. Any discrete part of a tree can be abscised under appropriate circumstances (Table 12.1).

12.1.2. Values of abscission

In the course of evolution, trees have developed the ability to control abscission and to induce it particularly when the abscission has obvious benefits:

1. A major function of abscission is to remove injured, infected, or senescent organs.
2. Trees commonly produce more leaves, branches, and especially flowers and fruits than they can fully support. Abscission functions to maintain homeostasis within a plant, keeping shoots in balance with roots, and flowers and fruits in balance with foliage (Sections 12.2.3, 12.5).
3. The protective layers that develop during abscission seal underlying tissues and prevent the entry of many disease-causing organisms (Section 12.1.4).
4. The architecture of many trees is determined largely by the pattern of abscission of buds, branches, and fruits (Section 12.4.6).
5. Nutrient recycling is facilitated by the regular abscission of leaves, branches, bark, and other structures (6–9).

Table 12.1. Tree parts that are abscised

Vegetative bud	Flower buds	Fruits
Bark	Flowers	Seeds
Branches	Sepals (calyx)	Prickles
Cotyledons	Petals (corolla)	Spines
Leaves	Stamens	Glochids
Leaflets	Style	Trichomes
Leaf stalks	Ovaries	Roots
Stipules	Mesocarp	Galls

6. Dispersal of tree species is facilitated by abscission of fruits and seeds (6,10) and of vegetative propagules such as leaves, buds, stem segments, and offsets. In some species flowers and fruits are made more visible to potential pollinators and dispersal agents by the prior abscission of leaves (Section 12.5.1).
7. Allelopathic substances leached from abscised leaves or other structures of one species can inhibit the germination and/or development of competing species.
8. Some tree species prevent the establishment of epiphytes and parasites by the abscission of bark.

12.1.3. The origin and evolution of abscission

The origins of abscission can be traced back to the algae from which the land plants evolved. The ability to separate (abscise) vegetative or reproductive cells is an essential aspect of the life cycle of even those relatively simple plants, and involves the controlled separation of cells by the dissolution of pectin-like cementing substances. The process is physiologically, if not chemically, identical with the cell separation that occurs during abscission in higher plants. As land plants evolved, their notable advance was to localize separation activity to precise, restricted positions, thus enabling the abscission of particular organs or structures.

Even more remarkable has been the evolution of the abscission control system in higher plants. Hormonal, nutritional, and other physiological factors interact, often in complex ways, to control the onset and rate of abscission (Section 12.2.2). Further, the process is sensitive to a wide variety of ecologic factors that impinge on and act through the physiological controls (Section 12.2.3). Consequently, trees show a tremendous array of abscission patterns not only in their foliage, but in their flowering and fruiting behavior as well (Sections 12.3, 12.4 & 12.5). Many of these behavior patterns are the result of coevolution with pollinators and disseminators. Spontaneous genetic variations in cultivated plants enable selection of desirable new abscission traits.

12.1.4. Morphology, anatomy, and cytology

The processes of abscission take place almost exclusively in readily identifiable regions, the *abscission zones*. These are usually found at the base of organs such as leaflets, leaves (Fig. 12.1), petals, seeds, fruits, internodes, and branches (11). Externally, abscission zones differ from adjacent regions. They may be constricted, but more commonly they are expanded, sometimes markedly so, as in the leaf abscission zones of palm trees (Fig. 12.2) and the branchlets of species of *Quercus*, *Populus*, and Araucariaceae.

Anatomically, tissues in the abscission zone are less differentiated than in adjacent regions. In the course of development, tissues in the adjacent regions differentiate and mature. While in the abscission zone the cells remain small,

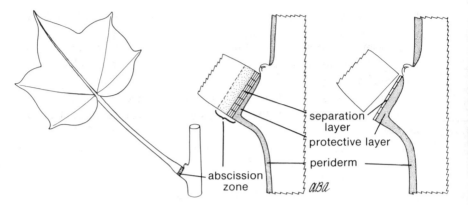

FIG. 12.1. Diagram of a leaf abscission zone showing location and arrangement of tissues. (Reproduced with permission from copyright owner, A. B. Addicott.)

with dense cytoplasm, and often contain starch. Cell walls are thin and usually unlignified. Fiber cells are absent, and some resin canals and laticifers may not cross the zone (Fig. 12.3). The relatively undifferentiated state of the cells in the abscission zone facilitates the development and functioning of the separation and protective layers, and of adventitious buds, as in *Picea abies* (12).

The *separation layer* differentiates within the abscission zone usually from a single layer of cells commonly at right angles to the axis of the zone. Cytologic changes within the cells of the layer include substantial increases

FIG. 12.2. Leaf scars of palms: (A) *Cocos nucifera*; (B) *Roystonea regia*. Note separation of the leaf sheath and separation in progress at the leaf base. (Photographs courtesy of J. A. McKinnon and A. B. Addicott, respectively.)

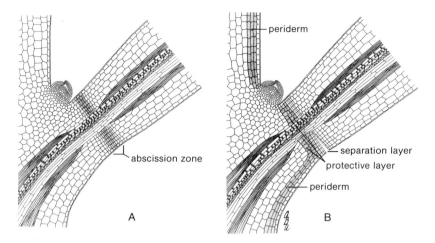

FIG. 12.3. Diagram of tissues in a typical leaf abscission zone: (A) shortly before separation; (B) at the time of separation. Note continuity of the protective layer with the periderm. (Reproduced with permission from copyright owner, A. B. Addicott.)

in endoplasmic reticulum, dictyosomes, vesicles, and microtubules (13). Soon after those changes, the middle lamellae of the cell walls swell and disintegrate, permitting the fall of the subtending organ. Often there is also swelling and partial erosion of primary cell walls. The cytolytic activities can involve more than one layer of cells and can be so extensive as to bring about complete dissolution of the primary cell wall and the cytoplasm, as in leaf abscission of *Prunus persica* (14).

In woody tissues the physiological action in the separation layer is often incomplete and actual separation is aided by external physical factors such as wind. Further, in many instances, such as the abscission of twigs and small branches, there is little evidence of a separation layer. Nevertheless, because the tissues of the abscission zones at the base of twigs and branchlets are less lignified and have weaker cell walls, separation occurs in the abscission zone. Thus in abscission among tree species we see a wide series of manifestations intergrading from the physiological to the mechanical, e.g., *Picea* leaves (15).

The tissues exposed by the abscission of an organ become the *primary protective layer* by the deposition of suberin and lignin and often by the division of cells, to form a layer that usually becomes continuous with the adjacent periderm (Fig. 12.3). In some cases a *secondary protective layer* can develop beneath the previous one. The rapid and complete development of protective layers is important for the prevention of infection following abscission.

Adventitious abscission of senescent portions of leaves occurs in a few instances, e.g., *Streptocarpus* spp., *Aloe asperifolia*. In such cases the location of abscission activity is determined by physiological factors rather than the morphology of the plant. Other examples include the shot-hole diseases such as *Clasterosporium carpophilium* on *Prunus amygdalus*. Adventitious abscission has followed bud grafts to midpetiole positions. Treatment with the hormones indoleacetic acid (IAA), gibberellin (GA), ethylene (ETH), or cytokinin (CK) have induced the formation and functioning of adventitious separation layers in internodes and/or pedicels, as have triiodobenzoic acid (TIBA) and NaClO.

12.2. Physiology of abscission

12.2.1. Metabolic events

Early experiments with explants (excised abscission zones) showed that abscission requires oxygen, and that abscission zones undergo a climacteric rise in rate of respiration during separation. The increased respiratory activity provides energy for the synthesis of hydrolytic enzymes that attack cell walls and especially the middle lamellae (2). Polygalacturonases have been identified in several situations, including an exopolygalacturonase in *Citrus* leaflet explants. Also, in some investigations, pectin methylesterase activity decreased during abscission. Such a decrease should permit increased esterification leading to fewer of the strengthening calcium bridges in the pectins. In the leaf and fruit abscission zones of *Citrus*, increased uronic acid oxidase is correlated with abscission (16).

In some investigations swelling and at least partial dissolution of primary cell walls has been observed. Since the primary cell wall contains cellulose, the involvement of cellulases has been studied. Synthesis of one such hydrolase designated, 9.5 cellulase, is correlated with abscission. However, it should be noted that the appearance of 9.5 cellulase is correlated with separation in some experimental materials and with the postseparation development of the protective layer in other materials. Further, in cellulase studies the enzyme preparations are assayed against carboxymethylcellulose. Thus, it is not yet known which of the many polysaccharides of the primary cell wall the cellulases are attacking.

Deposition of callose in and near abscission zones is correlated with abscission (17,18). By its plugging of phloem sieve plates, callose could contribute to alteration of the chemical signals moving to the abscission zone.

A common misconception in the literature is that lignified cells do not separate physiologically during abscission and are broken physically as the subtended organ falls. From herbaceous materials there is little evidence to support such a view other than the fact that the lignified cells are the last to separate and a few may be stretched and broken by the abscising organ before they could separate. On the contrary, the literature contains a number of anatomic illustrations showing lignified cell walls in the separation and protective layers that have been distorted and compressed as adjacent parenchyma cells have expanded or as they have been penetrated by tyloses. It appears unlikely that the observed distortions could have occurred without the participation of ligninases. Also, in the separation layer, the pectinases secreted by parenchyma cells could easily diffuse to the narrow ring of pectic materials between the end walls of adjacent xylem vessels, enabling separation at those locations. Thus the present evidence, although limited, indicates that separation of lignified cells is accomplished largely by enzymatic action with very little, if any, actual breakage (see also Section 12.4).

12.2.2. Hormonal and nutritional influences

Abscission is influenced by many physiological factors, internal and external, not the least of which are carbohydrate and nitrogen nutrition. Plants that are high in carbohydrates retain their leaves and fruits longer than do those that are deficient, primarily by increased deposition of cell wall materials.

Plants that are high in nitrogen are vigorous and retain their leaves much longer than do plants that are deficient. High-nitrogen plants are high-auxin plants, and high auxin is strongly inhibitory to abscission (see below). Further, high nitrogen facilitates the synthesis of proteins, nucleic acids, enzymes, and related substances utilized in vigorous growth.

Mineral nutrition, in general, must be normal to prevent premature or excessive abscission. Deficiencies of nitrogen, phosphorus, potassium, sulfur, calcium, magnesium, iron, zinc, and boron can lead to considerable leaf and/ or fruit abscission. For example, N- and Zn-deficient plants are low in auxin and prone to leaf abscission. Calcium, when applied to explants, can inhibit abscission. Possibly it acts by maintaining the calcium bridges in the pectic substances of the middle lamellae, and/or by retarding the membrane changes associated with enzyme secretion (19,20).

Shortly before abscission senescent changes in the subtending organ result in the solubilization and export of some carbohydrate and nitrogenous compounds as well as certain of the mineral components (21).

Auxin (IAA), the major plant growth hormone, is the central hormone in the control of abscission. While the supply of auxin reaching the abscission zone from the subtending organ remains high, abscission does not occur. However, when leaves become senescent, their ability to produce auxin diminishes and abscission follows (e.g., *Hevea*; Refs. 22,23). When a leaf is debladed, abscission of the remaining petiole is initiated, but if IAA is applied to the petiole stump, abscission can be delayed indefinitely. In contrast, auxin reaching the abscission zone from the proximal side promotes abscission. When varying amounts of IAA are applied simultaneously to the distal and proximal sides of explants, the rate of abscission is determined by the ratio between the two applications. When the amount of IAA applied to the distal side is greater than the amount applied proximally, abscission is retarded, but when the amount applied proximally is greater, abscission is accelerated. Thus it appears that the direction of the auxin gradient across the abscission zone is an important factor in the control of abscission. Although the extensive literature on auxin shows that it is the critical and dominant hormone in the control of abscission, other hormones and factors interact with it and can modify abscission responses in various ways (1,2).

Abscisic acid (ABA) is a plant hormone that occurs throughout the plant. In addition to its promotion of abscission it functions in a number of other processes, including stomatal closure, seed dormancy, and membrane transport (24). Levels of ABA increase greatly in leaves under stress, in aborting young fruit, and generally in leaves, flowers, and fruits as they mature and senesce. These are all conditions that commonly precede abscission. In such conditions levels of IAA, GA, and CK are falling while levels of ABA are rising. When applied to explants either distal or proximal to the abscission zone ABA strongly accelerates abscission. When applied to intact plants, the abscission response varies with dosage and growth status of the plants. Vigorous young plants may show little abscission in response to applied ABA, they contain high levels of IAA and other growth-promoting hormones that tend to counteract ABA. Also, plant tissues generally will rapidly conjugate ABA into relatively inactive glucose ester and glucoside. It is noteworthy that ABA can promote abscission in the absence of ETH (the common accelerator of abscission; see below). ABA has been found to affect the synthesis of a number of enzymes, promoting the synthesis of some (e.g., acid phosphatase, phenylalanine ammonia-lyase, IAA-oxidase, cellulase) inhibiting the synthesis of others (e.g., α-amylase, fatty acid synthetase, transaminase, invertase). In abscission, the cytological evidence indicates that a primary action of ABA is to promote the synthesis of pectinase(s).

Gibberellins (GA) are widely involved in growth-promoting processes in plants. Levels of GA in leaves and fruits fall during senescence or abortion; however, GA seldom appears to be directly involved in the control of abscission. In the many applications of GA to intact plants few abscission responses have been observed. However, there is a notable exception: sprays of GA to flowers during hand pollination have improved fruit set, preventing the abscission that often follows such manipulation. Applied either distally or proximally to the abscission zones of explants, GA is usually promotive of abscission. Although the action of GA is often similar to that of IAA, the interactions of the two hormones indicate that they act by different pathways.

Cytokinin (CK), when applied to young fruit, stimulates development and tends to prevent abscission. When applied directly to the abscission zone of an explant, CK retards abscission, but when applied even a short distance from the abscission zone, it promotes abscission. In the latter situation the CK appears to induce a strong local sink that is competitive with the abscission zone and weakens it speeding the changes of abscission.

Ethylene (ETH) is produced by many, but not all, senescent and abscising tissues. Further, many plants can be defoliated by exposure to ETH, but others not at all. Nevertheless, ETH has found wide use in the investigation of abscission because of its ability to speed abscission in common experimental materials (25) and because of the relative ease with which it can be assayed by gas chromatography. Careful investigations have found that increased production of ETH often follows, rather than precedes, abscission. Also, abscission can be initiated and completed under hypobaric conditions in the virtual absence of ETH (2,26). Thus for the present, ETH should be considered a useful accelerator of abscission and not an essential initiator. The action of ETH in speeding abscission is related to several properties, such as its ability to enhance IAA destruction, inhibit IAA transport, and increase ABA synthesis. Also, exposure to ETH has long been known to stimulate oxidative respiration in plant tissues possibly via increasing permeability of cell membranes to oxygen.

In addition to the five hormones discussed above, a number of other naturally occurring substances have been found to influence abscission. These include amino acids, peptides, phenolics, indoles, and still unidentified substances (27).

Thus many internal physiological factors influence the process of abscission. Each of the five major plant hormones (IAA, ABA, GA, CK, ETH) elicits a unique pattern of responses, which vary with the physiological state of the experimental material. Interactions and counteractions among the five are complex and modified especially by factors that affect cell wall deposition, oxidative respiration, and enzyme synthesis. The evidence indicates that the control of abscission lies in the balance of interacting hormonal influences at the abscission zone (2,3,22,25,28,29).

12.2.3. Physiological ecology

The influence of ecological factors on abscission of leaves, flowers, fruits, and other structures have received considerable attention in the literature of the plant sciences (e.g., see Ref. 30). This section will survey those factors and where possible, suggest the internal physiology of their action.

Light is essential for photosynthesis and accumulation of carbohydrate assimilates. High levels of carbohydrates in the plant make for heavier cell walls in abscission zones and enable a plant to carry more fruit. For example, the amounts of carbohydrates deposited in twigs of deciduous fruit trees are directly related to the amount of young fruit retained the following season. Conversely, low light intensities or darkness promote abscission.

A shortening *photoperiod* is an important factor stimulating autumnal defoliation of deciduous trees. Maintenance of long photoperiods has greatly delayed leaf abscission, e.g., in *Acer, Platanus, Plumeria, Populus, Salix*, and *Ulmus*. The response can be rather precise (Section 12.3.1), and apparently involves the phytochrome system as red light is inhibitory to abscission (31,32).

Under some circumstances *extremes of temperature* initiate abscission. For example, in *Citrus* a moderate frost can injure the leaf blades sufficiently to initiate abscission but seldom will damage the abscission zones, which then proceed to abscise the injured leaves. However, in such trees a severe frost can injure the abscission zones to the extent that they fail to function and the killed leaves then remain attached indefinitely. In some situations cold (freezing conditions) appears to contribute to the initiation of autumnal leaf abscission.

Likewise, excessive *heat* can contribute to abscission, although it is difficult to separate the effects of heat from those of the water stress that almost invariably accompany it. Following a period of hot weather many trees, e.g., *Eucalyptus*, *Citrus*, abscise a portion of their leaves within a few days. It is something of a paradox that in response to the heat of the sun it is not the leaves that receive the most direct rays that are abscised, but rather the older and innermost leaves. This supports the view that it is water stress rather than heat itself that is the important factor in heat-induced leaf abscission.

Fire is a potent defoliating agent and is sometimes used as such in agriculture and forestry. Also, in forests that are subject to understory fires the lower branches can be fire-injured and fall away early in the life of the tree. Such abscission contributes to the architecture of mature *Pinus ponderosa*, *Sequoiadendron giganteum*, and similar trees (see also Section 12.4).

Water stress is the most widespread factor that induces leaf abscission. Depending on circumstances, water stress will induce anything from abscission of a few leaves, e.g., *Theobroma* (33), to complete defoliation (see Section 12.3). The stress initiates a rapid rise in ABA content of leaves, decrease in IAA and CK, and increase in ETH. Each of these changes tends to promote abscission, and collectively they form an extremely strong stimulus to abscission. Prompt leaf abscission in response to water stress can protect the tree from further injury, e.g., *Coffea* (34), *Eucalyptus* (35), and *Juglans* (36).

Flooding of roots, if prolonged, can lead to considerable abscission of leaves, flowers, or fruits (37). The principal effect of flooding is to reduce levels of oxygen available to the roots, which in turn reduces the ability of the roots to absorb mineral nutrients and leads to lower levels of IAA, GA, and CK in the plant. At the same time the stress from flooding leads to higher levels of ABA and ETH. This combination of changes is quite promotive of abscission.

Wind and other physical forces act to bring about separation of leaves, branches, fruits, and other organs earlier than would otherwise occur. This action is especially noticeable in the abscission of branches and branchlets in which the physiological processes of separation do not go to completion. In such trees a strong wind will bring about branchlet separation months or even years sooner than otherwise. Abrasion by wind-blown volcanic ash induced considerable leaf abscission in *Populus*, *Acer*, and *Catalpa* (38).

Deficiency of any one of the *essential elements* can impose sufficient stress on a plant to induce at least some abscission (Section 12.2.2).

Excessive amounts of minerals and other chemicals can be deleterious to plant growth and induce abscission in sensitive species. Among these are borax, iron, zinc, copper, chlorine, iodine, saline soils, salts applied to roadways in winter, and detergent-polluted ocean spray (39). A common symptom of these toxicities is water stress, which, among other effects, stimulates the synthesis of ABA, thereby promoting abscission.

Atmospheric pollutants that can injure plants and sometimes induce abscission include illuminating gas, ETH, CO, fluorides, H_2S, ozone, nitrogen oxides, peroxyacetyl nitrates, NH_3, Cl_2, and mercury vapor (Ref. 40; see also Chapter 14 in this book). Except for ETH (Section 12.2.1), physiology of the abscission responses to these pollutants has received little attention. However, it is reasonable to assume that injury from pollutants includes reduced vigor and changes in the levels and balance of the controlling hormones.

Pathogenic insects and microorganisms can have devastating effects on their host plants (41), so it is not surprising that infected leaves, fruits, and other structures are often abscised (42–44). Some responses appear to be purely mechanical, caused by the physical removal of tissue. In other cases abscission is affected via (a) changes in metabolism of IAA, ABA, CK, and/or ETH or (b) secretion of toxic substances (2).

12.3. Leaf abscission

The abscission of leaves is sensitive to many influences, not the least of which is competition among the leaves for factors such as light, water, and nutrients. Thus leaf abscission is an important aspect of the *homeostasis* of a tree, serving to keep the foliage in balance with the other parts of the tree and to keep the tree in balance with the environment.

There is wide variation in both leaf production and abscission (6). Species of *Opuntia* and *Euphorbia* abscise their ephemeral leaves after a few weeks. The vast majority of trees retain leaves for a few months to a few years. For example, *Cocos nucifera* retains its leaves for 3–3.5 years and maintains a crown of 30–40 leaves (45). *Araucaria* is said to retain its leaves for up to 25 years. *Pinus longaeva* retains its needles for 25–30 years or more (46). The two leaves of *Welwitschia* grow slowly from the base and are never abscised even by plants 1000 or more years of age. Chabot and Hicks (47) discuss the ecologic implications of the lengths of lifespans of leaves.

The phenologic aspects of leaf abscission are related primarily to seasonal changes in water stress (drought), photoperiod, and temperature, and may be modified secondarily by any of the many other environmental factors affecting abscission (e.g., Ref. 48; see also Section 12.2).

The patterns of leaf abscission have been grouped variously; the following discussion utilizes the four categories suggested by Longman and Jeník (49).

12.3.1. Deciduous growth habit

This is a broad category characterized by the trees being free of leaves for an extended period, up to several months. Although the trees are vegetatively dormant while leafless, some species flower and fruit during this phase (50).

Shortening photoperiod is a major factor initiating defoliation in both temperate regions and the tropics. Conversely, experimental maintenance of long photoperiods delayed leaf abscission in many deciduous species. The response to shortening photoperiod can be quite striking even near the equator. In Peradeniya, Sri Lanka (7°N) species of *Hevea, Bombax, Manihot,* and *Erythrina* abscise their leaves between December and March, whereas in Bogor, Indonesia (7°S), those species abscise their leaves between June and August. Similar species in Costa Rica (10°N) defoliate in January–March and in Peru (10°S) and Bahia, Brasil (15°S) in July–September (51). In the northern hemisphere defoliation starts first in the northernmost forests and moves southward as the season progresses. The actual time of abscission varies and will come later than usual in years of good summer growing conditions and earlier in years when the first autumnal frosts are severe.

In the arid tropics and other regions with hot, dry summers the onset of drought is the major factor initiating seasonal defoliation. Most of the deciduous trees in these regions are *facultatively deciduous*; i.e., they retain their leaves until water stress increases to the point of initiating abscission. Thus, in dry years leaves abscise early and trees are bare for a long period, while in wet years trees will be bare for a shorter period. In these regions there are some trees that are *obligately deciduous* and appear to respond primarily to photoperiod and only secondarily to water stress. The adaptive nature of the facultatively deciduous habit is well known: Theophrastus (52) reported that a *Platanus orientalis* growing beside a spring on Crete was evergreen, while all other trees in the neighborhood were deciduous. Trees that are deciduous in their native regions but behave as evergreens in the uniformly wet climate of Singapore, include *Duabanga sonneratioides, Ficus plastica, Trema orientalis, Melia azedarach, Mimusops elengi,* and *Tectona hamiltoniana. Hevea brasiliensis* is an example of sensitivity to climate; in Ceara, Brasil, and southern Malaysia it is deciduous, bare for 2 months, and holding its leaves for 10 months, while in northern Malaysia it holds its leaves for 12 months and in Singapore holds them for 13.3 months (53). A striking example of the facultatively deciduous habit is *Fouquieria splendens* of the deserts of southwestern North America. It is bare most of the year, but shortly after a rainfall it produces leaves and holds them for a few weeks, abscising them after the return of hot dry weather. It can undergo several such cycles in the course of a year if the sporadic rains of the region come at appropriate intervals.

In contrast, a few tree species shed their leaves in the wet season, a response called *hygrophobic* leaf abscission. Examples include *Spondias mangifera* and *Tetramelis nudiflora* of Indonesia, *Melanorrhoea* sp. of Malaysia, and *Jacquinia pungens* of Central America. In Sri Lanka about 2% of the trees show this behavior (48,53,54).

Leaves of a few trees are *marcescent,* dying and withering in the autumn and tending to remain attached through the winter, abscising in early spring. This habit is shown by certain species of *Quercus, Fagus, Carpinus,* and *Ostrya.* In these species the cells of the abscission zone do not die in the autumn as do those of the rest of the leaf, but remain alive. At the end of winter the separation layer develops and abscission proceeds in the typical manner (2). The habit is more pronounced in young trees (that have higher levels of auxin and the other growth-promoting factors than do old trees). In some palms and tree ferns marcescent leaves remain attached for many years.

The ways in which environmental factors influence abscission of leaves of deciduous trees are only partially understood. For many species short photoperiods lead to a loss of leaf vigor and favor abscission. The levels of the growth hormones IAA, GA, and CK are high under long days and are low during short days, while ABA either increases or remains constant as days shorten: a combination of changes that promote abscission. As noted in Section 12.2.3, the involvement of phytochrome and the red–far-red system appears likely. Responses to water stress can develop quite rapidly. They appear to be brought on primarily (but not necessarily exclusively) by the rapid increase in ABA induced by stress. Preabscission increases in leaf ABA have been determined in *Acer* spp., *Citrus sinensis*, *Euonymus* spp., *Malus hupehensis*, and *Populus tremula* (24). There are, of course, other physiological changes that accompany shortening photoperiod, water, and other stresses. These changes are yet to be identified and their influence on abscission determined. Also worthy of study are the factors controlling deciduous behavior under the uniform photoperiod and rainfall conditions at locations such as Singapore, where some deciduous species are nonseasonal and defoliate at intervals ranging from 6.5 months to 20 or more months (53).

12.3.2. Evergreen, leaf-exchanging habit

Close to the time of annual budbreak, many trees abscise all the old leaves, which are soon replaced by new leaves from the expanding buds. This complete replacement of foliage is called *leaf exchange*; the trees are essentially evergreen. In temperate climates the exchange takes place in the spring as temperatures rise after a cool winter. Examples include *Dillenia indica, Entandrophragma angloense, Ficus variegata, Parkia roxburghii, Cinnamomum camphora, Magnolia grandiflora, Persea americana, Swietenia macrophylla,* and "live" oaks such as *Quercus suber* and *Q. agrifolia*.

The time relationship between leaf abscission and the appearance of new buds is not precise. Varying with species and other factors, leaf fall may precede or follow the actual appearance of new buds. In a few cases, e.g., *Sapium discolor, Terminalia subspathulata*, leaf fall extends for a 2–4-month period after budbreak. *Peltophorum pterocarpum* is often completely bare for a few days just before budbreak. There can be considerable genetic variation within the same species. Among specimens of *Quercus suber* at Davis, California, where the environment is quite uniform, the peak of leaf abscission varies from a week or more before budbreak to a week or more after budbreak. Thus some specimens are almost completely defoliated for a brief period.

The control of leaf exchange appears to be related to the physiology of its two components, leaf senescence and budbreak. Active leaves of many trees have the ability to inhibit budbreak. In some leaf-exchanging trees the old leaves show symptoms of senescence before budbreak and the appearance of new leaves. In these trees it appears that senescence of old leaves provides the signal for budbreak and the completion of leaf exchange (49). In other trees the development of buds and new leaves may be the required first step in leaf exchange. An example of the latter relationship was observed in *Quercus agrifolia* in California after the unusually dry winter and spring of 1968. That spring the buds did not break, and the trees retained almost all their old leaves; that is, there was no leaf exchange (55). Thus it appears that in *Q. agrifolia* budbreak is the essential first step in the leaf-exchange process. Leaf senescence includes decline in photosynthesis, low levels of auxin and other growth hormones, export of many nutrients, and usually increased ABA. Such changes favor abscission. In contrast, breaking buds produce high levels of auxin and growth hormones and are import sinks for nutrients. The resulting changes in auxin and other gradients at the abscission zones strongly promote abscission.

12.3.3. Evergreen, periodic growth habit

Trees in this category periodically abscise a portion of their leaves but always retain a substantial number. Typically, abscission comes either after the appearance of new leaves of a budbreak or after a period of dry weather. Examples among tropical trees include *Clusia rosea, Fagraea fragans, Mangifera indica,* and many dipterocarps; among subtropical and temperate zone trees are *Citrus* spp., *Buxus sempervirens, Picea excelsa, Taxus baccata, Pinus* spp., and other conifers (53,56). There is considerable variation in growth behavior among the trees showing periodic growth. Flushes of new leaves may be seasonal and come once, twice, or even three times a year, or they may come at irregular intervals, as for example with rains following a period of dry weather. In *Theobroma cacao* at Bahia, Brasil, the amount of leaf abscission is correlated with the amount of preceding new growth (33). *Camellia sinensis* retains two flushes of growth, abscising the leaves of the oldest flush as the next flush develops (57).

In genera such as *Eucalyptus* and *Pinus* leaf abscission takes place a few days after a period of hot dry weather. In these trees leaf abscission functions to maintain the homeostasis of the trees' water relations and appears to result from drought-induced increases in leaf ABA and the lowered levels of IAA in the oldest leaves.

12.3.4. Evergreen, continuous growth habit

Trees in this category show relatively steady production of new leaves and abscission of old leaves. The rates of growth and of abscission vary with many factors (Section 12.2), but abscission of old leaves results essentially from competition with the new leaves. There are many trees in this category, including *Casuarina equisetifolia, Dillenia suffruticosa, Trema guineensis, T. micranthum, Rhizophora mangle, Cycas, Pandanus, Carica papaya,* and treeferns, palms, *Sequoia,* and other conifers (see also Ref. 53). Some palms maintain a nearly constant number of leaves, by abscising old leaves as new leaves develop.

12.3.5. General comments

While the four categories above are convenient for the discussion of leaf abscission behavior, their boundaries are not firm and there are exceptions, intergrades, and complications to be recognized. For many trees, leaf abscission is a function of the environment as well as of genetic makeup. Trees that are deciduous in their native, seasonal habitats may behave as evergreens in more uniform environments, and vice versa (48,53). Further, different branches of the same tree can abscise leaves at different times so that leaf exchange may extend over a period of several weeks, e.g., *Mangifera indica*. At Singapore, the Asiatic subspecies of *Ceiba pentandra* behaves in a similar way, but the African–American subspecies is evenly deciduous. Similarly, *Pterocarpus indicus* at Singapore exchanges its leaves one or two branches at a time, while in northern Malaysia it is fully deciduous (48). In California *Quercus wislizenii* abscises more than half its leaves in early autumn and the balance at leaf exchange in midspring.

The behavior patterns of juvenile trees often change as the trees mature. For example, a number of trees that have the evergreen continuous growth habit when young become periodic as they mature (49). In *Fagus sylvaticus* the retention of marcescent leaves through the winter is a juvenile character that disappears completely with age (58).

12.4. Bud and branch abscission

12.4.1. Shoot tip abortion and abscission

A number of trees abort their shoot tips and abscise them at the end of a growth period. This habit is in contrast with the formation of resting buds enclosed in scales, and with continuous growth of shoot tips. After shoot tip abortion the resumed growth displays a sympodial pattern. This behavior is characteristic of many genera, including *Ailanthus, Albizia, Betula, Catalpa, Carpinus, Castanea, Citrus, Diospyros, Platanus, Rhamnus, Salix, Tilia, Ulmus*, and also *Crataeva roxburghii, Semecarpus sinensis*, and *Pistacia formosana* (53,59–61). The length of shoot tips that are abscised varies from 2 or 3 mm in *Citrus* to 4 cm in *Tilia americana* and may include up to seven or eight young leaves.

Abortion and abscission of shoot tips is sensitive to a number of physiological factors much as is leaf abscission. Water stress and mineral deficiencies will bring on abortion earlier, and conversely ample water and mineral nutrients tend to delay it. In *Ulmus* short days accelerate abortion and abscission.

12.4.2. Cladoptosis

Although sometimes used more broadly, in this review the term *cladoptosis* will be restricted to the abscission of discrete leafy branchlets, the leaves and stem abscising as a unit (Fig. 12.4A). Such behavior is common among the conifers but rare in flowering trees.

In a few trees cladoptosis is deciduous, with all of the leafy branchlets abscising at the end of summer, e.g., *Taxodium distichum, Glyptostrobus heterophyllum*, and *Metasequoia glyptostroboides*. More commonly, only a

FIG. 12.4. (A) Cladoptosis, abscission of leafy branchlets: (1) *Sequoia sempervirens*, (2) *Taxodium distichum*, (3) *Metasequoia glyptostroboides*. (B) Abscised branchlets of (1) *Quercus suber* with swollen base and smooth abscission scar and (2) *Zelkova serrata* broken through the abscission zone. (Photographs by the author.)

portion of the branchlets of an evergreen tree are abscised during a period of abscission. As with leaf abscission, cladoptosis often results from environmental stresses and/or competition within the tree.

Usually the branchlets that are abscised contain growth of 3 or more years, e.g., *Sequoia sempervirens*, *Thuja occidentalis*, *Juniperus virginiana*, and *J. communis* (60). Age of branchlets at cladoptosis has not been determined for *Araucaria*, *Calocedrus*, *Chamaecyparis*, *Libocedrus*, and most other genera. In *Pinus* the branchlets are in the form of needle clusters and usually are abscised when a few years old. Trees in the subsection *Balfourianae* of *Pinus* retain their needle clusters much longer, up to 30 years or more in *P. longaeva* (46).

In *Agathis*, leaf and branch abscission varies. Some species shed branches with leaves as a unit, in typical cladoptosis. On the other hand, *A. macrophylla* regularly abscises leaves and later abscises the branchlets that bore them. In

A. alba, A. australis, and *A. palmerstoni* some branches are abscised while still bearing a few green leaves but in these trees most branchlets fall leafless. Similarly, in *Podocarpus vitiensis* and *Salix tetrasperma* at least some of the branchlets still have green leaves when they are abscised (62). These latter examples are considered borderline and not cladoptosis in the strict sense.

12.4.3. Branchlet and branch abscission

Almost all trees abscise weakened twigs, branchlets, and branches in what is called "self-pruning." The pattern of abscission can be distinctive as in *Lagerstroemia microcarpa* where club-shaped main branches remain after branchlet abscission (63).

In a number of trees the bases of branches where they join the main stem are swollen and contain an abscission zone within which a separation layer develops and functions, e.g., species of *Agathis, Canangium, Gnetum, Populus,* and *Quercus.* Tissues of the abscission zone are mainly parenchymatous, fibers are usually absent and even vascular strands unlignified (64). In these abscission zones the separation layer secretes enzymes that digest middle lamellae and portions of primary cell walls, thereby enabling separation and leaving a smooth surface on the branch scar. Usually branches abscised in this manner are relatively small, up to a centimeter or more in diameter and half a meter or more long. *Agathis australis* abscises branches 5 cm or more in diameter (64). *Anthocephalus chinensis* abscised a branch 10 cm in diameter and 5 m long (J. Dransfield, personal communication).

In many trees bases of branches and branchlets are not swollen and a separation layer does not develop. However, an abscission zone is present to the extent that the tissues at the bases of the branches are less differentiated, with weaker cell walls and little or no lignin. Consequently, when such branches fall, separation occurs in the abscission zone. Branch abscission of this kind is shown by species of *Eucalyptus, Pinus,* and *Zelkova* (Fig. 12.4B), among others.

12.4.4. Unusual examples

In a few trees branch abscission involves disarticulation by separation in an abscission zone at the base of each node. Such abscission is characteristic of *Casuarina* and *Ephedra,* which commonly abscise their small branchlets and sometimes larger branches with numerous branchlets (62).

Abscission of very large branches can occur during wind or ice storms from sheer physical forces. However, "summer branch drop" also occurs, in good summer weather when large branches of up to 50 cm in diameter have been observed to break away. This has been observed in *Platanus, Cedrus, Ficus, Eucalyptus, Pinus, Quercus,* and *Ulmus* growing in well-watered areas of California, England, Australia, and South Africa. The separation commonly occurs late on a hot (35–40°C), still, summer afternoon. Reasons for summer branch drop are not clear; little evidence of injury or disease has yet been detected (65).

12.4.5. Branch stump extrusion

When branch abscission takes place without the participation of a separation layer a stump of broken tissues remains exposed and is slowly covered by the expansion growth of the stem. However, in a number of species of *Eucalyptus*, including many of the smooth-bark species, stumps remaining after the abscission of small branches are extruded, in a process that expedites healing and the development of smooth bark. In these trees abscission of a small branch leaves a stump usually 1 or 2 cm long. Over a period of 2 or more years the portion of the stump that is enclosed by the bark of the main branch is eroded and replaced in part by kino. The process continues until the xylem and other lignified connections of the stump to the wood of the main branch are eroded away, presumably by the action of ligninases. During the same period, bark of the main branch grows and constricts about the base of the stump forcing it outward, eventually to the point that the stump falls away. The resulting scars heal easily and the covering bark shows a minimum of distortion (66, Fig. 12.5).

12.4.6. Abscission and tree architecture

The form of a mature tree is influenced by many factors (59,67), among which the most important are (1) which buds develop, (2) orientation of the de-

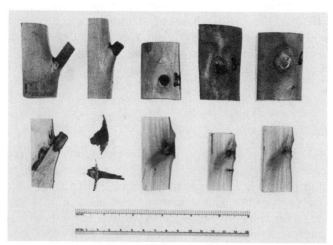

FIG. 12.5. Branch stump abscission and scar healing in *Eucalyptus viminalis*. Upper row, surface views; lower row, longitudinal sections and two extruded stumps with shields of bark that sometimes remains attached. The dark material in the stump sockets is reddish kino. The stages shown are estimated to cover a period of about 5 years. (Photograph by the author.)

veloping branches, and (3) which parts are abscised (Fig. 12.6). For example, in some sympodial growth patterns the terminal bud aborts at the end of a flush of growth and is abscised. For the next flush of growth, one or more of the nearby lateral buds develop into active shoots, e.g., *Citrus sinensis* and *Gleditsia triacanthis* (67). In *Magnolia grandiflora* the flowers are terminal on the branches. After abscission of the fruit two lateral buds usually develop; one grows more or less horizontally, extending the branch, and the other grows upward. Each of those branches may, in turn, produce flowers and eventually two more branches. Hallé et al. (59) present a comprehensive treatment of the many aspects of tree architecture (see also Chapter 1 in this book).

12.5. Flowers, fruits, and seeds

12.5.1. Flowering

There are several patterns of flowering and fruiting in trees, often correlated with leaf production or leaf abscission (51,53,68). For example, many deciduous trees flower when leafless, with the obvious advantage of making the flowers more visible and readily accessible to pollinators.

In the deciduous fruit trees of temperate regions, flowering may not be directly related to autumnal leaf abscission. In these trees, such as species of *Prunus*, *Malus*, and *Pyrus*, flowering comes at the end of winter (after an

FIG. 12.6. A mature tree of *Quercus lobata* in winter, leafless phase. Note that abscission of large, intermediate, and small branches is a major factor in determining the architecture of this species. (Photograph by the author.)

adequate period of cold), and is then a response to the warm temperatures of spring. In the tropics of Costa Rica most deciduous trees flower soon after leaf abscission, during the early part of the dry season. Exposure to sunlight appears to be a major requirement of such flowering; shaded branches, e.g., of *Tabebuia chrysantha, T. pentaphylla, Cordia alliodora,* and *Enterolobium cyclocarpum,* rarely flower (50).

In crop trees that show alternate bearing, e.g., apple, orange, pear, pecan, and prune the presence of a heavy crop inhibits the formation of flower buds for the following year (69). In contrast, *Pistacia vera* is an alternate-bearing tree that produces abundant flower buds every year, but abscises the buds during the summer of a heavy crop, which leads to a light crop the following year (70,71). The evidence suggests that one of the causes of alternate bearing is competition for limited supplies of carbohydrate.

12.5.2. Abscission of flowers and flower parts

The parts of flowers are abscised in many different patterns. For example, the abscission sequence in the flower of *Magnolia grandiflora* is as follows: floral bracts, stamens, sepals, petals, and eventually seeds (from the dehiscent follicles), and finally the peduncle with the empty follicles. In *Eucalyptus* the

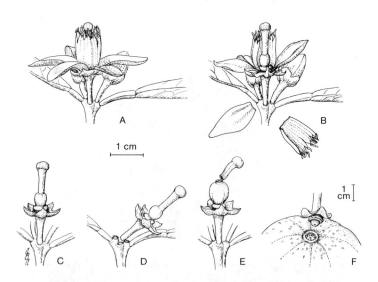

FIG. 12.7. Abscission of the flower and fruit of *Citrus sinensis*, cultivar "Washington" navel: (A) flower at anthesis; (B,C) during and after petal and stamen abscission; (D) young fruit abscission at the base of the pedicel; (E) style abscission of a young fruit that has set; (F) abscission of a mature fruit, between fruit and receptacle. (Reproduced with permission from copyright owner, A. B. Addicott.)

calyx and petals form a woody calyptra that is abscised. In *Prunus* spp. the floral cup holding withered remnants of sepals, petals, and stamens is abscised as a unit. Often the style is abscised from developing young fruit, e.g., *Prunus* and *Citrus* (Fig. 12.7).

Many trees produce far more flowers than they are able to maintain and develop into mature fruit (72,73). In some situations, especially when weather is adverse, flower buds may be abscised. However, most flower abscission takes place after anthesis. For example, the inflorescence of *Persea americana* contains 1000 or more flowers, from which it is rare for more than one or two fruits to develop. The aborted flowers abscise, and the stalks of the inflorescence also abscise in a kind of disarticulation. Similarly, more than 99.9% of the flowers of *Mangifera indica* abscise without maturing into fruit (74). *Cocos nucifera* develops about 30% of its flowers into mature fruit (45). In the deciduous fruit trees 90% or more of the flowers often abscise; the remainder are sufficient to develop into an adequate crop. Although production and abscission of such proportions of flowers and young fruit may seem wasteful, there are ecologic advantages (75). In particular, the habit often enables a tree to compensate for temporary adverse conditions.

12.5.3. Abscission of fruits

Abscission is one of many complications in the reproductive behavior of trees (76). Although some trees may abscise a few fruit at any time during fruit development, e.g., *Macadamia integrifolia* (77) and *Litchi chinensis* (78), for most trees fruit abscission is concentrated in three periods: (a) immediately after flowering, (b) at onset of rapid growth, "June drop," and (c) at maturity.

The abortion and abscission of small fruit immediately after flowering is usually the result of failure of pollination and/or fertilization. Adverse weather conditions such as water stress or frost also can induce such abscission. There is an underlying hormonal factor (79); application of auxin regulators can sometimes reduce abscission from adverse conditions (see Chapter 20 of this book).

In the northern hemisphere many fruit trees show an abscission of young, developing fruit, commonly in the month of June (hence "June drop"). The abscission is largely the result of competition for nutrients among young fruit (80–82). The number of abscised fruits can be large if the tree is deficient in carbohydrate or in nitrogen, or under water stress, or if zinc or other mineral nutrients are deficient. Conversely, young fruit abscission is minimal if the tree is well supplied with carbohydrate, mineral nutrients, and water (69). Thus the abscission serves to maintain homeostasis, keeping the number of fruits in balance with the ability of the tree to nourish them. At this stage, control of abscission is largely through the influence of the above physiological factors on the hormones in the young fruit (Section 12.2.2). Application of auxin regulators can delay June drop, but rarely affects final yield.

At maturity, fruits of many trees are abscised. This is especially true for fleshy fruits where abscission facilitates dispersal of seeds. As fruits mature and ripen levels of auxin decline, levels of ABA rise (24) and there is sometimes an increase in ETH as well. Together these changes function to initiate abscission. In some fruit trees, such as apple, peach, and pear, certain varieties tend to abscise their fruit prematurely. In these varieties the hormonal changes proceed too rapidly, and the result is an undesirable "preharvest drop." In such cases, application of auxin regulators can delay abscission and permit harvest when the fruits are fully mature (see Chapter 20 in this book).

Among the cones of conifers, as among the fruits of angiosperms, there is considerable variation in abscission behavior (83). Some cones remain closed and attached to the tree indefinitely (e.g., *Pinus attenuata*), while others open and shed seeds early abscising the empty cone later (e.g., *Pinus contorta, P. lambertiana, P. ponderosa*). Still others abscise scales and seeds quite early, followed shortly by peduncles with cone axes (e.g., *Agathis, Araucaria, Cedrus*) (64).

Many mangroves (e.g., *Bruguiera, Rhizophora*), are viviparous, the seeds germinate while still in the fruit. The seedlings abscise and usually float for a time before settling in the mud and continuing growth (84).

12.5.4. Dehiscence

This is the process whereby anthers and some fruits open and permit pollen and seeds to escape. Usually dehiscence takes place along sutures that open as longitudinal slits. However in some plants (e.g., *Rhododendron*), the anthers abscise a small disk exposing a pore through which the pollen escapes. Also some fruits open in a circumscissile manner. Notable among these is *Lecythis usitata*, whose large, woody fruit abscises a cap several centimeters in diameter to permit the seeds to escape.

There are many similarities between abscission and dehiscence. In particular, the cytologic changes of dehiscence in anthers and in herbaceous fruits include dissolution of middle lamellae and weakening of primary cell walls. The hydrolytic processes can be cytologically extensive, so that in some instances a number of the smaller cells in the dehiscence zone disintegrate completely. In other cases hydrolysis is less complete, and opening involves participation of physical as well as chemical factors (2).

In abscission, especially of leaves and bark, mechanical factors such as expansion of the stem and shrinkage of abscising tissues often facilitate separation. In anther dehiscence the walls desiccate and curl back as the sutures break down, thereby facilitating exposure of the pollen. Similarly, opening of dry fruits usually involves desiccation and shrinkage of the fruit walls. In some of such species opening is explosive and scatters seeds considerable distances: *Bauhinia purpurea*, 15 m; *Hura crepitans*, 45 m. In a few species with fleshy fruit walls, dehiscence is facilitated by the turgor of the wall (see also Ref. 10).

12.6. Bark abscission

Bark is abscised by a number of trees in various patterns of scales, long strips, or papery layers (48,85). Anatomic studies have detected no evidence of physiological activity in connection with bark separation; the tissues involved are dead and physiologically inactive. The patterns of bark abscission are determined by distribution of layers of thin-walled cells within the bark. Abscission commonly occurs after a period of stem increase in diameter, with the rupture of a layer of the weaker cells.

12.7. Root shedding

Although present-day trees do not actively, i.e., physiologically, abscise roots, there is considerable death and loss of small roots and of root tissues (8). The average lifespan of small roots of *Abies* and *Pinus* has been estimated to be 3.5–4.0 years. In a 50-year-old forest of *Picea excelsa* 20% the small absorbing rootlets were lost during the winter. The annual death and loss of small roots appears to be a counterpart to annual senescence and abscission of leaves (86).

Root caps remain in place at the tips of growing roots and are continually producing and sloughing off of cells and mucilage. Thus root caps may be considered to be in a steady state of abscission (2). On roots that persist, the cortex and outer primary tissues are eventually lost, as is the bark of older roots. Organic material from all these root sources contributes substantially to the chemical and physical quality of soil.

12.8. Cultural and genetic control of abscission

Abscission of leaves, young fruit, mature fruit, and dehiscence of fruit can be much greater or sometimes much less than what is economically desirable in practical horticulture and forestry. Undesired abscission can often be prevented by careful cultural practices. Deficits of water, nitrogen, and other mineral nutrients are common causes of abscission, and correcting these deficits is often the most practical way to prevent the abscission.

The genetic patterns of abscission can vary even among cultivars of the same species (36,87,88). Hence it is possible by hybridization to combine useful abscission characteristics with other desirable traits. Also, from time to time mutants are found that are superior to the parent cultivar. An example of the latter occurred in the apple, *Malus sylvestris*, cultivar "McIntosh." Although the fruit is highly regarded, that cultivar is quite prone to preharvest drop, i.e., to abscising a considerable portion of the fruit shortly before they are fully mature. Recently a mutant was found that retains all the desirable fruit qualities of McIntosh but also abscises normally, after the fruit is fully mature (C. G. Forshey, personal communication). Such a genetic solution to an abscission problem is greatly preferred to the risks involved with the use of regulator chemicals.

12.9. References

1. F.T. Addicott, "Plant hormones in the control of abscission," *Biol. Rev.*, **45**, 485–524 (1970).
2. F.T. Addicott, *Abscission*, Univ. California Press, Berkeley, 1982.
3. L.S. Jankiewicz, "Mechanism of abscission of leaves and reproductive parts of plants—a model," *Acta Soc. Bot. Pol.*, **54**, 285–322 (1985).
4. T.T. Kozlowski, ed., *Shedding of Plant Parts*, Academic Press, New York, 1973.
5. R. Sexton and J.A. Roberts, "Cell biology of abscission," *Ann. Rev. Plant Physiol.*, **33**, 133–162 (1982).
6. E.G. Leigh, A.S. Rand, and D.M. Windsor, eds., *The Ecology of a Tropical Forest*, Smithsonian Inst. Press, Washington, DC, 1982.
7. S.H. Spurr, *Forest Ecology*, 3rd ed., Wiley, New York, 1980.
8. J.P. Kimmins, *Forest Ecology*, Macmillan, New York, 1987.
9. L.S. Risley, "The influence of herbivores on seasonal leaf-fall: Premature leaf abscission and petiole clipping," *J. Agric. Entomol.*, **3**, 152–162 (1986).
10. L. van der Pijl, *Principles of Dispersal in Higher Plants*, 3rd ed., Springer-Verlag, Berlin, 1982.
11. K.G. Weis, R. Goren, G.C. Martin, and B.D. Webster, "Leaf and inflorescence abscission in olive. I. Regulation by ethylene and ethaphon," *Bot. Gaz.*, **149**, 391–397 (1988).
12. E. Jansson and C.H. Bornman, "In vitro initiation of adventitious structures in relation to the abscission zone in needle explants of *Picea abies*: Anatomical considerations," *Physiol. Plant.*, **53**, 191–197 (1981).
13. F.T. Addicott and S.M. Wiatr, "Hormonal controls of abscission: Biochemical and ultrastructural aspects," in P.E. Pilet, ed., *Plant Growth Regulation*, Springer-Verlag, Berlin, 1977, p. 249.
14. N. Rascio, A. Ramina, A. Masia, and C. Carlotti, "Leaf abscission in peach, *Prunus persica* (L.) Batsch: Ultrastructural and biochemical aspects," *Bot. Gaz.*, **148**, 433–442 (1987).
15. H.B. Sifton, "On the abscission region in leaves of the blue spruce," *Can. J. Bot.*, **43**, 985–993 (1965).
16. M. Huberman and R. Goren, "Is uronic acid oxidase involved in the hormonal regulation of abscission in explants of citrus leaves and fruits?," *Physiol. Plant.*, **56**, 168–176 (1982).
17. M.J. Jaffe and R. Goren, "Deposition of callose in relation to abscission of citrus leaves," *Physiol. Plant.*, **72**, 329–336 (1988).
18. B.W. Poovaiah, "Formation of callose and lignin during leaf abscission," *Am. J. Bot.*, **61**, 829–834 (1974).
19. B.W. Poovaiah and H. P. Rasmussen, "Effect of calcium, (2-chloroethyl) phosphonic acid and ethylene on bean leaf abscission," *Planta*, **113**, 207–214 (1973).

20. B.W. Poovaiah and A.S.N. Reddy, "Calcium messenger system in plants," *CRC Crit. Rev. Plant Sci.*, **6**, 47–103 (1987).

21. C. Côté and J.O. Dawson, "Autumnal changes in total nitrogen, salt-extractable proteins and amino acids in leaves and adjacent bark of black alder, eastern cottonwood and white basswood," *Physiol. Plant.*, **67**, 102–108 (1986).

22. S.E. Chua, "Role of growth promotor and growth inhibitor in foliar senescence and abscission of *Hevea brasiliensis* Muell. Arg.," *J. Rubber Res. Inst. Malaysia*, **24**, 202–214 (1976).

23. V.H.F. Moraes, "Rubber," in P. de T. Alvim and T.T. Kozlowski, eds., *Ecophysiology of Tropical Crops*, Academic Press, New York, 1977, p. 315.

24. F.T. Addicott, ed., *Abscisic Acid*, Praeger Publishers, New York, 1983.

25. R. Sexton, L.N. Lewis, A.J. Trewavas, and P. Kelly, "Ethylene and abscission," in J.A. Roberts and G. Tucker, eds., *Ethylene and Plant Development*, Butterworths, London, 1985, p. 173.

26. J.E. Watts and O.T. de Villiers, "The effect of 2,4,5-TP and ethylene on the abscission of bean explants," *S. Afr. J. Bot.*, **54**, 507–508 (1988).

27. R.W. Curtis, "Detection and characterization of abscission-inhibiting substances in leaves of malformin-treated cuttings," *Plant Cell Physiol.*, **25**, 1367–1377 (1984).

28. P. Montalti, G. Cristoferi, and S. Sansavini, "Effect of gibberellins 4 + 7 and shoot pinching on hormonal levels in 'Conference' pear," *Acta Hort.*, No. 161, 163–170 (1984).

29. S. Prakash and S. Ram, "Naturally occurring auxins and inhibitor and their role in fruit growth and drop of mango 'Dashehari,'" *Sci. Hort.*, **22**, 241–248 (1984).

30. P. de T. Alvim and T.T. Kozlowski, eds., *Ecophysiology of Tropical Crops*, Academic Press, New York, 1977.

31. R.W. Curtis, "Phytochrome involvement in the induction of resistance to dark abscission by malformin," *Planta*, **141**, 311–314 (1978).

32. D.W. Greene, L.E. Craker, C.K. Brooks, and P. Kadkade, "Inhibition of fruit abscission in apple with night-break red light," *HortScience*, **21**, 247–248 (1986).

33. R. Alvim, P. de T. Alvim, R. Lorenzi, and P.F. Saunders, "The possible role of abscisic acid and cytokinins in growth rhythms of *Theobroma cacao* L.," *Rev. Theobroma*, **4**, 3–12 (1974).

34. M. Maestri and R.S. Barros, "Coffee," in P. de T. Alvim and T.T. Kozlowski, eds., *Ecophysiology of Tropical Crops*, Academic Press, New York, 1977, p. 249.

35. E.M. Pook, "Canopy dynamics of *Eucalyptus maculata* Hook. III. Effects of drought," *Aust. J. Bot.*, **33**, 65–79 (1985).

36. W.C. Parker and S.G. Pallardy, "Drought-induced leaf abscission and whole-plant drought tolerance of seedlings of seven black walnut families," *Can. J. For. Res.*, **15**, 818–821 (1985).

37. T.T. Kozlowski, ed., *Flooding and Plant Growth*, Academic Press, New York, 1984.

38. R.A. Black and R.N. Mack, "Aseasonal leaf abscission in *Populus* induced by volcanic ash," *Oecologia*, **64**, 295–299 (1984).

39. J. Fraser, ed., *Trees and Salt*, Annotated Bibliography No. F33, Commonwealth Agricultural Bureaux, Slough SL2 3BN, England, 1983.

40. P. Schütt and E.B. Cowling, "Waldsterben, a general decline of forests in central Europe: Symptoms, development and possible causes," *Plant Disease*, **69**, 548–558 (1985).

41. H.M. Kulman, "Effects of insect defoliation on growth and mortality of trees," *Ann. Rev. Entomol.*, **16**, 289–324 (1971).

42. D.M. Kahn and H.V. Cornell, "Folivors, parasitoids, and early leaf abscission: A tritrophic interaction," *Ecology*, **70**, 1219–1226 (1989).

43. C.T. Maier, "Effect of the apple blotch leafminer (Lepidoptera: Gracillariidae) on apple leaf abscission [*Phyllonorycter crataegella*]," *J. Econ. Entomol.*, **76**, 1265–1268 (1983).

44. A.G. Williams and T.G. Whitham, "Premature leaf abscission: An induced plant defense against gall aphids," *Ecology*, **67**, 1619–1627 (1986).

45. D.B. Murray, "Coconut palm," in P. de T. Alvim and T.T. Kozlowski, eds., *Ecophysiology of Tropical Crops*, Academic Press, New York, 1977, p. 383.

46. D.K. Bailey, "Phytogeography and taxonomy of *Pinus* subsection *Balfourianae*," *Ann. Mo. Bot. Gard.*, **57**, 210–249 (1970).

47. B.F. Chabot and D.J. Hicks, "The ecology of leaf life spans," *Ann. Rev. Ecol. Syst.*, **13**, 229–259 (1982).

48. P.W. Richards, *The Tropical Rain Forest*, Cambridge Univ. Press, Cambridge, 1952.

49. K.A. Longman and J. Jeník, *Tropical Forest and Its Environment*, 2nd ed., Longman, London, 1987.

50. D.H. Janzen, "Synchronization of sexual reproduction of trees within the dry season in Central America," *Evolution*, **21**, 620–637 (1967).

51. P. de T. Alvim, "Tree growth and periodicity in tropical climates," in M.H. Zimmermann, ed., *The Formation of Wood in Forest Trees*, Academic Press, New York, 1964, p. 479.

52. Theophrastus, *Enquiry into Plants*, English translation by A. Hort, Putnam's, New York, 1916.

53. K. Koriba, "On the periodicity of tree growth in the tropics, with reference to the mode of branching, the leaf fall and the formation of the resting bud," *The Gardens' Bull. (Singapore)*, **27**, 11–81 (1958).

54. D.H. Janzen, "*Jacquinia pungens*, a heliophile from the understory of tropical deciduous forest," *Biotropica*, **2**, 112–119 (1970).

55. J.R. Griffin, "Xylem sap tension in three woodland oaks of central California," *Ecology*, **54**, 152–159 (1973).

56. J. Wiesner, "Über den Treiblaubfall und über Ombrophilie immergrüner Holzgewächse," *Ber. Dtsch. Bot. Ges.*, **22**, 64–72 (1904).

57. D.N. Barua, "Tea," in M.R. Sethuraj and A.S. Raghavendra, eds., *Tree Crop Physiology*, Elsevier Science Publishers, Amsterdam, 1987, p. 225.

58. M. Schaffalitzky de Muckadell, "Environmental factors in development stages of trees," in T.T. Kozlowski, ed., *Tree Growth*, Ronald Press, New York, 1961, p. 289.

59. F.R. Hallé, A.A. Oldeman, and P.B. Tomlinson, *Tropical Trees and Forests*, Springer-Verlag, Berlin, 1978.

60. W.F. Millington and W.R. Chaney, "Shedding of shoots and branches," in T.T. Kozlowski, ed., *Shedding of Plant Parts*, Academic Press, New York, 1973, p. 149.

61. J.A. Romberger, *Meristems, Growth and Development in Woody Plants*, USDA For. Serv. Tech. Bull. No. 1293, 1963.

62. L. van der Pijl, "The shedding of leaves and branches of some tropical trees," *Indonesian J. Nat. Sci.*, **109**, 11–25 (1953).

63. K.V. Bhat, T. Surendran, and K. Swarupanandan, "Anatomy of branch abscission in *Lagerstroemia microcarpa* Wight," *New Phytol.*, **103**, 177–183 (1986).

64. R. Licitis-Lindbergs, "Branch abscission and disintegration of the female cones of *Agathis australis* Salisb.," *Phytomorphology*, **6**, 151–167 (1956).

65. R.W. Harris, "Summer branch drop," *J. Arboric.*, **9**, 111–113 (1983).

66. A.J. Ewart, "Disarticulation of the branches of *Eucalyptus*," *Ann. Bot.*, **49**, 507–511 (1935).

67. M.H. Zimmermann and C.L. Brown, *Trees, Structure and Function*, Springer-Verlag, New York, 1971.

68. R.B. Foster, "The seasonal rhythm of fruitfall on Barro Colorado Island," in E.G. Leigh, A.S. Rand, and D.M. Windsor, eds., *The Ecology of a Tropical Forest*, Smithsonian Inst. Press, Washington, DC, 1982, p. 151.

69. W.H. Chandler, *Deciduous Orchards*, Lea & Febiger, Philadelphia, 1951.

70. J.C. Crane and B.T. Iwahori, "Morphology and reproduction of pistachio," *Hort. Rev.*, **3**, 376–393 (1981).

71. J.C. Crane and B.T. Iwahori, "Reconsideration of the cause of inflorescence bud abscission in pistachio," *HortScience*, **22**, 1315–1316 (1987).

72. W.H. Chandler, *Evergreen Orchards*, Lea & Febiger, Philadelphia, 1950.

73. S.P. Monselise, ed., *CRC Handbook of Fruit Set and Development*, CRC Press, Boca Raton, FL, 1986.

74. R.N. Singh, "Mango," in M.R. Sethuraj and A.S. Raghavendra, eds., *Tree Crop Physiology*, Elsevier Science Publishers, Amsterdam, 1987, p. 287.

75. A.G. Stephenson, "Flower and fruit abortion: Proximate causes and ultimate functions," *Ann. Rev. Ecol. Syst.*, **12**, 253–279 (1981).

76. G. Browning, "Reproductive behaviour of fruit tree crops and its implications for the manipulation of fruit set," in M.G.R. Cannell and J.E. Jackson, eds., *Attributes of Trees as Crop Plants*, Inst. Terrestrial Ecology, Midlothian, Scotland, 1985, p. 409.

77. W.S. Sakai and M.A. Nagao, "Fruit growth and abscission in *Macadamia integrifolia*," *Physiol. Plant.*, **64**, 455–460 (1985).

78. Sohan Singh and B.S. Dhillon, "Fruit drop pattern in litchi (*Litchi chinensis* Sonn) cultivars and its control by use of auxins," *Progressive Hortic.*, **13**, 91–93 (1981).

79. H. Fukui, S. Imakawa, and T. Tamura, "The relationship between early drop of apple fruit, cytokinin and gibberellin," *J. Jpn. Soc. Hort. Sci.*, **54**, 287–292 (1985).

80. J.L. Guardiola, F. García-Marí, and M. Agustí, "Competition and fruit set in the Washington navel orange," *Physiol. Plant.*, **62**, 297–302 (1984).

81. P.A. Nazeem, P.C. Nair, and P.C. Sivaraman, "Fruit set, fruit development and fruit drop in nutmeg (*Myristica fragrans* Houtt.)," *Agric. Res. J. Kerala*, **19**, 10–14 (1981).

82. L. Rallo and R. Fernandez-Escobar, "Influence of cultivar and flower thinning within the inflorescence on competition among olive fruit," *J. Am. Soc. Hort. Sci.*, **110**, 303–308 (1985).

83. G.B. Sweet, "Shedding of reproductive structures in forest trees," in T.T. Kozlowski, ed., *Shedding of Plant Parts*, Academic Press, New York, 1973.

84. P.B. Tomlinson, *The Botany of Mangroves*, Cambridge Univ. Press, Cambridge, 1986.

85. G.A. Borger, "Development and shedding of bark," in T.T. Kozlowski, ed., *Shedding of Plant Parts*, Academic Press, New York, 1973, p. 205.

86. G.C. Head, "Shedding of roots," in T.T. Kozlowski, ed., *Shedding of Plant Parts*, Academic Press, New York, 1973, p. 237.

87. A.G. Desai, V.P. Limaye, and R.T. Gunjate, "Studies on fruit set and fruit drop in Alphonso, Gaomankur and Kesar varieties of mango (*Mangifera indica* L.)," *Maharashtra J. Hort.*, **2**, 37–42 (1985).

88. H.B. Kriebel, "Maternal control over premature cone abscission of pines," *Genetika (Yugoslavia)*, **13**, 215–222 (1981).

13 Temperature Stress

JAN-ERIK HÄLLGREN, MARTIN STRAND, and
TOMAS LUNDMARK
Department of Forest Genetics and Plant Physiology, The Swedish
University of Agricultural Sciences, Umeå, Sweden

Contents

13.1. Introduction

Temperature is one of the most important uncontrollable climatic factors of the plant environment and is influencing tree performances and physiology in a number of ways. It is well known that temperature has a strong impact on the natural geographic distribution of plants and function as a determinant of plant productivity (1,2). Temperature also affects the rate of biochemical processes and temperature stress may induce imbalances in metabolic pathways. There is therefore a need for research on temperature stress to increase our knowledge in order to improve plant resistance and tolerance of temperature extremes. Adjustments to temperature regimes are seen in most plant processes such as growth and development, photosynthesis, and respiration.

In this chapter we will summarize direct stress effects, of low and high temperatures, on plant physiological processes, specifically photosynthesis. We will omit lengthy discussions about adaptation and acclimation to different temperature regimes since the literature about mechanisms of plant life in cold and warm climates is extensive (for some recent books and reviews, see Refs. 1–10).

13.2. Chilling stress

Plants of tropical and subtropical origin, including many important crop species, show physiological dysfunctions on exposure to low temperatures in the range of about 12–0°C (11). These so-called chilling-sensitive plants may be dramatically restricted in germination, growth, and reproduction at low temperatures. The susceptibility to chilling temperatures varies between species and there appears to be no sharp distinction between chilling-sensitive and chilling-resistant species. Physiological damage to plant tissues by low temperatures above 0°C is commonly referred to as *chilling injury* (for reviews, see Refs. 4, 11–15). The extent of chilling injury increases with increasing time of exposure. Physiological damage induced by short-term exposure to chilling temperatures is usually reversible after return to nonchilling temperatures. The development of chilling injury depends on the temperature, the photon flux density (PFD), and the relative humidity during chilling. Symptoms of injury, such as necrotic lesions in developing vegetative tissues and discoloration in fruits, usually develop more rapidly if the tissue is returned to warm temperatures. Such manifestations are probably the end result of a complex series of events.

13.2.1. Chilling stress; effects on physiological processes

13.2.1.1. Water relations. It is well known that transpiration decreases when roots are subjected to low temperatues, while the temperature of the shoots are held constant and near optimal (16,17). The reduction in transpiration is caused by both an increase in the viscosity of water and a decrease in the permeability of the root cells to water (17). The consequent decrease in hydraulic conductivity of the roots may result in a reduction in water potential and turgor of the leaves that is sufficient to partly close the stomata and hence reduce transpiration (see Chapter 6 in this book; also Refs. 16–18). Stomatal conductance in some plants, e.g., Sitka spruce (*Picea sitchensis*), may decrease sharply below a critical temperature, which can be shifted downward by preconditioning the plants at low temperatures (16,19). Chilling-sensitive species are probably more sensitive to low root temperatures than are chilling-resistant ones (17). For example, a break in the Arrhenius plot of water flow through the roots occurred in soyabean (*Glycine max*) but not in broccoli (*Brassica oleracea*) when the root systems were subjected to a constant pressure (20).

When whole plants of chilling-sensitive species are exposed to chilling temperatures under conditions favoring transpiration, rapid wilting is one of the earliest manifestations of chilling injury in many chilling-sensitive plants (21–23). About 40% of the leaf area became necrotic on return to warm temperatures when *Phaseolus vulgaris* plants were chilled at 5°C and 85% RH for 24 h (21). Apparently, cell death could be a result of leaf dehydration in this case. The primary reason to leaf dehydration is a reduced ability of the stomata in these chilling-sensitive plants to close at chilling temperatures in response to the water deficit (21–23), which develops as a result of a decrease in the water conductivity of the roots. Leaf dehydration and damage can be minimized by chilling the plants in darkness (22) or in an atmosphere saturated with water vapor (21).

13.2.1.2. Photosynthesis. Photosynthesis is likely to be one of the first processes that is adversely affected when chilling-sensitive plants are subjected to low temperatures (24). Low temperatures not only decreases the instantaneous rate of CO_2 assimilation at a moderate to high PFD (3), but may also significantly reduce the ability of leaves to assimilate CO_2 after return to warmer temperatures.

13.2.1.2.1. Chilling in darkness. An inhibition of net photosynthesis has frequently been observed when chilling-sensitive plants are transferred to warmer temperatures after exposure to chilling temperatures in darkness (for a review, see Ref. 7). For example, the light-saturated rate of CO_2 assimilation (A_{sat}) at a normal atmospheric concentration of CO_2 and a leaf temperature of 24°C was reduced by about 50% after exposure of the above-ground parts of coffee (*Coffea arabica*) plants to 4°C for 12 h (25). From the response of A_{sat} to intercellular CO_2 concentration (C_i) (Fig. 13.1) it was deduced that stomatal closure accounted for about 25% of this reduction. Consequently, about 75% of the inhibition was attributed to nonstomatal factors. The ~60% inhibition of A_{sat}, which occurred after chilling of tomato (*Lycopersicon esculentum*) plants at 1°C for 16 h, was also due predominantly to an impairment at the cellular level (26). Furthermore, both the initial slope of the response of A_{sat}

to C_i (i.e., the carboxylation efficiency) and A_{sat} at high C_i were reduced in *Coffea arabica* (Fig. 13.1). Carbon dioxide assimilation A_{sat} at saturating C_i was inhibited by about 25% after exposure of plants of *Lycopersicon esculentum* to 1°C for 16 h whereas the quantum yield (ϕ) at limiting PFDs was reduced by only about 10% (27). Similarly, exposure of whole plants of olive (*Olea europaea*), an evergreen crop of the Mediterranean, to 5°C in dim light (95 μmol m^{-2} s^{-1}) for 20 h reduced the rate of CO$_2$ assimilation at a PFD of 400 μmol m^{-2} s^{-1} to a greater extent than ϕ (28). Changes in relative water content and water potential of the leaves of *Coffea arabica* and *Lycopersicon esculentum* were small probably because chilling treatments were performed in an atmosphere saturated with water vapor.

The light-saturated rate of photosystem (PS) II electron transport in thylakoids isolated from prechilled leaves was only slightly reduced after exposure of plants of *Lycopersicon esculentum* to 1°C for 16 h (27). However, chilling for more than 16 h at 1°C caused a significant inhibition of the light-saturated rate of whole-chain and PS II electron transport, whereas PS I-mediated electron transport was not impaired (29). PS II appeared to be inhibited on the water-oxidizing side. Although the electron transport capacity was reduced, it was always in excess of that necessary to support the light- and CO$_2$-saturated rate of CO$_2$ assimilation (29). Although changes in the structure and activity of certain enzymes in the photosynthetic carbon reduction (PCR) cycle have been reported after exposure of leaves to chilling temperatures, very little is known about how these changes are related to inhibitions of CO$_2$

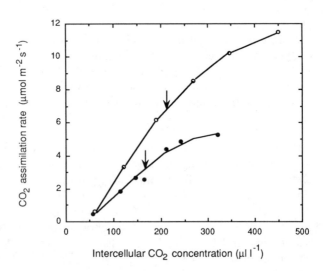

FIG. 13.1. Light-saturated rate of CO$_2$ assimilation as a function of intercellular CO$_2$ concentration before ($\bigcirc$) and after ($\bullet$) chilling (12 h in darkness at 4°C and 100% RH) of plants of *Coffea arabica*. Measurement conditions: PFD 300 μmol m^{-2} s^{-1}, leaf temperature 24°C. The arrows indicate C_i and A_{sat} at an external CO$_2$ concentration of 300 μl liter^{-1} (Redrawn after Ref. 25.)

assimilation in the intact leaf (7). The activation in the light as well as the deactivation in the dark of stromal fructose-1,6-bisphosphatase (FBPase) in *Lycopersicon esculentum* seemed not to be affected by 16 h of treatment at 1°C (30). Stromal FBPase is one of the enzymes in the PCR cycle, which shows a large degree of light activation (31). The mechanism for the inhibition of A_{sat} in *Lycopersicon esculentum* and other plants after chilling in darkness has not been clarified yet.

Complete recovery of A_{sat} at saturating C_i was obtained in the dark within 12 h when plants of *Lycopersicon esculentum* were transferred to 25°C after chilling at 1°C (32). In contrast, net photosynthesis in *Coffea arabica* required up to 6 days at growing conditions to completely recover from a single 12-h treatment at 4°C (25).

13.2.1.2.2. Chilling in light. It is well established that inhibition of photosynthesis may occur when the absorption of visible light energy by the light-harvesting pigment antennae in leaves exceeds the amount that can be orderly dissipated by the photosynthetic apparatus (33–35). Plants acclimated to low light or genotypically adapted to shaded habitats are especially susceptible to photoinhibition (33,35). Furthermore, a number of studies have shown that the inhibition of photosynthesis on return to normal temperatures is more severe after chilling in high light than after chilling in low light or darkness (36).

A typical feature of photoinhibition is a decrease in ϕ of CO_2 uptake (37) or O_2 evolution (38). A_{sat} is usually also reduced (37). Furthermore, photoinhibition is accompanied by altered chlorophyll fluorescence characteristics at room temperature (39) and 77 K (38), which are particularly useful in detecting photoinhibitory damage to photosynthesis in intact leaves. The main effect of photoinhibition is a substantial reduction in the variable fluorescence (F_V) and the maximum fluorescence (F_M) of PS II. The initial fluorescence yield (F_0) sometimes increases. Analyses of fluorescence induction kinetics at 77 K have indicated a primary site of damage at or close to the reaction centre of PS II (36). The efficiency of PS II photochemistry given by the ratio of F_V to F_M at 77 K has been found to be correlated with ϕ of O_2 evolution after photoinhibitory treatments (38).

The susceptibility to photoinhibition increases with increasing PFD and increasing time of exposure. Furthermore, decreases in ϕ or F_V/F_M of leaves of both chilling-sensitive plants (40–42) and chilling-resistant plants (42,43) are especially evident when the leaves are exposed to light at chilling temperatures. However, photoinhibition at chilling temperatures is generally more pronounced in chilling-sensitive species than in chilling-resistant species when grown under the same conditions (42,44).

Several factors may contribute to the increased sensitivity of photosynthesis to photoinhibition at low temperatures (36). Low temperatures reduce the rate of CO_2 fixation and photorespiration; metabolic reactions important for the orderly dissipation of light energy. Maintenance of some minimum rate of carbon turnover throughout exposure to a high PFD appears to be necessary for avoidance of photoinhibition, at least at temperatures optimum for growth (35). Furthermore, there is evidence indicating that the capacity of the recovery process(es) is reduced at low temperatures (45). Other protective mechanisms against excessive light may also be less efficient at low temperatures. These mechanisms include (35,46): thermal dissipation of excitation energy, reduction of oxygen in a Mehler reaction, and removal of destructive species of oxygen by various scavengers.

Recovery from chilling-dependent photoinhibition has been studied both in chilling-sensitive and chilling-resistant species. A major part of the inhibition of φ in tomato plants disappeared within 4 h in the dark after rewarming to 25°C (32). A similar degree of inhibition of φ (ca. 50%) in detached leaves of chilling-resistant spinach (*Spinacia oleracea*) was fully reversed within 3 h in dim light at 18°C (47). However, φ did not fully recover within 5 days when whole plants of *Olea europaea* were returned to growth conditions after a chilling treatment, which reduced φ by about 70% (28). Recovery in the chilling-sensitive *Phaseolus vulgaris* did not occur at 10°C and below (45), whereas partial recovery took place at 4°C in *Spinacia oleracea* (47). Leaves of *Phaseolus vulgaris* recovered more slowly from photoinhibition in darkness than in dim light (45). It has been shown that recovery and photoinhibitory processes occurs concomitantly (36).

13.2.1.2.3. Chilling of roots. Stomatal closure as a result of low root temperatures (see Section 13.2.1.1) would tend to decrease C_i and A_{sat}. However, stomatal closure was only partially responsible for the reduction in net photosynthesis when seedlings of *Picea sitchensis* were exposed to low root temperatures (19). In Engelmann spruce (*Picea engelmannii*), C_i was actually higher after 5 days of root chilling at 0.7°C than before the start of the treatment (48). The reduced mesophyll capacity for CO_2 uptake in seedlings of *Picea engelmannii* was further supported by measurements of A_{sat} at different CO_2 concentrations (48).

13.2.1.3. Respiration. A sudden change in the temperature coefficient (Q_{10}) for succinate oxidation in mitochondria, isolated from fruits or roots of chilling-sensitive plants, has been observed below about 9–12°C (49). The respiration rate of intact tissues may not always follow this pattern (50). Nevertheless, a reduction in the respiration rate below a critical temperature might lead to a decreased availability of adenosine triphosphate (ATP) and hence to a decrease in the synthesis of products necessary for maintaining cellular integrity (50). Furthermore, a suppression of mitochondrial respiration might lead to metabolic imbalances, such as the accumulation of toxic concentrations of glycolytic products (4,50).

The rate of dark respiration at normal temperatures may increase substantially in chilling-sensitive tissues, such as fruits, after a chilling treatment (11). If the exposure to chilling temperatures is brief, the rate of respiration will later return to a normal level. The increase in respiration rate in cucumber (*Cucumis sativus*) hypocotyls after chilling at 2°C was due partly to an increased activity of the cyanide-insensitive alternative pathway of electron transport (51). In contrast, a reversible decrease in the rate of O_2 uptake at 25°C was observed in mung bean (*Vigna radiata*) hypocotyls after exposure of intact, etiolated seedlings to 0°C in darkness for 24 h (52). Furthermore, the ATP content of the chilled hypocotyls was decreased. The respiratory activity in isolated mitochondria was, however, not affected.

13.2.2. Mechanism of chilling injury

Phase changes in the membrane lipids has been proposed as a primary event initiating chilling injury (11,49). Such phase transitions may lead to conformational changes in membrane-associated enzymes. When mitochondria were isolated from tissues of chilling-sensitive plants an abrupt increase in the activation energy (E_a) of oxidative activity, as judged from an Arrhenius-type plot, was observed below ~9–12°C (49). The change in E_a below a critical temperature seems to be correlated with a structural change in the polar lipids of mitochondrial membranes (53,54). Only a small proportion of membrane lipid with a high melting point appears to be involved in the transition down to 0°C (54). The temperature for these changes in the structure and function of mitochondria are near the critical temperature, below which injury may become visible.

The thermotropic lipid phase-transition hypothesis has been extensively discussed (for reviews, see Refs. 4,7,12,55). The relationship between structural and functional changes at low temperatures in the thylakoid membranes of higher plants seems to be particularly unclear (7). An increased leakage of solutes from chilling-sensitive tissues at low temperatures has been observed (4,7). This is an indication of an increased permeability of the plasma membrane. However, the increased loss of electrolytes in some species may be a secondary event associated with degenerative changes in the tissue rather than a phase transition in the plasma membrane (15,21). In chilled seedlings of *Vigna radiata*, an increased loss of electrolytes from the hypocotyls after rewarming was associated with a severely reduced regrowth capacity (52). Instead, one of the earliest cellular responses to chilling in hypocotyls of *Vigna radiata* was a reversible inhibition of the activity of the tonoplast H^+-ATPase (52). Phase transitions have been detected at chilling temperatures in total lipid fractions extracted from the plasma membrane and the tonoplast of hypocotyls of *Vigna radiata* (56). Unfavorable and direct effects of low temperatures on proteins and enzymes, which are not associated with membranes, has also been proposed as a primary event in chilling injury (13).

13.3. Freezing stress

Minimum temperatures below 0°C occur annually over about two-thirds of the earth's land masses (6). Leaves of tropical woody plants may be killed or severely injured by temperatures slightly below 0°C (1). These plants are likely to be permanently freezing-sensitive. In addition, some of them are chilling-sensitive. In contrast, plants of temperate origin have the ability to develop a freezing resistance, which enables them to survive low winter temperatures. The freezing resistance develop differently in different organs. Roots are, for example, not as hardy as the above-ground parts of the plant and young actively growing roots might not be able to achieve full cold-hardiness in the autumn. Resistance to freezing temperatures involves the ability to avoid ice formation and/or the ability to tolerate ice formation in the tissues (4).

Plants have developed different mechanisms to avoid freezing in their cells and tissues. Some plants exhibit freezing-point depression by an accumulation of sugars or other solutes in their cells. In addition, supercooling may occur when the temperature decreases below the freezing point. Supercooling is usually an unstable state and ice nucleation is initiated after 3–8°C super-cooling (1). This may give protection against brief radiation frosts. However, some plants have the ability to persistent supercooling (1). For example, floral bud meristems and xylem parenchymal cells of many temperate trees may supercool to very low temperatures.

Ice formation may occur either extracellularly or intracellularly (1,4,57,58). The probability for intracellular ice formation increases with the rate of cool-ing but decreases as a result of frost hardening. However, the occurrence of intracellular ice formation is probably rare under natural climatic conditions (4). Extracellular ice formation, which occur on the surface of the cell or between the protoplast and the cell wall, results in a withdrawal of water from the cell. Ice nucleation in the extracellular solution is facilitated by the low solute concentration there, which gives a high freezing point. In addition, effective ice-nucleating structures may be present in the cell walls (59). In organs containing xylem tissue, ice formation is likely to begin in the water-filled conduits (1). Ice nucleation results in a difference in the chemical po-tential of water between the ice and cellular solution. During extracellular ice formation, an equilibrium is achieved by diffusion of water from the cell to the extracellular ice. The onset of ice formation after supercooling is evident as a sudden rise (exotherm) in the temperature of the tissue.

Many chilling-resistant plants can acquire a freezing tolerance of varying degree by acclimation (hardening) under appropriate environmental condi-tions, e.g., low temperatures and/or short days (1,4). The potential freezing tolerance of a higher plant depends on its genetic constitution. Transitions between lower and higher levels of tolerance are especially evident in areas with a seasonal climate (1,4,6). Frost hardening has been suggested to be the result of integration of many diverse alterations in the cellular membranes and/or their environment (57). Since intracellular freezing is considered to be lethal, the ability of plants to tolerate freezing depends on their ability to tolerate extracellular ice (4).

13.3.1. Freezing stress; effects on physiological processes

13.3.1.1. Photosynthesis. The rate of CO_2 assimilation (A_{sat}) decreases with decreasing leaf temperature below an optimum, which varies with the species and the state of acclimation (3). When ice is formed in the leaves, net photosynthesis usually ceases (60). Furthermore, the rate of CO_2 assimilation after a freeze–thaw cycle or after a frost night may be reduced, especially in woody plants, in comparison with the rate of CO_2 assimilation before such an event.

13.3.1.1.1. Freezing in darkness. Exposure of leaves of unhardened plants to temperatures at or below their freezing point often results in a substantial reduction in the rate of CO_2 assimilation after thawing. This inhibition of CO_2 assimilation has been documented for unhardened seedlings or shoots of conifers of temperate origin (61–63). Growth at warm temperatures seemed to increase the susceptibility to frost (62); A_{sat} only partly recovered after exposure of seedlings of *Picea engelmannii* to $-5°C$ for 10 h (62), which indicates that the seedlings were permanently injured. In contrast, exposure of leaves of frost-hardened, woody plants to freezing temperatures above a certain critical level often results in a reversible inhibition of CO_2 assimilation after thawing (6,64,65). The sensitivity to freezing temperatures seems to decrease with increasing freezing tolerance, as in Silver fir (*Abies alba*) (66). CO_2 assimilation is unhardened and cold-acclimated herbaceous plants seems to be little affected until irreversible damage occurred (67,68).

Stomatal conductance is normally reduced after a frost treatment (6,62,63,65), which could reduce the supply of CO_2 to the chloroplasts. However, the stomatal contribution to the impairment of CO_2 assimilation seemed to be small, according to calculations (62,65). Furthermore, measurements of A_{sat} at different CO_2 concentrations clearly indicated that inhibition of photosynthesis occurs at the cellular level since both the initial slope of the response of A_{sat} to C_i and A_{sat} at saturating C_i were decreased (62,65).

On illumination of a dark-adapted leaf at room temperature, the chlorophyll fluorescence yield of PS II changes in a typical manner (69). During steady-state photosynthesis, the fluorescence yield is determined by the photochemical and nonphotochemical components of fluorescence quenching (70–72). Photochemical quenching (Q quenching; q_Q) is due to oxidation of the primary electron acceptor (Q_A). The major type of nonphotochemical quenching is normally energy-dependent quenching (q_E), which is assumed to be related to the transthylakoid pH gradient. The inhibition of A_{sat} at 12°C after exposure of frost-hardened seedlings of Scots pine (*Pinus sylvestris*) to $-7°C$ was not accompanied by any significant changes in the *in vivo* fluorescence yield of PS II at room temperature and at 77 K (73). A later study showed that the F_V of PS II was essentially unaffected after frost treatments above $-30°C$, which did not cause any visible symptoms of damage to the needles (74). The light- and CO_2-saturated rate of O_2 evolution was, however, substantially reduced. Furthermore, steady-state q_E increased while steady-state q_Q remained largely unchanged (Ref. 74; see also Fig. 13.2). The increase in q_E might be attributed to a low utilization of ATP and NADPH in the PCR cycle when the rate of CO_2 assimilation is low (72,75). Alternatively, the

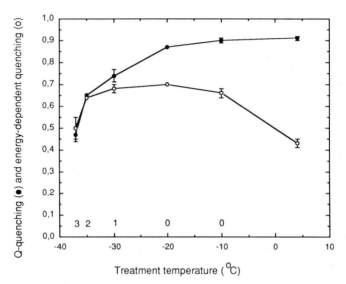

FIG. 13.2. Q Quenching (q_Q) and energy-dependent quenching (q_E) at steady state of primary needles of *Pinus sylvestris* as a function of the minimum temperature of treatment. Needles were excited with a PFD of 75 μmol m^{-2} s^{-1} at room temperature in the presence of 5% CO_2. SE is indicated for $n = 3$–15. Figures at the bottom indicate frost injury as assessed by chlorophyll bleaching on a scale of 0 (no damage) to 3 (severe damage). (Redrawn after Ref. 74.)

increase in q_E might reflect an energy-transfer inhibition of photophosphorylation. Largely based on these *in vivo* studies of chlorophyll fluorescence, it was proposed that an inactivation of enzymes in the PCR cycle and/or an inhibition of photophosphorylation caused the initial suppression of CO_2 assimilation in frost-hardened shoots of *Pinus sylvestris* after freezing and thawing in darkness (73,74). Studies of the mechanism of freezing damage to the photosynthetic apparatus in detached leaves and protoplasts of herbaceous plants have also shown that an inhibition of CO_2 fixation appears to be the earliest indication of freezing damage to photosynthesis (76). This inhibition may be due to an impaired light activation of enzymes in the PCR cycle (76,77).

Exposure of frost-hardened shoots or leaves to temperatures below a critical level results in irreversible damage to the photosynthetic apparatus. For example, irreversible damage to frost-hardened primary needles of *Pinus sylvestris* after freeze–thaw treatments below $-30°C$, which was later manifested as extensive chlorophyll bleaching, caused a reduction in the yield of F_V of PS II (74). The decreased yield of F_V resulted from both an increase in F_0 and a decrease in F_M. Furthermore, changes in the fluorescence kinetics from F_0 to the peak level (P) at room temperature were interpreted as an impairment of electron flow from Q_A to the plastoquinone pool (78). It was therefore suggested that severe freezing injury to primary needles of *Pinus sylvestris* involved damage to the Q_B protein (74). This hypothesis was supported by measurements of fluorescence relaxation kinetics following application of a single turnover flash (79; see also Ref. 80). In leaves and isolated protoplasts of herbaceous plants, injury to the thylakoid membranes after freeze–thaw treatments was manifested as an inhibition of photophosphorylation and electron transport (67,81). The most sensitive sites in the electron transport chain were located to oxidizing side or the water-splitting complex of PS II. Hence, the thylakoid membranes seems to be affected at several sites, primarily in PS II, when leaves are irreversibly injured. Furthermore, it cannot be excluded that damage to other cellular membranes, such as the plasma membrane and the tonoplast, more or less simultaneously results in a disturbance of cellular compartmentation. For example, Senser and Beck (82) proposed that frost damage to the thylakoid membranes of Norway spruce (*Picea abies*) was due to a liberation of membrane-toxic substances and/or lytic enzymes from the vacuole and other cellular compartments.

13.3.1.1.2. Freezing in light. The ability to dissipate absorbed light energy by assimilation of CO_2 appears to be severely restricted at subzero temperatures (61,83). Under such conditions photoinhibition might easily occur (see Section 13.2.1.2.2). Furthermore, the low temperature limit for net uptake of CO_2 is correlated with the onset of ice formation (60). Exposure of frost-hardened seedlings of *Pinus sylvestris* to a moderate PFD at a day/night temperature of $-5/0°C$ for 3 days reduced both ϕ and A_{sat} (84). Later measurements of CO_2 assimilation at $12°C$ and a saturating CO_2 concentration showed that the apparent ϕ of photosynthesis in frost-hardened seedlings of *Pinus sylvestris* was more inhibited after subzero treatments in high light (1300 μmol m^{-2} s^{-1}) than in darkness (65). Inhibition during the high light treatment increased with decreasing temperature below $0°C$, but ice formation had no dramatic effects on the degree of inhibition. However, treatment in darkness below the freezing point also caused an inhibition of ϕ. This inhibition increased markedly below $-10°C$ (Fig. 13.3).

Photoinhibition of photosynthesis is usually also evident as an inhibition of electron transport capacity, caused mainly by a decrease in electron transfer through PS II (35). A light-dependent decline in photosynthetic electron transport of seedlings of *Pinus sylvestris* during frost hardening at subzero temperatures was documented by Martin et al. (85). Exposure of frost-hardened shoots of *Pinus sylvestris* to a PFD of 1300 μmol m^{-2} s^{-1} at $-7°C$ for 4 h caused a substantial reduction of F_M and F_V of PS II at both room temperature and 77 K (73) when the fluorescence emission was measured from the upper exposed surface of needles. The changes were less pronounced when the fluorescence emission was measured from the lower, shaded surface of the needles, which confirmed the expected gradient of photoinhibitory damage across the needles. The lowered yield of F_V at 77 K indicates that exposure to high PFDs at freezing temperatures causes a modification in or near the reaction centres of PS II (see Section 13.2.1.2.2).

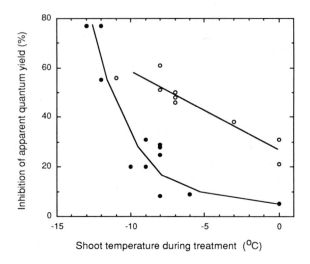

FIG. 13.3. The percentage inhibition of the apparent quantum yield for CO_2 assimilation after a 3-h exposure of seedlings of *Pinus sylvestris* to different temperatures in darkness (●) and at a PFD of 1300 μmol m^{-2} s^{-1} (○). Ice formation in the needles started at -4.3 (± 0.7)°C. Measurement conditions: $C_i \geq 85$ Pa, leaf–air vapor pressure deficit 0.4–0.5 kPa, leaf temperature 12 (± 0.5)°C. (Redrawn after Ref. 65.)

13.3.1.1.3. Freezing stress under natural climatic conditions. Night frosts during the growing season may have significant aftereffects on net photosynthesis in the following day(s). The effects of low night temperatures during summer and autumn on photosynthesis in seedlings of *Pinus sylvestris* have recently been studied in an area of northern Scandinavia where night frosts are frequent during the growing season (86–89). A reversible inhibition of A_{sat} and leaf conductance in *Pinus sylvestris* occurred after nights with minimum air temperatures below the freezing point of the needles (88). Significant reductions in leaf conductance have also been observed in other conifers on days following nights with freezing temperatures (90). The inhibition of A_{sat} in seedlings of *Pinus sylvestris* was not a result of stomatal closure since C_i increased (88). Both the initial slope of the response of A_{sat} to C_i and A_{sat} at saturating C_i decreased after night frosts (89). DeLucia and Smith (63) found that the sensitivity of A_{sat} to freezing temperatures in 1-year-old shoots of *Picea engelmannii* was highest in the middle of the growing season, i.e., when A_{sat} was at a maximum.

Frost at night followed by days with bright sunlight also seemed to predispose naturally regenerated and planted seedlings of *Pinus sylvestris* to photoinhibition (87). Photoinhibitory damage to PS II was assessed by measurements of *in vivo* chlorophyll fluorescence. Until the first severe frost night in autumn, F_V of PS II of current-year needles from shaded seedlings remained largely unchanged, whereas F_V of needles from unshaded seedlings decreased on clear days following night frosts. The decrease in F_V may be accompanied by an increased quenching of F_0 and a decreased q_E at steady state (89). Recovery from photoinhibition occurred on cloudy days. Full recovery seemed to require several days during the summer. The recovery is dependent on protein synthesis and temperature and is inhibited in the autumn with lower day temperatures (87).

A number of studies in regions with severe winters have revealed that the photosynthetic capacity (measured under standard conditions) of evergreen trees decreases during the autumn and winter (for reviews, see Refs. 7,91). Studies of *Picea abies* and Cembra pine (*Pinus cembra*) in alpine areas of Austria indicated that the potential for CO_2 assimilation decreased in the autumn as a result of night frosts (92,93). The extent of this depression was, furthermore, related to the severity and frequency of the frosts. The inhibition of photosynthetic capacity in evergreen conifers during the winter seems to be accompanied by a substantial decrease in the capacity for photosynthetic electron transport (82,94). It has been suggested that this inhibition is partly caused by an interaction between light and freezing temperatures (91). The more pronounced decline in F_V for unshaded seedlings of *Pinus sylvestris* than for shaded seedlings during the autumn (87), which coincided with freezing temperatures at night, seems to support this hypothesis. Numerous other alterations in the composition of the thylakoid membranes and in the structure of the chloroplasts also occurs during the winter (for reviews, see Refs. 7,91). Little is known about the potential activity of enzymes in the PCR cycle during the winter. The activity of Rubisco isolated from *Pinus sylvestris* decreased during the autumn and winter (95). However, the inactivation of Rubisco appears to be less pronounced than the inhibition of electron transport (94).

The recovery of photosynthetic capacity after the winter under natural climatic conditions can be slow. For example, the recovery in 1-year-old shoots of *Pinus sylvestris* during spring and early summer required several months in central Sweden (96) and similar results was observed in northern Sweden (97). The low photosynthetic capacity during spring depended on a low mesophyll capacity for photosynthesis rather than a low stomatal conductance (98). The recovery of photosynthetic capacity appears to be accompanied by an increase in the quantum yield for CO_2 uptake and in the activity of photosystem II (97,99). The recovery rate seems to be closely related to the temperature conditions (97,100). Subfreezing night temperatures and low daytime air temperatures might substantially delay recovery in early summer (88,96,97).

13.3.1.2. Respiration. Dark respiration in leaves of herbaceous plants generally seems to be less susceptible to inhibition by freezing and thawing than photosynthetic CO_2 uptake or O_2 evolution (68,101). A marked increase in the rate of dark respiration after freeze–thaw treatments has been observed, e.g., in shoots of *Abies alba* (64). Provided the leaf tissue is not permanently injured during the treatment, the stimulation of dark respiration increases with decreasing minimum temperature during the treatment. The transient increase in dark respiration has been considered to be a result of repair processes (102).

13.3.2. Mechanisms of freezing injury

Dehydration of cells during extracellular freezing has several secondary effects such as a loss of turgor, an increase in cellular solute concentration, and a reduction in cell volume and cell surface area. Since cellular dehydration causes a multitude of effects, many hypothesis on the mechanism of freezing damage have been presented. However, it seems generally accepted that cellular membranes are primary sites of freezing injury (58).

All cellular membranes are probably vulnerable to destabilization during a freeze–thaw cycle, and different membrane systems may be affected simultaneously. For example, electron micrographs of spinach leaves with a slight inhibition of CO_2 assimilation revealed small groups of strongly damaged mesophyll cells (103). Both the plasma membrane and the tonoplast appeared to be affected. In addition, the stroma of the chloroplasts was swollen and the envelopes were partly ruptured (67). When mitochondria and thylakoids were isolated from unhardened spinach leaves after freeze–thaw treatments between -5 and $-7°C$, respiratory and photosynthetic activities were inactivated to a similar extent (104). However, respiratory functions of mitochondria isolated from coleoptiles of unhardened and frost-hardened winter rye (*Secale cereale*) were not affected after freezing of the coleoptiles to lethal temperatures (105).

The plasma membrane has received special attention because of its central role in cellular behavior during freezing and thawing (4,58,106). The diffusion of water during extracellular freezing occur across this semipermeable membrane, which is also thought to be an effective barrier to nucleation of the intracellular solution (58). The water-soaked appearance of tissues is at least partial evidence for an alteration of the semipermeable characteristics of the plasma membrane after a freeze–thaw treatment. In leaves of *Spinacia oleracea* and *Valerianella locusta*, water infiltration was related to an inhibition of CO_2 assimilation (67,81). Several manifestations of freezing injury have been described in isolated protoplasts of unhardened and frost-hardened *Secale cereale* (58). Formation of endocytotic vesicles from the plasma membrane during slow cooling, which causes lysis of the protoplasts during subsequent warming, may be a lethal form of injury in unhardened protoplasts. In frost-hardened protoplasts, loss of osmotic responsiveness during warming due to altered semipermeable characteristics of the plasma membrane may be a predominant form of injury during slow cooling to lethal temperatures. Altered semipermeable properties of the plasma membrane after slow cooling of isolated protoplasts to sublethal temperatures may lead to an altered osmotic behaviour during warming. This may be related to a modification of the plasma membrane ATPase, which has been suggested as an early event during extracellular freezing injury (107). In unhardened and frost-hardened seedlings of *Pinus sylvestris*, the activity of plasma membrane ATPase decreased after freeze–thaw treatments of the seedlings at or below their killing point (108).

The liberation of membrane-toxic substances from the vacuole by damage to the tonoplast may affect other membrane systems, e.g., the thylakoid membranes, as previously mentioned. Furthermore, denaturation of proteins, e.g. Rubisco, after freeze–thaw treatments of needles of Norway spruce (*Picea abies*) was attributed to a release of toxic compounds from the vacuole (109). According to the results of Pukacki and Pukacka (110), damage to the tonoplast in needles of *Picea abies* occurred at freezing temperatures, which subsequently caused irreversible browning of the needles.

13.4. Heat stress

Heat stress as a factor limiting the survival of trees has been recognized for some time (4,5,111–114). High temperature can occur in the absence of other environmental stresses, although it is more common for high temperatures to accompany both atmospheric and edaphic water stress. The effects of heat stress are therefore often confounded with those of water stress. High-temperature conditions are furthermore often accompanied by clear skies and high solar radiation. The combination of drought, high light, and high temperature have a much greater potential than does high temperature alone in predisposing inhibition of photosynthesis (115). These drought high-temperature conditions can occur seasonally in monsoonal areas or intermittently in arid areas and last during periods of months to years. Two major types of environments can be distinguished on the basis of thermal regime: (a) permanent high temperatures and (b) a range of temperature variations, including extreme temperature stress. Kappen (5), in his comprehensive review of resistance to high temperature, distinguished between plants growing continuously at high temperature and those submitted to intermittent high temperatures.

Trees and shrubs in deserts (116) and savannas (117) are high-temperature stress-adapted, and this adaptation may be based on any aspect of the life cycle and physiological process, for example, the architecture of the tree, the pattern of allocation of nutrients and their reserves, phenological strategy, assimilatory and biochemical pathways (118). The variation in heat tolerance between species and ecotypes can be modified by hardening other adjustments, and developmental changes or through effects of water and nutrition (5). General principles of adaptive models have been described by several authors (4,5,119–123).

13.4.1. High air temperatures

Under natural conditions it is difficult to discriminate between high-temperature stress and other stress effects, such as drought. Direct heat injury seems to be less common, but exposed tree trunks may experience the highest thermal load because of the mass. Exposure to high temperature may cause stem lesions known as "stem girdle," "heat cancer," "sunscald," and various other names. Whitewashing of tree trunks is also a well-known precaution against heat damage. Direct injury is much more common in seedlings and young transplants than in older trees. The heat injury of the stem can occur not only after forest fires when the soils are dark but also in temperate climates after absorption of solar radiation. Scorching of leaves and fruits of high temperature impact, are described effects by horticulturists. Greater bark thickness and corky bark are also frequently observed, e.g., in the Brazilian cerrados (124). Similar features has been noticed for *Curatella americana*, *Bowdichia virgilionides*, and *Caeseria sylvestris* (123).

Heat injury of leaves in desert plants have been observed in trees and herbs (125–129). Heat injury of leaves differs between leaves at different stages of growth and during different periods of the year. Evidence of thermoadaptation by short heat shocks has been presented for *Populus deltoides* × *simonii* (5), but the response was not evident during the whole year (130). Other factors such as water content, photoperiod, and light intensity will influence the heat tolerance (5).

A single plant will not react uniformly to a heat stress; for example, young leaves can be more susceptible than older leaves. Usually trees will keep their growing points sheltered; for instance, the seeds are protected inside the fruits even if the fruits may suffer from heat stress. Stress avoiding mechanisms may permit deciduous tree species with relatively low heat tolerance to survive in hot environments. The stress avoiding mechanisms are therefore of great ecologic significance.

13.4.2. High soil temperatures

The energy balance at the soil surface is well understood, but the plant response to soil temperature is much more complex and hence less well understood. Great differences in tolerance to high soil temperatures exist between species as well as between provenances of trees. Seedlings of trees are generally more sensitive than mature trees. For many species the emerging seedlings are subjected to the high temperature of the top layer of the soil, which can reach temperatures exceeding the tolerance of the emerging plant. Under conditions with open spare vegetation, the strong heat absorption by soils with high humus content can create injurious conditions for seedlings even in high alpine regions (131). Soil temperature extremes may reach 65–75°C. Desert soils can reach even higher temperatures. The symptoms on the plants are varied, but necrotic lesions on stems and hypocotyls are usually observed.

A feature of trees in hot climates is the relative high root:shoot ratio. A low total leaf biomass and a high leaf:shoot biomass ratio has been shown for *Grewia flavescens* and *Ochna pullcra* by Rutherford (132). Deep-rooted systems are reported for various woody plant species in African, Australian, and South American savannas (133). The relatively high root:shoot biomass ratios can be a result of a strategy of the tree to economize carbon in environments where nutrient and water are limited. There will be a greater return on carbon by investigating in roots for gathering more of the limited resources then in making more leaves (134). Reported root:shoot biomass ratios can also be dependent on other factors, such as frequencies of fires. Root branching and elongation of root axis have optimum temperature responses. Typical values are 25 and 27°C for *Pinus taeda* and *Pinus banksiana*, respectively. Soil temperatures at shallow depths often exceed 50°C, which can also kill woody seedlings. Orchards in California have long been shown to suffer from high temperatures down to 30 cm below the surface. Several mechanisms for injury has been suggested: exhaustion of reactants or accumulation of reaction products, accelerated breakdown or inactivation of metabolites, enzymes, growth-regulating substances, and imbalance of reaction rates for various processes (135). Soil temperature affects nutrient transformations in the soil, root absorption, and assimilation. Different nutrients may follow different mineral uptake response curves. Differences between species exist; for example, *Malus* and *Coffea* trees differ considerably in their nitrogen uptake at different temperatures. Increased thermal tolerance of native plants is often correlated with decreased osmotic potential of their tissue (136). However, all trees do not show osmotic adjustments.

13.4.3. Heat stress; effects on physiological processes

13.4.3.1. Water relations. The cooling effect of transpiration has been known for a long time. The energy loss due to transpiration amounts to a considerable part of the incoming heat and is much greater than that from convection (137). The transpiration cooling of leaves have been discussed in detail in several reviews (138–140). Well-watered plants are usually able to transpire and dissipate energy as latent heat. The leaf types and leaf sizes (141) are features of importance. Small leaves with high convective heat exchange, divided leaves or torns, and leaves that display seasonal dimorphism are well-known adaptive mechanisms of plants in hot environments. Sclerophylls, e.g., plants of Mediterranean-type vegetation, can show overtemperatures of 20°C (5). These responses are called "overtemperature types" in comparison with "undertemperature types," in which temperature decreases below ambient as a result of transpiration cooling. It was concluded by Kappen (5) that the difference between under- and over-temperature species may be due to their different stomatal sensitivity to heat. Some factors that improve the evaporative cooling from transpiration when water is available might increase the high-temperature tolerance. Stems that can store water are only one example.

Sclerophyllous leaves with high specific leaf weight ratio (i.e., more xeromorphic leaf structure) are often seen in areas subjected to high temperatures and when the climate becomes drier and hotter (141). Sclerophyllous features such as thick cuticle, deep stomatal chambers, varied pubescence and colourless parenchyma or hypodermis has been mentioned as adaptive anatomic features (123). Other features such as increase in leaf thickness, number of stomates, small intercellular spaces, large vascular bundles, trichomes, and thick cuticles are shown in trees such as *Curatella americana*, *Bowdicia virgilioides*. Some bushes in the desert display leaves that may reflect as much as 70% of the incoming infrared radiation. The protective effects of reflectance and leaf angel has been described (140,142,143). Avoidance mechanisms such as arrangement of leaves to parallel the incident sunrays, curling and rolling of the leaves, and eventual shedding of primarily older leaves are well known. A few trees and bushes show paraheliotropic leaf movements. Chloroplast movements within the cells have also been observed, especially in lower plants.

In North American deserts numerous species shed leaves in response to summer drought, and a seasonal leaf dimorphism often occur. Deciduous shrubs such as *Ambrosia* spp., *Cercidium* spp., *Fouqieria splendens*, and *Lycium* spp. become leafless every year. Other perennial shrubs may loose the majority of their leaves. The reason for the reduction in leaf area might however be different for different trees, although seasonal water stress might be the dominating factor (116). For example, *Encelia farinosa* will decrease the leaf size in response to lower water potentials, while the increase in specific leaf weight is a response to irradiance. Increased temperature leads to smaller leaf size, increase in pubescence, and a higher specific leaf weight (116).

It is evident that an extremely important component in the response to heat stress is the stomata reaction. The observation that a number of plants such as soybean fail to thrive in the Death Valley in southern California despite being provided with ample water is an example. Spring annuals, for example *Cammasonia claviformis*, do not have any greater tolerance for high temperature than do plants from the subtropics, yet they survive in the desert. There seems to be an intrinsic difference between the responses of the stomata of a desert plant and those of a plant such as soyabean that permits the desert plant to remain productive at the low air humidity of the desert (see Fig. 1 in Carnegie Institution, *Year Book 1988*, p. 50). What physiological mechanism that underly these responses are not known.

Many of the trees and shrubs in arid regions are evergreens. Hence evergreens must possess adaptations to cope with extreme stress. The principal features of these plants are a tolerance to high temperatures, a xeromorphic structure, a capacity to tolerate low water potentials during extended periods, and an extreme stomatal regulation of water loss. Leaf renewal often takes place during the dry season (e.g., in *Larrea tridentata*), and the shoot-elongation–leaf-expansion period is relatively short. As stated above, many species are functionally leafless, although relatively high productivity rates can be noticed. True evergreens can retain some photosynthetic surface and remain metabolically active throughout the entire life cycle (144). Trees and shrubs with no leaves at all, the so-called Rutenssträucher, have green axes with temperatures close to the air temperature (125,145). In some cases (e.g., *Psorthamus spinosus*) stem photosynthesis make a substantial contribution to carbon gain after leaf abscision and during periods of low water availability and high temperatures. Savanna trees often show a completely opposite trend to grasses and herbs as they are actively growing and leaves are expanding when the grass layer shows high mortality rates and appears as a dead standing crop.

13.4.3.2. Photosynthesis.

The effect of high temperature on plants is primarily on photosynthetic functions, and photosynthesis seems to be the most sensitive physiological process. Tolerance varies with genotypes but is also subject to acclimation. High-temperature tolerance is usually considered to be correlated with maintenance of a high photosynthetic rate as shown, for example, in *Cammasonia claviformis*.

High-temperature acclimation stems at least partially from an increased heat stability of several chloroplast components (3). Long-term acclimations might be superimposed on rapid adaptive adjustments of thermal stability. Weis and Berry (146) conclude that reversible effects of temperature on rate and efficiency of photosynthesis are the main factors determining the long-term adaptation of the plants. Heat-adapted species have much higher rates of A_{sat} at higher temperatures then cold-adapted species and vice versa. The upper limit of photosynthesis varies with the temperature regime as much as 10°C in desert species compared with 3°C in temperate species (5). The high-temperature inhibition of photosynthesis is mostly reversible. If heat stress is sublethal, the photosynthetic capacity will recover in about 1–10 days (64,147). The recovery is not influenced by temperatures between 10 and 30°C (148).

13.4.3.2.1. High-temperature effects on photosynthetic reactions.

The steep decline in photosynthetic rate at high temperature is related to an irreversible inactivation of photosynthesis. It has been concluded that heat effects on the light reactions rather than thermal denaturation of enzymes or alterations of compartmentation are primarily responsible (146,149–152). The electron transport through photosystem II (PS II) in the thylakoid membranes seems to be most sensitive process (149). Heat inactivation of the oxygen-evolving system is prevalent, although a slow recovery has been observed (153,154). High temperature will also block the reaction center of PS II and disturb the lateral movements of pigment complexes in the thylakoid membranes (146). Since the high-temperature effect is primarily on the light reactions of photosynthesis, a decline in photosynthesis is correlated with a decline in the quantum yield (115).

Gas exchange and chlorophyll fluorescence studies has been used to study the energetic balance between carbon metabolism and light reactions. A blockage of the photochemical reaction center of PS II at high temperature can easily be observed by a sharp increase in the basal chlorophyll fluorescence (F_0). In leaves a correspondence between an abrupt change in F_0 versus temperature and a decline in photosynthetic capacity is well established (155–158). At moderately high temperatures a decrease in A_{sat} is observed. This is usually explained by an increase of photorespiration with temperature. In

C_3 plants, to which all trees belong, the increase in the ratio of photorespiration to CO_2 assimilation with an increase in temperature results partly from changes in the affinity of ribulose-1,5-bisphosphate carboxylase/oxygenase (Rubisco) for CO_2 in relation to O_2. The sharp decline in CO_2 assimilation at high temperatures cannot, however, be fully explained by the increase in photorespiration. The inhibition might also be related to a decline in the activation state of Rubisco (159). The mechanism behind this temperature-induced "down-regulation" of Rubisco is not known. Weis and Berry (146) recently extended the analyses of temperature stress causing a decrease in the quantum efficiency of CO_2 assimilation. The reversible temperature-induced rearrangement of pigment–protein complexes within the thylakoid membrane appeared to interfere with the efficiency and regulation of membrane-bound photochemical reactions. The disturbances in the balance between different pathways of carbon metabolism also seemed to be of great importance (146).

The effects of high temperature on proteins and the differential lability of enzymes are described *in vitro*, but the stability often exceeds that of photosynthesis. It was concluded by Björkman et al. (151) that thermal inhibition of photosynthesis occurs at temperatures where membrane-bound processes are affected and substantially below the temperatures required for thermal disruption of the Calvin cycle enzymes. Photophosphorylation, which is one of the membrane-bound processes, is relatively sensitive to heat stress, with noncyclic photophosphorylation more sensitive than cyclic photophosphorylation (149). However, the temperature effects on the ATP-synthesizing enzyme complex and its regulation is not well known (146). Denaturation of proteins and aggregations of proteins may occur at high temperatures (114) as well as changes in enzyme properties (160). Light-activated proteins involved in photosynthesis such as NADP glyceraldehyde 3-P dehydrogenase and ribulose 5-P kinase show stabilities similar to that of photosynthesis. Alterations in membranes with temperature is also described in higher plants (161); there is not much information from membrane-bound proteins and protein–lipid interactions in membranes at high temperature. The irreversible inhibition of photosynthesis may be related to the lipid properties of the membranes. The strength of hydrophobic bonds increase and the strength of hydrophilic bonds decrease at high temperature, and this may be an important factor for the explanation of the disruption of thylakoid membranes (161). Raison et al. (162) analyzed the lipid composition of chloroplasts isolated from *Nerium oleander* grown at high temperatures and observed a decrease in linolenic acid. The change could be attributed to a decrease of fatty acids in the galactolipid fraction in which linolenic acid predominates. The change in phospholipids was much less than those in the glycolipids. The structural changes, e.g. destacking of the grana at higher temperatures, cause a phase separation of nonbilayer lipids into stable aggregates. The factors responsible for the destacking of the grana membranes have been discussed by Quinn (55), and according to the model of Barber (163), the effects of cations on electrostatic charges on the surface of the membrane play a major role. The underlying reason for the change in photosynthetic function is a phase change of monogalactosyl diacylglycerol (MGDG) and a package of light harvesting protein chlorophyll (LHPC) a/b complexes together with photosystem II protein complexes into efficient functional units. This functional role of MGDG and other nonbilayer forming lipids has been proposed from several studies (55). Temperature stabilization at high temperature can also be achieved by other mechanisms, such as saturation of the membrane lipids. This observation is consistent with the observation that the proportion of unsaturated fatty acids in plants adapted to warmer temperatures tends to decrease (164). Changes in thylakoid protein:lipid ratios also support this mechanism stabilizing the photosystem II complex (165).

13.4.3.2.2. Interaction between light and high temperature. It is often observed that light causes an increase in tolerance to heat. However, effects of different levels and wavelengths of light are complex. Short heat stress caused by sunflecks may therefore in some cases cause injury, and in other cases acclimation to high temperature. Photoinhibition at high temperatures has been described in detail by Ludlow (115). In the absence of other stresses prolonged exposure to high photon flux densities may cause photoinhibition if the minimum temperature for reversible high-temperature injury is exceeded. The recovery process is light-saturated at lower photon flux densities and high temperatures may block the recovery (115). Water stress will predispose leaves to photoinhibition. High-temperature photoinhibition in water-stressed leaves results from differences between the relative temperature sensitivities of the rates of damage and repair. However, there is still controversy about the extent to which reductions in photosynthetic capacity is due to direct or indirect effects of water stress or water-stress-induced photoinhibition (115). The degree of high-temperature exacerbated photoinhibition depends on both leaf temperature and photon flux density. The effects are additive. Mild heating may cause two types of damage (158). Bilger et al. (158) suggested that a shift of energy distribution in favor of photosystem I was first manifested. A deactivation of Calvin cycle enzymes was suggested as a second type of inhibition.

As discussed by Ludlow (115), light stress at high temperature can be demonstrated in both unstressed and water-stressed leaves, but we have little evidence that it does occur under natural conditions. There is a close correlation between the quenching of chlorophyll fluorescence, often used as a direct measure of nonradiative energy dissipation, and the reversible formation of the carotenoid zeaxanthine from violaxanthin (xanthophyll cycle). If zeaxanthine is a mediator of excessive energy dissipation, this carotenoid should increase with increased excessive light energy. However, there seem yet to be no reports on the direct interaction between high temperature and light on zeaxanthine formation. The conclusions drawn from the results presented by Weis and Berry (146) indicate that photoinhibition is not often observed at high temperature and much less severe than at low temperature. The eventual effects on growth, yield, or survival of the plants are, therefore, basically unknown.

13.4.3.3. Respiration. At high temperatures respiratory rates are increased and photosynthetic rates decreased, which may eventually lead to reduction of photosynthates for assimilatory processes. The general increase in rate of respiration with temperature is well known; however, Q_{10} values for different processes differ and different enzymes have different temperature sensitivity. Respiration is clearly less sensitive than photosynthesis to heat stress (152). Abrupt inhibition of respiration can occur at near-lethal heat stress (166). Generally the change in respiration is not significant in response to heat stress in comparison with other stress factors (167). In most cases a decrease or cessation of respiration is observed when temperatures reach injurious levels (64). The degree of cellular injury will also affect the recovery of respiration.

13.4.4. Cellular manifestations of heat injury

Beside the effects of high temperature on photosynthesis and respiration described above, several manifestations of heat injury have been described. The cellular manifestations of high-temperature stress has been described by Steponkus (57). Cytologic changes include coagulation of the protoplasm, cytolysis, nuclear changes, and altered mitosis. That protein denaturation of the cytoplasm at high temperature is the cause of direct temperature injury was first suggested by Sachs in 1864 (cited in Ref. 168). Alexanderov (114) suggests that the various manifestations occur in a succession and that the protoplasmatic streaming is the most sensitive.

Numerous biochemical changes have been observed and correlated to heat injury, including protein content and nucleic acid content. The effects on rRNA content with a reduction in chloroplast ribosomes have been reported (169). Other more subtle repercussions have been proposed (135). These include accelerated breakdown of metabolites and metabolic rate imbalances. Example of such temperature-induced lesions are adenin and vitamin B synthesis (170). It was later shown that accelerated senescence of leaves and roots can be prevented by application of adenin and cytokinins (57).

13.5. Molecular mechanisms of temperature tolerance

The molecular mechanisms that render some plants tolerant to high or low temperature remain poorly understood, and several mechanisms have been suggested, especially alterations of the membranes with temperature. Chloroplast membranes are the best studied and have already been mentioned above (see also Ref. 151), changes in other organelle membranes and the plasmalemma have been suggested. Soluble enzymes in chloroplasts, mitochondria, and cytoplasm are also shown to be altered both structurally and functionally. However, the differences in thermostability of malic dehydrogenase of different cultivars, for instance, does not necessarily correlate with the differences in heat tolerance between the cultivars (171). Parallel to the changes in the proteins in membranes there are distinctive changes of the lipids. There is some evidence that an increase in the ratio of saturated to unsaturated fatty acids in the membranes can increase the tolerance to high temperature. Raison et al. (161), suggested that the relative strength of hydrophobic and hydrophilic interactions between proteins, lipids, and the aqueous environment of the membranes play a key role. Changes in lipid biosynthetic pathways and in specific enzymes in these pathways may play an important role (172). It is very likely that differences in membrane composition may account for the differences in sensitivity to chilling stress. Chilling-sensitive plants generally contain higher proportions of palmatic and *trans*-Δ^3-hexadecanoic acid (*trans* 16:1) (173). The studies by Raison and Wright (174) provide evidence that chilling injury is induced by small amounts of lipids form minor phase separation within the membranes. The synthetic pathways of lipids are also of interest. Recently, Murata et al. (175) isolated genes for isomeric glycerol-P acyltransferases and transformed a chilling-sensitive algae into a chilling-resistant one. Whether the same is true also for higher plants is not yet known.

Plant tissue generally respond rapidly to sudden increases in temperature by abolishing normal protein synthesis and producing new polypeptides called *heat shock proteins* (HSPs). HSPs are described from a number of plants, and their role in protecting the plants is currently being investigated at the molecular level but the information on the whole-plant level is not equally well understood. HSPs are described in recent review articles (176,177). The responses are best known from investigations of tropical cereals, and the localization of HSPs has been demonstrated in the chloroplast, mitochondria, plasmalemma and ribosomes. Investigations on cells of trees are lacking. The organization and regulation of HSPs are fairly well known, but the mechanistic function of HSPs is not yet clear. It may have a function in protecting cell components such as ribonuclear proteins from high temperatures (178). Similarly, low temperatures also change the protein synthesis, and some new peptides are produced while other proteins disappear. The role of these proteins and small peptides is also unclear in this case. Recent experiments provide evidence that mechanical stress on biomembranes is the primary cause to frost injury (106,179–181). The molecular mechanisms underlying freeze–thaw damage are complex, as pointed out by Steponkus (57). To understand the mechanisms of frost damage, factors such as frost-induced redistribution of solutes (179,180), membrane alterations (i.e., displacements of proteins), lateral phase separation (106), and damage caused by osmotically induced contraction and/or expansion of the cells (58). The complex physiological and metabolic effects of temperature are documented, however, only a few mechanistic explanations to the observed effects can be given. At this moment we suggest that the observed changes in plant membranes and their composition and in physiological processes relate to both increased resistance per se and improved function of trees during acclimation to temperature stress.

13.6. References

1. A. Sakai and W. Larcher, *Frost Survival of Plants. Responses and Adaptation to Freezing Stress* (*Ecological Studies*, Vol. 62), Springer-Verlag, Berlin, 1987.

2. J. Grace, "Temperature as a determinant of plant productivity," in S.P. Long and F.I. Woodward, eds., *Plants and Temperature* (*Symp. Soc. Exp. Biol.*, Vol. 42), Company of Biologists, Cambridge, 1988, pp. 91–108.

3. J. Berry and O. Björkman, "Photosynthetic response and adaptation to temperature in higher plants," *Ann. Rev. Plant Physiol.*, **31**, 491–543 (1980).

4. J. Levitt, *Chilling, Freezing and High Temperature Stresses* (*Responses of Plants to Environmental Stresses*, Vol. 1), 2nd ed., Academic Press, New York, 1980.

5. L. Kappen, "Ecological significance of resistance to high temperature," in A. Pirson and M.H. Zimmermann, eds., *Encyclopedia of Plant Physiology, New Series, Physiological Plant Ecology I*, Vol. 12A, Springer-Verlag, Berlin, 1981, pp. 439–474.

6. W. Larcher and H. Bauer, "Ecological significance of resistance to low temperature," in A. Pirson and M.H. Zimmermann, eds., *Encyclopedia of Plant Physiology, New Series, Physiological Plant Ecology I*, Vol. 12A, Springer-Verlag, Berlin, 1981, pp. 403–437.

7. G. Öquist and B. Martin, "Cold climates," in N.R. Baker and S.P. Long, eds., *Photosynthesis in Contrasting Environments*, Elsevier, Amsterdam, 1986, pp. 237–293.

8. P.H. Li, "Subzero temperature stress physiology of herbaceous plants," *Hort. Rev.* **6**, 373–416 (1984).

9. Ch. Körner and W. Larcher, "Plant life in cold climates," in S.P. Long and F.I. Woodward, eds., *Plants and Temperature* (*Symp. Soc. Exp. Biol.*, Vol. 42), Company of Biologists, Cambridge, 1988, pp. 25–57.

10. J.-E. Hällgren and G. Öquist, "Adaptations to low temperatures," in R. Alscher and J. Cumming, eds., *Stress Responses in Plants: Adaptation Mechanisms* (*Plant Biology Series*), Alan R. Liss, New York, 1990, pp. 265–293.

11. J.M. Lyons, "Chilling injury in plants," *Ann. Rev. Plant Physiol.*, **24**, 445–466 (1973).

12. J.M. Lyons, J.K. Raison, and P.L. Steponkus, "The plant membrane in response to low temperature: An overview," in J.M. Lyons, D. Graham, and J.K. Raison, eds., *Low Temperature Stress in Crop Plants. The Role of the Membrane*, Academic Press, New York, 1979, pp. 1–24.

13. D. Graham and B.D. Patterson, "Responses of plants to low, nonfreezing temperatures: Proteins, metabolism, and acclimation," *Ann. Rev. Plant Physiol.*, **33**, 347–372 (1982).

14. C.Y. Wang, "Physiological and biochemical responses of plants to chilling stress," *Hort. Sci.*, **17**, 173–186 (1982).

15. J.M. Wilson, "Chilling injury in plants," in B.W.W. Grout and G.J. Morris, eds., *The Effects of Low Temperatures on Biological Systems*, Edward Arnold, London, 1987, pp. 271–292.

16. D. Whitehead and P.G. Jarvis, "Coniferous forests and plantations," in T.T. Kozlowski, ed., *Water Deficits and Plant Growth*, Vol. 6, Academic Press, New York, 1981, pp. 49–152.

17. P.J. Kramer, *Water Relations of Plants*, Academic Press, New York, 1983.

18. S.W. Running and C.P. Reid, "Soil temperature influences on root resistance of *Pinus contorta* seedlings," *Plant Physiol.*, **65**, 635–640 (1980).

19. N.C. Turner and P.G. Jarvis, "Photosynthesis in Sitka spruce (*Picea sitchensis* (Bong.) Carr.). IV. Response to soil temperature," *J. Appl. Ecol.*, **12**, 561–576 (1975).

20. A.H. Markhart, III, E.L. Fiscus, A.W. Naylor, and P.J. Kramer, "Effect of temperature on water and ion transport in soybean and broccoli systems," *Plant Physiol.*, **64**, 83–87 (1979).

21. J.M. Wilson, "The mechanism of chill- and drought-hardening of *Phaseolus vulgaris* leaves," *New Phytol.*, **76**, 257–270 (1976).

22. J.R. McWilliam, P.J. Kramer, and R.L. Musser, "Temperature-induced water stress in chilling-sensitive plants," *Aust. J. Plant Physiol.*, **9**, 343–352 (1982).

23. D. Eamus, R. Fenton, and J.M. Wilson, "Stomatal behaviour and water relations of chilled *Phaseolus vulgaris* L. and *Pisum sativum* L.," *J. Exp. Bot.*, **34**, 434–441 (1983).

24. D.R. Ort and J.S. Boyer, "Plant productivity, photosynthesis and environmental stress," in B.G. Atkinson and D.B. Walden, eds., *Changes in Eukaryotic Gene Expression in Response to Environmental Stress*, Academic Press, Orlando, FL, 1985, pp. 279–313.

25. H. Bauer, R. Wierer, W.H. Hatheway, and W. Larcher, "Photosynthesis of *Coffea arabica* after chilling," *Physiol. Plant.*, **64**, 449–454 (1985).

26. B. Martin, D.R. Ort, and J.S. Boyer, "Impairment of photosynthesis by chilling-temperatures in tomato," *Plant Physiol.*, **68**, 329–334 (1981).

27. B. Martin and D.R. Ort, "Insensitivity of water-oxidation and photosystem II activity in tomato to chilling temperatures," *Plant Physiol.*, **70**, 689–694 (1982).

28. G. Bongi and S.P. Long, "Light-dependent damage to photosynthesis in olive leaves during chilling and high temperature stress," *Plant Cell Environ.*, **10**, 241–249 (1987).

29. S.C. Kee, B. Martin, and D.R. Ort, "The effects of chilling in the dark and in the light on photosynthesis of tomato: electron transfer reactions," *Photosynth. Res.*, **8**, 41–51 (1986).

30. G.F. Sassenrath, D.R. Ort, and A.R. Portis, Jr., "Effect of chilling on the activity of enzymes of the photosynthetic carbon reduction cycle," in J. Biggins, ed., *Progress in Photosynthesis Research*, Vol. 4, Martinus Nijhoff Publishers, Dordrecht, 1987, pp. 103–106.

31. B.B. Buchanan, "Role of light in the regulation of chloroplast enzymes," *Ann. Rev. Plant Physiol.*, **31**, 341–374 (1980).

32. B. Martin and D.R. Ort, "The recovery of photosynthesis in tomato subsequent to chilling exposure," *Photosynth. Res.*, **6**, 121–132 (1985).

33. O. Björkman, "Responses to different quantum flux densities," in A. Pirson and M.H. Zimmermann, eds., *Encyclopedia of Plant Physiology, New Series, Physiological Plant Ecology I*, Vol. 12A, Springer-Verlag, Berlin, 1981, pp. 57–107.

34. C.B. Osmond, "Photorespiration and photoinhibition. Some implications for the energetics of photosynthesis," *Biochim. Biophys. Acta*, **639**, 77–98 (1981).

35. S.B. Powles, "Photoinhibition of photosynthesis induced by visible light," *Ann. Rev. Plant Physiol.*, **35**, 15–44 (1984).

36. G. Öquist, D.H. Greer, and E. Ögren, "Light stress at low temperature," in D.J. Kyle, C.B. Osmond, and C.J. Arntzen, eds., *Photoinhibition*, Elsevier, Amsterdam, 1987, pp. 67–87.

37. N.R. Baker, S.P. Long, and D.R. Ort, "Photosynthesis and temperature, with particular reference to effects on quantum yield," in S.P. Long and F.I. Woodward, eds., *Plants and Temperature* (*Symp. Soc. Exp. Biol.*, Vol. 42), Company of Biologists, Cambridge, 1988, pp. 347–375.

38. O. Björkman, "Low-temperature chlorophyll fluorescence in leaves and its relationship to photon yield of photosynthesis in photoinhibition," in D.J. Kyle, C.B. Osmond, and C.J. Arntzen, eds., *Photoinhibition*, Elsevier, Amsterdam, 1987, pp. 123–144.

39. N.R. Baker and P. Horton, "Chlorophyll fluorescence quenching during photoinhibition," in D.J. Kyle, C.B. Osmond, and C.J. Arntzen, eds., *Photoinhibition*, Elsevier, Amsterdam, 1987, pp. 145–168.

40. S.P. Long, T.M. East, and N.R. Baker, "Chilling damage to photosynthesis in young *Zea mays*. I. Effects of light and temperature variation on photosynthetic CO_2 assimilation," *J. Exp. Bot.*, **34**, 177–188 (1983).

41. S.B. Powles, J.A. Berry, and O. Björkman, "Interaction between light and chilling temperature on the inhibition of photosynthesis in chilling-sensitive plants," *Plant Cell Environ.*, **6**, 117–123 (1983).

42. S.E. Hetherington, J. He, and R.M. Smillie, "Photoinhibition at low temperature in chilling-sensitive and -resistant plants," *Plant Physiol.*, **90**, 1609–1615 (1989).

43. E. Ögren, G. Öquist, and J.-E. Hällgren, "Photoinhibition of photosynthesis in *Lemna gibba* as induced by the interaction between light and temperature. I. Photosynthesis in vivo," *Physiol. Plant.*, **62**, 181–186 (1984).

44. T.C. Peeler and A.W. Naylor, "A comparison of the effects of chilling on leaf gas exchange in pea (*Pisum sativum* L.) and cucumber (*Cucumis sativus* L.)," *Plant Physiol.*, **86**, 143–146 (1988).

45. D.H. Greer, J.A. Berry, and O. Björkman, "Photoinhibition of photosynthesis in intact bean leaves: role of light and temperature, and requirement for chloroplast-protein synthesis during recovery," *Planta*, **168**, 253–260 (1986).

46. G.H. Krause and G. Cornic, "CO_2 and O_2 interactions in photoinhibition," in D.J. Kyle, C.B. Osmond, and C.J. Arntzen, eds., *Photoinhibition*, Elsevier, Amsterdam, 1987, pp. 169–196.

47. S. Somersalo and G.H. Krause, "Photoinhibition at chilling temperature. Fluorescence characteristics of unhardened and cold-acclimated spinach leaves," *Planta*, **177**, 409–416 (1989).

48. E.H. DeLucia, "Effect of low root temperature on net photosynthesis, stomatal conductance and carbohydrate concentration in Engelmann spruce (*Picea engelmannii* Parry ex Engelm.) seedlings," *Tree Physiol.*, **2**, 143–154 (1986).

49. J.M. Lyons and J.K. Raison, "Oxidative activity of mitochondria isolated from plant tissues sensitive and resistant to chilling injury," *Plant Physiol.*, **45**, 386–389 (1970).

50. J.A. Berry and J.K. Raison, "Responses of macrophytes to temperature," in A. Pirson and M.H. Zimmermann, eds., *Encyclopedia of Plant Physiology, New Series, Physiological Plant Ecology I*, Vol. 12A, Springer-Verlag, Berlin, 1981, pp. 277–338.

51. C.M. Kiener and W.J. Bramlage, "Temperature effects on the activity of the alternative respiratory pathway in chill-sensitive *Cucumis sativus*," *Plant Physiol.*, **68**, 1474–1478 (1981).

52. S. Yoshida, C. Matsuura, and S. Etani, "Impairment of tonoplast H^+-ATPase as an initial physiological response of cells to chilling in mung bean (*Vigna radiata* [L.] Wilczek)," *Plant Physiol.*, **89**, 634–642 (1989).

53. J.K. Raison and E.A. Chapman, "Membrane phase changes in chilling-sensitive *Vigna radiata* and their significance to growth," *Aust. J. Plant Physiol.*, **3**, 291–299 (1976).

54. J.K. Raison and G.R. Orr, "Phase transitions in liposomes formed from the polar lipids of mitochondria from chilling-sensitive plants," *Plant Physiol.*, **81**, 807–811 (1986).

55. P.J. Quinn, "Effects of temperature on cell membranes," in S.P. Long and F.I. Woodward, eds., *Plants and Temperature* (*Symp. Soc. Exp. Biol.*, Vol. 42), Company of Biologists, Cambridge, 1988, pp. 237–258.

56. S. Yoshida, K. Washio, J. Kenrick, and G. Orr, "Thermotropic properties of lipids extracted from plasma membrane and tonoplast isolated from chilling-sensitive mung bean (*Vigna radiata* [L.] Wilczek)," *Plant Cell Physiol.*, **29**, 1411–1416 (1988).

57. P.L. Steponkus, "Responses to extreme temperatures. Cellular and subcellular bases," in A. Pirson and M.H. Zimmermann, eds., *Encyclopedia of Plant Physiology, New Series, Physiological Plant Ecology I*, Vol. 12A, Springer-Verlag, Berlin, 1981, pp. 371–402.

58. P.L. Steponkus, "Role of the plasma membrane in freezing injury and cold acclimation," *Ann. Rev. Plant Physiol.*, **35**, 543–584 (1984).

59. S. Kaku, "Analysis of freezing temperature distribution in plants," *Cryobiology*, **12**, 154–159 (1975).

60. A. Pisek, W. Larcher, and R. Unterholzner, "Kardinale Temperaturbereiche der Photosynthese und Grenztemperaturen des Lebens der Blätter verschiedener Spermatophyten. I. Temperaturminimum der Nettoassimilation, Gefrier- und Frostschadensbereiche der Blätter," *Flora B*, **157**, 239–264 (1967).

61. R.E. Neilson, M.M. Ludlow, and P.G. Jarvis, "Photosynthesis in Sitka spruce (*Picea sitchensis* (Bong.) Carr). II. Response to temperature," *J. Appl. Ecol.*, **9**, 721–745 (1972).

62. E.H. DeLucia, "The effect of freezing nights on photosynthesis, stomatal conductance, and internal CO_2 concentration in seedlings of Engelmann spruce (*Picea engelmannii* Parry)," *Plant Cell Environ.*, **10**, 333–338 (1987).

63. E.H. DeLucia and W.K. Smith, "Air and soil temperature limitations on photosynthesis in Engelmann spruce during summer," *Can. J. For. Res.*, **17**, 527–533 (1987).

64. H. Bauer, W. Larcher, and R.B. Walker, "Influence of temperature stress on CO_2-gas exchange," in J.P. Cooper, ed., *Photosynthesis and Productivity in Different Environments*, Cambridge Univ. Press, Cambridge, 1975, pp. 557–586.

65. M. Strand and G. Öquist, "Inhibition of photosynthesis by freezing temperatures and high light levels in cold-acclimated seedlings of Scots pine (*Pinus sylvestris*). I. Effects on the light-limited and light-saturated rates of CO_2 assimilation," *Physiol. Plant.*, **64**, 425–430 (1985).

66. A. Pisek and R. Kemnitzer, "Der Einfluss von Frost auf die Photosynthese der Weisstanne (*Abies alba* Mill.)," *Flora B*, **157**, 314–326 (1968).

67. R.J. Klosson and G.H. Krause, "Freezing injury in cold-acclimated and un-hardened spinach leaves. I. Photosynthetic reactions of thylakoids isolated from frost-damaged leaves," *Planta*, **151**, 339–346 (1981).

68. G.H. Krause and R.J. Klosson, "Effects of freezing stress on photosynthetic reactions in cold acclimated and unhardened plant leaves," in R. Marcelle, H. Clijsters, and M. van Poucke, eds., *Effects of Stress on Photosynthesis*, Martinus Nijhoff/W. Junk Publishers, The Hague, 1983, pp. 245–256.

69. U. Schreiber, "Chlorophyll fluorescence yield changes as a tool in plant physiology. I. The measuring system," *Photosynth. Res.*, **4**, 361–373 (1983).

70. G.H. Krause and E. Weis, "Chlorophyll fluorescence as a tool in plant physiology. II. Interpretation of fluorescence signals," *Photosynth. Res.*, **5**, 139–157 (1984).

71. J.-M. Briantais, C. Vernotte, G.H. Krause, and E. Weis, "Chlorophyll *a* fluorescence of higher plants: Chloroplasts and leaves," in Govindjee, J. Amesz, and D.C. Fork, eds., *Light Emission by Plants and Bacteria*, Academic Press, Orlando, FL, 1986, pp. 539–583.

72. U. Schreiber, U. Schliwa, and W. Bilger, "Continuous recording of photochemical and non-photochemical chlorophyll fluorescence quenching with a new type of modulation fluorometer," *Photosynth. Res.*, **10**, 51–62 (1986).

73. M. Strand and G. Öquist, "Inhibition of photosynthesis by freezing temperatures and high light levels in cold-acclimated seedlings of Scots pine (*Pinus sylvestris*). II. Effects on chlorophyll fluorescence at room temperature and 77 K," *Physiol. Plant.*, **65**, 117–123 (1985).

74. M. Strand and G. Öquist, "Effects of frost hardening, dehardening and freezing stress on *in vivo* chlorophyll fluorescence of seedlings of Scots pine (*Pinus sylvestris* L.)," *Plant Cell Environ.*, **11**, 231–238 (1988).

75. K.-J. Dietz, U. Schreiber, and U. Heber, "The relationship between the redox state of Q_A and photosynthesis in leaves at various carbon-dioxide, oxygen and light regimes," *Planta*, **166**, 219–226 (1985).

76. G.H. Krause, S. Grafflage, S. Rumich-Bayer, and S. Somersalo, "Effects of freezing on plant mesophyll cells," in S.P. Long and F.I. Woodward, eds., *Plants and Temperature* (*Symp. Soc. Exp. Biol.*, Vol. 42), Company of Biologists, Cambridge, 1988, pp. 311–327.

77. S. Rumich-Bayer, C. Giersch, and G.H. Krause, "Inactivation of the photosynthetic carbon reduction cycle in isolated mesophyll protoplasts subjected to freezing stress," *Photosynth. Res.*, **14**, 137–145 (1987).

78. M. Bradbury, C.R. Ireland, and N.R. Baker, "An analysis of the chlorophyll-fluorescence transients from pea leaves generated by changes in atmospheric concentrations of CO_2 and O_2," *Biochim. Biophys. Acta*, **806**, 357–365 (1985).

79. M. Strand, *Photosynthetic Responses of Seedlings of Scots Pine* (*Pinus Sylvestris L.*) *to Low Temperature and Excessive Light*, Ph.D. thesis, University of Umeå, Umeå, Sweden, 1987.

80. U. Schreiber, "Detection of rapid induction kinetics with a new type of high-frequency modulated chlorophyll fluorometer," *Photosynth. Res.*, **9**, 261–272 (1986).

81. S. Rumich-Bayer and G.H. Krause, "Freezing damage and frost tolerance of the photosynthetic apparatus studied with isolated mesophyll protoplasts of *Valerianella locusta* L.," *Photosynth. Res.*, **8**, 161–174 (1986).

82. M. Senser and E. Beck, "On the mechanisms of frost injury and frost hardening of spruce chloroplasts," *Planta*, **137**, 195–201 (1977).

83. A. Pisek, "The normal temperature range. 1. Photosynthesis," in H. Precht, J. Christophersen, H. Hensel, and W. Larcher, eds., *Temperature and Life*, Springer-Verlag, Berlin, 1973, pp. 102–127.

84. G. Öquist, L. Brunes, J.-E. Hällgren, K. Gezelius, M. Hallén, and G. Malmberg, "Effects of artificial frost hardening and winter stress on net photosynthesis, photosynthetic electron transport and RuBP carboxylase activity in seedlings of *Pinus silvestris*," *Physiol. Plant.*, **48**, 526–531 (1980).

85. B. Martin, O. Mårtensson, and G. Öquist, "Effects of frost hardening and dehardening on photosynthetic electron transport and fluorescence properties in isolated chloroplasts of *Pinus silvestris*," *Physiol. Plant.*, **43**, 297–305 (1978).

86. T. Lundmark and J.-E. Hällgren, "Effects of frost on shaded and exposed spruce and pine seedlings planted in the field," *Can. J. For. Res.*, **17**, 1197–1201 (1987).

87. M. Strand and T. Lundmark, "Effects of low night temperature and light on chlorophyll fluorescence of field-grown seedlings of Scots pine (*Pinus sylvestris* L.)," *Tree Physiol.*, **3**, 211–224 (1987).

88. T. Lundmark, J.-E. Hällgren, and C. Degermark, "Effects of summer frost on the gas exchange of field-grown *Pinus sylvestris* L. seedlings," *Scand. J. For. Res.*, **3**, 441–448 (1988).

89. J.-E. Hällgren, T. Lundmark, and M. Strand, "Photosynthesis of Scots pine in the field after night frosts during summer," *Plant Physiol. Biochem.*, **28**, 437–445 (1990).

90. W.K. Smith, D.R. Young, G.A. Carter, J.L. Hadley, and G.M. McNaughton, "Autumn stomatal closure in six conifer species of the Central Rocky Mountains," *Oecologia*, **63**, 237–242 (1984).

91. G. Öquist, "Effects of low temperature on photosynthesis," *Plant Cell Environ.*, **6**, 281–300 (1983).

92. W. Tranquillini, "Standortsklima, Wasserbilanz und CO_2-Gaswechsel junger Zirben (*Pinus cembra* L.) an der alpine Waldgrenze," *Planta*, **49**, 612–661 (1957).

93. A. Pisek and E. Winkler, "Assimilationsvermögen und Respiration der Fichte (*Picea excelsa* Link.) in verschiedener Höhenlage und der Zirbe (*Pinus cembra* L.) an der alpinen Waldgrenze," *Planta*, **51**, 518–543 (1958).

94. B. Martin, O. Mårtensson, and G. Öquist, "Seasonal effects on photosynthetic electron transport and fluorescence properties in isolated chloroplasts of *Pinus silvestris*," *Physiol. Plant.*, **44**, 102–109 (1978).

95. K. Gezelius and M. Hallén, "Seasonal variation in ribulose biphosphate carboxylase activity in *Pinus silvestris*," *Physiol. Plant.*, **48**, 88–98 (1980).

96. E. Troeng and S. Linder, "Gas exchange in a 20-year-old stand of Scots pine. I. Net photosynthesis of current and one-year-old shoots within and between seasons," *Physiol. Plant.*, **54**, 7–14 (1982).

97. T. Lundmark, J.-E. Hällgren, and J. Hedén, "Recovery from winter depression of photosynthesis in pine and spruce," *Trees*, **2**, 110–114 (1988).

98. S. Linder and E. Troeng, "Photosynthesis and transpiration of 20-year-old Scots pine," in T. Persson, ed., *Structure and Function of Northern Coniferous Forests—An Ecosystem Study (Ecol. Bull.*, Vol. 32), Berlings, Arlöv, 1980, pp. 165–181.

99. J.W. Leverenz and G. Öquist, "Quantum yields of photosynthesis at temperatures between $-2°C$ and $35°C$ in a cold-tolerant C_3 plant (*Pinus sylvestris*) during the course of one year," *Plant Cell Environ.*, **10**, 287–295 (1987).

100. P. Pelkonen and P. Hari, "The dependence of the springtime recovery of CO_2 uptake in Scots pine on temperature and internal factors," *Flora*, **169**, 398–404 (1980).

101. K.L. Steffen, R. Arora, and J.P. Palta, "Relative sensitivity of photosynthesis and respiration to freeze–thaw stress in herbaceous species. Importance of realistic freeze–thaw protocols," *Plant Physiol.*, **89**, 1372–1379 (1989).

102. W. Larcher, "Effects of low temperature stress and frost injury on plant productivity," in C.B. Johnson, ed., *Physiological Processes Limiting Plant Productivity*, Butterworths, London, 1981, pp. 253–269.

103. G.H. Krause, R.J. Klosson, A. Justenhoven, and V. Ahrer-Steller, "Effects of low temperatures on the photosynthetic system in vivo," in C. Cybesma, ed., *Advances in Photosynthesis Research*, Vol. 4, Martinus Nijhoff/W. Junk Publishers, The Hague, 1984, pp. 349–358.

104. R. Thebud and K.A. Santarius, "Effects of freezing on spinach leaf mitochondria and thylakoids *in situ* and *in vitro*," *Plant Physiol.*, **68**, 1156–1160 (1981).

105. J. Singh, A.I. de la Roche, and D. Siminovitch, "Relative insensitivity of mitochondria in hardened and nonhardened rye coleoptile cells to freezing *in situ*," *Plant Physiol.*, **60**, 713–715 (1977).

106. P.L. Steponkus and D.V. Lynch, "Freeze/thaw-induced destabilization of the plasma membrane and the effects of cold acclimation," *J. Bioenerg. Biomembr.*, **21**, 21–41 (1989).

107. J.P. Palta and P.H. Li, "Cell membrane properties in relation to freezing injury," in P.H. Li and A. Sakai, eds., *Plant Cold Hardiness. Mechanisms and Crop Implications*, Academic Press, New York, 1978, pp. 93–115.

108. J. Hellergren, S. Widell, and T. Lundborg, "Freezing injury in purified plasma membranes from cold acclimated and non-acclimated needles of *Pinus sylvestris*: Is the plasma membrane bound ion-stimulated ATPase the primary site of freezing injury?," in P.H. Li, ed., *Plant Cold Hardiness*, Alan R. Liss, New York, 1987, pp. 211–220.

109. P. Ziegler and O. Kandler, "Tonoplast stability as a critical factor in frost injury and hardening of spruce (*Picea abies* L. Karst.) needles," *Z. Pflanzenphysiol.*, **99**, 393–410 (1980).

110. P. Pukacki and S. Pukacka, "Freezing stress and membrane injury of Norway spruce (*Picea abies*) tissues," *Physiol. Plant.*, **69**, 156–160 (1987).

111. H. Precht, J. Christophersen, and H. Hensel, eds., *Temperatur und Leben*, Springer, Berlin, 1955.

112. J. Levitt. *The Hardiness of Plants* (*Agronomy*, Vol. 6), Academic Press, New York, 1956.

113. R. Biebl, "Protoplasmische Ökologie der Pflanzen. Wasser und Temperatur," in *Protoplasmatologia, Handbuch der Protoplasmaforschung*, 12.1., Springer, Vienna, 1962.

114. V.Y. Alexanderov, *Cells, Molecules and Temperature. Conformational Flexibility of Macromolecules and Ecological Adaptation* (*Ecological Studies*, Vol. 21), Springer-Verlag, Berlin, 1977.

115. M.M. Ludlow, "Light stress at high temperature," in D.J. Kyle, C.B. Osmond, and C.J. Arntzen, eds., *Photoinhibition*, Elsevier, Amsterdam, 1987, pp. 89–109.

116. W.K. Smith and P.S. Nobel, "Deserts," in N.R. Baker and S.P. Long, eds, *Photosynthesis in Contrasting Environments* (*Topics in Photosynthesis*, Vol. 7), Elsevier, Amsterdam, 1986, pp. 13–62.

117. E. Medina, "Forests, savannas and montane tropical environments," in N.R. Baker and S.P. Long, eds., *Photosynthesis in Contrasting Environments* (*Topics in Photosynthesis*, Vol. 7), Elsevier, Amsterdam, 1986, pp. 139–172.

118. J.P. Grime, *Plant Strategies and Vegetation Processes*, Wiley, Chichester, UK, 1979.

119. H.A. Mooney and E.L. Dunn, "Convergent evolution of mediterranean-climate evergreen sclerophyll shrubs," *Evolution*, **24**, 292–303 (1970).

120. G.H. Orians and O.T. Solbrig, "A cost–income model of leaves and roots with special reference to arid and semi-arid areas," *Am. Nat.*, **11**, 677–690 (1977).

121. F.S. Chapin, "The mineral nutrition of wild plants," *Ann. Rev. Ecol. Syst.*, **11**, 233–260 (1980).

122. J.T. Gray, "Nutrient use by evergreen and deciduous shrubs in southern California. I. Community nutrient cycling and nutrient-use efficiency," *J. Ecol.*, **71**, 21–41 (1983).

123. G. Sarmiento, G. Goldstein, and F. Meinzer, "Adaptive strategies of woody species in neotropical savannas," *Biol. Rev.*, **60**, 315–355 (1985).

124. M.S. Ferri, *Plantas do Brasil. Especiés do cerrado*, Editora Edgard Blücher, Sao Paolo, 1969 (cited in Sarmiento et al. Ref. 123).

125. O.L. Lange, "Untersuchungen über Wärmehaushalt und Hitzeresistens mauretanischer Wüsten- und Savannenpflanzen," *Flora*, **147**, 595–651 (1959).

126. O.L. Lange, "Investigations on the variability of heat resistance in plants," in A.S. Troshin, ed., *The Cell and Environmental Temperature*, Pergamon Press, New York, 1967, pp. 131–141.

127. E.O. Hellmuth, "Eco-physiological studies on plants in arid and semi arid regions in Western Australia: V. Heat resistance limits of photosynthetic organs of different seasons, their relation to water deficits and cell sap properties and the regeneration ability," *J. Ecol.*, **59**, 365–374 (1971).

128. R. Karshon and L. Pinchas, "Variations in heat resistance of ecotypes of *Eucalyptus camaldulensis* Dehn. and their significance," *Aust. J. Biol.*, **19**, 261–272 (1971).

129. B. MacBryde, R.L. Jeffries, R. Alderfer, and D.M. Gates, "Water and energy relations of plant leaves during periods of heat stress," *Oecol. Plant.*, **6**, 151–162 (1971).

130. L. Kappen and A. Zeidler, "Seasonal changes between one- and two-phasic response of plant leaves to heat stress," *Oecologia*, **31**, 45–53 (1977).

131. E. Dahl, "On the heat exchange of a wet vegetation surface and the ecology of *Koenigia islandica*," *Oikos*, **14**, 190–211 (1963).

132. M.C. Rutherford, "Aboveground biomass subdivisions in woody species of the savanna ecosystem project study area, Nylsvley," *S. Afr. Nat. Sci. Progr. Rep. (Pretoria)*, **36**, (1979).

133. C.F. Creswell, P. Ferrar, J.O. Grunow, D. Gossman, M.C. Rutherford, and J.P. van Wyk, "Phytomass, seasonal phenology, and photosynthetic studies," in J.B. Huntley and B.H. Walker, eds., *Ecology of Tropical Savannas (Ecological Studies*, Vol. 42), Springer-Verlag, Berlin, 1982, pp. 476–497.

134. H.A. Mooney and J.L. Gulmon, "Environmental and evolutionary constraints on the photosynthetic characteristics of higher plants," in O.T. Solbrig, S. Jain, G.B. Johnson, and P.H. Raven, eds., *Topics in Plant Population Biology*, Columbia Univ. Press, New York, 1979, pp. 316–337.

135. J. Langridge, "Biochemical aspects of temperature response," *Ann. Rev. Plant Physiol.*, **14**, 441–462 (1963).

136. J.R. Seemann, W.J.S. Downton, and J.A. Berry, "Temperature and leaf osmotic potential as factors in the acclimation of photosynthesis to high temperature in desert plants," *Plant Physiol.*, **80**, 926–930 (1986).

137. D.M. Gates, *Biophysical Ecology*, Springer-Verlag, Berlin, 1980.

138. J.B. Passioura, "Water in the soil plant atmosphere continuum," in A. Pirson and M.H. Zimmermann, eds., *Encyclopedia of Plant Physiology, New Series, Physiological Plant Ecology II*, Vol. 12B, Springer-Verlag, Berlin, 1982, pp. 5–33.

139. E.-D. Schulze and A.E. Hall, "Stomatal responses, water loss and CO_2-assimilation rates of plants in contrasting environments," in A. Pirson and M.H. Zimmermann, eds., *Encyclopedia of Plant Physiology, New Series, Physiological Plant Ecology II*, Vol. 12B, Springer-Verlag, Berlin, 1982, pp. 181–230.

140. G.S. Campbell, "Fundamentals of radiation and temperature relations," in A. Pirson and M.H. Zimmermann, eds., *Encyclopedia of Plant Physiology, New Series, Physiological Plant Ecology II*, Vol. 12B, Springer-Verlag, Berlin, 1982, pp. 11–40.

141. E. Medina, "Physiological ecology of neotropical savanna plants," in J.B. Huntley and B.H. Walker, eds., *Ecology of Tropical Savannas, Ecological Studies* 42, Springer-Verlag, Berlin, 1982, pp. 308–355.

142. F.B. Salisbury, "Responses to photoperiod," in A. Pirson and M.H. Zimmermann, eds., *Encyclopedia of Plant Physiology, New Series, Physiological Plant Ecology I*, Vol. 12A, Springer-Verlag, Berlin, 1981, pp. 135–168.

143. J.R. Ehleringer and J. Comstock, "Leaf absorbtance and leaf angle: Mechanisms for stress avoidance," in J.D. Tenhunen, F.M. Catarino, O.L. Lange, and W.C. Oechel, eds., *Plant Response to Stress*, NATO ASI Series, Vol. G15, Springer-Verlag, Berlin, 1987, pp. 55–76.

144. H.A. Mooney, "Seasonality and gradients in the study of stress adaptation," in N.C. Turner and P.J. Kramer, eds., *Adaptation of Plants to Water and High Temperature Stress*, Wiley, New York, 1980, pp. 279–284.

145. O. Stocker, "Der Wasser- und Photosynthese-Haushalt von Wüstenpflanzen der mauretanischen Sahara. II. Weschselgrüne, Rutenzweig- und Stammsukkulente Bäume," *Flora*, **160**, 445–494 (1971).

146. E. Weis and J.A. Berry, "Plants and high temperature stress," in S.P. Long and F.I. Woodward, eds., *Plants and Temperature* (*Symp. Soc. Exp. Biol.*, Vol. 42), Company of Biologists, Cambridge, 1988, pp. 329–346.

147. W. Larcher and J. Wagner, "Temperaturgrenzen der CO_2-Aufnahme und Temperaturresistenz der Blätter von Gebirgspflanzen im vegetationsaktiven Zustand," *Oecol. Plant.*, **11**, 361–374 (1976).

148. L.I. Egorova, O.A. Semikhatova, and O.S. Yudina, "Influence of temperature on the reactivation of photosynthesis after heat injury," *Bot. Z.*, **63**, 356–362 (1978).

149. K.A. Santarius, "Sites of heat sensitivity in chloroplasts and different inactivation of cyclic and noncyclic photophosphorylation by heating," *J. Term. Biol.*, **1**, 101–107 (1975).

150. J.A. Berry, D.C. Fork, and S. Garrison, "Mechanistic studies of thermal damage to leaves," *Carnegie Inst. of Washington Year Book*, **74**, 751–759 (1975).

151. O. Björkman, M.R. Badger, and P.A. Armond, "Response and adaptation of photosynthesis to high temperatures," in N.C. Turner and P.J. Kramer, eds., *Adaptation of Plants to Water and High Temperature Stress*, Wiley-Interscience, New York, 1980, pp. 233–249.

152. R. Thebud and K.A. Santarius, "Effects of high temperature stress on various biomembranes of leaf cells *in situ* and *in vitro*," *Plant Physiol.*, **70**, 200–205 (1982).

153. H. Bauer and M. Senser, "Photosynthesis of ivy leaves (*Hedera helix* L.) after heat stress. II. Activity of ribulose bisphosphate carboxylase, Hill reaction and chloroplast ultrastructure," *Z. Pflanzenphysiol.*, **91**, 359–369 (1979).

154. E. Weis, D. Wamper, and K.A. Santarius, "Heat sensitivity and thermal adaptation of photosynthesis in liverwort thalli," *Oecologia*, **69**, 134–139 (1986).

155. U. Schreiber and J.A. Berry, "Heat-induced changes in chlorophyll fluorescence in intact leaves correlated with damage of the photosynthetic apparatus," *Planta*, **136**, 233–238 (1977).

156. U. Schreiber and P. Armond, "Heat induced changes of chlorophyll fluorescence in isolated chloroplasts and related heat damage at the pigment level," *Biochem. Biophys. Acta*, **502**, 138–151 (1978).

157. J.R. Seemann, J.A. Berry, and W.J.S. Downton, "Photosynthetic response and adaptation to high temperature in desert plants in comparison of gas exchange and fluorescence methods for plant studies of thermal tolerance," *Plant Physiol.*, **75**, 364–368 (1984).

158. W. Bilger, U. Schreiber, and O.L. Lange, "Chlorophyll fluorescence as an indicator of heat induced limitation of photosynthesis in *Arbetos unedo* L.," in J.D. Tenhunen, F.M. Catarino, O.L. Lange, and W.C. Oechel, eds., *Plant Response to Stress*, NATO ASI Series, Vol. G15, Springer-Verlag, Berlin, 1987, pp. 391–399.

159. J. Kobza and G.E. Edwards, "Influences of leaf temperature on photosynthetic carbon metabolism in wheat," *Plant Physiol.*, **83**, 60–74 (1987).

160. J.A. Teeri, "Adaptation of kinetic properties of enzymes to temperature vari-

ability," in N.C. Turner and P.J. Kramer, eds., *Adaptation of Plants to Water and High Temperature Stress*, Wiley, New York, 1980, pp. 251–273.

161. J.K. Raison, J.A. Berry, P.A. Armond, and C.S. Pike, "Membrane properties in relation to temperature stress," in N.C. Turner and P.J. Kramer, eds., *Adaptation of Plants to Water and High Temperature Stress*, Wiley, New York, 1980, pp. 221–233.

162. J.K. Raison, J.K.M. Roberts, and J.A. Berry, "Acclimation of the higher plant *Nerium oleander* to growth temperature: correlations between the thermal stability of chloroplast (thylakoid) membranes and the composition and fluidity of their polar lipids," *Biochem. Biophys. Acta*, **688**, 218–228 (1983).

163. J. Barber, "Influence of surface charges on thylakoid structure and function," *Ann. Rev. Plant Physiol.*, **33**, 261–295 (1981).

164. J.A. Berry and W.J.S. Downton, "Environmental regulation of photosynthesis," in Govindjee Ed., *Photosynthesis: Development Carbon Metabolism and Plant Productivity*, Vol. 2, Academic Press, New York, 1982, pp. 263–345.

165. D.J. Chapman, J.C. De-Felice, and J. Barber, "Growth temperature effects on thylakoid membrane lipid and protein content of pea (*Pisum sativum* cultivar Feltham First) chloroplasts," *Plant Physiol.*, **72**, 255–258 (1983).

166. W. Larcher, "Limiting temperatures for live functions," in H. Precht, J. Christophersen, H. Hensel, and W. Larcher, eds., *Temperature and Life*, Springer, Berlin, 1973, pp. 195–231.

167. H. Bauer, "CO$_2$-Gaswechsel nach Hitzestress bei *Abies alba* Mill. und *Acer pseudoplatanus* L.," *Photosynthetica*, **6**, 424–434 (1972).

168. P.J. Kramer and T.T. Kozlowski, *Physiology of Trees*, McGraw-Hill, New York, 1960.

169. J. Feierabend and M. Mikus, "Occurrence of a high temperature sensitivity of chloroplast ribosome formation in several higher plants," *Plant Physiol.*, **59**, 863–867 (1977).

170. J. Langridge, "Temperature-sensitive, vitamin requiring mutants of *Arabidopsis thaliana*," *Aust. J. Biol. Sci.*, **18**, 311–321 (1965).

171. E.J. Kinbacher, "Relative thermal stability of malic dehydrogenase from heat-hardened and unhardened *Phaseolus* sp.," *Proc. Am. Soc. Hort. Sci.*, **90**, 163–168 (1970).

172. N. Murata, "Low-temperature effects on cyanobacterial membranes," *J. Bioenerg. Biomembr.*, **21**, 61–75 (1989).

173. N. Murata, N. Sato, M.A. Takahashi, and Y. Hamazaki, "Compositions and positional distributions of fatty acids in phospholipids from leaves of chilling-sensitive and chilling-resistant plants," *Plant Cell Physiol.*, **23**, 1071–1079 (1982).

174. J.K. Raison and L.C. Wright, "Thermal phase transitions in the polar lipids of plant membranes. Their induction of disaturated phospholipids and their possible relation to chilling injury," *Biochim. Biophys. Acta*, **731**, 69–78 (1983).

175. N. Murata, O. Ishizaki, and I. Nishida, "Glycerol-3-phosphate acyltransferase and its complementary DNA," in P.A. Blacks, K. Gruitz, and T. Kremmer, eds., *Biological Role of Plant Lipids*, Akadémiai Klado', Budapest and Plenum Publishing Corp., New York, 1989, pp. 351–360.

176. H.J. Ougham and C.J. Howarth, "Temperature shock proteins in plants," in S.P. Long and F.I. Woodward, eds., *Plants and Temperature* (*Symp. Soc. Exp. Biol.*, Vol. 42), Company of Biologists, Cambridge, 1988, pp. 259–280.

177. S. Lindquist and E.A. Craig, "The heat shock proteins," *Ann. Rev. Genet.*, **22**, 631–677 (1988).

178. H. Pelham, "Activation of heat-shock genes in eucaryotes," *Trends Genet.*, **1**, 31–35 (1985).

179. D.K. Hincha and J.M. Schmitt, "Mechanical freeze–thaw damage and frost hardening in leaves and isolated thylakoids from spinach. I. Mechanical freeze–thaw damage in an artificial stroma medium," *Plant Cell Environ.*, **11**, 41–46 (1988).

180. D.K. Hincha and J.M. Schmitt, "Mechanical freeze–thaw damage and frost hardening in leaves and isolated thylakoids from spinach. II. Frost hardening reduces solute permeability and increases excessibility of thylakoid membranes," *Plant Cell Environ.*, **11**, 47–50 (1988).

181. P.L. Steponkus, M. Uemura, R.A. Balsamo, T. Arvinte, and D.V. Lynch, "Transformation of the cryobehavior of rye protoplasts by modification of plasma membrane lipid composition," *Proc. Natl. Acad. Sci. (USA)*, **85**, 9026–9030 (1988).

14 Air Pollutants

THEO KELLER

Swiss Federal Research Institute for Forest, Snow and Landscape,
Birmensdorf, Switzerland

Contents

14.1. Introduction

Increasing human population and its increased activity (industrialization, mining, and use of fossil fuels) have lead to a growing pollution load. Because humans depend on their environment, the ECE (Economic Commission for Europe of the United Nations) has proposed critical levels for some common air pollutants (1). As the latter vary widely with time and locality, "critical

Table 14.1. Critical levels (1) and sources of some major air pollutants

	Crit. level	Remarks	Sources
SO_2	$20\ \mu g\ m^{-3}$	Annual mean, sensitive plants	Industry, thermal power plants, household heating
	$30\ \mu g\ m^{-3}$	Annual mean expected to cause productivity declines in sensitive forest stands	
	$70\ \mu g\ m^{-3}$	Estimated daily mean	
O_3	$50\ \mu g\ m^{-3}$	Mean for growing season, daily 7 h; is within natural range of ozone	Complex reactions of NO_x, HC, etc., in the air under influence of solar radiation
NO_2	$30\ \mu g\ m^{-3}$	Annual mean in presence of O_3 + SO_2	Motor traffic, industry

level" means the concentrations of atmospheric pollutants above which direct adverse effects on receptors may occur according to present knowledge (Table 14.1).

Because pollutants cause very complex physiological reactions, the given references should be regarded as selected examples.

In order to get quick results, high concentrations for a short time were often used, whereas in forested areas low concentrations prevail over an extended period. This change of constellation, however, leads to different reactions since the demand for detoxification differs. Thus it was shown in Scots pine (2) that tolerance for SO_2 depended on the concentration and on the time lag between fumigation and judgment of effect. In addition, a fumigation over 650 days caused different growth injury (3) depending on duration of peaks and regeneration periods (Table 14.2). Although the same average concentration resulted, long occasional peaks (L peaks) with long regeneration periods caused a more severe growth reduction than constant low concentration, short peaks (S peaks) or increased peak concentrations.

Table 14.2. Weight increase of Scots pine seedlings over 650 days with different SO_2 fumigations[a]

Treatment[b]	Average $\mu l \cdot l^{-1}\ SO_2$	Maximum $\mu l \cdot l^{-1}\ SO_2$	Interval of regeneration (days)	Dry-weight increase (g)
Clean air	—	—	—	118.5
Constant fumigation	0.04	0.04	—	101.9
S peaks	0.04	0.12	1	101.8
S peaks	0.04	0.30	1	100.9
L peaks	0.04	0.12	22	92.8
L peaks	0.04	0.30	22	91.2

[a]Data from Ref. 3.
[b]S peaks—short, frequent peaks; L peaks—long, occasional peaks.

Trees, particularly evergreens, usually possess photosynthetic tissue which is hardier than that of annuals. Therefore when it is asked why trees are so sensitive for air pollutants, the following points should be considered:

1. Large volume of tree crowns (with increased leaf area index and takeup of pollutants).
2. Trees grow into zones of increased wind velocity and filter greater air volumes.
3. Longevity of photosynthetic tissue (the same tissue may be exposed several times and the sensitivity, when, e.g., CO_2 uptake is used as an indication, varies with season; Fig. 14.1).
4. Inadequate supply of water and nutrients (in many areas forests have been degraded to poor land unsuitable for agriculture).

The impact of air pollution is often considered injurious only if the tree is visibly damaged. However,many physiological reactions may be affected even if the tree does not show any symptom or lethal effect.

In some cases the pattern of ring formation in the woody stem allows detection of air pollution either over or after many years (4,5). Growth is

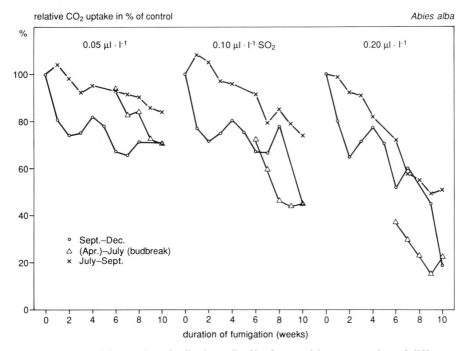

FIG. 14.1. The CO_2 uptake of a fir clone (in % of controls) as expression of different sensitivity to different SO_2 concentrations at different seasons. The early 5 weeks in April–July are not shown because they are more influenced by budbreak than by SO_2.

one of the many aspects of the vitality of an affected tree. Since gas exchange is a basic factor determining growth it is used as an entry for this chapter on the physiological effects of pollutants.

14.2. Carbon budget and water relations

14.2.1. CO_2 uptake

The uptake of CO_2 from the air has early been proposed as a sensitive measure of detecting pollutant effects in the absence of visible injury (6). Conifers were widely studied for their response to air pollution by SO_2 (Refs. 7–9; see also Fig. 14.1), fluorides (Refs. 10,11; Fig. 14.2), ozone (13–15), automobile exhaust (16), mixtures of different gases (17,18), or acid precipitation (19). There are also many reports on broad-leaf species (Ref. 20; see also Fig. 14.3).

In hybrid poplars exposed to low ozone concentrations for many weeks decreased photosynthesis was at least partly due to accelerated aging as the foliage had a shorter life cycle (Fig. 14.3). In young, still expanding leaves (6 days old) response of CO_2 uptake to light was practically the same in controls and in fumigated leaves. With increasing leaf age the decline of photosynthesis in fumigated leaves became more rapid and light saturation was reached at lower light intensities. That pollutant effects are enhanced by aging has also been detected in spruce (22).

Measurements of photosynthesis with increasing CO_2 concentrations showed a reduction in the carboxylation capacity of Scots pine under the influence of SO_2 (23). Carboxylation efficiency has recently also been found to be decreased in 2-week-old aspen leaves fumigated with low ozone concentra-

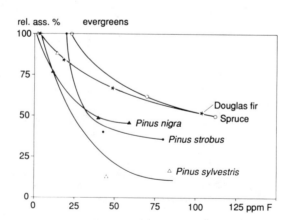

FIG. 14.2. The relative CO_2 uptake (calculated as net amount for 24 h) of several conifer species in early fall as related to the F content of the youngest needles. (Adapted from Ref. 12.)

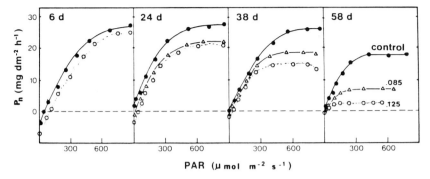

FIG. 14.3. The photosynthetic light response of hybrid poplar leaves of different age exposed to either 0.025 $\mu l\,l^{-1}$ (control), 0.085, or 0.125 $\mu l\,l^{-1}$ ozone. (Adapted from Ref. 21.)

tions, particularly when the leaves were visibly influenced (Dr. R. Matyssek, personal communication). Many previous studies have shown that the pigment contents decrease in most cases under the influence of pollutants, even in the absence of visible symptoms.

Carbohydrate metabolism depends directly on photosynthetic activity. Usually the depression of photosynthesis causes a diminished content of carbohydrates, but a generalization is hardly feasible since not only processes of synthesis but also those of translocation and dissimilation are involved. Reference is made to recent reviews on this subject (24,25).

Carbon dioxide as a "normal" component of the air is not usually considered as a pollutant. However, the CO_2 content of the air has been rising distinctly in the last decades. Although such a rise is considered stimulating for plant productivity, it was recently shown that at light saturation a photosynthetic increase may occur only to about a doubling of the present CO_2 concentration (26). And another study over more than two years detected that seedlings of ponderosa pine showed mottling and early senescence at such CO_2 concentrations (27).

14.2.2. Dark respiration

Respiration amounts to only a small percentage of CO_2 uptake and has rarely been measured in the past. It is essential for growth, maintenance, and repair and is affected by many internal and external factors (not only fumigation condition and pollutant dose). At high SO_2 concentrations respiration seemed to increase as shown for Scots pine (28). This may have been caused by repair needs or by detoxification. Also, ozone has been reported to increase the respiratory rate in several conifers (22,29) and in hybrid poplar (Fig. 14.4). On the other hand, significant decreases in a sensitive white pine clone were detected (30). Detailed information on this subject can be found in reviews (31–33).

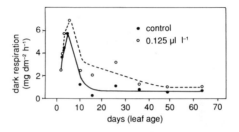

FIG. 14.4. Dark respiration of hybrid poplar leaves of different age exposed to either $0.025 \ \mu l \ l^{-1}$ (control •) or $0.125 \ \mu l \ l^{-1}$ ozone. (After Ref. 21.)

14.2.3. Translocation, carbon allocation, and growth

The carbon gain of a plant is dependent not only on the rate of photosynthesis and respiration per unit leaf tissue but also on the total amount of photosynthesizing tissue. Pollutants reduce leaf size (34) as well as the lifespan of a leaf (35), both resulting in a decreased leaf area per tree. Figure 14.5 shows the development of foliage in a poplar clone during the growing season under a continuous fumigation with different ozone concentrations. Although the number of formed leaves remained the same in all treatments (Fig. 14.5A) the earlier leaf drop (Fig. 14.5B) particularly diminished the active foliage area at higher ozone doses. In addition aging diminishes net photosynthesis (see Fig. 14.3).

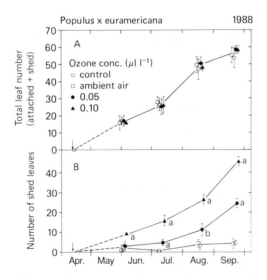

FIG. 14.5. The effect of different continuous ozone concentrations from April to September on a poplar clone (5 replicates): (A) total leaf number per shoot; (B) number of shed leaves per shoot (premature senescence). Significance from controls: (a) $P < .001$; (b) $P < .01$; (c) $P < .05$. (Courtesy Dr. R. Matyssek.)

A gain in dry matter depends greatly on the amount of carbon that is allocated to photosynthesizing tissue (36). This is particularly important if only the harvested part instead of the whole plant is considered. The carbon exceeding metabolic requirements is translocated and allocated to different plant parts. About 30–80% of the energy captured by photosynthesis may be consumed by allocation processes (19). The decreased translocation played a more significant role than suppression of photosynthesis in altering the carbon economy (34), especially considering that translocation regenerates more slowly than photosynthesis (37). Carbohydrates accumulated in tops while such substances were present in decreased amounts in roots (22, 29). Root processes are therefore important sinks of carbon, and translocation may also be influenced by interference with phloem loading (19).

As an example for growth reductions, Fig. 14.6 shows the effect of ozone doses on hardwoods and pines. When tree growth is determined, it is important to measure gain in dry weight as an integrative parameter that includes diameter growth, height growth, and cell wall thickness. Figure 14.7 shows the effect of a prolonged SO_2 fumigation on ring width (decreased cell formation) and latewood formation in a spruce clone.

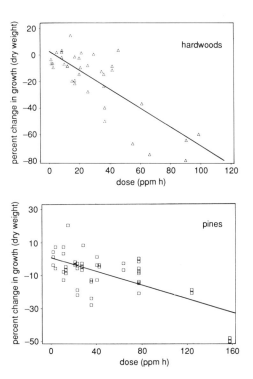

FIG. 14.6. The change of growth in hardwoods and pines as affected by ozone dose. (Reproduced with permission from Ref. 38.)

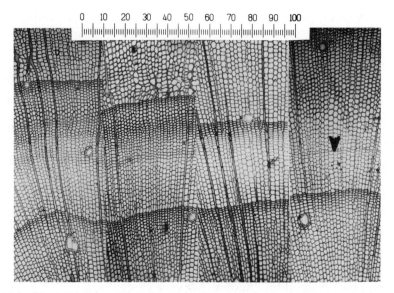

FIG. 14.7. The inhibitory effect of a 10-week fumigation (April–July) on ring width and formation of latewood in a spruce clone (from left to right: control, 0.05, 0.10, and 0.20 μl l^{-1} of SO$_2$; scale = 1 mm. Arrow points to the lack of latewood at 0.2 μl l^{-1}). (Adapted from Ref. 39.)

It seems that any environmental factor that causes a reduction of photosynthesis may alter allocation patterns and root/shoot ratio (40). Thus several papers document greater growth reductions in roots than in shoots (29,41,42). Yet such response may depend on the time of harvest as shown in Fig. 14.8.

14.2.4. Transpiration (including stomatal behavior)

Stomata are known as primary entries for air pollutants (and to be largely responsible for water loss), whereas the cuticle is hardly permeable for pollutants. The cuticular permeability to NO$_2$, however, may be much higher

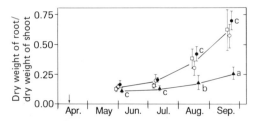

FIG. 14.8. The effect of different continuous ozone concentrations from April to September on the root:shoot ratio of a poplar clone. (Significance as in Fig. 14.5; courtesy Dr. R. Matyssek.)

than that to other gases (e.g., H_2O vapor, CO_2, O_3, SO_2), and NO_2 seems to be easily bound to the cuticle (43). The stomata, as important regulators of gas exchange, are subject to a great many internal and external factors (44). Stomatal closure may be beneficial by depressing pollutant uptake and water loss or harmful by decreasing CO_2 uptake. Depending on the existing conditions the stomata therefore react differently to pollutants as shown in several reviews (45–47). In addition their efficiency may be impeded by clogging with wax or dust particles. A loss of lignin was found in the walls of guard cells and subsidiary cells due to SO_2, which may be related to a malfunctioning of the stomata (48). But wax erosion, collapse, and melting of wax structures are considered to be characteristic for an influence of air pollutants (49).

Because stomatal behavior affects leaf conductance, the latter is used to determine stomatal reaction to a particular fumigation. Stomatal conductance may be altered in two ways (47):

- Direct action of the pollutant on the stomatal opening, which alters photosynthesis
- Absorption of the pollutant into the mesophyll, decreasing photosynthesis and subsequently causing stomatal closure

Stomatal movement may become sluggish through an extended ozone fumigation (50), or stomatal conductance may remain high even in darkness (51,52) when stomata are assumed to be closed.

Water availability is among the many factors that determine the effects of pollutants on transpiration. Present opinion holds that air pollutants increase transpiration. In birch, after a prolonged fumigation with $SO_2 + NO_2$, water loss per unit leaf area increased in both light and darkness (53). Transpiration in fumigated plants was higher initially than that in controls but was reduced earlier (Fig. 14.9). The abscission of leaves implied that there was no mechanism for water conservation when shortage of available water arose in fumigated plants, whereas in controls water loss was markedly reduced long before the onset of leaf loss.

14.3. Plasmatic changes

14.3.1. Buffering capacity

Sulfur dioxide peaks may alter the buffering capacity of needles depending on the needle age and season (54). Since organic acids, phenolic OH groups, and amphoteric electrolytes also play a role, any decrease in buffering, e.g., due to malnutrition, may facilitate the establishment of an optimum pH value for pathogens (55); for a review, see Ref. 56.

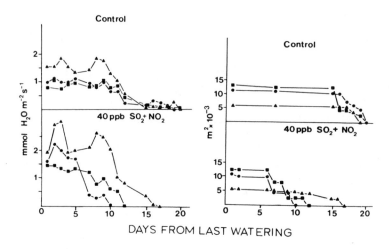

FIG. 14.9. Transpiration rates (left) and functional leaf area (right) in three plants of a birch clone. After a 35-day fumigation plants were not watered any more. (Reproduced with permission from Ref. 53.)

14.3.2. Membrane leakage

Ozone increases membrane leakiness and alters the ion permeability (57,58). The very reactive ozone may attack SH groups, aromatic metabolites, and olefinic bonds (e.g., unsaturated fatty acids) by forming free radicals (49,59). Although unsaturated fatty acids are often considered to be ozone targets, the evidence increasingly suggests that effects on membrane-bound proteins are responsible for changes in permeability (60). Lipid peroxidation may also cause membrane leakage (61).

Several field studies have reported an increased leaching of nutrient ions from conifer needles, especially after a combined effect of different pollutants, including acid mist (62). This leaching (although small; see Table 14.3) is considered to play an important role in forest decline in connection with nutrient deficiency on poor sites where the available supply of nutrients in the soil (and impaired root system) may prevent quick replacement of leached elements. Throughfall in forest stands, however, contain dust, ions leached from old needles, etc., and is hardly proof of membrane injury. In addition, the hydrophobic needle surface counteracts leaching. Therefore, in laboratory experiments surface waxes were removed and leaching (measured by soaking the needles in a water bath) was greatly increased, especially in comparison to the minute fraction of several nutrients leached from unwashed needles (Table 14.3). Although chloroform may be hard on the membranes, it was found to decrease leaching after an ozone fumigation.

The electrical conductance in the diffusate from foliage sometimes has been used to detect an effect of pollutants (63,64). It is, however, rather a bioindication than a proof of increased membrane leakiness. Membrane

Table 14.3. Element contents in spruce needles[a]

	Ca	K	Mg	Mn	P	Zn
Control						
nc (μg g^{-1})	7860	8094	1130	55	1955	48
df (%)	0.12	1.23	0.26	0.53	0.33	3.40
cl (%)	3.54	36.20	23.00	34.70	45.00	49.60
Ozone–fumigant						
nc (μg g^{-1})	9304	7795	1511	62	2051	54
df (%)	0.15	1.36	0.28	0.60	0.40	4.48
cl (%)	2.12	29.92	10.64	16.12	23.20	28.20

[a]Some element contents in spruce needles (nc) at the end of their first growing season and the percentage leached (diffused into a waterbath of pH 5.6 within 24 hs) from unwashed needles (df) or from chloroform-washed needles (cl). The needles had been fumigated continuously for 5 months (June–November) with 100 nl l^{-1} of ozone (all values are the average of 5 replicates).

injury might be determined more reliably by, e.g., measurements of turgor pressure.

14.4. Filtering action and element contents

14.4.1. Filtering action

Vegetation, especially trees, is capable of filtering the air, and this action is enhanced by the following factors:

- Enormous surface of tree crowns (sticky surface wax and tiny hairs increase the adsorption of dust). Particles of the size 5 μm have been found to be much better retained by rough than by smooth surfaces (65).
- For gaseous pollutants also the "inner" surface (air spaces and cavities in the mesophyll) is of great absorptive importance.
- Increased sedimentation of particles (a consequence of the decreased wind velocity inside a tree crown or forest stand).
- Increased turbulence with increased dust fall before and behind crowns.

By means of radioactive tracers it has been calculated that an aerosol (particle size 10 μm) would suffer a loss of about 95% by fallout over 5 km of a mixed forest as compared to about 15% over grass (66). Depending on their character, pollutants may be growth-stimulating or harmful. Positive effects may result if the pollutant improves nutrition (e.g., nitrogen-containing aerosols), if it warms up foliage (dark dust in a cool climate) or if it shields foliage from excessive insolation. Harmful effects, on the other hand, may result from corrosive dust, if photosynthesis is impeded by excessive shading, if respiration is increased by overheating, or if transpiration becomes excessive by stomatal clogging or by accumulation of hygroscopic compounds that dehydrate the tissue.

14.4.2. Tissue contents of major nutrient elements

The pollutants filtering into the canopy may increase the nutrient contents in foliage samples. In case of good nutrient supply it was found that SO_2 peaks raised the contents of Ca, Mg, and K in spruce needles (67). Ozone may also increase nutrient contents of needles (e.g., Ref. 68; see also Table 14.3). On the other hand, acidified rain is considered to leach many cations out of the tissue (51) and to give rise to an imbalanced nutrition. Particularly on poor sites, fertilization is therefore promoted to counteract "forest decline" (69).

According to the "nitrogen hypothesis," NO_x and other N-containing compounds may increase the N content of foliage. Without tracer studies it is probably hardly possible to distinguish between root uptake and direct foliar uptake of N from the air. For sulfur, present in the foliage in much smaller concentrations than N, it has been shown that SO_2 pollution generally causes an increase of inorganic S (SO_4–S) to levels higher than those found due to uptake of this essential element from the soil (49).

14.4.3. Tissue contents of other elements

The pollutants filtered from the air accumulate in the foliage. Therefore, air pollution is often detectable by foliar analysis, especially in the case of heavy metals, which have found increasing attention due to their restricted mobility. When they remain on the surface of the tissue they are particularly well suited for the detection of an environmental load if they are removed by washing (70).

Distribution of lead from the exhaust fumes of modern traffic near a highway is shown in Fig. 14.10. Several other elements, like vanadium or antimony, have been considered to be key elements for anthropogenic pollution. Also iron, manganese, and lead have been found to be widespread pollutants.

In deciduous trees it may be possible to detect even a wintertime pollution by mobile elements, e.g., fluorine, if they are taken up by bark, bud scales, etc., and translocated to the foliage in spring (72).

14.5. Biochemical reactions

Pollution affects the physiology of plants even at the molecular level. An "impressive list" of metabolic pools and enzymes affected is available (73). It has been concluded that biochemical results may create misunderstanding and misinterpretation since the alterations of metabolism or of levels of compounds are unspecific for pollutants and depend on many environmental parameters (74). Because many contradictory results have been presented only some important reviews are mentioned: Ref. 75, several chapters in Refs. 76 and 77 (for amino acids), Ref. 59 (scavenging processes of free radicals), Ref. 49 (mechanisms of detoxification), Ref. 78 (secondary metabolism), and Refs. 79 and 80 (stromal metabolism).

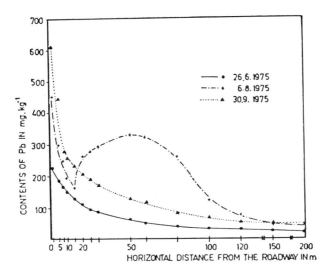

FIG. 14.10. Lead contents of spruce needles at 3 dates during the growing season in relation to the horizontal distance from a road. (Reproduced with permission from Ref. 71.)

14.6. Ecological interaction

14.6.1. Susceptibility to drought

Air pollutants probably increase the susceptibility of plants to drought, as they raise transpiration, possibly due to changes in the epidermal layer (including stomatal behavior) and interference with translocation (e.g., reduction of root growth) (53). Saturation of the cuticle with NO_x may strongly increase the epidermal permeability to water vapor (43). However, NO_x pollution is widespread nowadays in the vicinity of roads with heavy traffic. The epicuticular wax layer of spruce was decreased by an ozone fumigation (81) just as is often found due to aging and climatic factors. A structural degradation, however, was not seen in the 1-year-old needles, in contrast to some descriptions from field observations (82). In fumigated birch leaves stomata remained largely open because the subsidiary cells collapsed, which probably prevented the stomata from closing. The effect of SO_2 pollution on proteins of cell membranes was also aggravated by drought (60).

On the other hand, a drought stress during SO_2 fumigation increased resistance in spruce (83) and in fir a combination of ozone and water stress decreased transpiration in contrast to ozone alone (52).

14.6.2. Susceptibility to frost

In polluted forests it has been observed that frost resistance of conifers decreased particularly after harsh winters (84) or after sudden drops of temperature (85). Experimental SO_2 fumigations increased frost injury even after "normal" winters (86) and also a summer fumigation (60 days) of a sensitive spruce clone with 200 μg O_3 m^{-3} caused a drop of old needles after a later frost period, although no visible injury occurred during fumigation or on youngest needles (87).

The buildup of frost-hardiness is a very complex metabolic process that involves an osmotic adjustment. Any harm to that by pollutants may therefore raise winter injury, particularly when hardening is delayed (88). Accelerated weathering of the epicuticular waxes, injured cell membranes, delayed development of the cuticula, as well as N fertilization (prolonging growth), or low potassium contents (delaying carbohydrate conversion) are all known or suspected to favor frost damage (89,90).

14.6.3. Susceptibility to biotic agents

Many interrelationships between factors make also this susceptibility so complex that reviews should be consulted for details (91–93). Air pollution may affect either the host or the pathogen through the following possibilities:

1. Influence on host plant.
   a. Alteration of the surface mechanically or chemically, e.g., through corrosion of wax layer. A change of hygroscopic peculiarities may affect spore germination.
   b. Surface accumulation of pollutants that may have a toxic, complexing, nutritive, or leaching effect. This may also lead to a different epiphytic flora.
   c. Change in the appearance (e.g., color).
   d. Modification of stomatal behavior which may affect penetration by fungal hyphae.
   e. The environmental conditions may weaken the vitality and internal resistance of the host, e.g., by water stress or reduced photosynthesis (78).
   f. Reduction in allocation of resources to the formation of protective compounds, such as tannins or phenolics (19).

2. Influence on the pathogen.
   a. The pollution may affect its vitality or its enemies.
   b. The pollutant may alter the production of toxic compounds.

Secondary insect parasites suddenly tended to reproduce massively, which indicated either a weakening of the host or a reduced attack by their enemies. In fungi it seems that obligate parasites are impeded, whereas nonobligate parasites (e.g., *Armillaria*) appear to be favored by air pollution.

14.6.4. Susceptibility of pollen germination

Plant reproduction depends considerably on the allocation of photosynthate to flowers and fruit–seed formation. Flowering and fruiting have been extensively studied (94), while very little is known regarding the effect of pollution on pollen function, particularly in forest trees. Thus, for decades only a lack of natural reproduction was observed in "smoke-affected" forest stands.

The existing pollution on two forest sites was related to the reproduction of two pine species. Pollen germination was significantly affected in both species, whereas the percentage of filled seed or of seed germination was significantly lowered in white pine only (95). In a controlled experiment on the germination of conifer pollen less than 0.1 μl SO_2 l^{-1} had a significant depressive effect after $16-24$ h (96).

14.7. Concluding remarks

Pollutant-induced injuries usually start with alterations at the physiological or biochemical level. Since all metabolic processes may be affected, there are normally no specific reactions that might be used as an unequivocal determination of an effect of air pollution. The latter may rather cause reactions similar to those found after the influence of many other stresses. One must bear in mind that not only fumigation regime but also many external (climatic, edaphic) or internal (genetic) influences may alter the effects of pollution. In addition, we have to recognize that there are also many interrelationships between different organs of one and the same plant (e.g., between root tip and foliage). Therefore, we have to know more about mechanisms in trees. Thus there is still a wide field of research in front of us.

ACKNOWLEDGMENTS

The author thanks Drs. J.B. Bucher, M.S. Günthardt-Goerg, and R. Matyssek for valuable criticism and suggestions.

14.8. References

1. ECE, *Critical Levels Workshop*, Bad Harzburg, 1988, 146-p. mimeo.
2. S.P. Garsed and A.J. Rutter, "The relative sensitivities of conifer populations to SO_2 in screening tests with different concentrations of sulphur dioxide," in M.H. Unsworth, and D.P. Ormrod, eds., *Effects of Gaseous Air Pollution in Agriculture and Horticulture*, Butterworths, London, 1982, pp. 474–475.
3. S.P. Garsed, P.W. Mueller, and A.J. Rutter, "An experimental design for studying the effects of fluctuating concentrations of SO_2 on plants," in M.H. Unsworth, and D.P. Ormrod, eds., *Effects of Gaseous Air Pollution in Agriculture and Horticulture*, Butterworths, London, 1982, pp. 455–457.
4. E. Haselhoff and G. Lindau, *Die Beschädigung der Vegetation durch Rauch*, Bornträger, Leipzig, 1903.
5. S.B. McLaughlin and O. Bräker, "Methods for evaluating and predicting forest growth responses to air pollution," *Experientia*, **41**, 310–319 (1985).
6. A. Wieler, "Ueber unsichtbare Rauchschäden," *Z. Forst-u. Jadgwes.*, **35**, 204–225 (1903).

7. W. Koch, "Der Tagesgang der "Produktion der Transpiration." *Planta*, **48**, 418–452 (1957).

8. S. Börtitz, "Physiologische und biochemische Beiträge zur Rauchschadenforschung. I. Mitteilung," *Biolog. Zentralbl.*, **83**, 501–513 (1964).

9. T. Keller, "Einfluss niedriger SO_2-Konzentrationen auf die CO_2-Aufnahme von Fichte und Tanne," *Photosynthetica*, **12**, 316–322 (1978).

10. S.B. McLaughlin and R.L. Barnes, "Effects of fluoride on photosynthesis and respiration of some south-east American forest trees," *Environ. Pollut.*, **8**, 91–96 (1975).

11. T. Keller, "Der Einfluss von Fluorimmissionen auf die Nettoassimilation von Waldbaumarten," *Eidg. Anst. Forstl. Versuchswes. Mitteilung*, **53**, 161–198 (1977).

12. T. Keller, "Über die schädigende Wirkung des Fluors." *Schweiz, Z. Forstwes.*, **124**, 700–706 (1973).

13. P. Miller, J.R. Parmeter, Jr., B.H. Flick, and C.W. Martinez, "Ozone dosage response of ponderosa pine seedlings," *J. Air Pollut. Contr. Assoc.*, **19**, 435–438 (1969).

14. W.H. Smith, *Air Pollution and Forests*, Springer-Verlag, New York, 1981.

15. G.H.M. Krause and B. Prinz, "Zur Wirkung von Ozon und saurem Nebel auf phaenomenologische und physiologische Parameter," in F. Führ et al., eds., *Wirkungen von Luftverunreinigungen auf Waldbäume und Waldböden*, Statusseminar KFA Jülich, Jül-Spez-**369**, 208–221, Jülich (Germany 1986).

16. H. Kammerbauer, H. Selinger, R. Römmelt, A. Ziegler-Jöns, D. Knoppik, and B. Hock, "Toxic effects of exhaust emissions on spruce and their reduction by the catalytic converter," *Environ. Pollut.* (A), **42**, 133–142 (1986).

17. D.P. Ormrod, "Air pollutant interactions in mixtures," in M.H. Unsworth and D.P. Ormrod, eds., *Effects of Gaseous Air Pollution in Agriculture and Horticulture*, Butterworths, London, 1982, pp. 307–331.

18. Y.S. Yang, J.M. Skelly, and B.I. Chevone, "Whole tree physiology and air pollution effects on forest trees," *Can. J. For. Res.*, **12**, 803–808 (1982).

19. S.B. McLaughlin, "Clonal response of eastern white pine to low doses of O_3, SO_2, and NO_2, singly and in combination," in J. Bervaes et al., eds., *Relationships between above and below Ground Influences of Air Pollutants on Forest Trees*, CEC Air Pollut. Rep. **16**, 8–26 (Brussels, 1988).

20. P.B. Reich and R.G. Amundson, "Ambient levels of O_3 reduce net photosynthesis in tree and crop species," *Science*, **230**, 566–570 (1985).

21. P.B. Reich, "Effects of low concentrations of O_3 on net photosynthesis, dark respiration, and chlorophyll contents in aging hybrid poplar leaves," *Plant Physiol.*, **73**, 291–296 (1983).

22. K. Küppers and G. Klumpp, "Effects of ozone, sulfur dioxide, and nitrogen dioxide on gas exchange and starch economy in Norway spruce," *Geo J.*, **17(2)**, 271–275 (1988).

23. J.E. Hällgren, "Photosynthetic gas exchange in leaves affected by air pollutants," in M.J. Koziol and F.R. Whatley, eds., *Gaseous Air Pollutants and Plant Metabolism*, Butterworths, London, 1984, pp. 147–159.

24. M.J. Koziol, "Interactions of gaseous pollutants with carbohydrate metabolism," in M.J. Koziol and F.R. Whatley, eds., *Gaseous Air Pollutants and Plant Metabolism*, Butterworths, London, 1984, pp. 251–273.

25. M.J. Koziol, F.R. Whatley, and J.D. Shelvey, "An integrated view of the effects of gaseous air pollutants on plant carbohydrate metabolism," in S. Schulte-Hostede et al., eds., *Air Pollution and Plant Metabolism*, Elsevier, London, 1988, pp. 148–168.

26. O.L. Lange, G. Führer, and J. Gebel, "Rapid field determination of photosynthetic capacity of cut spruce twigs at saturating ambient CO_2," *Trees*, **1**, 70–77 (1986).

27. J.L.J. Houpis, K.A. Surano, S. Cowles, and J.H. Shinn, "Chlorophyll and carotenoid concentrations in two varieties of *Pinus ponderosa* seedlings subjected to long-term elevated carbon dioxide," *Tree Physiol.*, **4**, 187–193 (1988).

28. J. Oleksyn, "Effects of SO_2, HF and NO_2 on net photosynthetic and dark respiration rates of Scots pine needles of various ages," *Photosynthetica*, **18**, 259–262 (1984).

29. D.T. Tingey, R.G. Wilhour, and C. Standley, "The effect of chronic ozone exposure on the metabolite content of ponderosa pine seedling," *For. Sci.*, **22**, 234–241 (1976).

30. Y. Yang, J.M. Skelly, B.I. Chevone, and J.B. Birch, "Effects of long-term ozone exposure on photosynthesis and dark respiration of eastern white pine," *Environ. Sci. Techn.*, **17**, 371–373 (1983).

31. V.J. Black, "The effect of air pollutants on apparent respiration," in M.J. Koziol and F.R. Whatley, eds., *Gaseous Air Pollutants and Plant Metabolism*, Butterworths, London, 1984, pp. 231–248.

32. P. Dizengremel and A. Citerne, "Air pollutant effects on mitochondria and respiration," in S. Schulte-Hostede, et al., eds., *Air Pollution and Plant Metabolism*, Elsevier, London, 1988, pp. 169–188.

33. D.J. Ballantyne, "Phytotoxic air pollutants and oxidative phosphorylation," in M.J. Koziol and F.R. Whatley, eds., *Gaseous Air Pollutants and Plant Metabolism*, Butterworths, London, 1984, pp. 223–230.

34. S.B. McLaughlin, R.K. McConathy, D. Duvik, and L.K. Mann, "Effects of chronic air pollution stress on photosynthesis, carbon allocation and growth of white pine trees," *For. Sci.*, **28**, 60–70 (1982).

35. J. Mooi, "Influence of ozone on growth of two poplar cultivars," *Plant Disease*, **64**, 772–773 (1980).

36. H.A. Mooney and W.E. Winner, "Carbon gain, allocation and growth as affected by atmospheric pollutants," in S. Schulte-Hostede, et al., eds., *Air Pollution and Plant Metabolism*, Elsevier, London, 1988, pp. 272–287.

37. G. Lorenz-Plucinska, "Effect of sulphur dioxide on the partitioning of assimilates in Scots pine seedlings," *Eur. J. For. Pathol.* **16**, 266–273 (1986).

38. P.B. Reich, "Quantifying plant response to ozone: A unifying theory," *Tree Physiol.*, **3**, 63–91 (1987).

39. T. Keller, "The effect of a continuous springtime fumigation with SO_2 on CO_2 uptake and structure of the annual ring in spruce," *Can. J. For. Res.*, **10**, 1–6 (1980).

40. T.A. Mansfield, "Factors determining root-shoot partitioning," in J.N. Cape and P. Mathy, eds., *Scientific Basis of Forest Decline Symptomatology*, CEC Air Pollut. Rep. **15**, 171–180 (Brussels, 1988).

41. W.E. Winner, H.A. Mooney, K. Williams, and S. von Caemmerer, "Measuring and assessing SO$_2$ effects on photosynthesis and plant growth, in W.E. Winner et al., eds., *Sulfur Dioxide and Vegetation*, Stanford Univ. Press, Stanford, CA, 1985, pp. 118–132.

42. P.H. Freer-Smith, "The responses of six broadleaved trees during long-term exposure to SO$_2$ and NO$_2$," *New Phytol.*, **97**, 49–61 (1984).

43. H. Ziegler, "Interactive effects of dry and wet deposition on structure and function of canopies, in particular interactive effects SO$_2$, NO$_x$, and O$_3$," in *Direct Effects of Dry and Wet Deposition on Forest Ecosystems—in particular Canopy Interactions*, CEC Air Pollut. Rep. **4**, 102–109 (Brussels, 1987).

44. W. Larcher, *Physiological Plant Ecology*, 2nd ed., Springer-Verlag, Berlin, 1980.

45. V.J. Black, "SO$_2$ Effects on stomatal behavior," in W.E. Winner et al., eds., *Sulfur Dioxide and Vegetation*, Stanford Univ. Press, Stanford, 1985, pp. 96–117.

46. T.A. Mansfield and P.H. Freer-Smith, "The role of stomata in resistance mechanisms," in M.J. Koziol and F.R. Whatley, eds., *Gaseous Air Pollutants and Plant Metabolism*, Butterworths, London, 1984, pp. 131–146.

47. W.E. Winner, C. Gillespie, W.-S. Shen, and H.A. Mooney, "Stomatal responses to SO$_2$ and O$_3$," in S. Schulte-Hostede et al., eds., *Air Pollution and Plant Metabolism*, Elsevier, London, 1988, pp. 255–271.

48. U. Maier-Maercker and W. Koch, "Delignification of subsidiary and guard cell walls by SO$_2$ and probable implication on the humidity response," *Eur. J. For. Pathol.*, **16**, 342–351 (1986).

49. H.J. Jäger, H.J. Weigel, and L. Grünhage, "Physiologische und biochemische Aspekte der Wirkung von Immissionen auf Waldbäume," *Eur. J. For. Pathol.*, **16**, 98–109 (1986).

50. T. Keller and R. Häsler, "The influence of a fall fumigation with ozone on the stomatal behavior of spruce and fir," *Oecologia*, **64**, 284–286 (1984).

51. W. Flückiger, S. Leonardi, and S. Braun, "Air pollutant effects on foliar leaching," in J.N. Cape and P. Mathy, eds., *Scientific Basis of Forest Decline Symptomatology*, CEC Air Pollut. Rep. **15**, 160–169 (Brussels, 1988).

52. J.B. Bucher, G. Schiller, and R.T.W. Siegwolf, "Effects of ozone and/or water stress on xylem pressure, transpiration, and leaf conductance in fir," in J. Bervais et al., eds., *Relationships between above and below ground influences of air pollutants on forest trees*. CEC Air Pollut. Res. Rep. **16**, 83–88 (Brussels, 1988).

53. T.A. Mansfield, E.A. Wright, P.W. Lucas, and D.A. Cottam, "Interactions between air pollutants and water stress," in S. Schulte-Hostede et al., eds., *Air Pollution and Plant Metabolism*, Elsevier, London, 1988, pp. 288–306.

54. D. Grill, "Pufferkapazität gesunder und rauchgeschädigter Fichtennadeln," *Z. Pflanzenkrankh.*, **78**, 612–622 (1971).

55. D. Grill, W. Lindner, and H.J. Jäger, "Säuren in SO$_2$-belasteten und von *Chrysomyxa* befallenen Fichtennadein," *Phyton (Austria)*, **20**, 65–72 (1980).

56. E. Nieboer, J.D. MacFarlane, and D.H.S. Richardson, "Modification of plant cell buffering capacities by gaseous air pollutants," in M.J. Koziol and F.R. Whatley, eds., *Gaseous Air Pollutants and Plant Metabolism*, Butterworths, London, 1984, pp. 313–330.

57. R.L. Heath, "Initial events in injury to plants by air pollutants," *Ann. Rev. Plant Physiol.*, **31**, 395–431 (1980).

58. J.B. Mudd, S.K. Banerjee, M.M. Dooley, and K.L. Knight, "Pollutants and plant cells: Effects on membranes," in M.J. Koziol and F.R. Whatley, eds., *Gaseous Air Pollutants and Plant Metabolism*, Butterworths, London, 1984, pp. 105–116.

59. R.G. Alscher and J.S. Amthor, "The physiology of free-radical scavenging: Maintenance and repair processes," in S. Schulte-Hostede et al., eds., *Air Pollution and Plant Metabolism*, Elsevier, London, 1988, pp. 94–115.

60. H. Mehlhorn, G. Seufert, A. Schmidt, and K.J. Kunert, "Effect of SO_2 and O_3 on production of antioxidants in conifers," *Plant Physiol.*, **82**, 336–338 (1986).

61. H.J. Kunert and G. Hofer, "Lipidperoxidation als phytotoxische Folge atmosphärischer Schadstoffwirkung," in F. Horsch et al., eds., Vol. 3, Statuskolloquium PEF, Kernforschungszentrum Karlsruhe, 1987, pp. 177–188.

62. G.M.H. Krause, K.D. Jung, and B. Prinz, "Experimentelle Untersuchungen zur Aufklärung der neuartigen Waldschäden," *VDI-Berichte*, **560**, 627–656 (1985).

63. D.T. Tingey, R.G. Wilhour, and O.C. Taylor, "The measurement of plant responses," in W.W. Heck et al., eds., *Methodology for the Assessment of Air Pollution Effects on Vegetation*, Air Pollution Control Assoc., Philadelphia, 1978, Chapter 7.

64. T. Keller, "The electrical conductivity of Norway spruce needle diffusate as affected by certain air pollutants," *Tree Physiol.*, **1**, 85–94 (1986).

65. P. Little, "Deposition of 2.75, 5.0 and 8.5 μm particles to plant and soil surfaces," *Environ. Pollut.*, **12**, 293–305 (1977).

66. R. Jonas, M. Horbert, and W. Pflug, "Die Filterwirkung von Wäldern gegenüber staubbelasteter Luft," *Forstwiss. Cbl.*, **104** 289–299 (1985).

67. J. Materna, "Der Einfluss des Schwefeldioxyds auf die mineralische Zusammensetzung der Fichtennadeln," *Naturwiss.*, **48**, 723–724 (1961).

68. R.A. Skeffington and M.T. Roberts, "Effect of ozone and acid mist on Scots pine and Norway spruce—an experimental study," *VDI-Berichte*, **560**, 747–760 (1985).

69. R.F. Hüttl, "Jüngste Waldschäden, Ernährungsstörungen und diagnostische Düngung," *VDI-Berichte*, **560**, 863–886 (1985).

70. A. Wyttenbach, S. Bajo, L. Tobler, and T. Keller, "Major and trace element concentrations in needles of *Picea abies*," *Plant and Soil*, **85**, 313–325 (1985).

71. B. Mankovska, "The content of Pb, Cd and Cl in forest trees caused by the traffic of motor vehicles," *Biologia (Bratislava)*, **32**, 477–489 (1977).

72. T. Keller, "Translocation of fluoride in woody plants," *Fluoride*, **7**, 31–35 (1974).

73. O. Queiroz, "Air pollution, gene expression and post translational enzyme modifications," in S. Schulte-Hostede et al., eds., *Air Pollution and Plant Metabolism*, Elsevier, London, 1988, pp. 238–254.

74. B. Lüthy, W. Landolt, and I. Pfenninger, "Biochemical effects of an ozone fumigation in Norway spruce," in *Direct Effects of Dry and Wet Deposition on Forest Ecosystems—in Particular Canopy Interactions*, CEC Air Pollut. Rep. **4**, 110–116, (Brussels, 1987).

75. H.J. Jäger, "Biochemical indication of an effect of air pollution on plants," in L. Steubing and H.J. Jäger, eds., *Monitoring of Air Pollutants by Plants. Methods and Problems*, Junk, The Hague, 1982, pp. 99–107.

76. M.J. Koziol and F.R. Whatley, eds., *Gaseous Air Pollutants and Plant Metabolism*, Butterworths, London, 1984.

77. A.J. Rowland, A.M. Borland, and P.J. Lea, "Changes in amino-acids, amines and proteins in response to air pollutants," in S. Schulte-Hostede et al., eds., *Air Pollution and Plant Metabolism*, Elsevier, London, 1988, pp. 189–221.

78. E.J. Pell, "Secondary metabolism and air pollutants," in S. Schulte-Hostede et al., eds., *Air Pollution and Plant Metabolism*, Elsevier, London, 1988, pp. 222–237.

79. M.A.J. Parry and C.P. Wittingham, "Effects of gaseous air pollutants on stromal reactions, " in M.J. Koziol and F.R. Whatley, eds., *Gaseous Air Pollutants and Plant Metabolism*, Butterworths, London, 1984, pp. 161–168.

80. L.E. Anderson, G. Muschinek, and I. Marques, "Effects of SO_2 and sulfite on stromal metabolism," in S. Schulte-Hostede, et al., eds., *Air Pollution and Plant Metabolism*, Elsevier, London, 1988, pp. 134–147.

81. M.S. Goerg-Günthardt and T. Keller, "Cuticular features and conductivity of needle diffusate in spruce," in J.N. Cape and P. Mathy, eds., *Scientific Basis of Forest Decline Symptomatology*, CEC. Air Pollut. Rep. **15**, 316–322 (Brussels, 1988).

82. J.J. Sauter and J.U. Voss, "SEM-observations on the structural degradation of epistomatal waxes in spruce," *Eur. J. For. Pathol.*, **16**, 408–423 (1986).

83. M. Tesche, H. Ranft, S. Feiler, G. Michael, and C. Bellmann, "Zur Komplexwirkung von Schwefeldioxid und Trockenheit auf Fichte," *Wiss. Z. Techn. Univ. Dresden*, **35**, 209–215 (1986).

84. S. Huttunen, "The effects of air pollution on provenances of Scots pine and Norway spruce in northern Finland," *Silva Fennica*, **12**, 1–16 (1978).

85. J. Materna, "Zusammenhang zwischen Schäden an Fichte und Kiefern und Temperaturstürzen in immissionsbelasteten Gebieten," *Gesellschaft f. Strahlenforschung*, Bericht 10/87, pp. 265–268 (1987, Neuherberg, Germany).

86. T. Keller, "Folgen einer winterlichen SO_2-Belastung für die Fichte," *Gartenbauwissensch.*, **46**, 170–178 (1981).

87. K.A. Brown, T.M. Roberts, and L.W. Blank, "Interaction between ozone and cold sensitivity in Norway spruce: A factor contributing to forest decline in Europe?," *New Phytol.*, **105**, 149–155 (1987).

88. A.J. Friedland, R.A. Gregory, L. Kärenlampi, and A.H. Johnson, "Winter damage to foliage as a factor in redspruce decline," *Can. J. For. Res.*, **14**, 963–965 (1984).

89. A.W. Davison and J.D. Barnes, "Effects of winter stress on pollutant responses," in *How Are the Effects of Air Pollutants on Agricultural Crops Influenced by the Interaction with Other Limiting Factors?* Proceedings COST CEC Workshop Roskilde 23.–25.3.86, pp. 16–32 (Brussels, 1986).

90. A.W. Davison, J.D. Barnes, and C.J. Renner, "Interactions between air pollutants and cold stress," in S. Schulte-Hostede et al., eds., *Air Pollution and Plant Metabolism*, Elsevier, London, 1988, pp. 307–328.

91. P.R. Hughes and J.A. Laurence, "Relationship of biochemical effects of air pollutants on plants to environmental problems: insect and microbial interactions," in M.J. Koziol and F.R. Whatley, eds., *Gaseous Air Pollutants and Plant Metabolism*, Butterworths, London, 1984, pp. 361–377.

92. P. Dowding, "Air pollutant effects on plant pathogens," in S. Schulte-Hostede et al., eds., *Air Pollution and Plant Metabolism*, Elsevier, London, 1988, pp. 329–355.

93. W. Flückiger, S. Braun, and M. Bolsinger, "Air pollution: Effect on host-plant–insect relationships," in S. Schulte-Hostede et al., eds., *Air Pollution and Plant Metabolism*, Elsevier, London, 1988, pp. 366–380.

94. J. Bonte, "Effects of air pollutants on flowering and fruiting," in M.H. Unsworth and D.P. Ormrod, eds., *Effects of Gaseous Air Pollution in Agriculture and Horticulture*, Butterworths, London, 1982, pp. 207–223.

95. D.B. Houston and L.S. Dochinger, "Effects of ambient air pollution on cone, seed, and pollen characteristics in eastern white and red pines," *Environ. Pollut.*, **12**, 1–5 (1977).

96. T. Keller and H. Beda, "Effects of SO_2 on the germination of conifer pollen," *Environ. Pollut.*, **33** (A), 237–243 (1984).

15 Adaptation to Salinity

YOAV WAISEL

Department of Botany, Tel Aviv University, Tel Aviv, Israel

Contents

15.1. Introduction

Trees constitute an exceptional group among halophytes, mostly because of their mass, size, and age. Because of their large size, the quantities of minerals that are transported through trees, or accumulate in their tissues, are immense. Hundreds of kilograms of NaCl would be transported through a ma-

359

ture tree of *Tamarix* during its lifetime (1). However, it is not only the large quantities of minerals that pose a problem but also the distances that such elements have to travel. Roots of some species of *Tamarix* reach distances of some 50 m from the base of the trunk. Ions taken up by such roots would travel through some 60–70 m of xylem vessels before reaching their final destination. Because of the old age, exclusion strategies, which are common among herbaceous plants, are of little use for trees. Salt resistance of trees must be based on endurance of the salts in the shoot tissues, which increase with time.

Most halotrees are permanently affected by salinity throughout their life cycle. Nevertheless, exposure to salinity may vary in time and space, e.g., in habitats at that are periodically inundated by saline water, or in roots that pass through a salty horizon in the soil profile.

Salt resistance of trees varies not only during different phases of their growth but also among different tissues and organs. In order to cope with such heterogenous conditions several mechanisms of salt resistance have developed in trees. Adaptation may depend on one dominant mechanism or on multiple traits (2).

Several aspects of the behavior of halotrees had been extensively discussed in the literature (3,4). In the present chapter, we shall try to concentrate on some aspects only, i.e. on the functional aspects of adaptation of halotrees to saline environments.

15.2. Reproduction

Salinity can influence the sex expression, pollination, fruit development and seed production of plants. Staminate specimens of *Populus* sp. and *Salix* sp. were more frequent than the pistillate ones on salt-affected soils (5). This might be a direct response to NaCl, but also a result of the developmental stage and the size of the trees. Abundance of male individuals of several species under stress conditions was thought to represent an attempt to reduce the cost of production of such plants (6).

Fruits and seeds of halotrees are unique among the organs of those plants by having, in most cases, only low concentrations of NaCl. Osmotic adjustment of those organs is achieved by other means, i.e., by the accumulation of various organic compatible solutes.

15.2.1. Germination

Germinating seeds differ from adult plants in their salt tolerance. The higher sensitivity to salinity of germinating seeds represents a major factor in the determination of plant distribution in saline habitats and prevents the establishment of several tree species.

Among the halotrees of Israel, the genus *Tamarix* is exceptional in its high salt tolerance during germination (7). Germination of seeds of *Tamarix* sp. occurs even at NaCl concentrations of >1 kmol m^{-3}. The sensitivity of the seeds to NaCl increased with age, and their viability was strongly reduced by salinity. Seeds of other trees seem to be more salt-sensitive. Although seeds of most mangroves will germinate in full seawater, seeds of *Suaeda monoica* Forssk. ex J.F. Gmel. are unable to germinate above the concentration of 0.4 kmol m^{-3} NaCl. Such a limit of salinity restricts the time of germination of several terrestrial halophytes to periods when salts are leached. Germination of many halophytes is little affected by temperature (in the 20–30°C range), although their capability to cope with salinity is narrower at the high-temperature treatments.

15.2.2. Vegetative reproduction

Many of the halotrees, e.g., *Tamarix*, are capable of vegetative reproduction. However, vegetative reproduction is possible only under a limited combination of environmental conditions. Cuttings of various saltmarsh species of *Tamarix* require good aeration, low salinity, and protection from evaporation for optimal establishment (8). Cuttings of the psamohalophyte *Tamarix aphylla* (L.) Karst. develop in NaCl concentrations of up to 200 mol m^{-3}, provided transpiration is kept low and the temperature is relatively high (30°C). At concentrations above 200 mol m^{-3}, the cuttings may sprout but rooting is severely inhibited.

15.3. Salinity and shoot growth

15.3.1. Extension growth

There is limited information for the growth responses of most species of halotrees. The little we know includes information regarding few species of mangroves and some species of *Tamarix*, *Populus*, and *Suaeda*.

Growth of most plant species is inhibited by salinity. The critical concentrations of NaCl that cause the first inhibitory symptoms and determine the viability of the plant differ for each taxon. The highest salt concentrations tolerated by *Avicennia marina* (Forssk.) Vierh. are about 1500 mol m^{-3} NaCl, but growth is affected even at 250 mol m^{-3} NaCl. *Rhizophora mangle* L. grows best in 25% seawater (9). Also other species of mangroves exhibit higher growth rates in diluted seawater (10). Growth of *Tamarix aphylla* decreases at NaCl concentrations of >100 mol m^{-3}, although growth can still proceed until the concentration of NaCl reaches 700 mol m^{-3}. The final lethal limits are dependent not only on the NaCl content but also on the ionic composition of the solution (pCa^{2+}, pNO_3^-, etc.), on temperature, water availability, and transpiration demands.

Leaves of several tree species that grow on saline media become thicker and more succulent than those that grow on a salt-free medium. Such a phenomenon was believed to help in salt resistance by reducing the internal concentrations of NaCl. The validity of such an explanation is questionable since succulence may reduce the mechanical strength of large-sized cells (11,12).

Table 15.1. Effects of NaCl on various parameters of leaf growth of *Eucalyptus occidentalis* Endl.[a]

Parameter	Treatment: NaCl (mol m^{-3})		
	2 (control)	30	90
Total plant weight (mg)	7700	6622	3003
Total leaf weight (mg)	3500	3185	1715
Average leaf weight (mg)	140	211	174
Average leaf area (cm^2)	10.1	15.4	12.1

[a]After Ref. 13.

Leaf growth of *Eucalyptus occidentalis* Endl. is reduced considerably by 90 mol m^{-3} NaCl. The size of the canopy was reduced because of the reduction in the number of leaves (13). Yet, under the very same conditions of salinity, the expansion of the individual leaves was accelerated (Table 15.1).

Many halophytic trees survive during periods of high salinity, with no net growth; production of new tissues of those plants is balanced by the death of an equivalent mass of old tissues. When better conditions are reestablished growth is resumed.

Growth responses of salt-affected plants vary with the constancy of the salinity level. Fluctuations in salinity, typical of habitats with seasonal changes in water potential, are reflected by a concomitant change in the osmotic potential of the shoots and by their metabolism (14).

15.3.2. Radial growth

Trees, including the halophytes, are characterized by their capability for massive radial growth. However, some of the halotrees have unusual types of cambia with anomalous radial growth. Nevertheless, such a behavior may be due to their tropical origin or family characteristics, and not because of the exposure to salinity.

Development of successive cambia of the mangrove *Avicennia marina*, and the subsequent differentiation of their derivatives, follow a typical sequence (15): (a) parenchyma cells are produced by the cambium; a few of them are produced inward, but most are produced outward; (b) several files of vessels are formed inward; (c) rings of sclereids develop from the outer border of the secondary parenchyma files; (d) the cambial initials lose their activity and phloem strands develop; and (e) new cambial initials develop from the outer parenchyma layer, next to the outermost sclereid band (Fig. 15.1). The new cambia originate from the first parenchyma cells to develop from the previous cambium. About two to six cycles of such activity can be observed annually. As this pattern was shown to be independent of leaf and branch initiation (15), and as it is not seasonally determined, activity of the cambium seems to be endogenously controlled (16). Similar types of anomalous ring formation

Bark

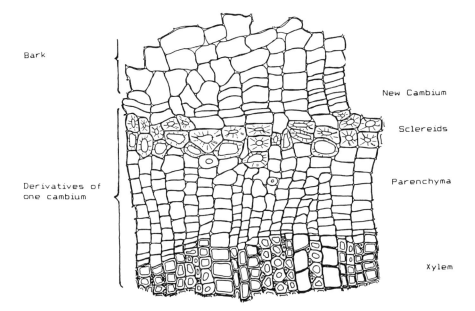

New Cambium

Sclereids

Parenchyma

Derivatives of
one cambium

Xylem

FIG. 15.1. New cambium development and a preceding anomalous wood ring of *Avicennia germinans*. Former ring ended by sclereids. (Adapted from Ref. 15.)

were described for *Atriplex halimus* L. (17,18). The first additional cambium of *Atriplex* develops in the pericycle and is a continuation of the intrafascicular cambium. Successive cambia are connected with the preceding cambia. Initiation of the successive cambia seems to be triggered by hormonal signals that are submitted by the young leaves.

The seasonal pattern of cambial activity of halotrees is determined by the plants' inherited characteristics as well as by the prevailing climatic conditions. Many of the tropical halotrees maintain their activity during a good part of the year. Species of the temperate regions exhibit seasonal activity with one, or sometimes with two, peaks per year. The water conductivity of the tree trunks and their annual pattern of transpiration reflect in a certain way those patterns of development of the new xylem.

The xylem vessels in halotrees are more dense and have smaller diameter and thicker walls than those in mesophytic trees (19,20). Furthermore, the xylem of halophytic trees have short vessel members, small pits, and highly dense fibers and rays (21). Such features play an important role in their water relations.

Salt stresses affect cambial activity and tissue differentiation of several trees. Under saline conditions the cambial activity of *Populus euphratica* Oliv. was restricted, the annual rings became narrow, and the type of wood changed from a diffused porous type into a ring-porous one (22) (Fig. 15.2). Such

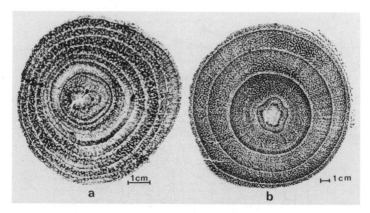

FIG. 15.2. Cross sections of branches of *Populus euphratica* from a salt-stressed plant (a) or a well-watered plant (b). (Adapted from Ref. 22.)

effects seem to be connected with the low water potentials of the salty medium. However, there is no direct evidence for specific ionic effects on cambial activity.

15.4. Salinity and root growth

15.4.1. Root distribution

Root mass, shoot:root ratio, and the pattern of root distribution in the soil are of prime importance for the adaptation of plants to saline habitats. The scanty data available on this aspect are limited to shrubs. Measurements made in the USSR indicate that the root volume of the salt-recreting *Reaumuria* shrubs may exceed that of the shoot by 12–400 times (23), depending on the soil texture, salinity, and the age of the plants.

The final shape and size of a root system of a tree is a result of the extension growth of each individual root, of the site of lateral root formation, and the rates of their development. Little is known of such processes in trees in general and in halophytic trees in particular. However, from what is known for her-baceous plants (24), it appears as if salinity affects the three growth processes differently. Initiation of lateral roots is least affected by salinity, whereas extension growth of the laterals seems to be the most sensitive root growth process. Preservation of the normal number of lateral root initials (25), in spite of a general decrease in growth, would secure the plants with the essential supply of cytokinins, and thereby improve their salt resistance (26). On the other hand, inhibition of the subsequent growth of lateral roots would reduce the horizontal spread of the root system of salt-affected trees and compel them to depend on the deep soil layers for the supply of water and nutrients.

15.4.2. Structure and root performance

Salinity affects the structure and development of roots. Casparian strips, i.e., these essential endodermal structures that control ion transport into the stele, are formed, in salt-affected plants, several millimeters beyond the tips of fast-growing main roots but appear much closer to the tips in fine laterals (27). As a result of that, transport of ions into fast-growing roots would be less selective because a significant fraction of the solutes would be dragged into the xylem via the apoplast of the gap between the mature endodermis and the root tip. Selectivity is regulated much better in fine roots because of the smaller gap in free space. Halotrees seem to prefer such roots (28,29). Thus, selectivity of ions by salt-affected plants is determined not only by the average physiological traits of the roots but also by the individual characteristics of each root and by the ratio of long roots to short ones.

Roots of *Avicennia marina* and *Bruguiera gymnorhiza* (L.) Lam. differ in length and thickness of their root caps, in the site of development of the Casparian strips, by the rates of differentiation of the vascular system, and by the content of phenolic substances (30).

15.4.3. Adaptation to inundation

Diffusion of gas from the leaves of trees into their roots, via the intercellular spaces of the stems, is usually too slow to supply enough oxygen for root respiration. Additional mechanisms exist to promote the capacity for gas flow into roots exposed to anoxic environment. In mangroves, O_2 is pumped into the roots via the lenticels of the pneumatophores. Pumping is facilitated by the negative pressures that develop inside the air spaces of the roots during the inundation period (31).

Oxygen transport into roots of trees of flooded habitats depends on the creation of a temperature gradient of at least $2-10$ K between the leaves and their environment (32,33). Compared to diffusion rates (1.5 µl air min^{-1} in leafless *Alnus glutinosa* Gaertn. trees and 4-µl air min^{-1} in leaf-covered trees), the so-called thermoosmotic gas transport may account for flows of $6-10$ µl air min^{-1}. Thus, the development of a temperature gradient between the leaves and the roots raises the air transport through the intercellular air spaces by a factor of 4. Such rates are high enough to supply the roots with oxygen not only for root respiration but also for oxidation of the rhizosphere. Such a transport system has so far been shown only in *Alnus* trees. However, a similar mechanism probably operates in all types of swamp plants, including halotrees.

Inundation, with the aftermath of anaerobiosis and reducing conditions, influences plant behavior in concurrence with salinity and other environmental parameters. There is a strong interaction between the tolerance of *Eucalyptus camaldulensis* Dehn. trees to inundation and the salinity of their medium (34). Flood tolerance of an ecotype from Lake Albacutya (a dry salt lake in the interior of Victoria, Australia), depended considerably on the salinity level of the water. Growth of those trees was superior, when flooded with low-salt water (2 mol m^{-3} NaCl), over the growth of plants that were irrigated daily. Growth of flooded and growth of normally irrigated plants were similar in the 30-mol m^{-3} NaCl treatment. However, growth of plants with flooded roots was strongly inhibited in the 80-mol m^{-3} NaCl solution, where it reached only 10% that of the controls. Thus, investigations of salt tolerance of halotrees must be related to their response to flooding.

15.5. Salinity and tree–water relations

Salinity affects the ionic balance of trees as well as the water–tree relations, depending on water availability, the conducting capability of the plants, and transpiration.

One of the most basic needs of salt-affected trees is the rapid establishment of osmotic adjustment of either the whole plant or its tissues. Differences in the osmotic potential between closely related organs (e.g., fruits, seeds, leaves) can be frequently observed in mangrove trees (35). The question of how the developing embryos of such species obtain water against an osmotic potential gradient needs further investigation.

15.5.1. Uptake and transport

The distribution of available water among the various soil horizons of the root zone determines the quantities of water that can be absorbed by trees. Thus, knowing the structure of the soil profile, soil water status, and the pattern of root distribution is a prerequisite for understanding the relationships between water and plants. Because of the extremely high variability of most saline habitats, determination of such parameters by soil sample analysis are practically impossible and other methods must be sought. Using the split-root technique, Waisel and Pollak (36) have estimated the water potentials around the active roots of some Israeli native halophytes. Trees of *Tamarix jordanis* Boiss. of the Dead Sea population tolerate great seasonal variations in the water potentials around their roots (poikilohydric species). Such a behavior seems to be due to the multilayered nature and the uneven distribution of their roots in the soil profile. Growth and flowering of *Tamarix* trees occurred during wintertime, when their water potential was -0.3 MPa, but has continued even when the equilibration point of the roots with the soil reached -3.4 MPa. Growth at such low water potentials was also observed for *Suaeda monoica*, although this species has exhibited only minor annual fluctuations in its water potentials (between -2.1 and -4.8 MPa). As both species grow side by side in one plant community, their roots apparently exploit different soil horizons.

The hydraulic conductivity of roots changes considerably following their exposure to NaCl (37,38). An increase in salinity (up to 100 mol m^{-3} NaCl) around maize roots has reduced their hydraulic conductivity by some 80% (from 4.7 m s^{-1} MPa 10^{-8} to 1.0) (39). The addition of Ca^{2+} to the medium (10 mol m^{-3} $CaCl_2$) had an ameliorating effect, and conductivity, under the same concentration of NaCl, was reduced by only 47%. Root growth was reduced by 54% in a NaCl solution without Ca^{2+} but by 33% only when Ca^{2+} was present. The promotion of root growth by Ca^{2+} under saline conditions may be due to the improvement in the hydraulic conductivity (39). The reduction in hydraulic conductivity of roots usually has negative effects on the water balance of plants. However, reduction of root conductivity may prevent exosmosis and dehydration, where roots are exposed to an abrupt increase in salinity.

Reduction in root resistance to water transport was caused, in various halophytes, also by infection with vesicular-arbuscular mycorrhizae (40). This is another aspect of halotree ecology that should be looked into.

The distances for water transport increases with the size of the plants. Trees of saline habitats, therefore, tend to develop small and hemispheric crowns (41).

Halotrees are usually subjected to extremely high negative pressures in their xylem, with values of up to -6.0 MPa reported for mangroves (42,43). Under such high water strains inside the xylem, air may enter the water-conducting elements and cause embolism, thereby disrupting water transport (44). In well-adapted trees, embolized vessels can be refilled with water, as soon as their water potential becomes positive (45,46). Because halotrees seldom experience high environmental water potentials, they must have a high resistance to entry of air, via the pits, into their water conducting system. For mangroves, the highest feasible water potentials are below -2.7 MPa, i.e., that of the seawater. Indeed, the vulnerability of the xylem vessels to embolism of the mangrove *Rhizophora mangle* L. was found to be much less than that of tropical rainforest species, where high water tensions are rare (21). Water conductivity of *Rhizophora* roots is affected at water potentials of > -6.0 MPa. Vulnerability depended on the permeability of the pits to air. Thus, resistance to embolism seems to be an adaptive trait of trees of salt-affected habitats.

The ascent of water in the stems of halotrees is determined by the negative pressures that develop in their shoots (47) and also depends on the structure and arrangement of the xylem vessels. The best distribution of water throughout the canopy reported for trees of humid habitats is achieved by a xylem structure that ensures a spiral pattern. The less effective sectorial ascent of water, either winding or straight, is common in woody species of arid regions. Very little is known regarding the pattern of water ascent in halotrees. The patterns described for *Tamarix aphylla*, *Populus euphratica*, and *Avicennia officinalis* L. have shown sectorial ascent, either straight or turning into ring ascent (48). Water ascent in chenopods, either trees or shrubs, exhibits an interlocked–sectorial pattern that is typical to the structural characteristics of most members of that family (1). The capacity for water transport also depends on the seasonal pattern of cambial activity and the size and number of xylem elements that differentiate.

15.5.2. Transpiration

High rates of transpiration were observed for various halotrees. The rates of transpiration of field-grown *Tamarix* trees were 350–1000 mg water [g DW (dry weight)]$^{-1}$ h^{-1}, but were as high as 5 g water (g DW)$^{-1}$ h^{-1} in hydroponically grown plants. Phreatophytes, thus need an abundant supply of water and are undesirable for afforestation of arid zones (49).

Transpiration of *Tamarix* trees is negatively affected by salinity. Among several taxa investigated, only one ecotype of *Tamarix jordanis* showed an increase in transpiration at NaCl concentrations of 100 mol m^{-3} (Solomon and Waisel, unpublished observations). Transpiration of *Tamarix aphylla* was negatively correlated with the salinity of the ambient water or soil water potential and was also affected by the presence of heavy metals, such as cadmium in the medium. The presence of Cd^{2+} affects the hydraulic conductivity of the roots of such plants rather than their stomatal aperture (50).

15.5.3. Circadian rhythms

Transpiration of trees exhibit day–night fluctuations. In most cases this is the direct response of the stomata to the change in light. However, in some species, transpiration is also governed by an internal circadian rhythm (Ref. 51; Solomon and Waisel, unpublished observations). The mean period of each cycle varies from 19 to 22 h, depending on the species and the salinity of the medium (Fig. 15.3). Such an endogenous rhythm may have an ecological significance: the stomata become fully open at dawn, when evaporative demand is still low. Moreover, they close daily early in the afternoon and by that shorten the time of transpiration.

15.6. Mineral metabolism

As salts are the constituents of large-sized perennial organisms, a gradual infiltration of salts results in a steady buildup of salt in the tissues of trees. Trees cope with such situations by regulating the content of Na and Cl of their tissues. This is done by restricting ion uptake at the root level but can also be achieved at the leaf end of the ion route by active recretion.

Several mechanisms can be employed for limitation of ion uptake or transport. For example, the negative pressures that prevail in the xylem of halotrees induce a forced ultrafiltration of the saline soil solution through the root cell membranes, enabling the uptake of water but leaving the salts outside the roots' surfaces. This is a very efficient process that remains functional even when roots had been exposed to metabolic poisons such as CO, DNP, or

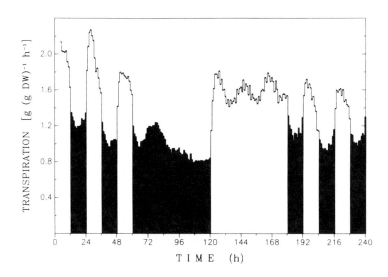

FIG. 15.3. Time course of transpiration of *Tamarix jordanis* (Sodom population). Illumination regime: 12 h light; 12 h dark, except for the marked period of continuous light or darkness. Plants treated with a basic nutrient solution (N) or nutrient solution plus 100 mol m^{-3} NaCl. (Courtesy of A. Solomon and Y. Waisel.)

anoxia (52). It seems, thus, that the membrane characteristics of mangrove root cells, which enable ultrafiltration of seawater, are static–structural rather than flexible–metabolic.

15.6.1. Ion composition and salt resistance

The effects of salinity are either direct, e.g., ion toxicity to the cells, or indirect, i.e., disturbing the uptake and transport of water and essential minerals. Salt resistance involves a certain component of ion selectivity. The barriers for sodium and for chloride ions are located at the root surface, at the endodermis, along the conducting system of the stem or inside the leaves. These barriers are related to the ionic composition at each site. For example, low-potassium roots have a higher preference for sodium than do high-potassium roots. A luxurious supply of potassium to plant roots, or to leaf cells, would increase its competitive inhibition of Na uptake and, thus, may contribute to the plants' salt resistance (53,54). Similarly, Ca^{2+} counteracts the effects of sodium or of other toxic ions by reducing their uptake and/or their influence (Refs. 55, 56; Hagemeyer and Waisel, unpublished data).

Salt resistance is dependent on the salt content of the plants, and large variations in salt content exist among various taxa and even within closely related species (57).

15.6.2. Ion localization

The precise distribution of ions in leaf cells of halotrees constitutes the basis for distinction between the various mechanisms of salt resistance that depend on avoidance, removal, or compartmentation of ions. Nevertheless, only little information regarding those aspects is available for halotrees.

Ultrastructural observations of mesophyll cells of the mangrove *Aegiceras corniculatum* Blanco has indicated that Cl^- is accumulated inside the cytosol of the leaf cells. The vacuoles in the leaves of *Aegiceras* are of two types: (a) a type low in Cl^- but high in organic solutes and (b) a type high in Cl^- but low in organic solutes. The high-chloride cells may play a role in the transport of inorganic ions from the xylem across the mesophyll and into the salt glands (58).

Considerable accumulation of Na^+ and Cl^- occurs in the cytosol of leaves of *Suaeda monoica* (59,60). Thus, salt resistance of salt tolerant plants does not always depend on the removal of surplus Na^+ or Cl^- from the cytoplasm.

Localization of Na and Cl in cells of the different types of assimilating tissues of *Suaeda monoica* further complicates the situation. Result of X-ray microanalysis of cross sections of such leaves (Fig. 15.4) have shown low Na signals for cells of the inner chlorenchyma as well as for those of the water tissue. Sodium content was high only in the outer chlorenchyma, where it reached over 50% of the cells dry mass. Distribution of Cl was different, with the highest signals detected in inner chlorenchyma (15–25% of the cells' dry mass). Inverse relationships between the two ions were found for the outer chlorenchyma and for the epidermis (60). Estimation of the concentrations in the outer chlorenchyma cells have yielded 1 kmol m^{-3} Na^+ and 0.3 kmol m^{-3} Cl^-. The concentrations of the inner chlorenchyma cells were only 0.3 kmol m^{-3} of Na^+ but 0.6 kmol m^{-3} for Cl^-. Thus, precise localization of ions in the succulent leaves of *Suaeda* shows that despite the high concentrations of Na^+ and Cl^- accumulate in the assimilating tissues, no interference with their functions was found. Moreover, the selective distribution of the various ions indicates that the enzymes of each of the cell types are exposed to different internal chemical environments (61). In some cases it was shown that Na can be employed in the regulation of stomatal opening and thus as a substitute for the unavailability of K (62).

15.6.3. Interactions with microorganisms

Roots of *Rhizophora mangle* L., *Avicennia germinans* L., and *Laguncularia racemosa* L. Gaertn. are heavily colonized by several types of bacteria. Some of the populations are concentrated in the intercellular spaces of the outer layer of the cortex, but most are found in the mucigel layer and in the sloughed cells (63).

The most important interaction between halotrees and bacteria concerns the biological fixation of nitrogen; the roots deliver carbon and energy while the bacteria supply fixed nitrogen. Although this is an essential feature in natural habitats, very little is known about characteristics of such symbiosis

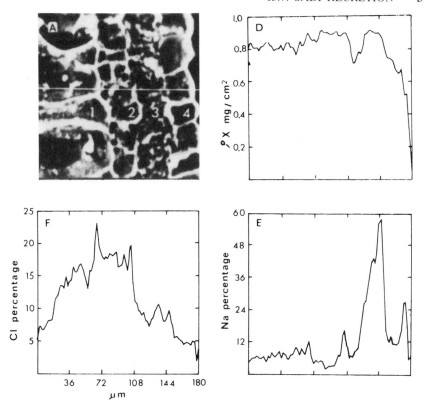

FIG. 15.4. Electron probe X-ray microanalysis of a leaf cross section of *Suaeda monoica*: (A) secondary electron image, with the analysis line crossing; (1) water tissue, (2) inner chlorenchyma, (3) outer chlorenchyma, (4) epidermis; (D) profile of ρ_x values; (E) Na percentage profile; (F) Cl percentage profile. (Adapted from Ref. 60.)

in halophytic species. *Casuarina equisetifolia* J.R.&G. Forst., a halotree of the eastern coast of Australia, has nitrogen-fixing nodules. The development of the nodules was positively correlated with NaCl concentrations in the 50–100-mol m^{-3} range but was reduced at NaCl concentrations of >200 mol m^{-3}. However, the rates of nitrogen fixation were negligibly affected by salinity up to a concentration of 200 mol m^{-3} NaCl. Even at 500 mol m^{-3} NaCl, N fixation was reduced to only 40% of the control (64). This is not unique for *Casuarina* since roots of mangroves also live in close association with several N-fixing bacteria (63). Thus, nitrogen fixation by halotrees can occur even under highly saline conditions and should be further studied in detail.

15.7. Salt recretion

Ions that enter the plant through its roots move with the transpiration stream upward via the stems and into the crowns. Unless such ions are removed from sensitive sites, the leaves and meristems might become salt-poisoned. Some halotrees are capable of overcoming the injurious effects of high internal salt concentrations, or extending the threshold of lethality. This is achieved by recretion of excess salts via salt glands or by accumulation in salt bladders (1,65,66).

Salt glands, initially described as "chalk glands," were first discovered for halotrees in the midnineteenth century (67,68). Salt glands are common in several tree species, mostly among the hydrohalophytes. In some species salt is recreted by epidermal salt glands, whereas in others, it is accumulated in bladder cells that are later sloughed off. In the past, recretion was interpreted as the major mechanism responsible for regulation of the salt content of halophytes. However, a quantitative evaluation of the role of salt glands in the salt balance of *Avicennia marina* has shown that the control of the salt content of those trees is primarily dependent on the exclusion of salts outside their roots (43). Exclusion at the root surface controls some 80% of the sea salts that are carried toward the roots by the transpiration stream, and which would have entered the plants otherwise. Of the ions that still pass the root barriers and reach the leaves, the salt glands are capable of recreting only 40%. The rates of salt transport into the shoots and the rates of their recretion by salt glands, show diurnal fluctuations with one peak occurring during noon and another one around midnight (43,69).

Preconditioning of plants in low salt solutions improves the subsequent capability of the plants to balance their ion content and tolerate higher salt concentrations (70). Mangrove trees that had been subjected to full-strength seawater, recrete and exclude NaCl better, than those grown on 10% seawater (71). The energy costs for such an increased efficiency were negligible, since plants of both salt treatments were similar in their photosynthetic activity and water-use efficiency.

At the cellular level, recretion starts with accumulation of ions in microvacuoles, followed by their movement to the outer cell surface. There, the microvacuoles fuse with the plasmalemma, and their brine content is subsequently emptied outward (72).

The structure of the salt glands may vary in different species. The salt glands of *Avicennia* consist of 2–4 collecting cells, one disklike stalk cell, and 8–12 recreting cells. There are some differences between the cells of the abaxial and those of the adaxial sides of the leaves. The recreting cells have a dense cytoplasm, with numerous microvacuoles and a large amount of endoplasmic reticulum (73). They also have large nuclei, numerous mitochondria and Golgi bodies, and a perforated cuticle on top. The stalk cell is characterized by cutinized side walls and several plasmodesmata. The collecting cells look almost like the other epidermal cells, although their nuclei are often large (74).

Two types of leaves are found on *Avicennia* trees: pilose and hairless. Salt recretion by the pilose type is high, because they recrete from both sides. Salt is recreted by the hairless leaves only from one side of the leaf. Recretion is nearly equal during the day or during the night (75).

The salt glands of *Tamarix* are constituted of four pairs of cells: two collecting cells and six recreting ones (Fig. 15.5). Salt glands of *Tamarix aphylla* trees, grown on saline media, contain more ribosomes and polysomes than do glands of salt-free plants (76). The collecting cells are highly vacuolated, and the recreting cells are rich with microvacuoles (72). The salt gland of *Aegiceras* consists of one large collecting basal cell with several recretory cells. The recretory cells resemble those of *Tamarix*, except for the wall protuberances that are absent in *Aegiceras*. There are many plasmodesmata between the recreting cells and the collecting one. The basal cell of *Aegiceras* is surrounded by a cuticular cover (77).

The salt gland of *Aegialitis*, like all the glands of the Plumbaginaceae, is multicellular, consisting of 16 cells. The collecting cells are connected with the recreting cells by numerous plasmodesmata. The cuticle of the outer walls of the gland cells is thick and is perforated on the upper and lower sides (77).

Several factors determine the rate of salt recretion. These include salt composition and age of the tissues, water status, temperature, light, and oxygen availability. The salt content of the shoot is often determined by the salt concentration in the root medium. However, the concentration of the recreted fluid is in many cases higher than that of the root medium (1,78–80). Large quantities of concentrated brine (e.g., 100 mg brine 100 mg leaf DW^{-1} 24 h^{-1}) are recreted. Under dry atmospheric conditions, the water of the recreted brine evaporates and the salts crystallize to form "salt scales" (e.g., in *Avicennia*) or "salt whiskers" (e.g., in *Tamarix*). Maximal rates of recretion was obtained when the salt concentrations of the root zone exceeded the critical value for the species (e.g., 400 mol m^{-3} NaCl and 2.5 mol m^{-3} $CaCl_2$ for *Tamarix aphylla*).

In most species, the recreted solution consists mainly of NaCl. Nevertheless, many other inorganic and organic substances are also present. Phosphate, K^+, Ca^{2+}, Mg^{2+}, SO_4^{2-}, NO_3^-, Fe, and Cd were found in the recreta of *Tamarix aphylla*, whenever the plants were exposed to those elements in the root medium (51,53,81). In general, the preference of recretion was in the order Na > K > Ca >, although the rates depended on the relative concen-

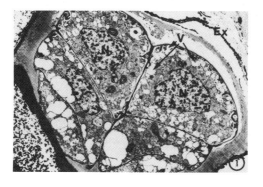

FIG. 15.5. Cross section of a salt gland of *Tamarix aphylla*. (Courtesy W.W. Thomson.)

trations of those ions in the medium (1,78,81). Only one population of *Tamarix jordanis* recreted more K^+ than Na^+ (Solomon and Waisel, unpublished data).

In some mangrove trees, e.g., in *Aegialitis annulata* R. Br., significant amounts of Ca^{2+} were recreted when the concentration of NaCl in the root medium was reduced (75,82).

The Na^+/Cl^- ratio in the recreted brine increases with increasing NaCl concentration of the root medium, with Na recretion becoming more prominent (83).

Salt can be removed from sensitive sites in plant leaves, also by salt bladders (84). A salt bladder is an epidermal structure, consisting of a huge bladder cell supported by 1–4 stalk cells (Fig. 15.6). In some species the bladders are produced only by very young leaves, whereas in others they are continuously produced, almost throughout the lifespan of those leaves. Salt is accumulated inside the bladder until it reaches maturation. Then, either the whole bladder cell breaks and falls off its stalk, or it collapses *in situ* and its brine content is spread over the outer surface of the leaf. Both types of bladders would relieve the leaf mesophyll of the surplus salts.

Salt accumulating bladder cells are common in various genera of the Chenopodiaceae, i.e., *Atriplex, Halimione, Obione, Chenopodium,* and *Salsola* (85). However, they also occur in several genera of other families.

15.8. Salinity and metabolism

Since trees cannot avoid salt uptake completely, the metabolic activity of their cells must withstand an environment of high ionic activity. Indeed, in halophytes all metabolic systems respond to salinity.

Salinity, even at relatively low concentrations, reduces the photosynthesis of many plants. The effects of salinity involve the induction of a higher

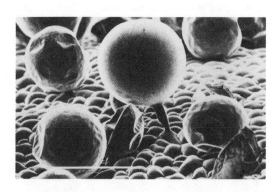

FIG. 15.6. A bladder hair of *Atriplex hortensis*. (Adapted from Ref. 85. Courtesy of Ms. Ute Schirmer and Prof. S.W. Breckle.)

resistance to gas diffusion. Only subsequently can one observe a decrease in the metabolic capability of the leaf cells to fix CO_2 (86). Salt stress increases respiration, routing assimilates from a growth path into an increased use for maintenance.

Another major effect of salinity, or of water stress, on plants is the promotion of senescence, which is further accelerated by the subsequent production and release of abscisic acid and ethylene. ABA affects the transport and use of water and, therefore, also plant growth under stress conditions (87). A decrease in the availability of cytokinins may also cause growth inhibition of salt-stressed trees. Exogenous addition of cytokinins to salt-treated plants improved their performance and raised metabolic activity to the levels of nonstressed plants (88).

Early senescence is accompanied by low rates of plant growth, as well as by a short growth season. Under high salinity, trees of *Populus euphratica* develop only the preformed leaves of their buds. No additional leaves are produced after the expansion of the preexisting ones, and the buds become dormant by early summer (22). Concomitantly, under conditions of low salinity, growth of neighboring trees continues for several months, extension growth is substantial, and many more leaves are produced on each branch.

Some halotrees have developed unique systems for adaptation to salinity, and the efficient system for carbon trapping of *Suaeda monoica* can be used as an example. Leaves of this species have three distinct layers of photosynthesizing cells. The outer, subepidermal, layer is characterized by a high activity of phosphoenol pyruvate carboxylase (PEPcase, EC 4.1.1.31), but with no apparent activity of ribulose bisphosphate carboxylase (RuBPcase, EC 4.1.1.39). The second layer of chlorenchyma is characterized by a very high activity of RuBPcase, but with only traces of activity of PEPcase. The inner layer of the photosynthesizing cells consists of the water tissue, where both enzymes are active, although at slower rates (61). During photosynthesis, CO_2 is fixed by the PEPcase of the outer photosynthesizing cell layer, is accumulated as aspartate, and is then transported into the inner chlorenchyma. There it is decarboxylated, and the resulting CO_2 is refixed *in situ* by the RuBPcase to produce sugars. Thus, the leaves of *Suaeda* can trap not only CO_2 from the atmosphere but also most of the CO_2 that is released by respiration inside their own tissues. Indeed, *Suaeda* plants have a very low compensation point, which is similar to that of all other C_4 plants.

Certain enzymes that are regarded as salt-sensitive can be modified into "salt tolerant" forms. Such a modification would raise the resistance of salt affected plants, and would permit normal metabolic activity despite the high content of salt in the cytosol. In some halophytes, the activity of certain enzymes (e.g., glutamine synthetase EC 1.4.7.1) can be even salt-stimulated (89). This is a result of production of new isoenzymes and the accumulation of protectants. Changes in the characteristics of PEPcase of *Suaeda monoica* were obtained *in vitro*, following the addition of NaCl and of various organic protectants into the extraction and reaction mixtures (Table 15.2). Similar

Table 15.2. Effects of NaCl on some properties of PEP-pretreated PEPcase from *Suaeda monoica*[a]

Parameter[b]	Concentration of NaCl (mol m^{-3})		
	0	100	300
n_H	0.83	1.08	1.23
V_{max}	0.68	1.36	0.42
K'	2.60	5.09	5.16

[a]After Ref. 91.
[b]V_{max} given in μmol CO_2 (mg protein)$^{-1}$ min^{-1}; K' in mol m^{-3} PEP; K' and n_H were estimated from the Hill plot, where n_H is the slope and $K' = [S] \times 0.5$.

changes were obtained when the concentration of the substrate had been elevated. Such treatments changed the K_m and V_{max} of the enzyme and modified it from a salt-sensitive configuration into a salt-tolerant one (90, 91).

The osmotic potential of halophyte cells is adjusted following the accumulation of inorganic ions as well as the production of organic compatible solutes. Betaine is one of the most common compatible solutes whose accumulation is typical for salt-resistant trees. Betaine occurs mostly in the shoots, where its concentrations may reach 1 kmol m^{-3}, much more than those in the roots (92). Such a high accumulation of compatible solutes, under salt stress, was thought to be a basic process of adaptation, especially for plants with a low content of inorganic ions.

Salt tolerance of plant cells can be increased by the use of such compatible solutes, which act as osmoregulators and enzyme protectants. Such a role will enable salt-sensitive enzymes to operate despite the massive presence of salts. One should, however, distinguish between the general protectants (betaine, proline, polyols etc.), that are active only when present in high concentrations (0.2–1.0 kmol m^{-3}) and the specific stabilizers (including the substrates of the very same enzymes) that operate in minute concentrations (mol m^{-3}) (Paleg, personal communication). In some cases, also the products, and not only the substrates, may serve as protectants.

The *in vitro* salt tolerance of PEPcase depends on its preconditioning as well as on the concentration of PEP in the medium. At high PEP concentrations, PEPcase of *Suaeda monoica* is more tolerant to NaCl and its activity is even accelerated (91). Similar protection of several other enzymes by their substrates has been reported. PEP and pyruvate protect the activity of pyruvate kinase. Glutamate protects the activity of glutamate synthetase whereas 2-PGA preserves the activity of enolase (93).

Even full protection of the operating enzymes within a plant cell may not furnish a comprehensive answer for plant salt resistance. For example, salinity had increased also the activity of the degrading enzymes, RNAase and DNAase (94). Acceleration of such activities would not contribute to the salt resistance of those plants. Protection of all enzymes might, therefore, involve certain problems.

15.9. Resistance to salt spray

Exposed habitats along wind-swept seacoasts are, as a rule, amply sprayed with seawater. Plants of such habitats suffer from direct exposure of their shoots to the spray, and salt-scorched trees can be detected as far as several kilometers from stormy coasts. As a result, exposed coasts are poor in trees, especially under arid and semiarid climates.

The few trees that exist in exposed coastal habitats are mostly salt-avoiders, since their main growth season is restricted to the spray-free summer months. During winter time, the plants are not affected by the spray, because most of the salt is washed off their shoots by the rains. The most severe damage to the trees is caused during the spring season, when storms cause an intensive spray but there is no more rain to wash the salt off.

Resistance to soil salinity and tolerance to salt spray seem to involve two different systems. Intraspecific and interspecific variations in spray tolerance among coastal trees have no relation to their resistance to soil salinity. Most trees of the genus *Tamarix* are sensitive to salt spray. Nevertheless, when several populations of this genus were planted together on the Mediterranean coast of Israel, one of them (the Nitzanim ecotype) exhibited conspicuous spray tolerance with growth rates far above those of others (95). Thus, the heterogeneity in spray tolerance of various taxa of trees, could form a good basis for selection of halotrees for coastal habitats.

15.10. Epilog

Salt resistance is a coordinated effort of plants to adapt to an external stress. The resistance can be based on avoidance, which would be dependent on the structural and physiological characteristics of the whole plant, and on the capability of the cellular organelles to confront high concentrations of ions (Table 15.3).

Protection of plants against Na inflow cannot yield a feasible solution. Some ions always penetrate into the xylem via uncontrolled gaps of the apoplast and eventually concentrate in the shoot. The size of such gaps in the endodermal cylinder of roots tends, in many crop plants, to increase under salt stress, because of the damage to root-cell membranes by NaCl (96). Therefore, salt exclusion might play a limited role in the salt resistance of only a few plant species. Many halophytes have a tendency to accumulate NaCl in their shoots, rather than to exclude it. Such plants have an obligatory salt requirement, and some of their enzymes are negatively affected when salt is lacking.

Thus, what might be the reasonable alternatives for increasing salt resistance of trees? Apparently, such systems should include not only the capability to manipulate their structure and metabolism but also the ability to change the microenvironment within their cells. The employment of efficient com-

Table 15.3. Modes of plant adaptation to salinity[a]

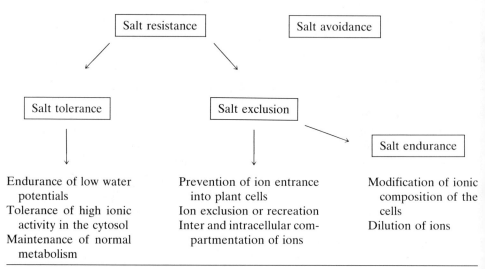

Salt tolerance	Salt exclusion	Salt endurance
Endurance of low water potentials	Prevention of ion entrance into plant cells	Modification of ionic composition of the cells
Tolerance of high ionic activity in the cytosol	Ion exclusion or recreation	Dilution of ions
Maintenance of normal metabolism	Inter and intracellular compartmentation of ions	

[a]Adapted from Refs. 1 and 97.

patible solutes to the cells of halotrees to provide suitable osmotica and to protect the metabolic systems against NaCl seems at present to be the best plant characteristic for selection and breeding of future halotrees.

15.11. References

1. Y. Waisel, *Biology of Halophytes*, Academic Press, New York 1972.
2. Y. Waisel, "Screening for salt tolerance," *Proc. IPI Symp. Lauvaine*, June, 1989, pp. 117–129.
3. H. Walter and S.W. Breckle, *Ecological Systems of the Geobiosphere*, Springer-Verlag, Berlin, 1986.
4. R.J. Reimold and W.H. Queen, *Ecology of Halophytes*, Academic Press, New York, 1974.
5. A.A. Shakhov, *Salt Resistance of Plants: an Ecologo-biological and Ecologo-physiological study*, Akad. Nauk (Academy of Science) USSR, Moscow, 1952.
6. E. Arieli, R. Arieli, and S. Lev-Yadun, "Female ratio of *Salix acmophylla* trees growing in the Upper Jordan valley," *Rotem*, **21**, 39–48 (1986).
7. Y. Waisel, "Germination behavior of some halophytes," *Bull. Res. Counc. Israel*, **6D**, 187–189 (1958).
8. Y. Waisel, "Ecological studies of *Tamarix aphylla* (L.) Karst. I. Distribution and reproduction," *Phyton*, **15**, 7–17 (1960).

9. F.P. Pannier, "El efecto dez distintas concentraciones salinas sobre el desarrollo de *Rhiziphora mangle* L.," *Acta Cient. Venez.*, **10**, 68–78 (1959).

10. B.F. Clough, "Growth and salt balance of the mangroves *Avicennia marina* (Forssk.) Vierh. and *Rhizophora stylosa* Griff. in relation to salinity," *Aust. J. Plant Physiol.*, **11**, 419–430 (1984).

11. J.J. Oertli, "Extracellular salt accumulation, a possible mechanism of salt injury in plants," *Agrochimica*, **12**, 461–469 (1968).

12. J.J. Oertli, "Gains of water potential in plants," *Studia Biophysica*, **115**, 95–103 (1986).

13. Y. Zohar, *The Autecology of Eucalyptus occidentalis Endl.*, Ph.D. thesis, Tel Aviv University, 1974.

14. Y. Vaadia and Y. Waisel, "Physiological processes as affected by water balance," in R.M. Hagen, H.R. Haise, and T.W. Edminster, eds., *Irrigation of Agricultural Lands*, Am. Soc. Agr., Madison, Wisconsin, 1967, pp. 354–372.

15. E. Zamski, "Does successive cambia differentiation in *Avicennia* depend on leaf and branch initiation?, *Israel J. Bot.*, **30**, 57–64 (1981).

16. E. Zamski, "The mode of secondary growth and the three-dimensional structure of the phloem in *Avicennia*," *Bot. Gaz.*, **140**, 67–76 (1979).

17. A. Fahn, *Plant Anatomy*, Pergamon, Oxford, 1974.

18. A. Fahn and M.H. Zimmermann, "Development of the successive cambia in *Atriplex halimus* (Chenopodiaceae)," *Bot. Gaz.*, **143**, 353–357 (1982).

19. B.P. Strogonov, *Physiological Basis of Salt Tolerance of Plants (as Affected by Various Types of Salinity)*, Akad. Nauk USSR; translated by the Israel Progr. Sci. Trans., Jerusalem, 1964.

20. G.J.C.M. van Vliet, "Wood anatomy of Rhizophoraceae," *Leiden Bot. Ser.*, **3**, 20–75 (1976).

21. J.S. Sperry, M.T. Tyree, and J. Donnelley, "Vulnerability of xylem to embolism in a mangrove vs. inland species of Rhizophoraceae," *Physiol. Plant.*, **74**, 276–283 (1988).

22. N. Liphschitz and Y. Waisel, "Effects of environment on relations between extension and cambial growth of *Populus euphratica* Oliv," *New Phytol.*, **69**, 1059–1064 (1970).

23. S. Bairamov and G. Rzakuliev, "The growth and development of the root systems of *Reaumuria oxiana* and *R. turkestanica*," *Izv. Akad. Nauk Turkm. USSR*, 1979, pp. 82–84 (Biosis No. 70022465).

24. Y. Waisel and S.W. Breckle, "Differences in responses of various radish roots to salinity," *Plant and Soil*, **104**, 191–194 (1987).

25. W.A. Charlton, "Lateral root initiation," in Y. Waisel, A. Eshel and U. Kafkafi, eds., *Plant Roots: The Hidden Half*, Marcel Dekker, New York, 1991.

26. Y. Waisel and A. Eshel, "Multiform behavior of various constituents of one root system," in Y. Waisel, A. Eshel, and U. Kafkafi, eds., *Plant Roots: The Hidden Half*, Marcel Dekker, New York, 1991.

27. D.T. Clarkson, "Root structure and sites of ion uptake," in Y. Waisel, A. Eshel and U. Kafkafi, eds., *Plant Roots: The Hidden Half*, Marcel Dekker, New York, 1991.

28. W. Macnae, "A general account of the fauna and flora of mangrove swamps and forests in the Indo-West-Pacific region," *Adv. Mar. Biol.*, **6**, 73–270 (1968).

29. M.A. Hajibagheri, A.R. Yeo, and T. Flowers, "Salt tolerance in *Suaeda maritima*. Fine structure and ion concentration in the apical region of roots," *New Phytol.*, **99**, 331–344 (1985).

30. J.R. Lawton, A. Todd, and D.K. Naidoo, "Preliminary investigations into the structure of the roots of the mangroves *Avicennia marina* and *Bruguiera gymnorhiza* in relation to ion uptake," *New Phytol.*, **88**, 713–722 (1981).

31. P.F. Scholander, L. van Dam, and S.I. Scholander, "Gas exchange in the roots of mangroves," *Am. J. Bot.*, **42**, 92–98 (1955).

32. W. Grosse and P. Schroder, "Oxygen supply of roots by gas transport in Alder trees," *Z. Naturforsch.*, **39**, 1186–1188 (1984).

33. P. Schroder, Proc. 6th Congr. FESPP, Split. poster No. 3.16 (1988).

34. R. Karschon and Y. Zohar, *Effects of Flooding and of Irrigation Water Salinity on Eucalyptus camaldulensis Dehn. from Three Seed Sources*, ARS Volcani Center, Israel, Leaflet No. 54 (1975).

35. F.P. Pannier, "Estudio fiziologico sobre la viviparia de *Rhiziphora mangle* L.," *Acta Cient. Venez.*, **13**, 184–197 (1962).

36. Y. Waisel and G. Pollak, "Estimation of the water stresses in the active root zone of some native halophytes in Israel," *J. Ecol.*, **57**, 789–794 (1969).

37. J.M. O'Leary, "The effect of salinity on permeability of roots to water," *Israel J. Bot.*, **18**, 1–9 (1969).

38. R.S. Ownbey and B.E. Mahall, "Salinity and root conductivity: differential responses of a coastal succulent halophyte *Salicornia virginica* and a weedy glycophyte *Raphanus sativus*," *Physiol. Plant.*, **57**, 189–195 (1983).

39. P. Neumann, "The effects of salinity, Ca and osmotic pressure on hydraulic conductivity and growth of roots," *Bot. Soc. Israel Proc. 1989 Meeting* (1989).

40. J. Rozema, W.A.J. van Diggelen, M. van Esbroek, R. Broekman, and H. Punte, "Occurrence and ecological significance of vesicular–arbuscular mycorrhiza in the salt marsh environment," *Acta Bot. Neerl.*, **35**, 457–467 (1986).

41. G.W. Paltridge, "On the shape of trees," *J. Theor. Biol.*, **38**, 111–137 (1973).

42. Y. Leshem and E. Levison, "Regulation mechanisms in the salt mangrove *Avicennia marina* growing on the Sinai littoral," *Ecol. Plant.*, **7**, 167–176 (1972).

43. Y. Waisel, A. Eshel, and M. Agami, "Salt balance of leaves of the mangrove *Avicennia marina*," *Physiol. Plant.*, **67**, 67–72 (1986).

44. J.J. Oertli, "The stability of water under tension in the xylem," *Z. Pflanzenphysiol.*, **65**, 195–205 (1971).

45. M.T. Tyree and M.A. Dixon, "Water stress induced cavitation and embolism in some woody plants," *Physiol. Plant.*, **66**, 397–405 (1986).

46. J. Sperry, J.R. Donelly, and M.T. Tyree, "Seasonal occurrence of xylem embolism in sugar maple (*Acer saccharum*)," *Am. J. Bot.*, **75**, 1212–1218 (1988).

47. P.F. Scholander, H.T. Hammel, E.D. Bradstreet, and E.A. Hemmingsen, "Sap pressure in vascular plants," *Science*, **148**, 339–346 (1965).

48. Y. Waisel, N. Liphschitz, and Z. Kuller, "Patterns of water movement in trees and shrubs," *Ecology*, **53**, 520–523 (1972).

49. Y. Waisel, "Ecological studies of *Tamarix aphylla* (L.) Karst. II. The water economy," *Phyton (Buenos Aires)*, **15**, 17–27 (1960).

50. J. Hagemeyer and Y. Waisel, "Influence of NaCl, Cd(NO₃)₂ and air humidity on transpiration of *Tamarix aphylla*," *Physiol. Plant.*, **75**, 280–284 (1989).

51. J. Hagemeyer and Y. Waisel, "An endogenous circadian rhythm of transpiration in *Tamarix aphylla*," *Physiol. Plant.*, **70**, 133–138 (1987).

52. P.F. Scholander, "How mangroves desalinate seawater," *Physiol. Plant*, **21**, 251–261 (1968).

53. Y. Waisel, "Ecological studies of *Tamarix aphylla* (L.) Karst. III. The salt economy," *Plant and Soil*, **13**, 356–364 (1960).

54. D.W. Rains and E. Epstein, "Preferential absorption of potassium by leaf tissue of the mangrove *Avicennia marina* an aspect of halophytic competence in coping with salt," *Aust. J. Biol. Sci.*, **20**, 847–857 (1967).

55. Y. Waisel, "The effect of calcium on the uptake of monovalent ions by excised barley roots," *Physiol. Plant.*, **15**, 709–724 (1962).

56. P.A. LaHaye and E. Epstein, "Salt toleration by plants: Enhancement with calcium," *Science*, **166**, 395–396 (1969).

57. N.A. Mirazai and S.W. Breckle, "Salzverhaltnisse in Chenopodiaceen Nord-Afganistan," *Bot. Jahrb. Syst.*, **99**, 565–578 (1978).

58. R.F.M. van Steveninck, W.D. Armstrong, P.D. Peters, and T.A. Hall, "Ultrastructural localization of ions. III. Distribution of chloride in mesophyll cells of mangrove (*Aegiceras corniculatum* Blanco). Aust.," *J. Plant Physiol.*, **3**, 367–376 (1976).

59. Y. Waisel and A. Eshel, "Localization of ions in the mesophyll cells of the succulent halophyte *Suaeda monoica* Forssk. by X-ray microanalysis," *Experientia*, **27**, 230–232 (1970).

60. A. Eshel and Y. Waisel, "Distribution of sodium and chloride in leaves of *Suaeda monoica*," *Physiol. Plant.*, **46**, 151–154 (1979).

61. A. Shomer Ilan, R. Neumann-Ganmore, and Y. Waisel, "Biochemical specialization of photosynthetic cell layers and carbon flow paths in *Suaeda monoica*," *Plant Physiol.*, **64**, 963–965 (1979).

62. A. Eshel, Y. Waisel, and A. Ramati, *Proc. 7th Interntl. Colloq. "Plant Analysis and Fertilizer Problems,"* Supp. Hannover, Germany, 1974.

63. D.A. Zuberer and W.S. Silver, "Nitrogen fixation (acetylene reduction) and the microbial colonization of mangrove roots," *New Phytol.*, **82**, 467–472 (1979).

64. B.H. Ng, "The effects of salinity on growth, nodulation and nitrogen fixation of *Casuarina equisetifolia*," *Plant Soil*, **103**, 123–125 (1987).

65. G. Pollak and Y. Waisel, "Ecophysiology of salt excretion in *Aeluropus litoralis* (Graminae)," *Physiol. Plant.*, **47**, 177–184 (1979).

66. N. Liphschitz and Y. Waisel, "Adaptation of plants to saline environments: salt excretion and glandular structure," in D. Sen and K.S. Rajpurohit, eds., *Contribution to the Ecology of Halophytes*, W. Junk, The Hague, 1982, pp. 197–214.

67. G. Volkens, *Die Flora der Aegiptisch-Arabischen Wuste auf grundlage Anatomische-Physiologiscer Forschungen dargestelt*, Gebrunder Borntraeger, Berlin, 1887.

68. R. Marloth, "Zur bedeutung der Salz abscheidenen Drusen der Tamariscineen," *Ber. d. Bot. Ges.*, **5**, 319–324 (1887).

69. Y. Waisel, "Salt excretion by *Avicennia marina*," in A.J. Davy, ed., *Ecological Processes in Coastal Environments*, Univ. East Anglia, Norwich, 1977.

70. A.J. Trewavas, "Resource allocation under poor growth conditions. A major role for growth substances in developmental plasticity," in D.H. Jenings and A.J. Trewavas, eds., *Plasticity in Plants*, Soc. Exp. Bot. Symp., **40**, 31–76 (1986).

71. O. Bjorkman, and B. Demmig, *Carnegie Inst. of Washington Yearbook 1985*, pp. 21 (1985).

72. K.A. Platt-Aloia, R.D. Bliss, and W.W. Thomson, "Lipid–lipid interactions and membrane fusion in plant salt glands," in W.W. Thomson, J.B. Mudd, and M. Gibbs, eds., *Biosynthesis and Function of Plant Lipids*, Am. Soc. Plant Physiol., Rockville, MD, 1983.

73. P.M. Drennan, P. Berjak, J.R. Lawton, and N.W. Pammenter, "Ultrastructure of salt glands of the mangrove, *Avicennia marina* (Forssk.) Vierh., as indicated by the use of selective membrane staining," *Planta*, **172**, 176–183 (1987).

74. A. Fahn and C. Shimony, "Development of the glandular and nonglandular leaf hairs of *Avicennia marina* (Forssk.) Vierh.," *J. Linn. Soc.*, **74**, 34–46 (1977).

75. M.L. Schnetter, "Investigations on salt secretion of the leaves of *Avicennia germinans*," *Flora*, **177**, 157–165 (1985).

76. W.W. Thomson and L.L. Liu, "Ultrastructural features of the salt gland of *Tamarix aphylla* (L.) Karst.," *Planta*, **73**, 201–220 (1967).

77. S. Cardale and C.D. Field, "The structure of the salt gland of *Aegiceras corniculata*," *Planta*, **99**, 183 (1971).

78. P.F. Scholander, H.T. Hammel, E.A. Hemmingsen, and W. Grey, "Salt balance in mangroves," *Plant Physiol.*, **37**, 722–729 (1962).

79. W.L. Berry, "Characteristics of salts secreted by *Tamarix aphylla*," *Am. J. Bot.*, **57**, 1226–1230 (1970).

80. W.W. Thomson, "The structure and function of salt glands," in A. Poljakof-Mayber and J. Gale, eds., *Plants in Saline Environments*, Springer-Verlag, Berlin, 1975, pp. 118–148.

81. W.W. Thomson, W.L. Berry, and L.L. Liu, "Localization and secretion of salt by the salt glands of *Tamarix aphylla*," *Proc. Natl. Acad. Sci. (USA)*, **63**, 310–317 (1969).

82. C.D. Faraday and W.W. Thomson, "Functional aspects of salt glands of the Plumbaginaceae," *J. Exp. Bot.*, **37**, 1129–1135 (1986).

83. J. Hagemeyer and Y. Waisel, "Excretion of ions (Cd^{2+}, Li^+, Na^+, and Cl^-) by *Tamarix aphylla*," *Physiol. Plant.*, **73**, 541–546 (1988).

84. U. Berger-Landefeldt, "Beitrage zur Okologie der Pflanzen nordafrikanischer Salzpfanen," *Vegetatio*, **2**, 1–48 (1959).

85. U. Schirmer and S.W. Breckle, "The role of bladders for salt removal in some Chenopodiaceae (mainly *Atriplex* species)," in D. Sen and K.S. Rajpurohit, eds., *Contribution to the Ecology of Halophytes*, W. Junk, The Hague, 1982, pp. 215–231.

86. Z. Plaut, "Control of photosynthesis under salt and drought stress," *Bot. Soc. Israel Proc.* 1989 Meeting (1989).

87. L.J. Jovanovic, S. Pekic, S.A. Quarrie, and M. Ivanovic, *Proc. 6th FESPP Congress* Abstr. Nos. 9–12 (1987).

88. D. Kuiper, J. Schuit, P.J.C. Kuiper, and H. Lambers, "Actual cytokinin concentrations in plant tissue as screening method on salt resistance in cereals," in *Genetic Aspects of Plant Mineral Nutrition*, Proc. 3rd Interntl. Symp. FAL. Braunschweig (1988).

89. J. Boucaud, and J.P. Billard, "The glutamate synthetase EC. 6.3.1.2 of *Suaeda macrocarpa* var macrocarpa *in vivo* and *in vitro* action of NaCl," *Physiol. Plant.*, **53**, 558–564 (1981).

90. A. Shomer Ilan and Y. Waisel, "Effects of stabilizing solutes on salt activation of phosphoenolpyruvate carboxylase from various plant sources," *Physiol. Plant.*, **67**, 408–414 (1986).

91. A. Shomer Ilan, D. Moualem-Beno, and Y. Waisel, "Effects of NaCl on the properties of phosphoenol pyruvate carboxylase from *Suaeda monoica* and *Chloris gayana*," *Physiol. Plant.*, **65**, 72–78 (1985).

92. R. Storey and R.G.W. Jones, "Quaternary ammonium compounds in plants in relation to salt resistance," *Phytochemistry*, **16**, 447–454 (1977).

93. D. Beno and A. Shomer Ilan, "Effects of salinity on the activity ratio of two glycolytic enzymes," *Bot. Soc. Israel Proc.* 1989 Meeting (1989).

94. G.V. Udovenko and L.A. Chudinova, "Effect of salinization in plants differing in salt resistance," *Fiziol. Rast.*, **33**, 1166–1172 (1986).

95. Y. Waisel and J. Friedman, "Selection of *Tamarix* trees for planting on exposed coasts," *La Yaaran (The Forester)*, **15**, 1–4 (1965).

96. A.R. Yeo, M.E. Yeo, and T.J. Flowers, "The contribution of apoplastic pathway to sodium uptake by rice roots in saline conditions," *J. Exp. Bot.*, **38**, 1141–1153 (1987).

97. J. Levitt, *Responses of Plants to Environmental Stresses*, Academic Press, New York, 1980.

16 Sap Exudation

J.A. MILBURN

Department of Botany, The University of New England, Armidale,
New South Wales, Australia

and

J. KALLARACKAL

Plant Physiology Division, Kerala Forest Research Institute, Peechi,
Kerala, India

Contents

16.1. Introduction

Exudation can be natural or manipulated. Nectar secretion, exudation from salt glands, guttation, etc. fall into the former group. Examples of manipulated exudations are phloem sap exudation obtained by tapping palms or other plants and tapping of rubber tree.

Various structures are involved in the process of exudation, especially the vascular system, consisting of xylem and phloem, which transport water and assimilates. Laticifer systems perform functions, not yet understood. Resin ducts in gymnosperms carry oleoresins. In plants with natural exudation systems there are special structures, e.g., hydathodes for guttation, nectaries, salt glands, and other glands. In manipulated exudation, the collection of sap is achieved by slicing a part of the plant stem or inflorescence stalk or skillfully tapping the bark. Some insects like aphids suck plant sap using devices of amazing sophistication.

In the following paragraphs, we have attempted to review briefly recent advances in present knowledge of various types of exudation, indicating characteristic similarities and differences.

16.2. Watery sap containing solutes—from leafy plants

16.2.1. Guttation

Guttation is the secretion of liquid water from the leaf often through special structures called *hydathodes*. Hydathodes are usually located at the ends of xylem elements, often at the margins of leaves. Frey-Wyssling (23) reported guttation in 350 genera belonging to 115 families.

Guttation can also occur through stomata, as in some grasses and also from twigs and branches of trees. In red maple, it has been reported to occur from lenticels (24). Guttation is caused by root pressure built up by active ion transport into the xylem vessels of the root stele. Guttation occurs when the plant root system is active, provided external conditions are favorable. This is probably the reason why guttation is seen from young growing plants, usually at night when the air is very humid and transpiration is virtually zero. Nevertheless, it is rather surprising that many plants, especially trees, seldom exhibit guttation even when conditions are optimal.

Since guttation is driven by root pressure (ca. 0.1 MPa in most plants), the potential for guttation is unequivocal in plants up to a height of 10 m. It is probable that in trees, because of their large hydraulic capacitance, the equilibration of the plant's water potential with that of the soil takes so long that guttation cannot occur as in herbaceous plants. However, experimental evidence is needed to support this view. Guttation is partially controlled by internal factors, e.g., ion gradients and phytohormones (15) and environmental factors.

The rate of fluid exudation by guttation can be measured by absorbing the drops on weighed strips of filter paper or by measuring the flow in microcapillaries. Care should be taken not to mistake condensation for guttated fluid. Atmospheric precipitation occurs frequently under natural conditions.

Guttation fluid characteristically contains few inorganic ions. These ions resemble those of xylem fluid but are more dilute. This occurs because guttation fluid is exuded from a plant *after* absorption of the ions required for metabolism. The guttation fluid has an acidic pH, resembling xylem sap. Milburn and McLaughlin (52) suggested that guttation could be a mechanism of removing gas emboli following cavitation. Plants such as *Plantago* and *Tussilago* can cavitate severely by day and guttate freely by night.

16.2.2 Exudation due to root pressure

Exudation of fluid from detopped plants is a widely observed phenomenon. Root pressure is explained as a standing osmotic flow in which salt release to the xylem provides the osmotic pressure for water flow (2,3,37). The flow equation for root pressure is usually given as

$$J_v = \kappa(\psi_{si} - \psi_{so})\qquad(16.1)$$

where J_v is the exudation flux, ψ_{si} is the solute potential in the root cells, ψ_{so} is the solute potential outside, and κ is an hydraulic coefficient. This equation treats a root as a simple osmometer. Although this relationship can be supported by many experiments, it represents an oversimplification. Diurnal rhythms, inhibitors, temperature, respiration, pressure, etc. all seem to have a great influence on root pressure exudation (51).

Most measurements have been made on exuding root system of herbaceous plants and a few trees. Root pressures normally do not exceed 0.2 MPa. Exudate volumes have been found to vary greatly depending on the size of the root system, the species, soil moisture availability, and temperature. Birch trees yield 20–100 liters of sap in spring (38). Root exudation has rarely been cited for conifers but experimental induction of root pressure has been achieved in detopped conifers like *Abies, Picea,* and *Pinus* (40).

Root exudate consists mainly of ionic forms of micro and macro elements with small organic molecules like amides, amino acids, organic acids, and sugars, and very low concentrations of growth regulators such as gibberellins and cytokinins (30,64,77). The presence of inorganic ions in the root pressure exudates is understandable. However, the occurrence of organic substances like sugars, organic acids, and growth regulators reported in certain species needs further explanation. Among the various analytical studies done on xylem sap from woody plants, the most comprehensive are those on *Actinidia chinensis* (12), *Vitis rotundifolia* (1), and *Nicotiniana glauca* (30). The root exudate collected from the base of the stem cannot be considered to be true xylem sap in the plant because of influx and efflux of various solutes in wood, bark and root cortex (19) and also tapping of solutes by various sinks as the sap moves toward the top of the plant.

Although researchers have considered root exudation as a simple osmotic flow of fluid, the diurnal rhythm exhibited by a detopped root shows that it is not a simple osmometer. Metabolic processes must be involved in this phenomenon. Inhibitors such as KCN reduce the uptake of water and inhibit salt uptake. Milburn (57) argued that if water transport is affected in unison with ion secretion, the proposed osmometer is being affected through its capacity to regulate ψ_{si} via transport linked to metabolism and respiration. Other external factors which regulate the root pressure exudation are temperature, respiration, and pressure. Temperature may affect exudation by causing changes in the hydraulic conductivity of root cell membranes. The effect of respiration on root pressure exudation can be shown under anaerobic conditions. Exudation is reduced but is restored or enhanced by aerating the roots. The influence of pressure on exudation of the detopped root was demonstrated by Mees and Weatherley (46). When the root system was pressurised the exudation rate increased. Thus the hydraulic conductance of the root system increases as the pressure gradient increases.

16.2.3. Natural root exudation

Natural root exudation is of certain organic substances from the surface of intact roots. A wide range of substances, including carbohydrates and vitamins, are exuded from plant roots (66). This process is mainly responsible for the concentration of microorganisms including mycorrhizas in the rhizosphere (11). The quantity of substances exuded by the roots is dependent on both the respiration of microorganisms and the physical environment of the root (7,57).

Root exudation is difficult to study physiologically. Measurements on exudates sampled from plants grown hydroponically are criticized because they measure only water-soluble, diffusible exudates, taking no account of water-insoluble and nondiffusible substances. Nevertheless, most studies on root exudation have been made on hydroponic plants. Microorganisms consume the exudates rapidly. Sterile cultures overcome this problem. However, microorganisms are also believed to interact and stimulate root exudation by releasing hormones or similar substances (8). Hence sterile cultures are inappropriate systems to study root exudation as *in vivo*.

Little is known about the mechanism of exudation from roots or the site of release of the substances into the root apoplast. The movement of sugars within the root cortex has been shown to be via the symplast (13,57). Few studies are available on tree roots (66); our understanding of the phenomenon is mainly based on work with herbaceous plants.

16.2.4. Exudation of nectar

Nectar is an exhaustively studied aspect of plant exudation, mainly because of its commercial significance and interest to both botanists and apiculturists (9). The relation between nectar and pollinating insects has been appreciated for centuries.

Nectaries on floral parts are classified as floral nectaries; others are termed *extrafloral nectaries*. Nectaries may be provided with special vascular tissue or they may contact the regular vascular system of the plant. Structurally, a nectary consists of an epidermis with or without trichomes and subtended by a specialized parenchymatous tissue. For details on the structural aspects of nectaries, see Durkee (16) and Fahn (18).

The most common sugars present in the nectar are sucrose, glucose, and fructose. Apart from these, several other sugars (in minor quantities), vitamins, minerals and organic acids are present in the nectar (4,18,42). The physiological basis of nectar secretion is not fully understood. Wolff (81) put forward the view that the nectaries secrete excess nutrients. Frey-Wyssling (22) supported this view by citing the example of *Hevea*, where the extrafloral nectaries are most active when the growth is slow.

The technique of monitoring the excised nectaries in controlled environmental conditions has greatly helped in understanding their physiology (4,10,21,59). Isolated nectaries continue to secrete nectar showing that the secretory process is not dependant on a direct connection with the phloem sieve tubes. A continual supply of sugars to the secretory glands is essential for maintaining secretion of nectar. Nectaries cultured on distilled water cease to secrete nectar within a few hours (59).

Labeling studies have indicated that nectar secreted by extrafloral nectaries is modified phloem sap (4). Modification seems to be related to the anatomic specialization of nectary (43). The presence of glucose and fructose along with sucrose in the nectar indicates that sugar interconversion occurs in nectaries.

Factors influencing nectar secretion are still not defined conclusively. Earlier, studies stated that nectar secretion is greatly enhanced by high atmospheric humidity. Nectar is very hygroscopic, and the large volumes of "nectar" are caused by condensation of water from the atmosphere. Increased soil moisture also has a long-term effect on nectar secretion (18). Similarly, increased temperature can enhance nectar secretion. Nichol and Hall (59) found that optimum temperatures ranged from 5 to 35°C with a temperature coefficient of 1.8 for total sugar production between 20 and 30°C (lower than the 2.3 earlier reported by Findlay et al., Ref. 21). Sugar conversion, a temperature coefficient of 1.8, inhibition of secretion by metabolic inhibitors and anaerobiosis indicate that metabolic energy is expended during secretion. The sugar transport into the nectary is through either the apoplast (78) or the symplast (17,25,39) or both (59). Recently, the symplastic pathway has gained wider acceptance because there are plamodesmata in the walls separating the nectary parenchyma from the secreting cells.

Nectar is finally secreted via the plasmalemma (20). The plasmalemma is rich in ATPase (17,59), probably indicating that transport is active. Cytochalasin B and colchicine inhibit nectar secretion. The energy requirement for nectar secretion is met from respiration (43), and is estimated as 1–5 organic phosphate bonds, per sugar molecule moved through the nectary (21).

Since this is the only measurement of this kind, comparisons are difficult. Lüttge (42) attempted to link sugar transport in nectaries with proton co-transport but the results of his experiments are not conclusive.

16.2.5. Salt glands

Salt glands occur in several angiosperms; the most notable are halophytic mangroves, e.g., *Tamarix*, *Avicennia*, *Aegiceras*, and *Aegialitis*. Exudation from salt glands must not be mistaken for vascular exudation. Direct connection between the cells of the salt glands and the vascular elements is lacking.

Salt glands are embedded on the leaf surface, and their frequency range is $300–1000$ cm^{-2}. Those found in halophytes are generally multicellular. For example, the salt glands of *Tamarix aphylla* consist of only 8 cells, whereas those of *Avicennia* consist of more cells. Basically they consist of a few collecting cells to which the secretory cells are connected. The collecting cells have a large vacuole, and the secretory cells are densely cytoplasmic. For more details on the structural aspects of salt glands, see reviews by Fahn (18), Hill and Hill (29) and Chapter 15 in this book.

Physiologically, salt glands are of two types. The first type are on halophytes, which exude salt and water from the leaves. Water is lost by evaporation and salt is crystallized and is later redissolved in rainwater (e.g., *Tamarix*, *Aegiceras*, *Limonium*). The second type has salt hairs accumulating excess salts from the plant body (e.g., *Atriplex*). Here, water is not lost by evaporation. The entire gland with accumulated salts dies, and salts are shed with the gland. Some halophytes lack salt glands. The xylem fluid in the glandular species contain $\frac{1}{4}$ the salt concentration of that in seawater, whereas in nonglandular species it is $\frac{1}{30}$th of the seawater concentration (29). The rate of secretion via salt glands is in the range of $0.004–0.86$ mm^3 cm^{-2} leaf h^{-1} depending on the plant (29).

The mechanism of salt transport into the glands is relatively well understood. Salts absorbed by halophytes move through the vascular system and are finally translocated into the salt gland through the mesophyll cells. Lüttge (41) discussed in detail the uptake of ions from the xylem and their transport into the salt glands. The salt glands of mangroves should be seen as an important adaptation for excluding salts from plants. Such plants are continuously under physiological water stress; their survival depends on the successful elimination of toxic ions.

16.2.6. Pathological exudation

Several plants exude, as a result of pathological infection or physiological malfunctioning of the system. In the first category is a phenomenon termed *gummosis* because it results in the exudation of gumlike substances. This may be caused by microorganisms, insects, mechanical injury, or physiological disturbances in the plant. Gummosis is frequent in species belonging to Pru-

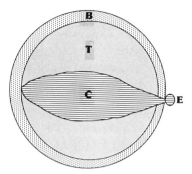

FIG. 16.1. Cross section of a "water blister" of a teak tree at the point of exudation E where there is a split in the bark B, allowing liquid in the crevice C to escape. The split causes a crevice in the heart-wood T.

noideae and Meliaceae (18) in which the cambium, instead of forming normal wood elements, gives rise to groups of parenchyma cells. Gummosis starts in the core of these parenchymatous groups, which then proceed to the periphery. A cavity is formed in the center and then fills with gum, and the cells disintegrate. In several species of *Acacia*, gummosis is a common phenomenon, e.g., *A. senegal*, from which gum-arabic is commercially extracted.

However, similar sap exudation occurs in the bark. A watery sap exudes from a hole created by damage in the main tree trunks of teak (*Tectona grandis*; Ref. 6). Fluid starts oozing from an oval hole on the main trunk of trees, more than 25 years old. The teak tree is deciduous and the maximum flow rate is found during the leafless state (Kallarackal and Seethalakshmi, unpublished data) and mainly at night. The flow rate has been monitored diurnally, and 100–200 ml of the fluid could be collected in a single night.

The condition begins with the formation of a "water blister" on the trunk that later exudes. When affected trees are felled, a large crevice can be seen in the trunk that is probably formed by splitting the wood (Fig. 16.1). Affected trees hold several litres of fluid inside this crevice. Possibly water collects in this crevice as root pressure exudate and later exudes through a crack due to pressurization. Chemical analysis of the fluid have shown that the cationic concentration is several times that of the xylem fluid (Kallarackal and Seethalakshmi, unpublished data). A high concentration of phenols noted in the fluid probably originates from the heartwood of the tree. The manner by which the crevice forms in the tree is not understood. It may arise from strains during growth.

16.3. Enriched sap—from leafless perennials

16.3.1. Enriched exudation driven by root pressure

Several species exhibit a pronounced root pressure (see Section 16.2.2) in the springtime before buds burst into leaf. Two mechanisms seem to be involved.

One is concerned with the refilling of xylem after winter freezing conditions; the other is the transport of reserve materials from winter storage in roots and ray tissue of trunks toward the developing buds.

Vines have been notorious for bleeding in the early spring and were subjected to quantitative physiological measurements by Hales (26). Vines became a favourite subject of Scholander et al. (65), who measured sap pressure gradients in the early spring. More recently Sperry et al. (70) studied the sap pressurisation as a means to restore conduction in the winter-embolized xylem, a suggestion made previously by Milburn (51). The pressurization generated in the roots drove sap vertically through the embolized vines, pushing air before it through the dry pit membranes. Eventually the pressure was sufficient to restore conduction in the xylem conduits; any entrapped bubbles would dissolve under the combined effects of root pressure and the effects of surface tension (see Chapters 6 and 7 in this book).

Birches (*Betula*) are cold-temperate trees that seem to be specially adapted to survive snowfall and freezing temperatures. Snow and ice storms can bend the branches to an incredible degree without serious breakage. With the onset of spring they exhibit considerable root pressures. In the USSR this phenomenon has been used as a small industry for many years. Russian peasants have traditionally tapped the trees to obtain the sap, which is slightly sugary in much the same way as sugar maple in the USA (described in detail, below). Sap is often fermented to produce "birch beer." The functional significance of these two processes are very similar, i.e., mobilization of assimilates utilizing the transpiration stream. But the means by which the flow is pressurised is quite different. Apparently, *Betula* is pressurized by osmosis that operates via root pressure. In *Acer*, the pressurisation arizes from ice formation within the trunks themselves (see below).

16.3.2. Maple sap exudation

Maple sap was being tapped by the Indians of North America at the time of European conquest. The system continued with few changes for about 300 years. Leafless maple trees (*Acer saccharum*—the sugar bush) were tapped from midwinter until budburst in the spring. The procedure was quite simple: holes were bored about 1 m above the ground in the tree trunks. Short metal pipes, ca. 15 mm in diameter, were then hammered into the holes. Several liters of sap, consisting of 2–4% solids, were collected in the warm part of the day. Tree branches were used to boil the sap so as to concentrate the solids (consisting mainly of sugars) to about 60%, thus forming the familiar maple syrup, a luxury food.

In later years, improvements in technique included the substitution of oil as fuel to evaporate and caramelize the sap. Trees were connected by tubing to a centralized collection hut. Sanitation and disinfectants were used to control growth of microorganisms in this system. Yield was further increased by the application of vacuum to the collection tubes.

The mechanism of maple sap exudation remained an intriguing mystery for about 200 years. A number of points were established beyond dispute. First, the exudate arose from the wood, the sap of which became positively pressurized. The cause of pressurization was not the familiar exudation caused by root pressure because the roots were unnecessary: frozen twigs cut from a tree would exude if warmed in the fingers. There seemed to be a remarkably good correlation between the amounts of exudate collected and the environmental conditions. Tappers claimed that sharp frosts followed by warm sunny days were ideal for good collections. Scientists dismissed the requirement for freezing and argued in favor of an osmotic mechanism depending on the sugar content of the sap (44,45). This osmotic mechanism was never clearly defined but held sway until the 1960s even though Stevens and Eggert (71) had strongly emphasized that the mechanism *must* be located within wood because sawn logs exuded in much the same way as trees.

Milburn and Zimmermann (55) studied maple sap flow in Massachussets in whole trees. A twig in a potometer was used to model the whole tree. Although the trees were leafless, they did sustain transpiration, which induced sap to ascend the tree by day. A clear correlation was found with the incidence of freezing and exudation except when trees were actually frozen and flow was arrested. A picture emerged of the tree as an hydraulic unit most strongly pressurised near ground level but with a peak of pressurization around midday. Sugar was added to the sap stream as it passed up the tree until it reached a maximum concentration in the upper branches. Water was absorbed from the soil to replenish transpired or exuded water (55).

Milburn and O'Malley (54,60) continued the research in Scotland on the European species *Acer pseudoplatanus*, which resembled *A. saccharum* in its behavior. Twigs of the tree were studied in detail under laboratory conditions while monitoring the sap temperature and pressurization. Freezing induced the uptake of water without which exudation could not occur in response to thawing. It was possible to follow freezing and thawing of twigs in the laboratory using thermocouples that detected endotherms or exotherms associated with ice formation and thawing (60). Exudation from whole trees was monitored and could be explained entirely in terms of freezing and associated pressurization after thawing. On the basis of their evidence Milburn and O'Malley (54) postulated that the mechanism was driven by gas contained in the xylem fibres (Fig. 16.2). During freezing crystals built up in the fibres causing uptake. On thawing, the decompressed gas drives the thawed sap from the trunk from bore holes. In contrast with earlier hypotheses, the role of osmotica as the primary mechanism was dismissed because the system could operate perfectly with pure water, virtually devoid of solutes.

Tyree, called on to advise on quantitative aspects of sycamore flow, repeated the work back in Canada on the sugar maple. The mechanism already discovered from *Acer pseudoplatanus* was found to apply to *A. saccharum* exactly (74,75). This work effectively completed the cycle proving that all members of the genus *Acer* probably operate in the same way and this remains

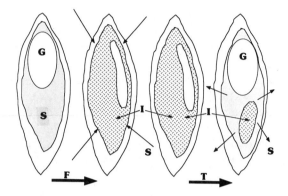

FIG. 16.2. The mechanism of sap exudation in *Acer*. On freezing (F) of wood fibers, entrained gas bubbles (G) are compressed as crystalline ice forms (I), causing sap to be absorbed. The reverse operation causes sap to exude when the ice thaws (T). Sap (S) can move laterally across ray cells collecting sucrose until it enters the xylem conduits, where it can move upward or exude via a wound. During freezing bubbles contract; sap is absorbed. During thawing bubbles expand; sap exudes.

the main hypothesis today. Exudation is a consequence of wounding. In the intact tree, the sap becomes pressurized but cannot escape. One benefit of this pressurization may be the reversal of winter cavitation damage when emboli in conduits are dissolved. Probably the main function of the flow of sap, however, is to carry sugars from storage in the ray tissue in the wood via the transpiration stream to the developing buds and twigs in preparation for the new growth season. Sugars are not a primary requirement for maple flow but are passively transported by it.

16.4. Sugary sap, high in solutes—from phloem

16.4.1. Monocotyledon phloem sap

Phloem sap, called 'toddy,' is collected from several palms of which the major ones are *Arenga, Borassus, Caryota, Cocos, Corypha, Nipa, Elaeis, Raphis, Copernicia, Judaea* and *Mauritia* (76). Apart from these palms, *Agave* and *Yucca* also exude considerable quantities of phloem sap. Apparently phloem sieve tubes, although under positive pressure often seal when cut or injured. Collection of sap requires suitable manipulation usually of the inflorescence of the palm. Several treatments probably inhibit sealing. These include massaging, beating with a mallet, kicking, smearing with clay, and finally slicing the inflorescence to yield phloem sap (53,61,76).

The phloem sap from the palms is characterized by its high sugar content (10–20%), high K^+ content, very low Ca^{2+} content, and high amino acid content. The sugar present is mostly sucrose. The sap shows an alkaline pH of ca. 8.0. More details on the analysis of phloem sap of monocotyledons can be found elsewhere (47,72,82,83).

The mechanism of sap exudation in palm is not fully understood despite the work of several investigators (53,76). Based on measurements of the physiological parameters of *Cocos*, Milburn and Zimmermann (53) proposed a model to explain the palm sugar exudation. Accordingly, the slicing operation induces a progressive reduction in the sealing process. In response to slicing, assimilates originating in the source leaves flow to the sink region. According to Milburn and Zimmermann (53) massage and other similar manipulative techniques partially isolate the inflorescence so that phloem turgor pressure is reduced locally. Later, when the conducting capacity is restored, a rapid surge of sap occurs into the deprived sink.

Experiments have shown that it is not the massage or beating that directly affects the rate of flow, but rather the flexing of the inflorescence stalk, which reduces the flow. The claim that phloem exudation can be induced without such pretreatments is certainly a challenge to an age-old technique of tapping palms for toddy. Our recent observations in India have shown that in tapping certain species of palms, no flexing of the inflorescence is involved. For example, in *Caryota*, which yields up to 25 dm^3 of sap per day, the inflorescence is in a suspended position. It is tapped after being given several days of massage to the individual "threads" (subbranches) of inflorescence are then sliced. More work is needed to establish the scientific basis for the many different manipulative techniques practiced in different countries. The exuding inflorescences of palms demonstrate the phenomenal transporting ability of sieve tubes. Tammes (73) measured an exuding *Arenga* fruit stalk with a specific mass transfer (SMT) of 95.5 g h^{-1} cm^{-2} of sieve tube cross-sectional area. The fruit stalk studied was bleeding sap up to 308 cm^3 h^{-1}.

16.4.2. Dicotyledon phloem sap

The phloem sap exudation in dicots is restricted to the bark because the sieve tubes are located in the bark. Commercial quantities of phloem sap have been collected from the manna ash (*Fraxinus ornus*) in Sicily, Italy, since antiquity. An incision is made on the bark and is renewed every day for 100 days in succession. The evaporated sap is commercially marketed as "manna."

One of the most remarkable and well understood systems is that of castor bean, *Ricinus communis*. The main advantage of *Ricinus* is its size and the capability of its different parts to exude phloem sap. Many studies have been done on the stem bark (27,48–50,67–69,79), inflorescence stalks (33–35), and seedling exudation (32,80). The fact that the mechanism was osmotic and strongly dependent on water supply was shown by Hall and Milburn (28).

Phloem sap exuding from the bark was the result of current photosynthesis (27). Although *Ricinus* bark normally exudes with skillful slicing alone, the exudation is enhanced by massage as practiced in palms (48) and also by repeated slicing of the bark or inflorescence stalk in succession (34,49). Pores in sieve plates of exuding sieve tubes of *Ricinus* were demonstrated to be without P-protein plugs (33). The phloem crossectional area of massaged bark had increased nearly three-fold when compared with unmassaged bark. This probably contributes to enhanced exudation due to massage (35). Studies on the exuding seedlings of *Ricinus* (31) have shown that the cotyledons operate a proton cotransport system of sugar loading. Sugars could be collected after loading by slicing the hypocotyl (32).

16.5. Nonsugary sap, high in solutes, usually acid—from wounded bark

16.5.1. Latex

Laticifers occur in about one-third of rainforest trees and are commonly found in other plants, including many small herbs and vines. The laticifer is a cell that has been specially modified to contain latex, which may be clear or colored though the predominant form is milky white. Laticifers may be single cells as in *Parthenium argentatum*, the guayule. In other species laticifers are articulated, forming long straight tubes, e.g. *Musa* (banana), *Nerium olean-der*, or interlinked to form a meshwork, e.g., *Ficus elastica* (the India rubber plant) or *Hevea brasiliensis* (commercial rubber). (Latex exudation from *Hevea* is covered in Chapter 17, this book.)

Although laticifers may be found in any tissue within the plant they predominate in the phloem and are usually situated in close proximity to the sieve tubes. Despite this their roles are very different. Sieve tubes usually contain sweet, slightly alkaline sap and are concerned with transport of assimilates of *all* higher plants. In contrast, many plants do not have laticifers; they appear to have no transport function except possibly as water storage, contain a bitter, acid sap that may exude in large amounts in contrast with sieve-tube sap. Bitterness and acidity of latex combined with the fact that latex often promotes sealing of coagulation and polymerization has suggested that it may be simultaneously a store for waste products, a toxic deterrant to sucking insects seeking to tap sieve tubes, and a natural sealing system to repair wounds. Since laticifers occur only in a minority of species, we can infer that they are not essential for survival.

Since some latex is colorless or only slightly opalescent, it can easily be confused with phloem exudate, as in *Bryonia dioica* or (during winter) *Musa sapientum*. However, its true nature is revealed by measuring the pH or tasting for the presence of sugars. Latex exudation also resembles phloem exudation from *Fraxinus* (84) in undergoing rapid dilution following wounding. This phenomenon is well understood in *Hevea* tapping and has been used in banana to study the water relations of the crop under normal and drought conditions (5,36,56).

16.5.2. Resins and mucilages

The chemistry of secretions, which we call resins and mucilages, varies considerably. Resins from plants, more properly described as oleoresins because the resin may include essential oils, contain high proportions of terpenes. Although resin may be rather watery when freshly exuded, it becomes viscous through drying and loss of volatile oils. This process is accelerated industrially by heating native resin from which a residue (rosin) remains; turpentine is obtained by condensation. Generally mucilages are gummy condensations of sugar residues, such as pentosans, which can also be concentrated by drying as occurs in gum-arabic, which is collected by slashing the bark of *Acacia arabica*. Incense, of value since antiquity, is collected in a similar manner from *Acacia duboisia*.

Resins are collected commercially from coniferous trees, e.g., *Pinus pinaster* and *Larix europea*. The former is golden brown (Bordeaux turpentine) when concentrated; the latter greenish (Venice turpentine). The trees are slashed in a manner similar to that for *Hevea* tapping and exuding resin is collected as it dries from the bark via resin canals, of which are ducts surrounded by cylinders of parenchymatous secretory cells. Several species of *Abies* lack resin ducts, but the resin collects in pockets or "blisters" that may be tapped producing the Canada balsam of histologic fame. Resin canals may be widely distributed in both xylem and phloem and slashing into the xylem is apt to kill both cambium and tree if over extensive.

Another form of resin is produced in gums (*Eucalyptus*) in "kino veins," which run longitudinally through the wood. Sometimes these ducts form a dense anastomozing network. They are regarded as traumatic ducts produced by injury and typically develop from the cambial stage of development (18). Kino is especially rich in polyphenols, the oxidation of which often turns it into a black tar-like deposit.

16.6. Indirectly obtained and modified plant sap

16.6.1. Xylem-derived fluids

Somewhat surprisingly in spite of the low solute content of xylem and its negative pressure, xylem has nevertheless been tapped successfully by a range of predaceous insects. Froghoppers, members of the Hemiptera, extract xylem sap with piercing mouth parts, that penetrate the xylem. Plants being attacked, often grasses and leguminous herbs, characteristically have foamy globules on the stem nodes (locally called "frog" or "cuckoo spit"). Within this liquid cocoon is an immature larval stage that maintains the foam globule and its own nutrition by tapping the supporting stem. Foam is stabilized by a proteinaceous exudate from the insect. This gives a clue to the essential mechanism because it appears that the xylem sap is relatively rich in nitrogenous substances (amines and amides) generated in roots and transported passively in the xylem to the growing shoots and leaves. Indeed, the same solutes appear to nourish plant predators, e.g., *Olax*, which is a hemiparasite (62) like the more familiar mistletoes.

Apparently cicadas too derive most of their nutrition from the organic nitrogen fraction in xylem sap. In this case, the extraction is possible through a powerful cibarial pump situated in the head of the insect (63). After a very slow larval phase (ca. 17 years), in which the grub feeds on xylem root exudate, it pupates just above soil level and metamorphoses into a giant flying insect that continues to feed, often in large noisy groups, on xylem sap from tree trunks. A watery faeces is ejected visibly with some force at frequent intervals. Exactly how the cibarial pump is able to function so well in extracting xylem sap even from *Eucalypts* under drought stress remains a puzzle. Theoretically one would expect cavitation, but this must be prevented in some way. Closely paralleling cicadas are the smaller sharp-shooters (*Hordnia*), which also eject forcibly jets of aqueous faeces (58). Presumably the physiological processes closely resemble those of adult cicadas.

Thus, animals extract xylem sap from plants to benefit from the organic nitrogenous solutes. Exactly how they do this without inducing cavitation, yet applying the power required for extraction, has not yet been clearly explained. From a plant physiologist's point of view the process is intriguing and a challenge for future research. Collection of the "exudate" of watery faeces can give only tentative information on the original plant sap composition. Phloem sap, sometimes collected from punctures, must also be suspect since it may be contaminated by injected insect saliva.

16.6.2. Phloem-derived fluids

"Honeydew" is the familiar "greenfly" faeces from aphids (*Aphis*). These insects pierce the bark until they reach sieve tubes using specially modified mouthparts. A single sieve tube is tapped for a considerable time. The aphid removes nitrogenous materials from the sap for its metabolism but voids the excess, which is mainly sugars.

Even when the insect has been removed, the isolated stylets continue to exude, demonstrating that the source turgor pressure can maintain flow without pumping. Maximum rates of exudation are about $1-4$ mm^3 h^{-1}. For further details, see Dixon (14).

16.7. Concluding Remarks

It is obvious that exudates can be obtained in many ways from a large variety of systems. Some products support industries, e.g. rubber, resins, maple syrup, palm sugar. Others are invaluable to researchers because exudates are easy to collect and study. Exudation studies described in this chapter illustrate the profound differences between natural and induced exudation and the dangers of diagnosing the cause of exudation without knowledge of the tissue of origin or the chemical composition of the exudate.

16.8. References

1. P.C. Anderson and B.Y. Brodbeck, "Diurnal and temporal changes in the chemical profile of xylem exudate from *Vitis rotundifolia*," *Physiol. Plant.*, **75**, 63–70 (1989).

2. W.P. Anderson, D.P. Aikman, and A. Meiri, "Excised root exudation: A standing gradient osmotic flow," *Proc. Royal Soc. Lond. Ser. B. Biol. Sci.*, **174**, 445–458 (1970).

3. W.H. Arisz, R.H. Helder, and R. Van Nie, "Analysis of the exudation process in tomato plants," *J. Exp. Bot.*, **2**, 257–297 (1951).

4. D.A. Baker, J.L. Hall, and J.R. Thorpe, "A study of the extrafloral nectaries of *Ricinus communis*," *New Phytol.*, **81**, 129–137 (1978).

5. D.A. Baker, J. Kallarackal, and J.A. Milburn, "Water relations of the Banana. II. Physico-chemical aspects of the latex and other tissue fluids," *Aust. J. Plant Physiol.*, **17**, 69–77 (1990).

6. B.K. Bakshi and J.S. Boyce, "Water blisters in teak," *Indian For.*, **85**, 589–591 (1959).

7. D.A. Barber and K.B. Gunn, "The effect of mechanical forces on the exudation of organic substances by the roots of cereal plants grown under sterile conditions," *New Phytol.*, **73**, 39–45 (1974).

8. D.A. Barber and J.M. Lynch, "Microbial growth in the rhizosphere," *Soil Biol. Biochem.*, **9**, 305–308 (1977).

9. B.L. Bentley and T. Elias, eds., *The Biology of the Nectaries*, Columbia Univ. Press, New York, 1983.

10. R.L. Bieleski and R.J. Redgwell, "Sorbitol metabolism in nectaries from flowers of Rosaceae," *Aust. J. Plant Physiol.*, **7**, 15–25 (1980).

11. F.E. Clark, "Soil micro-organisms and plant roots," *Adv. Agron.*, **1**, 241 (1949).

12. C.J. Clark, P.T. Holland, and G.S. Smith, "Chemical composition of bleeding xylem sap from Kiwi fruit vines," *Ann. Bot.*, **58**, 353–362 (1986).

13. P.S. Dick and T. Rees, "The pathway of sugar transport in roots of *Pisum sativum*," *J. Exp. Bot.*, **26**, 305–314 (1975).

14. A.F.G. Dixon, *Biology of Aphids*, Edward Arnold, London, 1973.

15. H. Dieffenback, U. Luttge, and M.G. Pitman, "Release of guttation fluid from passive hydathodes of intact barley plants. II. The effect of abscisic acid and cytokinins," *Ann. Bot.*, **45**, 703–712 (1980).

16. L.T. Durkee, "The ultrastructure of floral and extrafloral nectaries," in B.L. Bentley and T. Elias, eds., *The Biology of Nectaries*, Columbia Univ. Press, New York, 1983, pp. 1–9.

17. E.P. Eleftheriou and J.L. Hall, "The extrafloral nectaries of cotton. I. Fine structure of the secretory papillae," *J. Exp. Bot.*, **34**, 103–119 (1983).

18. A. Fahn, *Secretory Tissues in Plants*, Academic Press, New York, 1979.

19. A.R. Ferguson and N.A. Turner, "Mobilization of macro nutrients in cuttings of kiwi fruit (*Actinidia chinensis*) Planch.)," *Ann. Bot.*, **47**, 229–237 (1981).

20. N. Findlay, "Secretion of nectar," in F.A. Loewus and W. Tanner, eds., *Encyclopaedia of Plant Physiology, New Series*, Vol. 12A, Springer-Verlag, Berlin, 1982, pp. 677–683.

21. N. Findlay, M.L. Reed, and F.V. Mercer, "Nectar production in *Abutilon*. III. Sugar secretion," *Aust. J. Biol. Sci.*, **24**, 665–675 (1971).

22. A. Frey-Wyssling, *Die Stoffausscheidung der höheren Pflanzen*, Springer, Berlin, 1935.

23. A. Frey-Wyssling, "Die Guttation als allgemeine Erscheinung," *Ber. Schweiz. bot. Ges.*, **51**, 321–325 (1941).

24. R.C. Friesner, "An observation on the effectiveness of root pressure in the ascent of sap," *Butler Univ. Bot. Stud.*, **4**, 226–227 (1940).

25. B.E.S. Gunning and J.E. Hughes, "Quantitative assessment of symplastic transport of pre-nectar into the trichomes of *Abutilon* nectaries," *Aust. J. Plant Physiol.*, **3**, 619–637 (1976).

26. S. Hales, *Vegetable Staticks*, Oldbourne, London, 1727.

27. S.M. Hall, D.A. Baker, and J.A. Milburn, "Phloem transport of ^{14}C-labelled assimilates in *Ricinus*," *Planta*, **100**, 200–207 (1971).

28. S.M. Hall and J.A. Milburn, "Phloem transport in *Ricinus*. Its dependence on the water balance of the tissues," *Planta*, **109**, 1–10 (1973).

29. A.E. Hill and B.S. Hill, "Mineral ions," in U. Lüttge and M.G. Pitman, eds., *Encyclopedia of Plant Physiology, New Series*, Vol. 28, Springer-Verlag, Berlin, 1976, pp. 225–243.

30. P.J. Hocking, "The composition of phloem exudate and xylem sap from tree tabacoo (*Nicotiana glauca* Grah.)," *Ann. Bot.*, **45**, 633–643 (1980).

31. J. Kallarackal and E. Komor, "Transport of hexoses by the phloem of *Ricinus communis* L. seedlings," *Planta*, **177**, 336–341 (1989).

32. J. Kallarackal, G. Orlich, C. Schobert, and E. Komor, "Sucrose transport into the phloem of *Ricinus communis* L. seedlings as measured by the analysis of sieve-tube sap," *Planta*, **177**, 327–335 (1989).

33. J. Kallarackal and J.A. Milburn, "Studies on the phloem sealing mechanism in *Ricinus* fruit stalks," *Aust. J. Plant Physiol.*, **10**, 561–568 (1983).

34. J. Kallarackal and J.A. Milburn, "Specific mass transfer and sink-controlled phloem translocation in castor bean," *Aust. J. Plant Physiol.*, **11**, 483–490 (1984).

35. J. Kallarackal and J.A. Milburn, "Phloem sap exudation in *Ricinus communis*: Elastic responses and anatomical implications," *Plant Cell Environ.*, **8**, 239–245 (1985).

36. J. Kallarackal, J.A. Milburn, and D.A. Baker, "Water relations of the banana. III. Effects of controlled water stress on water potential, transpiration, photosynthesis and leaf growth," *Aust. J. Plant Physiol.*, **17**, 79–90 (1990).

37. P.J. Kramer, *Water Relations of Plants*, Academic Press, New York, 1983.

38. P.J. Kramer and T.T. Kozlowski, *Physiology of Trees*, McGraw-Hill, New York, 1979.

39. J. Kuo and J.S. Pate, "The extrafloral nectaries of cowpea (*Vigna unguiculata* (L.) Walp.) I. Morphology, anatomy and fine structure," *Planta*, **166**, 15–27 (1985).

40. W. Lopushinsky, "Occurrence of root pressure exudation in Pacific Northwest conifer seedlings," *For. Sci.*, **26**, 275–279 (1980).

41. U. Lüttge, "Structure and function of plant glands," *Ann. Rev. Plant Physiol.*, **22**, 23–24 (1971).

42. U. Lüttge, "Nectar composition and membrane transport of sugars and amino acids," *Aphidologie*, **8**, 305–319 (1977).

43. U. Lüttge and E. Schnepf, "Elimination processes by glands. Organic substances," in U. Lüttge and M.G. Pitman, eds., *Encyclopedia of Plant Physiology, New Series*, Vol. 2, Part B, Springer-Verlag, Berlin, 1976, pp. 244–277.

44. J.W. Marvin, "The physiology of maple sap flow," in K.V. Thimann, W.B. Critchfield, and M.H. Zimmermann, eds., *The Physiology of Forest Trees*, 1958, pp. 95–124.

45. J.W. Marvin, "Mechanism of sap flow," *Rec. Adv. Bot.*, **2**, 1305–1308 (1959).

46. G.C. Mees and P.E. Weatherley, "The mechanism of water absorption by roots. I. Preliminary studies on the effects of hydrostatic pressure gradients," *Proc. Roy. Soc. London B*, **147**, 367–380 (1957).

47. J.A. Milburn and D.A. Baker, "Physico-chemical aspects of phloem sap (Appendix)," in D.A. Baker and J.A. Milburn, eds., *Transport of Photoassimilates*, Longmans, Harlow, Essex, UK, 1988.

48. J.A. Milburn, "Phloem exudation from castor bean: induction by massage," *Planta*, **95**, 272–276 (1970).

49. J.A. Milburn, "An analysis of the response in phloem exudation on application of massage to *Ricinus*," *Planta*, **100**, 143–154 (1971).

50. J.A. Milburn, "Phloem transport in *Ricinus*. Concentration gradients between source and sink," *Planta*, **117**, 303–319 (1974).

51. J.A. Milburn, *Water Flow in Plants*, Longman, London, 1979.

52. J.A. Milburn and M.E. McLaughlin, "Studies of cavitation in isolated vascular bundles and whole leaves of *Plantago major* L.," *New Phytol.*, **73**, 861 (1974).

53. J.A. Milburn and M.H. Zimmermann, "Preliminary studies on sapflow in *Cocos nucifera* L. II. Phloem transport," *New Phytol.*, **79**, 543–558 (1977).

54. J.A. Milburn and P.E.R. O'Malley, "Freeze-induced sap absorption in *Acer* pseudoplantanus: A possible mechanism," *Can. J. Bot.*, **62**, 2101–2106 (1984).

55. J.A. Milburn and M.H. Zimmermann, "Sapflow in the sugar maple in the leafless state," *J. Plant Physiol.*, **124**, 331–334 (1986).

56. J.A. Milburn, J. Kallarackal, and D.A. Baker, "Water relations of the banana. I. Predicting the water relations of the field grown banana using the exuding latex," *Aust. J. Plant Physiol.*, **17**, 57–68 (1990).

57. P.E.H. Minchin and G.S. McNaughton, "Exudation of recently fixed carbon by non-sterile roots," *J. Exp. Bot.*, **35**, 74–82 (1984).

58. T.E. Mittler, "Water tensions in plants—an entomological approach," *Ann. Entomol. Soc. Amer.*, **60**, 1074–1076 (1967).

59. P. Nichol and J.L. Hall, "Characteristics of nectar secretion by the extrafloral nectaries of *Ricinus communis.*," *J. Exp. Bot.*, **39**, 573–586 (1988).

60. P.E.R. O'Malley and J.A. Milburn, "Freeze-induced fluctuations in xylem sap pressure in *Acer pseudoplatanus*," *Can. J. Bot.*, **61**, 3100–3106 (1983).

61. A.E.A. Päivöke, "Tapping practices and sap yields of the nipa palm (*Nipa fruticans*) in Papua New Guinea," *Agric. Ecosyst. Environ.*, **13**, 59–72 (1985).

62. J.S. Pate, N.J. Davidson, J. Kuo, and J.A. Milburn, "Water relations of the root hemiparasite *Olax phyllanthi* (Labill) R.Br. (Olacaceae) and its multiple hosts," *Oecologia* **84**, 186–193 (1990).

63. J. Raven, "Phytophages of xylem and phloem: A comparison of animal and plant sap feeders," *Adv. Ecol. Res.*, **13**, 135–234 (1983).

64. P.T. Richardson, D.A. Baker, and L.C. Ho, "The chemical composition of cucurbit vascular exudates, *J. Exp. Bot.*, **33**, 1239–1247 (1982).

65. P.F. Scholander, W.E. Love, and J.W. Kanwisher, "The rise of sap in tall grapevines," *Plant Physiol.*, **30**, 93–104 (1955).

66. W.H. Smith, "Release of organic materials from the roots of trees," *For. Sci.*, **15**, 138–143 (1969).

67. J.A.C. Smith and J.A. Milburn, "Osmoregulation and the control of phloem-sap composition in *Ricinus communis* L.," *Planta*, **148**, 28–34 (1980a).

68. J.A.C. Smith and J.A. Milburn, "Phloem transport, solute flux and the kinetics of sap exudation in *Ricinus communis* L.," *Planta*, **148**, 35–41 (1980b).

69. J.A.C. Smith and J.A. Milburn, "Phloem turgor and the regulation of sucrose loading in *Ricinus communis* L.," *Planta*, **148**, 42–48 (1980c).

70. J.S. Sperry, N.M. Holbrook, M.H. Zimmermann, and M.T. Tyree, "Spring filling of xylem vessels in wild grape-vine," *Plant Physiol.*, **83**, 414–417 (1987).

71. C.L. Stevens and R.L. Eggert, "Observations on the causes of the flow of sap in red maple," *Plant Physiol.*, **20**, 636–648 (1945).

72. P.M.L. Tammes and J. Van Die, "Studies on phloem exudation from *Yucca flaccida* (Haw) I. Some observations on the phenomenon of bleeding and the composition of the exudate," *Acta Bot. Neerl.*, **13**, 75–83 (1964).

73. P.M.L. Tammes, "On the rate of translocation of bleeding sap in the fruit stalk of *Arenga*," *Proc. Konikl. Ned. Akad. Wetenschap*, **C55**, 141–143 (1952).

74. M.T. Tyree, "Freezing induced sap uptake and exudation in excised branches of dormant sugar maple trees," *Plant Physiol.*, **69** (Suppl.), 97 (1982).

75. M.T. Tyree, "Maple sap uptake, exudation, and pressure changes correlated with freezing exotherms and thawing endotherms," *Plant Physiol.*, **73**, 277–285 (1983).

76. J. Van Die and P.M.L. Tammes, "Phloem exudation from monocotyledonous axes," in M.H. Zimmermann and J.A. Milburn, eds., *Encyclopedia of Plant Physiology, New Series*, Vol. I, Springer-Verlag, Berlin, 1975, pp. 196–222.

77. J. Van Die and P.C.M. Willemse, "Mineral and organic nutrients in sieve tube exudate and xylem vessel sap of *Quercus rubra* L.," *Acta Bot. Neerl.*, **22**, 446–451 (1975).

78. A.E. Vasiliev, "New information on the ultrastructure of flower nectary cells (Russian)," *Botanicheskii Zhurnal*, **56**, 1292–1306 (1971).

79. D. Vreugdenhil, "Source-to-sink gradient of potassium in the phloem," *Planta*, **163**, 238–240 (1985).

80. D. Vreugdenhil and E.A.M. Koot-Gronsveld, "Characterization of phloem exudation from castor-bean cotyledons," *Planta*, **174**, 380–384 (1988).

81. G.P. Wolff, "Zur vergleichenden Entwicklungsgeschichte und biologischen Bedeutung der Blütennektarien," *Bot. Arch.*, **8**, 305–344 (1924).

82. B. Wolterbeek and J. Van Die, "The contents of some hitherto not reported trace elements in phloem exudate from *Yucca flaccida* Haw. determined by means of non-destructive neutron activation analysis," *Acta Bot. Neerl.*, **29**, 307–309 (1980).

83. H. Ziegler, "Nature of transport substances," in M.H. Zimmermann and J.A. Milburn, eds., *Encyclopedia of Plant Physiology, New Series*, Vol. 1, Springer-Verlag, Berlin, 1975, pp. 59–100.

84. M.H. Zimmermann, "Translocation of organic substances in trees. II. On the translocation mechanism in the phloem of white ash (*Fraxinus americana* L.)," *Plant Physiol.*, **32**, 399–404 (1957).

17 Latex Exudation from Rubber Tree, *Hevea brasiliensis*

A. S. RAGHAVENDRA

School of Life Sciences, University of Hyderabad, Hyderabad, India

Contents

17.1. Latex: location and composition

Latex (meaning juice in Latin) refers to the white or colored liquid contained in specialized cells within the plant, called *laticifers* (22). Although latex is often milky or white in appearance, its color and composition are highly variable. In most plants, latex is clear (e.g., in *Morus, Nerium*) or milky (e.g., in *Ficus, Asclepias, Euphorbia*). It could also be yellow-brown (e.g. *Cannabis*) or yellow or orange, as in the members of Papaveraceae (10).

The turbidity and milkiness of latex is due to the suspension of numerous particles in a liquid medium. The refractive index of the particles is greatly different from that of surrounding liquid matrix, in which the particles are dispersed. The liquid medium can be regarded as the cell sap of the laticifer, and contains carbohydrates, organic acids, salts, alkaloids, sterols, fats, tannins, and mucilage. The dispersed particles, which are usually terpenes, could be essential oils, balsams, resins, camphor, or rubber. Some of the important commercial products from the latex of trees are rubber (*Hevea brasiliensis, Ficus elastica*), gutta (*Palaquium gutta, Mimosops balata*), and chicle (*Achras sapota*). Apart from hydrocarbons, the latex could be rich in protein (*Ficus callosa*), sugar (Asteraceae), tannins (*Musa*), alkaloids (*Papaver somniferum*), or papain, a proteolytic enzyme (*Carica papaya*).

The laticifers also vary in structure. They could be articulated or nonarticulated, branched or unbranched. Readers interested in structural features of laticifers are referred to the classic monographs on plant anatomy (22,23).

The best known latex is that of rubber yielding plants. The plants are screened regularly, since several years, for the presence of rubber and other hydrocarbons in latex. When latex is released from the plant, rubber particles of different sizes and shapes clump together and the latex coagulates. This property is used in the commercial preparation of natural rubber from latex. Out of more than 2000 species known to contain rubber, at least 500 species have been used as rubber-yielding plants (11). The rubber content of the latex in these plants varied from less than 1% to more than 20% of the dry weight. In *Hevea*, the rubber may constitute 40–55% of the latex.

The phenomenon of latex exudation is extensively studied in pararubber tree, *Hevea brasiliensis*, because of the great economic importance of the tree. *Hevea* is the only viable commercial source of natural rubber. This chapter therefore deals primarily with literature on latex exudation in *Hevea*. The topic of sap exudation from trees is covered in more detail in Chapter 16 (this volume).

17.2. Latex exudation

The laticifers are quite turgid *in vivo*, but in equilibrium with the adjacent parenchymatous tissue. When the laticifers are cut or torn open, as occurs when a twig or stem is cut, the laticifers release latex toward the cut end because of the release of pressure. Thus the latex exudation is a pressure flow phenomenon. The flow of latex eventually ceases because of the reduction in pressure as well as the sealing of the cut. Slowly, the turgor in the laticifers is restored. There have been several excellent reviews on the physiology of growth and latex production in *Hevea*, which appeared since 1965 (7,9,15,29,43,45,48,51), apart from two monographs (18,26). Readers interested in general aspects of the rubber tree are referred to the monographs of Dijkman (20) and the Rubber Research Institute of India (36).

Very high turgor pressures exist in the laticifers of several plants (Table 17.1). For example, the turgor pressures could be as high as 1.5 MPa in laticifers of *Hevea*. Further, the turgor pressure shows marked diurnal variations. The turgor of laticifers is maximum during dawn, falls during day, and increases in the evening and night (14). Such strong diurnal variations are due primarily to the changes in water deficit in the air (33). There is a gradient of turgor pressure with height in *Hevea* stem, with greater pressures at the

Table 17.1. The range of turgor pressures in laticifers of different species

Species	Maximum turgor pressure (MPa)	Ref.
Hevea brasiliensis	1.5	13,28,38
Ficus elastica	1.0	13
Euphorbia pulcherrima	0.8	13
Bursera microphylla	0.7	21
Nerium oleander	0.6	21
Cryptostegia grandiflora	1.2	A.S. Raghavendra, unpublished data

base of the stem than those in the upper region. The gradient is up to 0.6 MPa 10 m^{-1} during the day but decreases to 0.1 MPa 10 m^{-1} in the night (13).

17.2.1. Pattern and kinetics of latex flow

Because of the very high turgor pressure in the laticifers (12,38), when a cut is made on the trunk of the tree, latex flows out quite rapidly. The rapid initial flow is due to the elastic contraction of the walls, as the fluid cell sap of the laticifers is expelled after a sudden release in their turgor (9,15,26,51). As the turgor pressure falls to low levels, further flow is regulated by capillary forces until the flow stops because of the coagulation and plugging of the latex vessels (8,28). In several clones, the course of latex exudation exhibits two distinct phases (38). In the first few minutes, the expulsion of latex is rapid but the rate also decreases rapidly. During the second phase, the latex is exuded at a slow rate for several minutes until the flow finally stops. The extent and proportion of these two phases depends on the clones. For example, in clone RRII 105, the rates of initial flow and the duration of flow are much higher than those in clones such as Tjir 1 (Fig. 17.1). There is a steady dilution of latex during flow.

The area of the bark on the stem from which the latex flows out is hypothetically designated as the "drainage area" (27,41). Several studies made in *Hevea*, indicate that the drainage area is an oval region, which extends 40–120 cm below the cut to about 20–100 cm above the cut (26). In *Hevea*, it is a normal practice to make a half spiral cut on the trunk of the tree to extract the latex (see also Section 17.2.4). The structure and the extent of drainage area are of great importance in any tree because it is the site of not only storage but also biosynthesis of latex.

17.2.2. Modeling latex flow

The pattern of latex flow in rubber trees has been an interesting item for modeling by plant physiologists, and several models and mathematical equations have been proposed (24,26,32,41). The best equation to describe the

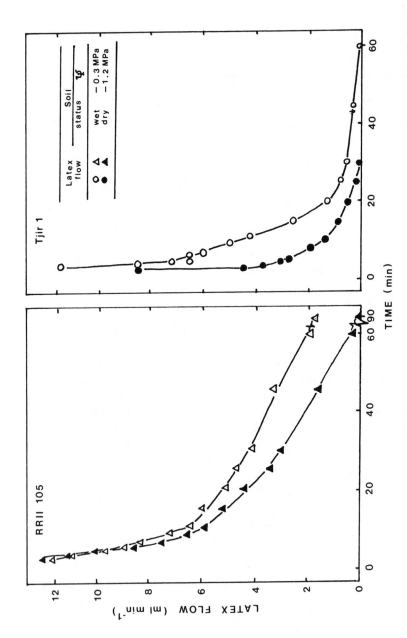

FIG. 17.1. The pattern of latex flow in two clones of *Hevea*, which are in strong contrast to each other. The clone RRII 105 is slow in plugging and yields much more latex does than that by Tjir 1, a fast-plugging clone. Further, the clone Tjir 1 is much more sensitive to the decrease in soil water status than is RRII 105. The latex flow in these trees at two soil moisture levels is presented.

latex exudation in *Hevea* is the die-away expression, derived by Pardekooper and Samosorn (32). As per their equation, the rate of flow of latex (y) at a given time (t) is a function of initial flow rate (b) and a time–flow constant (a). The equation, in a logarithmic transformation, is expressed as $y = be^{-at}$, where e is the base of natural logarithm.

The hypothetical flow curves reflecting the elasticity of the laticifers or capillary force are indicated in Fig. 17.2. None of the models described thus far can account for the very high initial flow rates, particularly during the first 2 min. The two phases of latex flow may have to be treated separately, since the first phase (≤4 min) fits into a curvilinear equation while the second phase (from 5th minute onward) is an exponential curve (38).

A detailed discussion on this subject can be found elsewhere (26).

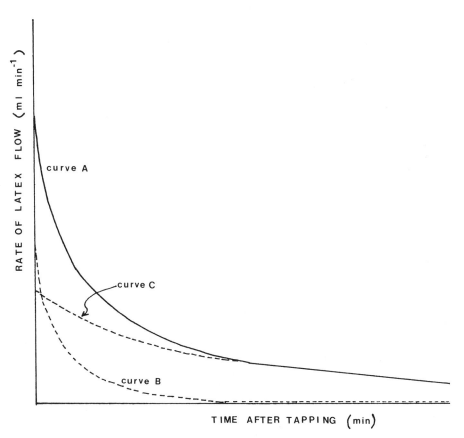

TIME AFTER TAPPING (min)

FIG. 17.2. A typical model of latex flow in *Hevea*. The normally observed pattern of latex flow (curve A) can be differentiated into at least two components. The initial phase of latex exudation is due to the elastic flow (curve B, theoretical), which ceases soon after the loss of high turgor in the laticifers. The second slow phase is due to capillary forces (curve C, theoretical) and is promoted by the dilution of latex by movement of water from adjacent tissues.

17.2.3. Mechanism of plugging

A physical plug forms near the cut end of laticifers and restricts further flow of latex and finally stops the exudation itself (8,51). The rapidity of such plugging, along with the initial rate of flow, are the major factors that would determine the total yield of latex from any given tree. The plugging index, which is an important factor, is formulated as given below (28), and corresponds to the time–flow constant a, referred to in Section 17.2.2:

$$a = \frac{\text{mean flow rate within the first 5 min (ml min}^{-1})}{\text{total latex yield (ml)}} \times 100$$

The plugging index is a clonal characteristic (32) but could be modified by the environmental stresses (particularly water stress) and the exploitation techniques (see also Sections 17.3 and 17.4).

The main components of latex in *Hevea* are the rubber particles, lutoids (equivalent to vacuoles), and other cell organelles suspended in the fluid matrix, called *C-serum*. The plugging or latex vessel closure is brought out by a classic interaction between the rubber particles and lutoid vesicles. The triglyceride layers around the rubber particles contribute to their stability (26,49). On the other hand, the lutoids, when broken, destabilize the rubber phase and lead to the formation of a coagulum (52,53). The lutoids are intact within the laticifers, but burst open when the laticifers are cut open.

The typical pattern of events during latex exudation and plugging in *Hevea* are represented in Fig. 17.3. There is a rapid flow of latex, on cutting the latex vessels, due mainly to the very high turgor pressure in the laticifers. The turgor pressure falls steeply. Although the turgor pressure recovers to increase after 15 min, the latex flow is further lowered. The decrease in latex flow during the first phase is due to the lowering of the internal turgor while the restriction of latex exudation in the second phase is due to the plugging of the laticifers, initiated by the bursting lutoids.

The fluid contents of lutoids (called *B-serum*) cause the flocculation of rubber particles. The exact agents are not identified, but factors such as acid pH, high levels of divalent cations (e.g., magnesium), or cationic proteins might be involved in such B-serum activity (26,51). Lutoids should therefore be intact to maintain the fluid state of latex. On the other hand, the C-serum of latex helps to keep lutoids intact by providing an isotonic osmoticum as well as a suitable microenvironment (high monovalent ions, basic proteins, neutral or basic pH). C-serum promotes the dispersion of rubber phase, while counteracting against B-serum.

Thus, the plugging of latex vessels is caused by flocs of rubber particles and broken lutoids. There is a marked increase in the population of damaged lutoids during latex flow (34). Factors that could cause lutoid damage might be osmotic (dilution), mechanical (shearing), electrical (wound induced potentials), or chemical (bark components) effects encountered during tapping (26,56).

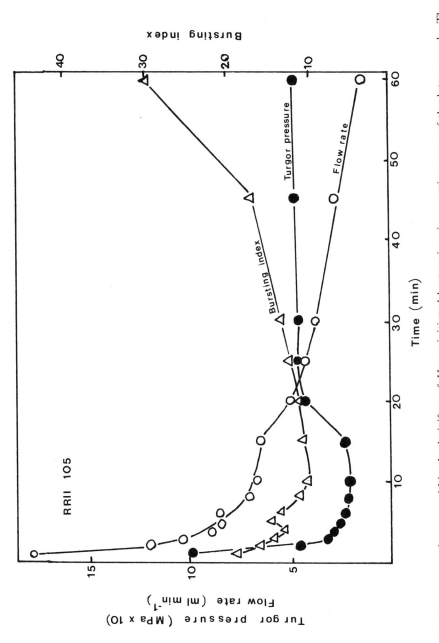

FIG. 17.3. The course of events within the laticifers of *Hevea* initiated by tapping, i.e., cutting open of the latex vessels. The rate of latex flow, turgor pressure in the laticifers, and the bursting index of lutoids were monitored simultaneously. The experiment was performed with the clone RRII 105. Further details are described in the text.

The extent of lutoid damage is usually expressed as the "bursting index." Acid phosphatase is located only in lutoids. The level of free acid phosphatase in the C-serum therefore represents the proportion of damaged lutoids. The total activity of acid phosphatase in the latex is assayed by disrupting all lutoids with detergents like Triton X-100 (40). The bursting index is estimated as

$$\text{Bursting index} = \frac{\text{free acid phosphatase activity}}{\text{total acid phosphatase}} \times 100$$

17.2.4. Tapping: the technique of commercial exploitation

In the trunk of *Hevea* tree, the articulated anastomosing laticifers are located as concentric rings in the phloem (25). The laticifers are oriented longitudinally. The exploitation of the tree for the commercial product (rubber, the component of latex) therefore aims at cutting open the maximum number of latex vessels. The technique of such cutting the laticifers on the trunk of rubber tree is called "tapping." The most common method of tapping is to cut a half-spiral groove near the base of the tree trunk, at an angle of 25–30° from left to right. This is done with a special knife so as to cut the bark deep without affecting the cambial tissue. Latex flows down along the cut and is then directed by a metal spout into a collection cup.

The latex may exude and/or flow for 1–3 h, depending on the clone and season. When the flow ceases, the latex is collected and processed. On the next tapping day, the cut is reopened by slicing away 1–2 mm of bark, thereby removing the coagulum that blocks the cut end of latex vessels. There are different tapping systems, based on the variation in the length of the cut (spiral or half spiral or quarter spiral), frequency of tapping (daily, alternate, or every third day), or number of cuts (one or more). Further details on tapping can be found elsewhere (26,36).

17.3. Factors affecting latex flow

The amount of latex that exudes on each tapping determines the rubber yield from a tree and has therefore been of great interest. The three major factors that affect the latex flow are the length of the cut, the initial flow rate, and the plugging index (44). The length of the cut is proportional to the girth of the stem, which depends on the growth of the tree. Apart from affecting the growth of the tree, several internal and external factors modify the latex flow by modulating the initial flow rate, plugging index, or both.

17.3.1. Clonal and diurnal variation

The extent and pattern of latex flow varies among different clones. A typical example is illustrated in Fig. 17.1. The duration of flow is more while the speed of plugging is less in clones like RRII 105 than in those such as Tjir 1. Factors that contribute to such marked clonal variations include extent and pattern of drainage area, duration of flow, initial rates, and plugging index. Structural features and assimilatory capacity of the tree may also result in an indirect effect on latex yield from rubber tree (45,50).

The best time for tapping rubber trees is just before sunrise. The latex yield is maximum and is only marginally affected between the nighttime and early morning, but decreases markedly as the day progresses. For example, the latex yield at 1:00 P.M. is only about 70% of the maximum (33). The diurnal variation in yield is inversely proportional to the saturation deficit in the air (31). Such marked decrease in latex exudation during the day is because of the severe drop in the turgor pressure in the laticifers, caused by the increase in loss of water through transpiration (12,13).

17.3.2. Environmental stress

The latex is predominantly watery. The exudation of latex from rubber tree is greatly affected by the water status of the tree (15). Latex yields are generally reduced at low soil moisture levels, prevalent in summer months or after a prolonged drought. It is been shown that both the duration and the pattern of latex flow are affected by water stress (47). There are variations in the sensitivity to water stress among the clones of *Hevea* (42). A typical example is illustrated in Fig. 17.1. The duration of flow and the total yield of latex were markedly reduced in clone Tjir 1, when the soil moisture decreased. The latex flow was only slightly affected in clones like RRII 105 or Gl 1. In fact, the rate of latex flow was enhanced during initial stages of water stress and was reduced only at later stages of stress (38).

The reduction in the yield of latex (total flow) under soil moisture stress is due primarily to enhanced plugging and to a certain extent to the decrease in drainage area (46). It is also possible that the relative stability of rubber particles as well as the lutoids is affected by a decrease in their protective layers of triglycerides and phospholipids, respectively (37). The drought-tolerant clones of *Hevea* (e.g., RRII 105) are known to maintain a high solute potential in their C-serum even during dry summer months (48). The ability of osmotic adjustment in these clones is also reflected in the relatively small decrease in their leaf water potential in the afternoon compared to predawn values.

17.3.3. Relationship between growth and exploitation of tree

The processes of tapping and the chemical stimulation of latex exudation from the tree (see Sections 17.2.4 and 17.4) collectively constitute the exploitation of rubber tree. Intensive exploitation of the tree affects the growth, including the girth of the tree stem. A reduction in the growth of the tree results in a marked decrease in the subsequent yields of latex. Further, the physiological factors that influence the growth, during the preexploitation phase, also continue to exert their effect on trees.

The extent of annual biomass production in trees, which are tapped (or exploited), is much less than that in untapped trees (54). Although still debated (50), the reduction in biomass cannot be completely accounted for by the rubber yields, even after taking into account the high energy value of rubber (2.5 times that of carbohydrates). In an extensive study, Templeton (54) reported a large variation among the clones in the extent of biomass reduction due to the exploitation of the trees. The ideal clones therefore exhibit minimum reduction in biomass after the tapping phase.

17.3.4. Brown bast

Some trees, while being tapped, suddenly overreact to the exploitation so much that they stop yielding latex (i.e., become "dry"). This phenomenon, called "brown bast," is believed to be a physiological disorder (39). The bark, when cut, does not exude latex and usually becomes dark brown in color. The only known way to overcome this problem is to considerably reduce the intensity of exploitation, or to completely stop tapping the affected trees (17).

There have been attempts to induce brown bast in trees by simulating overexploitation and tapping on areas of bark that are isolated by grooves around ("bark islands"). However, none of the following factors could be confirmed as the possible reasons for the malady of brown bast: carbohydrate depletion (16), loss of protein or RNA (17), altered osmotic potential of laticifers (9), or the reduction in the permeability of latex vessels (5).

The phenomenon of brown bast (reasons for the onset of dryness and ways to overcome it) remains one of the greatest challenges to tree physiologists working with *Hevea*.

17.4. Chemical stimulation of latex exudation

The latex exudation from rubber trees can be markedly enhanced by the application of growth regulators on to the bark. Such chemical stimulation of latex flow from rubber trees is a widely used commercial practice. Several chemicals are known to have a stimulatory effect on latex flow in *Hevea* (Table 17.2). The most effective among these are compounds related to ethylene. Several ethylene-releasing compounds are routinely employed in rubber plantations to increase the latex flow from rubber trees. The next best are those related to auxins, but it is quite possible that auxin-like compounds are resulting in an increased production of ethylene inside the plant tissue. A detailed discussion on the use of growth regulators to enhance latex yield from rubber trees can be found elsewhere (1,19,48). Ethylene is known to stimulate sap exudation in other plants as well.

Considerable work has been done to understand the mechanism of action of ethylene on latex exudation in *Hevea* (26). The growth regulator (ethylene containing formulation) is normally applied just below the tapping cut, after scraping the surface of the bark. Scraping helps in a rapid penetration of the

Table 17.2. Plant growth regulators and other chemicals reported to be capable of stimulating latex exudation in rubber tree, Hevea[a]

Ethylene-related compounds

Acytelene
2-Chloroethyl phosphonic acid (Ethephon)
Ethad
Ethylene
Ethylene oxide
1-Aminocyclopropane-1-carboxylic acid (ACC)
Calcium carbide

Auxin-type regulators

2,4-Dichlorophenoxy acetic acid (2,4-D)
2,4,5-Trichlorophenoxy acetic acid (2,4,5-T)
1-Naphthyl acetic acid (NAA)
Indole butyric acid (IBA)
4-Amino-3,5,6-trichloro picolinic acid (Picloram)
4-Chlorophenoxy propionic acid (CPA)
2,4-Dichloro-5-fluorophenoxy acetic acid (2,4-Cl-FPA)
α-Naphthoxy acetic acid (α-NOXA)
β-Naphthoxy acetic acid (β-NOXA)

[a]Further details of other chemicals can be found in Refs. 1, 19, and 48.

growth regulator into the bark tissue. Ethylene decreases the plugging capacity and thus extends the duration of flow. The exact reasons are not identified, but ethylene action might be a result of several effects, such as changes in stability of lutoids (40), increase in pH of latex (55), enlargement of drainage area (35,45), and alterations in biophysical and/or rheologic properties of latex (57).

Excess stimulation by chemicals of latex flow is harmful as it affects the growth of the tree by draining away too many assimilate towards latex production. The use of chemicals to stimulate latex flow should also be done judiciously. Further discussion on this subject can be found in the monograph by Gomez (26).

17.5. Concluding remarks

Although laticifers have been known for a long time, their role in plants is not yet identified. Earlier the laticifers were thought to be analogous to blood vessels of animals. Suggested roles of latex include food conduction, food storage, regulation of water balance, transport of oxygen, protection against animals, and excretion of excess secondary products (22). It is possible that the laticifers have more than one function.

The *Hevea* latex has also been extensively used for studying the biosynthesis of rubber. There are several excellent reviews on the biochemistry of rubber (polyisoprene) biosynthesis (2–4). It is not known whether there is any relationship between the rubber biosynthesis and the water potential of laticifers and the pattern of latex exudation.

The search for new chemicals that would be capable of stimulating latex flow from rubber trees continues. There is as yet no ideal stimulant that enhances latex flow but does not affect the biomass production of the tree. The ethylene- or auxin-related chemical stimulants of latex flow, known thus far, markedly reduce the tree growth. A new direction is initiated in enhancing the capacity of rubber biosynthesis, but in another rubber-yielding plant, guayule (*Parthenium argentatum*). Several enzymes of polyisoprene biosynthesis were stimulated on exogenous application of DCPTA, 2-(3,4-dichlorophenoxy)-triethyl amine in guayule (6).

Further studies should be made on the mechanism of plugging and, in particular, the reasons for lutoid damage during latex exudation. The observed dilution of latex is too minimal to disrupt lutoids. The large variation among different clones in the pattern of latex flow and their tolerance to water or temperature stress could be used to study and understand the physiology and regulation of latex exudation. The importance of *Hevea* as the only source of natural rubber remains unchallenged, since the commercial viability of alternate sources such as guayule (30) is yet to be established.

17.6. References

1. P.D. Abraham, S.G. Boatman, G.E. Blackman, and R.G. Powell, "Effects of plant growth regulators and other compounds on flow of latex in *Hevea brasiliensis*," *Ann. Appl. Biol.*, **62**, 159–173 (1968).

2. B.L. Archer, "Polyisoprene," in E.A. Bell and B.V. Charlwood, eds., *Encyclopaedia of Plant Physiology, New Series*, Vol. 8, *Secondary Plant Products*, Springer-Verlag, Berlin, 1980, pp. 309–328.

3. B.L. Archer and B.G. Audley, "New aspects of rubber biosynthesis," *Bot. J. Linn. Soc.*, **94**, 181–196 (1987).

4. B.G. Audley and B.L. Archer, "Biosynthesis of rubber," in A.D. Roberts, ed., *Natural Rubber Science and Technology*, Oxford University Press, Oxford, 1988, pp. 34–60.

5. F.J. Bealing and S.E. Chua, "Output, composition and metabolic activity of *Hevea* latex in relation to tapping intensity and the onset of brown bast," *J. Rubber Res. Inst. Malaya*, **23**, 204–231 (1972).

6. C.R. Benedict, P.H. Reibach, S. Madhavan, R.V. Stipanovic, J.H. Keithly, and H. Yokoyama, "The effect of 2-(3,4-dichlorophenoxy)-triethylamine on synthesis of *cis*-polyisoprene in guayule plants (*Parthenium argentatum*)," *Plant Physiol.*, **72**, 897–899 (1983).

7. G.E. Blackman, "Factors affecting the production of latex," in L. Mullins, ed., *Proceedings of Natural Rubber Producers Research Association Jubilee Conference, Cambridge 1964*, Maclaren, London, 1965, pp. 43–51.

8. S.G. Boatman, "Preliminary physiological studies on the promotion of latex flow by plant growth substances," *J. Rubber Res. Inst. Malaya*, **19**, 243–258 (1966).

9. S.G. Boatman, "Physiological aspects of the exploitation of rubber trees," in L.C. Luckwill and C.V. Cutting, eds., *Physiology of Tree Crops*, Academic Press, New York, 1970, pp. 323–333.

10. J. Bonner, *Plant Biochemistry*, Academic Press, New York, 1950.

11. J. Bonner and A.W. Galston, "The physiology and biochemistry of rubber formation in plants," *Bot. Rev.*, **13**, 543–596 (1947).

12. B.R. Buttery and S.G. Boatman, "Turgor pressure in the phloem. Measurements on *Hevea* latex," *Science*, **145**, 285 (1964).

13. B.R. Buttery and S.G. Boatman, "Manometric measurement of turgor pressures in laticiferous phloem tissues," *J. Exp. Bot.*, **17**, 283–296 (1966).

14. B.R. Buttery and S.G. Boatman, "Effects of tapping, wounding and growth regulators on turgor pressure in *Hevea brasiliensis*," *J. Exp. Bot.*, **18**, 644–659 (1967).

15. B.R. Buttery and S.G. Boatman, "Water deficits and flow of latex, in T.T. Kozlowski, ed., *Water Deficits and Plant Growth*, Vol. 4, Academic Press, New York, 1976, pp. 233–288.

16. S.E. Chua, "Physiological changes in *Hevea brasiliensis* tapping panels during the induction of dryness by interruption of phloem transport. I. Changes in latex," *J. Rubber Res. Inst. Malaya*, **19**, 277–281 (1966).

17. S.E. Chua, "Physiological changes in *Hevea* trees under intensive tapping," *J. Rubber Res. Inst. Malaya*, **20**, 100–105 (1967).

18. J. d'Auzac, J.L. Jacob, and B. Marin, *Physiology of Rubber Tree Latex: The Laticiferous Cell and Latex—a model of Cytoplasm*, CRC Press, Boca Raton, FL, 1988.

19. P.B. Dickenson, "The application of growth modifiers to the production of latex," *Outlook Agric.*, **9**, 88–94 (1976).

20. M.L. Dijkman, *Hevea: Thirty Years of Research in the Far East*. Univ. Miami Press, Coral Cables, FL, 1951.

21. W.J.S. Downtown, "Water relations of laticifers in *Nerium oleander*," *Aust. J. Plant Physiol.*, **8**, 329–334 (1981).

22. K. Esau, *Plant Anatomy*, 2nd ed., Wiley, New York, 1965.

23. A. Fahn, *Plant Anatomy*, 3rd ed., Pergamon Press, Oxford, 1982.

24. A. Frey-Wyssling, "Latex flow," in A. Frey-Wyssling, ed., *Deformation and Flow in Biological Systems*, North Holland Publishing Co., Amsterdam, 1952, pp. 322–349.

25. J.B. Gomez, *Anatomy of Hevea and Its Influence on Latex Production*, Monograph No. 7, Malaysian Rubber Research Development Board, Kuala Lumpur, 1982.

26. J.B. Gomez, *Physiology of Latex (Rubber) Production*, Monograph No. 8, Malaysian Rubber Research Development Board, Kuala Lumpur, 1983.

27. E.G.B. Gooding, "Studies on physiology of latex. II. Effects of various factors on the concentration of latex of *Hevea brasiliensis*," *New Phytol.*, **51**, 11–29 (1952).

28. G.F.J. Milford, E.C. Pardekooper, and C.Y. Ho, "Latex vessel plugging: Its importance to yield and clonal behaviour," *J. Rubber Res. Inst. Malaya*, **21**, 274–282 (1969).

29. V.H.F. Moraes, "Rubber," in P.T. Alvim and T.T. Kozlowski, eds., *Ecophysiology of Tropical Tree Crops*, Academic Press, New York, 1977, pp. 315–331.

30. National Academy of Sciences, *Guayule: An Alternate Source of Natural Rubber*, National Academy of Sciences, Washington, DC, 1977.

31. F. Ninane, "Evapotranspiration reelle et croissance de jeunes heveas soumis a differentes humidites du sol," *Rev. Gen. Caout. Plast.*, **44**, 207–212 (1967).

32. E.C. Paardekooper and S. Samosorn, "Clonal variation in latex flow patterns," *J. Rubber Res. Inst. Malaya*, **21**, 264–273 (1969).

33. E.C. Paardekooper and S. Sookmark, "Diurnal variation in latex yield," *J. Rubber Res. Inst. Malaya*, **21**, 341–347 (1969).

34. S.W. Pakianathan, S.G. Boatman, and D.H. Taysum, "Particle aggregation following dilution of *Hevea* latex: A possible mechanism for the closure of latex vessels after tapping," *J. Rubber Res. Inst. Malaya*, **19**, 259–271 (1966).

35. S.W. Pakianathan, R.L. Wain, and E.K. Ng, "Studies on displacement area on tapping in mature *Hevea* trees," *Proceedings of International Rubber Conference 1975*, Vol. II, Rubber Research Institute of Malaysia, Kuala Lumpur, 1975, p. 225.

36. P.N.R. Pillay, ed., *Handbook of Natural Rubber Production in India*, Rubber Research Institute of India, Kottayam, Kerala, India, 1980.

37. D. Premakumari, P.M. Sherif, and M.R. Sethuraj, "Variations in lutoid stability and rubber particle stability as factors influencing yield depression during drought in *Hevea brasiliensis*," *J. Plantation Crops*, **8**, 43–47 (1980).

38. A.S. Raghavendra, S. Sulochanamma, G.G. Rao, S. Mathew, K.V. Satheesan, and M.R. Sethuraj, "The pattern of latex flow in relation to clonal variation, plugging and drought tolerance," *Proceedings of International Rubber Research Development Board Colloquium on Exploitation Physiology and Amelioration of Hevea*, Montpellier, 1984, pp. 205–226.

39. R.D. Rands, "Brown bast disease of plantation rubber: Its cause and prevention," *Arch. Rubber Cult. Ned.-Indie.*, **5**, 235–271 (1921).

40. D. Ribaillier, "Importance des lutoides dans l'ecoulement du latex: Action de la stimulacion," *Rev. Gen. Caout. Plast.*, **47**, 305–310 (1970).

41. J.P. Riches and E.G.B. Gooding, "Studies in the physiology of latex. I. Latex flow on tapping. Theoretical considerations," *New Phytol.*, **51**, 1–10 (1952).

42. C.K. Saraswathyamma and M.R. Sethuraj, "Clonal variation in latex flow characteristics and yield in the rubber," *J. Plantation Crops*, **3**, 14–15 (1975).

43. M.R. Sethuraj, "Studies on the physiological aspects of rubber production. I. Theoretical consideration and preliminary observations," *Rubber Board Bull.*, **9**, 47–62 (1968).

44. M.R. Sethuraj, "Yield components in *Hevea brasiliensis*—theoretical considerations," *Plant Cell Environ.*, **4**, 81–83 (1981).

45. M.R. Sethuraj, "Physiology of growth and yield in *Hevea brasiliensis*," *International Rubber Conference 1985 Proceedings*, Rubber Research Institute of Malaysia, Kuala Lumpur, 1985.

46. M.R. Sethuraj and M.J. George, "Drainage area of the bark and soil moisture content as factors influencing latex flow in *Hevea brasiliensis*," *Indian J. Plant Physiol.*, **19**, 12–14 (1976).

47. M.R. Sethuraj and A.S. Raghavendra, "The pattern of latex flow from rubber tree, *Hevea brasiliensis*, in relation to water stress," *J. Cell Biochem.* (suppl.), **8B**, 236 (1984).

48. M.R. Sethuraj and A.S. Raghavendra, "Rubber," in M.R. Sethuraj and A.S. Raghavendra, eds., *Tree Crop Physiology*, Elsevier Science Publishers, Amsterdam, 1987, pp. 193–223.

49. P.M. Sherif and M.R. Sethuraj, "The role of lipids and proteins in the mechanism of latex vessel plugging in *Hevea brasiliensis*," *Physiol. Plant.*, **42**, 351–353 (1978).

50. N.W. Simmonds, "Some ideas on botanical research on rubber," *Trop. Agric.* (*Trinidad*), **59**, 1–8 (1982).

51. W.A. Southorn, "Physiology of *Hevea* (latex flow)," *J. Rubber Res. Inst. Malaya*, **21**, 494–512 (1969).

52. W.A. Southorn and E.E. Edwin, "Latex flow studies. II. Influence of lutoids on the stability and flow of *Hevea* latex," *J. Rubber Res. Inst. Malaya*, **20**, 187–200 (1968).

53. W.A. Southorn and E. Yip, "Latex flow studies. III. Electrostatic considerations in the colloidal stability of fresh *Hevea* latex," *J. Rubber Res. Inst. Malaya*, **20**, 201–215 (1968).

54. J.K. Templeton, "Partition of assimilates," *J. Rubber Res. Inst. Malaya*, **21**, 259–263 (1969).

55. J. Tupy, "Modification of pH of latex cytoplasm by ethylene," *Phytochemistry*, **19**, 509–511 (1980).

56. E. Yip and J.B. Gomez, "Characterization of cell sap of *Hevea* and its influence on cessation of latex flow," *J. Rubber Res. Inst. Malaysia*, **32**, 1–19 (1984).

57. E. Yip, W.A. Southorn, and J.B. Gomez, "Latex flow studies. IX. Effects of application of yield stimulants on rheology of *Hevea* latex and on concentrations of charged components in its sera," *J. Rubber Res. Inst. Malaysia*, **24**, 103–110 (1974).

18 Modeling: Canopy, Photosynthesis, and Growth

PERTTI HARI, EERO NIKINMAA, and
EEVA KORPILAHTI
Department of Silviculture, University of Helsinki, Helsinki, Finland

Contents

18.1. Principles of modeling

Modeling serves as a tool in ecological and physiological research. The effective use of modeling in the analysis of living systems requires knowledge of mathematics, system analysis, and the concerned biological processes. The difficulties in the transformation of the biological information into appropriate mathematical expressions seem to have been a major obstacle in the building of models.

The basis for functioning of living systems is flows of material. These can, for example, be the photosynthetically induced flow of CO_2 from atmosphere into a plant or through plant back to atmosphere or to forest soil, or the flows of water and nutrients from soil to plant and to atmosphere or back to soil. Dynamic models are mathematical expressions of continuously changing systems. They offer a rather simple description of these seemingly complicated systems, the state of which can always be different at any given moment.

Dynamic models are, therefore, effective tools for analyzing the CO_2 flows into a tree and the flow of carbon compounds within a tree.

There are two strategies in constructing a dynamic model: (a) one can either model the inputs and outputs of the system or (b) in addition, one can include the structure of the system into the models. The former approach is simpler, but the latter reveals a deeper insight of the system.

We treat alternative approaches to model canopy, photosynthesis, and growth. The main focus is to understand the formation of annual photosynthetic production and its allocation for growth. Mathematically this can be expressed as follows. Let p denote photosynthetic rate and ρ the leaf area density. Both photosynthetic rate and leaf area depend on spatial coordinate, x, and time, t. The photosynthetic production, $P(t_1,t_2)$ by a tree during time interval $[t_1,t_2]$ is obtained by integration of the product of photosynthetic rate and leaf area density over space and time:

$$P(t_1 t_2) = \int_V \int_{t_1}^{t_2} \rho(x,t)\, p(x,t)\, dt\, dV \qquad (18.1)$$

The growth is the difference between inflow (photosynthesis) and outflow (respiration, which is denoted by R). Denote the change of biomass compartment by ΔW_i, the allocation coefficient of compartment i by a_i, and the senescence of the compartment by S_i. A simple mass balance equation connects the different processes together:

$$\Delta W_i = a_i(P - R) - S_i \qquad (18.2)$$

The sum of allocation coefficients is one. Equations 18.1 and 18.2 form the backbone of this chapter. We first treat the canopy, i.e., the leaf area density ρ, and associated phenomena, thereafter photosynthetic rate p, and finally growth.

18.2. Canopy

The flow of carbon into trees occurs in leaves, which are distributed in a rather large space. The environmental factors within this space also vary because of the effect of leaves. This is why both leaves and environmental factors must be considered as spatial distributions.

The leaves are distributed into three-dimensional space. Their description requires functions describing leaf mass or area per unit volume. These distribution functions are mappings from three-dimensional space to one-dimensional space. A detailed description of the canopy structure, however, involves various parameters that are difficult to measure and to express in a generalized way (1).

The one-dimensional height pattern of leaves is often a sufficiently accurate description of the leaf distribution. In this case the horizontal coordinates are clumped together by integration. The height distribution involves two components: the leaf mass or area and the shape of the distribution.

The function describing height distribution should include one or two parameters that determine the location of the maximum leaf mass or area at any point between the lower and upper limits of the crown. In addition, the value of the distribution function should equal zero at the lower and upper limits of the crown. These requirements are, for example, fulfilled by the expression

$$\rho(z) = c\bar{z}^{\alpha}(1 - \bar{z})^{\beta} \tag{18.3}$$

where the parameter c determines the leaf mass, the parameters α and β represent the shape of the distribution, and $\bar{z}$ is the relative height within the crown:

$$\bar{z} = \frac{z - z_{max}}{z_{max} - z_{min}} \tag{18.4}$$

where z_{max} and z_{min} are respectively the upper and lower limits of the crown. The values of the parameters c, α, and β can be determined with normal statistical procedures when fitting the leaf mass distribution.

The reduction of irradiance toward lower parts of the canopy is the most dominant spatial feature of environmental factors within the plant canopy. Solar irradiance, being the only energy source of plants, is very important. The interception of radiation by the plant canopy has therefore been a subject for modeling. The sky as a source of light energy is rather well known in clear sky and standard overcast situations. The irradiance distribution is determined by the location of the sun, the transmittance properties of the atmosphere, the properties of cloud cover, and the shading in the canopy above the point or plane.

The radiation falling on a point within a canopy may be divided into three components: (a) direct solar radiation penetrating through gaps in the stand, (b) diffuse radiation penetrating through gaps in the stand, and (c) complementary radiation due to scattering of radiation on the foliage and reflection from the ground. Since the latter is often only a minor part of the radiation involved in photosynthesis, it is often neglected in the analysis.

Beer's law has been applied to plant canopies to estimate the attenuation of radiation. It states that the relative attenuation rate of direct radiation is proportional to the amount of foliage along the path of a solar beam. It gives a well-known formula for the mean irradiance $\overline{I(z)}$ at height z:

$$\overline{I(z)} = I_o e^{-k\text{LAI}(z)} \tag{18.5}$$

where $\text{LAI}(z)$ is the leaf area index along the path of radiation and k is the extinction coefficient. Beer's law can also be applied for estimating the diffuse component of radiation, although the attenuation of diffuse radiation is not strictly exponential (1). However, a mean extinction coefficient for diffuse radiation can be calculated, and thus a mean extinction coefficient for the attenuation of total radiation can also be calculated. Differentiating Eq. 18.5 with respect to LAI gives the mean radiation absorbed by an unit of leaf area at different heights in the plant canopy.

The mean irradiance is frequently used in approximation of photosynthetic production. This is justified if the dependence of photosynthetic rate on irradiance was linear. But it is well known that the dependence of photosynthesis on irradiance is nonlinear. This error results in biased estimates of photosynthetic production. For diffuse radiation the error is rather small, but for direct radiation there may be considerable overestimates of photosynthetic production.

The problem may be reduced if the horizontal mean and the variance are known. Another alternative is to treat the diffuse and direct radiation separately and use the mean radiation for the diffuse component and the mean angle or angle distribution between the solar beam and the leaf normal for direct radiation. However, the latter method gives underestimates of photosynthetic production of sunlit leaves caused by the penumbra effect (1).

Our solution to avoid the bias caused by the nonlinear dependence of photosynthesis on light is to directly measure how photosynthesis is decreased by the shading canopy. The close relationship between photosynthesis and irradiance (see Eq. 18.8) provides an indirect method for estimating the effect of shading on photosynthetic production by constructing an integrating electric device.

The effect of shading on photosynthetic production can then be analyzed using the measuring results of the device. Exponential extinction caused by shading leaf area seems to give satisfactory fit with empirical observations (2):

$$P(x,t_1,t_2) = P(x_o,t_1,t_2)e^{-a\text{LAI}(z)} \tag{18.6}$$

where x_o is a point above the canopy, $\text{LAI}(z)$ is the leaf area above the point in consideration, and a is a parameter. The acclimization of canopy structure and the within-shoot shading cause problems in this approach, which have to be considered.

18.3. Photosynthesis

18.3.1. Basic features

The measurements of gas exchange have guided the modeling of photosynthetic rate. This is unsatisfactory, however, since the measured gas exchange is a result of two different processes, photosynthesis and respiration, which have their own responses to environmental factors. Photosynthesis is driven mainly by irradiance and respiration by temperature. Consequently, the difference of photosynthesis and respiration, which is measured in the gas-exchange measurements, cannot be linked with environmental factors; instead, both processes have to be modeled separately. This is why we use the following terminology: photosynthesis is the formation of carbohydrates, respiration is consumption of carbohydrates for metabolic needs, and CO_2 exchange is the consumption or release of CO_2.

The models describing gas exchange include at least four parameters, two for photosynthesis and two for respiration. Reliable estimation of the value of a parameter requires more than 10 measurements per parameter. Thus at least 40 measurements are needed to identify the model. When there is only one measurement from several objects available, as is often the case when sampling large populations, an additional variance component is introduced that strongly disturbs the analysis.

Data of good quality can be produced by monitoring the same leaf or twig for a period long enough to produce over 40 measurements. If the focus of the research is to study changes in the model describing photosynthesis, the number of measurements should be even larger.

Measurements of gas exchange often take >10 s. Because this interval is so long, changes in environmental factors may occur. The variation in photosynthetic rate due to the changes in environment generates problems in linking the model and measurement, which must be taken into account in the arrangement of measurements (3).

18.2. Input–output model of photosynthetic rate

The input–output model covers the photosynthetic response to environmental factors and has several ecological applications. It is also the simplest among the models. Irradiance is the source of energy for photosynthetic processes, while temperature determines the rates of biochemical reaction. These parameters form the input for the model. The output of the system is the amount of carbohydrates formed indicated by the consumption of CO_2 by the leaf in consideration.

Let I denote irradiance, T temperature, and p photosynthetic rate per leaf area. The simple multiplicative input–output model links irradiance and temperature with photosynthetic rate:

$$p = f_I(I)f_T(T) \tag{18.7}$$

where f_I describes the effect of irradiance and f_T, that of temperature. Assuming that a Michaelis–Menten-type model can be used for f_I, we obtain

$$f_I(I) = \frac{P_{max}I}{I + \beta} \tag{18.8}$$

where P_{max} is a parameter describing the level of maximal photosynthesis and β introduces the saturating effect of photosynthesis. The effect of temperature can be approximated as

$$f_T(T) = \begin{cases} 0 & \text{if} & T \leq a_2 \\ 1 - (e^{-a_1(T-a_2)}) & \text{if} & T > a_2 \end{cases} \tag{18.9}$$

where a_1 and a_2 are parameters

Since we can measure only CO_2 exchange, the respiration also has to be considered in order to allow for proper parameter estimation and testing of the model with empirical data. Let r denote respiration rate per leaf area. Temperature is the dominating factor affecting the respiration. Its effect is exponential. Thus, the following model is applied for approximation the dependence of respiration rate on temperature:

$$r(T) = \begin{cases} 0 & \text{if} & T \leq c_3 \\ c_1[e^{c_2(T-c_3)} - 1] & \text{if} & T > c_3 \end{cases} \tag{18.10}$$

where c_1, c_2, and c_3 are parameters.

The environmental factors, especially irradiance, exhibit a strong spatial and temporal variation. Thus, environmental factors have to be introduced into the analysis as functions of time t and spatial coordinates x. Now the following model for gas exchange g is obtained:

$$g(t,x) = f_I[I(t,x)] \, f_T[T(t,x)] - r_T[T(t,x)] \tag{18.11}$$

The validation of the model and the parameter value estimation are somewhat difficult since the measurements provide temporal and spatial integrals of gas exchange. This is a technical problem that can be solved with proper arrangement of measurements (3).

Field measurements at the Forestry Field Station, Helsinki University revealed the following values for the parameters for Scots pine: $P_{max} = 6.2$ mg (CO_2) dm^{-2} h^{-1}, $\beta = 160$ W m^{-2}, $a_1 = 0.32°$C^{-1}, $a_2 = -5°$C, $c_1 = 0.5$ mg (CO_2) dm^{-2} h^{-1}, $c_2 = 0.036°$C, and $c_3 = -5°$C. The fit of the model in prediction with independent data is demonstrated in the Fig. 18.1. The model is able to explain in prediction about 90% of the variance of measurements of gas exchange performed during a given day (4).

18.3.3. Input–output model assuming system properties

The applicability of the simple input–output model can be improved by introducing the structure of the photosynthetically active tissue into the analysis. This can be done with two approaches: either by detailed description of the system and its functions or by assuming that the system as whole has some functional regularities that are modeled. These two alternatives results in different types of models.

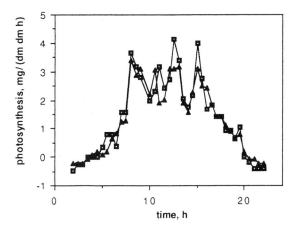

FIG. 18.1. Measured (squares) and calculated (Eq. 18.11) (triangles) photosynthesis during May 20, 1982 at Forestry Field Station University of Helsinki.

The photosynthetic system is under a complicated regulation during periods of drought and during wintertime. Although the functions of the biochemical regulation can, in principle, be modeled using concentrations of regulating substances, such an approach has not been possible because of insufficient knowledge of the system and limited data.

Another alternative is to assume that the status of the biochemical regulation can be described with a state variable, W. Now the model for photosynthesis, e.g., under water stress, can be expressed as

$$f(I,T,W) = f_I(I)\, f_T(T)\, f_W(W,T) \tag{18.12}$$

where f_I and f_T are (as previously) effects of irradiance and temperature on photosynthesis and f_W is the interacting effect of the status of biochemical regulation system and temperature.

The term f_W equals one, when the photosynthetic system is operating without symptoms of water deficit. Laboratory and field experiments have shown that increasing temperature causes symptoms of water deficit, particularly when the soil is dry (4,5). Such an affect is reasonable since the water-vapor deficit in the air is determined by temperature to a great extent in field conditions. The following approximation seems to work reasonably well:

$$f_w(W,T) = \begin{cases} 1 & \text{when} \quad T \le W \\ e^{-a(T-W)} & \text{when} \quad T \ge W \end{cases} \tag{18.13}$$

where a is a parameter.

As can be seen from Eq. 18.13, W can be interpreted as a threshold temperature for signs of water stress. The value of W changes slowly. It can be assumed to be constant during a day. It cannot be measured directly, but can be estimated using normal statistical procedures, such as minimizing the residual sum of squares. The model (Eq. 18.12) includes three functions to be determined using empirical results. The functions f_I and f_T can be determined in non-water-stressed conditions. The parameter a in the function f_W is constant during summer. The status of the biochemical control system (W) is the only quantity to be estimated when analyzing measurements of photosynthesis during water deficit. If the number of measurements during a given day exceeds 15–20, then the estimation can be done easily.

The model (Eq. 18.12) has proved to be an effective tool in analyzing field data. The fit of the model is demonstrated in Fig. 18.2. The value of the variable W decreases when the water deficit becomes more severe. This means that the stomata begin to close at low temperatures during increasing water deficit. In addition, the water vapor concentration may have a minor effect on W (4).

The linkage between threshold temperature and soil water concentration S_W is a key to understanding the behavior of trees during water deficit. The stomata regulate transpiration and also photosynthesis. This generates linkage between the depletion rate of water pool in the soil and the amount of water in the soil. Let E denote the transpiration rate of the stand and U the rainfall rate reaching the ground. The structure of the models connecting soil properties and gas exchange is

$$\frac{dS_W}{dt} = U - E \tag{18.14}$$

$$W = aS_W + b \tag{18.15}$$

$$E = \int_V \rho(x)cf_w(W,T)(w_a - w_i)\,dV \tag{18.16}$$

where ρ is leaf area distribution, V is the volume of the crown of the tree, f_w is (as mentioned earlier) the interacting effect of the status of the biochemical control system and temperature on photosynthesis, w_a is water-vapor concentration in the air, w_i is water-vapor concentration in the intercellular space, and a,b,c are parameters.

The regulation system of trees also reacts to the annual cycle of environment at least in the temperate zone. A scalar variable, M, is introduced to describe the annual stage of development. According to Pelkonen (6,7), the photosynthetic rate in the spring depends on irradiance, temperature, and annual stage of development. The model is a modification of the model describing photosynthesis during water deficit:

$$p(I,T,W,M) = f_I(I)f_T(T)f_w(W,T)f_M(M) \tag{18.17}$$

The function f_M describing the effect of annual cycle equals one during active

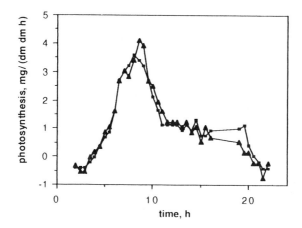

FIG. 18.2. Measured (squares) and calculated (Eq. 18.12) (triangles) photosynthesis during July 17, 1982 at Forestry Field Station University of Helsinki.

period and it is close to zero in the winter time. This requirement can be fulfilled with the following function

$$f_M(M) = \begin{cases} M/d_1 & \text{when} \quad M < d_1 \\ 1 & \text{when} \quad M > d_1 \end{cases} \tag{18.18}$$

where d_1 is a parameter.

The rate of development, m, defined as the time derivative of the annual stage of development, is determined primarily by temperature. Also, the annual stage of development seems to have an effect on the rate of development. The following approximation seems to be in satisfactory agreement with field measurements (7):

$$\frac{dM}{dt} = m(T,M) = \frac{100}{1 + 100 \, d_2^{-(T-M/d_3)}} - \frac{100}{1 + 100 \, d_2^{(T-M/d_3)}} \tag{18.19}$$

where d_2 and d_3 are parameters.

The annual stage of development changes so slowly that it can be assumed to be constant during a given day. The daily value of M can be estimated if measurements of CO_2 exchange are available. The water deficit effect f_W can be detected only on warm days in the spring. According to Pelkonen (8), there seems to be a clear linear relationship between the annual stage of development and the status of biochemical regulation system of water deficit W in the spring.

The models of photosynthesis, including the status of biochemical control systems, have the advantage that the photosynthetic rate can be predicted accurately using only environmental variables, i.e., irradiance, temperature, soil water concentration, and water-vapor concentration. This model has, however, the disadvantage that the structure of the system is characterized by aggregated description of components.

18.3.4. System properties based on leaf structure

Gaastra (9) introduced the Ohm's law analog approach in the analysis of photosynthesis. The physical background is flow of gas between two reservoirs having different gas concentrations. If the flow of gas is caused by diffusion, then the flow rate is linearly proportional to the concentration difference between the two reservoirs. The coefficient linking the flow rate and the concentration difference is called *conductance*. When the analogue of Ohm's law is especially stressed, the term *resistance* is used, which is the reciprocal of conductance.

The flow of CO_2 from atmosphere into the intercellular space of a leaf is diffusion of gas. Consequently, the Ohm's law analog is well justified. Let C_a denote the ambient CO_2 concentration, C_i the intercellular CO_2 concentration, and p the photosynthetically induced flow of CO_2 into the leaf. The Ohm's law analog links C_a, C_i, and p together

$$p = g_s(C_a - C_i) \tag{18.20}$$

where g_s is the stomatal conductance.

This above model has the disadvantage that C_i should be known in order to calculate photosynthesis. This problem is solved by applying the Ohm's law analog once again and introducing the mesophyll conductance. The definition of mesophyll conductance is, however, rather problematic since the CO_2 concentration close to chloroplasts varies strongly. This is usually omitted. Despite this theoretical weakness, the mesophyll conductance is frequently used. An alternate possibility is to assume that mesophyll CO_2 concentration is zero; then the mesophyll conductance is well defined.

Mesophyll conductance is needed for describing the effect of irradiance on photosynthesis. This is modeled by assuming that the mesophyll conductance depends on the irradiance. This may result in a rather satisfactory agreement with empirical results (10).

The problem of applying the Ohm's law analog in a situation that implicitly assumes zero concentration can be avoided by analyzing and modeling the CO_2 concentration at the site of fixation as Marshal and Biscoe (11) have shown. The construction of the model is based on three assumptions: (a) the photosynthetic rate is assumed to depend on a Michaelis–Menten type of function of irradiance and the CO_2 concentration at the site of fixation, (b) the net photosynthetic rate is the photosynthetic rate plus the respiration rate, and (c) the net photosynthetic rate is the concentration difference between ambient CO_2 and CO_2 concentration at the site of fixation divided by resistance. From these three equations, net photosynthetic rate can be determined.

The model describing the functions of light and CO_2 receptors (12,13) has a dynamic character. It allows the study of the effects of changing irradiance and other environmental factors on photosynthetic process. A very detailed description of the biochemical reactions of Calvin cycle is included into the model presented by Laisk (14,15). These dynamic models give a deeper insight into the photosynthetic process and should be utilized in the research.

18.3.5. Optimal control of gas exchange

The optimality hypothesis offers a third alternative to modeling the regulation of photosynthesis in plants. Then it is assumed that plants regulate their gas exchange in such a way that the photosynthesis is maximized within the limitations imposed by the availability of water (16,17). The optimality hypothesis is further developed by Hari et al. (18).

The flows of CO_2 are driven by photosynthesis and respiration. These flows of carbon dioxide determine the intercellular CO_2 concentration. For modeling purposes let us consider a leaf element, so small that environmental factors do not include spatial variation within the element. Let A denote the area of the element, C_i the intercellular CO_2 concentration, and C_a the ambient CO_2 concentration, p the photosynthetic rate, r the respiratory rate, and h the mean thickness of intercellular space. The amount of CO_2 in the intercellular space is the volume multiplied by the concentration: hAC_i. The volume of intercellular space can be considered to be constant. Now, the inflow plus the respiratory production minus the photosynthetic consumption equals the change in intercellular CO_2 concentration. This can be described by a differential equation describing the time development of intercellular CO_2 concentration:

$$hA \frac{dC_i}{dt} = A[g(C_a - C_i) - p + r] \qquad (18.21)$$

where g is the stomatal conductance.

Assume the photosynthesis is proportional to the product of the two limiting factors, irradiance and intercellular CO_2 concentration:

$$p = \alpha d I C_i \qquad (18.22)$$

This assumption is a simplification of that presented in Marshall and Biscoe (11). The time constant of intercellular CO_2 concentration seems to be a few seconds (19). Assuming that for short intervals the intercellular CO_2 concentration is in steady state, the time derivative equals zero and Eq. 18.1 results in

$$A[g(C_a - C_i) - p + r] = 0 \qquad (18.23)$$

The intercellular CO_2 concentration C_i can be solved

$$C_i = \frac{gC_a + r}{g + \alpha I} \tag{18.24}$$

The dependence of the photosynthetic rate p on the irradiance and ambient CO_2 concentration can be determined using Eqs. 18.22 and 18.24:

$$p = \frac{\alpha I(gC_a + r)}{g + \alpha I} \tag{18.25}$$

For steady-state conditions the resulting function is of Michaelis–Menten type for irradiance and linear for ambient CO_2 if the small respiratory term is neglected.

The stomatal functioning is introduced into the analysis with the degree of stomatal opening, u. Let g denote stomata conductance and g_o conductance when stomata are fully open. The degree of stomatal opening, u is defined as

$$g = ug_o \tag{18.26}$$

When g is replaced with ug_o in Eq. 18.25, the model for photosynthetic rate now includes the functioning of stomata.

Let e denote transpiration rate, w_i intercellular water vapor concentration, and w_a ambient one. Using these notations, the "classical" model for transpiration (9) is

$$e = aug_o(w_i - w_a) \tag{18.27}$$

where a is constant ($a = 1.6$).

Assume that there is a transpiration cost λ for maintaining a sufficient water stream per unit amount of water. The λ is expressed as grams of carbon dioxide consumed per gram of transpired water. The stomatal control is considered to be optimal if the amount of photosynthesis minus transpiration costs is maximized during the time interval under consideration:

$$\max_u \left\{ \int_{t_1}^{t_2} \frac{\alpha I(t)[ug_oC_a + r(T(t))]}{ug_o + \alpha\, I(t)}\, dt - \lambda \int_{t_1}^{t_2} aug_o[w_i(t) - w_a]dt \right\} \tag{18.28}$$

where t_1 is the beginning instant and t_2 the cessation instant of the period under consideration.

The maximization problem can be solved using a slight modification of the solution by Hari et al. (18). The optimal degree of stomatal opening u is

$$u^* = \begin{cases} 1 & \text{when stomata are fully open} \\[2mm] \left(\sqrt{\dfrac{C_a - (r\alpha I)}{\lambda a\,(w_i - w_a)}} - 1\right)\dfrac{\alpha I}{g_o} & \text{when stomata are partially closed} \\[2mm] 0 & \text{when stomata are closed} \end{cases} \tag{18.29}$$

According to this solution, the stomata may be fully open also during limited availability of water. This occurs if environmental factors are favorable for photosynthesis and unfavorable for transpiration. The degree of stomatal opening depends on irradiance, water-vapor pressure deficit, and respiration rate.

If the stomata are fully open, the photosynthetic rate is determined by irradiance according to the Eq. 18.25. This dependence is of the Michaelis–Menten type. If the stomata are partially closed, the photosynthetic rate is determined by irradiance and leaf temperature, which determines the intercellular water-vapor concentration. The dependence on irradiance is linear, which can be seen after algebraic manipulation. The dependence on temperature is rather complicated because the intercellular water-vapor concentration appears in Eq. 18.29 under a square root. The preliminary analysis of field data show a rather close agreement with measured and calculated photosynthetic rates (20).

18.4. Growth

Growth is considered to be an accumulation of organic material. Carbon, the principal structural component of plants—e.g., 50% of the total dry weight in Scots pine (21), is also an indirect measure of energy gain and expenditure in plants (22). Therefore, the models of stand growth are often based on the carbon balance (23–30). In stand growth models based on carbon budget, the rates of photosynthesis and respiration determine the new growth. However, the net growth is the difference between the growth and the senescence of different parts of trees.

The factors affecting photosynthesis as discussed in Section 18.3 include the amount of intercepted photosynthetically active radiation (PAR), water, and nutrient availability (31). The effect of these factors on photosynthetic production can be caused by decrease in the foliage area (32,33) or decreases in the process rates (see Section 18.3). For modeling, the respiration is often considered to result from maintenance, growth, or transport processes (34,35). As these processes determine the nonstructural carbon outflow from the system, their accurate description in the models is important. The proportion of the respiration from the total photosynthetic production has been estimated to be 40–50% in the boreal *Pinus sylvestris* forests and may go up to 90% in Australian *Pinus radiata* forests (36).

The biomass production by a tree is partitioned between the tree organelles. It has been shown experimentally that there are considerable changes in the carbohydrate partitioning of trees in response to a changing environment (21,32,37).

For shoot:root partitioning of carbohydrates the concept of functional balance between the foliage and fine roots has been developed (38–40). The shoot:root partitioning models have been further developed by Thornley (41) and Reynolds and Thornley (42). The variation in the shoot to total dry weight between the models is small, which would suggest that the more simple formulation by Davidson could be used as a simple approximation of the more detailed models (29).

The assimilate partitioning in woody plants, particularly into transport tissue, is a very complex and difficult topic. The branches, stem, and transport roots take up a considerable proportion of the total carbohydrates used for growth (28,43–47). However, it is not well known how the rate of substrate supply and control through plant growth substances affect the cambial activities and cell enlargement (48). It seems that auxin plays a major role in controlling the rate of cambial differentiation (49), but more work is needed to predict the xylem growth in relation to environmental conditions, especially when whole trees in stands are considered.

Similarly as with foliage and fine roots, an assumption of functional balance between foliage and transport structure can be made (25,50,51). This assumption is supported by observed regularities in the structure of tree between foliage and cross-sectional area of transporting wood (52–56), which is formulated as the "pipeline" model theory (57,58).

The carbohydrate partitioning on woody structure can be derived from the above-mentioned structural regularities (25,59,60). The same idea can be used to derive the carbon balance for a stand (61) or to stimulate the crown-form dynamics of trees within a stand (62).

The model described below uses the principles mentioned above and is based on the work at the Department of Silviculture, Helsinki University (23,27), but the allocation of carbohydrates is modified to correspond to the cost–benefit principle presented elsewhere (62). The actual structure of the model is presented in the Fig. 18.3.

The carbon inflow is a function of potential annual photosynthetic production of unshaded conditions and the shading of the existing biomass of the stand. The former is determined from field measurements (4). The growth and maintenance respiration depend on the growth rate and on the length of growing period and biomasses of different plant parts, respectively. The accumulation of biomass is the difference between the growth and senescence of different biomass compartments. In the model the needles die after reaching a certain age, and the branch senescence is connected to needle biomass decrease within a branch. The stem sapwood turnover into heartwood is a function of needles dying below the new living crown. The coarse- and fine-root senescence is a linear function of their total biomass. The height growth of trees is a function of carbohydrates allocated to the stem, the light position of trees, and the lifetime-long height growth rhythm, which gives the maximum height growth at any age of the stand.

The new needles are distributed within the crown in such a way that the ratio between their photosynthetic production and the structural carbohydrate consumption is the same within the crown (62). On the structural cost are

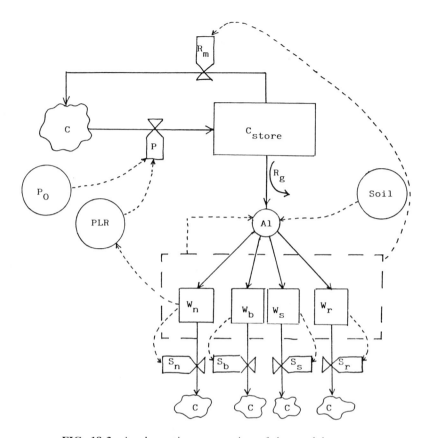

FIG. 18.3. A schematic presentation of the model structure.

calculated the needle biomass, the root biomass required to supply the needles with enough nutrients (functional balance), and the "pipeline" connecting these organs together. A detailed presentation of the equations, variables used in the model, and the parameter values are presented in Section 18.7.

Figure 18.4 present the simulated development of different biomass compartments. The stem biomass development from simulations is compared with the values taken from growth and yield studies (63) in Fig. 18.5. The starting point for the curve in Fig. 18.4 was chosen so that the yield tables corresponded with the stem biomass value of the simulations, since the simulations did not start from the age 0. The development of the needle biomass height distribution is shown in Fig. 18.6.

The simulated pattern of biomass accumulation in different compartments agrees quite well with the reported results on the development of needles (45) or the stem. When the root functioning was altered during simulations,

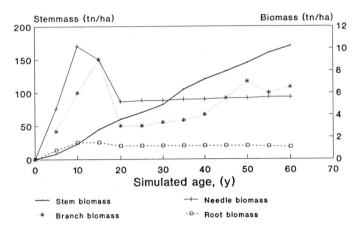

FIG. 18.4. The simulated development of different biomass compartments.

the changes in the height distribution of needles mass were similar, as reported in many fertilization experiments (21,32,64).

The present model is thus able to predict with certain accuracy the functioning and growth of a forest stand. A better description of the soil conditions and derivation of energy from the assimilates in relation to nutrient uptake is needed to improve the model. The pipeline model theory is a gross approximation of the formation of the stem. In the future a more accurate description of the woody structure is needed, especially the connection between foliage transpiration and the water transport through sapwood. The simulations indicated that the branching pattern and the heartwood formation have a considerable effect on carbon usage. Finally, the model used to describe light climate was very simple since it assumed horizontally homogeneous canopy. To predict the performance of single trees within a stand, a more detailed description of light climate is needed.

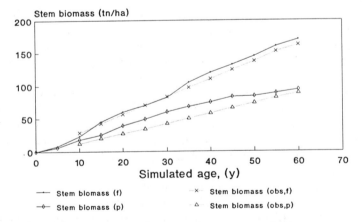

FIG. 18.5. The comparison between simulated and yield tables of stem biomass in fertile and poor soils.

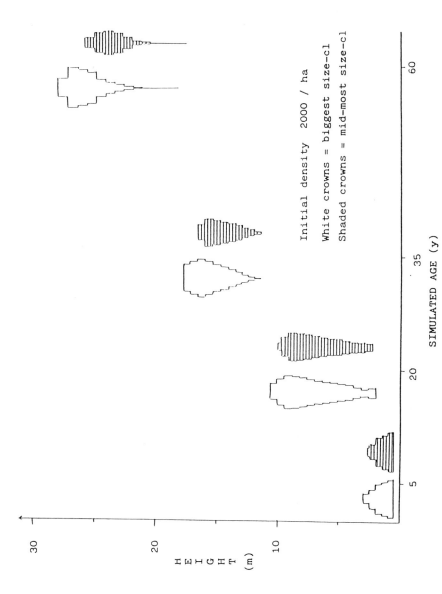

FIG. 18.6. Simulated development of vertical needle mass distribution. (The width of the crown is proportional to needle mass per unit length.)

18.5. Concluding remarks

The use of material flows offers a quantitative description of the functioning of a system that can be easily transformed into a mathematical expressions. In this chapter we have described a limited part of flows taking place in the forest ecosystem and the environmental factors affecting them. At the present the analysis is concentrated only on the energy capture and carbon flows. However, there does not seem to be any overwhelming reason why a similar approach could not be used to include the nutrient and water flows more explicitly.

The work presented here evolved mainly during a long period of continuous interaction between modeling and experimental work in the field. The object of the research has been a rather simple ecosystem of boreal even-aged *Pinus silvestris* stands. During the work it became clear that with a close cooperation between empirical work and modeling practices, the focus of the empirical work has improved. When we consider the below ground parts of the ecosystem that are more complicated and rather difficult to measure, the connection between modeling and empirical work is still more important for a rapid progress.

Once a simple but sufficiently extensive description of the dynamics of a forest ecosystem has been developed that includes the main processes, it can be used as a backbone to study practical problems or to study more heterogeneous systems with more disturbing variance. The material flows offer a possibility for a construction of a family of coherent models that can be applied in different situations, even outside the range of environmental variables in which the experimental work is done. This is important in the present situation, when we are experiencing the CO_2 increase and also an evident climate change.

The model structures used to analyze photosynthesis were assumed to be very simple; only the main features of the phenomenon was described. Despite this fact, the fit of the models were often within the measuring accuracy. Also, the predictive power of the models is good. The growth model is more complicated, but the ideas guiding the construction are simple and biologically well justified. Even with the present simple structure, the results obtained are in reasonable agreement with the rather limited empirical results available. It seems evident that with dynamic models, based on flows of material, the main features of the functions of a stand can be rather accurately described.

18.6. References

1. P. Oker-Blom, *Acta For. Fenn.*, **197**, 1–44 (1986).
2. S. Kellomäki, P. Hari, M. Kanninen, and P. Ilonen, *Silva Fennica*, **14**, 243–257 (1980).
3. P. Hari, R. Sievänen, and R. Salminen, *Flora*, **173**, 63–70 (1983).

4. E. Korpilahti, *Acta For. Fenn.*, **202**, 1–71 (1988).

5. P. Hari and O. Luukkanen, *Physiol. Plant.*, **29**, 45–53 (1973).

6. P. Pelkonen, *Flora*, **169**, 386–397 (1980).

7. P. Pelkonen and P. Hari, *Flora*, **169**, 389–404 (1980).

8. P. Pelkonen, *Recovery and Cessation of CO_2 Uptake in Scots Pine at the Beginning and at the End of the Annual Photosynthetic Period*, Univ. Helsinki, Dept. Silviculture, Research Notes No. 30, Helsinki, 1981, p. 95.

9. T. Gaastra, *Mededelningen van de Landbouwhoegeschool de Wageningen. Nederland*, **13**, 1–68 (1959).

10. T. Lohammar, S. Larson, S. Linder, and S. Falk, "Fast-simulation models of gas exchange in Scots pine," in T. Persson, ed., *Structure and Function of Northern Coniferous Forests*, Ecol. Bulletin, Stockholm, 1980, pp. 505–525.

11. B. Marshal and P. Biscoe, *J. Exp. Bot.*, **31**, 29–39 (1980).

12. J.H.M. Thornley, *Mathematical Models in Plant Physiology*, Academic Press, London, 1976, p. 318.

13. V. Kaitala, P. Hari, E. Vapaavuori, and R. Salminen, *Ann. Bot.*, **50**, 385–396 (1982).

14. A. Laisk and H. Eichelman, *Phil. Trans. Roy. Soc. London*, **323**, 369–384 (1989).

15. A. Laisk and D. Walker, *Proc. Roy. Soc. London*, **B227**, 281–302 (1986).

16. I.R. Cowan and G.D. Farquhar, "Stomatal function in relation to leaf metabolism and environment," in D.H. Jennings, ed., *Integration of Activity in Higher Plants*, Cambridge Univ. Press., Cambridge, 1977, pp. 471–505.

17. I.R. Cowan, *Adv. Bot. Res.*, **4**, 117–228 (1977).

18. P. Hari, A. Mäkelä, E. Korpilahti, and M. Holmberg, "Optimal control of gas exchange," in R.L. Luxmoore, J.J. Landsberg, and M.R. Kaufman, eds., *Coupling of Carbon, Water and Nutrient Interactions in Woody Plant Soil Systems*, Heron Publishing, Victoria, Canada, 1986, p. 169–175.

19. P. Hari, V. Kaitala, and R. Salminen, *Photosynthetica*, **22(2)**, 236–239 (1988).

20. P. Hari and F. Berninger, "Field testing of optimal control of gas exchange," in H. Jozefek and P. Pelkonen, eds., *Modelling to Understand Forest Functions*, Joensuu Univ., Joensuu, in press.

21. S. Linder and B. Axelsson, "Changes in carbon uptake and allocation pattern as a result of irrigation and fertilization in a young Pinus silvestris stand," in R.H. Waring, ed., *Carbon Uptake and Allocation in Subalpine Ecosystems as a Key to Management*, Forest Research Laboratory, Corvallis, OR, 1982, pp. 38–42.

22. F.S. Chapin III, *Am. Nat.*, **133(1)**, 1–19 (1989).

23. P. Hari, S. Kellomäki, A. Mäkelä, P. Ilonen, M. Kanninen, E. Korpilahti, and M. Nygren, *Acta For. Fenn.*, **177**, 1–39 (1982).

24. R. McMutrie and L. Wolf, *Ann. Bot.*, **52**, 437–448 (1983).

25. P. Hari, L. Kaipiainen, E. Korpilahti, A. Mäkelä, T. Nilson, P. Oker-Blom, J. Ross, and R. Salminen, *Structure, Radiation and Photosynthetic Production in Coniferous Stands*, Univ. Helsinki, Dept. Silviculture, Res. Notes No. 54, Helsinki, 1985, p. 233.

26. S. Linder, R.E. McMurtrie, and J.J. Landsberg, "Growth of eucalyptus: A mathematical model applied to *Eucalyptus globulus*," in P.M.A. Tigersted, P. Put-

tonen, and V. Koski, eds., *Crop Physiology of Forest Trees*, Helsinki Univ. Press, Helsinki, 1985, pp. 117–126.

27. A. Mäkelä and P. Hari, *Ecol. Modelling*, **33**, 205–229 (1986).

28. G.M.J. Mohren, *Simulation of Forest Growth, Applied to Douglas Fir Stands in the Netherlands*, Pudoc, Wageningen, 1987, p. 184.

29. A. Mäkelä, *Models of Pine Stand Development: An Ecophysiological Systems Analysis*, Univ. Helsinki, Dept. Silviculture, Research Notes No. 62, Helsinki, 1988, p. 267.

30. P. Hari, E. Nikinmaa, and M. Holmberg, "Implications of photosynthesis, transpiration and of water and nutrient uptake on the structure of trees," in R.K. Dixon, R.S. Meldahl, G.A. Ruark, and W.G. Warren, eds., *Process Modeling of Forest Growth Responses to Environmental Stress*, Timber Press, Portland, OR, in press.

31. J.P. Lassoie, T.M. Hinckley, and C.C. Grier, "Coniferous forest of the Pacific Northwest," in B.F. Chabot and H.A. Mooney, eds., *Physiological Ecology of North American Plant Communities*, Chapman and Hall, New York–London, 1987, pp. 127–161.

32. S. Linder, "Responses to water and nutrients in coniferous ecosystems," in E. Schultze and H. Zwölfer, eds., *Potentials and Limitations of Ecosystem Analyses*, Springer-Verlag, Berlin, 1987, pp. 180–202.

33. D. Whitehead, "A review of processes in the water relations of forests," in J.J. Landsberg and W. Parsons, eds., *Research for Forest Management*, CSIRO, Melbourne, Australia, 1985, pp. 94–124.

34. F.W.T. Penning de Vries, *Neth. J. Agric. Sci.*, **22**, 40–44 (1974).

35. F.W.T. Penning de Vries, A.H.M. Brunstig, and H.H. Van Laar, *J. Theor. Biol.*, **45**, 339–377 (1974).

36. S. Linder, "Potential and actual production in Austrian forest stands," in J.J. Landsberg and W. Person, eds., *Research for Forest Management, Division of Forest Research*, CSIRO, 1985, pp. 1–35.

37. T. Ingestad, *Physiol. Plant.*, **52**, 454–466 (1981).

38. H.L. White, *Ann. Bot.*, **1**, 649 (1935).

39. R. Brouwer, *Netherl. J. Agric. Sci.*, **10**, 361–376 (1962).

40. R.L. Davidson, *Ann. Bot.*, **33**, 561–569 (1969).

41. J.H.M. Thorley, *Ann. Bot.*, **36**, 431–441 (1972).

42. J.F. Reynolds and J.H.M. Thorley, *Ann. Bot.*, **49**, 585–597 (1982).

43. C.M. Möller, D. Müller, and J. Nielsen, *Forstl. Forsoekgsvaes. Dan.*, **21**, 327–335 (1954).

44. E. Mälkönen, *Commun. Inst. For. Fenn.*, **84(5)**, 1–87 (1974).

45. A. Albrektson, "Total tree production as compared to conventional forestry production," in T. Persson, ed., *Structure and Function of Northern Coniferous Forest—an Ecosystem Study. Ecological Bulletin*, Stockholm, 1980, pp. 315–328.

46. A. Albrektson and E. Valinger, "Relations between tree height and diameter, productivity and allocation of growth in a Scots Pine (*Pinus silvestris* L.) sample tree material," in P.M.A. Tigersted, P. Puttonen, and V. Koski, eds., *Crop Physiology of Forest Trees*, Helsinki Univ. Press, Helsinki, 1985, pp. 95–105.

47. E. Schultze and F.S. Chapin III, "Plant specialization to environments of different resource availability," in E. Schultze and H. Zwölfer, eds., *Potentials and Limitations of Ecosystem Analyses*, Springer-Verlag, Berlin, 1987, pp. 120–148.

48. E.D. Ford, "Can we model xylem production by conifers," in S. Linder, ed., *Understanding and Predicting Tree Growth*, Studia Forestalia Suecica, Stockholm, 1981, pp. 19–29.

49. L.W. Roberts, P.B. Gahan, and R. Aloni, *Vascular Differentiation and Plant Growth Regulators*, Springer-Verlag, Berlin, 1988.

50. P.G. Jarvis, "Water transfer in plants," in D.A. de Vries and N.G. Afgan, eds., *Heat and Mass Transfer in the Plant Environment*, Scripta Book Co., Washington DC, 1975, pp. 369–394.

51. D. Whitehead and P.G. Jarvis, "Coniferous forests and plantations," in T.T. Kozlowski, ed., *Water Deficit and Plant Growth*, Academic Press, New York, 1981, pp. 49–152.

52. M. Kaufman and C. Troendle, *For. Sci.*, **27**, 477–482 (1981).

53. J.N. Long, F.W. Smith, and D.R.M. Scott, *Can. J. For. Res.*, **11**, 459–464 (1981).

54. R. Waring, R. Schroeder, and R. Ohren, *Can. J. For. Res.*, **12**, 556–560 (1982).

55. L. Kaipiainen and P. Hari, "Consistencies in the structure of Scots Pine," in P. Tigersted, P. Puttonen, and V. Koski, eds., *Crop Physiology of Forest Trees*, Helsinki Univ. Press, Helsinki, 1985, pp. 32–37.

56. P. Hari, P. Heikinheimo, A. Mäkelä, L. Kaipiainen, E. Korpilahti, and J. Samela, *Silva Fenn.*, **20**, 205–210 (1986).

57. K. Shinozaki, K. Yoda, K, Hozuni, and T. Kira, *Japn. J. Ecol.*, **14**, 97–105 (1964).

58. K. Shinozaki, K. Yoda, K. Hozumi, and T. Kira, *Japn. J. Ecol.*, **14**, 133–139 (1964).

59. H.T. Valentine, *J. Theor. Biol.*, **117**, 579–584 (1985).

60. A. Mäkelä, *J. Theor. Biol.*, **123**, 103–120 (1986).

61. H. Valentine, *Ann. Bot.*, **62**, 389–396 (1988).

62. E.H. Nikinmaa and P. Hari, "A simplified carbon partitioning model for Scots pine to address the effects of altered needle longevity and nutrient uptake on stand development," in R.K. Dixon, R.S. Meldahl, G.A. Ruark, and W.G. Warren, eds., *Process Modeling of Forest Growth Responses to Environmental Stress*, Timber Press, Portland, OR, in press.

63. Y. Ilvessalo, *Acta For. Fenn.*, **15**, 1–96 (1920).

64. H. Brix, *Can. J. For. Res.*, **11(3)**, 502–511 (1981).

18.7. Appendix

The variables and equations used in the stand growth model (order as they appear in the equations) are as follows:

Variable	Meaning	Unit
P	Annual photosynthetic production	kg C yr^{-1} m^{-2}
P_0	Potential annual photosynthetic production in unshaded conditions	kg C yr^{-1} m^{-2}
PLR	Photosynthetic light ratio	
ρ	Needle area distribution	m^2 m^{-3}
h_t	Top height of a tree	m
l	Lower limit of the living crown	m
B	Total stand needle biomass	kg dW
R	Total annual respiration	kg (C) yr^{-1}
R_m	Total annual maintenance respiration	kg (C) yr^{-1}
R_g	Total annual growth respiration	kg C yr^{-1}
r_i	Maintenance respiration parameter	kg (C) yr^{-1} kg (dW)$^{-1}$
c	Growth respiration parameter	kg (C) yr^{-1} kg (dW)$^{-1}$
n,b,s,tr,r	Indexes referring to needles, branches, stem, transport roots, and fine roots	
W_i	Total biomass of a biomass compartment	kg (dW)
G	Annual growth	kg (dW) yr^{-1}
a_i	Allocation coefficient	
M_i	Growth of a biomass compartment	kg (dW) yr^{-1}
m_i	Density of growth of biomass connected to height h	kg (dW) m^{-1} yr^{-1}
l_{sh}	Length of new shoots at particular height h	m
l_b	Average length of branch at particular height h	m
L_b	Reuse of transport structure in branches at height h released by dying needles	m kg (dW)$^{-1}$
L_s	Reuse of transport structure in stem	m kg (dW)$^{-1}$
g_b	Sapwood:needle mass ratio for branches	cm^2 g (dW)$^{-1}$
C_c	Conversion of carbon to dry matter	kg (dW) kg (C)$^{-1}$

(*continued on next page*)

Variable	Meaning	Unit
g_s	Sapwood:needle mass ratio for stem	$cm^2\ g\ (dW)^{-1}$
g_{tr}	Sapwood:fine-root mass ratio for transport roots	$cm^2\ g\ (dW)^{-1}$
A	Age of a whorl	year
w_i	Density of biomass connected to height h	$kg\ (dW)\ m^{-1}$
par_1	Parameter relating root and foliage functioning efficiencies	
par_2	Root mortality fraction	
l_r	Average transport root length	m
C	Benefit–cost ratio	
γ	Mass specific needle area	$m^2\ kg\ (dW)^{-1}$
G_h	Annual height growth	m
PI	Position index	
Ag	Age of tree	
s	Diameter growth	m
t_{n1}, t_{n2}	Needle age transformation parameters	
S_i	Senescence of biomass compartments	$kg\ (dW)\ yr^{-1}$
NT	Density of the tree stand	number ha^{-1}

The equations are as follows.
Annual photosynthetic production:

$$P = P_0 \int_l^{h_t} PLR(z)\rho(z)dz$$

$$PLR(z) = \frac{1}{1 + e^{[-2(\log B(z) - \alpha]\beta}}$$

Respiration:

$$R = R_m + R_g$$

$$R_{mi} = r_i W_i \qquad (i = n,b,s,tr,r)$$

$$R_g = gG$$

$$G = (P - R) \cdot C_c$$

Growth of biomass compartments:

$$C_c \cdot a_i(P - R) = M_i \qquad (i = n,b,s,tr,r)$$

$$M_i = \int_l^{h_t} m_i(z)dz$$

At each height z for branches:

$$m_b = (l_{sh}m_n + l_b m_n - L_b)g_b$$

$$l_{sh} = \begin{cases} \dfrac{(bm_n + c)}{6! - (6 - A)! \times l_b/d} & \text{if} \quad A < 6 \\[2ex] \dfrac{(bm_n + c)}{6! \times l_b/d} & \text{if} \quad A > 6 \end{cases}$$

Stem:

$$m_s = (zm_n - L_s)g_s$$

Fine roots:

$$W_r = par_1 W_n$$

$$m_r = par_1(m_n - s_n) + par_2 w_r$$

Transport roots:

$$m_{tr} = \begin{cases} l_r g_r par_1(m_n - s_n) & \text{if} \quad m_n - S_n \geq 0 \\ 0 & \text{if} \quad m_n - S_n < 0 \end{cases}$$

Cost–benefit principle:

$$\frac{P_0 \, PLR(z) \, \rho(z)}{m_n(z) + m_b(z) + m_s(z) + m_r(z)} = C$$

in which

$$\rho(z) = m_n(z) \, \gamma(z)$$

where

$$\gamma(z) = N_1 PLR(z) + N_2$$

Since

$$\int_l^{h_t} \sum_i m_i(z)dz = (P - R) \cdot \alpha$$

We can solve the equation and obtain the allocation of carbohydrates and the height distribution of the new needle biomass. To calculate the stand growth, additional state variables need to be defined.
Height growth:

$$G_h = f_1(PI)f_2(S)f_3(AG)$$

where

$$f_1(PI) = 1 - c_1 PI$$

$$f_2(s) = \frac{s}{s + 1/c_2}$$

$$f_3(AG) = h_0 - h_1 AG$$

$$s = M_s h$$

$$PI = \frac{\int_l^h PLR(z)\, \rho(z)dz}{\int_l^h \rho(z)dz}$$

Senescence of needles:

$$m_{2n}(k + 1) = t_{n1}m_{1n}(k)$$

$$m_{3n}(k + 1) = t_{n2}m_{2n}(k)$$

$$s_n = [(1 - t_{n1})m_{n_1}(z) + (1 - t_{n2})m_{n_2}(z) + m_{n_3}(z)]dz$$

$$S_n = \int_l^{h_t} s_n(z)\, dz$$

Senescence of branches:

$$S_b = \int_l^h (1 - t_{n1})m_{n_1}(z)[l_{sh}(z) + l_b(z)]$$

$$+ (1 - t_{n2})m_{n_2}(z)l_b(z) + m_{n_3}(z)[l_{bp}(z) - L_b(z]dz$$

Senescence of roots:

$$S_r = \text{par}_2 W_i$$

Dynamic equation for each tree biomass compartment:

$$W_i^j(k + 1) = W_i^j(k) + M_i^j(k) - S_i^j(k)$$

The tree height changes as follows:

$$h^j(k + 1) = h^j(k - G_h(k)$$

$$B(z,k) = \sum_{j=1}^{m} NT_j(k) \int_{z}^{h} \rho_j(z)dz$$

The densities of the tree stands change as individual trees die:

$$NT_j(k + 1) = NT_j(k) - \alpha_j(k)NT_j(k)$$

$$\alpha_j(k) = \frac{M_n^j(k) - S_n^j(k)}{M_j(k)} \alpha_0$$

19 Use of Tissue Culture in Tree Physiology

PRAKASH P. KUMAR

Plant Physiology Research Group, Department of Biological Sciences, University of Calgary, Calgary, Alberta, Canada, *Botany Department, National University of Singapore, Republic of Singapore,

and

TREVOR A. THORPE

Plant Physiology Research Group, Department of Biological Sciences, University of Calgary, Calgary, Alberta, Canada

Contents

*Present address.

19.1. Introduction

Trees are structurally and physiologically complex organisms because of many unique features, such as long growth periods, the presence of juvenile and mature phases, and heterozygous genomes. In order to understand some of the metabolic problems associated with their growth and development one must study trees not only in their entirety but also in their parts, i.e., organs, tissues, and cells (1). Plant physiologists have long used excised plant parts, segments, disks, and slices of organs in numerous experiments (2). Such systems, in the past, were riddled with technical problems, e.g., (a) plant materials not suitable for continued growth and development and (b) frequent microbial contamination (1).

The concept of totipotency (potential of individual plant cells to develop into entire organisms) when subjected to proper conditions has provided a new powerful tool for plant research: plant cell, tissue, and organ culture. Although many workers attempted to culture plant tissues under aseptic conditions early in the twentieth-century, it was not until the mid-1930s when scientists were successful in maintaining excised plant parts for prolonged periods in vitro (3). After decades of research, we now have adequate knowledge on the aseptic techniques and the nutritive and environmental conditions required for the long-term culture of excised organs, tissues, cells, and protoplasts from a variety of plant species.

Over 1000 scientific reports have appeared concerning forestry species, wherein *in vitro* cell and tissue culture techniques have been used in this decade alone. However, many of the papers published before 1969 were concerned only with announcing the successful cultures of tissues and organs from various plant species (1). Some fundamental problems that can be studied using tissue culture systems are (a) nutritional and hormonal interrelationships between organs and tissues, (b) experimental embryology, (c) meristem organization and function, (d) organ initiation and development, and (e) juvenility and senescence (1).

In this chapter, a brief discussion of tissue culture methods will be followed by some recent studies in tree species that attempt to answer specific physiological problems associated with growth and development. In particular, studies dealing with the metabolism of carbon, nitrogen, phytohormones, nucleic acids, lipids, and secondary metabolites will be used to illustrate the usefulness of cell and tissue cultures in tree physiology.

19.2. Methods of tissue culture

For simplicity, the expression "tissue culture" will be used to describe the culture of plant cells, tissues, and organs *in vitro*. Detailed discussions of microspore and protoplast cultures are beyond the scope of this chapter. For complete details on the requirements of tissue culture laboratories, formulations of various nutrient media, obtaining aseptic explants or inoculum, as well as the protocols for culturing a variety of plant species *in vitro*, interested readers should refer to some of the excellent books that are currently available (4–10).

19.2.1. Nutrient medium

Excised tissues and organs of plants lack the capacity to synthesize all the nutrients required for their growth. Hence, to establish them in culture it is essential that in addition to the macro and micro elements they be provided with certain vitamins (e.g., thiamine, nicotinic acid, pyridoxine) and in some cases, selected amino acids (11). No single mineral formulation can support the growth and development of all plant species. When a fully defined medium fails to achieve the desired level of growth and development, complex addenda such as casein hydrolysate, yeast extract, and coconut milk (liquid endosperm of coconuts) may be incorporated into the medium. However, this should be done as a last resort because the compositions of these mixtures are not completely known. In a vast majority of the cases, about 3% (w/v) sucrose is generally added to the medium, part of which serves as a carbon source and the remaining portion serves as an osmoticum (12). In many cases my-oinositol (about 100 mg liter^{-1}) is added to the medium, the role of which is not clearly understood. In order to manipulate the growth and development of the plant tissues in vitro, various types and concentrations of phytohormones, empirically determined, are added to the medium. In general, an auxin such as indole-3-yl acetic acid (IAA), α-naphthaleneacetic acid (NAA), or 2,4-dichlorophenoxyacetic acid (2,4-D) and a cytokinin such as kinetin, N^6-benzyladenine (BA), 2-iP, or zeatin are incorporated into the culture medium.

The pH of the medium is generally adjusted to between 5.0 and 6.0 before autoclaving. If the culture is to be established on semisolid medium, gelling agents are added. Also, antioxidants such as sodium diethyl-dithiocarbamate, citric acid, or ascorbic acid may be added in specific cases (13). Addition of acid-washed activated charcoal to the medium is another common practice when culturing woody plant species (14–17). This is thought to promote growth of the tissues by adsorbing toxic metabolites that may exude from the tissues into the medium.

19.2.2. Explants

The choice of the right explant or inoculum is critical if plant regeneration is to be achieved (18–20). A variety of plant tissues or organs rich in meristematic or parenchymatic cells can be grown *in vitro* for various experimental purposes. Some of the explants of choice are shoot tips, apical meristems, axillary buds, petioles, leaf disks, stem segments, seedling tissues, and zygotic embryos. The physiological state of the donor plant may influence the response of the explants *in vitro* (21).

The explants can be obtained from aseptically grown plants, in which case they can be inoculated directly on to the medium. If the donor plants are not grown under aseptic conditions, the explants from such plants generally can be rendered aseptic by surface cleaning with chemical sterilizing agents, such as sodium hypochlorite (10–20%, v/v), mercuric chloride (0.01–0.1%, w/v), or hydrogen peroxide (6–12% peroxide). In cases where systemic infection is present (22,23), as is seen in tissues from some field-grown woody perennials, appropriate concentrations of antibiotics may be incorporated into the medium, especially for the first few subculture periods. In such cases additional controls with antibiotic treated tissues must be kept to assess any unwanted physiological changes induced by the antibiotic itself (24–26).

19.2.3. Culture conditions

The explants can be cultured under different conditions depending on the species and experimental needs. They can be kept immersed in liquid medium and incubated on rotary shakers or placed on filter-paper bridges over liquid medium. The most common type of culture is where the tissues are inoculated on semisolid media. The nutrient media are routinely solidified by adding gelling agents such as agar or Gelrite prior to autoclaving. Gelrite, which is a complex polysaccharide composed of glucuronic acid, glucose, rhamnose, and O-acetyl moieties (13), needs to be added at only about half the concentration of agar to obtain approximately the same degree of solidification. In some cases, mixtures of agar and Gelrite have been used (27).

The cultures are incubated either in darkness or under varying intensities of light from fluorescent tubes and incandescent light bulbs, alone or in combination. Temperature is generally maintained between 20 and 30°C. Plant cells and tissues in culture produce many gases such as ethylene, ethane, and CO_2, which may accumulate within the culture vessels and affect morphogenesis (28–30). The culture vessels are routinely closed with various sealants. These include plastic caps, aluminum foil, plastic film, Parafilm, and plugs made of cotton or foam. These closures, which have various degrees of permeability to the gases produced by the tissues in culture, should be selected experimentally for the culture of each plant species (31).

19.3. Advantages and limitations of using tissue cultures

19.3.1. Advantages

Advantages are as follows:

1. Excised tissues and organs are free of influence from other organs and tissues of the plant (absence of correlative influence) (32). Plant cells in culture

may therefore be considered to be "organisms" in their own right, analogous to microorganisms (33).

2. Tissue cultures tend to be relatively simple with limited number of cellular phenotypes in comparison to intact plants.

3. Rapid growth rates can be achieved with the proper conditions, especially in cell-suspension cultures.

4. *In vitro* cultures can be used as models for growth and differentiation occurring in the intact plants. Morphogenesis *in vitro* often follows the *in vivo* pathway; e.g., somatic embryogenesis essentially recapitulates all the phases of zygotic embryogenesis.

5. Plant organelles can be obtained relatively easily from protoplasts; e.g., the study of isolated vacuoles is facilitated by the use of protoplasts.

6. Study of metabolism in general is facilitated because cells and tissues are in an environment free of microbial contamination. Also, *in vitro* cultures on controlled nutrient media provide an excellent system for studying the physiological roles of micronutrients because their levels can be readily manipulated under these conditions (34).

7. Large quantities of specimen of the desired stages of development within a given pathway, e.g., somatic embryos of defined stages, can be obtained from *in vitro* cultures with relative ease for physiological and molecular analyses.

19.3.2. Limitations

Disadvantages are as follows:

1. The endogenous physiological gradients are often absent or disrupted in *in vitro* cultures.

2. The artificial environment to which the cells and tissues are subjected may alter their physiology. Therefore, comparison of data gathered from *in vitro* systems may not always be applicable directly to *in vivo* situations.

3. To date it has not always been possible to maintain specialized plant cells in their differentiated states *in vitro*. Cultured cells undergo dedifferentiation to the parenchymatous and/or meristematic state subsequent to the establishment of culture. Nevertheless, differentiated organs, such as somatic embryos, shoots and roots, can be maintained and propagated in their organized state.

Notwithstanding the above, physiological and biochemical studies have been carried out with cell suspension, callus, and organ cultures from both angiospermous and gymnospermous tree species.

19.4. Carbon metabolism

Cambium-derived cell suspension cultures of sycamore (*Acer pseudoplatanus* L.), maintained as continuous cultures in a chemostat or as batch cultures, have been used for most of the early physiological and biochemical research in tree species *in vitro* (35). Sycamore cell cultures exhibited invertase activity in the cell wall and soluble fractions of the cells (36), as did tissue cultures of *Libocedrus decurrens* Torr. and *Cupressus funebris* Endl. (37). Hence, invertase, which catalyzes the hydrolysis of sucrose into glucose and fructose, can play an important role in the uptake of sucrose from the nutrient medium by cells and tissues *in vitro* (35). Callus cultures of *Juniperus communis* were able to hydrolyze starch, sucrose, maltose, and raffinose extracellularly when grown on medium containing these carbohydrates independently of each other (38,39). These carbohydrates were broken down to the level of monosaccharides. Evidence for the secretion of enzymes, especially, amylase, was obtained (38).

The pattern of glycolysis and the pentose phosphate pathway (PPP) has been studied by examining the levels of relevant enzymes and related metabolites in sycamore cell cultures (40–42). These metabolic pathways were chosen because glycolysis provides ATP and precursors of tricarboxylic acid cycle, whereas the PPP is involved in supplying reducing power in the form of NADPH and pentose precursors for nucleic acid biosynthesis. In the cell-suspension cultures of sycamore there was a greater increase in the activities of the enzymes of the PPP than those of the glycolytic pathway (40,43). It is likely that during the initial 3–4 days after subculturing, the metabolism of the cells is directed toward biosynthetic activities in preparation for the ensuing cell divisions (35).

Pronounced increases in the intracellular levels of NADPH, ATP, and energy charge were observed during the lag phase of batch cultures of sycamore cells, followed by a decline in their levels when the cells began to divide (42). Presumably, by then the demand for these compounds decreases along with the decline in biosynthetic activities. Similarly, enhanced levels of glycolysis and PPP have been observed during growth and differentiation of shoot buds in tobacco callus, indicating that the stimulation of these two metabolic pathways may be a general phenomenon (44).

Carbon dioxide, at about 1% (v/v), was essential to the initiation of growth in sycamore cell suspension cultures (45). Addition of malate, citrate, glutamate, aspartate, and alanine at levels that did not inhibit growth in the presence of CO_2 failed to initiate growth when CO_2 was scrubbed from the flasks. This suggests that the role of CO_2 is not only in providing these products anaplerotically. The slight decrease in pH during the culture period did not affect growth, because buffered medium failed to maintain the growth rate in the absence of CO_2. When the cells were incubated with $^{14}CO_2$, malate and glutamate were the most predominantly labeled compounds, but aspartate and alanine along with two unidentified metabolites were also labeled.

Activities of NADP-dependent malic enzyme (ME), malate dehydrogenase and phosphoenolpyruvate carboxylase (PEPC) in sycamore cell cultures were highest during the early exponential growth phase, which decreased once the cells attained the stationary phase (46). The activity of ME would increase the availability of NADPH, required for the increased reductive biosynthesis during the active growth of the cells. Incorporation of label from $NaH^{14}CO_3$ closely paralleled the activity of PEPC in these cells. The incorporation into the acidic (organic acids) and the basic (amino acids) fractions were identical during growth under optimal conditions.

Metabolism of ^{14}C-labeled glucose, acetate, and bicarbonate were examined during culture of excised cotyledons of radiata pine (*Pinus radiata* D. Don) under shoot-forming (SF) and non-shoot-forming (NSF) conditions (47). Label was detected in the respired CO_2 and various metabolites such as lipids, amino acids, organic acids, sugars, proteins, starch, and the cell wall during the incubation. The pattern and amounts of label incorporated into the different fractions varied with the age in culture and the type of morphogenesis occurring at the time of feeding, with peaks corresponding to the period of rapid elongation (on day 3 in the NSF) and meristematic tissue formation and shoot bud differentiation (on days 10 and 21 in the SF) stages. The incorporation of label from ^{14}C-bicarbonate was higher in the NSF than in the SF cotyledons during the 3-week culture period.

Pulse-chase studies with ^{14}C-glucose followed by ^{12}C-glucose showed that the pattern of incorporation of ^{14}C was similar in SF and NSF cultures, and that only specific amino acids (glutamate/glutamine) and organic acids (malate/citrate) were appreciably labeled (48). However, the presence of BA enhanced synthesis from the beginning of culture. Furthermore, metabolically long-lived lipids were also synthesized. The labeling of malate and citrate increased as the meristematic nodule and shoot bud formation progressed (49), as did the amount of $^{14}CO_2$ released. Incorporation of label into proteins was also nearly 2-fold higher in the SF than in the NSF cotyledons of radiata pine later in culture compared to the early culture periods.

The cotyledons of radiata pine used as explants for initiation of shoot buds *in vitro* are green at the time of inoculation and have an absolute requirement of BA for bud induction, and BA and light for bud differentiation (50,51). Also, during day 21 of the bud induction period the cotyledons produce high levels of CO_2 and ethylene (30). Therefore, to understand the role of CO_2 fixation in the process, the activities of ribulose bisphosphate carboxylase/ oxygenase (RuBPC) and PEPC were measured along with the short-term fixation of $NaH ^{14}CO_3$ (52). During the initial 5 days the PEPC activity in the SF tissues increased about 2.5-fold over that in the freshly excised tissues, but there was no appreciable rise in the PEPC activity in the NSF tissues during this period, leading to 3-fold higher levels of malate plus aspartate in the SF cotyledons. In contrast, the level of RuBPC activity increased initially in both tissues, but it leveled off in the SF cotyledons and continued to increase in the NSF cotyledons. The changes in the total chlorophyll content in these tissues were more or less parallel to that of RuBPC activity (52). These observations suggest that photosynthesis probably plays a lesser role than nonphotosynthetic CO_2 fixation in providing C skeletons and energy for metabolic events associated with de novo shoot bud differentiation. The increased PEPC activity observed in the SF cotyledons (52) corresponds to periods of intense, localized cell division activity (51). Thus PEPC might be needed to provide C skeletons anaplerotically to the tricarboxylic acid cycle and to amino acid synthesis as has been reported in other systems (53–55). The higher level of malate, resulting from an increased synthesis by PEPC activity, may be decarboxylated by NADP-malic enzyme to generate the extra energy and reductant postulated to be required for de novo organogenesis (56,57).

Lipids and free sugars were depleted about 10-fold and 6-fold, respectively, during the 3-week bud induction period in cotyledons of radiata pine cultured *in vitro* (58). Although there was a steady decline in the soluble amino-N during culture, the protein-N pool remained relatively high. Free sugars were also rapidly metabolized early in the bud induction process. Respiration initially declined, coincident with the depletion of reserve nutrients, but as the meristematic nodules developed, respiration rate increased. The cotyledons of radiata pine cultured *in vitro* contained starch grains at the time of inoculation (59). When cultured in the absence of BA (NSF), starch grains disappeared from the cells within 3 days. In contrast, cells of the SF layer in the BA-treated (SF) cotyledons of the same age retained abundant starch grains, although starch from the rest of the cells in these cotyledons was eliminated. When the organogenic centers were formed as the SF process progressed, these starch grains were slowly used up.

Mannitol is one of the sugar alcohols that is used as a metabolically inert osmoticum in physiological studies (60). However, [U-^{14}C]-mannitol was absorbed and metabolized within 14 h of incubation by cultured cotyledons of radiata pine and cell suspension cultures of tobacco and carrot (61). Therefore, one should exert extreme caution while using the so-called inert osmotica in long-term studies of plant tissues (63).

19.5. Nitrogen assimilation and metabolism

Some of the early research on nitrogen metabolism in plant tissues cultured *in vitro* was again with sycamore cell suspension cultures. The levels of activities of nitrate-(NR) and nitrite-(NiR) reductases in batch cultures of sycamore cells were dependent on the form of nitrogen present in the culture medium (35,62). When these cells were transferred to fresh medium, the activities of both these enzymes increased appreciably. However, if NO_3^- was replaced by glutamate as the sole nitrogen source in continuous cultures, the activity of NR remained very low and constant, but the activities of glutamine synthetase, glutamate–oxaloacetate transaminase, and glutamate–pyruvate transaminase increased (62). This suggests that NR or NiR may be limiting nitrogen assimilation when NO_3^- is the sole nitrogen source. The activity of glutamate dehydrogenase was about 25-fold higher when sycamore cells were grown in the presence of NO_3^- plus NH_4^+ as compared to its level in medium supplemented with NO_3^- alone (63). It was speculated that the increase in the enzymatic activity might be due to the availability of high levels of NH_4^+. However, the NO_3^--grown cells when transferred to medium containing only NH_4^+ failed to grow and enzymatic activity declined with time.

As NH_4^+ stimulates nonautotrophic CO_2 fixation in isolated cells, there has been a dispute over whether NH_4^+ has to be metabolized to bring about the observed stimulation (64). In sycamore cell suspension cultures, addition of NH_4Cl caused an almost immediate stimulation of CO_2 fixation coincident with the stimulation of PEPC (65). Although to a smaller extent, a similar enhancement occurred when the nonmetabolized analog, methylamine, was added. This indicates that the stimulation does not depend on the metabolism of NH_4^+, which takes place mostly by the activity of glutamine synthetase (65). This was further proved by the observation that PEPC activity was stimulated in the presence or the absence of an inhibitor of glutamine synthetase, namely, methionine sulfoximine. There was no indication of selective stimulation of any group of metabolites as indicated by the incorporation of radioactivity from NaH $^{14}CO_3$ by the cultured cells (65).

Multiple-shoot bud formation on excised vegetative buds of *Picea glauca* cultured *in vitro* requires both NH_4NO_3 and KNO_3 in the nutrient medium (66). Metabolism of N-containing compounds in SF cultures of vegetative buds of *Picea glauca* was studied using ^{14}N and ^{15}N nuclear magnetic resonance (NMR) spectrometry (67). Nitrogen-15 NMR spectra indicated peaks for α-amino groups, including that of glutamate as well as for proline, alanine, and the side-chain groups in glutamine, arginine, ornithine, and γ-aminobutyric acid. Resonance peaks for α-amino groups, proline, NO_3^-, and NH_4^+ could be identified in ^{14}N NMR spectra also. Perfusion experiments conducted for up to 20 h in the NMR spectrometer showed that ^{15}N-labeled NO_3^- and NH_4^+ are first incorporated into the amide group of glutamine and then enter the α-NH_2 pool. Eventually alanine and arginine were also labeled with ^{15}N. These results suggest that the glutamine synthetase/glutamate synthase pathway of N assimilation functions under these culture conditions (67). Further, NH_4^+ was assimilated faster than NO_3^-, and consequently more than 70% of the newly synthesized internal free amino acid pool derived its N from NH_4^+ rather than from NO_3^-. They observed that the tissues failed to take up NO_3^- if NH_4^+ was absent in the medium, resulting in limited growth of the buds during the 9-week culture period. The use of NMR spectroscopy allows the study of *in vivo* metabolism without involving disruptive and often complex tissue extractions. Thus, one can expect increased use of this technique for a better understanding of the metabolite levels, kinetics of processes and intracellular environment of intact cells and tissues.

19.6. Phytohormone metabolism

The majority of studies involving phytohormones in tissue culture have been concerned with examining the effects of exposing tissues to different types and concentrations of these compounds. Consequently, we know very little about the physiological bases of the modes of action of these substances. However, attempts are being made to elucidate the metabolism of various phytohormones in plant tissue cultures, and we can expect useful information in the future, particularly through the use of ELISA (enzyme-linked immunoabsorbent assay) techniques.

19.6.1. Auxins

Auxins, especially 2,4-D, restrict the process of abscission in cultures of *Citrus* pistils (68). Rapid transport and slow metabolism of the auxin are necessary in order to render the auxin an effective inhibitor of abscission. In olive (*Olea europea*) it was found that while the levels of free IAA did not increase following exposure of intact leaves or bark-derived callus to ethylene, there was a 3-fold increase in the concentration of bound IAA in the treated tissues when compared to the levels in the untreated controls (69).

19.6.2. Cytokinins

The uptake and metabolism of ^{14}C-BA have been examined in cultured shoots of elm (70), two Japanese plum cultures (71) and apple (72), and excised embryos of *Picea abies* (73,74) and *Pinus sylvestris* (73). These studies showed, inter alia, that when these explants were grown in BA-containing medium, the cytokinin was rapidly taken up (70,72), apparently passively (73), and was found in the apices within 30 min (70). The label accumulated and the level of radioactivity only declined when the elm shoots were transferred to a BA-free medium (70), or in plum when BA decreased in the medium (71). In apple most of the BA in the tissue remained in the basal region of the shoots, from where multiple shoots originated (72); ^{14}CO$_2$ was released (70,71), and most of the label appeared in the ethanol-soluble fraction (71). However, the rate of shoot proliferation in two varieties of plum could not be correlated with the amount of label in that fraction, but only with a decline of label toward the end of the culture period (71). Metabolism to a BA-nucleotide, which was biologically active, was the major process in *Picea abies* embryos (74), but degradation into a metabolite, which cochromatographed with adenine, was observed in elm shoots (70). Radioactive metabolites (mainly ribosyl-BA and various BA-glycosides) were observed in the medium (74).

19.6.3. Ethylene

Cultured cotyledons of radiata pine produced significant levels of CO$_2$ and the gaseous phytohormone, ethylene (30). Under NSF conditions, the accumulation of these gases was very low. To establish the role of these gases in morphogenesis, the composition of the headspace gas was manipulated (30). This involved (a) allowing the gases to accumulate within the flasks by sealing them with gastight serum caps on various days and replacing the caps with foam plugs on various days during incubation, (b) absorbing the gases by setting up chemical traps singly and in combination, and (c) incubating the cultures under a continuous flow of gas mixtures of known composition. The results indicated that both CO_2 and ethylene, which build up during the initial 10–15 days of culture, promote shoot bud differentiation. Excessive accumulation of these gases beyond this stage caused slight dedifferentiation. When both the gases were eliminated from the flasks, shoot bud induction and growth were inhibited.

In contrast, accumulation of ethylene and CO_2 in the headspaces of the culture vessels inhibited growth of the cells and multiplication of proembryos in cell-suspension cultures of white spruce (75). Ethylene can influence the orientation of cellulose microfibrils in plant cells (76) and is known to induce partial synchrony in cell-suspension cultures (77). Also, ethylene may have an entirely independent, as yet unidentified, role in influencing the process of organogenesis. Carbon dioxide, on the other hand, may be required during shoot formation to modify the biosynthesis and action of ethylene at various stages (30). Also, CO_2 is required for the maintenance of high activity of the nonphotosynthetic carbon-fixing enzyme, PEPC, observed in these cotyledons during the early stages of shoot bud induction (52).

19.6.4. Polyamines

Polyamines, mainly putrescine, spermidine, and spermine, are required for growth and differentiation in many plant species (78). Spermidine was found to be the major polyamine in cultured cotyledons of radiata pine (79,80). However, putrescine, spermidine, or spermine could not replace the requirement for the cytokinin, BA, in the medium (Kumar and Thorpe, unpublished observations). Pulse-fed ^{14}C-putrescine was metabolized primarily to γ-aminobutyric acid, aspartate, and glutamate in the excised cotyledons of radiata pine, and only traces of ^{14}C were found in the higher polyamines, spermidine and spermine (80). However, when the cotyledons were cultured for extended periods in the presence of ^{14}C-putrescine, the higher polyamines were labeled to appreciable levels after 2 days in culture (79). During the pulse-feeding period, $^{14}CO_2$ was also released by the cotyledons, indicating that the derivatives of putrescine catabolism enter the tricarboxylic acid cycle (80). Therefore, putrescine, and possibly other polyamines, may serve as reserves of carbon and nitrogen during de novo organogenesis. The activity of arginine decarboxylase, an enzyme involved in the biosynthesis of putrescine, was maintained at 3- to 5-fold higher levels in the SF tissues than in the NSF cotyledons early in culture (Kumar and Thorpe, unpublished observations), suggesting the possible importance of polyamines in de novo organogenesis.

19.7. Nucleic acid metabolism

The changing pattern of nucleotides in sycamore cell suspension cultures was examined during the lag phase (0–4 days), rapid cell division phase (4–8 days), and stationary phase (8–21 days) (81). The predominant nucleotide was ATP in the stationary-phase culture. The level of UDP-glucose, which is needed for the synthesis of new structural polysaccharides on cell division, increased 46-fold, and it became the major nucleotide toward the end of the lag phase. During this period, the levels of other nucleotides examined also increased, presumably in preparation for the ensuing cell division phase. By day 8, when most of the divisions were completed, the levels of ATP, UDP-glucose, and other nucleotides fell. However, the levels of NAD, UMP, and ADP rose slightly by day 8, before falling to the day 0 level at the end of the 21-day culture period. The observed changes in nucleotide levels closely paralleled the growth pattern of the cells (81). There were no detectable levels of nucleotides in the culture medium in which the cells were grown, indicating that there was no leaching or secretion from the cells. Both RNA and DNA contents increased 2- and 4-fold, respectively, during the lag phase of sycamore cell suspension cultures (82). The DNA level fell rapidly with the onset of cell divisions, but the decline in the RNA level was slower but continued until the contents of these nucleic acids reached a stable value in the stationary phase of the cell cultures. No appreciable changes in the species of RNA or its nucleotide concentration could be detected during the entire culture period.

   Autoradiographic studies of incorporation of radioactive precursors into protein (^3H-leucine), RNA (^3H-uridine) and DNA (^3H-thymidine) by excised cotyledons of radiata pine cultured under SF and NSF conditions revealed that during the initial 2 days in culture there were no significant differences in the patterns of incorporation (50). But by days 3–5 labeling became concentrated in the epidermal and subepidermal cells of the SF cotyledons; these are the cells that give rise to adventitious shoot buds later in culture. In contrast, the cells of the NSF cotyledons incorporated very little of the labeled precursors. ^3H-thymidine labeling of the plastids was found in the latter tissues, in which plastids matured earlier than in the SF cotyledons (50). These observations were confirmed by histochemical studies, where increased staining for RNA, DNA, and nuclear and cytoplasmic proteins in the SF cotyledons as compared to their NSF counterparts was observed (59).

19.8. Lipid metabolism

The major reserve foods stored in the cotyledons of radiata pine are lipids and proteins, which decline during de novo shoot formation (58,83). Lipids constituted the major reserve food at the time of excision (57%), but these declined rapidly in culture; most dramatic was the reduction in triglycerides (58), as in the cotyledons during germination. There were also qualitative changes as well in the lipids. Thus, linolenic acid content of the polar lipids increased, and stigmasterol, a component of plant membranes, was synthesized at higher levels during the early stages of shoot initiation. However, the overall changes of the lipid profile of the cultured cotyledons did not differ noticeably from those that occurred during germination and seedling growth, suggesting that lipid mobilization serves primarily for supplying energy in the cultured cotyledons (83). In a complementary study, increased staining for several enzymes including lipase, acid phosphatase, ATPase, and succinate dehydrogenase was observed when the SF cotyledons were examined histochemically (59). Although lipase was distributed evenly in the cotyledons at the time of inoculation, the activity became restricted to the SF cell layers by day 3 in culture. Interestingly, during the later stages of bud differentiation, lipase activity was highest in the mesophyll cells internal to the SF layer, indicating mobilization of lipids from the mesophyll tissue by the SF cells (59), which are in need of an increased energy supply (84).

19.9. Secondary metabolism

Plant tissue and cell cultures can be used for the study of their secondary metabolites, many of which are commercially valuable. There are certain problems associated with this, e.g., cell and tissue cultures of some plants fail to produce secondary metabolites (35). Occasionally, they may produce novel metabolites not seen in intact plants.

The synthesis of phenolic compounds is one of the most extensively studied secondary metabolites in forest tree species. Raising the level of sucrose in the medium led to an increased accumulation of phenolics in sycamore cells (85). Exhaustion of nitrogen from the medium also led to the accumulation of tannins, which were the major class of phenolics in cultured sycamore cells. That the nitrogen supply can adversely affect production of phenolics was further confirmed when it was observed that by doubling the medium nitrogen content, the production of phenolics was delayed by 6 days (85).

Lignin was synthesized at a higher level when sucrose was increased from 1 to 15% in sycamore cell cultures (86). Also, increased levels of auxin (2,4-D) and cytokinin in the medium stimulated lignin production. Similar treatments led to enhanced production of anthocyanin in poplar cell cultures, which was preceded by an increase in the activity of phenylalanine ammonia lyase (PAL) (87). Increase in PAL activity occurred parallel to the increase in the production of phenolics in cultured sycamore cells (85).

Callus derived from the albedo tissue of *Citrus paradisi* Macf. (grapefruit) and four other *Citrus* species exhibited PAL activity (88). It increased by about 10-fold within 2 days after subculture and decreased gradually during the next 10 days to near day 0 level. The conversion of ^{14}C-phenylalanine to cinnamic acid was observed when the callus was incubated with the labeled amino acid. However, label from ^{14}C-phenylalanine was not incorporated into the citrus flavonoids.

Cell-suspension cultures of white spruce maintained under constant light and temperature (22.5°C) exhibited a lower tannin production than did those maintained at alternating light/dark conditions (89). Electron microscopic observations suggested that tannins arose in small cytoplasmic vacuoles, which, in turn, were derived from the endoplasmic reticulum (ER). No tannin inclusion was observed in the starch grains, contrary to earlier reports suggesting that tannins probably arose in degenerating starch grains (89). However, there was circumstantial evidence suggesting some kind of interrelationship between starch and tannins as the cells rich in starch had little tannin, and vice versa. No conclusive evidence was obtained in another study using embryo-derived callus cultures of *Pinus elliottii* with respect to the involvement of plastids in the synthesis of tannins (90). The latter study supported the earlier observation that the accumulation of tannins in the cultured cells occurred mainly in the central vacuoles and that ER-derived vesicles were involved in the transport of tannin within the cells. Some of the cells exhibiting tannin synthesis showed generalized disorganization of their cytoplasm and organelles. However, minor deposition of tannins, especially in the vacuoles and membrane-bound vesicles, did not cause cell death. Excessive accumulation of certain types of tannins in the callus cells resulted in death of the cells, probably due to the precipitation of proteins (90).

Certain phenolics such as pinosylvin (3,5-dihydroxystilbene) and its monomethyl ether are associated specifically with the heartwood in red pine (*Pinus resinosa* Ait.) (91). Also, they were formed in response to wounding and fungal penetration of the sapwood in red pine. Actively growing callus initiated from the cambium of red pine shoots was devoid of these heartwood phenolics (92). However, when the callus was subjected to desiccation, significant levels of these phenolics could be detected in the callus pieces. This indicates that the heartwood-specific phenolics may be formed by a shift in metabolism associated with starvation and slow dying. Similar observations were made in callus cultures of white elm (*Ulmus americana* L.), suggesting that the process may be wide spread among woody plants and that callus cultures can be used for studying the metabolism associated with the process of heartwood formation (92). However, later studies along this line apparently were not undertaken.

19.10. Miscellaneous studies

The mechanism of uptake of inorganic phosphate (P_i) by sycamore cells in suspension cultures was energy-dependent at P_i concentrations < 10 mM in the external medium, and at higher concentrations it occurred mainly by passive diffusion (93). Privation studies indicated that P_i uptake was stimulated by low intracellular concentrations of P_i and phosphate esters in sycamore cells (93). Using ^{31}P NMR it was found that the cytoplasmic P_i pool was maintained fairly constant (2–3 mM) at the expense of the vacuolar P_i pool in sycamore cells (94). This occurred when the cells were incubated in either phosphate-deficient or phosphate-rich medium, supporting the hypothesis that the vacuolar P_i pool is primarily a storage pool. Phosphorus–31 NMR has also been used to estimate the cytoplasmic pH of sycamore cells in suspension culture (95) and in the study of cytoplasmic pH regulation associated with acid-load effects (96).

The anatomy of the root–shoot junction of tissue-culture-derived plantlets of eastern white cedar (*Thuja occidentalis* L.) was compared with that of greenhouse-grown seedlings (97). In both plant types the xylem was well developed and smooth, and the vascular connection was continuous. Also, the uptake and translocation of anions and cations ($^{32}PO_4^{2-}$ and $^{86}Rb^+$, respectively) were comparable in the two plant types despite the different origins of the root system (97).

Protoplast cultures of white spruce (*Picea glauca*) have been used for transformation studies. The gene for chloramphenicol acetyltransferase (CAT) was introduced into protoplasts of white spruce by electroporation, and its transient expression was observed (98). The transient expression of β-glucuronidase gene as well as the CAT gene was also reported in protoplasts derived from embryogenic cell-suspension cultures of white spruce (99). In the latter study, the introduction of plasmids containing the reporter genes was mediated by treating the protoplasts with polyethylene glycol. Protoplasts from cell cultures of Douglas fir (*Pseudotsuga menziesii*) and loblolly pine (*Pinus taeda*) also have been used in similar studies using luciferase as the reporter enzymes (100). These reports are particularly exciting because regeneration of somatic embryos from protoplasts derived from cell suspension cultures of white spruce has also been achieved (101). Therefore, the ultimate goal of studies such as those mentioned above, namely, obtaining transgenic conifers with desirable qualities, appears to be achievable in the not-too-distant future.

19.11. Conclusions

There is limited information on the physiology of growth and differentiation of tree species, as gleaned from studies of tissues cultured *in vitro*. These studies indicate the superiority of using cell, tissue, and organ cultures over traditional tissue slices for physiological investigations. Some of the constraints imposed on the research by the complexity of the tree species can be overcome by using tissue culture. Also, the information available suggests that there are no fundamental differences in primary metabolism between the tree species and the herbaceous species (84,102). Thus, tree physiologists will indeed benefit immensely from using tissue cultures as an experimental tool. As has been pointed out, "the tendency to isolate from one another whole plant physiology, organ, tissue and cell culture, cell physiology and molecular biology is myopic" (1). The need for more research with cell and tissue cultures of woody species to expand the currently limited knowledge of their physiology should be considered a matter of high priority.

19.12. References

1. H.E. Street, "Growth in organized and unorganized systems," in F.C. Steward, ed., *Plant Physiology: A Treatise*, Vol. 5B, Academic Press, New York, 1969, pp. 3–224.

2. C.E. Yarwood, "Detached leaf culture," *Bot. Rev.*, **12**, 1–56 (1946).

3. R.J. Gautheret, "History of plant cell and tissue culture: A personal account," in I.K. Vasil, ed., *Cell Culture and Somatic Cell Genetics of Plants*, Vol. 2, Academic Press, Orlando, FL, 1985, pp. 1–59.

4. T.A. Thorpe, ed., *Plant Tissue Culture: Methods and applications in agriculture*, Academic Press, New York, 1981.

5. I.K. Vasil, ed., *Cell Culture and Somatic Cell Genetics of Plants*, Vol. 1, Academic Press, Orlando, FL, 1984.

6. I.K. Vasil, ed., *Cell Culture and Somatic Cell Genetics of Plants*, Vol. 2, Academic Press, Orlando, FL, 1985.

7. I.K. Vasil, ed., *Cell Culture and Somatic Cell Genetics of Plants*, Vol. 3, Academic Press, Orlando, FL, 1986.

8. D.A. Evans, W.R. Sharp, P.V. Ammirato, and Y. Yamada, eds., *Handbook of Plant Cell Culture*, Vol. 1, Macmillan, New York, 1983.

9. W.R. Sharp, D.A. Evans, P.V. Ammirato, and Y. Yamada, eds., *Handbook of Plant Cell Culture*, Vol. 2, Macmillan, New York, 1984.

10. P.V. Ammirato, D.A. Evans, W.R. Sharp, and Y. Yamada, eds., *Handbook of Plant Cell Culture*, Vol. 3, Macmillan, New York, 1984.

11. O.L. Gamborg, T. Murashige, T.A. Thorpe, and I.K. Vasil, "Plant tissue culture media," *In Vitro*, **12**, 473–478 (1976).

12. D.C.W. Brown, D.W.M. Leung, and T.A. Thorpe, "Osmotic requirement for shoot formation in tobacco callus," *Physiol. Plant.*, **46**, 36–41 (1979).

13. R.L.M. Pierik, *In Vitro Culture of Higher Plants*, Martinus Nijhoff, Dordrecht, 1987, p. 344.

14. P.-J. Wang and L.-C. Huang, "Beneficial effects of activated charcoal on plant tissue and organ cultures," *In Vitro*, **12**, 260–262 (1976).

15. G. Fridborg, M. Pedersen, L. Landstrom, and T. Eriksson, "The effect of activated charcoal on tissue cultures: Adsorption of metabolites inhibiting morphogenesis," *Physiol. Plant.*, **43**, 104–106 (1978).

16. M.A. Weatherhead, J. Burdon, and G.G. Henshaw, "Some effects of activated charcoal as an additive to plant tissue culture media," *Z. Pflanzenphysiol.*, **89**, 141–147 (1978).

17. M.A. Weatherhead, J. Burdon, and G.G. Henshaw, "Effects of activated charcoal as an additive to plant tissue culture media: Part 2," *Z. Pflanzenphysiol.*, **94**, 399–405 (1978).

18. J. Aitken, K.J. Horgan, and T.A. Thorpe, "Influence of explant selection on the shoot-forming capacity of juvenile tissue of *Pinus radiata*, *Can. J. For. Res.*, **11**, 112–117 (1981).

19. J. Aitken-Christie, A.P. Singh, K.J. Horgan, and T.A. Thorpe, "Explant developmental state and shoot formation in *Pinus radiata* cotyledons," *Bot. Gaz.*, **146**, 196–203 (1985).

20. P.S. Rao, "Plant regeneration," in F. Constabel and I.K. Vasil, eds., *Cell Culture and Somatic Cell Genetics of Plants*, Vol. 4, Academic Press, Orlando, FL, 1987, pp. 229–254.

21. T. Murashige, "Plant propagation through tissue cultures," *Ann. Rev. Plant Physiol.*, **25**, 135–166 (1974).

22. Z.A. Wilson and J.B. Power, "Elimination of systemic contamination in explant and protoplast cultures of rubber (*Hevea brasiliensis* Muell. Arg.)" *Plant Cell Rep.*, **7**, 622–625 (1989).

23. P.M. Young, A.S. Hutchins, and M.L. Canfield, "Use of antibiotics to control bacteria in shoot cultures of woody plants," *Plant Sci. Lett.*, **34**, 203–209 (1984).

24. K. Pollock, D.G. Barfield, and R. Shields, "Toxicity of antibiotics to plant cell cultures," *Plant Cell Rep.*, **2**, 36–39 (1983).

25. R. Shields, S.J. Robinson, and P.A. Anslow, "Use of fungicides in plant tissue culture," *Plant Cell Rep.*, **3**, 33–36 (1984).

26. R. Phillips, S.M. Arnott, and S.E. Kaplan, "Antibiotics in plant tissue culture: Rifampicin effectively controls bacterial contaminants without affecting the growth of *Helianthus tuberosus*," *Plant Sci. Lett.*, **21**, 235–240 (1981).

27. B.J. Nairn, "Significance of gelling agents in a production tissue culture laboratory," *International Plant Propagation Soc.*, Pacific Section, Combined Proceedings, 1986, pp. 200–205.

28. C.C. Dalton and H.E. Stret, "The role of the gas phase in the greening and growth of illuminated cell suspension cultures of spinach (*Spinacea oleracea* L.)," *In Vitro*, **12**, 485–494 (1976).

29. D.S. Thomas and T. Murashige, "Volatile emissions of plant tissue cultures," *In Vitro*, **15**, 654–658 (1979).

30. P.P. Kumar, D.M. Reid, and T.A. Thorpe, "The role of ethylene and carbon dioxide in differentiation of shoot buds in excised cotyledons of *Pinus radiata* in vitro," *Physiol. Plant.*, **69**, 244–252 (1987).

31. P.P. Kumar and T.A. Thorpe, "Alteration of growth and morphogenesis by endogenous ethylene and carbon dioxide in conifer tissue cultures," in V. Dhawan, ed., *Application of Biotechnology in Forestry and Horticulture*, Plenum Press, New York, 1989, pp. 205–214.

32. M. Tran Thanh Van, H. Chlyah, and A. Chlyah, "Regulation of organogenesis in thin cell layers of epidermal and subepidermal cells," in H.E. Street, ed., *Tissue Culture and Plant Science*, Academic Press, New York, 1974, pp. 101–139.

33. D.K. Dougall, "The use of tissue cultures in studies of metabolism," in D.D. Davies, ed., *The Biochemistry of Plants*, Vol. 2, Academic Press, New York, 1980, pp. 627–642.

34. R.D. Teasdale, "Micronutrients," in J.M. Bonga and D.J. Durzan, eds., *Cell and Tissue Culture in Forestry*, Vol. 1, Martinus Nijhoff, Dordrecht, 1987, pp. 17–49.

35. D. Grey, G. Stepan-Sarkissian, and M.W. Fowler, "Biochemistry of forest tree species in culture," in J.M. Bonga and D.J. Durzan, eds., *Cell and Tissue Culture in Forestry*, Vol. 2, Martinus Nijhoff, Dordrecht, 1987, pp. 31–61.

36. L.G. Copping and H.E. Street, "Properties of the invertase of cultured sycamore cells and changes in their activity during culture growth," *Physiol. Plant.*, **26**, 346–354 (1972).

37. J. Straus, "Invertase in cell walls of plant tissue cultures," *Plant Physiol.*, **37**, 342–348 (1962).

38. F. Constabel, "Zur Amylasesekretion pflanzlicher Gewebeculturen," *Naturwissenschaften*, **47**, 17–18 (1960).

39. F. Constabel, "Quantitative untersuchungen uber die extracellulare hydrolyse von kohlenhydrate durch *Juniperus communis* gewebekulturen," *Planta*, **59**, 330–337 (1963).

40. M.W. Fowler and A. Clifton, "Activities of enzymes of carbohydrate metabolism in cells of *Acer pseudoplatanus* L. maintained in continuous (chemostat) culture," *Eur. J. Biochem.*, **45**, 445–450 (1974).

41. W. Jessup and M.W. Fowler, "Interrelationships between carbohydrate metabolism and nitrogen assimilation in cultured plant cells. III. Effect of the nitrogen source on the pattern of carbohydrate oxidation in cells of *Acer pseudoplatanus* L. grown in culture," *Planta*, **137**, 71–76 (1977).

42. T. Shimizu, A. Clifton, A. Komamine, and M.W. Fowler, "Changes in metabolite levels during growth of *Acer pseudoplatanus* (Sycamore) cells in batch suspension culture," *Physiol. Plant.*, **40**, 125–129 (1977).

43. M.W. Fowler, "Studies on the growth in culture of plant cells. XIV. Carbohydrate oxidation during the growth of *Acer pseudoplatanus* L. cells in suspension culture," *J. Exp. Bot.*, **22**, 715–724 (1971).

44. T.A. Thorpe and E.J. Laishley, "Glucose oxidation during shoot initiation in tobacco callus cultures," *J. Exp. Bot.*, **24**, 1082–1089 (1973).

45. R.W.E. Gathercole, K.J. Mansfield, and H.E. Street, "Carbon dioxide as an essential requirement for cultured sycamore cells," *Physiol. Plant.*, **37**, 213–217 (1976).

46. C. Vanderhoven and J.-P. Zryd, "Changes in malate content and in enzymes involved in dark CO_2 fixation during growth of *Acer pseudoplatanus* L. cells in suspension culture," *Physiol. Plant.*, **43**, 99–103 (1978).

47. H. Obata-Sasamoto, V.M. Villalobos, and T.A. Thorpe, "[14]C-Metabolism in cultured cotyledon explants of radiata pine," *Physiol. Plant.*, **61**, 490–496 (1984).

48. L. Bender, R.W. Joy IV, and T.A. Thorpe, "Studies on [14C]-glucose metabolism during shoot bud induction in cultured cotyledon explants of Pinus radiata," *Physiol. Plant.*, **69**, 428–434 (1987).

49. L. Bender, R.W. Joy IV, and T.A. Thorpe, "Studies on [14C]-glucose metabolism during shoot bud induction in cultured cotyledon explants of Pinus radiata," *Plant Cell Physiol.*, **28**, 1335–1338 (1987).

50. V.M. Villalobos, M.J. Oliver, E.C. Yeung, and T.A. Thorpe, "Cytokinin-induced switch in development in excised cotyledons radiata pine cultured in vitro," *Physiol. Plant.*, **61**, 483–489 (1984).

51. V.M. Villalobos, D.W.M. Leung, and T.A. Thorpe, "Light–cytokinin interaction in shoot formation in cultured cotyledon explants of radiata pine," *Physiol. Plant.*, **61**, 497–504 (1984).

52. P.P. Kumar, L. Bender, and T.A. Thorpe, "Activities of ribulose bisphosphate carboxylase and phosphoenolpyruvate carboxylase and ^{14}C-bicarbonate fixation during in vitro culture of *Pinus radiata* cotyledons," *Plant Physiol.*, **87**, 675–679 (1988).

53. L. Bender, A. Kumar, and K.H. Neumann, "On the photosynthetic system and assimilate metabolism of *Daucus* and *Arachis* cell cultures," in K.H. Neumann, W. Barz, and E. Reinhard, eds., *Primary and Secondary Metabolism of Plant Cell Cultures*, Springer-Verlag, Berlin, 1985, pp. 22–42.

54. E. Latzko and G.J. Kelly, "The many-faceted function of phosphoenolpyruvate carboxylase in C_3 plants," *Physiol. Veg.*, **21**, 805–815 (1983).

55. E. Melzer and M. O'Leary, "Anaplerotic CO_2 fixation by phosphoenolpyruvate carboxylase in C_3 plants," *Plant Physiol.*, **84**, 58–60 (1987).

56. P.L. Plumb-Dhindsa, R.S. Dhindsa, and T.A. Thorpe, "Non-autotrophic CO_2 fixation during shoot formation in tobacco callus," *J. Exp. Bot.*, **30**, 759–767 (1979).

57. T.A. Thorpe, "Morphogenesis and regeneration in tissue culture," in L.D. Owens, ed., *Genetic Engineering: Applications to Agriculture* (Beltsville Symposium 7), Rowman & Allanheld, Totowa, NJ, 1983, pp. 285–303.

58. S. Biondi and T.A. Thorpe, "Growth regulator effects, metabolite changes, and respiration during shoot initiation in cultured cotyledon explants of *Pinus radiata*," *Bot. Gaz.*, **143**, 20–25 (1982).

59. K.R. Patel and T.A. Thorpe, "Histochemical examination of shoot initiation in cultured cotyledon explants of radiata pine," *Bot. Gaz.*, **145**, 312–322 (1984).

60. W.J. Cram, "Mannitol transport and suitability as an osmoticum in root cells," *Physiol. Plant.*, **61**, 396–406 (1984).

61. M.R. Thompson, T.J. Douglas, H. Obata-Sasamoto, and T.A. Thorpe, "Mannitol metabolism in cultured plant cells," *Physiol. Plant.*, **67**, 365–369 (1986).

62. M. Young, "Studies on the growth in culture of plant cells. XVI. Nitrogen assimilation during nitrogen-limited growth of *Acer pseudoplatanus* L. cells in chemostat culture," *J. Exp. Bot.*, **24**, 1172–1185 (1973).

63. M.W. Fowler and R.J.D. Barker, "Assimilation of ammonia in nonchlorophyllous tissue," in E.J. Hewitt and C.V. Cutting, eds., *Nitrogen Assimilation of Plants*, Academic Press, London, 1979, pp. 484–500.

64. K.E. Hammel, K.L. Cornwell, and J.A. Bassham, "Stimulation of dark CO_2 fixation by ammonia in isolated mesophyll cells of *Papaver somniferum* L." *Plant Cell Physiol.*, **20**, 1523–1529 (1979).

65. K.M. Wright and C.V. Givan, "Regulation of non-autotrophic carbon dioxide assimilation by ammonia in cultured cells of *Acer pseudoplatanus* L." *Plant Sci.*, **58**, 151–158 (1988).

66. D.I. Dunstan, G.H. Mohammed, and T.A. Thorpe, "Shoot production and elongation on explants from vegetative buds excised from 17- to 20-year-old *Pseudotsuga menziesii*," *NZ J. For. Sci.*, **16**, 269–282 (1986).

67. T.A. Thorpe, K. Bagh, A.J. Cutler, D.I. Dunstan, D.D. McIntyre, and H.J. Vogel, "A ^{14}N and ^{15}N NMR study of nitrogen metabolism in shoot-forming cultures of white spruce (*Picea glauca*) buds," *Plant Physiol.* **91**, 193–202 (1989).

68. J.W. Einset, J.L. Lyon, and D.L. Sipes, "Citrus tissue culture: Auxins in relation to abscission in excised pistils," *Plant Physiol.*, **67**, 1109–1112 (1981).

69. E. Epstein, "Levels of free and conjugated indole-3-acetic acid in ethylene-treated leaves and callus of olive," *Physiol. Plant.*, **56**, 371–373 (1982).

70. S. Biondi, L. Cancini, and N. Bagni, "Uptake and translocation of benzyladenine by elm shoots cultured in vitro," *Can. J. Bot.*, **62**, 2385–2390 (1984).

71. G. Marino, "In vitro [^{14}C]-labelled 6-benzyladenine uptake and $^{14}CO_2$ evolution in two Japanese plum cultivars," *Plant Cell Tissue Organ Cult.*, **13**, 49–59 (1988).

72. A.-C. Nordstrom and L. Eliasson, "Uptake and translocation of [^{14}C]-labelled benzylaminopurine in apple shoots grown in vitro in relation to shoot development," *Physiol. Plant.*, **68**, 431–435 (1986).

73. T.C. Vogelmann, C.H. Bornman, and P. Nissen, "Uptake of benzyladenine in explants of *Picea abies* and *Pinus sylvestris*," *Physiol. Plant.*, **61**, 513–517 (1984).

74. J. Van Staden, C. Forsyth, L. Bergman, and S. von Arnold, "Metabolism of benzyladenine by excised embryos of *Picea abies*," *Physiol. Plant.*, **66**, 427–434 (1986).

75. P.P. Kumar, R.W. Joy IV, and T.A. Thorpe, "Ethylene and carbon dioxide accumulation, and growth of cell suspension cultures of *Picea glauca* (white spruce)," *J Plant Physiol.* (in press).

76. J.M. Lang, W.R. Eisinger, and P.B. Green, "Effects of ethylene on the orientation of microtubules and cellulose microfibrils of pea epicotyl cells with polylamellate cell walls," *Protoplasma*, **110**, 5–14 (1982).

77. F. Constabel, W.G.W. Kurz, K.B. Chatson, and J.W. Kirkpatrick, "Partial synchrony in soybean cell suspension cultures induced by ethylene," *J. Cell Res.*, **105**, 263–268 (1977).

78. R.D. Slocum, R. Kaur-Sawhney, and A.W. Galston, "The physiology and biochemistry of polyamines in plants," *Arch. Biochem. Biophys.*, **235**, 283–303 (1984).

79. S. Biondi, P. Torrigiani, A. Sansovini, and N. Bagni, "Inhibition of polyamine biosynthesis by dicyclohexylamine in cultured cotyledons of *Pinus radiata*," *Physiol. Plant.*, **72**, 471–476 (1988).

80. P.P. Kumar and T.A. Thorpe, "Putrescine metabolism in excised cotyledons of *Pinus radiata* cultured in vitro," *Physiol. Plant.*, **76**, 521–526 (1989).

81. E.G. Brown and K.C. Short, "The changing nucleotide pattern of sycamore cells during culture in suspension," *Phytochemistry*, **8**, 1365–1372 (1969).

82. K.C. Short, E.G. Brown, and H.E. Street, "Studies on the growth in culture of plant cells. VI. Nucleic acid metabolism of *Acer pseudoplatanus* L. cell suspensions," *J. Exp. Bot.*, **20**, 579–590 (1969).

83. T.J. Douglas, V.M. Villalobos, M.R. Thompson, and T.A. Thorpe, "Lipid and pigment changes during shoot initiation in cultured explants of *Pinus radiata*," *Physiol. Plant.*, **55**, 470–477 (1982).

84. T.A. Thorpe, "Organogenesis in vitro: Structural, physiological and biochemical aspects," *Int. Rev. Cytol.* (suppl.), **11A**, 71–111 (1980).

85. R.J. Westcott and G.G. Henshaw, "Phenolic synthesis and phenylalanine ammonia-lyase activity in suspension cultures of *Acer pseudoplatanus* L.," *Planta*, **131**, 67–73 (1976).

86. M. Carceller, M.R. Davey, M.W. Fowler, and H.E. Street, "The influence of sucrose, 2,4-D, and kinetin on the growth, fine structure, and lignin content of cultured sycamore cells," *Protoplasma*, **73**, 367–385 (1971).

87. T. Matsumoto, K. Nishida, M. Noguchi, and E. Tanaki, "Some factors affecting the anthocyanin formation by *Populus* cells in suspension culture," *Agric. Biol. Chem.*, **37**, 561–567 (1973).

88. T.A. Thorpe, V.P. Maier, and S. Hasegawa, "Phenylalanine ammonia-lyase activity in citrus fruit tissue cultured in vitro," *Phytochemistry*, **10**, 711–718 (1971).

89. S.C. Chafe and D.J. Durzan, "Tannin inclusions in cell suspension cultures of white spruce," *Planta*, **113**, 251–262 (1973).

90. P.S. Bauer and C.H. Walkinshaw, "Fine structure of tannin accumulations in callus cultures of *Pinus elliotti* (slash pine)," *Can. J. Bot.*, **52**, 615–619 (1974).

91. E. Jorgensen, "The formation of pinosylvin and its monomethyl etherin the sapwood of *Pinus resinosa* Ait.," *Can. J. Bot.*, **39**, 1765–1772 (1961).

92. E. Jorgensen and D. Balsillie, "Formation of heartwood phenols in callus tissue cultures of red pine (*Pinus resinosa*)," *Can. J. Bot.*, **47**, 1015–1016 (1969).

93. F. Rebeille, R. Bligny, and R. Douce, "Regulation of Pi uptake by *Acer pseudoplatanus* cells," *Arch. Biochem. Biophys.*, **219**, 371–378 (1982).

94. F. Rebeille, R. Bligny, J.-B. Martin, and R. Douce, "Relationship between the cytoplasm and the vacuole phosphate pool in *Acer pseudoplatanus* cells," *Arch. Biochem. Biophys.*, **225**, 143–148 (1983).

95. J.-B. Martin, R. Bligny, F. Rebeille, R. Douce, J.-J. Leguay, Y. Mathieu, and J. Guern, "A ^{31}P nuclear magnetic resonance study of intracellular pH of plant cells cultivated in liquid medium," *Plant Physiol.*, **70**, 1156–1161 (1982).

96. J. Guern, Y. Mathieu, M. Pean, C. Pasquier, J.-C. Beloeil, and J.-Y. Lallemand, "Cytoplasmic pH regulation in *Acer pseudoplatanus* cells," *Plant Physiol.*, **82**, 840–845 (1986).

97. L. Bender, I.S. Harry, E.C. Yeung, and T.A. Thorpe, "Root histology, and nutrient uptake and translocation in tissue culture plantlets and seedlings of *Thuja occidentalis* L.," *Trees*, **1**, 232–237 (1987).

98. F. Bekkaoui, M. Pilon, E. Laine, D.S.S. Raju, W.L. Crosby, and D.I. Dunstan, "Transient gene expression in electroporated *Picea glauca* protoplasts," *Plant Cell Rep.*, **7**, 481–484 (1988).

99. S.M. Wilson, T.A. Thorpe, and M.M. Moloney, "PEG-mediated expression of GUS and CAT genes in protoplasts from embryogenic suspension cultures of *Picea glauca*," *Plant Cell Rep.*, **7**, 704–707 (1989).

100. P.K. Gupta, A.M. Dandekar, and D.J. Durzan, "Somatic proembryo formation and transient expression of a luciferase gene in Douglas fir and loblolly pine protoplasts," *Plant Sci.*, **58**, 85–92 (1988).

101. S.M. Attree, F. Bekkaoui, D.I. Dunstan, and L.C. Fowke, "Regeneration of somatic embryos from protoplasts isolated from an embryogenic suspension culture of white spruce (*Picea glauca*)," *Plant Cell Rep.*, **6**, 480–483 (1987).

102. M.R. Thompson and T.A. Thorpe, "Biochemical perspectives in tissue culture for crop improvement," in K.R. Khanna, ed., *Biochemical Aspects of Crop Improvement*, CRC Press, Boca Raton, FL, 1990, pp. 328–358.

20 Use of Growth-Regulating Chemicals

LOUIS G. NICKELL

Nickell Research Inc., Hot Springs Village, Arkansas, USA

Contents

20.1. Introduction

The number of trees per acre is being increased to capitalize on improved production in the early years of fruit tree plantings. However, crowding and increased pruning may become problematic as trees mature.

Many plants produce more leaves than are needed for maximum photosynthesis, and the shade from one or two leaves markedly reduces photosynthesis in the shaded leaves. The control of excessive shoot growth and shading in fruit trees is a major concern of fruit growers. As trees age, heavy, dense canopies shade lower portions of the tree and result in low vigor spurs with inferior flowers and fruit (1).

Tree size of pecan is a major concern to pecan growers. The absence of dwarfing rootstocks or dwarflike scion cultivars and the general inadequacy of mechanical pruning techniques as practical methods of size control have created a need for other size-control methods (2).

467

Seed-orchard trees would be more accessible for spraying, pollinating, and seed harvesting if their height could be controlled without reducing seed yield. Even if yield per tree were reduced, the closer spacing possible with smaller trees might offset this disadvantage. One major problem in pear cultivation is the delay in bringing trees into full production. Increasing production costs have made management of perennial crops more stringent. Among the solutions for deciduous orchard managers are high, early, and sustained production from small trees (3).

The intent of short-rotation intensive silviculture is the rapid production of shoot biomass. Rapidly growing trees such as hybrid poplar or willow are utilized for this purpose. However, the initial establishment of trees can be slow, creating problems, including poor competition with weeds (4).

All of these problems with trees and tree crops have been and are being addressed through the use of plant growth regulators (PGRs; Ref. 5). In most cases, the problems have been solved or substantially overcome. In the rest, sufficient progress has been made to be optimistic about the resolution of the problems.

20.2. Rooting

One of the oldest commercial uses of plant growth regulators has been to initiate or accelerate the rooting of cuttings. Following the discovery that IAA promoted rooting, the search for more active compounds, both naturally occurring and synthetic, began. The strong root-promoting properties of IBA and NAA were reported by Zimmerman and Wilcoxon in 1935 (6). Probably the best known chemical for rooting is IBA, which is destroyed relatively slowly by the auxin-decomposing enzyme systems in plants. Because this compound moves very slowly within the plant, much of it is retained near the site of application—another desirable characteristic. In 1947 Avery and Johnson (7) summarized the uses of plant hormones in horticulture to that date, emphasizing rooting. Since that time many compounds have been found to initiate and/or stimulate rooting, but IBA remains the most commonly used to date for commercial purposes. For example, Table 20.1 lists the trees from which cuttings have been successfully rooted using IBA during the 1980s.

In 1979, aryl esters of IAA and IBA were reported to be superior to the free acids of these compounds in promoting root initiation (8,9).

20.3. Abscission

Abscission is a botanical term meaning shedding. It is a process in which leaves, flowers, or fruits become detached from the parent plant body (see Chapter 12, this book). The timing as well as the process of abscission is important for many agricultural crops. For example, in fruit and nut trees, premature abscission results in an unripe and useless crop. On the other hand, an overabundance of flowers that persist and set fruit can result in an inferior crop of small fruit or place such a strain on the tree that it will produce an

Table 20.1. Rooting of tree cuttings with IBA reported during 1980s

Abies fraseri (Fraser fir)	*Malus malus* (*Malus domestica*)
Acacia flexifolia	(apple)
Acer ginnala (Amur maple)	*Malus pumila* (red vein crabapple)
Acer palmatum (Japanese maple)	*Malus sylvestris*
Acer pseudoplatanus (sycamore maple)	*Mangifera indica* (mango)
Acer rubrum (red maple)	*Olea europea* (olive)
Acer saccharum (sugar maple)	*Persea americana* (avocado)
Anacardium occidentale (cashew nut)	*Philadelphus virginialis* (mock orange)
Betula pendula (European birch)	*Physocarpus opulifolius* (ninebark)
Betula platyphylla (Japanese white birch)	*Picea sitchensis* (Sitka spruce)
Betula pubescens (birch)	*Pinus banksiana* (Jack pine)
Carya illinoensis (pecan)	*Pinus densifolia* (Japanese red pine)
Castanea mollissima (Chinese chestnut)	*Pinus radiata*
Casuarina cunninghamiana	*Pinus strobus* (eastern white pine)
Casuarina equisetifolia (Australian pine)	*Pinus sylvestris* (Scotch pine)
Casuarina junghuhniana	*Pinus thunbergii* (Japanese black pine)
Casuarina montana	*Platanus occidentalis* (sycamore)
Casuarina papuanum	*Pongamia pinnata*
Casuarina suberosa	*Populus alba* (white poplar)
Ceratonia siliqua (carob)	*Populus gamblei*
Citrus fortunella (kumquat)	*Populus grandidentata*
Citrus sinensis (Valencia orange)	*Prosopis juliflora*
Cornus kousa (Japanese dogwood)	*Prunus avium* (sweet cherry)
Corylus avellana (filbert)	*Prunus cerasifera* (cherry plum)
Cotinus coggygria (*Rhus cotinus*) (smoke tree)	*Prunus cerasus* (sour cherry)
Cotoneaster acutifolia (Peking cotoneaster)	*Prunus domestica* (plum)
Cotoneaster dammeri	*Prunus fruticosa* (ground cherry)
Cryptomeria japonica	*Prunus mahaleb* (ripe mahaleb cherry)
Cupressus sempervirens (Italian cypress)	*Prunus persica* (peach)
Cupressus leylandii (Leyland cypress)	*Prunus persica* var. *nectarina* (nectarine)
Fagus sylvatica (European beech)	*Prunus triloba* (flowering almond)
Ficus carica (fig)	*Prunus ulmifolia*
Fraxinus excelsior (ash)	*Pseudotsuga menziesii* (Douglas fir)
Hevea brasiliensis (rubber)	*Psidium Guajava* (guava)
Juniperus chinensis	*Quercus alba* (white oak)
Juniperus virginiana (eastern red cedar)	*Quercus coccinea* (scarlet oak)
Liriodendron tulipifera (tulip tree)	*Quercus petraea*
Maclura pomifera (Osage orange)	*Quercus rubra*
Magnolia kobus	*Quercus robur* (English oak)
Magnolia liliflora	*Sequoiadendron giganteum* (giant tree)
Magnolia soulangiana	*Simmondsia chinensis* (jojoba)
Magnolia stellata	*Syringa vulgaris* (common lilac)
Malpighia punicifolia (West Indian cherry)	*Taxus cuspidata* (Japanese yew)
	Taxus media (yew)
	Thuja occidentalis (American arbor vitae)
	Thuja plicata (giant arbor-vitae)
	Tilia argentea (silver linden)
	Tilia cordata (small-leafed linden)

inferior crop, or no crop at all, during the next season. Thus, the control of abscission is extremely important commercially. Both the induction and the prevention or delay of abscission are valuable tools to the grower.

The value of controlling abscission to increase both the quality and the quantity of crop plants has been appreciated for centuries. The traditional hand thinning of fruits, to improve size and quality of fruit in some tree crops and to overcome the problem of alternate bearing, has now essentially been replaced by the use of chemicals. The reduction in labor and its cost have been impressive. The ability to remove unwanted leaves at harvest or at other appropriate times is most important in cotton and in tree nursery stock, as is the removal of nuisance fruit in wood pulp trees.

In addition to the prevention of preharvest fruit drop in tree fruits such as apples and pears, the prevention or delay in abscission is important in flower, fruit, and foliage preservation in Christmas trees, holly, mistletoe, and the like, as well as in on-tree storage of certain citrus crops, particularly Navel oranges.

Table 20.2 summarizes the recent literature showing the array of chemicals that have been used on a number of trees for the control of abscission—in some instances leaves; in others, flowers and/or fruit; and in still others, both vegetative and reproductive organs. The widespread usage of ethephon, NAA, and Sevin is evident.

For a detailed discussion of the use of chemicals for leaf and fruit abscission control, the reader is referred to the articles by Bukovac (10), Morgan (11), Looney (12,13), and Williams and Edgerton (14). For in-depth consideration of the physiology of abscission, reference should be made to the articles by Osborne (15,16) and Addicott (Chapter 12, this book).

20.4. Flowering

Trees, being perennial, are quite valuable, whether for ornamental or horticultural purposes. The control of flowering by trees, especially fruit and nut trees, is very important. Such control of flowering has three objectives: (a) to prevent flowering when young in order that the energy produced goes into vegetative growth and development, (b) to induce flowering when mature to increase yield, and (c) to regulate cropping and increase overall long-term yields by increasing "return flowering" of those varieties and cultivars that tend to bear every other year or alternate between heavy- and light-bearing years.

The ability to manipulate flowering in conifers with chemicals has been known since the late 1950s. A large number of conifers can be made to flower in response to applications of gibberellins. A detailed discussion of this subject can be found in the articles by Ross et al. (17) and Owens (Chapter 11, this book).

Table 20.3 presents the chemicals tested on a number of tree species for the control of flowering—to either prevent or induce flowering or both. The effect may vary with the concentration and timing of application.

Table 20.2. Chemicals tested on trees for control of abscission of leaves, flowers, and/ or fruit

Tree	Acti-Aid	Alar	AOA	A-Rest	Atrinal	AVG	BA	CGA-15281	3-CIIPC	CPA
Alnus incana										
Apple		F				F	F	FL		F
Apricot										
Banyan				L						
Betula pendula										
Carpinus betulus										
Cherry										
Sour		F					F	F		
Sweet		F								
Citrus										
Grapefruit										
Kumquat										
Lemon					F	F			F	
Mandarin orange										
Orange	FL	F					F	FL		
Tangelo										
Tangerine							F			
Coffee										
Guava										
Macadamia			F				F			
Mango	F									
Oak		L								
Olive		F								
Peach		F						F	F	F
Nectarine										
Pear								L		
Pecan								F		
Pine, loblolly										
Pistachio										
Platanus × hispanica										
Plum		L								F
Walnut										

[a]L = leaves; F = flowers or fruit.

Table 20.2. (*Continued*)

Tree	CuEDTA	2,4-D	DEF	Dichlorprop	Dinoseb	DNOC	DWK	Elgetol	Ethephon	GA$_3$
Alnus incana			L						L	
Apple	L	F		F		F	L	F	FL	F
Apricot		F			F	F		F		
Banyan									L	
Betula pendula			L						L	
Carpinus betulus			L						L	
Cherry										
Sour									F	F
Sweet			L				L		F	F
Citrus										
Grapefruit		F							F	F
Kumquat									F	
Lemon		FL							F	F
Mandarin orange		F							F	
Orange		F							F	F
Tangelo									F	
Tangerine									F	F
Coffee									F	F
Guava									FL	
Macadamia		F							F	F
Mango		F							F	
Oak	L									
Olive										
Peach						F	FL		F	F
Nectarine							L		L	
Pear	L						L		F	
Pecan									FL	
Pine, loblolly	L									
Pistachio									F	F
Platanus × *hispanica*									L	
Plum	FL				F	F			FL	
Walnut									F	

^{a}L = leaves; F = flowers or fruit.

Table 20.2. (*Continued*)

								Chemical							
GA_{4+7}	Harvade	MCPA	MH-30	MITS	NAA, NAAm	Octylamine	Pik-Off	Release	RH-2915	Sevin	Sweep	2,4,5-T	Terbacil	2,4,5-TP	Triclopyr
									L						
F	L	F			F					F		F	F	F	F
					F					F		F		F	
								L							
								L							
					F					F					
L					F					F					
		F													
	F						F	F				FL			
			F		F							F			
				F	F	F	F	F			F				
F															
					F										
					F										
	L		L												
				F											
	L				F								F		F
	L				F										
					F										
								L							
	L	L	L		F					F	F				

Table 20.3. Chemicals tested for control of flowering in trees[a]

Plant or crop	Alar	A-Rest	AVG	BA	BOA	CCC	Ethephon	GA3	GA4	GA7	GA4+7	GA5	GA9	Hyvar X	Maintain	NAA	Phosphon D	Promalin	TIBA	2,4,5-TP
Almond	X																			
Apple	X			X			X	X	X	X	X			X	X				X	
Apricot	X	X					X	X												
Cherry																				
Sour	X	X					X	X												
Sweet							X	X												
Citrus																				
Lemon	X				X			X												
Lime	X					X		X												
Mandarin orange								X												
Orange	X				X	X		X												

Coffee	X		X	X	X	X
Conifers						
Cypress			X	X		
Larch	X	X	X	X	X	X
Spruce	X	X	X	X	X	X
Pine	X		X	X	X	X
Fir	X	X	X	X	X	X
Cedar	X		X	X		
Hemlock			X	X		
Holly		X		X		
Lychee	X	X		X		X
Mango		X		X		
Olive			X			
Papaya	X	X	X	X	X	
Peach	X					
Pear	X	X	X	X	X	X
Pecan		X	X	X		
Plum		X	X			X

[a]Symbol X (here and in Tables 20.3–20.6) indicates that the chemical was tried on the tree.

20.5. Fruit-set and development

The regulation of fruiting processes is a key element in the successful production of tree fruit (10). Considerable success has been achieved in fruit thinning with chemicals. Much less success has been obtained in finding effective chemicals for the promotion of fruit set in both pome and stone fruits, although some progress has been made with pears. Table 20.4 presents a group of chemicals that have been evaluated for their effects on fruit-set and development of a number of crops. Emphasis has been placed on citrus, pome, and stone fruit crops. Varietal differences, vicissitudes of nature (particularly in the spring), and geographic variations, added to a list of other variables, has made this particular usage a primary research target for continuing studies.

20.6. Size and shape of canopy

There are a number of reasons to control the size of a tree—to either retard or increase its growth. In bearing trees, suppression of vegetative growth often enhances fruit yield and quality. For ornamentals, restriction of size is often desirable. Along power lines, suppression of woody growth saves huge amounts of hand labor. A troublesome characteristic of certain fruit rootstocks and of some ornamentals is the tendency to initiate root suckers. For all of these and other reasons, the ability to control the size of trees is an important tool.

As can be seen in Table 20.5, gibberellic acid is the most widely used chemical to increase vegetative growth of a number of trees, whereas the most commonly used growth retardants are Atrinal, MH-30, and PBZ (paclobutrazol).

The ability to control the shape of trees has important implications for both horticulture and agriculture. The promotion of branching can improve both plant quality for horticultural purposes and plant yield for agriculture. The use of chemicals to replace labor has substantial cost advantages.

The induction of branching in many varieties of maiden fruit trees can result in a higher grade of tree at the time of sale and in increased numbers of fruit the following year. Young orchards planted with well-branched trees flower more abundantly and yield more than do those planted with less branched trees. The use of growth regulators for "chemical pruning" results in additional cost savings.

Such control of tree shape fits the needs for high-density plantings and more intensive orchard management by supplying smaller, better-branched trees for closer planting and earlier cropping, both increasing orchard value.

The value of chemical control of fruit tree shape and size has been repeatedly shown by Quinlan and others (18,19). Table 20.6 gives a list of chemicals that induce changes in tree shape. The most effective appear to be BA, M&B 25-105, NC-9634, and PBZ. All these chemicals have been evaluated on apple trees, indicating both the importance of that crop and the success achieved in its control.

Table 20.4. Chemicals tested for effects on fruit set and development

Plant or crop	Alar	AVG	BA	CCC	2,4-D	DPU	Ethephon	GA₃	GA₄₊₇	IAA	IBA	IZAA	NAA	NOA	PBZ	Promalin	Sevin	2,4,5-T	2,4,5-TP	Triadimefon
Apple	X	X	X			X	X	X	X			X	X	X	X	X	X			X
Banyan							X						X	X	X	X				
Cashew					X					X	X									
Cherry																				
Sour	X	X	X						X									X	X	
Sweet	X					X	X	X					X	X				X	X	
Citrus																				
Grapefruit					X													X		
Lime					X													X		
Mandarin orange			X		X		X	X				X						X		
Orange			X		X		X	X	X									X		
Tangelo								X												
Coffee							X	X												
Loquat			X					X												
Mango							X													
Olive							X													
Palm, date			X					X		X			X							
Peach							X	X											X	
Pear	X		X	X			X	X	X				X		X					
Persimmon, Japanese												X								
Plum		X	X		X	X	X	X	X				X	X		X			X	
Walnut							X													

Table 20.5. Chemicals tested for effects on tree size

Plant or crop	Alar	Amo-1618	A-Rest	Atrinal	BA	CCC	Chlorfurenol	Dichlobenil	EHPP	EL-500	Ethephon
Alder				X							
Almond					X						
Apple	X				X			X	X		X
Ash	X			X							
Aspen				X							
Banyan											
Citrus											
Lemon						X					X
Orange											
Tangelo											
Birch				X							
Cherry											
Sour											
Sweet				X							
Coconut					X						
Coffee	X					X					
Cottonwood	X			X							
Elm	X		X	X		X	X				
Eucalyptus	X		X	X							
Fig				X			X				
Fir											
Hackberry				X							
Hemlock											
Hibiscus						X					
Locust				X							
Macadamia					X						
Maple	X		X	X		X					X
Malaleuca				X							
Oleander			X								
Oak	X			X	X						
Olive				X							
Peach										X	
Nectarine											
Pecan										X	
Pear	X					X					
Pine	X	X	X	X	X	X			X	X	X
Plum											
Poplar	X			X							
Spruce	X	X	X	X	X	X			X	X	X
Redwood				X							
Rubber											
Sweetgum				X							
Sycamore	X			X						X	
Tulip tree										X	
Walnut				X							
Willow											

Table 20.5. (*Continued*)

Fluoridamid	GA$_3$	GA$_{4+7}$	IBA	Krenite	Maintain	Mefluidide	MH-30	NAA	PBZ	Promalin	Phosphon D	RH-531	TIBA	Uniconazol
	X							X						
		X	X					X	X	X			X	X
							X	X	X					
							X							
									X					
	X			X						X				
	X													
					X				X					
							X							
	X						X		X					
	X							X						
	X												X	
						X	X						X	
							X	X						
					X		X							
	X						X							
				X										
							X	X						
X						X	X	X	X					
							X							
							X							
	X					X		X	X					X
								X	X					X
									X					
									X					
X					X	X	X		X		X	X		
									X					
	X						X							
X			X	X	X	X	X					X	X	
							X							
			X										X	
							X	X	X	X				
							X		X					
							X							
							X							

479

Table 20.6. Chemicals tested to change shape of trees.

Plant or crop	A-820	Alar	Atrinal	BA	Ethephon	GA$_{4+7}$	KT-30	M&B 25-105	NAA	NC-9634	Off-Shoot-O	PBZ	PP-528	Promalin	SD-4901	SD-8339
Almond	X							X	X							
Apple		X	X	X	X	X	X	X	X	X	X	X	X	X	X	X
Cherry		X						X					X	X		
Cherry, Jerusalem				X	X											
Citrus				X												
Coffee				X												
Crabapple				X												
Fir				X												
Holly										X						X
Macadamia				X												
Orange				X												
Peach			X						X							
Nectarine									X							
Pear	X							X		X	X		X	X		
Pine			X	X												
Plane, London																
Plum										X						
Rubber										X						
Sorbus aucuparia	X	X														
Spruce		X		X												
Tilia euchlora	X															

20.7. Fruit shape

Two compounds have been shown to control the shape of the apple fruit. The desirable characteristics for the most salable apple are an elongated body with pronounced calyx lobes. Fruit with such attributes are termed "typey." The two products that produce "typiness" in apples are Promalin (20–22) and forchlorfenuron (CPPU, KT-30) (23). Both also produce larger fruit. Such combination of effects is most helpful for the marketability of fruits.

20.8. Latex flow

Over half a century of organized applied research has produced a spectrum of innovations for the rubber industry. One of these innovations is the use of plant growth regulators to enhance the flow of latex from the rubber tree. Results of early investigations on this process resulted in the use of 2,4,-D, 2,4,5-T, or NAA as stimulants for latex flow. Work since that time with many chemicals has resulted in the use of ethephon applied to the tree bark, enabling the trees to express their full genetic potential by reducing or removing the physical barriers to flow. The use of ethephon has now become an estate practice in most rubber-producing countries (see Chapter 17 in this book).

For an in-depth review of the physiology of latex production and the influence of plant growth regulators on that process, the reader is referred to the articles by Bridge (24) and by Sethuraj and Raghavendra (25).

20.9. Oleoresin accumulation in pine

In the early 1970s, it was reported that the application of paraquat to the exposed wood of several species of pine caused the accumulation of oleoresin in the boll of the trees. Paraquat enters the transpiration stream and causes the living xylem cells to synthesize large quantities of oleoresin that are subsequently transferred (secreted or leaked) in large amounts to neighboring cells until the entire area is saturated. The commercial attractiveness is because the hydrocarbon supplied by the oleoresin represents a renewable resource. This potential also serves as a boost to the naval stores industry, which has been on the decline.

A detailed discussion of the increase in oleoresin accumulation through the use of paraquat can be found in the article by Schwarz (26).

20.10. Chemical composition of fruits

There have been a number of studies concerning the effects of plant growth regulators on the chemical composition of fruit. As would be expected, most of the studies have been concerned with apple and the various citrus fruits.

Several chemicals have been evaluated for their effect in increasing the anthocyanin level in apple, thus making their color more intense. Most of the major varieties have been included in these studies, particularly Delicious, Jonathan, and McIntosh. The chemicals studied include Alar, CGA-15281, 2,4-D, ethephon, NAA, Promalin, and 2,4,5-TP.

TIBA, PBZ, and Alar have been found to increase the mineral content of apple fruit, while Alar, CCC, and PBZ do the same for their polyamine content. 2,4,5-TP reduces russetting.

Increasing the carotenoid content, especially of the rind, is a desirable effect for citrus fruit. CPTA, ethephon, and MPTA have been found to be effective in this action for grapefruit, kumquat, lemon, and several Mandarin oranges, as well as Navel and Valencia oranges.

Treatment of Mandarin oranges with GA_3 or ethephon increases the vitamin C content of the fruit. IZAA accelerates the degreening of Navel oranges and increases the total sugar content.

In stone fruit, CPTA has been shown to increase the carotenoid content of peach and apricot, while GA_3 increases the vitamin C content of sweet cherries and delays the formation on anthocyanins. Alar increases the anthocyanins in sweet cherries (27).

Treatment of papaya with ethephon increases the sugar content of the fruit, both reducing and total sugars (28).

20.11. Resistance to environmental stress

Two of the most harsh environmental stresses on trees are cold and drought. Progress has been made in alleviating both of these pressures through the use of plant growth regulators (29,30). Those found to be effective for inducing cold-hardiness in crop trees and those helpful in relieving water stress or as antitranspirants are given in Table 20.7.

20.12. Concluding Remarks

Space does not permit a more detailed discussion of a number of other uses for plant growth regulators in trees and tree crops. The most important other uses include the postharvest preservation of the harvested crop (31), the induction of resistance to diseases (32), and the induction of resistance to insect and other pests.

Successful agriculture, horticulture, and forestry are all based on the control of plant growth, for various advantages, such as for beauty, fiber, food, or shelter. The advances in crop control, through the use of plant growth regulators, have been quite important over the past few decades. The optimal production of tree fruit and nuts is dependent on maintaining a delicate balance between all the vegetative and reproductive processes involved in the

Table 20.7. Chemicals effective under stress conditions

Plant or crop	Inducing cold hardiness	Alleviating water stress
Apple	Alar, A-Rest, BA, Dropp, CGA-15281, EL-500, GA_3, GA_{4+7}, Fluoridamid, IBA, Promalin	PBZ
Apricot	DHAHA, PBZ	
Ash		ABA
Cherry	PBZ	
Citrus		ABA
Cocoa		CCC
Coffee	TMHEA	
Grapefruit	BA, 2,4-D, GA_3	
Maple, sugar		ABA
Orange, Valencia	Amo-1618	
Peach	DHAHA, PBZ	
Pear	HDHPA	
Pine, red		ABA

growth of trees. Plant growth regulators offer a great potential in the control of these processes. The success obtained thus far promises an increasing possibility to find even more active, cheaper, and safer chemicals to aid in feeding and protecting an ever-expanding population.

20.13. References

1. M.M. Williams, "Use of bioregulators to control vegetative growth of fruit trees and improve fruiting efficiency," in R.L. Ory and F.R. Rittig, eds., *Bioregulators: Chemistry and Uses*, American Chemical Society Symp. Ser. No. 257, 1984, pp. 93–99.

2. B.W. Wood, "Paclobutrazol, uniconazole, and flurprimidol influence shoot growth and nut yield of young pecan trees," *HortScience*, **23**, 1026–1028 (1988).

3. G.C. Martin, F. Yoshikawa, and J.H. LaRue, "Effect of soil applications of paclobutrazol on vegetative growth, pruning time, flowering, yield, and quality of 'Flavorcrest' peach," *J. Am. Soc. Hort. Sci.*, **112**, 912–921 (1987).

4. S.B. Rood, G. Daicos, and T.J. Blake, "Gibberellin acid induced growth acceleration in *Populus* hybrids," *Can. J. For. Res.*, **14**, 850–854 (1984).

5. L.G. Nickell, *Plant Growth Regulators: Agricultural Uses*, Springer-Verlag, Berlin, 1982.

6. P.W. Zimmerman and F. Wilcoxon, "Several chemical growth substances which cause initiation of roots and other responses in plants," *Contrib. Boyce Thompson Inst.*, **7**, 209–229 (1935).

7. G.S. Avery and E.F. Johnson, *Hormones and Horticulture*, McGraw-Hill, New York, 1947.

8. B.E. Hassig, "Influence of aryl esters of indole-3-acetic and indole-3-butyric acids on adventitious root primordium initiation and development," *Physiol. Plant.*, **47**, 29–33 (1979).

9. B.E. Haissig, J.R. Gaines, and G. Giacoletto, "Tree rooting using synthetic auxins," U.S. Patent 4,297,125. Oct. 27, 1981.

10. M.J. Bukovac, "Plant growth regulators in deciduous tree fruit production," in J.L. Hilton, ed., *Agricultural Chemicals of the Future*, 8th Beltsville Symp. Agric. Res., Rowman & Allanheld, Totowa, NJ, 1985, pp. 75–90.

11. P.W. Morgan, "Chemical manipulation of abscission and desiccation," in J.L. Hilton, ed., *Agricultural Chemicals of the Future*, 8th Beltsville Symp. Agric. Res., Rowman & Allanheld, Totowa, NJ, 1985, pp. 61–74.

12. N.E. Looney, "Growth regulator usage in apple and pear production," in L.G. Nickell, ed., *Plant Growth Regulating Chemicals*, Vol. I, CRC Press, Boca Raton, FL, 1983, pp. 1–26.

13. N.E. Looney, "Growth regulator use in the production of *Prunus* species fruits," in L.G. Nickell, ed., *Plant Growth Regulating Chemicals*, Vol. I, CRC Press, Boca Raton, FL, 1983, pp. 27–39.

14. M.W. Williams and L.J. Edgerton, "Fruit thinning of apples and pears with chemicals," USDA Agric. Inform. Bull. No. 289. 1981.

15. D.J. Osborne, "Abscission in agriculture," *Outlook Agric.*, **13**, 97–103 (1984).

16. D.J. Osborne, "Abscission," *CRC Crit. Rev. Plant Sci.*, **8**, 103–129 (1989).

17. S.D. Ross, R.P. Pharis, and W.D. Binder, "Growth regulators and conifers: Their physiology and potential uses in forestry," in L.G. Nickell, ed., *Plant Growth Regulating Chemicals*, Vol. II, CRC Press, Boca Raton, FL, 1983, pp. 35–78.

18. J.D. Quinlan, "New chemical approaches to the control of fruit tree form and size," *Acta Hort.*, **120**, 95–106 (1981).

19. J.D. Quinlan and E.M. Pakenham, "Effects of manual and chemical control of lateral shoots on the growth of young ornamental trees," *J. Hort. Sci.*, **59**, 45–56 (1984).

20. M.W. Williams and E.A. Stahly, "Effect of cytokinins and gibberellins on shape of 'Delicious' apple fruits," *J. Am. Soc. Hort. Sci.*, **94**, 17–19 (1969).

21. M.W. Williams and H.D. Billingsley, "Suggested commercial use of Promalin to improve Delicious apple shape and size," *Proc. Ann. Mtg. Wash. St. Hort. Assn.*, **74**, 36–40 (1978).

22. R.J. Cibulsky, "Response of seven strains of Red Delicious apples to bloom applications of Promalin (GA_{4+7} and 6-BA)," *Proc. 5th Ann. Mtg. Plant Growth Regulator Working Group*, 227–234 (1978).

23. L.G. Nickell, "Effects of N-(2-chloro-4-pyridyl)-N'-phenylurea on grapes and other crops," *Proc. 13th Ann. Mtg. Plant Growth Regulator Soc. Am.*, 236–241 (1986).

24. K. Bridge, "Plant growth regulator use in natural rubber (*Hevea brasiliensis*)," in L.G. Nickell, ed., *Plant Growth Regulating Chemicals*, Vol. I, CRC Press, Boca Raton, FL, 1983, pp. 41–58.

25. M.R. Sethuraj and A.S. Raghavendra, "Rubber," in M.R. Sethuraj and A.S. Raghavendra, eds., *Tree Crop Physiology*, Elsevier, Amsterdam, 1987, pp. 193–223.

26. O.J. Schwarz, "Paraquat-induced light wood formation in pine," in L.G. Nickell, ed., *Plant Growth Regulating Chemicals*, Vol. II, CRC Press, Boca Raton, FL, 1983, pp. 79–97.

27. S.R. Drake, E.L. Proebsting, G.H. Carter, and J.W. Nelson, "Effect of growth regulators on ascorbic acid content, drained weight and color of fresh and processed 'Rainer' cherries," *J. Am. Soc. Hort. Sci.*, **103**, 162–164 (1978).

28. R.K. Battacharya and V.N. Madhava Rao, "Effect of growth regulants on duration of maturation, physical characters and chemical constituents of CO.2 papaya (*Carica papaya* L.) fruit," *S. Indian Hort.*, **29**, 27–34 (1981).

29. J.T. Raese, "Conductivity tests to screen fall-applied growth regulators to induce cold hardiness in young 'Delicious' apple trees," *J. Am. Soc. Hort. Sci.*, **108**, 172–176 (1983).

30. W.J. Davies and T.T. Kozlowski, "Effects of applied abscisic acid and plant water stress on transpiration of woody angiosperms," *For. Sci.*, **21**, 191–195 (1975).

31. F.W. Liu, "Interaction of daminozide, harvesting date, and ethylene in CA storage on 'McIntosh' apple quality," *J. Am. Soc. Hort. Sci.*, **104**, 599–601 (1979).

32. D. Davis and A.E. Dimond, "Inducing disease resistance with plant growth regulators," *Phytopathology*, **53**, 137–140 (1953).

20.14. Appendix

An alphabetical list of chemicals cited by designation or name as used in text and tables, is as follows. Because of lack of space, especially in the tables, chemicals are referred by their shortest designations of their common name, trade name, chemical abbreviation, or even the code number. To assist the reader, all the forms of reference to the chemicals included in this chapter are listed here.

A-820; butralin, Tamex; 4-(1,1-dimethylethyl)-*n*-(1-methylpropyl)-2,6-dinitrobenzamine

ABA; abscisic acid; 3-methyl-5-(1-hydroxy-4-keto-2,6,6-trimethyl-2-cyclohexen-1-yl)-*cis,trans*-2,4-pentadienoic acid

Acti-Aid; actidione, cycloheximide

Alar; daminozide; B-9; butanedioic acid mono-(2,2-dimethylhydrazine)

Amo-1618

AOA; (aminooxy) acetic acid

A-Rest; ancymidol; EL-513; α-cyclopropyl-α-(4-methoxyphenyl)-5-pyrimidine methanol

Atrinal; dikegulac sodium; 2,3:4,6-di-*O*-(1-methylethylidine)-α-L-xylo-2-hexulofuranosonic acid

BA; BAP; 6-benzylaminopurine; 6-benzyladenine

BOA; benzothiazole-2-oxyacetic acid

CCC; Cycocel; chlormequat chloride; (2-chloroethyl)trimethyl ammonium chloride

CGA-15281; (2-chloroethyl)methyl-bis(phenylmethoxy)silane

Chlorflurenol; 2-chloro-9-hydroxy-9H-fluorene-9-carboxylic acid

3-ClIPC; 3-chloro-isopropyl-N-phenylcarbamate

CPA; 4-chlorophenoxyacetic acid

CPTA; 2-(4-chlorophenylthio)triethylamine

2,4-D; 2,4-dichlorophenoxyacetic acid

DEF; S,S,S-tributylphosphorotrithioate

Dichlobenil; 2,6-dichlorobenzonitrile

Dichloroprop; BAS-04418H; 2-(2,4-dichlorophenoxy)propanoic acid

DHAHA; 1,1-dimethyl-2-(3-(N-dodecyl-N-(2-hydroxypropyl)amino) pro-pionyl)-1-(2-hydroxypropyl) ammoniumimine

Dinoseb; dinitro-o-butylphenol

Dipterex; dimethyl (2,2,2-trichloro-1-hydroxyethyl)phosphate

DNOC; 4,6-dinitro-o-cresol

DPU; diphenylurea

Dropp; thidiazuron; N-phenyl-N'-1,2,3-thiadiazol-5-yl urea

DWK; DuPont WK, dodecyl ether of polyethyleneglycol (surfactant)

EDTA; ethylenediaminetetraacetic acid

EHPP; ethyl hydrogen 1-propyl-phosphonate

EL-500; flurprimidol; α-(1-methylethyl)-α-(4-trifluoromethoxy)phenyl-5-py-rimidine methanol

Elgetol; dinitro-o-cyclohexylphenol + dinitro-o-cresol

Ethephon; Ethrel; (2-chloroethyl)phosphonic acid

Fluoridamid; Sustar; 4-(4-methyl-3((trifluoromethyl)-sulfonyl)amino)phenyl)-phenylacetamide

GA_3; gibberellic acid; 2,4α,7-trihydroxy-1-methyl-8-methylene-gibb-3-ene-1,10-dicarboxylic acid-1,4α-lactone

GA_4

GA_5

GA_7

GA_9

GA_{4+7}; Pro-Gib 47

Harvade; dimethipin; N-252; 2,3-dihydro-5,6-dimethyl-1,4-dithiin-1,1,4,4-te-troxide

HDHPA; 4-hydroxy-3,6-dioxo-hexahydro-pyridazinyl-(4)-acetic acid

Hyvar X; bromacil; 5-bromo-3-sec-butyl-6-methyluracil

IAA; heteroauxin; 3-indoleacetic acid

IBA; 3-indolebutyric acid

IZAA; Figaron; J-455; ethyl 5-chloro-1*H*-3-indazolyl-acetate

Krenite; ammonium ethylcarbamoylphosphonate

KT-30; forchlorfenuron; CPPU; CN-11-3183; *N*-(2-chloro-4-pyridyl)-*N'*-phenylurea

M&B 25-105; *N*-propyl-3-*tert*-butylphenoxyacetate

Maintain; morphactin; chlofurenol methyl; methyl 2-chloro-9-hydroxy-fluorene-9-carboxylic acid

MCPA; 4-chloro-2-methylphenoxyacetic acid

Mefluidide; Embark; MBR-12325; 4-(2,4-dimethyl-5-(trifluoromethyl)sulfenyl)amino)phenyl)acetamide

MH-30; Slo-Gro; 1,2-dihydro-3,6-pyridazinedione

MITS; 5-methyl-2-iodoethyl-2-thienylsulphonate

MPTA; 2-(4-methylphenoxy)triethylamine

NAA; Phyomone; α-naphthaleneacetic acid

NC-9634; phenylthiadiazolyl thioacetate

NOA; BNOA; β-naphthoxyacetic acid

Octylamine

Off-Shoot-O; methyl esters of fatty acids

PBZ; PP-333; paclobutrazol; Cultar; (2*RS*,3*RS*)-1-(4-Chlorophenyl)-4,4-dimethyl-2-1,2,4-triazol-1-yl)pentan-3-ol

Phosphon D; 2,4-dichlorobenzyltributylphosphonium chloride

Pik-Off; CGA-22911; glyoxime; glyoxal dioxime

Promalin: BA + GA_{4+7}

Release; 5-chloro-3-methyl-1-nitro-1*H*-pyrazole

RH-531; 3-carboxy-1-(*p*-chlorophenyl)-4,6-dimethyl-2-pyridone

RH-2915; oxyfluorfen; Goal; Koltar; 2-chloro-1-(3-ethoxy-4-nitro-phenoxy)-4-(trifluoromethyl)benzene

Sevin; carbaryl; 1-naphthyl-*N*-methyl carbamate

Sweep; chlorothalonil; 2,4,5,6-tetrachloroisophthalonitrile

2,4,5-T; 2,4,5-trichlorophenoxyacetic acid

Terbacil; Sinbar; 3-*tert*-butyl-5-chloro-6-methyluracil

TIBA; Regim-8; triiodobenzoic acid

TMHEA; trimethyl-β-hydroxyethyl-ammonium chloride

2,4,5-TP; Fenoprop; Silvex; 2-(2,4,5,-trichlorophenoxy)propanoic acid

Triadimefon; Bayleton; 1-(4-chlorophenoxy)-3,3-dimethyl-1-(1*H*-1,2,4-triazol-1-yl)-2-buranone

Triclopyr; Grazon; 3,5,6-trichloro-2-pyridinyloxyacetic acid

Uniconazol; XE-1019; (*E*)-1-(*p*-chlorophenyl)-4,4-dimethyl-2-(1,2,4-triazol-1-yl)-penten-3-ol

X-45; Triton X-45 (surfactant)

INDEX